AMERICAN
POLITICAL
TERMS

AMERICAN POLITICAL TERMS

An Historical Dictionary

Hans Sperber
THE OHIO STATE UNIVERSITY

and

Travis Trittschuh
WAYNE STATE UNIVERSITY

DETROIT   WAYNE STATE UNIVERSITY PRESS   1962

Published simultaneously in Canada
by Ambassador Books, Limited, Toronto, Ontario, Canada

Library of Congress Catalog Card Number
62–11233
Printed in the United States of America

Grateful acknowledgement is made to
the Ford Foundation for financial assistance in making possible
the publication of this volume.

Preface

A politician who turns to this book in the hope of finding ammunition for his next campaign will probably find himself disappointed. He may stumble on one or two words that could be revived for propaganda purposes, but we suspect, or rather wish, that he will find himself considerably sobered by discovering that the catchwords he wants to use on his audience have been used before and very often been found wanting. In any case, we want to make very sure that nothing has been more foreign to our intentions than to offer a guide to the use and misuse of language in politics.

We hope we have succeeded in keeping ourselves detached from all political partisanship, but we can not claim to be neutral in the struggle against undue and dangerous restrictions that so many scholars impose upon themselves by becoming specialists in one narrow field, constantly shunning the temptation of looking beyond their fences. We quote an older publication:

> There is not a dean's office in the country where the problem of universality as against specialization of knowledge has not been the subject of lengthy and, we profoundly hope, fruitful discussions. But theory is a long way ahead of practice. Everybody is in a fair way of being convinced that the fences by which the vast field of knowledge is divided into cucumber beds and cabbage patches ought to give way. But as yet they stand as firm and forbidding as ever, and mere discussion will hardly remove them. In our opinion they will never be breached until some one is resolute enough to lay hands on that part of the fence that serves to limit his own backyard.[1]

The field of political language offers a typical example of what happens whenever an area of investigation stretches beyond the fences of just one branch of knowledge: nothing or next to nothing. The philologist feels that he is not competent to deal with a subject that with more justice may be claimed by the historian, and vice versa. What little anyone knows about the origin and history of American political words consists largely of occasional remarks, sometimes based on actual knowledge but more often on explanations made up at random or on anecdotes invented for

[1] R. M. Estrich and Hans Sperber, *Three Keys to Language*, p. v.

v

the purpose of explaining this or that colorful or puzzling expression. Under these conditions our first and most important task was to establish the historical facts behind each word. We are aware of our inability to take more than the first steps towards the fulfillment of this task. The sources on which we have based our findings, although in themselves adding up to a large body of printed material, appear to be very insignificant if compared to the enormous amount of material we have been forced to neglect. We want to be first to point out the sketchiness of our work. This applies not only to the articles included but in even higher degree to the probably very large number of political terms that have eluded us altogether—forced us by ignorance or lack of time to neglect. We do not consider this book a harvest but just a bagful of seeds.

A practical consequence of our disclaiming all pretentions to completeness is that we have taken pains to make at least some of our gaps plainly visible to the reader. This has been done by using the two symbols [ ] and ¿, the first indicating that we consider the material at hand more than excusably inadequate and the second that we have taken up statements we consider plausible without having been able to establish their correctness. We might have used them in many more places, but using them indiscriminately would have lessened their effectiveness.

The reader may well wonder why in view of the inevitable inadequacies of our book, we have devoted so much work and time to marginal material: remarks on European parallels, the cultural backgrounds of many words, literary influences on political vocabulary, the passing of political terms into the general vocabulary, and even words whose political character appears doubtful. Our defense against any such criticism we base on the same aversion to strict specialization that has prompted us to undertake this work. We do not want to present political language in artificial isolation. It is a product on the one hand of its social and cultural environment and on the other, a factor of no mean importance in the development of language in general. We thought ourselves justified in including quite a few politically "unimportant" words for the sole reason that we have not found them in the general dictionaries, such as the *Oxford English Dictionary,* the *Dictionary of Americanisms,* and the *Dictionary of American English.* We are, after all, philologists, and we did not think it necessary to deny ourselves the pleasure of adding a few minutiae to the findings of our great lexicographers.

Neither is an apology needed for the frequent inclusion of puns, snatches of song hits, anecdotes, and other marginal material of a similar type. Although this is not lexicographical material in the strict sense of the term, we feel that such items are of great help in reconstructing the atmosphere that pervades political language. Besides, the discovery of these side lights has largely contributed to the fact that the hunt for word material, although frequently a rather tiring task, has proved an extremely stimulating and often amusing activity. We can not see a valid reason why some of the fun we have had should not be passed on to the reader.

Since some of this type of material would have been lost if scattered among the separate articles, we have introduced bracketed items such as Polk and trade names. These items do not concentrate on any particular word but contain small and very insufficient listings of illustrative quotations. The same typographical device is used for items dealing with rhetorical and stylistic tricks common in political language, as, for instance, alliteration and allegory.

In a few cases we hope to have corrected widespread errors about historical facts. For example, a very large number of historical works state that the election of 1844 was fought and won by virtue of the slogan "Fifty-four forty or fight!" Our findings show that the history of this phrase begins in 1846 and therefore could not possibly have influenced the outcome of the preceding election.

For the benefit of our fellow linguists we would like to suggest that the present work may usefully contribute to removing the prejudices against historical linguistics that undoubtedly exist in some quarters. We are convinced that the preponderance of descriptive methods does not conform to the nature of language, which, although recreated in every actual utterance, is still the great link between ourselves and earlier generations and the most important means of utilizing the experiences of our forbears. To understand our own language habits without investigating their history appears to us an almost preposterous mistake.

It is hardly necessary to say that these remarks are not meant as a disparagement of sound descriptive methods. Any improvement in the presentation of language as it is must, of course, be hailed as an important gain; but we can not possibly stress description to a degree that lets us forget that the constant evolution of language makes it impossible to eliminate the diachronic approach. On the other hand, it must be admitted that historical linguistics has often been rather lax in its fact-finding methods; too often we are content with stating that this or that has taken place during the Middle English period, when a closer study of the sources might make it entirely possible to arrive at a much narrower chronological limitation. We flatter ourselves that our material, with much of it that can be dated not only to the year but sometimes to a single day, may curb the tendency to acquiesce in approximations where precise facts might and ought to be found.

It is our duty as well as our pleasure to acknowledge the help we have received from the Graduate School of the Ohio State University during many years, in particular to Prof. Paul N. Hudson, former Dean of the Graduate School, who as long as he was in office never failed in finding the necessary funds for our work (mainly through the Research Foundation) and to encourage us in every possible way. Later, when difficulties arose that threatened the completing of the dictionary, other faithful friends were instrumental in helping us overcome the obstacles. We mention with particular gratitude the names of Prof. James E. Fullington, former Dean of the College of Arts and Sciences; his successor, Prof. Osborn Fuller, who at a very critical stage granted us the necessary funds for putting our MS into printable form; Prof. Dieter Cunz, Chairman of the German Department; Prof. Robert M. Estrich, Chairman of the English Department; and Prof. George Havens of the Romance Language Department. The many friends who have contributed information can not be enumerated here, but we want to assure them that their help is gratefully remembered. Three names, however, cannot be omitted: Prof. James N. Tidwell, of San Diego State College, who for a short time was closely associated with our work at a period when his energy and scholarship were most needed; Prof. Mamie Meredith, University of Nebraska, who in a most generous way provided us with a lot of valuable material; and Prof. Mitford M. Mathews, formerly of the University of Chicago Press, who has aided us most efficiently by letting us profit of the rich store of experience accumulated during his work on the *Dictionary of Americanisms on Historical Principles* (2 vols., Chicago: University of Chicago Press, 1951)

Most of the titles have been quoted in a form that ought to make their identification easy. Abbreviations have been used sparingly and in accordance with Mathews' "List of Bibliographic Abbreviations," II, 1914–15. The same applies to symbols where they have been used. Our deviations from Mathews' usage are the symbols explained above.

H. S.
T. T.

Abbreviations

a. . . . .*ante*, before
Adv. . . . . .Advertiser; Advocate
Agric. . . . . .Agricultural; Agriculture
Am. Sp. . . . .*American Speech*
Amer. N. & Q. . . . .
       American Notes and Queries
Ann. . . . . .Annals; Annual
Antiq. . . . . .Antiquarian
app. . . . . .appendix
Arch. . . . . .Archeological; Archives
Assn. . . . . .Association
Autobio. . . . . .Autobiography
Bd. . . . . .Board (of)
Bio. . . . . .Biography
Bk. . . . . .Book
Bull. . . . . .Bulletin
C. . . . . .Century
c. . . . . .circa, about
Cal. . . . . .Calendar (of)
Cat. . . . . .Catalog
Cent. Mag. . . . .*Century Magazine*
Ch. . . . . .Chapter
Chi. . . . . .Chicago
Chron. . . . . .Chronicle (s)
Cinc. . . . . .Cincinnati
Cleve. . . . . .Cleveland
Co. . . . . .Company; County
Coll (s). . . . . .Collections; College
Comm. . . . . .Commercial
comp. . . . . .compiled (by) ; compiler
Cong. . . . . .Congress (ional)
Cong. Rec. . . . .*Congressional Record*
Corr. . . . . .Correspondence
Ct. . . . . .Court
Cyc. . . . . .Cyclopedia
D. . . . . .Daily
DA. . . . .*Dictionary of Americanisms*
DAB. .*Dictionary of American Biography*
DAE. . . .*Dictionary of American English*

Deb. . . . . .Debate (s)
Dem. . . . . .Democrat
Dept. . . . . .Department
Det. . . . . .Detroit
Dial. . . . . .Dialect
Dict. . . . . .Dictionary
DN. . . . .*Dialect Notes*
DNB. .*Dictionary of National Biography*
Doc. . . . . .Documentary; Documents
Econ. . . . . .Economics
ed. . . . . .edited (by) ; edition; editor
edit (sometimes, ed.) . . . . .editorial
EDD. . . . .*English Dialect Dictionary*
Encyc. . . . . .Encyclopedia
Eng. . . . . .England; English
Ess. . . . . .Essay (s)
Eve. . . . . .Evening
Ex. . . . .*Examiner; Express*
F. . . . . .Farmer, *Americanisms*
For. . . . . .Foreign
Gaz. .Gazette (er)
Gloss. . . . . .Glossary
Gt. . . . . .Great
Hist. . . . . .Historical; History
H.R. . . . . .House of Representatives
Ill. . . . . .Illustrated
Int. .International
Intell. . . . .*Intelligencer*
Jrnl (s). . . . . .Journal (s)
K.C. . . . . .Kansas City
Lang. . . . . .Language
Lect. . . . . .Lecture (s)
Legis. .Legislature
Lib. . . . . .Library
Lit. Digest. . . . .*Literary Digest*
Ltr (s). .Letter (s)
Mag. . . . . .Magazine
Man. . . . . .Manual
Mem. . . . .Memoirs; Memorial; Memories

Mess. ....Messages; Messenger	Reg. ....Register; Regulations
Misc. ....Miscellaneous	Relig. ....Religious
Mon. ....Monthly	Reminisc. ....Reminiscences
Morn. ....Morning	Rep. ....Report (er) ; Republican
MS (S) . ...Manuscript (s)	Repub. ....Republic (an)
Mus. ....Museum	rev. ....revised
N.A.; N. Amer. ....North America	Rev. ....Review (s)
Narr. ....Narrative	Sci. ....Science; Scientific
Nat. ....National	Sel. ....Selected
n.d. ....no date	Sen. ....Senate
N. Eng. ....New England	ser. ....series
No. ....Number	Sess. ....Session
N.O. ....New Orleans	S.F. ....San Francisco
n.p. ....no place	Sk. ....Sketches
n.s. ....new series	So. ....Southern
OED. ....*Oxford English Dictionary*	Soc. ....Society
P. ....Papers	Sp. ....Speech (es)
Phil. ....Philological	St. ....State
Phila. ....Philadelphia	Stats. ....Statutes
Phil (os) . .....Philosophical; Philosophy	Sun. ....Sunday
Pol. ....Political; Politics	Suppl. ....Supplement
p (p) . ...page (s)	sw. ....semi-weekly
pref. ....preface	Terr. ....Territorial; Territory
Pres. ....President (ial)	Th. ....Thornton
priv. pr. ....privately printed	tr. .....translated (by) ; translation (of)
Proc. ....Proceedings	Trav. ....Travels
Prog. ....Progress	Univ. ....Universal; University
Prov. ....Provincial	v.d. ....various dates
Pseud. ....Pseudonym (of)	vol (s) . ...volume (s)
pub. ....published (by) ; publisher	Vt. ....Vermont
Pub. ....Public	w. ....weekly
q.v. ....quod vide, which see	Wash. ....Washington
Rec. ....Record (s)	West. ....Western
Recoll. ....Recollections	Wks. ....Works

A

absenteeism.

In law, an absentee is one who has left his residence in a state, leaving no one to represent him, especially for the purpose of receiving legal papers, etc. This may apply either to individuals or corporations. At various periods, however, the word *absentee* has been given a specific significance which is invariably derogatory.

A. The landlords of Ireland resident in England gave the word *absentee* its most widespread and generally understood notoriety. The term has since been applied to all who own land or do business or in any way wield influence in one state, thereby drawing benefits from that state, but are never or rarely on hand to accept corresponding responsibilities.

1735 Swift *Drapier's Ltrs.* [*OED*]. The other articles by which we [the Irish] are altogether losers and England a gainer. ... The occasional absentees for business, health or diversion.

B. These English absentee landlords supplied the pattern for criticism of similar practices in America. The plantation owners in the South were among the chief offenders.

1854 Richard Hildreth *Memoirs of a Fugitive* 170. The absentee aristocracy congregates in Charleston, or dapples and astonishes the cities and watering places of the North by its profuse extravagance and reckless dissipation. The plantations are left to the sole management of overseers. ...

Later, the word was applied to those who enriched themselves in any way from the country's resources and spent their wealth abroad.

1875 Bret Harte *Gabriel Conroy* Bk. V. ch. 2. The rival paper ... had an editorial on "absenteeism," and spoke, crushingly, of those men who, having enriched themselves out of the resources of One Horse Gulch, were now seeking to dissipate that wealth in the excesses of foreign travel.

Because this passage is written satirically, we can assume that the topic of absenteeism was somewhat overworked. Nevertheless, the following quotation is patently sincere:

1875 in Barnes *Thurlow Weed* 509. And it is painful to reflect that in consequence of this lavish expenditure upon a class that never earned a dollar, there are other tens of thousands without employment, and suffering for food, fuel, and raiment. And last, though not least, are the millions of gold sunk by Americans who idle away both their time and their money in Europe. Ireland is not now the only country demoralized by absenteeism.

By 1919 a much less tangible type of absenteeism had come into being—absentee capitalism.

1919 Lyman P. Powell *The Social Unrest* 262. Corporate bargainers range from small concerns, which retain much of the old personal contact between master and man, to far-flung enterprises governed by wire, which have injected a system of absentee capitalism into American industrial life as definite in its effects as is absentee landlordism.

In times of war, *absentee* took on a special meaning peculiar to the circumstances.

DAE: A loyalist who absented himself from his residence during the American Revolution.

1783 in *Life of Zachariah Chandler* 30. The occasion is this; the return of those persons to this country, who are known in Great Britain by the name of loyalists, but in America by those of conspirators, absentees, and tories.

During the American Civil War, soldiers absent without leave were called *absentees*.

1863 Morford *Shoulder-Straps* 135. That terrible something was absenteeism. Thousands and tens of thousands who should have been in their places in the army, were shamelessly absent when their brothers-in-arms were being sacrificed from their very want of numbers.

The absentee of World War II was the factory worker who did not turn up regularly for work, and the word is still used in this sense.

1948 *Cols. Citizen* 8 July 15. Addressing a labor meeting, the premier [of Czechoslovakia] scolded factory workers for a sharp decline in May's production. He said workers were guilty of absenteeism, tardiness, job-quitting....

It may be assumed that the term has frequently been used, without any particular opprobrium, to designate those voters who stayed away from the polls. An early instance:

1837 *New Yorker* 2 Dec. 586/3. The republican absentees numbered upwards of forty-one thousand,... and were of course far greater proportionably than the federal absentees.

absolute money.

During the struggle against paper money, the theory was evolved that the government has absolute power of making money out of any worthless material by putting its stamp on it. (See SOAP)

1876 in Garfield *Works* II. 252. "Absolute money"; that is, printed pieces of paper, called dollars, to be the only standard of value, the only legal tender for all debts, public and private, the only circulating medium. The advocates of this kind of "money," though few in numbers, claim the highest place as philosophers. The ablest defence of this doctrine will be found in a *brochure* published in St. Louis during the present year, in which the author says: "If such national legal-tender money is not of itself sovereign and absolute, but must be convertible into some other substance or thing, before it can command universal circulation, what matters it whether that other substance or thing be interest-bearing bonds or gold or silver coin? ... The coin despotism cannot be broken by substituting in its place the despotism of interest-bearing bonds."*

* Britton A. Hill *Absolute Money* 53.

1878 Ben Butler in *Cleve. Plain Dealer* 4 Oct. 2/2. We want absolute money, not redeemable in anything, not valuable in itself.

1878 *Harper's W.* 17 Aug. 647/1. The growth of the Greenback Party ... springs from the general prostration of industry, which was largely due to the very thing which is now proposed as a remedy. "Absolute money"—that is, redundant paper, or paper at discretion—was the cause of the expansion and fatal collapse [of industry].

1878 *Ib.* 24 Aug. 667/2 [quoting a declaration submitted by the State Republican Committee of Wisconsin]. "The printed bits of paper which some wild theorists propose to employ as currency, and which they term 'absolute money,' containing no promise of payment and no intrinsic value, would soon become absolute in one respect only. They would be absolutely worthless."

1878 *Ib.* 19 Nov. 916. [Cartoon ridiculing the concept: Central is a Thanksgiving dinner table; on the platter is a printed placard "This is an absolute turkey," other dishes show similar placards: "absolute mince pie," "absolute potatoes," etc. A young woman shows her husband an "absolute baby"; an old man warms his hands before an "absolute fire"; an unhappy man holds some "absolute money," and so on.] AN ABSOLUTE FRAUD—THE LOGIC OF ABSOLU-TISM—IF DOLLARS, WHY NOT EVERYTHING ELSE?

abstractionist.

A. In reference to the anti-slavery movement:

1856 Cartwright *Autobiog.* 437. I have indulged in the fond hope that these Northern abstractionists [Methodist Episcopal preachers opposed to slavery] would, if they cannot be reconciled to conservative, consistent Methodism, . . . go and set up for themselves, and let the old conservative Methodist Episcopal Church alone. . . .
1875 Garfield in *Gt. Deb.* VIII. 228. The men who began this anti-slavery struggle forty years ago were denounced as dreamers, abstractionists.

B. Used specifically in Virginia politics, with patently no reference to anti-slavery sentiments.

1880 Congdon *Reminiscences* 80 [refers to Tyler as] a stiff Virginia abstractionist. . . .
1886 *Perley's Reminiscences* 71. Tazewell [a Senator from Va.] . . . was a first class Virginia abstractionist and an avowed hater of New England.

As neither Tyler nor Tazewell are admired by the respective authors, we may assume that *Virginia abstractionist* is not a term of approbation. It is not uncommon in America to apply the same term with opposite meaning to opposing factions, and therefore it may be that a Virginia abstractionist was a pro-slavery man, and Tyler's reputation bears this out; when the term is linked with "hating New England," agrarianism opposed to industrialism may also be inferred.

Accidency.

"His Accidency" was the derisive title applied, first to John Tyler, and later to Andrew Johnson, both of whom succeeded to the Presidency of the United States through being Vice President when their superiors died in office.

"His Accidency" is a happy blending of ingredients: the fortuitous manner of achieving to the presidency, the unfitness for such a position, and a play on "His Excellency," the approved form for addressing the President.

That the title "His Excellency" never fell trippingly from the American tongue, and that the office of Vice President did not in itself command great respect, is suggested in the following story; though the story may be apocryphal, its survival indicates that it contained a sentiment which had some appeal.

1925 Thomas R. Marshall *Hoosier Salad* 228. [When the first Senate of the United States convened, there was much discussion about how to address the President, avoiding "the trappings of royalty"; "His Excellency" was finally agreed upon.] While unrecorded, there is a legendary story that . . . one of the Senators from Virginia, who did not like Vice-President Adams, suggested *sotto voce,* that the official title of the vice-president of the United States should be His Superfluous Excellency.
1842 *Ohio Statesman* 29 March 3/2. "His Accidency," as the [Ohio State] Journal sometimes styles the acting President. . . .
1843 *Cleve. Herald* 16 Sept. 2/1. So much for John Tyler's popularity with the "rank and file" of the Locofoco party.

—Not even a Postmaster in the county could be found to deposit a vote for his Accidency!
1880 Congdon *Reminiscences* 80. They began to nickname him [Tyler] "His Accidency" at once.

"His Accidency" appears again when Andrew Johnson filled out Lincoln's second term of office.
1866 *Nation* 8 March 299 [ed.] "Excellency and Accidency."
1867 *Wash. D. Morn. Chron.* 2 Jan. 1/1. The last "dodge" of "His Accidency" is to threaten the interposition of the Supreme Court against such legislation [the ratification of the Amendment by three-fourths of the loyal States].

If it is not a mere coincidence that few cases of "His Accidency" have been discovered since Johnson's time, although four terms have been filled out by the Vice President, we may assume that it is due, at least in part, to the fact that "His Excellency" has fallen into disuse, and no special form of address for the President has common recognition.
1872 *Ann. of Cleve.* 20 July No. 2723. Who wouldn't choose the honest and noble Senator Wilson, of Massachusetts, before the scheming, trading demagogue Governor Brown, of Missouri, as 'his accidency,' in case of a Vice Presidential successor to the Presidency?

accountability.

The quality of being answerable for one's actions and conduct.
1794 S. Williams *Hist. Vermont* 140. No mutual checks and ballances [sic], accountability and responsibility.

Particularly prominent during Jackson's administration as a synonym for his widely-known doctrine of "responsibility."

1834 Jackson in *Reg. of Deb.* 31 May III. 18. No joint power of appointment is given to the two Houses of Congress; nor is there any *accountability* to them as one body.
1838 *Cong. Globe* 10 Dec. 21/1 ... the great Democratic doctrine of accountability.

adamantine.

A. An extreme faction of the hardshell (q.v.) democracy.
1853 *N.Y. Trib.* 15 Nov. 4/3. The "Adamantines" of the District of Columbia had a meeting last night in Washington City, to congratulate the "Hards" on the result of the recent election in this State.
1854 A. M. Murray *Ltrs from U.S.* I.197. Party terms ... such as Adamantines, Hard-shells, Soft-shells, Loco-focos, Rick-burners, and Pollywogs.

B. Later a faction in Illinois.
1874 *Chic. Times* 28 Aug. 1/2. Lamentations of the Adamantine Jeremiahs of Illinois. (head)

[advertisements.]

The great interest attached to political words is frequently exploited by business men in order to advertise their wares and products. A few characteristic examples:
1838 *Dayton Dem. Herald* 24 Feb. 4/2. Removal of the Deposites. D. Edwards. Wholesale and Retail Grocer Would inform the good citizens of Dayton and the country, that he has removed his stock of goods next door to Myers & Knode.
1861 *N.Y. D. Trib.* 29 June 3/1. UNION [ornamented] L.P.E.C. & C. Ladies Patent Electro Collars and Cuffs 6 sets for 50 cents.
1866 *Wash. D. Morn. Chron.* 15 Jan. 3/3. Shall the Negro Vote?
The "Rads" cry out with joyous shout, "Hurrah for the Suffrage Bill!"
While the Johnson men make ugly mouths
At such a nauseous pill.

But whether it be right or wrong to let
the Negro vote
I'm sure a man's of no account
With a badly fitting coat.

. . . .

Now Koppel is the very man
To meet your special case.
His suits are always sure to fit
With perfect ease and grace.

H. Koppel, 15th Street.

1868 *Harper's W.* 17 Oct. 670/3. A Scrub
Race.
Seymour, Seymour is the man;
Then elect him, if you can.
Grant and Colfax, Boys in Blue,
Blair himself is after you;
And the Wickedest of Men,
While in Water Street his den,
Has a host of voters too,
Good and bad, what will you do?
Then, in Broadway, Grecian Bend
Seeks for homage, and will send
Weakness, discord, and despair
In the ranks of Grant and Blair,
Vote for WOLCOTT and PAIN PAINT
Try this cure for your complaint;
For your efforts then shall be
Crowned with glorious victory.

See also [TRADE NAMES.]

agrarian(-ism).

A. The radical character of the
Roman agrarian law introduced
by Licinius in 367 B.C. and renewed by Tiberius Sempronius
Gracchus in 133 B.C., caused violent disturbances in consequence
of which the word *agrarian* even
before its use in America became
associated with the idea of extreme
leftism and demagogism.

1774 J. Adams *Works* IV. 527. Another
subject of dispute was soon introduced,
"which served to the last hour of the
[Roman] republic as an object of popular zeal and furnished a specious pretence
to ambitious and designing men to capti-
vate the ears of the populace—an equal
division of land, known by the name of
an agrarian law."

B. In early American politics
the word consequently is used as
a synonym of *Jacobinical* and *democratic* (in the Federalist sense) :

1787 Madison *Fed. Conv.* 26 June 243.
No agrarian attempts have yet been made
in this country; but symptoms of a levelling spirit . . . have sufficiently appeared.
1797 Paine *Works* III. 332. The fault is
in the system, and it has stolen imper-
ceptibly upon the world, aided afterwards
by the agrarian law of the sword.
1818 Birkbeck *Ltrs.* 82. I don't want an
Agrarian Law to define the limit of every
man's estate.
1837 Buckingham *America* I. 56. There
was no term of opprobrium too severe
for them [the Whigs] to apply to their
opponents, the Democratic Republicans.
They called them atheists, infidels, agrarians, incendiaries. . . .
1844 Seward *Writings* III. 263. Universal
education is the great agrarian agent—
the leveller we must use to prevent wealth
and power from building up aristocratic
institutions, and dividing society into unequal classes.

C. In particular, the word
was used against the workingman's
party:

1829 *Courier and Enquirer* in Werner
Tammany 41. There is a scandalous report about town that Miss Epicene
Wright has abstracted, or rather Agrari-
anized, a pair of Mr. Jennings's inexpres-
sibles, and means to appear in them at
her next lecture.
1829 *Workingman's Adv.* 14 Nov. 3/4. The
Commercial of last evening, in an article
headed "The Agrarians," by which title
he is pleased to denominate the working
men of this city, says. . . .
1829 *Ib.* 5 Dec. 3/1. On the subject of
the agrarian law, the most incorrect and
absurd opinions prevail; the general impression—an impression which our enemies have taken especial pains to incul-
cate—being that an agrarian law is
synonymous with a general system of
plundering the rich and sharing the spoils
by the poor.

1836 J. H. Perkins *Memoirs* I. 136. By Agrarianism we understand sometimes a disposition, and sometimes a system, that would attack the present rights of property. Not content with forbidding the law to aid individuals in the acquisition of wealth, it would make it strip them of their present possessions, and prevent future acquisition.

1838 *Ohio St. Jrnl.* 7 Nov. 3/5 ... still we think the only true course to pursue towards her [Fanny Wright] is to stay away from her brawlings and treat her with the sovereign contempt her outrages demand. This is the only way to put down such a poisonous scatter of Infidelity and Agrarianism.

1841 Buckingham *America* I. 124. "Agrarians" is the name here given to people who meet to recommend the government to keep the revenues in safe custody, in treasuries of their own, instead of intrusting it to speculating banks.

1844 *Wash. Intelligencer* 16 Aug. 3/3. Agrarians in the United States ... being nothing more than English Chartism transplanted to this country.

D. The anti-rent movement in New York State (1839 and the following years) caused a retrograde development in the meaning of the word, the connection of which with land problems had been forgotten during the preceding period but which was now revived:

1846 Cooper *Redskins* ch. ii. I certainly do not apprehend that any direct attempt is about to be made in New York, to divide its property; nor do I fear any open, declared agrarian statute....

E. In the debates on the Homestead Bill:

1852 Chandler in *Gt. Deb.* X. 45. Sir, let me say that this cry of "agrarian laws" and the Gracchi are inapposite. By agrarian laws people are led to understand a legislative attempt forcibly to equalize the possession of lands. Sir, no such attempt is made in this bill.

1852 Johnson in *Ib.* X. 48. The opponents of this bill seemingly think that they have erected a rampart that is impregnable ... to be sustained by three main barriers, or columns; on the center one they have written "unconstitutional"; on the right-hand column they have inscribed "diminution of the revenue"; on the left-hand one, "rank demagogism and agrarianism."

F. Later uses of the word take its status back to that before 1839, its connection with land problems again becoming obscure.

1855 Hambleton *H. A. Wise* 355. [The Republican party] will defend the state against agrarianism, freesoilism and abolitionism.

1859 *At. Mon.* April III. 394. Of late years we have heard much of Socialists, Communists, Fourierites and so forth; but the word Agrarians comprehends all these, and is often made to include men who have no more idea of engaging in social reforms than they have of pilgrimizing to the Fountains of the Nile.

1861 in *Northern Editorials* II. 606. Let those who would carp at this suggestion [land as payment for Southern wrongs] as too agrarian....

1866 Lowell *Pol. Essays* 242. We have heard enough of New England radicalism, as if that part of the country where there is the most education and the greatest accumulation of property in the hands of the most holders were the most likely to be carried away by what are called agrarian theories.

1875 Weed in Barnes *Weed* 513. Let it be remembered always that the real purpose of these combinations—for which we are unhappily indebted to the worst specimens of English, French, and German radicalism—is, first as "socialists" and then as "communists," to sow the seeds of agrarianism and infidelity among us.

1878 *Nation* 14 Nov. 296. An attack ... [on the gov't. credit] largely supported by avowed communists and agrarians, would probably succeed.

alarmist.

One addicted to raising alarms; a panic-monger.

A word which in the minds of most people probably suggests the periods before the first and second World Wars, but which is considerably older than that.

A. The European history of the word goes back to the end of the 18th century. It is of French origin and was coined during the French Revolution.

in Brunot *Histoire de la langue Française* IX. 807. "Alarmiste" est attribué a Barère. Il est frequent à l'epoche de la convention et du directoire pour désigner les gens qui répandent des nouvelles destineés à inquiéter et a justifié les violences.

In England Sheridan uses it in 1794:

Sp. III. 214. Will the train of newly-titled alarmists, of supernumerary negotiators, of pensioned paymasters, agents and commissaries, thank him for remarking to us how profitable their panic has been to themselves, and how expensive to the country?

Later the word seems to have been applied to those who anticipated disastrous consequences from the enactment of the pending parliamentary reform.

1827 Macaulay *Sp.* I. 57. But in all these cases, and in none more than the last, there were various differences of principle; not only were Whig and Tory, Alarmist and Reformer, to coalesce; but during the war, and for the sake of carrying it on to a better issue, they who were the authors of it, were united with its constant and sturdy opponents.

Again in the eighteen fifties, during the armament race between England and France, *alarmist* meant those who were afraid of a French invasion.

Cobden *Pol. Writings* II. 219–220. There is something very puerile in the recent attempts to frighten the country with stories about secret preparations in the French dockyards. . . . Such tactics on the part of the alarmists are novel, and not complimentary to the intelligence of the public.

B. In America the word must have been used much more frequently than we can show at the present time.

1840 White of Ky. in *Cong. Globe* App. 765/1. Sir, open and bold usurpations never alarm me. I fear no danger of the perpetuity of this Government, from the assaults of the manly tyrant or despot. I can look with some forbearance upon the unjust pretensions to power, asserted and defended upon principle; yet, whilst I protest, I am no alarmist.

1846 Clayton in *Niles Reg.* 2 Feb. 393/2. I entirely concur with the views which the senators from Michigan and Florida have expressed on this subject. They are not alarmists; but, in the high place they occupy, they have exposed the naked and unguarded condition of their country, and, so doing, they were strictly in the path of their duty.

1866 Julian *Sp.* 328. Sir, while I dislike the occupation of an alarmist, I must say that I have seen few darker seasons than the present since the first battle of Bull Run. The President has not kept the faith. He has not favored the hanging of a single rebel leader.

The following example shows an extension of meaning (alarmist: person of a timid or pessimistic mind) which could hardly have occurred unless the word had been in general use.

1904 Lynde *Grafters* 108. Contrary to the expectations of the alarmists and the lawyers, and somewhat to the disappointment of the latter, the vested interests showed no disposition to test the constitutionality of the act in the courts.

Algerine.

The colloquial name of a faction in Rhode Island politics at the time of the Dorr War.

1842 *Wash. Intell.* 17 May 3/4. It was rumored that the Algerines had laid a plan to arrest Gov. Dorr as soon as he arrived in the State, at Kingston, and imprison him in Washington or Newport county.

1842 *N.Y. W. Trib.* 10 Sept. 4/5. All those accused of being "Algerines" were cleared off the ground.

1844 *Cong. Globe* 11 March 360/1. The gentleman from Rhode Island had talked of "ruffianism" in that State, and of "Algerines"; but if the proposition he made to this house was not a specimen of "Algerineism," he apprehended it was not to be found in Rhode Island.

The name *Algerine* is explained by the fact that the Algerine War (1815), brought about by the enslavement of American prisoners in Algiers, was not forgotten by the middle of the 19th century, at which time the word *Algerine* still suggested the idea of slavery, and in particular, white slavery.

1820 *R.I. American* 8 Feb. 3/1. The very Algerines despise such conduct as this [imprisonment for debt].

1820 in *Ann. of Cong.* 11 Feb. 1244. To these suggestions I will only reply that they have been the arguments of aristocrats and tyrants in all ages of the world; that they are now used for the purpose of justifying all the usurpations which have ever been committed on the rights and liberties of mankind, and that by them the Algerines defend all their enormities.

1824 *Cinc. Nat. Rep.* 28 Sept. 2/4. The "Algerines" will have their own way. They cannot be gulled. They are determined

to support the Second Washington of America.

1848 (Salem, Ohio) *Anti-Slavery Bugle* 14 July 1/6. Who questions, said Mr. S. [Gerrit Smith] in substance, but Dr. Bailey would have exulted in the conduct of the men now imprisoned at Washington, if, instead of black men in American slavery, the persons they sought to liberate had been American white men in Algerine slavery?

1855 Hildreth *White Slave* 401. Shall America be what the fathers and founders of her independence wished and hoped—a free democracy, based upon the foundation of human rights, or shall she degenerate into a miserable republic of Algerines, domineered over by a little self-constituted autocracy of slave-holding lynchers and blackguards, utterly disregardful of all law, except their own will and pleasure?

aliunde (*L.* "from another place").

This term was popular for a few years, following its use by the electoral commission—probably by Judge Bradley—in its decision on the disputed election of 1876. The satirical effect of the term was brought about by the commission's statement that it would not investigate anything which may have been irregular in the elections or in the counting of the votes; it was concerned only with the returns.

1877 S. S. Cox *Thirty Yrs.* 658. Why, sir, everything as to testimony and facts and forging and perjury and force is *aliunde* —outside—not to be considered. Truth and justice and morality and fairdealing— *aliunde.* The House is *aliunde.* All its acts and the acts of its committees and their reports, all the facts gathered in these Southern States—*aliunde!*

1877 in *Cong. Rec.* 137/2. With one fell blow of his legal hammer, he [Sen. Edmunds] killed that veracious witness Mr. *Aliunde,* and would not let the people

of this land have the man for whom they had voted to be their ruler.
1880 *N.Y. World* 17 Nov. 4/1. To the Political Nomenclature of Republicanism, already enriched by Mr. Stoughton's "clerical error" and Judge Bradley's "aliunde"....
1889 Shapley *Mulhooley* 52. It does not require an inspiration of genius to perceive that when a man makes from twenty to a hundred thousand dollars a year out of an office that pays no salary and does not allow car-fare or postage stamps as perquisites, he makes it *aliunde*.

[allegory.]

Among the favorite devices of political satire is the use of elaborate allegories. The vicissitudes of an election may, for instance, be compared to a dangerous sea voyage; this idea furnishes a "master metaphor," around which a number of secondary nautical images will be grouped. The following are typical examples:
1788 in Hart *Source Book* 178. "The New Roof."
I. Come muster, my lads, your mechanical tools,
   Your saws and your axes, your hammers and rules;
   Bring your mallets and planes, your level and line,
   And plenty of pins of American pine:
   For our roof we will raise, and our song still shall be,
   Our government firm, and our citizens free.
II. Come, up with *the plates,* lay them firm on the wall,
   Like the people at large, they're the ground work of all;
   Examine them well, and see that they're sound,
   Let no rotten part in our building be found:
   For our roof we will raise, and our song still shall be

A government firm, and our citizens free.

. . . .

V. Our *king-posts* are *judges;* how upright they stand,
   Supporting the *braces;* the laws of the land:
   The laws of the land, which divide right from wrong,
   And strengthen the weak, by weak'ning the strong:
   For our roof we will raise, and our song still shall be
   Laws equal and just, for a people that's free.
VI. Up! up! with the *rafters;* each frame is a *state:*
   How nobly they rise! their span, too, how great!
   From the north to the south, o'er the whole they extend,
   And rest on the walls, whilst the walls they defend:
   For our roof we will raise, and our song still shall be
   Combined in strength, yet as citizens free.
1820 in *Gt. Deb.* IV. 92. Rather would he call slavery a contagious disease in the body politic. Like smallpox, it ought to be confined in the smallest possible limits. The Congress of 1787 introduced a sort of political vaccination into the constitutions of Ohio, Indiana, and Illinois, which effectually secured those States from the evil; and I am also for extending the same salutary process to our infant sister, Missouri. And why? Is it to injure her? Is it to mutilate or disfigure her? No, sir, it is to secure her health and to preserve her beauty!
1824 *Cinc. Nat. Rep.* 4 June 1/3. PRESIDENTIAL SQUADRON. The good ship, the JOHN QUINCY ADAMS, which set sail some time since for Port President under a fine breeze, lately put into Consideration Bay for recruit, being short of hands; some on board sea-sick, in consequence of having for the last six weeks of her voyage, to beat against wind and tide. Some think her ultimate success doubtful.

1824 *Cinc. Gazette* 26 Oct. 3/2. "STEAM-BOAT ACCIDENT." At the time the *Adams* passed the *Andrew Jackson,* the well known and beautiful Boat HENRY CLAY, having a full cargo of domestic manufactures, was lying to in a snug cove, taking in wood. Soon after getting under way, she came up with the wreck of the *Jackson, and found her a sheer hulk.* All on board was confusion, bluster, and dismay.... On the 24th she [the *Henry Clay*] overhauled the *Adams* which had *brought to all standing,* on the headland of TARIFF ISLAND, where it is supposed she had stranded. The Clay continued her route with a fine *head of steam,* and it is confidently believed she will make the Ohio lighthouse of Port President on the 29th.

1834 in Samuel J. May *Recoll. of the Antislavery Conflict* 118–119. Mr. Thompson then went on to give us a graphic, glowing account of the long and fierce conflict they had had in England for the abolition of slavery in the British West Indies. His eloquence rose to a still higher order. His narrative became *a continuous metaphor,* admirably sustained. He represented the antislavery enterprise in which he had been so long engaged as a stout, well-built ship, manned by a noble-hearted crew, launched upon a stormy ocean, bound to carry inestimable relief to 300,000 sufferers in a far-distant land. He clothed all the kinds of opposition they had met, all the difficulties they had contended with, in imagery suggested by the observation and experience of the voyager across the Atlantic in the most tempestuous season of the year. In the height of his descriptions, my attention was withdrawn from the emotions enkindled in my own bosom sufficiently to observe the effect of his eloquence upon half a dozen boys, of twelve or fourteen years of age, sitting together not far from the platform. They were completely possessed by it. When the ship reeled or plunged or staggered in the storms, they unconsciously went through the same motions. When the enemy attacked her, the boys took the liveliest part in battle, manning the guns, or handling shot and shell, or pressing forward to repulse the boarders. When the ship struck upon an iceberg, the boys almost fell from their seats in the recoil. When the sails and topmasts were wellnigh carried away by the gale, they seemed to be straining themselves to prevent the damage; and when at length the ship triumphantly sailed into her destined port with colors flying and signals of glad tidings floating from her topmast, and the shout of welcome rose from thousands of expectant freedmen on the shore, the boys gave three loud cheers, "Hurrah! Hurrah!! Hurrah!!!" This irrepressible explosion of their feeling brought them at once to themselves. They blushed, covered their faces, sank down on their seats, one of them upon the floor. It was an ingenuous, thrilling tribute to the surpassing power of the orator, and only added to the zest and heartiness with which the whole audience applauded (to use the words of another at the time) "the persuasive reasonings, the earnest appeals, the melting pathos, the delightful but caustic irony and enrapturing eloquence of Mr. Thompson."

[alliteration.]

The attractions of alliteration have frequently been used for propagandistic purposes. A few random examples:

1848 *Xenia* (Ohio) *Torchlight* 3 Aug. 2/6. Konsekently King and Kourt Kandidate Kass Kant Kwite Kome in.

1875 *Cinc. Enquirer* 10 Oct. 4/1 ... Hayes, hard money and hard times. There are too many H's in this business.

1880 *N.Y. Trib.* 9 Oct. 4/2. And yet the Democratic party appears to be in favor of "a full vote, free ballot and fair count."

1904 *Judge* 3 Sept. 1. The Three R's of Politics. Republican: Roosevelt, Republicanism and Reelection. Democrat: Resignation, Rejection and Retirement.

1928 *New Rep.* 7 Nov. 325/2 ... plunk for prosperity, protection, prohibition,

Protestantism and the freedom of the **P's**.

1954 *Cols. Citizen* 29 Oct. [U.P. release] In Trenton, N.J., Stevenson accused the Republicans of winding up the campaign with a "frenzied outburst of smut, smear and slander."

almighty nigger (democracy).

Characterized by an obsession to the maintenance of the status quo in regard to the Negro question. Based upon the formula of *almighty dollar.*

1857 *Ann. of Cleve.* 21 Aug. No. 1546. Very interesting, indeed, is this "game of brag" adopted by the Almighty Nigger Democracy.

amalgamate (amalgamation, amalgamationist, amalgamator).

Originally a chemical term meaning to soften or dissolve a metal by adding mercury, to combine mercury with another metal.

In politics a term meaning to unite classes, races, etc. into a whole.

A. The political history of the word begins in France (1793) when the regular army and the national guard were combined into one unit.

Brunot *Histoire de la langue Française* IX. 939. C'est ce mélange des volontaires des troupes de ligne qu'on a désigné par le mot amalgame.

Since this measure was definitely in line with the democratic tendencies of the time, the word, although principally administrative in significance, also has political implications.

Ib. L'armeé "amalgameé" fut passionément républicaine.

Also in England, where the word appears first in 1797, the political connotation is apparent.

Anti-Jacobin I. 169. Liberty's friends thus all learn to amalgamate.

By 1848 Bulwer uses the word in reference to the mixture of races by intermarriage.

Harold I, ii. 12. These turbulent invaders had amalgamated amicably with the native race.

B. Very likely this use is much older, since the specialized meaning later found in American political language (sexual relations between whites and negroes) seems to pre-suppose a more general meaning. In fact, Clay's use of *amalgamation* in 1829, although referring to the Negro problem, does not seem to stress sexual implications.

in Colton *Clay* I. 197. But if the dangers of the civil contest which I have supposed could be avoided, separation or amalgamation is the only peaceful alternative....

Still less are such implications to be found in 1834 in the *Liberator,* 21 June, 1/2, where the writer of an article entitled "Amalgamation" refers to the use of a church by both white and negro. However, in 1834, the word has already become a synonym of *abolitionist.*

1834 (Boston) *Liberator* 27 Sept. 1/1. It is generally known that fears have been entertained by many of our Southern fellow citizens that the Abolitionists, amalgamationists, Tappan-men, or by whatever other name they may be called, would be able to make so many converts in the Northern States as to put in jeopardy our only certain guarantee of liberty and independence, to wit, the *National Union.*

That from the beginning the word had an erotic connotation can be assumed from the following:

1835 in Hone *Diary* 181. So in Boston too ...a meeting of the Female Abolition Society was broken up by the mob. The lovely amalgamators were assembled to listen to the honeyed sounds of Mr. Garrison's voice, whose enmity to Southern slave-holders seems to be equal to his affection for the daughters of the "universal Yankee nation."

A similar connotation is evident in the use of the terms *practical amalgamation, practical amalgamationist.*

1839 *Alex. W. Mess.* 19 June 3/5. The populace became incensed at a most glaring instance of practical amalgamation. One of the parties was a huge negro man and the other a white girl.
1840 (Milledgeville) *Ga. Jrnl.* 15 Sept. 2/2. Now, sir! suppose ... that by the aid of the abolitionists, and the voice of the Union Electors, Martin Van Buren and Richard M. Johnson,—THE ONE AN ULTIMATE ABOLITIONIST IN PRINCIPLE AND AN ADVOCATE OF FREE NEGRO SUFFRAGE—THE OTHER [Johnson] A PRACTICAL AMALGAMATIONIST, who has been wedded to two negro women, and is now honored by half a dozen mulatto children, of his own get, are raised to the Presidency....

Similar attacks on Johnson are found frequently during the campaigns of 1836 and 1840 and certainly largely contributed to the popularity of the word. The word continued in frequent use as long as slavery was a living issue.

1865 Wendell Phillips in S. S. Cox *Eight Yrs. in Congress* 359. Now, I am going to say something that I know will make the New York "Herald" use its small capitals and notes of admiration, and yet no well-informed man this side of China but believes it in the very core of his heart. That is, "amalgamation," a word that the Northern apologist for slavery has always used so glibly, but which you never heard from a Southerner. Amalgamation! Remember this, the youngest of you, that on the 4th day of July, 1863, you heard a man say that in the light of all history, in virtue of every page he ever read, he was an amalgamationist to the utmost extent. I have no hope for the future, as this country has no past, and Europe has no past, but in that sublime mingling of races which is God's own method of civilizing and elevating the world.

C. Amalgamation also turns up as a synonym of *fusion* (q.v.): the merging of two or more parties into one.

1830 *N. Eng. w. Review* 1 March 2/1. Amalgamation. [Article on attempts to unite Conn. Jacksonmen and Adamsmen.]
1851 Seba Smith *Thirty Yrs.* 346. We can 'malgamate the twenty parties down into two.

America first.

A slogan popularized by Pres. Harding but first used by Pres. Wilson.

1914 Wilson *Public Papers* III. 158. My thought is of America. I am speaking, I feel sure, the earnest wish and purpose of every thoughtful American that this great country of ours, which is, of course, the first in our thoughts and in our hearts....
1915 *Ib.* III. 303. Our whole duty, for the present at any rate, is summed up in this motto, "America first." Let us think of America before we think of Europe, in order that America may be fit to be Europe's friend when the day of tested friendship comes.... 379. I would not be afraid upon the test of "America first" to take a census of all the foreign-born citizens of the United States, for I know that the vast majority of them came here because they believed in America.
?1919 in Daugherty *Harding Tragedy* 16. It [Harding sp. at Ohio Soc. of N.Y.] struck a keynote that was never changed throughout his campaign for the nomi-

nation, the deliberations of the National Convention, his speech of acceptance, and his campaign for election. He made "America First" the outstanding issue of the campaign.

1921 Harding *Our Common Country* 64. When the responsibility for leadership in putting America back on the main road was placed upon me, I said to myself that we must all unite under the slogan "America First." When I say America First I mean not only that America maintain her own independence and be first in fulfilling her obligations to the world ... but I mean that at home any special interest, any class, any group of our citizenship that has arrayed itself against the interests of all, must learn that at home, as well as abroad, America First has a meaning, profound, and, with God's aid, everlasting. **1921** *Ib.* 160. But we do ask all to think of "America First," to serve "America First," to defend "America First," and plight an unalterable faith in "America First."

Perhaps because of the association of *America first* with the isolationism of the 1920's, the slogan received connotations of bigotry and prejudice and later became the name of an American fascist group, thus having gone full circle from its early usage by Wilson. **1932** Carter *What We Are About to Receive* 172. Hence "America First!" is apt to prove a boomerang to the party which adopts it. **1943** Carlson *Under Cover* 146. True was the first to apply the fascist-nationalist phrase America First when in August, 1934 he organized America First, Inc. "for the protection of the Constitution, American Industry, and individual enterprise." ...260. The American First Committee had become the voice of American Facism and the spearhead aimed at the heart of Democracy, carrying to their doom many who were innocent and would have resigned in disgust had they known what went on behind the scenes.

America for the Americans.

A slogan of the Know-Nothing party. Suggested, perhaps, by Washington's order, the slogan is found in many variations.

1854 *N.Y. sw Trib.* 7 Nov. 4/1. Nothing is more untrue to the whole spirit and meaning of our history than the maxim, "America for the Americans." **1855** *Sons of the Sires* 19. Apprehensions which had a home in the mind of Washington, when he said to his staff, "Put none but Americans on guard to-night." **1855** *Ib.* 45. We regard, moreover, the principle that Americans should rule America a just one, for the reason that, circumstances being equal, Americans are better qualified to rule. **1855** "Phila. Plat." 9 June in *Young Sam* 7. Americans by birth, education and training—thus fulfilling the maxim, "Americans only shall govern America." **1855** in Hambleton *Wise* 92. It has been said, "Let Americans rule America." I say let American principles rule America. **1856** John P. Sanderson *Rep. Landmarks* 334. America for Americans, is a demand not based upon narrow sectarianisms, or mere party predilections. It is no new doctrine.... Did not Daniel O'Connell raise the talismanic cry among his countrymen of *Ireland for the Irish?* **1856** *Middletown Banner of Liberty* 53/4. Yet the Know Nothings, in spite of all these facts, persist in proclaiming their hypocritical doctrine, "Americans must rule America!" **1866** Sennoia Rubek *Chivalry, Slavery, and Young America* 30. "Americans this land must rule," The maxim of the native school—

Later use:

1896 in Depew *Memoirs* 149. And his [McKinley's] personality will carry into the presidential chair the aspirations of the voters of America, of the families of America, of the homes of America, protection to American industry and America for Americans.

Americanism.

From its early associations with the Know-Nothing party, *Americanism* has been a controversial word, its meaning always differently interpreted. No *one* positive element can be traced, but there does seem to be a common feeling that it should not be a label one hides behind.

1852 Webster *Works* XIII. 535. Well, gentlemen, let us adhere to that spirit of union, of nationalism, of Americanism, and let no narrow, selfish, local policy— no trifling concern of the day and the moment—influence the counsels of Massachusetts.
1856 *Ann. of Cleve.* 22 May No. 2302. There may be a great deal of Know Nothingism about the Fillmore-Donelson creed, but it contains precious little Americanism.
1860 *Iowa St. Jrnl.* in *Northern Eds.* II. 924. But within the last few years a spirit of intolerance, first developed under the cloak of Americanism, and rapidly merged into sectional hatred against the South....
1888 *Nation* 12 July 23/1. Men...who pride themselves upon their "Americanism" as being the only genuine brand.
1890 Roosevelt *Works* IX. 217. There is one point upon which I wish to lay especial stress; that is, the necessity for a feeling of broad, radical, and intense Americanism, if good work is to be done in any direction.
1894 *Ib.* XV. 15. There are plenty of scoundrels always ready to try to belittle reform movements or to bolster up existing iniquities in the name of Americanism; but this does not alter the fact that the man who can do most in this country is and must be the man whose Americanism is most sincere and intense.
1896 *Puck* 26 Feb. But he [Puck] will not plead to the charge of un-Americanism until the definition of that word as revised by the Jingos is the generally accepted one. When "buncombe" is a synonym for "Americanism" and "blatherskite" for "patriot," then Puck will plead guilty.
1896 Schurz *Writings* V. 259. There has, of late, been much loose speech about "Americanism." Is not this [peace with honor] good Americanism? It is surely to-day the Americanism of those who love their country most.
1908 Roosevelt *Works* XII. 478. Americanism is a question of principle, of purpose, of idealism, of character;...not a matter of birthplace, or creed, or line of descent.

American system.

A. The earliest usages indicate it is a term applying to principles of American government:

1787 Hamilton in *Federalist* No. 11. Let the thirteen States, bound together in a strict and indissoluble Union, concur in erecting one great American system, superior to the control of all transatlantic force or influence, and able to dictate the terms of the connection between the old and the new world.
1817 Jefferson in 1830 *Niles Reg.* 12 June 294. The history of the last twenty years has been a sufficient lesson for us all to depend for necessaries on ourselves alone; and I hope that twenty years more will place the American hemisphere under a system of its own....

B. In 1824 Henry Clay brought about a change of meaning by appropriating the phrase as a recommendation of his tariff bill:

Ann. of Congress 18th Cong. I Sess. II. 1978. That remedy consists in modifying our foreign policy, and in adopting a genuine American system.

This narrowed meaning prevailed during the following period:

1828 *Argus of West. Am.* (Frankfort, Ky.) 6 Feb. 1/2. The friends of the [Adams] administration claim to themselves the credit of being the supporters of the American system.
1830 *New Eng. W. Rev.* 23 Oct. 2/1. The great defender of the American System

is made the object of the most bitter hatred and abuse of the Anti-Tariff party. **1844** *Wash. D. Globe* 24 Jan. 83/4. The American-system lawyers in Congress under their minimum and specific duties levied in terms that none but the initiated can understand and the manufacturers by their technical description of the articles they propose for taxation, make the whole tariff to an unlearned man, as inscrutable as a doctor bill or prescription.

C. Partly restoring the old general meaning, Herbert Hoover in a speech of August 11, 1945, described the "American system of freedom."

Add. Upon the Am. Road 259. The American system of life is unique in the world.... Our American system also holds to economic freedom.... We have proved the American system by raising the standards of life higher than any nation on earth.

Ananias.

Epithet applied to a person or organization which is felt to be insincere or misleading in dealing with the public.

A. An expression based upon Acts 5:3:

But Peter said, Ananias, why hath Satan filled thine heart to lie to the Holy Ghost, and to keep back part of the price of the land? **1876** *Cinc. Enquirer* 2 June 4/2. It [Miss. Platform] is a matchless product of Uriah Heep "harmony," or of Ananias "harmony."

B. As used by Theodore Roosevelt:

1911 *Writings* (Mem. Ed.) XV. 637. The type of magazine which I condemn is what may be called the Ananias muckraker type. No paper ... can be viler, or can play a more contemptible part in American politics, ... than the Ananias muck-raker type of magazine, the type of magazine of which the proprietor, editor, and writer seek to earn their livelihood by telling that what they know to be scandalous falsehoods about honest men.

The term may have been suggested to Roosevelt by the book by J. F. B. Lillard, *Poker Stories as Told by Statesmen, Soldiers ... Members of the Ananias Club and the Talent* (1896).

C. However, the Ananias Club is found in politics before Lillard's book:

1884 *N.Y. Times* 2 Nov. ... a transparency on which was inscribed, "I did it with my hatchet.—James G. Blaine, President of the Ananias Club."

angle-worm nomination. [ ]

1880 in Chidsey *Gentleman from N.Y.* 291. Grant, said Senator Conkling. Nobody else but Grant. There must be "no angleworm nomination," said he, doubtless thinking of Rutherford B. Hayes.

Anglomania.

A passion for what is English; in American politics acceptance of a monarchical and aristocratic system of government or sympathy with England in her conflicts with France and other nations.

A. In France, *Anglomanie* appears in the 18th century primarily in its wider non-political meaning. (See Voltaire, *Oeuvres Complètes*, Paris, 1885, XXV. 219.)

After the outbreak of the French-English war in 1793, the word becomes sharply political.

1793 in Brunot *Histoire de la langue Française* IX. 922. La Nation, qui avait tant admiré l'Angleterre, devint passionnément "anti-anglicane," on disait aussi "anti-anglaise." Malheur á qui avait la réputation d'être "anglisé" ou "anglomane."

In a note Brunot quotes from an unprinted source of 1793: "pour surveiller at atteindre l'aristocratie, les fédéralistes, les royalistes, et les anglomanes." This political use was short-lived; Brunot points to the fact that the 1798 Supplement to the *Dictionaire de l'Académie* gives only the non-political sense "sans tenir compte du sens que le mot avait pris en 1793."

B. In America the word seems to have been a political word from the very beginning. The connection between the American use of *Anglomania* and its cognates and the French word quoted by Brunot becomes clear from the fact that beginning in 1793 the counterparts of these French words turn up in American writings.

1787 Jefferson *Writings* VI. 370. It will be of great consequences to France and England, to have America governed by a Galloman or Angloman.
1793 Madison *Works* I. 584. Every Gazette I see (except that of the United States) exhibits a spirit of criticism on the Anglified complexion charged on the Executive politics.
1794 *Ib.* II. 4. But if he [Fauchét] is not an uncommon fool, or a traitor, it is impossible he can play into their hands, because the Anglicism stamped on the Aristocratic faction must warn him of its hostility to his objects.
1795 Jefferson *Writings* IX. 314. A treaty of alliance between England and the Anglomen, against the Legislature and the people of the United States.
1796 *Ib.* IX. 335–6. ... an Anglican monarchical aristocratical party has sprung up, whose avowed object is to draw over us the substance, as they have already

done the forms, of the British government.
1810 *Ib.* XII. 373. The toryism with which we struggled in '77, differed but in name from the federalism of '99, with which we struggled also; and the Anglicism of 1808, against which we are now struggling, is but the same thing in still another form.
1813 *Ib.* XIII. 210. Anglomany, monarchy, and separation, then, are the principles of the Essex federalists. Anglomany and monarchy alone, those of the Hamiltonians, and Anglomany alone, that of the portion among the *people* who call themselves federalists.

(Note the forms *Angloman, Anglomen,* which in view of Jefferson's scholarship has to be considered a joke rather than a folk etymology.)

Anglo-federalist we have not found before 1840, but it is probably much earlier:
Cong. Globe 11 Feb. App. 314. Money, then, being the fundamental principle of the Anglo-Federalists, the paper system the adopted means of making the Government subservient to this end, and the country thus drawn within the central influence of that system in England, can it be surprising that the most intense sympathies should have always subsisted between *this* party and *that* country?

C. In modern usage the word *Anglomania* is used in a social rather than a political sense. (Cf. Harrison, *The Anglomaniacs,* a satire on people who ape British manners.)

1904 T. R. in Bishop *Roosevelt* I. 348. If an Anglomaniac in social life goes into political life he usually becomes politically an Anglophobiac, and the occasional political Anglophobiac whose curious ambition it is to associate with "vacuity trimmed with lace" is equally sure to become an Anglomaniac in his new surroundings.

See also BRITISH TORY, TORY, WHIG.

annexation.

A. In public affairs, the word is known in England since 1626: Bacon *The Union of Eng. & Scot.* [*OED*]. To make one compounded annexation . . . out of the lands of both nations.

B. Our expectation of finding the term in connection with the Louisiana Purchase has as yet not been verified. The common word seems to have been *acquisition* [*Jefferson Cyc.* 509, 510]. However, in 1810 Henry Clay used *annex, annexation,* and *reannex,* referring to the Florida question:
1810 Clay *Sp.* I. 206. It is urged, that he has assumed powers belonging to congress, in undertaking to annex the portion of West Florida, between the Mississippi and the Perdido, to the Orleans territory. But congress, as has been shown, has already made this annexation, the limits of the Orleans territory, as prescribed by congress, comprehending the country in question.
Ib. 203. She [Spain] reannexes it to the residue of Louisiana—extends the jurisdiction of that government to it. . . .
1820 *Ib.* 40. Annexed to the United States, and we should have to extend our line of defence so as to embrace Florida.
1820 *Ib.* 403. The difference between those who might be disinclined to its annexation to our confederacy. . . .

In 1836 the word is used in connection with the planned incorporation of Texas into the United States:
1836 James *Houston* [Swartwout to Houston]. We think your Independence will soon be acknowledged. . . . We shall press hard for annexation.

C. When in 1844 and later, Polk and his party made the annexation of Texas a campaign issue, the word became a controversial one.
1843 Tyler *The Tylers* 131 [Gilmore to Calhoun]. The effect of annexation on the interests of our country, however, is the point to which public attention will be chiefly directed.
1844 Polk in *Ib.* 137. . . . it will be utterly hopeless to carry the vote of this state [Tenn.] for any man who is opposed to immediate annexation.
1844 in Garraty *Wright* 323 [campaign song]. Against Bank machination And high-tariff taxation— They will go for Annexation And Dallas, Polk, and Wright.
1846 Hone *Diary* I. 774. Annexation is now the greatest word in the American vocabulary. "Veni-vidi-vici!" is inscribed on the banners of every Caesar who leads a straggling band of American adventurers across the prairies. . . . Take care, my dear countrymen, of this annexation. . . .

Later uses:
1898 *Cong. Record* App. 508., I am not disposed to think that any statement of reasons . . . will have any real weight in deciding American action or the action of Congress as to the annexation of Hawaii.
1922 *Canadian Ann. Rev.* [Harding in Vancouver]. Do not encourage any enterprise looking to Canada's annexation of the United States.

antediluvian.

Epithet characterizing politicians or other public figures whose ideas are held to be hopelessly outdated.
1870 *N. Y. Times* 9 Aug. 4/3 . . . the proposal of a few antediluvians in Tennessee and other states to revive the Whig organization. . . . They awake now, like so many Rip Van Winkles.
1903 C. Lloyd *H. D. Lloyd* II.230. These antediluvian captains of industry, who call themselves masters, walk on Market Street or on Wall Street as if it were

Mount Ararat, and they were just landed from the Ark.

1934 Carter *New Dealers* 121 ... he [Warburg] served as an admirable buffer between the White House and the antediluvian Senators and the Stone Age financial community in New York.

Anthony rule.

An order of procedure for the Senate framed by Senator Henry Anthony of Rhode Island. See 1870 quot.

1870 *Cong. Globe* 17 June 4541/3. The Chair will state the distinction between this and what was popularly known in the Senate as the "Anthony rule," under which the Calendar was gone over, subject to objection. That order stated that no other business whatever should be entertained.

1876 *Cong. Record* 8 Aug. 5299/1., I will see whether I cannot get the approbation of the Senate to take up the Calendar under the Anthony rule.

1882 *Ib.* 3 Feb. 870/2. [This proposition opposes] what is called the Anthony rule. That rule has been usually adopted at each session of the Senate for a number of years. It was first adopted ten or twelve years ago, and it has operated very well. A great number of bills were passed under the five-minute rule and the docket was very largely reduced.

anti-American.

See UN-AMERICAN.

anti-auction. [ ]

1828 Hone *Diary* 5 Nov. I.6. A new party called anti-auction has been organized and is very active. Their opposition has been principally exerted against Messrs. Cambreleng and Verplanck, but these gentlemen are nevertheless elected by large majorities.

anti-mason.

A political party which grew out of the opposition to Freemasonry, brought into special prominence by the mystery surrounding the disappearance of William Morgan in 1826 [see GOOD ENOUGH MORGAN]. The first state convention of the party was held at Utica, N.Y., August 4, 1828, and the first national in 1831.

1827 *Cinc. Sat. Eve. Chron.* 16 June 3/3. The masonic fraternity of Batavia, N.Y. ... The antimasons have as unwisely resolved to call a county meeting at the same place on the same day.

1828 *Anti-Masonic Rev.* I.70. It is made a reproach to Anti-Masonry that it seeks the fields of politics. . . . Anti-Masonry is a principle. . . . Free Masonry is deeply connected with politics and Anti-Masonry must be.

1828 Tracy to Weed in Barnes *Weed* 32 [letter, 19 June]. The administration party in this State is in the hands of men not able to steer it to a successful issue. This I have long known, and were it not for anti-Masons they would not have a loop to hang a hope on.

1829 *Anti-Masonic Rev.* I.377 ... they hum and thumb upon re-action, and unblushingly pronounce Anti-Masonry dead.

1831 Seward *Works* III.348. We rejoice that the question of masonry and antimasonry is thus presented fairly and openly to the people, stripped of all former political names and associations.

1854 *Wash. D. Union* 8 Sept. 2/2. In Ohio, the whigs are now republicans; in New York, they are anti-Nebraska men; and in Pennsylvania, they are mounted on the temperance, anti-Masonic, know-nothing, and anti-Nebraska hobbies.

anti-monopolist.

The question of privileges granted or to be granted to the banking interests brought the word *monopoly* into general use, particularly in New York, where William Leggett suggested an original method of opposition to bank notes.

1834 Leggett *Pol. Writings* 6 Aug. I.43. A cheap, and, to a certain extent, most effectual method of disseminating the principles of those opposed to incorporated rag-money manufactories, would be for them to write upon the back of every bank-note which should come into their possession, some short sentence expressive of their sentiments. For example— "No Monopolies!" "No Union of Banks and State!" "Jackson and Hard Money!" "Gold before Rags!" and the like.

The anti-bank men became known as anti-monopolists, Equal Rights men (q.v.), and Loco Focos (q.v.).

1838 Leggett *Pol. Writings* 24 Oct. II.336. To be an abolitionist is to be an incendiary now, as, three years ago, to be an anti-monopolist, was to be a leveller, and a Jack Cade.
1842 Byrdsall *LocoFoco* 17. John Windt, an ultra anti-monopolist, who would indeed do justice to the Banks, though the whole credit system should fall.

Naturally the term came back into vogue when the trust question became a burning one.

1888 Lane *Pol. Catchwords*. Anti-Monopolists, those who are opposed to the creation of corporations that have the control of any article of common use.

anti-rent (party).

The attempt by the heirs of Stephen Rensselaer to procure the rent which had not been collected in his lifetime created great unrest in upper New York and finally resulted in the formation of the Anti-Rent party. Although the trouble began in 1839, this word has not been found prior to 1844. [**1839** in Hone *Diary* 10 Dec. 440. The De Ruyters, the Van Tromps, and the Stuyvesants of the manor of Rensselaer re-

main still in an attitude of open rebellion to the laws of the land, equally opposed to good order as to good manors. They won't pay their rent to him whom they style as the pretended proprietor.]
1844 *N. Y. W. Trib.* 20 July 1/6. Anti-Rent Difficulties.—We understand ... that the Sheriff of Rensselaer County ... while attempting to serve a process upon some of the Manor tenants in Stephentown ... met with forcible resistance.
1844 in Hammond *Silas Wright* 480. There was still another party, which, at the election in November, 1844, exhibited itself at the polls, which is known as the anti-rent party.
1846 Webster *Works* II.320. That Anti-rentism in New York and some other ism in Pennsylvania have produced such important consequences, it is folly to say.... There were counties in New York in which there was no Anti-rentism.
1847 in *Mangum Papers* V.1. The region on the opposite side of the river in New York, which is also the chief seet [sic] of Anti-rentism.

anti-semitic (semitism).

Showing intolerance toward the Jewish people.

This particular form of religious prejudice is in evidence early in America (See Link, *Dem. Soc.*, p. 51n: he quotes from the *N. Y. Journal*, 19 Dec., 1795); however, the term did not come into existence until the late 19th century when affairs in Germany brought anti-semitism to the world's attention.

1880 Treitschke in *Nation* 22 Jan. 53 ... the anti-Semitic movement is powerful and deep in all the most enlightened and cultivated circles.
Ib. 29 Jan. 74. Herr Glagan ... has started an anti-Semitic monthly called Der Kulturkämpfer.
1882 *Harper's W.* 11 Feb. 93/3. The anti-Semitic outbreak in Germany has been

the inspiration of the rioters [in Russia], and the apathy of the government their encouragement.

1896 *Rev. of Rev.* XIII.52. The campaign which has been waged against the Jews in certain parts of Europe for the last 15 years has been disguised by the name anti-Semitism.

In 1896 anti-semitism became a problem of local concern in New York when a German preacher Ahlwardt attempted to recreate the German antagonism toward the Jews:

1896 *N. Y. Trib.* 7 April 1/3. Herr Ahlwardt, the anti-Semitic agitator...was mobbed last night by the Hebrews in Hoboken....

Ib. 4 May 12/2. It was reported at the meeting of the Central Labor Union yesterday that Herr Ahlwardt, the anti-Semite, had started a paper in Brooklyn.

Theodore Roosevelt, *Autobiography*, p. 192, describes this same episode:

While I was police commissioner an anti-Semitic preacher from Berlin, Rector Ahlwardt, came over to New York to preach a crusade against the Jews. Many of the New York Jews were much excited and asked me to prevent him from speaking and not to give him police protection. This, I told them, was impossible.... The proper thing to do was to make him ridiculous. Accordingly I detailed for his protection a Jew sergeant and a score or two of Jew policemen. He made his harangue against the Jews under the active protection of some forty policemen, every one of them a Jew!

anxious seat.

A position of uncertainty.

A. In early revival meetings a bench was provided near the pulpit for those who felt inclined to make public confession of their sins and frailties.

1832 Mrs. Trollope *Domestic Manners* I.iii. As the poor creatures approached the rail, their sobs and groans became audible. They seated themselves in the "anxious benches." ...

B. In politics, the position of an office holder or potential candidate:

1842 *Cong. Globe* 14 Feb. 231. Mr. Buchanan of Pennsylvania said he was on the anxious seat, and the senator from Kentucky had brought him to it.

1871 *N. Y. Times* 10 Sept. 5. So far as could be heard from other sources, if there is any intention of any of the heads of Departments to resign, they certainly keep the secret remarkably well. Most of their subordinates are, however, evidently on the "anxious seat," and seem to think that some great change is impending.

1876 *Ann. of Cleve.* 3 Aug. No. 2402. Mr. Hendricks was a long time upon the anxious seat.

Apollo Hall.

A faction of the Democratic party in New York City.

1872 *N. Y. Trib.* 2 Oct. 4/2. The application of the Democratic (Tammany Hall) Committee for the appointment of United States Inspectors of Election brought up representatives of the Apollo Hall faction, who claim to be the only true Democracy.

1873 *Nation* 30 Oct. 281/2. The organization known as Apollo Hall, which was composed in equal numbers of gentlemen who wished to "sell out" to Tammany, and gentlemen who would on no account sell out to Tammany for the very good reason that they desired to sell out to Tom Murphy, has effected an arrangement with the Custom-House, securing a share of offices on the Republican ticket.

apostle of hate.

Applied in the post-Civil War period to those who revived memories of the war to bolster their own political fortunes.

1876 *Harper's W.* 26 Feb. 162/1 ... and that anybody in this Centennial year ... who does not confine himself to rejoicing over our happy reunion, but looks to see the facts, is an apostle of hate, delighting to dabble his fingers in the gore of the bloody shirt.

See GOSPEL OF HATE.

arena.

The area of political combat, particularly the chambers of Congress.

The combination of *arena* with *gladiator* clearly indicates its classical allusions.

1827 (Xenia, Ohio) *Western Coronet* 2 Nov. 3/2. George Kremer that celebrated lump of Fanaticism ... has again made his appearance upon the political arena.
1828 J. Randolph in *Cong. Deb.* 25 Jan. 1165. No, Sir; if this House is to be converted into a political arena, and I shall be accused as one of the gladiators, whether the man with the trident or him with the net. ...
1828 Letcher in *Ib.* 31 Jan. 1290. I do not think it either complimentary to the members of this House, or to the People of this nation, to make the Representative Hall the arena of electioneering strife, and turmoil, and bustle.
1839 John Clark in *Ib.* 30 Jan. Shall this place be converted into an arena, in which political gladiators shall combat, with weapons steeped in poison?
1876 *Cleve. Leader* 17 June 1/5. Thompson of Indiana severely denounced the chairman for bringing into the arena of this Convention his personal differences.
1880 *Cleve. Plain Dealer* 2 June 2/1. Mr. Edmunds having withdrawn himself from the arena as a presidential contestant.

armed neutrality.

A state of being prepared for war but remaining neutral.

The phrase was frequently used in the early days of the Civil War, particularly in reference to the activities of the border states.

1859 *Ann. of Cleve.* 9 June No. 297 ... is it not the duty of the true National Democracy to maintain an "armed neutrality"?
1861 *Cinc. D. Times* 26 April in *Northern Editorials* II. 877. The gentlemen who represented Kentucky, pledged their word that we of Ohio could rely upon the fidelity of Kentucky in preserving an "armed neutrality."
1861 *Providence Eve. Press* 7 May in *Ib.* II.883 ... it is an "armed neutrality"; a phrase which implies preparation to repel by force of arms either the government or the revolutionists, if they do not respect it.

Arnold.

A traitor.

A. The name of Benedict Arnold continued to be a national epithet long after his action in the Revolutionary War.

1845 *St. Louis Reveille* 17 April 2/4. The "Arnolds of the Press" is the very appropriate appellation given to the papers which are literally inviting the hostilities of Mexico against this country, since the ... annexing of Texas.
1868 Moore *Life of Schuyler Colfax* 63. There are some Arnolds now as then, but the party is purged of them. Our ranks may be thinned by the desertion of the timorous and the recreant.

B. The middle name of Stephen Arnold Douglas was given special attention during the Civil War.

1862 *Cols. Crisis* 6 Aug. 223/2. They were wont to place his name thus: "Stephen ARNOLD Douglas," by which to associate him in the mind of the public with the traitor Arnold.

Artful Dodger.

The popularity of this character from *Oliver Twist* is attested by the fact that at various times certain politicians have been given this nickname.

1840 *Log Cabin* 1 Aug. 4/3. The Artful Dodgers Laboring in their Vocation [ed.].
1862 Anon. *The Impending Contest* 5 [pamph.]. Cox as an Artful Dodger. Mr. Cox was in the House, but dodged on the vote to postpone the action on the enlargement of the Erie....
1864 *Ann. of Cleve.* 27 Oct. No. 1694. The "artful dodger," as Pendleton is sometimes called in Congress, says.... Alas! for the dodger. It is too late now to dodge into the Vice Presidency.
1876 *Ann. of Cleve.* 13 July. He says he will not support the Artful Dodger [Tilden] for the Presidency.
1884 *N. Y. World* 7 Sept. 4/4. Let Mr. Blaine be known as the Artful Dodger.

According to an unverified statement by Russell in *Blaine of Maine* (p. 370), the nickname was applied to Garfield by the *New York Sun* and other Democratic papers in 1880.

as Maine goes, so goes the nation.

The formula for predicting election results on the basis of the returns from an earlier, particular section or state has undergone many variations and has not always been confined to any particular state.

1836 *Cinc. Rep.* 18 Oct. 2/3. As goes the Key Stone State, so goes the Union.
1848 *Ohio State Jrnl.* 27 Sept. 2/5. As Vermont goes, so goes all New England.
1854 *N. Y. Times* 6 Sept. 8/2. As goes Illinois this Fall, so goes the Union.
1872 *Harper's W.* 14 Sept. 714/4. It is not, however, true that as Maine goes so goes the country, for Maine was Republican in 1856, when Buchanan was elected.
1880 *Ib.* 53. [Nast cartoon showing schoolboys throwing snowballs at figure

"Alonzo Garcelon Caesar I" outside of school with sign: Public School. "As Maine Goes So Goes the Union."]
1880 *N. Y. Times* 21 Oct. 1/1. "As goes Indiana so goes the United States" had for days been their constant cry.

Following the election of 1936, in which Franklin D. Roosevelt won the electoral votes of all the states except Maine and Vermont, the phrase was given many humorous changes:

1936 in *Am. Speech* XII.9. As Maine goes, so goes Vermont. As Maine goes, so goes Maine.

assassin of character.

One who seeks to destroy the political effectiveness of an opponent by statements impugning his personal morality.

A. Formulas suggesting the phrase or related expressions—*assassinate character, character assassin*—are found early in English usages (all from *OED*):

1647 Wharton *Wks.* 263. Attempt to Assassine the Honour of a whole Nation with his Invectives.
1683 Dryden *Dk. Guise* v. Your rimes assassinate our fame.
1824 Dibdin *Libr. Comp.* 744. Lord Byron was the assassin of his own fame.

B. In American politics, usually found in connection with congressional investigations.

1876 Hereford in *Cong. Record* 17 June 3860/1. Say that our committees of investigation are intended to strike down some loyal man or "assassinate character."
?1924 in Allen *Only Yesterday* 154. The *New York Times,* despite its Democratic leanings, called them [oil scandal investigators] "assassins of character."
1927 Booth *Mad Mullah* 212. Evans and his followers at Atlanta ... were branded "character assassins" by Stephenson, in his fight against the Imperial Wizard.

1932 Daugherty *Harding Tragedy* 229. The thing that gave to Wheeler the deadly power which he wielded as an assassin of character were not the facts which he developed, but the impetus that his insinuations gave to venomous gossip.
1944 Hoover *Add.* 246. Their [European revolutionists] strategy is to make public opinion by falsehood and to destroy opposition by assassination of character through smearing.
1952 Stevenson *Camp. Speeches* 249. Because we have always thought of government as friendly, not as brutal, character assassins and slanderers in the Congress of the United States have a free hand in the methods they use.

associated wealth.

One of the phrases (see BLOATED BONDHOLDER) used against the moneyed class during the Jacksonian epoch. Apparently first used by President Van Buren. [ ]
1838 Bell in *Cong. Globe* 26 Dec. App. 359/3. Among the most prominent dangers to which our form of government is exposed, the President here enumerates "the anti-republican tendencies of associated wealth."
1840 Watterson in *Ib.* 2 April App. 370/2. I mean the influence of "associated wealth," of privileged corporations, ... against the policy of the Administration of the General Government.

availability.

Suitability for office frequently founded on the inoffensive character rather than the positive merits of the candidate.

Characteristic uses of the term, including *available,* adj., and *availables,* n., follow. Note the general tendency toward derogatory connotations.
1835 Clay *Writings* V.399. He [Harrison] was very respectful and cordial ... appeared to be in good spirits and I thought seemed confident. I adhere to the opinion ... that if Pennsylvania will give satisfactory demonstrations of an intention to support him, it will be expedient to run him as the most available candidate against Mr. Van Buren.
1835 *Ann. of Cleve.* 21 Oct. No. 311. It is said that he [Webster] is not an "available" candidate and therefore we dropped him. It proves that the American people have come to think that sterling integrity, splendid talents, a noble support of the constitution, an unflinching opposition to corruption and to every violation of the letter and spirit of that constitution do not constitute a man an "available" candidate for the highest office in their gift.
1836 *Cols. West. Hemisphere* 13 July 1/6. Of all apparent "availables" it is evident that the opposition could not have selected a more unpromising one than the individual whom they have dubbed "Hero of Tippecanoe."
1837 Leggett *Pol. Writings* II.270. We are tired of contending against "availables," men of no fixed political character, but ready to mould themselves to any new opinion and suit their doctrines to the varying hour.
1840 in Benton *Thirty Yrs.* II.204. Availability, to use their own jargon, was the only ability which these managers asked— that is, available for the purposes of the election, and for their own advancement.
1843 *Cleve. Herald* 18 Dec. The Locos used to jeer the Whigs in '39–'40 about running Mr. Availability for President.
1856 *Cinc. Enquirer* 17 May 4/2. [Republicans] will go off in search of what they call an "available candidate."
1876 *Harper's W.* 5 Feb. 122/4. Senator Sherman's argument for Governor Hayes is that of availability. The worst of this argument is that it is negative. It recommends a candidate on the ground that nothing is known to his discredit.

avalanche.

A landslide, tidal wave (q.v.). Particularly frequent during the campaign of 1840.

1840 *Harrison Dem.* 16 June 2/3. It was another of those glorious and enthusiastic Avalanches of the people that distinguish this contest from any other in our National History.

1840 *Straightout Harrisonian* 11 Sept. 3/3. His [Corwin's] progress through the State has been like the descent of an avalanche from the summit of Mount Blanc, irresistible and overwhelming.

1840 *Ann. of Cleve.* No.1788. Let the idea float, that Gen. Wm. Henry Harrison has been borne into the Presidential chair upon a thundering avalanche of popular opinion.

1844 *Cleve. Herald* 23 Feb. 3/1. Neighbor Bowers...threatens to roll an avalanche of Summit Whigs upon us at the 15th of May convention.

1844 *Ohio Coon Catcher* 17 Aug. 1/2. A perfect Avalanche from the Prairie State —The Suckers Awake. [head]

1888 *N. Y. Trib.* 5 Sept. The rout of the Democracy in the Green Mountain State is complete and thorough. The party is not only buried under an avalanche of Republican ballots in the State at large, but is dethroned from power in a number of local strongholds.

axe.

A. Synonymous with *guillotine* (q.v.) .

1858 *Ohio St. Jrnl.* 5 Oct. The Axe in Ohio. Buchanan, the headsman,...is about to consign Faran, the Postmaster of Cincinnati, to the guillotine.

B. Having an axe to grind: having private ends to serve.

The assumption that the phrase goes back to Benjamin Franklin (*OED*) is discussed and corrected in Walsh (*Handy-book of Lit. Cur.*) The story behind the phrase belongs to Charles Miner, who, influenced perhaps by Franklin's anecdote about paying too much for a whistle, tells of a boy induced by the flattery of a stranger to turn the grindstone until his hands blistered.

In politics the phrase is frequently used with the idea of doing somebody a service with the expectation that he will reciprocate. (See LOGROLLING.)

1855 J. H. Lee *Am. Party* 201. Each one of the little secret caucus had "an axe of his own to grind," and each was willing to play into the other's hands, if he was certain of having the favour returned.

1856 Goodrich *Rec.* 126...still, when I see a noisy politician crying out, "The democracy! ho, the democracy!" I consider it pretty certain—judging from long experience and observation—that, according to the proverb, "Somebody has an axe to grind," and desires to wheedle dupes into turning the grindstone, gratis.

1867 Nasby *Swinging Round the Cirkle* 202....all cood depend on all, each cood depend on the other, coz each faction, or ruther each stripe, had its little private axe to grind, which it coodent do without the others to turn the grind-stone.

1875 DeForest *Playing the Mischief* 105. Congress used to be a law-making body. Now it is mainly an axe-grinding body.

C. lay the axe to the root.

Reminiscent of the Biblical use of the phrase: Matt. 3:10. And now also the axe is laid unto the root of the trees....

1765 Dickinson *Writings* II.201. The Resignation of the Officers was judged effectual and the most decent Method of preventing the Execution of a Statute, that strikes the Axe into the Root of the Tree, and lays the hitherto flourishing Branches of American Freedom, with all its precious Fruits, low in the Dust.

1790 *Hist. of Cong.* 1818. If the principle be adopted of requiring no compensation from the exempted [from military duty], it will lay the axe to the root of the militia....

1823 *Del. Patron* 25 June 3/3...place his axe at the root of the tree and not be quite so harkless to the admonition of Editors or the patience of Anybody.

axis.

The alliance before and during World War II between Germany and Italy; later enlarged to include Japan; attributed to Mussolini (?).

1937 *N. Y. Times* 17 Jan. 33/3. He [Mussolini] repeats his previous assurances that the British-Italian agreement is intended to strengthen rather than to weaken the Rome-Berlin united front. "We have forced the axis to Berlin and Rome," he adds. "That is the beginning of European consolidation."
1937 *Ib.* 6 June iv.4/1. Last week's events had the effect of strengthening the Rome-Berlin axis at the very point where it had given some evidence of being the weakest.
1938 *Ib.* 19 May 14/5. There was a triangle in 1914—Berlin-Vienna-Rome. There is an axis in 1938—Berlin-Rome.
1942 in Hoover *Add. Upon the Am. Road* 11. It is a favorable and important sign that there is today active debate of the problems of peace throughout the Allied world. . . . I have noticed no such discussions in the Axis world.
1943 *Ib.* 100. The beginning of the Axis was made by Germany and Italy in 1936 and later extended to include Japan.
1943 *Ib.* 180. The United Nations have now closed iron rings around the European and the Asiatic Axis.

B

baby act, to plead the.

To defend one's actions on the ground of immaturity or inexperience. In politics, often used satirically.

1837 *New Yorker* 9 Dec. 593/2. We do not defend the conduct of any man who pleads usury in bar of an honest man, neither would we if he should plead the baby act, or minority.
1862 *Cinc. Comm.* 12 July 2/4. The friends of the Hon. E. M. Stanton, Secretary of War, plead the "baby act" for him.
1864 Carpenter *Logic of Hist.* 230. Then the Administration organs began to plead the "Baby Act." They declared the Administration knew nothing. . . .
1898 Schurz *Writings* V.508. It is also pretended that if we liberate the Spanish West Indies and the Philippines from Spanish misrule, we shall be responsible for their future welfare, and shall have to keep them, because we shall not be able to make other satisfactory arrangements for them. This is "pleading the baby act" to justify the keeping of the islands. . . .
1909 *N. Am. Rev.* cxc:542. The favors are obtained in two ways—by "influence" and by supplication of a kind for which there is no classical or strictly parliamentary assignation. In the vulgar, it is called "the baby act."
1914 White *Editor and People* 262 . . . the fellows whose factional toes are aching are bellowing lugubriously. And which same is the baby act. Politics is war. A man can't play both sides.

backbone.

Characterized by unfailing regularity to one party. [ ]

1856 *Ann. of Cleve.* No.2454 . . . the old Democratic "Backbone Counties" of Ohio are genuinely Democratic still.

backer.

One who gives political support, particularly financial.

1876 *Cinc. Gazette* 15 June 3/1. He has the great moral element of the party as his friends and backers.
1884 *Harper's W.* 86/2. The only sense of responsibility which is destroyed [by Reform] is that of responsibility to a boss, and the only negligence which is promoted is that of the commands and interest of a political "backer."

back seat.

A position of lesser importance.
1858 in Isely *Greeley and the Republican Party* 13 Sept. 252. The Americans were generally ready to fuse on one condition —this, namely, that Mr. Thurlow Weed should take a back seat in the new car.
1858 G. F. Train *Spread-eagleism* 121. The only difficulty is, when two ride the same horse, who shall take the back seat?
1900 *N. Y. Trib.* 4 Feb. 9. [cartoon "Inviting Teddy To Take A Back Seat" on the Republican elephant]

backstairs.

Quite old in England (see *OED*) backstairs influence became prominent during the debates in Parliament on the India Bill.
1770 Burke *Works* I.316. This parliament was to look on, as if perfectly unconcerned, while a cabal of the closet and backstairs was substituted in the place of a national administration. . . .
323. Set themselves, in the great concern of peers and commons, against a backstairs influence and clandestine government.
in Wright *Caricature Hist.* 375. Some strong remarks on backstairs influence . . . were made in the House of Lords. . . . On the 17th of December [1783], the very evening when this underhand influence was brought into play in the other House, a violent debate arose upon the subject in the Commons.
1784 *Ib.* 552. A figure representing Secret Influence was well-drest, and seasonable in its point . . . a ladder was painted down his back, entitled "The Back Stairs."

This is the event to which Randolph alludes in 1806, which gave currency to the phrase in American papers:
in Garland *Randolph* I.223. I allude to the case where the King's name was used for the purpose of throwing out Mr. Fox's India bill. I then reprobated this backstair influence, this double dealing, the sending one message for the journals and newspapers, and another in whispers to this House.
Ann. of Cong. 561. I speak of back-stairs influence—of men who bring messages to this House, which although they do not appear on the Journals govern its decisions.
1806 Jefferson *Corr.* IV.46. Our situation is difficult; and whatever we do is liable to the criticisms of those who wish to represent it awry. . . . If we express opinions in conversation, we have then our Charles Jenkinsons, and back door counsellors. If we say nothing, "we have no opinions, no plans, no cabinet."

Both Randolph himself and Jefferson took up the phrase on later occasions, and others followed suit:
1812 *Salem Gazette* 10 July [Thornton]. Should an Albany Caucus take our kingship in hand,
  Our veto would addle Dewitt's nomination;
For unmov'd on the backstairs D. Tompkins would stand,
  And send home the bolters by new prorogation.
1835 Byrdsall *Loco Foco* 17. Garrett Gilbert was also a malcontent, and the burden of most of his speeches was, "Go it my boys, against the old hunkers of Tammany Hall, who go up the backstairs."
1866 Grinnell *Men and Events* 164. Mr. Rousseau had the credit of a membership in the "back stairs cabinet."
1878 *N. Y. Trib.* 20 Sept. 4/5. Mr. Boutwell thinks Butler has made his defeat certain by his backstairs performance at Worcester.

See also KITCHEN CABINET, POWER BEHIND THE THRONE.

bagman.

The term is evidently suggested by *to hold the bag,* a phrase found much earlier in American politics.
1787 Tyler *Contrast* II.ii. General Shays has sneaked off and given us the bag to hold.

1793 Jefferson *Works* IV.7. If France collected within her own limits shall maintain her ground there steadily, ... and if the bankruptcies of England proceed to the length of an universal crush of their paper, ... she will leave Spain the bag to hold. ...
1954 Mockridge & Prall *The Big Fix* 234. Nobody believed, either, that Jim Moran kept all of the money he collected. For many years he had been known as a bagman, which in political jargon, is literally the man who carries the bag or boodle for somebody higher up. And the bagman never gets to keep the big money.

-bait(-er, -ing).

To attack or persecute a group or organization.

Bull, bear, and badger-baiting were all once popular sports in England (see *OED*), until condemned by a more humane society.

A. Modern use of baiting seems to begin with the anti-Jewish disturbances in Germany (see ANTI-SEMITIC).

1883 *N. Y. Eve. Post* 21 April. The Jew-baiting in Germany; the bloody persecutions in Russia.
1883 *Pall Mall Gaz.* 19 Nov. 3/1. [They] are now in full possession of the case of the German jew-baiters against the Jews.
1896 *Nation* 5 March 189/3. That pious Jew-baiter, Dr. Stöcker, is in disgrace, repudiated by his erstwhile enthusiastic admirer, the Emperor.

B. Following the Russian revolution of 1917 and the spread of Bolshevism, red-baiting came into prominence:

1922 in White *Editor and People* 331. During the fortnight passing, John D. Rockefeller, Jr., got himself in bad with the red baiters.
1923 *Sel. Ltrs. of W. A. White* 237. The red-baiters have so thoroughly scared the people with the bogie of Bolshevism, that

any public man who takes any public attitude in favor of organized labor ... does so at his tremendous peril politically.
1927 *Ib.* 278. In which we criticized the officers of the Daughters of the American Revolution for joining in the red-baiting endeavors of the ultra-conservative organizations centering around Washington.
1931 *Wash. Merry-Go-Round* 137. The administration, fifty years ago, of Hamilton Fish, grandfather of the Red-baiting Congressman.

C. In various other compounds:
1925 Coan *Red Web* 60. Radical organizations of all shades joined in the cry for the recognition of Russia and its "ambassador" and participated in the demand for the scalp of the "labor baiter," Attorney General Palmer.
1932 Carter *What We Are About To Receive* 204. The Bolshevik-baiters will make it uncomfortable, unprofitable and, if possible, painful, for any American citizen to advocate a real change in our methods of living and letting others live.
1953 *Nation* 24 Oct. 327/3. The old professionals who have now added U.N.-baiting to the profitable job of attacking Jews, Negroes, Catholics, and labor unions.

balance of power.

In international history the idea of a balance of power in Europe, a status in which no single state is powerful enough to interfere with the interests of others, has a long tradition. (Ladendorf, under *Europaische Gleichgewicht.*) According to J. J. Moser, *Europaisch Volkerrecht* (1750), p. 17, the concept goes back to Henry IV of France:
Zu Anfang des vorigen Jahrhunderts verfiehezwar König Heinrich IV in Franckreich auf die Gedanken dass er die Macht derer Europaisches souverainen Staaten in eine gewisse Art der Balance ... bringen wollte.

Repercussions of this use can, of course, be found in American political writers.

1846 *Democratic Rev.* April 273 ff. Great as have been the evils that have flowed from the theory of the "balance of power," it has never yet been defined, and is utterly incapable of definition. . . . It has been remarked, that the first instance in which this balance was alluded to by the kings of England, was in the speech of William III from the throne, Dec. 31, 1701, as follows: . . . to see England hold the balance of Europe. . . .

Much more frequently, however, the term in American usage refers to the equilibrium of powers within the state:

1644 John Cotton *Keyes of Heaven* 3. And accordingly the wisdome of the first Constitutors of Commonwealths is most seen in such a just balancing of power and priviledges. . . .

1776 Adams *Works* IV.384 . . . it might be immortal; and so perhaps would a political body, if the balance of power could be always held exactly even.

1789 J. Adams *Selected Writings* 18 July 116 . . . every project has been found to be no better than committing the lamb to the custody of the wolf, except that one which is called a balance of power.

1841 in *Mangum Papers* III.234 . . . they have not sufficient force to form a balance of power party.

Originally a term of sociological theory, *balance of power* took on a political significance during the period when free states and slave states were equally represented in the Senate:

1845 Lyon *Gov't of the United States* 139. Just half of the States hold slaves, the other half are opposed to it. . . . The effort to keep up this balance, at least in the Senate of the United States, is great, and hereafter will very like [sic] entangle them with foreign governments.

1856 B. F. Morris *Morris* 72. The balance of power has always been with the South.

1862 Christy *Pulpit Politics* 496 . . . no one doubts that the struggle of the southern States has been maintained to secure the balance of power in their own favor, that they might, under the guarantees of the Constitution, be able to protect their property in slaves.

ballot-box stuffing (ballot-box stuffer).

Fraudulent, multiple voting; one who casts many votes.

Bartlett (1859) calls attention to a specially constructed ballot-box into which any necessary number of spurious votes could be added. Early quotations suggest that this was a San Francisco invention.

1856 *Alta California* 24 May 2/2. This conclusion had been arrived at after reflecting upon the means used to elect the ticket, and the general disrepute of ballot-box stuffing of late.

1857 in Nevins *Emergence of Lincoln* I.230 . . . a set of broken-down political hacks, demagogues, fire-eaters, perjurers, ruffians, ballot-box stuffers, and loafers.

1866 *Cong. Globe* 10 Jan. 166/1. A few years since we heard much of a set of fellows in San Francisco who were designated as ballot box stuffers.

1873 in *Sen. Reports* 42nd Cong. 3rd Sess. No.1529 p. 706. I do not think there was one-third as much ballot-box stuffing as there was then [1870].

band-box statesman.

A politician of super-elegant manners and dress.

1875 *Kansas City Times* in *Cinc. Comm.* 7 May 2/5. They [reformers] will work out their logical consequences regardless of band-box statesmen like Charles Francis Adams.

banditti.

Outlaws; spec. Southern terrorists.

A. General uses of the term:

1803 in *Gt. Deb.* II.96. It is no less improper to represent our western brethern [sic] as a lawless, unprincipled banditti who would at once release themselves from the wholesome restraints of law and order.

1837 in Byrdsall *Loco Foco* 112. The banks are, in fact, legally authorized banditti.

B. In 1875 the term came into the popular vocabulary for a short time as the result of General Sheridan's reports from Louisiana. In Nast's cartoons (see *Harper's W.,* 30 Jan. et seq.) banditti are represented by peaked caps, connoting the Italian and Sicilian background of the word.

1875 Sheridan in *Harper's W.* 23 Jan. 71. I also know of the kidnapping by the banditti of Mr. Cousin, one of the members elect of the Legislature.

1875 *Ib.* 30 Jan. 89. If Congress would pass a bill declaring them banditti, they could be tried by a military commission.

1875 Logan in Fenton-Cooper *Am. Pol.* III.168. You are excited, your extreme wrath is aroused at General Sheridan because he called your White League down there [La.] "banditti."

bandwagon (get on the).

In investigating the origin of this phrase and variations, *jump on, rush on the bandwagon,* etc., we have clearly to follow the different lines: 1. the bandwagon used by circuses and later by political organizations in order to attract attention; 2. the metaphorical use of phrases like *to get on the wagon* (water wagon, bandwagon) meaning to join up. The circus bandwagon is mentioned in P. T. Barnum's *Life,* published in 1855 but describes an earlier event:

205. At Vicksburg we sold all our land conveyances excepting four horses and the "band wagon."
[see also May, *The Circus,* p. 51]

Political cartoonists adapted the circus idea to their own use as early as 1848:
John Donkey II.13 [cartoon showing the "Philadelphia Brass Band as it appeared on its way to the Taylor Meeting."]

Puck, 1884, depicts the presidential bandwagon driven by Arthur and carrying the other presidential hopefuls. *Puck,* 29 April, 1896, has a similar cartoon, the McKinley Bandwagon; somewhat more original is Gillam's broken down bandwagon (*Judge,* 19 Nov., 1892) showing the ruins of the Harrison bandwagon. [For the interesting history of this cartoon—it was originally intended to illustrate Cleveland's anticipated defeat—see Murrell, *History of American Graphic Humor,* II.119.]

Behind these cartoons is the fact that real bandwagons were used at conventions and during campaigns in order to promote the interests of certain candidates. A Blaine bandwagon is mentioned in connection with the Chicago convention of 1884. [ ]

In all these uses the central idea is that of a ballyhoo while the idea of joining a successful movement has not yet crystallized. Outside of politics, however, the notion of jumping into a wagon in order to join a common enterprise is quite old. A song published in 1851, but still a favorite around 1900, "Wait for the Wagon, A New Ethiopian Song and Melody" by

W. Loftin Hargrave, contains the stanzas:

Where the river runs so pretty, and the birds they sing so sweet,
I've got a cabin, Phillis, and something good to eat.
Come listen to my story, it's a load upon my heart,
So jump into the wagon, and off we will start.
   Wait for the wagon, wait for the wagon,
   Wait for the wagon, and we'll all take a ride.
Your lips are red as poppies, your hair so slick and neat,
All braided up with dahlias, and holly-hocks so sweet.
It's every Sunday morning, with Jacob by our side,
We'll jump into the wagon, and all take a ride.
   Wait for the wagon, etc.

Closer to politics is the temperance song, "The Prohibition Bandwagon" (*Prohibition Songs,* c. 1900) :

O, it won't be long, is the burden of our song,
Till we get our wagon started on the way;
   (on the way) ;
And our friends who vote for gin,
Will all scramble to jump in,
When we get our big band-wagon, some sweet day,
   some sweet day.

The temperance wagon is later replaced by the waterwagon (see *New York Evening Post,* 24 Aug., 1904, *Review of Reviews,* XXX Sept., 1907, *The Log of the Water Wagon,* by Bert Leston Taylor and W. C. Gibson, 1905) but not before the political bandwagon in its modern sense as a symbol of unified opinion has made its appearance. The merging of the old (ballyhoo) and the new (unity) idea is shown in a cartoon of 1902 (Albert Shaw,

Cartoon History of Roosevelt's Career, p. 81) . The wagon itself is of the old type—Roosevelt's friends making musical noises in his favor—but the main character is Senator Platt, running after the wagon in a frantic effort to board it, and, as the whip in his hand shows, to get into the driver's seat.

From 1902 on the phrase is well established in political terminology; the Roosevelt quotation of 1899, however, indicates that its origin may be in N.Y. local politics of the 1890's.

1899 Roosevelt *Ltrs.* II.999 . . . when I once became sure of one majority they tumbled over each other to get aboard the bandwagon.
1902 Brand Whitlock *The 13th District* 315. The bandwagon had taken them by surprise and rolled by too swiftly for them to climb in.
1903 Crissey *Retired Politician* 45. Every man who climbed into the bandwagon would get his share of the great consolidation water melon.
1904 *Cinc. Enquirer* 4 June 9/3. Refused To Climb into the Wagon. [Head on political article. Bandwagon has apparently been shortened for typographical reasons.]
1908 *Rev. of Rev.* XXXVII June 652/2. Naturally they [minority Republicans] will accept the situation, or, as the politicians say, they will clamber into the "band-wagon."
1960 *Time* 7 March 15/3. For a Kennedy sweep there would quickly bring most of the Northern fence-sitting Democratic bosses around the U.S. racing to get on the magnetic bandwagon.

See also other circus terms: ARENA, RING, SIDE SHOW, STRADDLE, WOOLLY HORSE.

bank bought (ridden, tyranny), bankism, bankarchy.

Under the control of the U.S.

Bank; a Democratic charge against the Whigs.

1834 Leggett *Writings* I.58. The people have groaned and sweated under Bank Tyranny long enough.
1838 *Ohio Statesman* 18 May 3/3. At work . . . to undermine the democracy and establish a federal bankarchy.
1838 *Hamilton Intelligencer* 31 May 3/2. All Democrats were warned to beware of it as a "Bank bought press."
1838 *Ib.* 6 Sept. 2/2. He [Allen] denounced it . . . as a meeting of the "Whig Bankers" and "Bank bought hirelings."
1840 *Harrison Dem.* 14 April 1/3. He preaches most vehemently against shinplasters—the cussed banks—and bankbought Whiggery.
1840 *Rough-hewer* 30/3. A Fact for the Bank-Ridden.
1841 *Ohio Statesman* 5 Jan. It is thus that the sacredness of contracts are observed by this Bank Ridden Legislature.
1843 *Ib.* 20 Jan. 3/5. The Reckless Spirit of Bankism.

Bank party (conservative, tory).

Those favoring the establishment of a national bank; later a Democratic nickname of the Whigs.

1808 *Phila. Aurora* 17 Feb. [Satirical analysis of Federal party] 5. The army and navy, place and profit[ing]-hunting party. 6. The funding, banking, and loan party.
1824 *Cinc. Nat. Rep.* 27 Aug. 2/1. What are called the Bank Party.
1825 *Nat. Crisis* 8 Aug. 3/2. And Gentlemen I say, I am no Bank Party, I don't belong to the Bank.
1834 Leggett *Pol. Writings* I.68. General Jackson is the object of the direct hatred of the Bank tories.
1834 *Ib.* I.155. Whoever is an observer of the signs of the times must have noticed the earnest and painful efforts of the Bank party to rid themselves of that appellation. . . . This then is the party which

claims to be called Whigs, and repudiates the name of the Bank party.
1842 *Ohio Statesman* 12 July 3/2. A new bank-conservative party has developed itself.

banner county.

1840 *Niles Reg.* 5 Dec. 210/2. The banner county.—Designation is claimed by Worcester, Massachusetts, which gave Harrison the largest aggregate majority, viz: 4,773.
1850 *N. Y. Trib.* 18 Oct. 4/4. In Old Genesee, formerly the Whig Banner County of the State. . . .
1888 in *Cong. Record* 15 Aug. 7598/1. Clay County is the banner Democratic county of my Congressional district.

banner district.

1843 *Memoir of Abel Brown* 172. In the Congressional District occupying the N.E. corner of Ill. the liberty vote was over 1200. . . . I think that is the *Banner District* in the U.S.
1885 *Century Mag.* Nov. 28/1. The visitors . . . were mostly . . . miners on their way to the "Banner district."

banner state.

The state most prominent in its support of a party in the national elections.

The designation arose during the campaign of 1840 when a Whig group in Louisiana offered a banner to the state which would show the greatest returns for Harrison.

1840 *Ohio Confederate* 26 Nov. 2/4. The Banner State. Mr. Editor:—I wish to know whether the banner provided by Louisiana is to be given to the State that has a plurality of votes in the Presidential questions; or to the state that distinguishes itself by giving its unqualified votes to "Old Tip." . . .
1840 *Log Cabin* 5 Dec. 2/3. The Banner State. It is known that the Ladies of New Orleans early in the late contest offered a

splendid Banner to the State which should give the largest relative majority for Harrison and Tyler. . . . It lies between Vermont and Kentucky. . . . It is a nice question which of these states is entitled to the Banner.

1841 Clay in *Cong. Globe* 1 March App. 332 . . . an attempt to prove that Vermont, and not Kentucky, was entitled to the honor of "the Banner State."
1843 *Ohio Statesman* 9 Feb. 3/1 . . . Kentucky, the Banner Whig State in the Union!!!
1862 *Knickerbocker* Oct. 371. Illinois is still the banner State.

barnacle.

Metaphor applied to office holders and spoilsmen (q.v.) whose only qualification for office is their party servitude.

1829 James *Jackson* 498. The Barnacles Shall Be Scraped Clean from the Ship of State. [head]
1852 T. Parker *Add. Speeches* 254. These barnacles clove to the great man's (Webster's] unprotected parts, and hastened his decay.
1867 *Cols. Morning Jrnl.* 13 April 4/3. He fastens upon the Democratic faith like a barnacle on the rotton [sic] bottom of a ship, and never opens his shell to a single generous emotion of sympathy with anything man-ward or God-ward above the line of his narrow horizon.
1880 Woolley *Life* 172. The insect of society, the barnacle of office miss the malaria of that lower air, in which they thrive, in the pure atmosphere of the White House home.

Also, one of the politicians in Dickens' Circumlocution Office (q.v.) (Curtis, *Sp.* II.23, 1869)

See HACK.

barnburner.

The left wing of the Democratic party in New York in the 1840's and later in other states.

There are two current explanations of the word, which we give in the words of Donovan's *Barnburners,* p. 32:

To the faction that demanded radical restriction of canal extension and the re-imposition of a direct tax, there now began to be applied the picturesque but scarcely clarifying name of "Barnburners." The use of the term is not common before 1843. . . . The term is said by some to have originated in the angry charge of their opponents that the Radicals were none too good to be guilty of burning barns; that, in fact, they had condoned such excesses when committed by the radical element in Rhode Island, during the Dorr Rebellion there. . . . Another explanation is, that the name grew out of a slighting remark that the policy of the Radicals in connection with public works resembled that of the legendary Dutch farmer who had burned down his barn to rid it of the rats—the implication being that the Barnburners were willing to destroy the public works and corporations to stop the abuses connected with them.

The first of these theories, which Donovan calls "fantastic," because there was "no clear connection between the Rhode Island troubles, which were constitutional and political, and New York's financial troubles," is still taken seriously by the *DAE* and other works. It must be rejected, however, not because of the reason given by Donovan, but because known uses of the term antedate the Dorr Rebellion.

1841 *Xenia Torchlight* 19 Aug. 2/2. The repeal meeting was a failure. The leaders in Philadelphia attempted it there, but like that of New York, it failed. The meeting was attended by about 400 men and boys—such as Gov. Porter's brother calls "barn-burners." . . . it dispersed without tearing up any railroad or burning any building.

1842 *N. Y. Trib.* 29 Jan. 7/3. The barnburners (as the ultra Loco-Focos are
called) are for Samuel Young for Secretary....

At first sight the anecdote about
the Dutch farmer seems to be one
of those *ex post facto* stories invented for the purpose of explaining a word of forgotten origin
(see SALT RIVER). However, the
story is accepted only a few years
after the first appearance of *barnburner*, and is told in 1848 with so
much detail that it is hard to discredit it.

1848 *Ohio St. Jrnl.* 7 June 2/4. The
origin of the term *barnburner* was, we
believe, this:—In the State of New York
it is well known that politics were for
many years arranged and directed by a
class of men called the *Albany Regency.*
They held the state offices and parcelled
them out as their own domain. The
young and new members of the party
could see neither justice nor propriety in
this sort of political aristocracy; and many
of the old ones, who had fought long un-
rewarded, took sides with them. This
manifested itself in the Legislature. A
radical faction was formed, and the great
point of dispute was, as it has always
been, *the offices.* "Ah, (said the radicals)
what right have these fellows—these
hunkers—to be forever sucking at the
public crib, while not a teat remains for
us?" ... At length, seeing there was no
chance without force, a leader of the faction rose and said: "Mr. Speaker:—I see
that the gentlemen who hold the Regency
power have taken their course, and are
not to be moved by persuasion or eject-
ment; they are no sooner driven out at
one corner than they come in at the
other. Sir, I see no way to get them out
but to serve them as some fellow did the
rats. He was troubled excessively by
rats in his barn; he tried all sorts of ways
to get them out; he set traps for them; he
got a terrier dog, he sent in a weasel, and

he put poison in their way; but all in
vain—no sooner did they go out one side
than they came in the other. The traps
they would not enter, the poison they
would not eat. He resolved what he
would no [read *do*]: *he set fire to the
barn, and burnt barn, rats and all!* This
is what we will do, sir. In the masterly
language of the immortal Jefferson, sir,
'few men die and none resign.' We must
try a summary method—we will *burn the
barn, rats and all!*"

If the quotation is correct, then accounts of this barnburning ought
to be found in New York papers
of 1841 and, as the quotation from
the *Xenia Torchlight* indicates, in
Pennsylvania papers of the same
period.

A late variant:

1932 Cobb in Hoover *Memoirs* III.378.
Merely let me say to you, sir, that we are
grateful because during your occupancy
of the White House you never got the
idea of burning down the temple of our
fathers in order to destroy a few cock-
roaches in the basement.

barnstorm.

To make a campaign tour, usually of a rather spectacular or
whirlwind nature. Originally applied to theatrical tours in both
England and America.

See *OED* 1884; *DAB,* biographies of James Lewis and Noah
Miller.

[c1895] *Kansas City Eve. World* in Salisbury *Career of a Journalist* 15. "The
Beggar Student" Butchered By a Troupe
of Comic Opera Barnstormers. [head]

In politics found in America as
early as 1896:

Cong. Record 7 April 3661/1. The last I
heard of him was barnstorming down in
Georgia in favor of a gold monometallism.
1916 in Barkley *That Reminds Me* 110.
[Wilson] simply did not think it was

dignified for a President in time of a threatening crisis to go "barnstorming"—that was his word for it—through the country.

1953 *Cols. Citizen* 25 Oct. They say Nixon is the logical man to carry the campaign load in view of Mr. Eisenhower's firm decision against barnstorming the country for GOP candidates for Congress.

(See also STUMP, SWING AROUND THE CIRCLE.)

barrel (bar'l).

A. Prior to the Democratic convention of 1876 reports were circulated that Tilden was prepared to spend $1,000,000 on the presidential campaign. (See *Cinc. Enquirer* 31 May, 1876, 1/5.) During the campaign, allusions to "Tilden's barrel of money" are extremely frequent. The phrase is said to have been coined by papers in St. Louis, where the Democratic convention took place.

in Lane *Pol. Catchwords* 16. It is said to have originated in a dispatch to the St. Louis Globe-Democrat from Jefferson City about two weeks before the meeting of the Democratic Convention, in 1876, in St. Louis.

1876 *Cinc. Enquirer* 5 June 4/1. The politicians who met at Jefferson City last week, and sold the party to a man who is understood to have a "barrel of money" to trade for the Presidency, are worse than cowards.

1876 *Fremont Courier* 13 July 2/1. Auf das blödsinnige Geschwatz der "Chicago Tribune" dass Tilden durch ein Fass voll Geld seine Ernennung ... erkauft habe, erwidert die "Chicago Times" Die Fasser voll Geld, welche Tilden's Ernennung bewirkten, sind jene Fasser voll Geld, welche Tilden ... den Bürgern des Staates New York gerettet und erspart hat.

1876 *Cinc. Enquirer* 17 July 4/1. He [A. B. Cornell] is worth $15,000,000, and

can put a "barrel of money" into the campaign.

1876 *N.Y. Trib.* 14 Aug. 4/6. There is evidently great alarm in Indiana about Gov. Tilden's much talked of "barrel of money."

1876 *Ann. of Cleve.* 16 Aug. No.2557 Tilden's "bar'l of money" is beginning to show up in Cleveland.

1876 *N. Y. Trib.* 18 Aug. 4/6. The chairman of the Democratic State Committee of Maine declares ... that he has received no intimation that any of Gov. Tilden's barrel of money is going to be sent to that state.

B. Undoubtedly the popularity of the "barrel" was increased by Nast's cartoons. It appears in those in *Harper's W.* of 26 Aug., 16 Sept., 30 Sept., 28 Oct., 11 Nov., etc.

The phrase persisted even after Tilden had retired from active politics.

1879 *N. Y. Trib.* 29 May 4/5. Judge Davis is advertised now as a millionaire. Another barrel in the field.

1880 *Ib.* 5 March 4/5. There is no sense in squandering the contents of the barrel, if it *is* full.

1880 *Ib.* 10 March 4/5. All the Democratic booms are out of sight, and the barrel holds the field alone.

1880 *Puck* 21 July 355/1. Thus the greatest of all the bar'ls is yet un-tapped—the real old original Tilden bar'l.

C. The barrel had a new vogue in 1884 when the candidacy of Blaine brought the corruption issue to the foreground.

1884 *Boston Jrnl.* 16 June 2/2. Mr. Flower was a Man-with-a-barrel and one who knows how to tap it.

1884 *Cinc. Enquirer* 2 July 4/1. Blaine has no barrel. He was nominated without the use of money.

1884 *Puck* 2 April 66/1. When the history of this turbulent century is written down, there will be a large chapter devoted to

"The Bar'l in American Politics." It is not the least of the ominous "signs of the times," that this word "bar'l" should have become a piece of common and common-place slang. It means a barrel—a barrel of money—a barrel of money to be used in various dark and dishonest ways, to procure the election to office of him who owns it.

Later uses:

1909 *Rev. of Rev.* Jan. XXXIX 36 [cartoon]. "The Barr'l Will Get Ye If Ye Don't Watch Out!"...Charles P. Taft His Barrel.

1931 Steffens *Autobio.* 525. There was an investigation in Wisconsin of the repurchase by a lumber senator of his seat in the Senate. He had "opened a barrel at both ends," and his agent who handled the money was snitching on the stand.

1932 Mencken *Making a President* 27. The second is that he lacked Lord Hoover's bar'l, could not find an angel to finance him, and hence had to keep out of the Southern States, where only cast money counts.

barren ideality.

An unrealistic proposal.

This euphemistic phrase was apparently coined by Gov. William Allen of Ohio.

1875 *Urbana* (Ohio) *Citizen and Gazette* 5 Aug. suppl. [interview with Gov. Allen]. I regard the whole doctrine of specie payments as an ideality, without practical foundation to rest on. I regard it as a *d----d barren ideality*, sir.

1890 Ingalls in *Gt. Deb.* XIV.261. It is a dream. It is a barren ideality, as has been said about another transaction.

bashaw.

A leading politician.

Though *bashaba* is the name of a chief in the Abnaki tribe of Maine (see *DA*), there is no doubt that the political *bashaw* is a variant of Turkish *pasha* (*OED*). The

reference to "three tails" and "six tails" is further evidence of this relationship; the number of horse tails on his standard being a mark of the pasha's rank.

1776 J. Adams *Works* IX.387. The dons, the bashaws, the grandees, the patricians, the sachems, the nabobs, call them by what name you please, sigh, groan, and fret.

1835 Crockett *Van Buren* 96. No bashaw with three tails ever had his slaves under more abject and servile control.

1840 *Ohio St. Jrnl.* 4 Feb. 3/5. We do not have the honor...to be represented in that august assembly [Dem. Conv.] of disinterested and pure patriots by a "Bashaw of six tails."

See MOGUL.

basket meeting.

A picnic-type political meeting.

1859 Bartlett *Dict.* 24. Basket-meeting, in the West, a sort of picnic, generally with some religious "exercises."

1862 *Lancaster* (Ohio) *Eagle* 4 Sept. 3/1. Grand Basket Meeting of the Democracy. ...The Democratic Ladies are expected to be present with their baskets filled with eatables.

Bastil(l)e.

A. The name of the Paris prison was symbolic of tyrannical oppression before the American Revolution.

1750 Mayhew in Thornton *Pulpit in Am. Revolution* ["Discourse Concerning Unlimited Submission"]. God be thanked! one may, in any part of the British dominions, speak freely ... without being in danger either of the Bastile or the Inquisition.

B. In America the word was used to describe the slave market in Washington.

1844 Giddings *Sp.* 137. Go to the Bastile of slavery on Maryland Avenue which is so distinctly in view from the windows of this hall.

C. When during the Civil War suspension of the writ of *habeas corpus* made imprisonment without trial possible, the word became the favorite catchword in the South and among the anti-administration forces of the North.

1862 Gray & Ropes *Ltrs.* 17 ... to justify his removal to the East to some "Bastille" there.

1862 *Cols. Crisis* 24 Sept. 1/1 ... they had Democrats arrested for *treason* and confined in the dungeons of Republican *Bastiles.*

1863 S. S. Cox *Eight Yrs.* 311. Bastiles of the Administration.

D. Characteristic of the popularity of the term is its frequent use in book and pamphlet titles.

1861 Anon. *The Bastille in America* [title].

1863 *The Bastiles of the North. By a Member of the Maryland Legislature* [title].

1865 Strong *Diary* IV.12. Two lamentable diatribes entitled "American Bastilles," or some such thing, I found particularly refreshing.

beershop politician.

1828 *Ohio St. Jrnl.* 13 March 3/5. Nor is a disquisition of public speeches and documents shrunk from by any—not even by the "Beer shop politicians."

bellmare. ¿

1889 Farmer *Americanisms* 50. A political leader. The term is a slang appropriation from the terminology of Western life, where it seems to be used in regard to mules much in the same way as bellwether is employed in England in reference to sheep.

bellwether.

A chief or leader of an unthinking crowd, attested in England from the 15th century. See *OED.*

In American politics:

1878 *Harper's W.* 7 Sept. 706/1. The "rank and file," as they are offensively called, will follow the bellwether over any wall and into any pasture, but the independent sheep will not.

The analogous use of German *Leithammel* goes back at least to 1848:

1848 Herwegh *Briefe* 151.... wir werden uns weder durch die reaktionären, noch durch die liberalen Leithammel zurückhalten lassen, welche, ... aus Konstitutionellen über Nacht Republikaner geworden.

betweenites.

Moderate Federalists during the administration of John Adams:

1800 in Dauer *The Adams Federalists* 28 June 276. [referring to *Columbian Centinel*] This [moderate] still carries more of an implication of non-partisanship than is actually the case. There was in use at the time a word which best expresses the actual situation, "Betweenites."

b'hoys.

A. The enthusiastic but rough-mannered elements in a party, especially the Democratic party in New York. The *h* indicates the prominence of the Irish in this class, and there is evidently a connection with names like White Boys, Peep o' Day boys, Oak Boys used by Irish organizations in the 18th and 19th centuries. Charles Lever uses *boys* without any additions in his novel *Tom Burke of "Ours,"* as a synonym for Irish underground men. The novel was published in 1872, but the wording probably reflects the usage of around 1800:

Lever *Works* I.256/7. "The boys," said Derby, thereby meaning his own party. ... "Ye must larn that air, Master Tom; and see, now, the yeos [Anglified landed proprietors] is as fond of it as the boys. . . ."

B. American political usage:

1841 *Sketches of Mike Walsh* 22. Here there was a tremendous uproar and a general fight, in which the "boys," as the Young Democracy are familiarly termed were triumphantly victorious.

1846 in *Mangum Papers* IV. 488 ... "the Boys" the spirit of which last expression the Whigs have always (except in 1840) neglected.

1848 *Ib.* V.123. The b'hoys have had little to do with Taylor's success.

1848 *Ann. of Cleve.* No. 1101. Mr. Whipple is one of the "b'hays" [sic] of a higher grade. He goes the whole figure without bolting.

1865 Sala *Diary* 260 ... who have dressed up the hobbledehoys of Brooklyn in the snowy turbans and scarlet breeches of Zouaves, and the "bhoys" of the Bowery in the tunics and plumed hats of Bersaglieri.

1870 Cozzens *Sayings* 52. "Let us," said the Doctor, "Take up the familiar, every day language—the language, sir, not of the drawing room, but of the street—the language, not of the b'hoy, sir, and dissect it."

big bug.

Humorous allusion to people of prominence and particularly to politicians of high rank in the party.

1820 *Phila. Aurora.* If we learn them more than their neighbors, when they grow up, they get saucy— ... which to be what some of our big bugs call genteel; that is, wear ruffles and fine clothes instead of homespun.

1824 *Cinc. Nat. Rep.* 29 Oct. 2/3. Hereafter, I would advise your big-bugs of Cincinnati to keep their political jackalls [sic] at home.

1829 Kendall *Autobio.* 280. You must know that the "big bugs" here pay no attention to the sun or the time of day in regulating their meals. They are above that.

1835 *Niles' Reg.* 4 July 311/1. A new piece will be produced [in Boston] called "Bugs, Big and Little.". . . No doubt, some of our big bugs will figure conspicuously.

1853 *St. Louis Morning Herald* 10 May. Who is that walking there with the big bugs in front? he eagerly asked. Why, don't you know? That is the Governor.

1865 *Three Yrs. Among the Working Classes* 14. Republican "big bugocracy" sports its jewels, silks, and drapery.

See BIG GUN.

big deal.

A variation of *square deal, new deal, fair deal,* with connotations associating it with *big business.*

In American slang *big deal* designates an undertaking of exaggerated importance or of doubtful benefit.

1953 *Cols. Dispatch* 15 Feb. A13. Former Gov. Adlai E. Stevenson of Illinois pledged support tonight to President Eisenhower's "business administration"— provided that the New Deal successor did not become "The Big Deal."

1954 *Nation* 26 June 543. The "Big Deal" Tax Bill. [head]

big gun.

A leading politician.

An allusion to the large cannons which were a decisive factor in all battles. The early use of *great* instead of *big* is probably an attempt to be literary.

1807 *Weekly Inspector* 318 ... from the doughty Cheetham, the great gun of democracy, down to that pitiful pop-gun, the Public Advertiser.

1828 *Niles Reg.* 5 April 97/2. It [McDuffie's essay] is regarded as the "great gun" or "long Tom," of the enemies of the American system.
1836 *Ohio St. Jrnl.* 12 April 3/4. He is, you know, one of the great guns of the precious party.
1842 *Ann. of Cleve.* No. 1703 ... the Whigs would have an opportunity of discussing issues with Burigh and other "big guns."
1856 *Darke County Dem.* 6 Aug. 2/1 ... Tom Spooner, the K.N. "Big Gun" at the Black-Republican ratification meeting in Dallas.

See also BIG BUG.

big stick.

A policy of threatening force.

A. Closely associated with Theodore Roosevelt, the phrase was apparently first used by him in 1900:

1900 Roosevelt *Ltrs.* II.1141. I have always been fond of the West African proverb: "Speak softly and carry a big stick; you will go far." If I had not carried the big stick the organization would not have gotten behind me.

The expression was probably given universal currency by its repeated usage in presidential speeches.

1901 in *T. Roosevelt Cyc.* 2 Sept. 42 [at Minnesota State Fair]. "Speak softly and carry a big stick—you will go far." If a man continually blusters, if he lacks civility, a big stick will not save him from trouble; and neither will speaking softly avail, if back of the softness there does not lie strength, power.
1903 *Ib.* 2 April 42 [at Chicago]. There is a homely old adage which runs: "Speak softly and carry a big stick; you will go far." If the American Nation will speak softly, and yet build, and keep at a pitch of the highest training, a thoroughly efficient navy, the Monroe Doctrine will go far.

While his contemporaries frequently considered Roosevelt's

"big stick" a symbol of a bullying attitude in internal affairs and in U.S. relations with weaker neighbors (cf. Shaw, *Cartoon History of Roosevelt's Career*, N.Y. 1910, pp. 131, 134, 135, 144), he himself insisted that the adage should be taken as a whole and that the big stick was certainly no more important than soft speech.

1914 in *Roosevelt Cyc.* One of the main lessons to learn from this war is embodied in the homely proverb: "Speak softly and carry a big stick." Persistently only half of this proverb has been quoted in deriding the men who wish to safeguard our national interest and honor. Persistently the effort has been made to insist that those who advocate keeping our country able to defend its rights are merely adopting "the policy of the big stick." In reality, we lay equal emphasis on the fact that it is necessary to speak softly; in other words, that it is necessary to be respectful toward all people and scrupulously to refrain from wronging them, while at the same time keeping ourselves in condition to prevent wrong being done to us. If a nation does not in this sense speak softly, then sooner or later the policy of the big stick is certain to result in war.

B. In spite of Roosevelt's own interpretation, the *big stick* part of the proverb is the one the public remembered and the one that still is used in political language.

?1909 *San Francisco Bulletin* in Train *Yankee Lawyer* 216.
"Dear Teddy, I [Taft] need you; come home to me quick,
I am worried and weary and worn.
And as hope long deferred only makes the heart sick,
I am sadly in need of your potent 'Big Stick';
So, Teddy, please haste your return."
1909 *Cols. Citizen* 20 Sept. [edit.]. Taft Resurrects "Big Stick" and Hits Railroads.

1936 Barry *Theme Song* 34. The Senate "bloc" of 22 votes, spectacularly arranged solely as a tactical gesture of power, under the leadership of Senator Kenyon was the big stick—but there had to be created a force to wield the big stick.
1946 *Time* 16 Nov. No union leader would say it, but labor's strategy over the next few months was to tread softly until it was clear how the other fellow [government] might use his big stick.

C. Roosevelt always insisted that the source of his phrase was the old proverb; however, *big stick* appears in New York politics at a much earlier period. The possibility of a connection between Mike Connolly's "big shtick" and Roosevelt's is suggested by the fact that Halpine's poetical works were edited by Robert Barnwell Roosevelt, uncle to Theodore.
1869 Halpine *Poetical Works* 259. Your heart is big, an' your brain is big—Out o' jail you 're our "biggest big thing," And 'tis Big Judge Mike, wid his big shtick, That'll break the Tammany "Ring."

billion-dollar Congress.

Applied exaggeratingly to the 51st Congress, ridiculing its extravagant appropriations. However, the term may already have been in use before that time. [ ]
1893 Henderson of Iowa in *Cong. Rec.* App. 3 March. You can now change the old tune of "a billion-dollar congress," and tell the story of a billion-dollar democratic house.... The Democratic press, after the work of the Fifty-first Congress was completed, came out with such headlines as these: "The Billion Congress" ... "The Indelible Billion" ... These are a few sample headlines of 1891.
1893 Champ Clark in *Cong. Rec.* 2667/2. I would much prefer to see this Congress pass into history as a million-volume Congress rather than a billion-dollar Congress. [Satirizes govt. publications.]

1897 *Cong. Rec.* 89/1. Mr. Dockery: After the wasteful appropriations of the "billion-dollar Congress," the annual expenditures of the government leaped from $303,792,115.07 to $305,342,188.30.
Mr. Lacey: Which "billion-dollar Congress"?
Mr. Dockery: The first "billion-dollar Congress."
Mr. Maguire: This is the second.
Mr. Dockery: No; the last Congress was the third.

bird dog.

The term enjoyed an ephemeral vogue when used by Secretary of Defense Charles Wilson in a speech on the unemployment situation.
1954 *N. Y. Times* 12 Oct. 13/4. "I've always liked bird dogs better than kennel-fed dogs myself—you know, one who'll get out and hunt for food rather than sit on his haunches* and yell." [*In the transcription of his remarks (*Times,* 13 Oct. 1/2) the word is "fanny."]
1954 *Ib.* 13 Oct. 1/2. Wilson Protests Remarks on "Bird Dog" as "Distorted" [head] ... "I certainly intended no individual comparisons nor insinuations likening people to dogs in any sense."
1954 in *Cols. Citizen* 14 Oct. 3/1. Republicans weighed today the political effects of ... Wilson's abject apology to the American people for his "inept remarks" about bird dogs and the unemployed. Wilson ... said: "I admit that I made a mistake—an unfortunate mistake—by bringing up those bird dogs at the same time I was talking about people."

The brief popularity of the metaphor led to secondary metaphors:
1954 *Cols. Citizen* 15 Oct. 14/1 [edit.]. Say one thing for Charley Wilson: He sure put the election on Page 1. It had been a dull campaign, and guileless Charley didn't intend to get mixed up in it when, without benefit of muzzle, he held that press conference where he made the off-hand remark that he preferred hunting dogs to kennel dogs.

1954 *Ib.* 19 Oct. AFL's No. 2 Chief Attacks Wilson's Bird-Dog Remark [head] ..."they [working people] wear no leash and they will not be muzzled—nor will they rest content with a diet of second-rate slogans and second-best statistics."

black abolitionist. [ ]

See BLACK REPUBLICAN.

? Douglas in Sandburg *Prairie Yrs.* II.11 ...those renegades from the party, Trumbull, Palmer, Judd, and Cook, who have formed an unholy alliance to turn the glorious old Democratic party over to the black Abolitionists.

Black and Tan.

Nickname for Southern Republicans.

1868 *Harper's W.* 25 April 258/3. The din about "Pan-African" or "Black and Tan" Conventions...are all parts of the efforts to throw the political power in those States wholly into the hands of the class most disaffected to the Union and the Government.

1868 in A. G. Ranck *Brown* 259. He [General Ord] brought into existence the "Black and Tan" Convention.

1868 in Garner *Reconstruction in Miss.* 186. The important political event of Gen. Gillem's administration was the session of the reconstruction convention locally known as the "Black and Tan" convention.

Evidently the name was directed against the negrophile tendencies of this group.

1868 Strong *Diary* 30 Jan. IV.184. Meanwhile, the "Reconstructing" Conventions seem to work hopefully....It is easy to write reports of the proceedings of "black and tan conventions"—"whitey-brown committees"—"Meade's Ministrels"—and the like.

1868 *Harper's W.* 2 May 283/4. Nicknames abound at the South, although it is difficult to see any points of beauty in them, even if they are ingenious. The Reconstruction Convention in Florida was

called "The Black and Tan Convention"; that of Georgia, "The Unconstitutional Convention"; that in Mississippi, "the Miscegenation Convention";...that in South Carolina, "The Ring Streaked and Striped Negro Convention"; that in North Carolina, "The Gorilla Bayonet Convention"; that in Virginia, "The Bones and Banjo Convention."

black cockade.

The Democratic fashion to wear the French cockade as an outward sign of their sympathy with republican France induced the Federalists to adopt the black (and white) cockade as their party badge. It is alleged that the suggestion came from William Cobbett (Meigs, *Ingersoll,* p. 31). The party badge was widely used, especially in New England.

1798 *Columbian Centinel* in Buckingham *Specimens* 4 July II.73. It has been repeatedly recommended that our citizens wear in their hats on the day of Independence, the American cockade, (which is a Rose, composed of black ribbon, with a white button, or fastening) and that the Ladies should add to the attraction of their dress (the Ladies cockade should be a white rose), this symbol of their attachment to the government, which cherishes and protects them....Every cockade will be another edition of the Declaration of Independence, and the demonstration of it, by this national emblem now, will be as highly laudable as the display of the immortal instrument of 1776 was then....

1840 *Georgia Jrnl.* 28 April 3/2. In 1826, John Randolph in the presence of Gen. Harrison in the Senate of the United States, declared that Gen. Harrison was a Federalist of the order of the Sedition Law and Black Cockade Administration.

1840 in Norton *Log Cabin* App. 86.

When my old hat was new, of Richard Rush 'twas said,

To figure well among the Feds he wore a black cockade.

1840 *Rough-hewer* 251. General Harrison's Black Cockade Standing Army Speech. The terrific scenes and sufferings of the democrats under the black cockade reign of terror of old John Adams.

Black Code.

Laws which were directed against the negro population, chiefly but not exclusively in the Southern states.

1840 *New Orleans Picayune* 30 July 2/1. A black man ... has been arrested and ... [will] be tried before Judge Preval, under the Black Code.

1857 Julian *Sp.* 127. The sad truth is, that Indiana is the most pro-slavery of all our Northern States. Her Black Code ... tells her humiliating pedigree far more forcibly than any words I can employ.

1866 in Lefler *North Carolina* 321. North Carolina's "Black Code" was one of the most tolerant.

black democracy.

The Democratic party in as far as it favored slavery.

1856 *We the People* (Indianapolis) 27 May 3/2. The Black Democracy.—For the purpose of casting odium upon those who desire to limit Slavery to the States where it now exists, they are called "Black Republicans". . . . The Republicans are opposed to the extension of *black* slavery into Kansas. The Democrats are in favor of it, and hence, if there is any propriety in using the word, it ought to be applied to the Democracy. Let them be hereafter called the "Black Democracy" so long as they apply the epithet to the Republican, or People's Party.

1856 *Marshall* (Mich.) *Statesman* 20 Aug. 2/3. The black democracy assert that he [Bingham] is "unfit" to be Governor of Michigan.

Black Horse Cavalry.

A. Following an English tradition, the government of Virginia organized a regiment of black horse cavalry, which among others took part in the first battle of Bull Run.

1862 S. S. Cox *Twenty Yrs.* 221. A cry was raised that the Black Horse, a formidable body of the rebel cavalry ... were charging upon us.

1861 *Harper's W.* 10 Aug. 510/4. The Fire Zouaves and the Black Horse Cavalry ... the famous Black Horse Guard, about which Governor Wise has so frequently spoken.

1862 *N.Y. Times* 26 April 2/5. The Black Horse and the Zouaves were at it pell mell, determined to conquer or die. . . . The strife had ceased and Black Horse and Zouave lay down together.

B. We may assume that the uniform color of the horses created an impression of compactness. It may have been this quality that caused the transfer of the phrase to parliamentary groups voting in unison at the command of a leader. Perhaps the first clique known by that name was organized by Boss Tweed; hence, the connotation of corruption that clings to the name.

1878 in Werner *Tammany* 176. There was an organization formed of men of both parties, Republicans and Democrats, called the Black Horse Cavalry, composed of twenty-eight or thirty persons, who would all be controlled by one man, and vote as he directed them.

1905 Riordan *Plunkett* 82 ... did me the honor to call me commander-in-chief of the "Black Horse Cavalry."

1913 Roosevelt *Autobio.* 70. The corrupt legislators, the "black horse cavalry," as they were termed, would demand payment to vote as the corporation wished.

1929 Smith *Up to Now* 113. The revelation of the Hughes insurance investigation silenced the so-called Black Horse Cavalry and put an end to the open operations of the lobby.

Black Know Nothing.

Evidently coined as a parallel to *Black Republican.*

1855 *Marshall* (Mich.) *Democratic Expounder* 29 Nov. 2/3. Black Know Nothings. . . . The colored population generally voted for the American ticket day-before yesterday.

1856 *Hancock Courier* (Findlay, Ohio) 7 June 2/3. The Abolitionists and Black Know Nothings in the House have a majority and they of course would not expel or censure one of their own midnight band.

black law.

Patterned on *blue law;* characterizing laws relating to slavery.

1836 Lydia Marie Child *An Appeal* 200. Fifty years hence, the *black* laws of Connecticut will be a greater source of amusement to the antiquarian, than her famous *blue* laws.

1842 *Ohio Statesman* 6 Aug. 3/2. The black laws of Ohio were a disgrace to our Statute books.

1850 Julian *Sp.* 20. All attempts to repeal our [Indiana] "black laws" (and some are much blacker than this) have thus far signally failed.

1855 in *Garrison Story* 24 Dec. III.418. Now I feel quite certain that the very people who will vote against the introduction of slavery [in Kansas] will also vote for a "Black Law." . . . I can find but few who dare to say that they are in favor of allowing the colored man to come here and buy land on an equality with the white man.

1856 *Cinc. Enquirer* 17 May 4/1. The Black-Law Negrophilists. . . . the silence and acquiescence of the negrophilists in laws excluding negroes from States in which they reside.

blackleg.

As a synonym for *gambler* or *horse jockey* the term apparently referred to the black boots which were a characteristic feature of their uniform.

1817 Paulding *Ltrs.* I.39 . . . it is not customary to dress fine at the Springs, or elsewhere; those who do, are apt to be taken for Black Legs, or Horse Jockeys.

182– Scott *Heart of Midlothian* ch.XIII. At a fair or market, you could not for a moment have doubted that he was a horse-jockey. . . . His dress was also that of a horse-dealer—close-buttoned jockey-coat, or wrap-rascal, as it was then termed, with huge metal buttons, coarse blue upper stockings, called boot hose, because supplying the place of boots, and a slouched hat.

1849 Melville *Redburn* 319. They seemed unanimous in believing that, by abandoning his country, Harry had left more room for the gamblers. Jackson even asked him to lift up the lower hem of his trowsers, to test the color of his calves.

The term created a sensation in politics when a reference by John Randolph to the collusion between Adams and Clay—

1826 in Garland *Randolph* II.254. I was defeated, horse, foot, and dragoons—cut up, and clean broke down by the coalition of Blifil and Black George—by the combination, unheard of till then, of the puritan and the blackleg.

—precipitated a duel between him and Clay.

We find references to this event long after:

1890 *N. Y. Sun* 8 Nov. 6/4 . . . "combine" of renegade Democrats, Republicans, Mugwumps and preachers—"Puritans and Blacklegs" to use an expressive John Randolphism.

There is evidence, however, that Clay had already been called a *blackleg* before Randolph's insult:

1825 *Alleghany Dem.* in James *Jackson* 443. Henry Clay . . . morally and politically a gambler, a blackleg and a traitor.

Occasional later uses of the expression:

1836 *Hamilton Intelligencer* 27 Oct. 1/6. Rush into the arena with fearless step & dauntless spirit, & never quit the ground until you have utterly subverted every scheme of the Black Leg Politicians. . . .
1844 in *Mangum Papers* IV.22. Not long since they were all of them, needy, shiftless, desperate and unscrupulous political black-legs, eagerly engaged in studying the tracks and chances.
1873 *N. Y. Times* 13 Feb. 4 . . . the Republican party stood for Mr. Havemeyer, but were denounced "as a party of gamblers and black-legs."

black line (er).

Reference to the division of sentiments over the Negro question. The meaning is not consistently clear nor is the association with actual black lines always obvious.
[ ]
1855 *Marshall* (Mich.) *Democratic Expounder* 25 Oct. 2/3. The free-soil papers, and the Whig papers, too, seemed to take a savage delight in publishing his name surrounded with black lines, and denouncing him [Douglas] as a "doughface" who proposed to draw a black line through the territory of the union. . . . Douglas was again denounced in unmeasurable terms by the same party, for moving the repeal of this same "black line" [36° 30']. . . .
1855 Choate *Life and Writings* II.329 . . . we have no new party tonight; that, when we have, we shall choose any other, aye, any other, than that which draws the black line of physical and social geography across the charmed surface of our native land. . . .
1876 44th Cong. 2 Sess. 45 *Sen. Misc. Doc.* 583. Warren County . . . made a clean sweep of the county officers for the blackliners, and today scores of their ignorant dupes lie buried in the ditches.

See COLOR LINE.

black list.

A listing of persons who are felt to deserve public censure.

A. Attested as early as 1692 in England (*OED*), the origin of the black list is suggested by a later incident:
1794 Erskine *Sp.* II.130. Two books should be opened, one of them (bound in black) in which should be entered all the enormities of those who deserve the censure.

B. In America opposition presses have printed black lists of politicians who advocate measures or policies contrary to their beliefs.
1820 *N. H. Patriot and State Gazette* 28 March 3/2 . . . arrayed their Black Lists to the gaze of their admiring readers.
1826 *Ann. of Cleve.* No.262. "Ohio Black List." The Anti-Administration presses have published for months past the names of Messrs. Whittlesey, Beecher, . . . under the above title.
1856 *Ohio St. Jrnl.* 3 July 2/2. The Black List [Record of vote in House for admission of Kansas]. It will be seen that Ohio presents a clean record in the affirmative, with the exception of one black sheep, John Scott Harrison, in the negative, and one absent, Richard Mott.
1860 Helper *Impending Crisis* 120. The black list of three hundred and forty-seven thousand slaveholders, who, as a body, have shocked the civilized world with their barbarous conduct.
1874 *N. Y. w. Trib.* 21 Oct. 3/2. Down to the end of the Tweed regime, the representatives of the people were commonly spoken of as "thieves." It was no uncommon thing to find in the morning's Tribune a "black list" containing the names of the more noted among them, and the prices they were supposed to have received for their votes on particular measures.

Black Republican (-ism).

The term *red republican* (q.v.) being current at the time of the foundation of the Republican Party, it must have been only a question of time when its negrophile tendencies would cause it to be denounced as black republican. According to Hudson (*Journalism in the U.S.*, p. 275) the men who actually coined this epithet were Major Heiss of the *Washington Union* and George N. Sanders:

The later name of "Black Republican" was given to the present Republican Party as one of reproach, just before the Rebellion, by Major Heiss of the Washington Union, and the well-known George N. Sanders.... "If the Republicans of France are red," said Sanders, "ours must be black."

In any case the word was used by Stephen Douglas as early as September, 1854:

Peoria Weekly Republican in *Lincoln Works* II.234. The Judge had called the new party Black Republican. He might call names, and thereby pander to prejudice, as much as he chose: he (Mr. L.) would not bandy such language with him.
1854 *Peru Daily Union City* 29 Sept. 2/2. To see Stephen A. Douglas...dealing in "niggerism," "fusionists," "black republicanism," and such slang phrases....

During the pre-Civil War years *black republican* was the most prominent term of abuse on the Democratic side:

1855 *Wash. Daily Union* 30 Sept. 2/6. How can the Union stand if this black "republican party" obtains the ascendency in the North?
1855 *Ann. of Cleve.* No.2931. Why is it that the Washington reporters of the AP, in their dispatches term our party the "black" Republicans? It is no part of their business to retail the low cant of such a paper as the N. Y. Herald.
1855 *Lancaster* (Ohio) *Eagle* 13 Dec. 2/5. Two parties have reared their hydra heads in opposition to the Constitution— the K.Nothings, with their dark lanterns and the Black Republicans with their woolly heads.

1856 *Cleve. Campaign Dealer* 31 Oct. 1/2. A Black Republican [under picture of Negro].
1856 *Hartford Courant* 6 March. Though some belittled the new party with taunts of "Black Republicanism," it was really an aristocratic, white man's party, for it intended to preserve as much of the land as it could from "the pestilential presence of the black race."
1856 *Middletown* (N.Y.) *Banner of Liberty* 47/3. The National Democrats and Whigs have met the cohorts of Black Republicanism in all their boasted strength and glory, and made the monster bite the dust; the lion of Fusion now lies crouching at the feet of the indomitable Democracy, with its blind devotees scattered and discomfited, cast, torn and bleeding from every pore, never, never to raise its hydra head to power in Indiana again.
1858 Douglas in Sparks *Lincoln-Douglas Deb.* 170...until I nail the responsibility of it upon the back of the Black Republican party throughout the State. ["White, white...."]
Ib. 193. After a copious volley of phrases from the cock-pit, he bellowed out "You Black Republicans" to his audience, who stopped him right in his tracks, and ordered him to say "white," or to leave off the adjective entirely. [See also pp. 93, 95, 168, 180, 188, 202, etc.]
1860 in *Sp. and Add. of Winter Davis* 130. That sagacious and learned body, the Senate...having before them this bill for the inauguration of that great modern convenience in the city of Baltimore, thought that there likewise they should protect themselves by law against this poison in the atmosphere. And therefore it was provided, and now stands as a part of that bill, "That no Black Republican, or indorser or approver of the Helper book (laughter) shall receive any of the benefits and privileges of this act, or be employed in any capacity by the said railway company." (Renewed laughter.)
1861 Brownlow *Sketches* 58. Any man saying...that I am an Abolitionist or a Black Republican is a liar and a scoundrel.
1862 Hayes *Diary* 5 June. General Sher-

man said he was "ashamed to acknowledge that he had a brother who was one of these damned Black Republicans."

Even in recent years *Black Republican* seems to be aggressive enough to make an accompanying apologetic gesture advisable if the term is used in the presence of a Republican friend.

1947 Helm *Truman* 25. "And there I saw the honored graves of Mr. Helm's father and grandfather.... They were all good Democrats. And how in the hell a man with that background can be a black Republican is more than I can understand." Having thus denounced me with twinkling eyes he then would take the curse off. "I'm afraid you can trust him, nevertheless...."

blackwash.

The counterpart of *whitewash* (q.v.).

1839 in *Cong. Globe* Jan. App. Every effort will be used by the committee to whitewash the black frauds and corrupt iniquities of Swartwout, and blackwash the administration.

bleeding Kansas.

A popular phrase of Northern orators to describe the violence of the slavery controversy in Kansas, 1854–1860. The use of *bleeding* to depict the devastation or bloodshed in a country is attested in English usage from the seventeenth century, when it was "bleeding Ireland" (*OED*).

According to Farmer (*Americanisms*, p. 62), "bleeding Kansas" was "believed to have been originally coined as a newspaper headline by the *New York Tribune*" but no actual record of such a headline has been found as yet.

However, the phrase is found in 1856 and with increasing frequency in the following years:

1856 *Cleve. Plain Dealer* 7 Nov. The ladies ... were on their kerchy-benders, too, sighing and sobbing for "bleeding Kansas."

1857 *Ohio Statesman* 14 Jan. 2. "B-l-e-e-d-i-n-g K-a-n-s-a-s!" Mr. McCurdy, yesterday, introduced into the House a resolution to appropriate $20,000 of the people's money for "the relief of the suffering citizens of the Territory of Kansas."

bloated bondholder (and others).

English phrases like *bloated minister* (1731), *bloated pluralist* (1863), *bloated aristocracy* (1868) (see *OED*) form the pattern for various American propaganda phrases directed against the privileged classes.

1851 *Liberator* in *Garrison Story* III.334. I was not putting my legs under the tables of the bloated planters of the South, or truckling politicians of the North of America.

1866 Browne *Artemus Ward, His Travels* 132. Of course I mean no disrespect to the United States of America in the remark, but I think I prefer a bloated monarchy!

1884 Hay *Breadwinners* 166. "We are Labor Reformers," said the spokesman. "We represent the toiling millions against the bloated capitalists and grinding monopolies; we believe that man is better...."

The most important phrase in this group is *bloated bondholder;* frequently used by those who advocated payment of the war debt in greenbacks:

1868 *Harper's W.* 31 Oct. 691/4. And these people are the bloated bondholders.

1877 in *Gt. Deb.* XIV.66 ... not that he is a "bloated bondholder," for, as in every such case, the bloated bondholder knows how to take care of himself.

1878 *Harper's W.* 24 Aug. 667/3. "Bloated bondholders" are made to take in this country the place held in other countries by the "bloated aristocrats."

1958 *Cleve. Press* 9 Dec. 6. Salty Harry S. Truman has got the White House dander up again—or still. Speaking at a National Press Club blowout in Washington, HST called the GOP the "bloated bondholder party."

bloc.

As the spelling indicates the word comes from France where Clemenceau organized the Bloc des Gauches toward the end of the 19th century and edited a paper called *Le Bloc* from 1900 on. (The electoral success of the Bloc des Gauches in 1902 brought Clemenceau back into the public eye. Jackson, *Clemenceau*, p. 123). After the first World War, Poincare created the Bloc National. The American press in referring to this later organization takes over the French term:

1923 *Rev. of Rev.* LXVIII.436. Poincare is solidly supported by the majority in the Chamber of Deputies, called the national Bloc. . . .

1924 *Ib.* LXIX 43 . . . the Bloc National, which supported Poincare, and the Bloc of the Left, which opposed him.

In American politics the first and still most frequent use of *bloc* applies to organizations of the farm interests.

1921 *Nation* 21 Sept. 308/2. The most interesting development in Congress up to the recess was the formation of the agricultural bloc which came close to holding the balance of power in the Senate.

1936 Barry *Theme Song* 24. One afternoon in early December, 1920, on a houseboat in the St. Johns River, Florida, Senator Harding sat with four advisers. In about ninety days he would be President of the United States, and he was casting a weather eye over his approaching empire.

By way of opening a major subject the Senator remarked: "What shall we do about the farm bloc?"

1935 Pollard *A Connotary* 12. Bloc—a minority group often led by a bloc-head.

blocks of five.

In the 80's floaters (q.v.), particularly in Indiana where it had become customary to lock up large numbers of unreliable voters until they were marched to the polls on election day, became a major problem. Of course, whiskey was served in large quantities in order to keep them in humor, a practice which occasionally led to serious disorders. According to Dabney (1888 *Nation,* 22 Nov. 412/3) on one occasion the floaters set fire to the building in which they were kept. In 1888 a letter ascribed to W. W. Dudley, treasurer of the Republican National Committee, but repudiated by him, proposed a change in these practices:

in Peck, *Twenty Years* 158. Divide the floaters into blocks of five and put a trusted man in charge of these five, with the necessary funds, and make him responsible that none get away, and that all vote our ticket.

From then on blocks of five are frequently mentioned as a feature of ward politics.

1888 *Nation* 22 Nov. 412/3 . . . the first batches of floaters (in "blocks of five," more or less) . . . .

1888 *N. Y. World* 27 Nov. 1/1. Blocks of Floaters. . . . Indiana, New Jersey and other States where the "blocks of floaters," in "bunches of fives," were driven to the polls like sheep.

1891 Roosevelt *Works* XIV.127 . . . a law which shall threaten the evils that exist in one State or section as much as those that exist in another which shall tell as heavily against "blocks of five" as against tissue ballots.

1892 *Nation* 16 June 442. No "blocks of five" can be marched to the polls on election day with their ballots held in sight of the man who has brought them till they are dropped into the ballot boxes.

bloodhound law.

The Fugitive Slave law of 1850.
[ ]
"Warrington" *Pen Portraits* 45. The Fugitive-slave Bill (Mason's), called the "Bloodhound Law," was signed Sept. 18, 1850. . . .

bloody chasm.

A. In his acceptance speech of May 20, 1872, Horace Greeley said:

1872 *N. Y. Trib.* 22 May 4/3. I accept your nomination, in the confident trust that the masses of our countrymen, North and South, are eager to clasp hands across the bloody chasm which has too long divided them.

During the campaign the phrase was used to mock Greeley's policy of conciliation toward the South. Particularly in the cartoons of Thomas Nast was the satirical aspect of the phrase brought forth:

1872 *Harper's W.* 3 Aug. [cartoon]. "Baltimore 1861–1872. 'Let us Clasp Hands over the Bloody Chasm.'" [Greeley is shaking hands with an Irish Democrat over a body representing the Massachusetts 6th.]
24 Aug. [He is extending his hand to take the blood-drenched one of a Southern Ku-Kluxer]
14 Sept. [He is shaking hands with John Wilkes Booth over the grave of Lincoln.]

B. In later campaigns when reconciliation with the South was still a major factor:

1876 *Cong. Record* 14 June 3791/1. This measure is one of conciliation. It reunites;

it fills up the "bloody chasm."

1880 *Cinc. Gazette* 23 June 4/3. A ticket composed of Hancock and Hampton would typify the shaking of hands across the bloody chasm, and would carry out that idea of the union of the blue and the gray.

bloody shirt.

A. "Bloody shirt, the. usually found in the expression, 'waving the bloody shirt.' It is used to describe the attempts made in political campaigns (especially in 1872 and 1876) by radical Republicans to defeat the Democrats by impassioned oratory designed to keep alive the hatreds and prejudices of the Civil War period.

"Perhaps the most reasonable explanation of the origins of the phrase is the Scottish tradition that after the massacre of Glenfurin, 220 widows rode to Stirling Tower, each bearing aloft on a spear the bloody shirt of her murdered husband, thus arousing the people to take vengeance on their enemies." (*DAH*)

This statement must be revised on several important counts.

A number of historical events and fictional situations can be quoted that have just as good a claim to be considered in connection with the phrase as has the story about the widows of Glenfurin. Gibbon (*Decline and Fall*, II.703) mentions that the bloody shirt of the murdered caliph Othman was displayed in the Mosque of Damascus as an incitement to vengeance. In a similar way, the bloody shirts of victims were used in France during the revolutions of the 1830's.

1840 Fourcher in *Dem. Rev.* 370. It is by spreading out the miseries of the workmen, the bloody shirt of some victim, the humiliation of all, that the people are excited to take arms.

Walsh points to the Corsican custom of the "gridata" in which the bloody shirt of the murdered man is waved.

Of literary works to be considered in this context we might mention *Julius Caesar* (III.ii), Sidney's *Arcadia,* and the *Laxdaela Saga* (XL). Something of the latter might have been known in connection with the great interest in Iceland aroused by its millenial celebrations in 1874—a year of especial importance in the history of *bloody shirt.*

B. More important than these instances from overseas are a few episodes from American history in which a bloody garment was or was said to be used to keep the memory of an outrage alive.

Stimpson *Handbook of Am. Pol.* On one occasion Patrick Henry placed the bloody clothes of a murdered man in the courtroom where they could be seen by the jurymen.

1855 in Haynes *James Baird Weaver* 24. To Weaver probably belongs the credit of being one of the originators of the expression "the bloody shirt." His own story of the origin of the phrase was that a "preacher by the name of McKinney ... got the Negroes together at Ft. Worth and preached to them. Word was passed around that an abolitionist was exciting the Negroes to insurrection and the citizens got together. They took McKinney out and whipped him with a rawhide blacksnake whip, cutting his shirt into shreds and lacerating his body. He re-

turned to Davis county in about '55 or '56, and an abolitionist meeting was held and I presided. McKinney had his shirt with him.

A few days later . . . I recounted the outrages on McKinney and had the shirt with me. I waved it before the crowds and bellowed: 'Under this bloody shirt we propose to march to victory'."

1874 Lester *Sumner* 539. [According to Lester, Sumner had preserved the coat he had worn when attacked by Preston Brooks and showed the blood on it to John Brown when the latter set out on his Virginia expedition.]

Another story in this category is claimed as the source of the phrase and its use in politics:

Robert Holzman *Stormy Ben Butler* 180. After an Ohio carpetbagger ... was flogged in Mississippi, his blood-stained shirt was sent to Washington as an exhibit. Butler carried it to the floor of Congress and waved the garment above his head as he warned of punishment to the South; and from this incident all Reconstruction ranting became known as "waving the bloody-shirt."

Unfortunately the authenticity of this story is subject to great doubts, as pointed out by:

Pub. of Miss. Hist. Soc. IX.66n. Some say the bloody shirt worn by Huggins was carried to Washington by an army officer, turned over to Gen. Butler and that he waived [sic] the ensanguined garment in an impassioned sectional speech and that the incident gave rise to what is called "waiving the bloody shirt." I have not been able to positively verify this statement though it is vouched for by no less an authority than Major S. A. Jones. Dr. Spofford, the learned ex-Librarian of Congress, says that no such incident occurred in the hall of the House of Representatives. Lieutenant Pickett is said to have carried the "bloody shirt" away from here.

This criticism does not entirely exclude the possibility that the story may have some factual core. Both Lt. Pickett and Huggins are mentioned in the Ku Klux Klan Report of 1871; the latter as a victim of a KKK flogging, but we have not been able to identify Major Jones.

While nothing in this material can be shown to have had any direct influence on the origin of the political phrase, it seems valuable as an indication of how widespread was the idea of the bloody shirt as a symbol of retribution. On the other hand, Biblical allusions of this sort can be shown to have influenced American political speech. The language of Isaiah 34:6; 63:1 and Jeremiah 2:34 is reflected in the following quotations:

1828 *Ohio St. Jrnl.* 9 Feb. 1/5. We shall not be reluctant to proclaim our error and to wash his [Jackson's] blood stained garments white.

1859 Davidson in *Cong. Globe* 21 Dec. 201/3. And yet this man, John Sherman, whose garments are dyed with the blood of its victims, you propose to make third officer in the political government.

1866 Schurz *Life* I.392. The South entered the Philadelphia wigwam with the blood of Memphis and New Orleans upon her garments.

1867 Stevens in *Cong. Globe* 13 Feb. 1214 ...hugging and caressing those whose hands are red and whose garments are dripping with the blood of our and their murdered kindred.

C. The fundamentally new element in the use of *bloody shirt* during the '70's is the satirical attitude toward politicians who, if they do not invent stories about Southern outrages against the Negro, at least exaggerate them for propaganda purposes. In this way *bloody shirt* becomes part of a whole family of synonyms within which *raw head* and *bloody bones* seem to be its nearest relatives. It seems to be significant that this latter phrase is repeatedly used by the *New York World,* the paper that apparently is the first to use *bloody shirt* in its later sense.

1874 *N. Y. World* 3 Sept. 4/4. Even the New York *Times* finds it rather hard to swallow its own stories of "outrages".... It says, for very shame's sake, after publishing a long string of these raw-head and bloody-bones narratives....

1874 *Ib.* 9 Sept. 4/6. The Northern people, disgusted with the Radical carpet-bag villainies in the South, are not going to have their attention diverted again by the regularly "put-up" display of raw heads and bloody bones.

D. While the *DAH* attributes *bloody shirt* to 1872 without giving any quotation from that date, and while on the other side the earliest example quoted in historical literature dates from 1875, it is quite clear that the critical year is 1874. It may be important that the first actual occurrence of the political *bloody shirt* follows closely upon a sensational murder in New York, in which a bloody shirt played an important part.

1874 *N. Y. World* 10 July 5/2. A Blood-Stained Relic. The Night-Shirt in which Mr. Nathan was Murdered Found in an Outhouse Behind His Residence.... 11 July 5/2. The Nathan Night-Shirt Sensation.

1874 *N. Y. Times* 11 July 4/1. The Nathan murder is surrounded with mysteries and among them must be included the affair of the "bloody shirt," now being duly worked up into a "sensation" by the journal of personal advertisements.

As we said before, the *N. Y. World* seems to be ahead of other papers in its use of the propaganda phrase:

1874 *N. Y. World* 5 Sept. 4/1. Its [govt. circular's] purpose is to rescue the falling fortunes of the Republican party at the fall elections by usurping a state police at the South and shaking a bloody shirt in the eyes of the North.

Ib. 10 Sept. 4/5. The Republican party itself laughs at Grant's frantic waving of the bloody shirt.... Some organs of a completely abject servility, like the Albany Journal and the Troy Times, roar and grimace when the red rag is fluttered from the White House.

Ib. 21 Sept. 4/6. The thieves at Wash. evidently have much to conceal.... the instant the New Orleans affair began it was announced.... It is not the first time a thief has put on the bloody shirt.

Ib. 25 Sept. 1/6. Conkling waves the Bloody Shirt....

8/1. The party orators, small and great, were in effect told, if they found any Republicans inclined to support the excellent Democratic ticket, to shake the bloody shirt in their faces.

In 1875 and later the phrase is frequently attributed to Morton; in his speeches, however, we have failed to discover the term.

1875 *Cinc. Enquirer* 9 Aug. 1/4. Sen. Morton's Speech at Urbana. He Waves the bloody shirt....

4/2. More than ten years ago, a terrible civil war closed, but Oliver P. Morton is waving the bloody shirt still.

1875 *N. Y. Trib.* 3 Sept. 1/1. Mr. Morton Shakes out the Bloody Shirt again. His efforts were in the main directed toward a revival of the old war feeling against the South, and the bloody shirt was shaken as in the campaign of 1872.

1875 *Cinc. Enquirer* 11 Oct. 2/3.

> Oliver P.
> Morton, he
> Waves his shirt
> But it don't suit me.

1875? in Rhodes *Am. Hist.* VII.178. The *Cinc. Enquirer*, the leading Democratic organ, charged him [Morton] with introducing into the canvass "the bloody shirt."

1876 *Harper's W.* 30 Nov. 946/2. The bloody shirt, in Mr. Morton's sense, can never again be unfurled successfully.

The campaign of 1876, of course, makes full use of the phrase:

Tucker in *Cong. Record* 17 April 2523/2. There are gentlemen in this House ... who seem to think that whenever I rise upon this floor it is for the purpose of discussing State Rights, whether I propose to discuss State rights, or not, because that is one of the great bugaboos which is to go along with the "bloody shirt" in the great contest which is approaching.

Cinc. Gazette 28 June 2/1. The Republicans have once more unfurled the bloody shirt, that piratical flag.

Storrs in Adams *Emery A. Storrs* 155. They [Democrats] complain of us that we are waving the "bloody shirt," that we will not let by-gones be by-gones, and that we are continually singing the same old song, and making the same old speeches.

Meridian Merc. 29 July in *Cong. Record* 5183/2. He [Lamar] and others who wanted to dress up in a nice starched and ironed white shirt that would shame the bloody shirt, established a laundry at Jackson, on the 4th of August, and a great many patronized it and came out in snowy white fronts to present themselves creditably before the Northern public sentiment.

Logan in *Ib.* 5258/1 ... it has come to be a saying in this Chamber and in some of the feeble-minded newspapers that we are "shaking the bloody shirt" if we call attention to brutal wholesale murder of colored republicans. All I have to say in answer to that is that when democrats will stop staining the shirt with blood, we will quit shaking it.

Gov. Kirkpatrick in *N. Y. World* 22 Aug. 1/1. A Bloody Shirt campaign with money and Indiana is safe.

Later examples:

1878 *Nation* 26 Sept. 189. The incongruity of the political situation is shown in nothing more clearly than in the fact that the Republican leaders have used every means in their power to carry on the present campaign with the old issues, the old war-cries and the worn out passions of the past. They wanted above all things to "make it hot under the old flag," to wave the bloody shirt, and to attack the "Solid South."

1879 *Ib.* 6 Nov. 301. He will now probably run for Congress again, as likely as not, on the "bloody-shirt" issue. . . .

1880 *Cinc. Gazette* 24 June 9/2. Under Allen G. Thurman there will be no bloody shirt to kill. He will send it to his laundry.

1888 *Ohio St. Jrnl.* 1 Oct. 4/3. Who is waving the bloody shirt—who is reviving the memories of the war?

1952 *Nation* 2 Aug. 86. The bloody shirt wavers may still bolt to Eisenhower or a plain Dixiecrat.

bluebacked locofoco.

1840 *Ohio St. Jrnl.* 4 Jan. 1/3. They are the hard currency men, the Benton men, the "Perish Credit, Perish Commerce" men . . . the "Red-dog, blue-backed, Locofocos."

Blue-backed evidently refers to some sort of wild cat money. During the Civil War Confederate money is called *bluebacks:*

1869 Mathews *Beginnings* 156. The Rebels had their "bluebacks" for money.

Whether there is a direct connection is doubtful, since as DeVere points out, *blueback* may be a new coinage to distinguish the Southern money from the Northern greenback.

DeVere *Americanisms* 47. During the Civil War . . . the original Blue Backs of the Confederacy (so-called in opposition to Green Backs of the Union) soon became known as **Shucks.**

blue light.

During the War of 1812 it was alleged that Federalists in New England installed blue lights along the coast in order to guide British ships to a safe landing (Goodrich, *Recollections,* 437ff, 485). The term *blue light* became a derogatory epithet aimed at the Federalists, suggesting traitorous activities:

1817 Fearon *Sketches* 6 Oct. 144. It is an unholy league between apostates and political traitors on the one part, and on the other the anglo-federalists, the monarchists, the aristocrats, the Hartford conventionalists, the blue-light men. . . .

1840 in Norton *Log Cabin* App. 86.

When my old hat was new, 'twas in the Granite State,

That Henry Hubbard asked each town to send a delegate

To meet in council at the time when Federalism blue

Made Hartford look like Indigo, when my old hat was new.

Ib. App. 51.

When war's deadly summons had led us to blows,

Where was Kinderhook Van to be found?

In the rear of all dangers, with Bluelights and foes,

He hated the battle's dread sound.

1840 *Georgia Jrnl.* 22 Sept. 3/2. Are not Niles, Hubbard, Buchanan, Wall, Gilpin, Ingersoll, and a host of others, FEDERALISTS?—black cockade, if you choose, or worse, "blue light Federalists?"

The term followed those Federalists who turned to the Whig party:

1838 *Ohio Statesman* 2 Oct. 2/2. From the Pioneer, a blue light Whig paper.

bogus baby.

A spurious or ill-advised bill, brought forth with no intent of its ever being seriously considered.

But of all "bogus babies," unboned and
    ungristled,
And of all merry tunes by "the dying cow
    whistled,"
And of all the vile fizzles that ever were
    fizzled,
    Commend us to Butler's impeachment.
1868 Halpine *Poetical Works* 326.

boiler plate campaign.

Printed material distributed free
to newspapers for republishing,
already on plates for the presses.
1912 *McClure's* XXXIX 323/2. The
Boiler-Plate Campaign. By Saturday of
each week the printed matter for the
weeklies was completed and printed on its
sheets. . . . Then, after the first rush was
past, came the "boiler-plate" campaign. A
great number of the country newspapers
of the United States . . . print a large percentage of the matter from already stereotyped plates, now furnished by two great
concerns with their headquarters in New
York and Chicago. For many years, in all
kinds of political campaigns for elections,
this plate matter has been furnished free
to country editors by political committees.

bolt (-er, -ing).

To desert a party or program;
also, to dodge a vote.

One of the many political terms
derived from the racetrack.
1884 E. L. Anderson *Mod. Horsemanship*
I.viii 44. Bolting is the quick, determined
movement, usually off the course and
often against some obstacle, that a horse
makes to break away from restraint.

The metaphorical background remained known for a long time and
perhaps has not entirely disappeared today.
The importance of the term is,
of course, greater when a major
party split occurs, as, for instance,
in 1860, 1884, 1912.
1821 in Brown *Missouri Compromises* 43.

Parker of Virginia, & some others, bolted.
1830 *Workingman's Adv.* 15 May 2/2 . . .
their opponents having already bolted, as
their fourth resolution respectfully and
earnestly urges upon their republican fellow citizens of the Fifth ward to abstain
from any participation in an expensive
and unnecessary election, should one be
ordered.
1840 *Hamilton Intelligencer* 28 Aug. 3/2
. . . the loco foco leaders ridiculed the idea
of our little whig poney [sic] running the
race alone, and said that he would certainly bolt the course when their big loco
foco stallion returned from Wash. and
took the track in person.
1843 *Lima Porcupine* 7 Oct. 3/3. We
should avoid petty jarring and discord in
our ranks, and above all we should so dis-
countenance the business of BOLTING
from the nominations of our country conventions, that. . . .
1848 *John Donkey* 222. Washington
Course. Presidential Sweepstakes. "General Scott" is a fine, noble animal, but apt
to bolt and given to queer tricks.
1852 *Scott Battery* 20 July 1/1. The Bolter's Manifesto. . . . Messrs Toombs and
Stephens bolted from the Whig party on
the election of Speaker. . . .
1866 *Wash. Morning Chron.* 10 July 2/3.
Of these 56, 45 are true Union men, so
that unless Andrew Johnson can secure
enough to make another "bolt," Tennessee will be among the first to ratify the
amendment of the national Constitution.
1868 Moore *Life of Colfax* 137. He has
carried every vote of his party in the
House—there is not a bolter or a dodger.
1874 *N. Y. W. Trib.* 14 Oct. 4/1. Indiana
appears to be in doubt, and develops a
very healthy amount of bolting and
scratching of tickets.
1884 *N. Y. Times* 9 May. A Philadelphia
paper predicts that Mr. Blaine's next
book will be "What I know about Bolts,
Bolters, and Being Bolted."
1884 *Boston Jrnl.* 23 June 2/2.
    "Pray, what's a bolter?" Johnny cried,
    "I hear of bolters every day."
    "A bolter's one," the sire replied,
    "Who can't command and won't obey."

bone and sinew.

One of many phrases designating the laboring classes. Its political effectiveness lay in its appeal to the pride of the workers who had usually not been considered worthy of a part in the government until Jacksonian democracy brought them into prominence.

1834 *Tipton Papers* III.7. The farmers and the mechanics—the real bone and sinew of the country.

1840 Kennedy *Quodlibet* 159. If he (the merchant) fails, as the greater part of the poor devils do, we can get a still worse cry against him, for turning the humble and honest laborers out of employment, grinding the faces of the poor, depriving the widow and the orphan of their bread, and coining the sweat of the Bone and Sinew's brow to feed Usurers, Brokers and Shavers.

1845 Mike Walsh in Werner *Tammany Hall* 48. There are many men in the party who fawn upon us and call us the bone and sinew of the country...and who would use us until there was nothing but bone and sinews left of us.

See GREASY MECHANIC, HUGE PAW.

bone-hunter.

A low class politician whose services may be had for either a gift or an easy job.

1905 Riordan *Plunkett* 76. Nowadays a new Democracy means nothin' at all except that about a dozen bone-hunters have got together for one campaign....A dinner to twelve bone-hunters—$12.00.

bone taker.

A servile politician, appeased by any money "thrown" at him.

1881 *N. Y. Times* 9 May 1/3. When a man appeared who had dangerous knowledge, a "bone" was thrown at him. The number of "bone-takers" necessarily increased.

boodle (-er, -ing, -ful).

Money used for graft or bribery.

Ultimately a Dutch word *boedel* (property). In 1858 it turns up as a euphemistic term for counterfeit money (*Harper's Weekly*, 3 April, 222/1. "Boodle" is a flash term used by counterfeiters.). In politics it is found first as the name of an imaginary politician:

1852 *N. Y. Trib.* 21 Aug. 4/3. Some citizens who know him refuse to vote the ticket, or perhaps stay away from the polls.... and so Boodle or Foodle (it matters not which) gets in, though equally void of fitness and popularity.

The vogue of *boodle* as a political term seems to start in New York in 1883, apparently in connection with dishonest proceedings among the Aldermen concerning construction of the Brooklyn Bridge and other projects:

1883 *Judge* 3 March 7/1. "The Bridge"
Yet forever and forever,
  As long as the people pay,
As long as there's "boodle" to capture,
  As long as they find a way,
Will the Brooklyn Bridge be a swindle,
  A shadow in each clear day,
The symbol of millions wasted,
  Which the people will have to pay.

1883 *Puck* 2 May 140/2. "The New Aqueduct" An informal discussion in the Board of Aldermen....Alderman Finnegan.—Annyhow, they say there's a power of boodle in the buildin' av it; so yous needn't bother about what they'll do wid it.

1884 *N. Y. World* 11 April 1/3. An active lobby has been here for weeks off and on, wining and dining members and spending money freely without ostensible motive. It has been a double-barrelled shot-gun of boodle, because the promoters have been met by an equally interested opposition. *Ib.* 6 Aug. 4/2. It is notorious that large amounts of money, bonds and stock have been set aside to buy some of these schemes through the Board [of Aldermen]. The name of the persons handling

the "boodle" and managing the bribery are as well known. . . .
Ib. 5 Sept. 4/2. It is said that the person who has acted as the "boodle" agent for the Aldermen is a prominent County Democratic politician.

The term received a fresh impetus during the presidential campaign of 1884, when James G. Blaine was charged with having received bribes:
N. Y. World 10 Sept. 4/1. New York Alderman, with "Boodle" in his pocket to Monopoly Sharp: "Well, Blaine did it. We are no worse than Blaine.". . .
Harper's W. 20 Sept. 611. [Nast cartoon] Blaine lampooned as defending Fort "Boodle."—a rampart constructed of money bags.
Ib. 15 Nov. 761. Enough of Boodle Blaine's Canvass Bag. [head]

Later uses:
1888 *Harper's W.* 466/3. Great fun was made of his "Bar'l," but nobody ever pretended to describe Mr. Tilden as a "Boodle" candidate.
1888 *N. Y. Trib.* 22 Oct. 2/4. Boodle poured into Indiana. [head]
1892 *Nation* 27 Oct. 313/2 . . . the Hackett boodle plan is to bribe as many Democrats as possible to refrain from registering.
1948 Clare Luce in *Newsweek* 24 Jan. (1955) 30. The wampum and boodle boys.

As verb:
1912 La Follette *Autobio.* 606. It found the aldermen of St. Louis organized to boodle the city with a criminal compact.

BOODLER:
1890 *N. Y. Times* 9 Feb. 10/1. Last of the Boodlers [head].
1896 *Cabinet Diary of W. L. Wilson* 112. John McLean, the notorious boodler and proprietor of the nasty, sensational, venal, Cincinnati Enquirer.

BOODLING:
1903 *McClure's* XXI. 564. But boodling, with its backing of "big men" and "Big

interests," is the hardest evil a democracy has to fight. . . .

BOODLEFUL:
1884 *Harper's W.* 15 Nov. 758 [cartoon]. That Boodleful Dinner at Delmonico's before the Election.

A reference in Melville (supported by an 1850 quot. in *DA,* see *public hydrant*) offers tantalizing evidence that *boodle* is to be found much earlier in local New York politics.
1849 Melville *Redburn* 231. I hurried to one of the Boodle Hydrants, which I remembered having seen running near the scene of a still smoldering fire in an old rag house.

boohoo.
A defeatist.
1856 *Bellefontaine* (Ohio) *Republican* 2 Nov. 2/1. These same demagogues and boohoos were talking of dissolution.

boom.
A sudden vogue of interest in a candidate.

The word presents a difficult problem since the many variations of meaning in older non-political language offer quite a number of possible connections between which it is hard to decide. One of these and perhaps the most important one is the frequent comparison of the hullabaloo accompanying a "boom" to the noise of a cannon. (See FIRST GUN.)

1840 Norton *Tippecanoe* App. 46.
But half our grateful task was done,
When the clock toll'd the hour so desiring;
And we knew by the boom of a Harrison gun
That the Whigs were merrily firing.

1840 *Harrison Dem.* 17 March 2/1. Gun after gun, announcing whig victories, comes booming upon our senses like the successive explosions of a thundercloud. 1866 Schurz *Writings* I.416. We have already heard the triumphant morning gun of Vermont, booming with increased volume.

When in the 1880's the noun *boom* and the accompanying verb became universally-used elements in the political vocabulary, many people clearly understood that they referred to the noise associated with the noise and hullabaloo created by the followers of certain politicians:

1880 *Cinc. Gazette* 21 June 4/5. A fitting attending boom was a four horse wagon, with a brass band inscribed "For President Stephen J. Field.". . .
1884 *Puck* [ ]. "A Song for the Slap-Bang Boom Campaign."

And why were they nominated?
D'ye hear that boys? Hurrah!
Why because—Bang! Boom!
Bang! Fizz! Boom! Bang!
Hail to the—Boom! Tigah-h-h!

1880 *Harper's W.* 1 May 288. "Boom! Boom! Boom!" [cartoon showing Blaine beating "Solid for Blaine" drum]

There are, however, definite indications that another connection played at least a contributing part. In the language of the lumber camp, *boom* means not only the barrier preventing logs from floating away, but also the accumulation of logs behind this barrier. It is important that the professional language of lumbermen also presents a metaphorical transfer of that second meaning that comes pretty close to the modern use of the word meaning business boom:

1879 *Lumberman's Gazette* 19 Dec. There has not been the "boom" upon lumber

experienced in many other articles of merchandise.

The possibility that the political use is secondary to the professional use is considered the most likely one in the *DAE*.

A third variation ties the political word *to boom* as describing the sudden rise of a river:

1831 Audubon *Ornith. Biog.* I.155. To give you some idea of a Booming Flood of these gigantic streams. . . .

This possibility is supported by an utterance of McCullagh:

1879 *San Diego Daily Union* 18 Oct. 1/4. Mr. McCullagh, editor of the St. Louis Globe-Democrat, who first applied the word "boom" to the Grant movement, says he used the term in the sense that it is applied to a sudden and irresistible rise in a river. He wanted a term to imply that the Grant movement was sweeping everything before it, and he chose the word "boom."

It has also been suggested that the political use ought to be related to maritime phrases, like *booming sails,* or *the ship comes booming* (cf. *OED,* boom, vi,2 and *Dialect Notes,* VI.145). We have found no material to support this theory.

To illustrate the use of *boom* in 1878 and 1879 and the following years, we quote:

1878 *Chic. Trib.* 23 Sept. 7/4. The returns from Maine will have the effect of giving an additional boom to the Grant movement.
1879 *Cols. Dem.* 12 May 1/4. His [John Sherman's] Recent Fence building in Ohio—Said to be a Boom for the Man on Horseback. [head]
1879 *Chic. Trib.* 15 May 11/5. The more the Democrats in Congress back down, the worse it is for the Grant boom.
1879 *Cols. Dem.* 27 May 11/3. The different booms are all representative but un-

less the beer becomes exhausted, it looks
as though the Taft boom will carry everything before it.

1880 *Puck* 21 April 106/3 . . . Davis's boom
and Sherman's boom, and Smith's boom,
and Jones's boom, and all the other
booms and alleged boomlets. . . .

1948 *Time* 10 May 21/1. The boom for
Justice William O. Douglas had collapsed.

boomerang.

An Australian weapon which
when thrown returns to the
thrower.

Holmes uses the word metaphorically in:

1845 *Mod. Req. Poems* 42.
Like the strange missile which the Australian throws,
Your verbal boomerang slaps you on the
nose.

In politics the word seems to have
been inaugurated by Thomas
Nast, who, in 1877, published a
cartoon aimed at Carl Schurz,
whose protest against the sale of
U.S. guns to France turned out to
his political disadvantage:

1877 *Harper's W.* 11 May [cartoon:
Schurz firing a gun which explodes in his
face]. "Carl's Boomerang. Little Children
Should Not Investigate (French) Fire-
Arms."

From then on the political use of
the word was by no means rare.

1878 *Harper's W.* 28 Sept. 766. The Democratic Boomerang. [ed.]
1882 *N. Y. Trib.* 2 Oct. 4/3. A First-Class
Boomerang. [ed.]

American politics seldom over-
looks the facetious value of a word,
particularly if it lends itself to a
pun:

1883 *N. Y. Trib.* 19 Sept. 4/3. That statesman's [Tilden's] refusal to be "boomed"
for 1884 is due not so much to his positive
purpose to remain in private life as to his

knowledge that the "boom" just now is a
"boomerang," and his unwillingness to get
far enough in front to draw the fire of
personal rivals and political opponents.

boondoggle.

On April 3, 1935, Robert Marshall excited the curiosity of a
New York Aldermanic committee
investigating the work relief projects in New York City by stating
"that he taught 'boondoggles.' "
Questioned about the meaning of
the word, he said:

1935 *N. Y. Times* 4 April 2. "I spend a
good deal of time explaining it. . . . 'Boon
doggles' is simply a term applied back in
the pioneer days to what we call gadgets
today. . . . That is an old time name; they
catch it out West. . . . No, it is not named
for Daniel Boone. It is boon doggles. It is
spelled differently."

The word spread with great rapidity since it proved useful in
characterizing certain useless and
unprofitable activities by govern-
mental relief organizations, such
as a study of the geographical distribution of safety pins, mentioned
in the same article in the *Times*.

1935 *N. Y. Times* 4 April 1/8. "Boon Doggles" Made. Alderman Find These Are
Gadgets. [head] [Also 5 April, 8/1; 6
April, 14/5]
1935 *Ib.* 13 Oct. iv.12/2. Like the word
boon-doggle which came out of the New
York City relief investigation to sweep the
nation only a few months ago, a new word
is being popularized by our current campaign against unnecessary noise—the
decibel.

The Western origin of the term
has not been verified and several
different origins have been suggested:

Mencken *Am. Lang. Suppl.* I.303n. Said
an anonymous contributor to *Word Study*,

Sept., 1935, p. 2: "Boondoggle was coined for another purpose by Robert H. Link of Rochester. Through his connection with scouting the word later came into general use as a name given to the braided leather lanyard made and worn by Boy Scouts."
1935 *Chic Trib.* 4 Oct. To the cowboy it meant the making of saddle trappings out of odds and ends of leather, and they boon doggled when there was nothing else to do on the ranch.

borer.

Mathews' definition of *borer* as a political lobbyist seems to need further widening to cover those uses in which a borer was not acting on behalf of some other person or group but was seeking a political advantage for himself.

Although the earliest examples are from the political vocabulary, it is probable that the term was first applied to the commercial salesman or drummer.

1823 *Cinc. Nat. Rep.* 22 April 1/1. They [Pennsylvanians] have applied to each other the elegant appellations of log-rollers and borers. . . .
1840 *Ohio Statesman* 17 July 3/3. These cliques are always great "borers." They are constantly besieging legislatures for some law. . . .
1851 Greeley in Barnes *Weed* 20 Dec. 197. I see the old set of borers for everything here.
1863 Dennett *Hay* 4 Oct. 98. He says Prof. McCoy, after a good deal of indirect boring, came at him flatfooted this evening urging the absolute necessity of uniting. . . .

bottleholder.

A close supporter or adviser.

Found already in the 18th century in England, the bottleholder was a prize fighter's second.

1838 Price *Clem. Falconer* I.144. He is to be my bottle holder, and had a great deal of good advice to give me as to the best mode of combatting the enemy.
1842 Hone *Diary* II.602. Dorr, the leader of the insurrection and Governor, as he styles himself, by the choice of the people, with his right-hand man and bottle-holder, Dutee J. Pierce, have been receiving company in form, as has been the practice with regular legitimate Governors and lawful Presidents.

bounce.

To discharge or dismiss summarily.

1876 *N. Y. Times* 23 June 1/5. Tilden is no stronger than he was, although his friends are already playing the "bounce" game that was so unsuccessful at Cincinnati.
1879 *Puck* 29 Jan. 3/3. And he [Hayes] has been justly rebuked. "Bounced" some of our political friends call it.
1880 *Cleve. Leader* 31 May 1/2. Should this plan be adopted it will save Don Cameron from the humiliation of being summarily deposed from his chairmanship. . . . should it not be agreed to by the Grant men the doughty Don will be bounced.

Bourbon.

An ultra conservative.

A. Talleyrand's *bon mot* that during their exile the Bourbons had neither learned nor forgotten anything caused ultra conservative politicians, mostly in the Democratic party, to be branded as Bourbons already in the 1820's.

1827 *Spirit of Seventy Six* 4 Jan. 3/3. What "Bourbons" ever existed in Kentucky? What "Bourbons" are restored?
1835 *N. Y. Herald* in Carlson *J. G. Bennett* 141. We have found the Irish people of this city tyrannized over and borne down by a Roman bishop and a Bourbon knot of ignorant uneducated priests.
1837 Kendall *Autobio.* 426 . . . our legiti-

mate souvereign [the bank] to whose restoration, through your secession and that of your friends, the friends of "the Bourbons" so confidently look.

1840 *Dem. Rev.* Jan. 87. "No one," he [L. Napoleon] often said, "shall have cause to say of me, as the Emperor did of the Bourbons, that during a long exile, they had learnt nothing, and forgotten nothing."

1844 in *Mangum Papers* IV.42. The Whigs —many of them—with that Bourbon spirit—"That forgets nothing, and learns nothing."

1848 *Urbana* (Ohio) *Citizen* 22 April 2/3. The Bourbons of Washington will learn only by the shots of the Ballot Box.

1852 *N. Y. Times* 15 Nov. 4/3. The old Bourbons of the Polk Administration will look for at least partial restoration.

1852 *N. Y. Trib.* 17 June 4/3. They Learn Nothing, They Forget Nothing! So said Napoleon of the obstinate and stupid faction of the Bourbons. The maxim is equally applicable to the men who in the United States assume the special guardianship of Slavery.

B. The Reconstruction Period brings Bourbon into new prominence and almost makes it a party name, denoting intransigent Democrats.

1866 *Cinc. Comm.* 1 March 4/4. They will learn, if the Bourbons of Ohio can learn, not to sprout prematurely.

1867 *Wash. Morn. Chron.* 10 Jan. 2/3. The poor antediluvian Intelligencer, which as Mad. de Stael said of the Bourbons "never learns and never forgets anything"....

1872 *Cinc. Enquirer* 3 Sept. 2. Edward F. Slates is the name of a noisy South Carolina idiot who aspires to the position of chaplain and "orator" of the Great Bourbon Democracy.

1872 Watterson *Editorials* 39. No wise man can desire to load the next generation with more of the burdens of the present generation than fairly belong to it. This is what the Bourbons [Toombs *et al*] are trying to do.

1874 *N. Y. Trib.* 21 Oct. 4/6. [The people] are unwilling to help in any revival of the old Bourbon and Tweed Ring Democracy.

1875 Robbings in *Cong. Record* 10 Feb. App. 37/2. If any American looks back to and longs for something like the republic of the fathers, he is hooted at as a "Bourbon."

C. Occasionally applied to Republicans:

1885 *Nation* 9 July 21/2. The Bourbons among the Republicans—and they seem to number a large portion of the party—cannot conceal their disappointment and disgust....

D. Inevitably, the double meaning of *bourbon* (bourbon conservative and bourbon whisky) led to innumerable puns made more effective for the Democrats than for their opponents. [See WHISKY DEMOCRATS.]

1868 *Harper's W.* 22 Aug. 539. Spirit(s) of the Democratic Party [cartoon showing bottle labelled "Bourbon."]

1872 *Cinc. Enquirer* 4 Sept. 2. People here call attention to the fact that neither James O'Brien nor Brick Pomeroy drink intoxicating liquors or lemonade. Like certain kinds of mollusks which possess but one sense, a single virtue, and yet it is called the Bourbon Convention.

1879 *Harper's W.* 21 June 496. Shaky Times [Nast cartoon showing "King Caucus" crown on "Bourbon Democratic" bottle.]

E. Later attempts to revive the phrase:

1944 R. S. Kerr (Keynote Add. Dem. Conv.) 19 July. Talleyrand said: "The Bourbons were incapable either of learning anything or forgetting anything." To give these modern Bourbons, these Republican leaders, control of the nation for the next four years would bring about a certain return of 1932.

1948 *Time* 28 June 10/3. The Democrats, she [Clare Booth Luce] said, were divided into a "Jim Crow wing led by lynch-loving Bourbons . . . a Moscow wing, masterminded by Stalin's Mortimer Snerd, Henry Wallace . . . and a Pendergast wing run by the wampum and boodle boys. . . ."

brag horse.

The favorite or leading candidate of a party.

1838 *Hamilton Intelligencer* 27 Sept. 2/5. The same nag who distanced "the brag horse," of the party. . . .

See WHEEL HORSE AND STALKING HORSE.

Brahmin.

A member of the "first families" of Boston.

Originally, a member of the priestly caste in India; Oliver Wendell Holmes applied the name to descendants of "the old historic scholars" of New England:

1860 *Elsie Venner* 3 [first published in *At. Mon.*, Jan.]. He comes of the Brahmin caste of New England. This is the harmless, inoffensive, untitled aristocracy referred to, and which many readers will at once acknowledge.
1863 "Warrington" *Pen Portraits* 293. He [Gov. Andrew] has taken great pains with its organization; and the "Brahmin caste," which Dr. Holmes tells us about in "Elsie Venner," is supposed to be more largely represented in its organization then even in the other fifty-three. . . .
1882 Tourgée *Hot Ploughshares* 69. The New England Brahmin and the nameless shoemaker's son struck hands in advocacy of the doctrine.
1955 Luthin *Am. Demagogues* 17. James M. Curley: The Boston Brahmin-Baiter [chap. head] 21. He developed into an indefatigable baiter of the Brahmins, now in the minority. "Jim," remarked one student of the Boston scene, "can make the term 'blue blood' sound like the vilest epithet known to man. He shows them [the people] why it would be a catas-

trophe to permit the 'Brahmins,' as he terms the wealthy and socially prominent, to obtain a foothold in politics."

brain trust.

A. According to some authorities, first used to designate the advisers of Franklin D. Roosevelt:

Mencken *Suppl.* I.304. *Brain trust* has been ascribed to Dr. James M. Kieran, president of Hunter College, New York, but it was actually invented by another James M. Kieran, a reporter for the New York *Times.* This was at Hyde Park, N.Y., where Roosevelt was preparing campaign speeches with the aid of three Columbia University professors, Raymond Moley, Rexford G. Tugwell and Adolph A. Berle, Jr. When informed at a press conference that they were in residence Kieran exclaimed, "The Brains Trust!" and soon afterward he used the phrase in a dispatch to the *Times.*
1939 Raymond Moley in *Am. Sp.* XIV. 246n. The term *brains trust* . . . was originally used by James Kieran during the campaign of 1932.

B. It is evident, however, that this is not the origin but an adaptation to politics of an older use in academic circles. In 1910 it is found as a synonym for *college faculty* and in 1928 for another group of professors:

1911 George Fitch *At Good Old Siwash* 85. I remember feeling very confidently that if I went up before that brain trust in the faculty room once more. . . . 201. The ponderous brain trust that sat on this case didn't decide it until the day before the big game with Muggledorfer. [First pub in *Sat. Eve. Post*, 1910.]
1928 *Time* 9 Jan. 28/3. Brain Trust [head to article on meeting of American Council of Learned Societies, where several papers on business and government were read.]
1960 *Detroit News* 16 Aug. 22A/5. Again the celebrated Kennedy "brain trust" of Ivy League professors will not long re-

main strictly an eastern seaboard enterprise.

brass band. (adj.) Loud and gaudy.

Usually describing campaign techniques in which the brass band or similar attractions played an important part.

1872 *Nation* 13 June 388/1 ... Senator Logan, the Hon. Mr. Lynch, and others, who inflicted on us the regulation brass-band speech, of which it is a hoary and current superstition that American audiences are very fond.
1876 *Cleve. Leader* 16 June 1/4. No more calcium lights, very little brass band business.
1880 *Ib.* 22 June 1/5. A busy day at Cincinnati Yesterday. Marked by Much Cocktail, Chin, Uncertainty, Brass Band and Oratory.
1884 *N. Y. World* 7 June 1/5. We don't want any plumed knight and brass-band Administration.

bread and butter.

Quarreling with one's bread and butter ("acting in a way that might cost one his job") is used in Swift's "Polite Conversation" [*OED*].

The earliest American quotation already shows clear political connotations:

Irving *Salmagundi* 180. These little, beardless, bread and butter politicians.

A speech by Felix Grundy seems to have popularized the phrase around 1835:

1840 *Straightout Harrisonian* 1 May 3/2. The Straight-Outs immediately sent the following quotation in reply: "When I see a public officer interfering with popular elections, I set him down as fighting for his bread and butter!"—Felix Grundy. [Compare *Ohio St. Jrnl.* 30 May, 1835, 3/1 ... men who (as Felix Grundy has it) were thinking of their bread.]

In 1840 the phrase got considerable publicity, at least in Ohio, when John Brough explained his change of heart in regard to the Sub-Treasury bill by saying, "I have my bread and butter to look after." [*Straightout Harrisonian,* 12 June, 2/5.]

1840 *Little Magician* 29 April 1/2. It is alleged that J. Brough opposed and denounced the Independent Treasury plan when first suggested—but afterwards came into its support for the reason that "he printed for his bread and butter."
1840 *Straightout Harrisonian* 9 Oct. 2/3.
   Oh why is it that John the Big
      Is now in such a splutter?
   It is because the filthy pig
      Has lost his "bread and butter!"
1912 Theo. Roosevelt in *Harper's W.* 29 June 8/3. They represent the bread-and-butter politicians and the office-holders. And we stand for the future.

bricks without straw.

The phrase belongs in that group of terms in which American slavery is compared with the bondage of the Israelites in Egypt.

Exodus 5:7. Ye shall no more give the people straw to make brick, as heretofore; let them go and gather straw for themselves.

In politics making bricks without straw means to be engaged in a hopeless or unprofitable cause.

1866 Nasby *Swinging Round the Cirkle* 74. He wuz the Moses wich I spected wood lead the Democrisy out uv the desolate Egypt into which we hev ben making bricks without straw for five long weary and dreary years. ...
121 ... it's us that's a-goin to quit brick making without straw, and go up into the Canaan wich is runnin with the milk and honey uv public patronage.
1880 Tourgée *Bricks Without Straw* [novel centered on the almost hopelessly entangled race problems of the South.]

brindle (tail).

The nickname of a Republican faction in Arkansas. (A brindled dog is spotted or streaked.)

1871 *Cong. Globe* 7 Jan. 350/1. The Republican party in the State of Ark. was divided, and the "brindle-tail party," as it is called, headed by Senators Rice and McDonall, went off and opposed Governor Clayton's usurpations and power.

1872 *N. Y. Trib.* 9 Oct. 4/4. It [Liberal ticket in Ark.] was nominated by the Reform Republicans, commonly known as "Brindles."

British Tories.

In American politics, unpatriotic persons, aping the behavior and fashions of British conservatives; British sympathizers.

A. Applied to Americans sympathizing with the British:

1813 *Salem Gazette* 12 March 2/4. To pronounce him a friend to Great Britain, or, in their language of vulgar abuse, a British Tory.

B. During the Tippecanoe campaign Van Buren was accused of being under the influence of the British aristocracy and of favoring British fashions. He had been seen dancing with the Countess of Westmoreland at Saratoga [Charles Ogle's speech in HR, 16 April, 1840, in Norton, p. 71] and was alleged to ride in an English coach [Holt, *Ohio Pol.* p. 51].

Consequently *British Tory* was used as a nickname of the Democrats:

1840 in Norton *Log Cabin Songs* 13.
> Let all de British Tory,
> Who feel very low,
> Keep stiff de upper lip,
> And give a loud crow.

1840 *Harrison Dem.* 4 June 2/2. The last Telegraph contains an article about "British Whigs." Does it know that the opponents of British Whigs, are *British Tories?*

Naturally the Democrats retaliated by calling their opponents "British Whigs":

1840 *Hickory Club* 11 July 4/4. The Wheling [sic] Times is a good specimen of British whig sincerity.

1840 *Wash. Nat. Intelligencer* 8 Oct. 3/1. "British Whigs," which the leading prints in the pay of the Executive have applied to the Whigs (or Republicans) of the United States is ... the most contemptible.

1840 Kennedy *Quodlibet* 218. In the meantime, it is the desire of the President and his managing friends here, that you not only continue to brand the opposition as Federalists, but call them British Whigs.

1846 in *Mangum Papers* IV.363. Why don't the whig party thunder against the war? are they afraid of a nick name—are they afraid of taking the responsibility of preserving the peace of the world and being called "British Whigs."

British Whigs.

See BRITISH TORIES.

broad gauge (narrow-).

Factions within the Prohibition Party; a metaphor based upon the lack of standardization in railroad tracks.

1896 *Rev. of Rev.* XIV.11. These candidates belong to the so-called "narrow-gauge" wing of the party, holding to the view that it is the business of the Prohibitionists to stick to the temperance question and not to make opinions upon other subjects a test of allegiance.

1896 *Ib.* XIV.12. The "broad-gauge" men were led by Ex-Governor St. John of Kansas.

1900 *Ib.* XXII.327/2. The split in the Prohibition ranks was caused by two radically different conceptions of the movement and its aims, the factions dividing under the designation of "broad-gauge" and "narrow-gauge." ... the

"broad-gaugers," disappointed and angered, left the party, led by ex-Governor St. John, and organized a new party, which they called the Liberty party.
1906 Peck *Twenty Yrs.* 504. Already [1896] a section of the Prohibition Party, known as the "broad gaugers," had adopted a platform favouring the free coinage of silver at the ratio of 16 to 1.
1906 Roosevelt *Ltrs.* V.354. He [Taft] is the kind of broad gauge American that Kansas ought to like.

Buchanier.

Nickname for advocates of the election of Buchanan in 1856.
1856 *Sandusky Comm. Reg.* 9 July 3/2. The Bucanier had a meeting last night at the Court House.
1856 *Ib.* 2/3. The Buchaneers of Madison County were circulating the story.
1856 *Ohio St. Jrnl.* 6 Oct. 2. The man who votes for the Buchanier State or County ticket ... votes to make the Territory we now have slave territory and gives a Free State endorsement to the murders and robberies committed by Border Ruffians upon their brethren in Kansas.
1856 Fröbel *Aus Amerika* I.476. Es ist eine der witzigsten Parteibezeichnungen welche in der jetzigen Präsidentschafts Wahlbewegung aufgekommen die Demokraten, deren Kandidat James Buchanan ist, Buchaneers (Buccaniere) zu nennen.

The term was still in use in 1860, but a split between the Buchanan and Douglas factions had given it a narrower meaning.
1860 *Stark County Republican* 23 March 2. We need the strengthening of the Republican element in this county, not only for the sake of securing a majority, but to insure an utter repudiation of the Negroe [sic] Extension, Buckaniers and Douglasites.

bucktail.

A. Originally an official part of the Indian dress of the Sons of Tammany worn on special occasions.
1813 *Niles' Reg.* IV.25/2. The society are requested to attend this morning, precisely at nine o'clock, with buck's tail in their hats.

B. During the governorship of Dewitt Clinton in New York the Tammany or anti-Clintonian faction were identified by the bucktail in their hats and became known as the Bucktail party.
1817 in Alexander *Pol. Hist. of N. Y.* I.251. It was during this contest [over the canal bill] that the friends of Clinton called his opponents "Bucktails"—the name growing out of a custom, which obtained on certain festival occasions, when leading members of Tammany wore the tail of a deer on their hats.
in Lynch *Pol. Parties* 51–2. In DeWitt Clinton's first year as governor, the Republicans opposed to him were called the Bucktail party. The name was rooted in the nucleus of the opposition, for the Tammanies were summoned to patriotic gatherings in newspaper advertisements always ending thus: "Each member will wear a Buck's tail in his hat, the distinguishing badge of Tammany, in honor of the day."
1821 in Barnes *Weed* 23 Sept. 19. A Bucktail paper was offered to me.
1822 *Liberty Hall* 21 Sept. 3/1 ... by a persevering display of the bucktail even when it had become a tag-rag emblem for boys to hoot and dogs to bark at.
1838 in Mackenzie *Van Buren* 198. You may remember when in 1817 we ran up the Bucktail flag we had but eighteen men with us in the legislature.

buffalo hunt.

The disguised plans of a group of expansionists, who after the treaty with Mexico wanted to organize an expedition for further territorial acquisitions.

1848 *Reserve Battery* 17 Aug. 2/5. The Buffalo Hunt. "For the able bodied a new field will soon be opened in the South. The Buffalo Hunt on the Rio Grande is not proposed in badinage." (From St. Louis Reveille) The Reveille enjoys superior advantages for obtaining correct information in regard to the project now on foot to further dismember Mexico.
1848 *The Battery* 21 Sept. 181/3. We see just now organizing "a Buffalo Hunt," as it is called, for the conquest of all that part of Mexico east of the Sierre Madre mountains.

buff and blue.

The Whig party organized in 1834 made great efforts to present itself as the direct heir of the English Whigs and their colonial adherents. (See OLD LINE WHIG.) This tendency is documented by their adoption of the traditional style of dress and on the linguistic side by the fact that *buff and blue* appears as a synonym of *whig*.

1840 in Norton *Tippecanoe* 107. Buff and Blue—Good and True—For Tippecanoe [banner].
1848 *John Donkey* I.69. In looking over a file of the Tribune the other day, we find the following in regard to Mr. Webster's "blue coat" and "buff vest with brass buttons." "This was the old Fox colors in England over fifty years since. The followers of Charles James Fox wore them to distinguish themselves from the Pittites. Mr. Webster has given this dress an almost equal reputation in this country.—He wore it, I have understood on the ever memorable day of the reply to Hayne.—He wore it when, in 1838, he repulsed, in the Senate, the premeditated attack of Calhoun; and again, in angry parle, when he smote Ingersoll and coadjutor, Dickinson...." By the by, a careful examination of our portrait, on the first page, will show that we also, like other great men, wear the blue coat and the buff vest, with brass buttons.

bugaboo.

An English source of 1740 (*OED*, s.v.) gives *buggybows* as a synonym of *hobgoblins, rawheads and bloody bones*. For the political use, not attested in England:

1835 Crockett *Martin Van Buren* 188... all they hear on this subject [Judge White and the bank question] from Blair and Ritchie is nothing but the bugaboo of an old coat and breeches hung up to scare them.
1841 *Georgia Jrnl.* 3 Aug. 3/2. Now if this convenience [sic] on the part of the Government officers, to screen others from the public censure, when they deserve it, is a "bugaboo"—a scarecrow alone to children—then the Standard may be contented with the use of such a term.
1878 *Cong. Globe* 9 April 2365/2. All the imaginary bugaboos which [Mr. Edmunds] has constructed out of his fertile imagination ... I propose to cut up by the roots.
1890 *Ib.* 1 May 4100/1. You use the "trust" as a bugaboo to frighten the people away from the Republican party into your ranks.

bugbear.

As early as 1581 *bugbear*, a sort of hobgoblin used by nurses to frighten children, is attested in England. Even in British politics its use antedates the American example by over a century:

1717 Kennett in Ellis *Original Ltrs.* [*OED*] The king of Sweden is every day a less bugbear to us.

American examples:

1835 Martineau *Retrospect of Western Travel* II.219. I thought Garrison the most bewitching person I had met in the United States. The impression cannot but be strengthened by his being made such a bugbear as he is.
1845 Lyon *Govt. of the U.S.* 46. The bug bears with which she humbugged

and alarmed the people were, consolidation, federal usurpation, federal courts, State sovereignty....
1853 Cass in *Cong. Globe* 15 Jan. App. 91/2. And we should thus be led, but how I know not, into entangling alliances, the bugbear of American politics.
1876 *Harper's W.* 1 Jan. 2/1. The New York Times says that "it is curious to consider what it is that gives the third-term bugbear its vitality," since nobody seems to desire a renomination of the President.

bulldoze.

The Proceedings of the Historical Society of East and West Baton Rouge has an article, "The True Etymology of Bulldoze," which ascribes the origin of the word to a German-born wag, Louis Wagner, with whom "bulldoozer mit der Hoozza" was a favorite expression. The only value of this anecdote is that it points to Louisiana and particularly to East Feliciana parish as a possible place of origin. According to the article quoted there actually existed in this country an organization called the "bulldozers."

The most probable etymology is the one given by *DA:*
"It app. consists of bull + dose, a dose suitable for a bull."

In support of this etymology we point to two versions of the same story in Trowbridge:
1866 *The South* 292. I sent to the stable for a trace, and gave him a hundred and thirty with it, hard as I could lay on.
1903 *My Own Story* 292. I sent to the stable for a trace, and gave him a bull-dose with it, hard as I could lay on.

It seems evident that to Trowbridge the difference between *dose* and *bull-dose* was one of degree rather than meaning. It may also be pointed out that some of the early uses of *bull-dose* clearly point to whipping rather than other maltreatment:
1876 *Senate Report* No.701. 617. What did the bull-dozers say? —They come to the people's houses all the time of the night, to whip them and to beat them and to make them join the democrats.
Ib. 1191 ... there was a man badly bulldozed or whipped.

At any rate in 1876 the word is frequently found in sources from different parts of the country, where it refers to the treatment of the Negroes.
1876 *N. Y. Trib.* 30 Nov. 1/4. I very much regret that I am unable to spend a few days in each of the "bull-dozed" parishes of the State.
1876 *Ib.* 16 Dec. 3/1. For a year or more there has existed in every one of the disturbed districts organizations known as "regulators" or "rifle clubs," and called by the negroes "bulldozers.".. .
1876 *Senate Report* No.701. 1181. He was on the wrong side to be a bull-dozer. (Q) That is limited to one side, is it? (A) So it seems, sir; in the literature of the day, and in the opinion of the people.
1877 *Harper's W.* 3 Feb. 82/3. [Common sense] will decide whether, under all the known circumstances in Louisiana, such a result is due to the bulldozing of negroes by each other, to Republican tactics of not voting, in order to create a presumption of bulldozing, or to the intimidation of the negroes by the whites.
1878 *Ib.* 23 Nov. 926/3. They were lately slaves, and they have not that sense of equality and the determination to resist injustice which would make bulldozing and red-shirting and Ku-Kluxery of every kind impossible on a great scale in the Northern States.

The great popularity of the word is shown by the fact that it also appears in a wider sense, meaning to bully or mistreat.

1877 *N. Y. Trib.* 17 Jan. 4/4 . . . they think it would be better to "bulldoze" some remote parish rather than undertake it on Congress at Washington. . . . Washington is not a good place for "bulldozing" just now.

1877 *Puck* April 3/1. We . . . will not be bulldozed into adopting a country exchange's notion of etiquette.

1878 *N. Y. World* 11 April 4/5. But he [Pomeroy] must not allow "municipal reformers" to "bulldoze" him, as in days of yore men as clever as he is were narcotized by lobbyists who wore the livery of good St. Peter Cooper in which to serve the unsaintly Tweed.

1878 *Harper's W.* 17 Aug. 646/3. Not wishing the return in your favor unless it is clear that it ought to be so, and not willing to be cheated out of it, or to be "bulldozed" or intimidated, the truth is palpable that you ought to have the vote of Louisiana. [Letter from John Sherman to Hayes, 23 Nov., 1876.]

1878 *N. Y. Trib.* 8 Oct. 1/3. Florida had been bullied and bribed, "bulldozed" and terrorized through a long and fierce campaign.

In testimony of the popularity of the word and as a sample of the "poetical" fad described in Mark Twain's "A Literary Obsession," we quote:

1877 *Cinc. Comm.* 2 Feb. 8/5
                Ye Bulldozaire
Is the scamp that in some dark cornaire
Waylays the man with the kinky haire,
Whom the Laws have made a free votaire
And, then, with his shot-gun persuadaire,
All ready for action, noosed haltaire,
And also a loaded revolvaire,
Coaxes Blacky to vote as a White-Legaire.

bullionist.
An advocate of metallic currency.

A. In English usage as early as 1811 *(OED)*. Its popularity as an American political word is probably influenced by the nickname of *Old Bullion* applied to Thomas Benton during the controversy over specie in 1837. Webster called himself a *bullionist* in 1852:

Works I.374. I profess to be a bullionist in the usual and acceptable sense of the word. I am for a solid specie basis for our circulation.

B. The term enjoyed a renewed vogue in 1875 when the Democratic party—particularly in Ohio —favored a policy of inflation and branded their opponents as *bullionists*.

1875 *Ann. of Cleve.* No.1924. I warn you, bankers and bullionists, that unless you desist from your plunder and robbing, a mob may be at your doors and a knife at your throat.

1875 *Urbana* (Ohio) *Citizen* (Suppl.) 5 Aug. "That . . . was rather in the nature of a compromise between my views and those of the bullionists," replied Gov. Allen.

1875 *M'Connelsville* (Ohio) *Dem.* 30 July 1/5. The term "bullionists" is used to designate the class who demand that specie payment be resumed at once. . . .

1875 *Ib.* 6 Aug. 1/1. Does Mr. Stanton, bullionist candidate for State Senator . . . still hold the same views . . . ?

The Republican press retaliated by reminding some of the inflation men—especially Gov. Allen—that they had once been on the other side of the fence.

1875 *Ohio St. Jrnl.* 25 June 2/1. Hard Money. William Allen as a Bullionist. Former Views of a Greenback Candidate [head].

1875 *Ann. of Cleve.* No.1921. The Plain Dealer has undertaken the task of explaining how Bullion Bill Allen can consistently be prancing around on the rag money platform.

bull moose.

A nickname of Theodore Roosevelt and his third party followers in 1912.

A. Evidently Roosevelt was impressed during his hunting expeditions in the West with the great strength and stamina of the bull moose, so that "as strong as a bull moose" became one of his favorite similes.

1895 Roosevelt *Ltrs.* 29 Oct. I.493. I feel as strong as a bull-moose.
1900 *Ib.* 27 June II.1342. I am as strong as a bull moose . . . and you can use me to the limit.

B. In 1912, when he refused to support Taft for reelection, *bull moose* became the nickname and symbol of the independent movement which he led.

1912 *Cinc. Enquirer* 25 June 4/2. The Burial of the Bull Moose.
Not a drum was heard, not a funeral note,
Save a squeal or a muttered curse.
When they buried him with Tim Woodruff's goat,
The band-wagon was the hearse.
1912 *Harper's W.* 6 July 4/1. When it comes to the part of bull-moose, it is evident that Brother Roosevelt has nothing on Brother Bryan. They are incontestably the two greatest bull-moose statesmen in the world.
1912 *Ib.* 20 July 7 [cartoon showing bull moose with face of TR]. The latest animal at the political zoo.

C. Later references to progressives or other independents.

1936 *Rev. of Rev.* CIV.23. Bull Moose Revival. In Governor Landon the Republican party revives and proposes to carry forward the progressive tradition implanted by Theodore Roosevelt.
1950 Elmer Davis in election broadcast of 7 Nov. referred to Sen. Duff of Pa. as a "bull-mooser."

bullwhack (-ing).

A. A bullwhacker is a political leader or whip who employs rough tactics to keep the party in line; a comparison to the driver of a bull team.

1880 *Cleve. Plain Dealer* 11 June 2/2. The big bullwhackers, to be sure, seemed to have been worsted in the end; but the secret history of the Chicago convention will yet show that a ring within a ring compassed the end that appeared so entirely the result of generous and unpartisan impulse.

B. Bullwhacking. A variant of *bulldozing* (q.v.).

1884 Tourgée *Appeal* 206. Ku Kluxing, bullwhacking, tissue-ballots, or any other form of fraud or violence by which the Southern Whites have asserted and maintained their right to rule.

bummer (-ing).

A loafer; a camp follower.

The often repeated suggestion that the word is derived from German *Bummler,* which in 1840 and thereafter was a semipolitical word (see Ladendorf), is hardly acceptable, since no side forms with *l* have been found in American sources (while such forms are found in Scottish dialects) and since *bumming* and *bummer* are older in English slang than in German.

Bummer occurs in Scott's *Pirate* (*N & Q,* 4 ser., i, 75) and *bumming* occurs already in 1700.

1700 Rhead *London Spy* 435.
And when his Youthful Days are past,
His only Refuge is at last,
To follow Theft or Bumming.

A. Nonpolitical American use:
1855 *Oregonian* 27 Jan. 1/4. Come clear

out, you trunken loafer! Ve don't vant
no bummers here!
1861 in *Art. Ward: His Wks. Complete*
113.
"My illustrious and patriotic Bummers!"
sez I, a gittin up and takin orf my Shappo,
"if you allude to A. Ward, it's my pleasin
dooty to inform you that he's ded.

Soldier slang knows the word already before Sherman's march to the sea. This event, however, made the word generally known and clearly tended to reinforce its derogatory sense.

1862 *Haversack* 11 Oct. 3/1. "How are
you old bummer?" "Hey—O yes, not very
well, been exposed to a terrible draft
which made me quite deaf."
1862 *Ib.* 11 Oct. 3/3.
> A "bummer," by a faithful hound,
> Half buried in the mud was found
> Still grasping tight the played-out rag
> The banner with the same old gag—
>   "Secession"!

1865 Nichols *Gt. March* 240. The origin
of this nickname [bummer] is unknown.
No English dictionary contains it; only
the "bummers" themselves know exactly
what it means, except, perhaps, inferentially. Probably the word originated
among themselves; they were certainly not
ashamed of it. If it be asked what a
bummer is, the reply is easy. He is a
raider on his own account—a man who
temporarily deserts his place in the ranks
while the army is on the march, and
starts out upon an independent foraging
expedition.

Occasionally in military usage the word seems to be under the influence of *boom.*

1862 Page *War Corr.* 28. The day wore
away until noon, with a continuance of
desultory shelling ("bumi'n" [sic] the
butternut prisoners call it.)

In Halpine's *Miles O'Reilly,* 36, *bummer* means gunboat.

B. Political use.

1866 *Nation* 1 March 262. The great host
of "bummers" with which every political
party surrounds itself on the approach
of great conflicts.
1868 "Warrington" *Pen Portraits* 116 . . . it
was a handsome success for the indomitable "Warrington," who had not
only the bummers of the P.L.L. faction
down upon him. . . .
1871 *Ann. of Cleve.* No.3581. Holden . . .
candidate for Mayor on the Bummer's
ticket.
1872 *Ib.* No.2346. . . . Those who opposed
him were mostly the shoulder-hitters,
gamblers, professional demagogues, dissolutes, bummers, thieves and the lowest
and most degraded portion of our population.
1872 *San Diego Daily World* 25 Aug. 2/2.
In their despair they turned their gaze
upon the Louisville Convention of played
out political bummers.
1872 T. Ewing in *Cinc. Enquirer* 2 Sept. 1.
We find ourselves associated in this campaign with the great reform leaders of
the Republican party. We are associating
with the heads of the Republican Party,
while they are associating with the tail of
ours. We are associating with their Corps
Commander and they with our bummers.
1876 *Ann. of Cleve.* No.1451. In the election in Chicago on Apr. 4, the respectable
business men administered a rousing defeat to bummerism in spite of attempts
by the bummers to carry the election by
organized rowdyism and fraud.
1880 *Cleve. Plain Dealer* 4 June 1/3. The
Grant men are particularly bitter on the
Chicago Tribune and the Chicago anti-
Grant bummers!

bushwhack (-er, -ing).
1826 T. Flint *Recoll.* 86. We began to
pull the boat up the stream, by a process,
which in the technics of the boatmen, is
called bush-whacking.

Reference to the hardy frontiersman:

18—Irving   *Knickerbocker*   265 . . . they

were gallant bushwhackers and hunters of raccoons by moonlight.

1817 Paulding *Ltrs.* I.140 ... in a few years a race of lusty *bushwhackers* rewards the labours of the industrious pair.

A type of primitive, no-holds-barred campaigning:

1836 Crockett *Exploits* 17. So I mounted the stump that had been cut down for the occasion and began to bushwhack in the most approved style.

1845 *Cong. Globe* 3 Feb. App. 152/1. All he asked for was a clear field and a fair fight—no bushwhacking, if he might be indulged in an expressive word, well understood in the border wars of the West; no masked batteries.

1859 Lincoln *Works* V.165. This is what I call bushwhacking, a sort of argument that they know any child can see through.

1874 *Ann. of Cleve.* No.2989. They are, so to speak, throwing up fortifications for the nation at Washington, while liable to be picked off by bushwhackers in their constituency.

1876 *N. Y. Times* 25 Aug. 4/4. But the wily old wire-puller himself never meant what he said, when he declared for an aggressive campaign; his forte is bushwhacking and secrecy.

1905 Riordan *Plunkett* 45. For several years he was a political bushwhacker. In campaigns he was sometimes on the fence, sometimes on both sides of the fence, and sometimes under the fence.

Used during the Civil War to characterize both methods of fighting and specific participants:

1861 *Cinc. Comm.* 18 July 2/2. It appears, however, that Gen. McClellan's skirmishes whipped the Georgians and Virginians in "bushwhacking" fights with great ease.

1862 *Lawrenceville* (Kans.) *Republican* 11 Sept. 4/1. That faction of Democracy who sympathise with the rebels are known in Ohio as "Vallandighamers," ... in Missouri as "butter-nuts," in Kansas as "jayhawkers," in Kentucky as "bushwhackers."

business man's campaign.

1880 *N. Y. Times* 23 Oct. 1/3. As Carl Schurz said in New York the other night, this is essentially a "business man's campaign."

1896 *Nation* 30 July 80/1. We have had feigned or fraudulent "Business Men's Campaigns" in this country, but this time it is the genuine article. The business interests of the country are for the first time almost absolutely solidified on one side in a Presidential election.

butt-ender.

A member of a N.Y. rowdy faction.

1839 Hone *Diary* 19 Dec. I.443. In this appointment the President, it is said, has given mortal offence to the butt-enders and indomitables who form the elite of his party in New York.

1840 *Boston Transcript* 4 Jan. 2/2. A riot was raised at New York, on New Year's Day, by a body of young men, called Butt-Enders, belonging to the noisy and turbulent portion of the Fire Department.

button-hole.

A. To solicit support; to detain for electioneering purposes.

Assumed to be a variant of *button-hold*.

1862 *Ann. of Cleve.* 15 Oct. No.3449. Quarreling, fighting, button-holeing [sic], "scratching," or taking under the sheds, and other pleasing features were quite wanting in the election yesterday.

1873 Mark Twain *Gilded Age* 226. Harry ... "buzzed" and "button-holed" Congressmen in the interest of the Columbus River scheme.

1881 *Home Jrnl.* 21 Jan. [*OED*]. Charles Lamb, being button-held one day by Coleridge ... cut off the button.

1881 *N. Y. Times* 5 Jan. 1/1. Although there is plenty of buzzing and button-holing about the hotel, it is more among the outsiders than among members of the Legislature. ...

B. A secondary meaning exists: to place a campaign button or emblem in the button hole.

1912 *Harper's W.* 29 June 612. The delegates as they come in are badged, tagged, and button holed.

buzzard dollar.

A derisive reference to the 90 cent dollar during the silver controversy of the 1870's, the lordly eagle being reduced to the status of a scavenging buzzard.

1878 *N. Y. Trib.* 18 March 4/5. If the buzzard dollar ever gets into circulation, it will not be hoarded. Nobody will wish to keep one long.

1878 *Ib.* 20 March 4/5. There is a loud demand for the substitution of an eagle for the buzzard on the 90-cent dollar.

1878 *Nation* 19 Sept. 170/2. The "buzzard dollar" [is] the designation applied by indignant holders of the trade dollar to the now standard dollar.

C

cabinet.

While according to the Constitution the heads of the executive departments act individually as advisers to the President, a tendency to make them a collegiate body rose early during Washington's first term. The term *cabinet* in common use in England since the 17th century was according to the *Cyc. of Am. Govt.* (I.199) first used in America in connection with the Genet imbroglio in 1792.

1796 Hamilton *Works* X.162. It will be an error to be too tame with this overbearing Cabinet.

1797 Jefferson *Works* VII.107. My letters inform me that Mr. Adams speaks of me with great friendship and with satisfac-

tion in the prospect of administering the government in concurrence with me.... If by that he means the Executive Cabinet, both duty and inclination will shut that door to me.

1823 *Cinc. Nat. Rep.* 16 May 1/2. And this opinion ... will save us from the *perpetual reign of a cabinet heir-at-law* who is elected by a Caucus in defiance of the opinions of the people to the contrary.

1824 *Niles' Reg.* 6 Nov. 148/1. A member of what is called the "cabinet."

Later examples continue to show mixed feelings in regard to the make-up and activities of the cabinet.

1877 Hamilton *Blaine* 23 Feb. 427. I presume that Hayes may be regarded now as the next President. Bring on a new relay of cabinet-makers.

1881 *N. Y. World* 2 March 1/4. Gen. Garfield ... is beset by Cabinet-Makers. 1/5. The Cabinet-Makers at Work. 5/1. Cabinet-making in the Past.

1900 *Rev. of Rev.* XXII.524/2. The President's cabinet is not merely a group of men charged severally with the management of particular departments of administration. It is also charged with the duty of advising the President in a general way on all subjects.

1930 *Outlook and Independent* 26 Nov. 493 in *Am. Sp.* VI.280 ... in despair at the Cabineteer's ignorance of legislative proceedings....

Caesarism.

A. Originally a French term characterizing the one-man government of Napoleon III, coined by Romieu, 1851 (see Ladendorf, p. 40f; also *Harper's W.*, 1867, 482), applied to Andrew Johnson, who in Nast's cartoon of 1867, (*Harper's W.*, 200–1) was depicted as a Roman Caesar.

B. *Caesarism*, itself defined by Orestes Brownson as "monarchial absolutism" (OED), becomes popular during the presidency of U. S. Grant in connection with Sumner's attacks on him and with his alleged intentions of seeking a third term:

1872 Sumner *Works* XX.125. Either he [Grant] did not see the responsibilities, or the Caesar began to stir in his bosom. **1874** Foote *Casket* 453 ... the subject of "Caesarism," now so vehemently agitated in certain sensational journals of a very extended circulation. **1874** *Cinc. Enquirer* 7 Sept. 4/4. The specter of Caesarism ... is by no means removed from sight by the proposition to re-elect Grant for a third term. **1876** *Harper's W.* 8 Jan. 23/2. The members of the Grant Central Club have probably sneered a great deal at the talk about Caesarism. Do they know what Caesarism is? ... It is the advocacy of personal government in a country of laws. It is the assertion that in a republic some one person is essential to the national safety.

C. The comparison of an ambitious politician with Caesar is, of course, much older, as for example:

1792 Hamilton *Works* X.22. In a word, if we have an embryo-Caesar in the United States, 'tis Burr. **1834** *Reg. of Deb.* I.803/1. That modern Caesar, Andrew Jackson, has driven away from the door of the Treasury, the modern Metullus, William J. Duane.

calico vote.

A type of fraudulent ballot. [ ]

1842 *Bro. Jonathan* I.lxvi. In the 8th [Ward], where the "calico votes" were thrown, a portion of them have been thrown out, and the opposition aldermen and assistants are declared elected.

Calmuck.

Term applied to members of a Republican faction.

1864 *Cinc. Comm.* 13 May 2/3 ... these political Calmucks, who wear their hair long and talk in rhapsodies.

See LONG-HAIRED, TARTAR.

campaign.

In England *campaign* seemed to have been a synonym for *session:* **1770** Junius *Ltrs.* No.39. [*OED*] The odium of measures adopted by the collective body sits lightly upon the separate members who composed it. They retire into summer quarters, and rest from the disgraceful labours of the campaign.

This shows how easily the military metaphor could be adapted into the political vocabulary but apparently has no connection with the later American usage.

A few representative examples of the term's early use in America:

1809 in *Steele Papers* II.601. The electioneering campaign having become much warmer than I had anticipated.... Col. Bodinhamer & myself have been under a forced march since Sunday last—We have left none of the enemies ground, in this quarter unexplored—and I think have succeeded in blowing up most of their strong places. **1817** J. Q. Adams *Writings* 31 March VI.171. The parliamentary campaign hitherto has been consumed in one laborious effort to suppress the reformers and their projects. **1817** *Cinc. Western Spy* 21 Nov. 3/1. Since the close of the several election campaigns, the principal subject of discussion.... **1823** in *Mangum Papers* 1.70. ... when we first met in the campaign & constantly afterwards when the subject was mentioned, you professed it to be your fixed resolution not to interfere in the Congressional contest in any respect whatever.... **1828** *Niles' Reg.* 21 June 266/1. Our readers will recollect that, for reasons stated at the commencement of the present electioneering campaign, we have steadily de-

clined to give place to papers of this
description. . . .
1834 in *Mangum Papers* II.74. The President is said to be up to that high pitch
of excitement that might be expected in a
real war campaign.
1835 Bradley *Isaac Hill* 60. He finally
thought the time had arrived for taking
an active part in the presidential campaign.

campaign fund.
1876 *N. Y. Trib.* 4 March 7/1. They don't
need any inflation in New Hampshire, so
far as campaign funds are concerned.
1878 *Ib.* 7 May 4/6. Some wag at Washington has suggested that Postmaster General
Key be asked to contribute to the Republican campaign fund.
1880 *San Diego Daily Union* 1 Sep. 1/1.
He has indicated that he will take care of
the Indiana campaign expenses, with the
understanding that he be not called on
to contribute to their campaign fund for
other states.
1884 *Nation* 30 Oct. 365/2. The great
controversy between Butler and Parsons
on the question of whether or not Butler
is running in the interest of Blaine, and
at the Blaine campaign fund's expense
is proceeding with much animation.
1884 *Puck* [in cartoons 2 April 72; 12 Aug.
376; 1 Oct. 72].
1905 *McClure's* XXV.49. They . . . gave the
seat for which he had sacrificed so much
to . . . the largest contributor in the new
public service crowd, to the Democratic
campaign fund.

campaign of confusion.
Satirical variant of *campaign of
education*.
1949 Truman in *N. Y. Times* 25 Feb.
18/6. The same die-hard reactionaries . . .
have also started a campaign of confusion
against all our other measures for the
welfare of the people.

campaign of education.
A campaign in which a great effort is made to inform the voters

by means of books, pamphlets,
speeches, etc.

The campaign of 1888 is cited as
one of great educational value for
the voter:
Summers *William L. Wilson and Tariff
Reform* 90. Nor is there room to doubt
that more than any other presidential
campaign in American history the election of 1888 was a battle of books.

This view is in part supported by
contemporary comments:
1888 *Nation* 30 Aug. 162/3. The Educational Value of the Present Campaign
[ed.]. . . . Altogether the most valuable
political education is furnished by just
such a campaign as that in which we
are now engaged.
1888 *N. Y. Trib.* 1 Oct. 6/3. The "campaign of intellect" gives place to the campaign of corruption.

However, a letter to the *Nation* in
1889 suggests that the educational
value of the campaign was of
doubtful quality or was at least
limited in its scope.
1889 *Nation* XLVIII. 10/3. I think it is
not impossible that the late Democratic
defeat resulted in part from the *dense
ignorance* of some of the voters. Yesterday
I met upon the streets of this city a
wealthy and respectable farmer, of average intelligence, who saluted me with the
remark, "Well, we laid you out at the
election"; to which I replied, "I think
you laid yourself out. A farmer who
votes to maintain the present protective
tariff, votes to tax himself for the benefit
of others, without any compensating advantage." "Why, how is that?" he asked.
"We farmers in Michigan cannot compete
with the cheap wool and beef of Texas
and our great West, unless the producers
there are compelled to pay a tariff tax
when they bring their products here to
sell in our market. It is the tariff upon
this Southern and Western wool and beef
that keeps up the price of ours"; and he
assured me that that was really what he

understood by our protective tariff. If this man is a fair average of his class, what missionary work can be undertaken to meet such ignorance?

By 1890 it is evident that the expression was quite current:

1890 in *Add. and Papers of G. Cleveland* 271f [Add. in response to toast, "The Campaign of Education"]. I suppose I have a correct understanding of what is meant by "The Campaign of Education." ... The grand and ultimate object of the campaign of education was the promotion of the welfare of the country and the relief of the people from unjust burdens. [Repr. in *Lit. Digest,* 14 March 1891.]
1892 Davenport *Crime of Caste* 56. The Atlanta *Constitution,* of November 17th, claims that "the leaders of the two great parties have had a good deal to say during the past few months about 'the campaign of education.' " In the main, this phrase very correctly describes the work of both parties. Republican speakers and journalists work night and day to convince the people of the benefits of high Protection. On the other hand, the Democrats are equally active in exposing the true inwardness of McKinleyism and class legislation. This educational literature covered the country, and the average voter got a clearer insight of the questions at issue than he ever had before.
1896 *Rev. of Rev.* XIV.553. It had been the fashion in previous presidential contests in this country to sneer at the phrase, "campaign of education," although it was said that in England, and in some other countries where popular suffrage prevailed, the words had a meaning which they had never possessed here. However that may be it is certain that from this time on the American people will fully understand what is meant by a campaign of education, for such a campaign we have had beyond question.
1902 *Am. Federationist* March 118/1. The "campaign of education" has just begun.
1914 *Cyc. of Am. Govt.* I.209. Although much of the campaign speaking is mere "buncombe," there have been times of

general and geniune interest in important public affairs when serious and able argumentation has directly affected national opinion—when a real "campaign of education" has been conducted (e.g., 1856, 1860, 1876, 1896).

camp follower.

A lesser politician who attaches himself to a party or a movement with the sole hope of financial gain.

The Civil War provided the impetus for the phrase's entry into the political vocabulary.

1860 *Ann. of Cleve.* No.2071. She (Charleston) will confer more watching than hospitality upon the "Camp followers," who have come to swarm at the assembly of the convention.
1869 G. W. Curtis *Works* II.14 ... to provide against his early removal either by the victory of the other party—in which case all the trimmers and camp-followers of the victors will enter upon the spoils. ...
1886 Peck *Twenty Yrs.* 87 ... no mercenary camp-followers fled for shelter to the bomb proofs of the Tenure of Office Act, no sublter [sic] crawled behind the fragile breastworks of civil service reform for protection.

candidate's disease. [ ]

1948 *New Rep.* 21 June 3/3. He is suffering from Candidate's Disease—the assumption that because people come to hear you, and applaud your appearance, they will vote for you in the fall.

candle-box returns.

Fraudulent votes. [ ]

1858 in Richardson *Beyond the Mississippi* 104 [describing events in Kansas]. Under the woodpile, buried in the earth, was discovered a box bearing McLean's name, and labelled "candles." Within it were the election returns. ... McLean escaped punishment by flight, but the "candle-box" achieved a notoriety that never candle-box won before.

1858 *Cong. Globe* 15 March 1122. Cincinnati directories and candle-box returns have been infinitely more potent than the real votes of the inhabitants.

Canvas Club.

In view of the fact that no other reference to Canvas Club has been found, we must suspect that this may be a misreading of someone's Caucus Club.

If this is true, the origin of *caucus* must be looked for earlier in the 18th century than is presently suggested. [ ]

1723 *New Eng. Courant* 21–28 Jan. 2/1. And Lastly, Beware of casting dirty Reflections on that worthy Society of Gentlemen, scoffingly call'd The CANVAS CLUB. Truly, they are Gentlemen of as good Credit and Reputation as any we have; and some of them are Men of Power and Influence, and (if you offend them) may contribute not a little to the crushing of your Paper.

canvass (noun).

A. The election.

1828 in *Cong. Deb.* 1290 ... the importance and consequence which some gentlemen seem to attach to what they may say in this Hall, tending to bear upon the Presidential canvass, is very greatly overrated.

1859 *N. Y. Trib.* 21 June 8/4. A Presidential canvass is approaching.

1888 Norton *Tippecanoe* 365. It will be seen from the foregoing that General Harrison's canvass was hotly contested.

B. The campaign.

1825 *Mangum Papers* I.170. Not having seen you during the canvass. . . .

1828 (Cinc., O.) *Liberty Hall* 17 April 4/1. The Canvass [head].

1835 *Scioto Gazette* 30 Sept. 2/4. If I had not known from observation and experience that a candidate, during the

canvass for an election, is liable to be accused of everything supposed to militate against his success. . . .

1860 *Ib.* 3 Jan. 2/2 ... we must all resolve ... that the canvass for a Republican triumph shall begin at once.

1876 *Cong. Record* 5464/2 ... it was not quite fair, certainly not exactly manly, that we should have a series of partisan investigations going on in vacation during a heated political canvass.

1879 *Nation* 31 July 67. Senator Sherman has gone up to Maine to speak in the canvass. . . . The Republicans generally say they will make an active canvass. . . .

canvass (verb).

From the earliest English meaning, "to toss in a canvas sheet" the word has undergone many semantic changes in English usage (See *OED*).

In American politics typical uses are:

A. To count the votes:

1807 *Weekly Inspector* 30 May 222. On canvassing the votes for governor, it was found that

Gov. Trumbull had	11,959
Mr. Hart	7,951.

B. To discuss or scrutinize matters relating to an election:

1823 in *Mangum Papers* I.89. The principal movements of the members here [Wash.] is in relation to the next presidency—there is considerable effort and canvassing on that subject. . . .

C. To solicit votes or information; to campaign:

1832 in Garrison *Garrison Story* 43. African colonization is directly and irreconcilably opposed to the wishes of our colored population, as a body. . . . I have never seen one of them who was friendly to this scheme; and I have not been backward in canvassing their opinions on this subject.

1859 *N. Y. Trib.* 25 Jan. 4/1. But, when brought to book, he dare not deny that

Gov. Seward canvassed for Mr. Clay, urged all he could influence to vote for him, and did so himself.
1860 *Ib.* 3 Jan. 2 ... Mr. Dennison, while canvassing for Governor on the Republican side....

Carbonari.

The name of a secret society aiming at the liberation and unification of Italy, first attested in 1802 but probably older as an offspring of the charbonnes, a similar French association of the 18th century (*Enciclopedia Italiana*, s.v.). Although the society was after 1831 overshadowed by *la giovine Italia* (see *Young America*), the mystery attached to it continued to be much discussed in Europe. In 1849 the *Columbus New Constitution*, p. 290, has an article reproduced from the *New York Albion* and dealing with the history of the Carbonari.

During the Civil War the name seems to have been adopted by an ultra-secessionist society.

1864 in Pollard *Secret Hist.* 412. I belong to the society of Carbonari! It sympathizes with the Southern Confederacy. ...I hold in my hand the life of Abraham Lincoln; the victim whom the Carbonari designates cannot elude them.

In 1880, the Virginia City, Nevada, *Territorial Enterprise* (20 Jan.) ascribes an attack on a railroad engineer to his troubles with a secret union called *Carbonari*.

caretaker of the White House.

Satirical reference to the presidency, particularly when the occupant is felt to be a weak or indecisive man.

1888 *Nation* 9 Aug. 101/1. It was very different in 1840, when the grandfather of the present Republican candidate for caretaker of the White House was running for the presidency.
1888 *Ib.* 23 Aug. 141/1. There was not even so much as a Harrison and Morton banner, or a picture of the man who is running for care-taker of the White House.

carry.

To win an election or a majority in a particular section.

Carry with the meaning of "to win" can be found in English usage as early as the 17th century (*OED*) but there is no evidence that it was used in its present political sense; thus we must assume that *to carry an election* first appears in American political terminology:

1828 *Liberty Hall* 17 April 4/1. But the day for this mode of carrying elections is passing rapidly away even in New York.
1858 in *Lincoln Cyc.* Under the Dred Scott decision squatter sovereignty squatted out of existence—tumbled down like temporary scaffolding—like the mould at the foundry, served through one blast, and fell back into loose sand, —helped to carry an election, and then was kicked to the winds.
1876 *Cinc. Daily Gazette* 10 June 5/1. Blaine cannot carry New York.
1880 *N. Y. Trib.* 18 March 4/2 ... the friends of particular candidates are busy trying to demonstrate that their man, and their man only, can "carry New York," or "carry Indiana," or break the Solid South.

A corollary meaning is to give a majority for a particular candidate:

1860 *N. Y. Trib.* 3 Jan. 2/2. If N.J., Penn., Ind., and Ill. should unitedly say, "we cannot carry" this or that statesman, then another should be selected; and he should be one of those whom these states, or a majority of them, believe they can carry.

carry the war into Africa.

To act aggressively. [ ]

1828 Randolph in *Cong. Globe* 1315/1. I shall not, as the gentleman said he would do, act in mere self-defence. I shall carry the war into Africa. **1838** *Ohio Statesman* 5 Jan. 2/3. To use Mr. Wise's borrowed and hackneyed allusion, he has found one ready to carry the war into Africa. **1844** in Julian *Recoll.* 44. He [C. M. Clay] had been sorely tried by Mr. Clay's Alabama letter and the Whig defeat, but he was now armed with fresh courage, and resolved to "carry the war into Africa" by the establishment of his newspaper, the "True American," in Lexington in his own State.

catchall.

A miscellaneous collection, of politicians or of legislative articles.

1838 *Cong. Globe* App. 275. [The Administration Party includes] old Federalists, the champions of the Hartford Convention, counterfeit Democrats, National Republicans, Antimasons, and Abolitionists. They have been a kind of catch-all, or omnium gatherum.

cavalry cabinet.

Variant of *kitchen cabinet* (q.v.) . [ ]

1931 *Wash. Merry-Go-Round* 116–7. He had surrounded himself with the famous "Calvary Cabinet"—military men who had become so biased against any human being with a brown skin that their advice was impossible.

cave in.

To yield or collapse; to withdraw one's political support.

A. The "caving in" of walls and banks may be found early in American usage:

1764 *Boston Eve. Post* 30 Jan. Nor was he missed till he had been buried an Hour, when the People found the Well caved in. **1796** Morse *Am. Geography* I.398. The cellars are walled with brick ... to prevent the loose sand from caving in. **1832** Williamson *Hist. of Maine* II.115. The heavy rains caused the banks of the trenches to cave in upon them.

B. In the political vocabulary:

1848 *N. Y. Trib.* 4 March. The South-Western and Western Locos, it is thought, will cave in. **1848** Webster *Works* II.438. But the moment it was ascertained that Mr. Polk was the favorite of the South [in 1844] ... these friends of Mr. Van Buren in the North all "caved in," not a man of them stood. **1852** *Scott Battery* 17 Aug. 3/1. Iowa, hitherto an unyielding Locofoco State, has caved in, and elected an entire delegation of Whig Congressmen. **1856** *Ill. St. Reg.* in Lincoln *Works* II.344. The same caving in as to the restoration of the Missouri restriction, marks the latter day policy of the sectional party, and he [Lincoln] has cautiously avoided it. **1860** "Warrington" *Pen Portraits* 94. Gov. Andrew was not in favor of the commission; but (says Mr. Robinson in his diary) "he afterwards caved in, as he did on the Personal-Liberty Bill."

centralization.

Used in France during the Revolution and later under Napoleon (See Brunot, IX.1024 and Ladendorf, 349) . Under foreign influence the word is found in American politics largely in place of the term *consolidation* (q.v.) .

1870 *Harper's W.* 658. Centralization.... He [Tilden] descries the imminence of the empire. We are becoming rapidly centralized. Centralization is the destruction of liberty.... **1872** Gen. Tom Ewing in *Cinc. Enquirer* 2 Sept. 1. The power of the government

is becoming centralized.... Now fellow-citizens... this tendency toward centralization....
1872 Adams *Storrs* 125. As to this point of local self-government, it is a mere sugar-coated method of administering the old "State Rights" dose. Great clamor is made over what is called "centralization," and one would think that there was a great deal in it.
1889 Farmer *Americanisms* 132. Centralization. The political creed which favors large powers for the general government, as opposed to the limitation of State Rights.

champagne statesmanship.

Policy-making by a small select group of politicians. [ ]
1880 *Harper's W.* 29 May 339/1. The protest of the Republican press of the State has been emphatic and universal against the "Champagne" statesmanship which proposes to deprive the Mayor of New York of his power of appointment, and to invest it in a ring of the political minority.... In this situation a Champagne caucus was held at Albany.

charcoals.

Nickname of a radical Republican party group in Missouri, clearly an intensification of *Black Republican:*
1856 *Cleve. Plain Dealer* 6 Aug. 2/1. He [McLean] has been besieged by Fremonters of every stripe, from the slightly *pinked,* up to the "thorough bred" coal black Republicans....

In contradistinction the conservatives are called "Claybanks," alluding to the yellow color of the banks of the Mississippi:
1862 *Cleve. Leader* 18 Nov. 1/1. More words for the political vocabulary. The emancipationists of St. Louis, who are opposed to Frank P. Blair, are denominated "Charcoals" and the supporters of that gentleman "Claybanks."
(See Thomas S. Barclay, *Liberal*

Movement in Missouri, p. 5, passim.)

A third faction is mentioned in a quotation from the *DA*.
1877 *Exchange Paper* [*DA*]. The members of the [Missouri] Legislature are divided into charcoals, Clay-banks, White-legs....

chip-in-porridge politician.

Older English phrases, *chip in pottage* and *chip in broth,* had the proverbial meaning of "an addition which does neither good nor harm." (*OED*) A chip-in-porridge politician was one who could do good or harm.
1842 *Bro. Jonathan* II.4... chip-in-porridge politicians—i.e. doubtful voters—have a great respect for prowess....

chisel.

To swindle or defraud.

Although Bartlett in 1848 calls this "a western word," and the *OED* calls its history obscure, it is probable that the word has a long English background since Jamieson included it in his dictionary of 1808. In America the first use of *chisel* (or *chizzle*) is attested from 1834:
Davis *Ltrs. of Jack Downing* 181. If you can chizzle them out of their property... without turnin' as red as a beet when you meet 'em, I for one say I can't, and I won't.

In politics:
1841 *Georgia Jrnl.* 26 July 3/1... combined together for the corrupt purposes of chiseling the Government....
1846 *Quarter Race of Ky.* 160. I ain't a goin' to be chizzled out of my fees for making the arrest, that way.

chivalry.

The aristocracy of the South claimed to be the true nobility of

America and boasted of their families and their virtues.

1838 Price *Clem. Falconer* II.62. I will never consent that the South, those sons of chivalry and high honor, ... shall be rendered mere hewers of wood and drawers of water, to the lordly manufacturers north of the Potomac.
1854 *Wash. Union* 20 Oct. 2/2. They admire that fearless chivalry which is the birthright of the southern man.
1888 Lane *Pol. Catchwords* 15. Chivalry. —A cant name for the Southern people, that was much in use about the time of the breaking out of the Civil War. The idea was that Southern emigration had been largely from the Royalist or Cavalier population of England, while the Northern emigration had been largely of the Roundhead or Puritan part. Hence the South was supposed to represent the blue blood or chivalrous portion of the country.

In the North, however, the association of chivalric ideals and slavery did not seem a reasonable one, and the term as a name for the South expressed contempt and satire.

1830's? Channing *Works* 738. Let it not be thought that I would recommend to the North, what in some parts of our country is called "Chivalry,"—a spirit of which the duelling pistol is the best emblem, and which settles controversies with blood.
1837 *Ann. of Cleve.* No.1700. Ritchie should advise Mr. Stevenson to resign, come home, & exhibit himself in retirement, as a dried specimen of modern Virginia chivalry.
1851 *N. Y. Trib.* 8 May 4/2. We are glad that this Convention [Charleston] is held because it must make an end of the whole wearisome stupidity of Disunion. Either the Chivalry will do nothing more than talk, and straightway collapse into insignificance, or else they will attempt rebellion.
1861 *Ohio St. Jrnl.* 3 June. Chivalry. Some of the best words in our language have been prostituted to the basest uses.

... Yet no more corrupt office does it [*affinity*] perform than the word written above.
1861 in *Northern Editorials* II.877. The "chivalry," as the sons of wealthy Virginians delight to call themselves, are only a little better than the peasants.
1862 Kirke *Among the Pines* 228 ... the fumes of bad whiskey, and the crowd of drunken chivalry, thru whom the Colonel with great difficulty elbowed his way....
1868 *Cong. Globe* 1153/3. He was one of the Hotspurs of the South, one of the pinks of southern chivalry, one of those who believed that one southern man could whip five northern men in a fair and equal fight.

See ROUNDHEAD, LOST CAUSE.

Choctaw. [ ]
A. A secret society in Georgia.
1861 *The Crisis* 31 Jan. 3/4. A correspondent of the New York *Times,* dating from Georgia, a short time ago, wrote that there "is a secret society called the Choctaws, numbering 25,000 men, who are sworn to secession or revolution."

B. A society in New Orleans and later a political organization.
1957 P. H. Howard *Pol. Tend in La.* 107. Organized in 1897, the New Orleans Choctaw Club, the Ring, or the "Old Regulars" as they became known to their friends, developed a machine along these lines and began to play an influential part in the state politics.

chow chow.
Chow chow is a relish, usually of chopped mixed pickles. Hence, in politics, it refers to a ticket or convention made up of various factions.
1872 *Ann. of Cleve.* No. 2483. There were the Blairs, eminent as moral examples, and enough others to make up a book which would leave no possible doubt

that the "Chow Chow" convention was a powerful instrument of "reform."

1872 *Ib.* No.2506 ... D. Vorhees, who the Plain Dealer had fondly hoped would go for Greeley and carry the western Democrats, bag and baggage, to the support of the "Chow Chow" ticket, has gone back on "H. G."

Christian party in politics.

A short-lived organization which attempted to fuse religion and politics. It is very doubtful that the name can be related to the later German *Christlich-Soziale Arbeiterpartei* of 1878.

1829 *Workingman's Adv.* 12 Dec. 3/2. The "Christian party in politics" are at last out in their might.... The "Christian party," (or, more properly, the *orthodox* party, for some denominations of Christians are almost universally opposed to their measures, as are the *liberal* among *all*) ....

1830 *Ib.* 2 Jan. 2/3. Those combinations which are aiming to get up "a Christian party in politics," through which to effect "a union of church and state."

1830 *Ib.* 9 Jan. 3/4. The effort now making, by the "Christian party in politics" to procure a stoppage of the mails on Sunday....

1830 *Ib.* 13 Feb. 2/5. Rev. Dr. Ezra Stiles Ely, the would be founder of the "Christian party in politics."

1830 *Ib.* 20 March 3/1. A fanatic and intolerant *"Christian party in politics,"* who are aiming to effect a *"Union of Church and State,"* and the establishment of *their own opinions* as the will of God and the law of the land.

1872 Wilson *Slave Power* I.545. Mr. Garrison, as early as 1834, advocated the organization of a "Christian party in politics."

church.

As a synonym for *party, church* has often been used in elaborate political metaphors.

1815 J. Adams *Works* X.117. One party reads the newspapers and pamphlets of its own church, and interdicts all writings of the opposite complexion. The other party condemns all such as heresy, and will not read or suffer to be read, as far as its influence extends, any thing but its own libels.

1834 *Mangum Papers* V.572. A good Jackson man, a member of the political church, in full communion.

1844 *Ib.* IV.10. Are his past political offences to be *sponged,* and the *Traitor* and his gang again to be taken in full-communion with the Whig Church?

1844 *Buckeye Eagle* 25 Sep. 3/3. A man was taken into the Locofoco Church, and *immersed* in the regular style, the administrator of the ordinance using the following ceremony:—I baptize thee in the name of Andrew Jackson, the Father! James K. Polk, the Son!! and Texas, the Holy Ghost!!

1858 Medill in Holister *Colfax* 124. My private opinion is that he [Douglas] will never be reinstated in the Democratic Church, and that he will gradually drift *toward* our side, and finally be compelled to act with us in 1860.

1859 Thompson in *Cong. Globe* 20 Jan. Sir, it is the glory of the Republican church, and its strength also, that it admits of unity in diversity; banded together in a common aim, and yet various in the character of its civic equipment; constructing no narrow plank on platforms, to operate as instruments of exclusion and elements of disunion and distrust.

1878 *Harper's W.* 12 Jan. 26/1. If he [Hayes] was to conquer in the inevitable struggle, it would be, so to speak, by making his Administration and the Republican conviction that supported it the Church, and by putting his antagonists in the position of Dissenters.

We also find *creed* and *sect* in the political vocabulary:

1808 in Robinson *W. R. Davie* 387 ... their political creed is entirely taken from the government papers ... while these are their bibles, you will be at a loss to discover the Gods they worship.

1834 Leggett *Pol. Writings* I.51. Their next step will be, not by mutual compromise and conciliation to name some candidate for the President on whom all the diversified sects of their composite party might unite . . .

1858 Douglas in Sheahan *Douglas* 342. It is a proposition in violation of the Democratic creed; in violation of the Republican creed; in violation of the American creed; in violation of the creed of every party which professes to be governed by the principles of free institutions and fair elections.

1889 Cleveland *Ltrs. and Add.* 169. Happily the party creed which we profess is not within such narrow lines.

church-burner.

American Speech, XXI.116, points out that the *DAE* is wrong in considering *church-burner* a humorous variant of *barn-burner.* On the basis of—

1849 *N. Y. Post* 14 May. It is now well known to the police that several persons from Philadelphia known as 'Killers' and 'Church Burners' were in the city participating with rioters on Thursday night.—

church-burner is considered a Philadelphia synonym of (Baltimore) *plug ugly* and (New York) *dead rabbit.* However, the word is originally an opprobrious nickname of the Native Americans, who were charged with having burned a church in Philadelphia in 1844.

1844 *Cleve. Herald* 26 Oct. 2/1. It is a well known fact that the Whigs of Philadelphia entered into a coalition with the Natives— (some of them called "churchburners") . . . .

1844 *The Madisonian* in Geary *Third Parties* 107. The so-called Native Americans, alias Churchburners united with the Whigs. . . .

1855 Lee *Am. Party in Politics* 133. And even until this time, they are condemned in certain quarters as rioters, churchburners, and woman-killers!

Ib. 211. But though the Whigs thus retained their name until 1852, they never, in the meantime, scorned alliance with the native American party, even after it had become known by the opprobrious but well deserved name of "churchburners."

ciderite.

A supporter of Harrison in the "hard cider" campaign of 1840:

1840 *Memoir of Abel Brown* 8 Sept. 101. I have made your expose of the urchedness of the ciderites public. . . .

circumlocution office (circumlocutionist).

The immense popularity of Charles Dickens is reflected in the history of several political words (see ARTFUL DODGER, DOLLY VARDEN) . *Circumlocution office* comes from *Little Dorrit.* Our oldest quotation (1869) clearly indicates that the word was used even before that with reference to the Civil Service Reform (q.v.) .

1869 G. W. Curtis *Orations* II.22. Then it is said that the reform would establish a circumlocution office and restore the great official practice of how not to do it. Now, I think it would be an extremely clever circumlocution office that would practise that principle more zealously than the present system does.

1876 T. W. Barnes *Weed* 25 July 532. The administration and Congress have been distinguished as "circumlocutionists." Their efforts toward resumption so far have been in the direction of "how not to do it"; and finally, when the proposed action of Congress on the silver question evinces a disposition to learn how to do it, resistance comes from influential journalists!

The arguments against Civil Service Reforms alluded to by Curtis are stated in almost the same words by Senator Oliver Morton (*Great Debates*, IX.300) :

1871 The amendment suggested by the Senator to his bill is that the President may, in writing, call upon a member of Congress to answer in writing in regard to a recommendation to office. That is the establishment of a circumlocution office—"how not to do it."

citizen.

A. Although *citizen* originally is a dignified word ("citizen of Heaven," Bunyan, see *OED*), it shows signs of degeneration in 18th century English: Johnson says "a man of trade, not a gentleman." This use must have been known in America since the abbreviation "cit" carries a depreciative sense.

1763 J. Adams *Works* II.141. He is, as that writer says, seventy years old; an honest man, but avaricious; a woollen draper, a mere cit; so ignorant of Court and public business, that he knew not where the public offices were. . . .

B. However, the Articles of Confederation and later the Constitution used the word without any admixture of derision or contempt.

1777 *Art.* IV . . . the free inhabitants of each of these states, paupers, vagabonds, and fugitives from justice excepted, shall be entitled to all privileges and immunities of free citizens in the several States.

1787 *Art.* IV. The Citizens of each State shall be entitled to all Privileges and immunities of Citizens in the several States.

C. A new epoch in the history of the word begins with the French Revolution, when *citizen* in democratic circles is recommended as a general term of address following the example of French *citoyen.*

1792–3 in McMaster *Hist.* II.94. Let us stop this, go to France for a Republican lesson, put aside the absurd epithets of Mr. and Sir, and use "the social and soul-warming term Citizen."

1793 *Conn. Courant* in Robinson *Jeff. Dem.* 98. There are such [rabble] among every people, no matter how they may be dignified by the French and Bostonians with the honorable title of citizen.

1793 in Robinson *W. R. Davie* 286. The illustration which he [Iredell] has drawn from the relation of the word subject to the word sovereign, as contradistinguished from the appelation of *citizen*, as a correlative of the American Government, is no better than a contemptible play upon words. . . .

1793 *Columbian Centinel* in Warren *Jacobin and Junto* 46. The procession, it stated would pass through certain streets, "thence to the dwelling house of Citizen Hancock, thence through Winter Street to the House of Citizen S. Adams. . . ."

1817 Birkbeck *Notes* 99. A good citizen is the common designation of respect, when a man speaks of his neighbor as a virtuous man—"he is a very good citizen."

1854 Lowell *Works* I.135. It is wonderful how soon a republican ear reconciles itself with syllables of this description [Lordship]. I think *citizen* would find greater difficulties in the way of its naturalization. . . .

1880 Congdon *Rem.* 24. I well remember several Jeffersonians and Madisonians who were dubbed Citizen this or Cit. that, and who were charged with holding Danton and Robespierre in high esteem.

D. A feminine, *citess* or *citness* was also suggested.

1793 *Indep. Gazetteer* in McMaster *Hist.* II.94n.

No Citess to my name I'll have, says Kate,
Tho' Boston lads about it so much prate;
I've ask'd its meaning, and our Tom, the clown,
Says, darn it, 't means, 'A woman of the town.'

[Another version in *The Centinel*, 16 March, 1793, has "citness."]

E. After the Emancipation Proclamation *citizen* was adopted as a title by the freed Negroes.

1863 Russell *Diary North and South* 19. A "citizen" who was kind enough to come in to shave me, paid me some easy compliments, in the manner of the "Barber of Seville"....
1868 *Putnam's Mag.* II.46. The freedmen were still [1863–4] called "contrabands," to their own great wonderment; but as their ideas crystallized, they began to call each other "citizens"....

citizens' ticket.

One which usually is made up for the purpose of combatting the undesirable candidates of the regular parties.

1855 *N. Y. Herald* 18 Dec. 3/1. One of the gentlemen on the citizens' ticket, in Boston ... had expressed himself not only in favor of the introduction of slavery into Kansas, but of introducing it into Massachusetts.
1884 Roosevelt *Ltrs.* 30 Oct. I.85. The success of the citizens' ticket will have a direct bearing upon the moral welfare of the city as a whole....

civil rights.

"Civil rights are those which belong to the individual as a result of his membership in organized society, that is, as a subject of civil government.... To a large extent, however, civil rights are nothing but natural rights which have been created and defined by the state." (*Cyc. of Am. Govt.* I.281) In politics *civil rights* has been mainly applied since the Civil War to the rights of Negroes as citizens.

1866 *Cong. Globe* 184/2 ... the bill (S.No.61) to protect all persons in the United States in their civil rights, and furnish the means of their vindication.
1866 Trumbull in *Ib.* 1755/3. Mr. President, I fully share with the President of the United States the regret expressed that he was unable to sign the bill "to protect all persons in the United States in their Civil Rights...."
1870 *Nation* 10 Feb. 81/1. On Wednesday week there was reported from the Senate Judiciary Committee a bill amendatory of the Civil Rights Act of 1866, and specially designed for the protection of the Chinese.
1871 Sumner *Works* XIX.231. The bill for Equal Rights is simply supplementary to the existing Civil Rights Law, which is one of our great statutes of peace, and it stands on the same requirements of the National Constitution.
1871 *Ib.* XIX.165. The Civil Rights Law needs a supplement to cover these cases [Negro rights in hotels, theaters, etc.].
1874 Hays of Ala. in *Cong. Record* 31 Jan. 1096/2. The discussion of this question of "civil rights" has brought about a state of feeling in the South which is to be deplored.... Newspapers, politicians, demagogues, and inciters of sectional hate have preached to the white masses of the South that Congress was upon the verge of enacting a law enforcing "social equality" and blotting out the lines between knowledge and ignorance.
1875 *Gt. Deb.* VIII.211. The opposition to civil rights in the South is confined almost exclusively to States under Democratic control, or States were the legislature has failed or refused to pass a civil-rights bill.

civil service reform.

A. The first suggestion of an organized attempt to reform the government civil service was in relation to the British political system.

1857? in Nevins *Emergence of Lincoln* I.130. Greeley's Tribune seized the opportunity to call attention to the British Civil Service Commission, which had begun work two years earlier, remarking that it was high time the United States followed this example.

B. Ten years later a civil service bill was introduced, and in the following decades *civil service reform* became a common phrase in the political vocabulary.

1867 *Nation* 10 Jan. 32/1. The civil service bill of Mr. Jenckes, of Rhode Island, submitted at the last session and renewed at this, is a matter that specifically deserves earnest study and careful discussion.
1869 Curtis *Orations* II.20. ["Civil Service Reform," Oct.] The Civil-Service Reform therefore begins with the assertion that there is no reason in the nature of things or of our form of government that the United States should not manage its affairs with the same economy, ability, and honesty that the best private business is managed. . . .
1871 Sherman in *Gt. Deb.* IX.289. I have regarded this measure for the last year as being not a complete civil service reform in itself, but as being an entering wedge indispensably necessary to bring about a civil service reform separating the civil service in the executive departments entirely from the legislative until the unconstitutional habit that has sprung up in this country of allowing members of Congress to control appointments is broken up.
1872 *Harper's W.* 402/1. The country demands . . . a radical civil service reform. . . .522/3 When Mr. Jenckes began, it was often necessary to explain what was meant by the words civil service.
1886 Ingalls in Peck *Twenty Yrs.* 28 March 89. A political system which illustrates in its practical operations the appointment by the same administration of Eugene Higgins and Dorman B. Eaton can properly be regarded as in the transition epoch and characterized as the pterodactyl of politics. It is, like that animal, equally adapted to waddling in the slime and mud of partisan politics, and soaring aloft with discordant cries into the glittering and opalescent empyrean of civil service reform.
1913 Roosevelt *Works* XXII.158. Civil service reform is designed primarily to give the average American citizen a fair chance in politics, to give to this citizen the same weight in politics that the "ward heeler" has.

claybanks.
See CHARCOALS.

Clay Whig.
An adherent of Henry Clay.

1854 *Wash. Union* 19 Oct. 2/6 . . . his speeches are cordially received and heartily responded to by the old Clay Whigs of twenty and thirty years' standing. . . . "genuine Clay whig". . . .
1859 R. B. Hayes letter in *Ohio Arch. and Hist. Qtrly.* LX.31. I understand Mr. Lincoln was an old Clay Whig of Kentucky parentage, and with a wholesome dislike of Locofocoism.

clean sweep.
A total victory; a change of officeholders.

In 1810 Governor Clinton used a similar phrase:

in Bobbe *Clinton* 140. No man here entertains any doubts as to the impunity of his [Williams'] motives. The consequences will be a general sweep of the Republicans from office.

However, the term seems to belong in the main to the Jackson campaigns which also brought the related metaphors *Augean stable* and *(hickory) broom* into prominence.

1829 James *Jackson* 488. Great efforts are being made to put him up to a general sweep as to all offices; springing from great doubts whether he is disposed to do it.
1837 *New Yorker* 554/2. The Whigs, of course, swept the board.
1840 Clay in Norton *Tippecanoe* 27 June 196. General Jackson was a bold and fearless reaper carrying a wide row, but he did not gather the whole harvest; he left some gleanings to his faithful successor, and he seems resolved to sweep clean the field of power.

1840 *Ohio St. Jrnl.* 30 Sept. 1/2 ... our friends seem to have made a clean sweep of the Legislative and Congressional tickets. ...

1848 *Old Zack* 29 July 1/3. The Whigs will sweep everything in this State.

1856 *Greenville* (Ohio) *Jrnl.* 13 Aug. 2/3. A Clean Sweep!! Republicans elected all candidates for State offices in Iowa.

1876 *N. Y. Trib.* 20 Sept. 4/4. We have made a clean sweep of all the Congressional districts.

1951 *Time* 19 March 25 ... when Bakewell was swept into Congress for one term by the new Republican broom.

In addition to describing a total victory in the elections *clean sweep* developed a new meaning after the Jackson inauguration of the spoils system. The term came to mean a thorough change of officeholders:

1840 *Cong. Globe* 2 April App.370/3. Did not the Ritner dynasty carry out the spoils principle, as my colleague has been pleased to call it, with a vengeance? He made a clean sweep.

184– Parton *Greeley* 246. The Loco-Foco House has ordered a clean sweep of all its underlings.

1876 *Harper's W.* 22 Jan. 62/2. There has been a "clean sweep." From the highest to the lowest position, from the Clerk's deputies to the pages on the floor, every Republican incumbent, Union soldiers disabled and impoverished in the war, with every man and boy in every place have been shot out like rubbish, that Democrats may be put in.

1877 *Puck* 12 May 10/3. If Hayes is wise, he'll sweep out every Jack in the department, from the Collector to the smallest of the Weigher's assistants.

1877 *Ib.* 31 Oct. 2/1. Puck hasn't yet seen the wholesome clean-sweep of corrupt officers which he was led to expect from Hayes's assurances.

1884 *Harper's W.* 6 Dec. 796/3. If Mr. Hendrick's "clean sweep" policy should prevail in the civil service there would be a clean sweep of his party at the next election.

clear the track.

Notice given that a particular candidate is going to make a strong and supposedly winning race.

The racing background of the phrase is clearly seen in a description of pre-race conditions at an English track:

1834 *N. Y. Sporting Mag.* II.152/2. The next step was to clear the Course [Ascot] preparatory to the commencement of the races—a task of no small difficulty from the crowd which was assembled; but it was at length effected, and the pedestrians either took their stand along the rails, or returned to their carriages. Between each race the promenade was resumed, and towards five o'clock the King and Queen ... were repeatedly cheered.

American political usage:

1844 in *Ohio Arch. Qtly.* (1948) 35. Clear the track for Emancipation! Cars can not run on a Clay Foundation.

1844 *Nat. Clay Minstrel* 44. Clear the track for old Kentucky.

1856 *Sandusky Comm. Reg.* 4 July 2/1. Clear the track for the Pathfinder of Empire.

Variants:

1848 *Ohio St. Jrnl.* 19 July 1/6 [campaign song]. Old Zack's on the track.

1876 *Ann. of Cleve.* No.1909. Hayes has already run Thurman, Pendleton, and Allen off the track.

No.1846 ... to get back fairly upon the track again.

closed (and open) shop.

Although the idea of excluding unorganized labor from the workshop goes back at least to the labor troubles in the Philadelphia shoe industry in 1806 (see SCAB), the terms *open* and *closed shop* themselves have not been found prior to the beginning of the 20th century. In 1896, however, we find *open office:*

Typographical Jrnl. IX.445. Our next efforts were directed to the Morning Leader, also an "open" office.

Both *open* (with its synonym *free shop*) and *closed shop* seem to have originated among the manufacturers, while the unionists prefer *union* and *non-union*.

1898 *Am. Federationist* December 207/2. The shoe manufacturers of Marlboro, Mass.,... have resorted to the usual ruse employed by unfair employers in the method to hoodwink both the employees and the general public; that is, have promulgated an order for so-called "free shops."

1901 *World's Work* III.914/2. The shop had previously been an "open" one—that is, union and non-union men were employed without distinction.

1903 *Am. Federationist* March 163. In line with this recognition of the union, which tacitly carries with it the "union shop," and when once admitted the battle for fair conditions is practically won.

1903 *Ib.* April 256. A partly organized, or what is called a free or open, shop is untenable....

1903 *Ib.* Nov. 1164. The unionist may not demand the union closed shop, but the employer may insist upon the non-union closed shop.

1903 Mitchell *Organized Labor* 201. A strike by a union against a trust which has non-union shops merely transfers the profits of the trust from one pocket to another....

1903 *Rev. of Rev.* XXVIII. 354. The "Union" Versus the "open" Shop.... The open shop is the place of natural selection; it is the free field for the play of economic forces.

1904 *Rev. of Rev.* XXIX.225. Since the "closed shop" means not only that none other than union laborers shall be employed, but that the rules of the shop shall be made by the unions, and that the foreman shall be a member of the union, it is clear that the management of the business is practically taken out of the hands of the employers.

1904 *Am. Federationist* March 213–4. The "open shop" lies between the union shop and the sweat shop.... The object of the union shop is not to create a monopoly of opportunity. *It is not a "closed shop."*

1904 *Weber's W.* 11 June 2. That "Closed Shop" agreements between employer and trades unionists ... is an interference with the property rights of the non-unionist.

1905 *Ib.* 11 March 4... it will easily be seen that the civil service law could be used by a trades union city administration to bring about a strictly "closed shop" condition in the city service.

1911 *Johns Hopkins Studies* XIX.13. Since 1905 there has been much objection on the part of trade unionists to the use of the term "closed shop".... They contend that this use of the term has been brought about by designing employers who wish to place the unions in a bad light.... The proper term, they claim, is "union shop." They assert that the union shop is "never a closed one."

coalition.

A. Eighteenth century English used *coalition* as a merely descriptive term designating a combination of parties for the achievement of common aims. Since such action is likely to cause sacrifices of principle, the word soon acquired an unpleasant flavor:

1749 Auckland *Corr.* III.220. [*OED*] I am sick of coalitions, royal, military, or ministerial.

1827 Macaulay *Sp.* I.13 [*OED*]. The writers and speakers of the Opposition repeat their favourite phrases—"deserted principles," "unnatural coalition," "base love of office." They have not, we must allow, been unfortunate in their choice of a topic. The English are but too much accustomed to consider every public virtue as comprised in consistency; and the name of coalition has to many ears a startling and ominous sound.

B. In America the critical year in the history of the word is 1824, when alliances between the various candidates were in the air and culminated in the alleged "corrupt bargain" between John Quincy Adams and Henry Clay. In April the word was used in a neutral way:

Cinc. Nat. Rep. 16 April 2/3. The Coalition.... we are now assured that a coalition of the most prominent adherents of these candidates is confidently expected, and the votes of New York guaranteed to Mr. Crawford.

In June we read:

Nat. Intelligencer 29 June 3/4. Despising the system of bargain and intrigue, they [followers of Crawford] have formed no coalitions, nor attempted any "holy alliance."

And by late summer the word had acquired definitely unpleasant connotations:

Clay Works IV.98 [letter of 31 Aug.]. The anticipated coalition in New York, I should suppose was very probable, unless it could be prevented by the apprehension of the imputation of corruption, bargaining, etc.

Cinc. Nat. Rep. 21 Sept. 2/2. The Coalition.... the Clay and Crawford coalition, which ought to arouse the exertions of every man who pretends to any concern for the public welfare, to put down an aristocratic combination formed for private benefit and personal objects.

1831 *Cinc. Liberty Hall* 3 Nov. 4/1. In the position now occupied by President Jackson ... no favorable effect can be produced by denouncing corruptions, coalitions and bargains.

See FUSION, HOLY ALLIANCE.

coattails.

Usually occurring in phrases, *to hide under the coattail, to hang onto the coattails, to ride on the coattails;* suggests that a lesser

known or weaker man is profiting by the presence on the ticket or in the party of a stronger, more popular man.

A. In his celebrated speech of July 27, 1848, on the political situation, Lincoln made frequent references to coattails:

Cong. Globe App.1042. But the gentleman from Georgia [Iverson] further says, we have dissected all our principles, and taken shelter under General Taylor's military coat tail.... Has he no acquaintance with the ample military coat tail of General Jackson? Does he not know that his own party have run the last five Presidential races under that coat tail, and that they are now running the sixth under the same cover? ... Mr. Speaker, old horses and military coat tails, or tails of any sort, are not figures of speech such as I would be the first to introduce into discussions here; but. ...

Despite Lincoln's apology and denial, the introduction of *coattail* into the debate does not appear to have been made by Iverson. His speech of the preceding day contains the idea but not the phrase:

App.965 ... now suddenly hides the light of its principles, as under a bushel, and arraying itself under the banner of a military chieftain....

Later variations:

1852 *Scott Battery* 1 Nov. 2/4. Be sure and hang fast to John's coat tail.

1860 *Bobolink Songster* 41.

He can't get de vote 'case de tail ob de coat
Is hung just a little too low.

1872 *Harper's W. passim.* [Gratz Brown appears in Nast cartoons as a tag on Horace Greeley's coat tail.]

1949 *Cols.* (Ohio) *Citizen* 16 Dec. That straight-ticket voting has enabled many a mediocre candidate to ride into office on the coat-tails of an able, popular man at the top.

1953 *Ib.* 5 Nov. 14/1. Results everywhere demonstrated that Republican candidates must have more to recommend them than a tight grip on Mr. Eisenhower's coattails. **1956** *Ohio State Lantern* 13 Jan. 2. Ike seems to be a bit cautious before making any statement that might be mistaken for a campaign speech. Could be that he's not interested in carrying a lot of dead wood around on his coat tails. Unless of course the wood happens to be a brassie or spoon.

codfish and cabbage ticket.

The Free Soil party slate of 1848 consisting of Martin Van Buren and Charles Francis Adams.

Van Buren raised cabbages in New York; Adams was from Massachusetts, which is frequently symbolized by the codfish.

1848 in Donovan *Barnburners* 107. The Free-Soil ticket was contemptuously denounced as the "codfish and cabbage" ticket.

codfish aristocracy.

The rich merchant families in New England, particularly in Boston, perhaps in allusion to the codfish in the Massachusetts Statehouse (see below).

First attested in 1844, but probably older since *codfish president* presupposes it:

1833 *Examiner* 18 Sept. 63/1 ... another the principle of turning out that cod-fish President [J. Q. Adams], and mortifying the Yankees. **1844** *Wash. Intelligencer* 15 Aug. 3/4. Is it to be the leader of the Subterraneans, who some time ago told us of "the codfish aristocracy of Democracy?" **1850** Butler of S.C. in *Cong. Globe* 9 July App.1248. We should regard it as somewhat strange if we should require a codfish aristocracy to keep us in order. **1852** *Ib.* 15 Dec. App.102. When Foote spoke, [the Russian Minister] looked on

with that expression of contempt ... with which one of our codfish aristocracy would regard a Democratic harangue from Mike Walsh. **1867** *Ib.* 12 Feb. App.105/3. The codfish aristocracy had bounties for fishing, in order to build up a navy. **1876** *Ib.* 19 May 3221/1. In the Statehouse at Boston, in the house of representatives ... there hangs swimming in air, the well-mounted effigy of an enormous codfish, suggesting the origin and giving a typical representation of what is called there "the codfish aristocracy."

Sometimes used and occasionally misunderstood outside of New England.

1849 *Bellville* (Ohio) *Rainbow* 30 Nov. 2/4. That evil is the instigation or giving rise to what is called Codfish Aristocracy, a class of persons who wish to appear before the public as though they were worth thousands. **1888** *Cong. Globe* 11 June 5115/2. [They wanted to get] into the society of the codfish aristocracy of the city of Columbus [Ohio].

coffee house politician.

1828 *Niles' Reg.* 16 Feb. 402/2. "Coffee House" Politicians.... proceedings of the "merchants and others," at the coffeehouses, in Philadelphia, to prevent the passage of any law for the further protection of domestic industry.

See BEER SHOP POLITICIAN.

coffin handbill.

During the campaign of 1828 one of the political maneuvers attempted to secure the defeat of Andrew Jackson was the printing of handbills charging him with the murder of various individuals while he was commander of the armed forces at New Orleans and in the Florida campaign. The striking thing about the handbills was their border of black coffins, always at least six and sometimes as many as eighteen. In the *Liberty Hall* of 3 April, 1828, 1/2, there is a detailed description of the handbills, concluding with

Such are the materials of "this infamous hand-bill." And why is it infamous? The coffins do but represent realities. The eighteen persons designated, were all put to death under the orders of Gen. Jackson.

John Binns, a Philadelphia publisher, is credited with having originated the handbill:

1828 *Spirit of '28* (Portland, Maine) 29 Oct. 1/2 . . . John Binns, the forger of the Harris letter and manufacturer of coffin hand bills.

But they appeared in many forms and in many different localities:

1828 *Liberty Hall* 3 July 1/2. Coffin Hand-bills. Preparations are making to publish a brief sketch of Gen. Jackson's cruelties, in pamphlet form, with plates, of which coffins will be a part.

The Jackson men tried to counteract their effect by various methods:

1828 *Liberty Hall* 9 April 3/1. One means of electioneering [by Jackson men] was to carry round the coffin hand-bill, and assert that it was the work of Mr. Clay.

In 1844 when Congress voted to refund Jackson's fine imposed by Judge Dominick Hall for his conduct at New Orleans, references to the coffin handbills are found:

1844 *Wash. Daily Globe* 11 Jan. 39/6. We notice his accomplished epistle because it is accompanied by one of those beautiful Coon memorials (the famous coffin handbill) which, we trust, will be adopted as an appropriate pictorial illustration in the approaching campaign.

cohesive power of public plunder.

Apparently an elaboration of Calhoun's statement; substitution made for his longer and less colorful phrase:

1836 Calhoun *Works* 28 May II.568. A power has risen up in the Government greater than the people themselves, consisting of many, and various, and powerful interests, combined into one mass, and held together by the cohesive power of the vast surplus in the banks.

1840 *Straight-Out Harrisonian* 17 July 2/5 . . . the movement of a party which, to use the words of John C. Calhoun . . ." is kept together by no other bond than the Cohesive Power of Plunder."

1844 *Niles' Reg.* 20 April 122/3. It is the "spoils party, held together by the cohesive power of public plunder!"

It is doubtful whether other identification of its originator can be supported by evidence.

1867 Warner in *Gt. Deb.* IX.12. It was feared by the radicals that he [A. Johnson] might build up a party united "by the cohesive power of public plunder"— in the classic phrase coined at this time by Representative Samuel L. Warner (Ct.) . . . .

1880 Congdon *Rem.* 66. For it [Dem. party] believed in what John Quincy Adams felicitously called "the cohesive power of public plunder."

Later use:

1912 Osborne in Chamberlain *No Truce* 183. Choose ye this day whom ye will serve. On the one side stand Woodrow Wilson and the principles of progressive Democracy; on the other, Charles F. Murphy and the cohesive power of public plunder!

cold water.

A. In the late 18th century the benefits of cold water were exploited as a remedy for many ailments, reaching the proportions of an international fad after the development of a specific medical treatment in 1825 by the German Preissnitz. (see *OED*)

1846–7 Beecher *Autobio*.II.505 [Advice to his son]. Ease up, Rest—sleep—exercise. Cold water—rub. No tobacco.—Father.

B. That the treatment had a long time vogue is suggested by evidence of its metaphorical use as early as 1785.

1785 Jay *Works* II.178. Hence it is that the most leading men in Congress from that quarter do not only not promote measures for vesting Congress with power to regulate trade, but, as the common phrase is, throw cold water on all such ideas.

C. Pertaining to total abstinence and the prohibition movement in American politics:

1839 *Liberator* 6 Dec. 196/1. The cold-water preachers will keep saying still, That Rum isn't good, and we'd best do without it.

1854 Bungay *Off-Hand Takings* 210. In politics he is a cold water Democrat; in religion he is a cold water Universalist.

1884 *Cent. Mag.* April 807/2. The cold-water regime [of Pres. Hayes] lasted four years. . . .

1900 *Rev. of Rev.* XXII.327. The high-water mark of the cold-water party (for a Presidential election) was reached in 1892.

collective bargaining.

Apparently coined by Beatrice Potter (Webb) in 1891.

1897 Webb *Industrial Dem.* I.174n. The phrase "Individual Bargaining" is used incidentally by C. Morrison in his *Essay on the Relations Between Labour and Capital* (London, 1854) . . . . We are not aware of any use of the phrase "Collective Bargaining" before that in *The Co-operative Movement in Great Britain* (London, 1891) . . . .

1891 Webb *Co-op. Movement in Gt. Brit.* 217. Individualist exchange must follow individualist production, and give place to collective bargaining.

B. American uses.

1903 Mitchell *Organized Labor* 4. Trade unionism thus recognizes that the destruction of the workingman is the individual bargain, and the salvation of the workingman is the joint, united, or collective bargain. . . .

10. Without the right to choose their representative, the men cannot enjoy the full benefit of collective bargaining; and without the right of collective bargaining, the door is opened to the individual contract and to the progressive debasement of the working classes, and to the deterioration of conditions of work to the level of conditions in the sweated and unregulated trades.

1910 Roosevelt *Works* XVIII.218. In the modern field of industrialism it is often an absolute necessity that there should be collective bargaining by the employees with the employer.

1923 Vandenberg *If Hamilton Were Here Today* 176. How has this "I.T.U." chiefly succeeded in making the vast gains for itself which it has recorded in years gone by? Through strikes? Oh, no! First by legitimate collective bargaining. . . .

1938 F. D. Roosevelt in *Homegrown Liberal* 251. We are seeking, of course, only legislation to end starvation wages and intolerable hours; more desirable wages are, and should continue to be, the product of collective bargaining.

In addition to the "individual bargaining" mentioned by Webb, the term "collective" was also early used in the labor movement.

1861 Wainhouse *Trades' Unions Justified* 24. The refusal to work alongside "unfair" workmen is a "legitimate interference of collective opinion."

cologne Whig.

Belonging to the group including such terms as *silk stocking* and *ruffled shirt, cologne Whig* referred to the aristocratic qualities which the Whigs assumed in contradistinction to the roughness associated with the Democrats of this period.

1836 *Cols. West. Hemisphere* 17 Aug. 1/7 ...since the cologne whigs and short horns of Pickaway had the *honaw* to present themselves to his North-Bend-ship.

The reference to the short horns is not clear, but it may be either a misuse of *short hairs* (q.v.) or an early example of the Western term meaning tenderfoot:

A. H. Lewis *Sunset Trail* chap.2. Don't let no shorthorn have my room, I may need it myself; an' in case I do, I don't want to be obleeged to bootcher no harmless stranger.

colonization.

A. Of Negroes. The plan of transferring freed Negroes to colonies in Africa goes back to the time of the Revolution (see Wilson, *Slave Power*).

The term *colonization* must have become generally known when on December 21, 1816, the American Colonization Society was organized.

1816 Jefferson *Works* (Ford ed.) X.290. Under this view, the colonization society is to be considered as a missionary society....

The Colonization Society became further popularized by the passionate criticism of the colonization idea by the abolitionists.

1832 Garrison *Selections* 39. The Colonization Society deters a large number of masters from liberating their slaves, and hence directly perpetuates the evils of slavery.

Child *An Appeal* 12. I object to the Colonization Society, because it tends to put public opinion asleep, on a subject where it needs to be wide awake.... The

Colonization Society are always reminding us that the master has rights as well as the slave: The Anti-Slavery Society urge us to remember that the slave has rights as well as the master.

B. Of voters.

The practice of influencing elections by temporary transfer of reliable voters to doubtful districts.

1839 *New Yorker* 13 April 2/1. "Colonization" or the removal of voters from certain to the doubtful wards.

1858 *Ann. of Cleve.* No.2997. That there was colonizing and frauds in the closely contested districts by the Douglas democracy, there is no doubt.

1880 *Puck* 17 Nov. 171/1. There has been a shameful colonization on the part of the Republican party.

(See BLOCKS OF FIVE.)

color line.

An invisible line of distinction between the races.

No evidence has been found as yet to bear out the plausible suggestion that color line referred originally to actual lines which were formed in the South to separate white and negro applicants for jobs and offices or for relief. (See, however, WHITE LINE.) Nor does there seem to be any connection between the military and political color lines.

1874 *House Report* 43rd Cong. 2nd sess. No.265.32. The "color line" means that the whites of this State have become satisfied that it is useless further to attempt to coalesce with the negro element in voting....All offices in the State of any importance...are filled by men who encourage the maintenance of the color-line....

1875 *Urbana* (Ohio) *Citizen and Gazette* 30 Sept. 1/5. The Mississippi Democrats abandoned the "color line" with considerable ostentation at their last convention, but the editor of the Columbus Index (Dem.) announces that a color-line club has been organized in that city.

1876 in *Cong. Record* 19 Jan. One excuse given for this [white line policy] is that the colored people had adopted a color-line, by which they sought to gain exclusive control of the government in Mississippi and other Southern States.

1896 *Cinc. Trib.* 9 June 1/7. The local committee promised that no color line would be drawn and no discrimination made by any of the hotels.

come-outer.

One who leaves his party over a difference of principle.

A. Originally, a religious dissenter:

1840 in Longfellow *Life of H. W. Longfellow* I.373. Not long after, came up from Cape Cod a new sect called the "Comeouters," who formed a holy alliance with the Transcendentalists.

B. In politics:

1844 *Ohio St. Jrnl.* 17 Aug. 2/2. "Come-outer." This is a term applied by the Locofocos to those whose names they use as having renounced their Whig principles.

1847 Garrison *Garrison Story* III.202–203. Two of the graduates took occasion, in their addresses, to denounce "the fanaticism of Come-outerism and Disunion.

coming man. [ ]

1860 Jones *Mirror of Democracy* 257 [Pierce to J. Davis]. Our people are looking for the "Coming Man." One who is raised by all the elements of his character above the atmosphere ordinarily breathed by politicians.

1860 *Ann. of Cleve.* No.1915 ... eulogized Douglas as the "coming man."

1861 Richardson *Secret Service* 141. In those days, every eye was looking for the coming man—the Hour must have its Hero.

common herd.

The masses.

As used by Shakespeare:

Julius Caesar I.i.264 [Casca]. Marry, before he fell down, when he perceived the common herd was glad he refused the crown, he pluckt me ope his doublet, and offer'd them his throat to cut....

American examples:

1836 *Ann. of Cleve.* No.841. The pompous manner in which his [Van Buren's] carriage, with his English horses, English drivers, and waiters in full livery, rolls down and up the avenues of Washington and New York seems to excite the special wonder of the "common herd," as they have been politely termed.

1954 *Cols.* (Ohio) *Citizen* 21 Oct. [Inez Robb, "Around the U.S.A."]. (In using the expression "common herd," I apologize in advance to owners and breeders of Black Angus, Hereford ... cattle, and wish to disassociate myself in any way from an invidious comparison between pure bred cattle and homo sapiens.)

communism.

The word *communism* is based upon the Bible where the Vulgate uses *communis* in regard to property—

Acts II.44. Omnes etiam qui credebant, erant pariter, & habebant omnis communia—

although it is a rather devious connection.

During the French Revolution, *communiste* refers to those benefiting from the socialization of the big estates (Brunot, IX, pt. 2, 1123). It is not a party name, nor does it allude to the adherents of a certain theory. It is not known that the theoretical communists of this period ever used the term. Goodwyn Barmy claims that in 1840 he first invented the term:

1848 *New Apostle* No.1. I also conversed [in 1840] with some of the most advanced minds of the French metropolis, and there . . . I first pronounced the name of Communism. . . .

According to Bestor the terms were introduced in America in connection with the various socialistic communities, an association which has continued:

1948 *Jrnl. of the Hist. of Ideas* 281. The word *communism* seems to have been first used in America in the Perfectionist, 15 July, 1843, as reprinted in Circular (Oneida Community), n.s. V,115 (29 June, 1868).
1844 Emerson *Writings* I.380–1. [7 Feb. lecture in Boston.] Witness the new movements in the civilized world, the Communism of France, Germany, Switzerland. . . . These communists [at Brook Farm, Fruitlands, and Hopedale] preferred the agricultural life as the most favorable condition for human culture.
The Communist. [Published by Skaneateles Community, N.Y., 1844–46.]
1848 *Webster's Dictionary*. Communism. A new French word, nearly synonymous with agrarianism, socialism, and radicalism.
1854 *Wash. Union* 24 Oct. 2/6. The Ebenezers are a communist, or common-property association.

Most of the criticism of communism up to 1871 consists chiefly of denunciations of the failures of the various utopian communities.

1871, however, seems to be a turning point with the setting up of the Commune in Paris, in which, as a matter of fact, the communists proper only played a limited part (Cole *Hist. of Soc.* II.148, 169).

1871 *Every Saturday* 13 May 450/3. Force, divorced from the free exercise of mind and will, will be dominant in the worst of conceivable despotisms. That is the ideal which the Paris Commune is now fighting to establish.

1871 *Ib*. 24 June 578/2. The full and vivid accounts of the doings of the Commune . . . enable us to form clear ideas of the purposes and the passions of that wretched combination of knaves, thieves, and fanatics, which assumed the right of governing France. . . . This is, we believe, the fundamental fact to be considered, that the Communists are the declared enemies of modern civilization.
1882 *Works of Garfield* II.585. J. A. MacGanah . . . was in Paris during the Commune, and was saved from death at the hands of the Communists by the United States Minister.

Communism becomes associated with robbery and lawlessness and is the arch-foe of capitalism.

1873 in Loth *Public Plunder* 186. A mild suggestion that a rent moratorium [in 1873] would ease the crisis was met by the World with the flat assertion that this was a communist plot to rob the landlords.
1878 *Harper's W.* 2 March 158 [cartoon]. Wolf, inscribed "Political Communism," shooting arrows "income tax" and "90/cent Silver Dollar" at beaver "Industry."
1878 *Nation* 4 July 1/1. [E. A. Storrs] concluded with a pointed nomination of Gen. Grant for the Presidency in 1880, with the view of stemming the tide of Communism in the United States, and assuring alike to capital and labor their just reward.
1878 *Harper's W.* 7 Sept. 706/1. The apparent expectation among many public men seems now to be that the Presidential election will present Communism, a reign of terror, the overthrow of society, and the annihilation of property on one side, and General Grant on the other. . . .
1880 Conkling in Ridpath *Garfield* 432. When he [Grant] refused to receive Denis Kearney in California, he meant that Communism, lawlessness, and disorder, although it might stalk highheaded and dictate law to a whole city, would find a foe in him.
1884 *Mansfield* (Ohio) *Shield* 2 Aug. 4/4. The tide of crime, violence, and commu-

nism, of contempt of authority and law, is high enough now.

Following the Russian Revolution in 1917, *communism* becomes almost exclusively identified with the Russian Communist Party.

1924 *Nation* 2 Jan. 6/1. The Russian Communist Party combines the secrecy of the Masons and the fanatic devotion of the Jesuits with the worldly adaptability of a modern political organization. . . . But the Russian Government is in reality so closely identified with the Russian Communist Party that an attempt to discover where the authority of the one ends and that of the other begins amounts to little more than academic hair-splitting.
1925 Coan *Red Web* 148. The "left wing" Reds—the Communists—and the "right wing" reds—the socialists—were in complete accord.
1932 *New Rep.* 10 Aug. 329/1. He [Hoover] issued a series of statements implying that the veterans were largely either criminals or Communists—two categories which in his mind are evidently identical.
1934 Carter *New Dealers* 58. The wage-scale had collapsed and the Communist bugaboo had lost its power to terrify the conservatives.
1946 *Ohio State Lantern* 21 Oct. 4. The act of howling "communist" every time someone points out the already known gaping holes in our economic system is a practice born of the dark ages.
1950 Lattimore *Ordeal* 223. The typical Communist is a man whose thinking is regimented with the thinking of other Communists, but has nothing whatever to do with the thinking of average Americans.
1952 Stevenson *Major Camp. Sp.* 161. Your effective fight against communism goes clear back to the time it was called bolshevism.

confidence game.

Political maneuvering in which the public seems to be the victim of a swindling operation.

1867 Blaine in *Cong. Globe* 26 Nov. 801/2 . . . for Congress . . . to step forward at this late day and declare itself not bound by the conditions published by the Secretary is simply to place the U.S. Gov't. in the position of a man playing a "confidence game" of the meanest description, in which the Treasury Dept. and Congress are confederate knaves, and the whole mass of bondholders the unfortunate victims.
1872 *Harper's W.* 27 July 578. But what an absurd and shadowy assembly that Johnsonian Convention [of 1866] seems to-day! What an imposture it was! What a wretched confidence game!
1872 *Ib.* 9 Nov. 866. The Failure of the Confidence Game. . . . There has been an attempted confidence game in politics, and it has ridiculously failed.

Congo creed.

A derogatory reference of the Democrats to the antislavery doctrines of the Republicans:

1857 *Ohio Statesman* 22 Aug. 2. Congo Creed. [placed at masthead; contains excerpts from *Ohio State Journal,* which, 7 Sept. 2, denied the excerpts]
1857 *Ann. of Cleve.* 11 Sept. No.1459. When the Democrats, from Payne down, become worried about the opposition, they resort to slang and misrepresentation. In an article in the Plain Dealer, they attack Governor Chase and his party with the cry, "creed of the Congo," saying that the Republicans would put into office Negroes and permit Negro suffrage.

conscience Democrat.

A title proposed for an antislavery Democrat:

1858 Theodore Parker in *N. Y. Antislavery St.* 27 Feb. 2/2. Soon there will be Conscience Democrats as once Conscience Whigs.

conscience Whig.

Conscience seemed to play an

important part in New England oratory, even before it became closely associated with *cotton* over the slavery question. See *cotton whig* for additional material.

1804 Channing *Memoirs* I.321. A just man appeals from the laws of the land to the dictates of conscience. He does not cling to every shadow of right.

1834 Choate in Bartlett *Quot.* 599. The courage of New England was the "courage of conscience." It did not rise to that insane and awful passion, the love of war for itself.

Webster speech in Niblo's Garden. ¿ Slavery is a question not only of politics but of conscience.

The term came into prominence in 1848:

1848 *Ohio Statesman* 5 Aug. 2/2. That portion of the Whig party, known as conscience whiggery....

1848 *Cong. Globe* 21 July App.814.2. Though there were Clay Whigs and Conscience Whigs, Native Whigs and Abolition Whigs, with a small dash of Antirentism, yet they never failed to come up here with the pro-slavery Whigs of the South.

1848 *N. Y. Herald* 10 July 3/2. The conscience whigs, to do them justice, do care something for the slave; whereas Van Buren and his gang would sell every negro to the devil, if they could make a shilling by the transaction.

1848 *Free Soil Banner* 21 Aug. 4/3.
For conscience whigs and liberty men
And every true barnburner
Here join to stay proud slavery's course
And from free soil to spurn her.

1851 in *Mangum Papers* V.205. These Whigs—the conscience Whigs—are so timid and so pure that they scarcely ever act.

consent of the governed.
A. The idea that lawful government must be based upon the con-

sent of the people is found in Plato:

Plato *Laws* III.690 [Loeb Classical Lib.] ...man without understanding should follow, and the wise man lead and rule. Nevertheless, my most sapient Pindar, this is the thing that I, for one, would hardly assert to be against nature, but rather according thereto—the natural rule of law, without force, over willing subjects.

B. English political philosophers of the 16th and 17th centuries developed Plato's idea and arrived at the formula *consent of the people.*

1593 Hooker *Eccl. Pol.* I.10. [*OED*] Strifes and troubles would be endless, except they gave their common consent all to be ordered by some whom they should agree upon.... The assent of them who are to be governed seemeth necessary.

1647 in Gough *Locke's Pol. Philos.* 63. [*OED*] It's clear, that every man that is to live under a government ought first by his own consent to put himself under that government.

1660 in *Ib.* 180. If the supreme authority be conferred on the magistrate by the consent of the people,... then it is evident that they have resigned up their liberty of action into his disposure....

1689 Locke *Second Treat. on Govt.* 104. The examples of history showing that the governments of the world ... were made by the consent of the people....

142. They must not raise taxes on the property of the people without the consent of the people given by themselves or their deputies.

Pufendorf was one of the few who objected to the logic of the theory.

1688 Pufendorf *Law of Nature and Nations* III.iv.4. Enimvero falsissimum est, omne imperium constitui consensu eorum, quibus imperatur. [But the statement that all government is based upon the consent of those who are governed is utterly false.]

C. Early American uses reflect the influence of the English philosophers. The variation of the phrase in the Declaration of Independence sets the pattern, in general, for later usage.

1676 in West *Sourcebook* 328. [Proclamation signed] Nath. Bacon. Genll by Consent of the people.

1638 T. Hooker in Hart *Sourcebook* 51. Because the foundation of authority is laid, firstly, in the free consent of the people.

1750 in Thornton *Pulpit in Am. Rev.* 89. He [Charles I] levied many taxes upon the people without consent of Parliament....

1774 in West *Sourcebook* 400. Taxes imposed without the consent of the people or their representatives.

1774 *Fairfax Co.* (Va.) *Res.* in *Ib.* 412. Resolved, That the most important and valuable part of the British Constitution, upon which its very existence depends, is the fundamental principle of the people's being governed by no laws to which they have not given their consent by Representatives freely chosen by themselves.

1776 *Dec. of Ind.* That to secure these rights, Governments are instituted among Men, deriving their just powers from the consent of the governed.

1787 *Federalist* No.23. The fabric of American empire ought to rest on the solid basis of the consent of the people.

1864 Dem. Platform in Stanwood *Hist. of the Presidency* 304...a perpetuation of a government deriving its just powers from the consent of the governed.

1874 in *Appleton's Ann. Cyc.* 479/1. Resolved, That, in our opinion, the true cause of the trouble in Louisiana is to be found in the fact that the people have no confidence in the present usurping Government, which does not command their obedience, and which fails to give protection, because it is not founded upon "the consent of the governed."

The expression was given renewed vigor in the debates on the imperialistic tendencies of the U.S. following the Spanish-American War.

1900 Roosevelt *Ltrs.* II.1401. The doctrine of "the consent of the governed," the doctrine previously enunciated by Jefferson in the Declaration of Independence, was not held by him or by any other sane man to apply to the Indian tribes in the Louisiana territory which he thus acquired.

1900 *Rev. of Rev.* XXI.219. A writer in *Education* for January asks several pertinent questions relative to the application of the phrase "consent of the governed" in American history. It is now charged by the "anti-imperialists" that the present administration at Washington is subverting our form of government in so far as it attempts to administer the Philippines without first obtaining the consent of the inhabitants.

1900 *Ib.* XXII.177/1. The wave of enthusiasm, amounting almost to frenzy, which swept through the convention hall when the platform-makers harked back to that good old phrase, "consent of the governed"....

1900 *Ib.* XXII.288 [cartoon showing donkey kicking Negro]. A Kick Without Consent of the Kicked. The Filipino: "That's worse than government without consent of the governed."

conservative.

The idea that the conservation of valued institutions and achievements of the past is a necessary complement to progressive reform found its expression in the creation of the Senat Conservateur by the French constitution of 1795 (see Brunot, IX, ii, 796) . In America this phrase was regularly rendered by *the conservative Senate:*

1803 *Mass. Spy* 27 July 1/4. Conservative Senate. Sitting of the 24th floreal.

1813 in Shipp *Crawford* 110. Visited the garden of the Luxembourg, which is an appendage to the palace of the Conservative Senate.

The same idea—conserving measures necessary to counterbalance but not necessarily to combat reform—is expressed in the famous article by J. W. Croker in the *Quarterly Review* of January, 1830, in which he launched *conservative* on its international career by suggesting that the Tories ought to adopt this name:

276 ... to what is called the Tory, and which might with more propriety be called the Conservative, party; a party which we believe to compose by far the largest, wealthiest, and most intelligent and respectable portion of the population of this country, and without whose support any administration that can be formed will be found deficient both in character and stability. Some of this party, we know, object to all change whatever—but these are neither considerable in numbers, in rank, or in influence.

In England this suggestion met with immediate success, conservative clubs springing up all over the country; while on the other hand, liberals branded the word as insincere:

1832 Macaulay *Essays and Biographies* V.618. [*OED*] If M. Dumont had died in 1799, he would have died, to use a new cant word, a decided "conservative."

In America the term was first applied to the Whig party:

1836 Donovan *Barnburners* 10. They [Whigs] speedily drew to themselves most of the friends of the small banks, and others who had suffered from the sudden stoppage of the Western land development. These people came to be called "Conservatives."
1837 *Ohio Statesman* 5 July 2/3. The *Pennsylvania Reporter,* speaking of a probable change in the name of the op-

position, from Whig to "Conservative," says the best cognomen they could adopt would be the "Fast and Loose" party.
1839 in *Cong. Globe* App.103/2 ... that the Government has been defrauded ... and that the Conservative Whig scoundrel, Samuel Swartwout, has done it.
1839 in *Ib.* 17 Jan. App.110/3. Conservatism is but another name for Whiggery, and both, but other names for Federalism. ... Above all isms on the face of the earth, conservatism is the last and tail-end-ism.
1840 *Rough-hewer* 11. In England, the Conservatives and Tories are identical; and so they are in the United States. In our revolutionary war, the Tories were the Conservatives; they were opposed to the levelling doctrines of equal rights and democratic liberty.
1840 Webster to Lord Ashley in Hodder *Earl of Shaftesbury* 27 May 156. Party denominations have changed often with us, and names do very little towards description. The Whigs are, in fact, the Conservative Party.
1844 *Wash. Globe* 22 Aug. 799/4 ... a nondescript class, called conservatives. ... but first a word about this new whig creation—the conservative party.
1852 Stanwood *Hist. of Presidency* 251. The Whigs of the United States, in convention assembled, adhering to the great conservative principles by which they are controlled and governed. ...

This adoption of the term by the Whigs did not remain unchallenged by the Democrats, especially when the slavery struggle gave them the chance of claiming this designation as the champions of anti-radicalism (see below). The first instance of *conservative* as a party name is its application to the bank faction of the Democrats:

1837 *Ohio Statesman* 13 Sept. 1/5. The Washington Correspondent of the Baltimore Merchant says that parties are now classed in the Metropolis: Conservative, LocoFoco, and Opposition.

1837 *Ib.* 20 Sept. 1/1. Many of the "Conservatives," (the "third party," who are said to have "more affinity" to the whigs than to the democracy) ....

1837 *Madisonian* 26 Sept. 3/6 ... the "Conservative Squad" as they are elegantly termed will be faithful ... by fighting against the errors of Radicalism and Locofocoism ... and United States Bankism.

1837 Jackson *Corr.* 13 Oct. V.515. The Conservatives are every moment dodging off into a committee room where, it is said, Rives and Talmadge have a little *Conservatory* and ply them with all sorts of good words and winning ways, to induce them to lay the [Divorce] Bill over to the next session.

1837 *Ib.* 26 Dec. V.522 ... the political tornado that has lately spread over the State of New York ... will open the eyes of the people to the apostacy of the conservatives....

1838 Hone *Diary* 12 July I.338. Honor and praise to the noble Whigs and Conservatives; they have saved the country!

During the breakup and realignment of parties during the 1840's and '50's *conservative* came to designate those who in both the Whig and Democratic parties held a middle ground between abolitionists and fire eaters (q.v.). Attempts to unite these elements into a "conservative union-exalting national party" are discussed in Nevins' *Emergence of Lincoln,* II.59.

1847 *N. Y. W. Trib.* 20 Oct. 1/3. An overwhelming defeat [of N.Y. Democrats] is necessary to purify the party from conservatism.... Just in proportion as defeat casts off Conservatism, will the radical and democratic portion of the Whig party ... be found among us.

1847 *Ib.* 27 Oct. 1/3. The successful attempts of the Conservatives and other allies in the Syracuse Convention to prevent an expression of the views entertained by an immense majority of the party in this

State, concerning one of the great political questions of the day....

1852 Sumner *Works* 9 Aug. III.249. Recognizing in the social and political system those essential elements of stability and progress, he [R. Rantoul] discerned at once the offices of Conservative and Reformer. But he saw also that a blind conservatism was not less destructive than a blind reform.... he seemed often to blend two characters in one, and to be at the same time a Reforming Conservative and a Conservative Reformer.

1853 in *Cong. Globe* 3 Jan. 190/2. Conservative myself, I represent a people who are strictly conservative—conservative in the highest sense in requiring a strict adherence to the Constitution and laws, and an unwavering regard for the rights of all nations. Conservative in the protection of property, and the preservation of individual rights.

1856 in Foner *Business and Slavery* 2 Aug. 125. Fremont is the conservative candidate in this campaign.

1858 *At. Mon.* II. 756/2. They [Democrats] are painting out the old name, letter by letter, and putting "Conservative" in its stead.

A new shade of meaning developed during the Civil War when the anti-administration forces in the North tried to offset charges of disloyalty by claiming to be just conservatives:

1862 *Ann. of Cleve.* No.3600. A strong opposition party is organizing all over the country. It takes various names. Its leaders are Democrats, "peace" Democrats, and "Conservatives."

1862 *Harper's Pict. Hist.* 502/2. The success of the Democratic—or, as it now styles itself, the Conservative party—has been so great....

1862 *Harper's W.* 22 March 179/1. Two kinds of conservatism. Number one conserves rattlesnakes; number two conserves the human race.

1863 Dennett *Hay* 94. The Conservatives in Missouri and the Copperheads in Illinois.

1863 *Harper's W.* 31 Jan. 67 ... all disturbance of public order and outrage of law, all pandering to the basest prejudice and denial of generous principle, is made by the most unscrupulous politicians and the most disreputable men [in Penn.] who call themselves "Conservative"....
1865 *Nation* 20 July 73/1 ... an ultra radical tendency in one direction was sought to be balanced by high claims to conservatism in another. Men began to call themselves "democratic conservative," or "conservative democrats"—phrases which would have been incomprehensible to Jefferson; and so, on the other hand, adherence to the fundamental ideas of the founders of the republic—a course which, in any other part of the world would have been regarded as the soundest conservatism—was stigmatized as radical, until it became difficult to tell where we were, since words supposed to be the most fixed in political language seemed to have lost all meaning.

During the Reconstruction period *conservative* was used in opposition to *radical* and sometimes as a party name:

1868 *Harper's W.* 14 March 163/2. The same excellent "Conservative" pride sees with pleasure that "the Mobile Tribune is publishing a list of the White scalawags and renegades who voted for the bogus Constitution...." If such judicious "conservative" measures, assisted by the efforts of Northern Conservatism ... do not secure conciliatory reconstruction the failure must be charged to the rascally radicals.
1867 *Appleton's Annual Cyc.* 550. On the 27th of September there was a mass meeting of Conservatives at Raleigh.
Ib. 28 On September 4th a Conservative State convention assembled at Montgomery. It convened under a call previously issued, of which the following is an extract; "The chairman ... suggests the holding of a State Conservative convention at the capitol, in the city of Montgomery, on Wednesday, the fourth day of September." [See also pp. 366, 537, 700.]

1870 *N. Y. Times* 24 Aug. 4/4. The so-called "Conservative" Party, which has recently been so cautiously organized in the South, will prove but a temporary affair.
1874 *House Report* No. 265.32. What party do you mean when you say "conservative"? ... I suppose it may be called the democratic party, but I do not think it is entitled in this country to that name, because all of us old-line Whigs are now acting with that party.
1874 *Ann. of Cleve.* No.3230. Amid the shouting and beating of big drums this week it would be interesting if some one would explain what this "Conservative" party of the South is. Why "Conservative"? What does it "Conserve," and how does it propose to do it? To the ordinary observer "Conservative" as applied to Southern politics means simply the Copperhead Democratic party of that section....

consolidation.

In the 16th century the term is used in reference to church politics, but the connection with later political uses is doubtful since the first prominent English application to public affairs clearly originates in business language:

1785 Burke *Works* IV.210. Collected in a second debt from the nabob of Arcot, amounting to two millions four hundred thousand pounds ... This is known by the name of the Consolidation of 1777.

In America the term was used in connection with the problems that led to a call for a Constitutional Convention of 1787, but although it expressed a vital necessity, it was from its very beginnings an unpleasant word to the advocates of state sovereignty.

1787 in West *Source Book* 30 June 540. Mr. Bedford (Delaware) contended, that there was no middle way between a perfect consolidation, and a mere confederacy of the States. The first is out of the question; and in the latter they must continue, if not perfectly, yet *equally*, sovereign.

In spite of such opposition the favorable connotations of the word were strong enough to make its use possible in places like Washington's letter of transmittal:

1787 in *The Federalist* 17 Sept. 586. In all our deliberations on this subject we kept steadily in our view, that which appears to us the greatest interest of every true American, the consolidation of our Union. . . .

Before the end of the century *consolidation* was on its way to rapid deterioration due to the sharpened contrast between federal and states rights. In 1781 an essay by Madison in the *National Gazette* "described the natural tendency of government to follow a self-directed course when 'the public mind' had no voice or was apathetic. This general tendency of consolidation could be countered only by an alert and united body of citizens whose devotion to local or state governments permitted them to express effectively the 'sense of the people.' 'Let it be the patriotic study of all,' Madison entreated, 'to maintain the various authorities established by our complicated system, each in its respective constitutional sphere; and to erect over the whole, one paramount Empire of reason, benevolence, and brotherly affection.' " (Koch, *Jefferson and Madison,* p. 120)

Jefferson's Kentucky Resolutions say:

1798 in *Basic Jefferson* 329 . . . it does also believe, that to take from the States all the powers of self-government and transfer them to a general and consolidated government without regard to the special delegations and reservations solemnly agreed to in that compact, is not for the peace, happiness or prosperity of these States.

In 1800 Jefferson uses much stronger words:

Works VII.451. I do verily believe that . . . a single consolidated government would become the most corrupt government on the earth.

[See *Jefferson Cyc.* for other quotations]

By 1811 *consolidation* had developed into a veritable scareword:

Graydon *Memoirs of a Life* 324 [Harrisburg, Penn.] The bugbear of consolidation stalked hideously among us, to the dismay of many federalists, no less than of the anti-federalists.

In 1824 Madison makes this interesting remark:

Works III.442. And that the language of our Constitution is already undergoing interpretations unknown to its founders will, I believe, appear to all unbiased inquirers into the history of its origin and adoption. Not to look farther for an example, take the word "consolidate" in the Address of the convention prefixed to the Constitution. It there and then meant to give strength and solidity to the union of the States. In its current and controversial application, it means a destruction of the States by transferring their powers into the government of the Union.

Our next witness is Webster:

1830 *Works* III.256. Consolidation!—that perpetual cry both of terror and delusion —Consolidation!

contraction (-ist).

The reduction of the volume of currency in circulation; one who supports that policy.

Arising first in the specie controversy of the Jackson era, the term was revived after the Civil War during the Greenback controversy:

1838 *Sp. of D. Bernard* 209. We are informed that all our alarms about expansions and contractions are quite useless, because the precious metals have been found to be more fluctuating than any thing else ever used as money.

1874 B. Butler in *Cong. Record* 4 April 2811/1 ... our contractionists—I do not use the term invidiously, because they will be very much ashamed of this title one of these days. ...

1875 *Cinc. Enquirer* 2 Aug. 4/3. [Thurman] says that the Democratic party of Ohio "plainly denounces contraction, but fail to expressly advocate inflation."

1892 Stewart in *Cong. Record* 30 June 5658/1. It was the duty of Senators to return here when a bill of this kind was pending; but they can defeat the will of the people, and serve the gold-standard contractionists. ...

convention.

A. In England *convention* as distinguished from *parliament* means an assembly not regularly elected but composed of members who appear on their own initiative or as delegates of local organizations. (Source material in Jameson, *Am. Antiq. Soc. Proc.*, 1899, 183–96.) A similar distinction is made in early American usage where occasionally the more democratic character of the convention is stressed.

1719 Jameson *Am. Antiq. Soc. Proc.* 184. That we cannot Act as an Assembly, but as a Convention, delegated by the People ... [in S. Car.].

1722 *Am. Hist. Leaflets* No. IV.5 [Coxe's Plan]. It is further humbly propos'd, That two Deputies shall be annually

Elected by the Council and Assembly of each Province, who are to be in the Nature of a Great Council, or General Convention of the Estates of the Colonies. ...

In connection with the French Revolution the word was on its way to lose its respectability as well in England (see *State Trials,* XXV, 67, 382, 385, 458) as in America.

1794? Cobbett *Works of Peter Pindar* I.63 ... mobs and conventions are devils. ... If a constitutional legislature cannot redress grievances, a mob never can.

1794 *State Trials* XXV.67. The difference between "meeting" and "convention" will be very difficult to discover.

1794 *Ib.* 458. The Latin word *convention* was omitted, and the Saxon word *meeting,* which is now our English word, was suffered to stand.

c.1794 Erskine in *Ib.* XXV.382. If I attended properly to the Duke of Richmond's examination, his grace proved that there was a meeting there—whether a convention, or what it was signifies nothing—there was a meeting of gentlemen of great distinction. ...

c.1794 Tooke in *Ib.* XXV.385. Were we not a convention—instead of meeting for the purpose of bringing about a convention? What was that meeting but a convention of delegates from different towns and counties throughout England?

1795 Sheridan *Sp.* IV.16,17. As to the phrases convention, &c, in which they had affected an imitation and approbation of the proceedings of the French, the worst that could be said of them was that they were contemptibly foolish.

1801 Jefferson letter to Monroe 15 Feb. The very word *convention* gives them the horrors, as in the present democratical spirit of America, they fear they should lose some of the favorite morsels of the Constitution.

1804–8 Jameson *Encyc. Dictionary.* Conventialists: In Penn. politics, Extreme Democrats.

B. When the custom of designating the presidential nominees by the party caucus came into disrepute, it was replaced by national party conventions, the earliest official presidential convention being the Anti-Mason Convention in Baltimore in 1831. It was, however, preceded by a meeting in New York City in September, 1812, which Stanwood (*Hist. of the Presidency*, 101) calls, "a highly interesting meeting, as being the first convention of the same sort as those which now present presidential candidates."

From 1831 on the term with its present meaning is well known.

1831 McClure *Half Cent.* 3 [first nat. conv. held by Anti-Masons].
1838 *New Yorker* 13 Jan. 681/1 ... the friends of the first two at least of these gentlemen are eagerly pointing to a National Convention as the appropriate and ultimate tribunal to decide between their favorites and select the candidate of their party. Indeed, there has been a serious dispute between the two sections respectively, each claiming to have been the earlier to propose a National Convention, and to be now the more loyal in its resolution to abide the decision of such a body.... We believe these Conventions have all the evil tendencies which have been ascribed to them, and are never, or very rarely, necessary.
1847 in *Mangum Papers* V.46. I am in principle opposed to Conventions and will not if I can help it give any countenance to them. They are a modern invention of Yankee conception, designed to stifle and suppress the popular voice—dangerous in my judgment to republican institutions— and almost always the instrument of foul play!
1850 *Harper's Mon.* I.563. An active canvass has been going on in Virginia for the election of members of a convention to revise the state constitution.
1868 *Ib.* XXXVII.567. "The Convention ... was denunciatory of the 'Radicals,'

who, elected in an evil hour, have placed the iron heel of the Conqueror upon the South."
These eloquent words were spoken at the July 4th dedicatory meeting of Democrats on the occasion of the new Tammany Hall in denunciation of the Republicans.
1935 Chidsey *Gentleman from N. Y.* 118. He could scheme like a cigar-chewing convention rigger.
1940 Stokes *Chip* 317. Standing by the hour, shifting from one foot to another, in front of rooms where conferences are held, in tiled hotel lobbies, brings on that disease known as "convention feet."

Coody.

In 1811 Gulian Verplanck wrote a satirical treatise, "Letter to the Hon. Saml. L. Mitchell ... by Abimalech Coody, Esq., Ladies' Shoemaker." (See Robert W. July, *The Essential New Yorker*, biblio.) When in 1814 he organized a faction of the Federalists in opposition to DeWitt Clinton, this new American Federalist party was called "the coodies" by the rival faction. Clinton himself may have suggested the name, and in January, 1815, he published a tract, "An Account of Abimaleck Coody and Other Celebrated Writers of New York," in which he wrote:

[in July *Ess. N. Yorker* 48] ... he has become the head of a political sect called the Coodies, of a hybrid nature, composed of the combined spawn of federalism and jacobinism, and generated in the venomous passions of disappointment and revenge, without any definite character....
1829 in Mackenzie *Van Buren* 218 .. the coodies, highminded, and Clintonians.

Also coodyitism

1815 *Columbian Centinel* 12 April 2/3. Our votes have fallen off; but there have been no converts to Coodyitism.

coonmandering. [ ]
1842 *Ohio Statesman* 7 Dec. 3/5. Coonmandering. The Trenton Emporium thus speaks of the Gerrymandering of the coons in New Jersey.

copperhead.

During the Civil War a Northerner who sympathized with the South.

As a general term of abuse *copperhead* can be found long before the Civil War. Some of the following quotations suggest that it was predominantly applied to extremists in the Democratic party:

1831 *Detroit Jrnl. and Mich. Adv.* 11 May 2/6. From the "Free Press."—"They (the Detroit newspapers) go by the name of the *rattlesnake papers*—but a friend suggests to us that they ought to be called *copperheads*." Very pointed, pungent, and withal polite, this.—What may we not expect from such rare beginnings?
1837 *Ohio Statesman* 29 Aug. 3/4. The few bank-ridden slaves at Reynoldsburg, writhe like a scorched copperhead, at their overwhelming defeat on Monday week.
1840 *Harrison Dem.* 22 Sept. 3/2. The Hickory Club is now mainly conducted by a sheepish looking locofoco of the copperhead tribe, whose name is Bartlett . . . he writhes in apparent distress . . . and this distress has risen to agony since his fangless bites have been received with contemptuous indifference.
1844 *Ann. of Cleve.* No. 1837 . . . we hope that Sammy's friends will make an early application for him, lest, like the copperhead, which he resembles, he turns his venom upon himself.
1844 *People's Paper* 20 Sept. 2/1. Like a copperhead in August . . . he strikes venomously around at all, but only wounds himself.

Only by inference can it be shown that the comparison between the sneaky copperhead and the rattle-snake which at least warns before striking must be quite old. In 1832 Ludwig Börne [*Briefe aus Paris, Werke,* Reclam ed., III.366] wrote: "Preussen klappert und warnt; Osterreich zischt nicht eher, bis es gebissen." This must go back, perhaps, through many intermediate links to an American pattern. It is of importance since the same comparison is the starting point of the use of *copperhead* during the Civil War. The new phase in the history of the word has been erroneously attributed to its use in the Detroit *Free Press* of May 5, 1861, but see 1831 quotation above.

For more than a year copperhead is only in sporadic use:

1861 *N. Y. Trib.* 9 July 6/3. The copperhead secessionists, as Frank Blair aptly termed our Maryland Traitors, have been scotched, but they are not dead.
1861 *Ib.* 20 July 7/3. The "Copperheads" [Southern sympathizers in Baltimore] are very irritable, and are growling savagely at the late success of Major-General McClellan.
1861 *Cinc. Comm.* 17 Aug. 1/1. Call them Copper Heads [head] . . . The Southern Confederacy, at the outset, symbolized itself in the eminently classic and tastefully chosen figure of the rattle snake. It would therefore be eminently proper that their "natural allies" should select their heraldry from the reptile kingdom, and since the rattlesnake's mate, or, (as it is sometimes called,) the copper head, is in all the essentials a fitting representative of common affinities . . . we therefore respectfully suggest that the term, "Copper Heads" be applied to the aforesaid party. . . .

But during the election campaign of 1862, when the attitude of each candidate to the "peace movement," was thoroughly discussed *copperhead* became an extremely frequent word. This phase is ably presented in Albert Matthews' "Origin of Butternut and Copperhead," *Mass. Col. Soc. Pub.* XX. 205–37. [Compare *American Historical Review*, XXXII, 799ff., and Estrich and Sperber, *Three Keys to Language*.]

Occasionally the word is used with strong indications that it is a local word, not necessarily known to the reader.

1862 Hayes *Diary* II.248, I send you enclosed a list of Captain Foley's men, the "Flat Top Copperheads."

1862 *Mahoning Reg.* 7 Aug. 1/7. Copper Heads—In Maine they call rebel sympathizers "copper heads."

1862 *Lawrence* (Kansas) *Republican* 11 Sept. 4/1. That faction of the Democracy who sympathize with the rebels are known in Ohio as "Vallandighamers," in Illinois as "guerillas," in Missouri as "butternuts," in Kansas as "jayhawkers," in Kentucky as "bushwhackers," and in Indiana as "copperheads."

The following quotations are only a very small selection from sources of 1862 and 1863:

1862 *The Haversack* 25 Oct. 3/3.
"Do you know that the same cent puts me in mind of a democrat?"
"How so."
"Because it's a copperhead."

1863 *N. Y. Trib.* 24 Jan. 4/2 . . . holding themselves ready to fight treason North as well as South, should Copperhead Golden Circle madness render such a step necessary.

1863 Kelso *Stars and Bars* 227 . . . the disloyal men of the North are cool, calculating knaves, snakes in the grass, and very appropriately called "copperheads."

Democratic attempts to counteract the effect of the new catchword are shown in the following quotations:

1863 Vallandigham speech 14 Feb. There are others here from the Northwest, all "Butternuts," "Copperheads" like myself. (Cheers)

1863 *Vallandigham Songbook* 5
They call us "traitors," "copperheads,"
  We care not what they do;
But they'd best not tread on copperheads,
  Or they will surely rue;
If they rouse us, "they'll wake up snakes";
  Believe it, for it's true.

Another counteraction, which has long confused the origin of *copperhead* was a badge issued by the Democrats. This was a copper penny with the head of the Goddess of Liberty inscribed upon it. Matthews has shown convincingly that these could not have been the origin of the term since they do not appear before the word had gotten into general use.

By a widening of meaning, very common in political words of abuse [see *Three Keys to Language*], *copperhead* finally became an opprobrious synonym of *Democrat*.

1870 in Gail Hamilton *Blaine* 198. [Mr. Blaine] . . . If the Committee of Election shall report that he is ineligible on that account, why of course then this copperhead competitor by this construction comes immediately in.
Eldridge.—I rise to a question of order. I insist that the term copperhead is not parliamentary.
Blaine.—I recall the word. I never used it before in a debate here. I will say his Democratic competitor.
The Speaker overruled the point of order on the ground that he was not speaking of any gentleman in the House, but Mr. Blaine refused to be thus upheld: "I did not withdraw the word as a question of order. I should have told the gentleman that he had made no point of order. As a question of taste I confess that I have transgressed, and as a question of taste I

change the word. It was in bad taste, as it always is, to use offensive political epithets in debate.

1900 *Cleve. Leader* 6 June 1/1. Sen. Hanna and Sen. Carter . . . administered to Pettigrew the worst drubbing that copperhead ever received. **1938** in Burns *Roosevelt* 360. Never before have we had so many Copperheads. **1943** Gordon *Wrecking the 18th Amend.* 131. Copperhead Fire in the Rear.

During the first World War Theodore Roosevelt compared the peace-at-any-price men with the Civil War copperheads [See *Roosevelt Cyc.*].

cormorant.

A politician greedy for the spoils of office.

The metaphorical transfer from the large voracious sea-bird to the politician hungering for the "loaves and fishes" is an obvious one.

1817 Fearon *Sk.* 145. Take notice who are the friends of William Findlay—1. Traitors and apostates. 2. Inveterate aristocrats. 3. Office-holders and office-hunters. 4. Cormorants for the loaves and fishes. 5. Fugitives from British gaols and justice. **1840** *Straight-out Harrisonian* 1 May 1/1. The cormorants of the national administration are awake, and not only awake but active. **1866** *Trial of Johnson* I.327. This gang of office-holders—these bloodsuckers and cormorants—had got fat on the country. **1880** *Harper's W.* 450/3. The Democratic platform says, in pot-house slang, that the party pledges itself to protect the laboring-man "against the cormorants and the communes."

corn dodger.

A Whig. [ ]

The word appears among other nicknames on a cartoon in the *Coon-Catcher,* a Democratic campaign paper, Columbus, 1844, No. 1. From the quotation below it appears that corn dodgers (cakes made of wheat or corn) were among the accessories of the log cabin.

1850 Olds of Ohio in *Cong. Globe* 24 July App. 946. Who was it, sir, that in 1828 could condemn the erection of hickory poles, yet in 1840 could build log cabins, drink hard cider, and nibble corn dodgers?

cornerstone.

Based on various passages in the Bible (for instance: Job 38:6 Whereupon are the foundations thereof fastened? or who laid the cornerstone thereof [cf. Ephesians, 2:20]) , *cornerstone* means metaphorically a fact or issue of paramount political importance. The most significant use of this metaphor is its application to slavery from 1835 to the Civil War period:

1835 in Wilson *Slave Power* I.324. In his message to the legislature of South Carolina, in December, 1835, Governor McDuffie elaborately defended slavery as "the cornerstone of the republican edifice"; declared the laboring population, "bleached or unbleached, a dangerous element in the body politic". . . . **1852** *Scott Battery* 20 July 4/3. The Fugitive Slave Law is the Corner-Stone of the Democratic Party! **1861** in Greeley *Conflict* 21 March I.416 [speech of Alexander Stephens at Savannah]. Our new government is founded upon exactly the opposite idea; its foundations are laid, its corner-stone rests upon the great truth, that the negro is not equal to the white man. **1863** Kelso *Stars and Bars* 238 . . . just come back into the Union and help us beat the Republicans and we'll make slavery the chief corner-stone of the government.

Ib. 31. As to Missouri, we contemplate nothing short of an empire,—an empire, of which slavery is to be the chief corner-stone.

Applied to other issues:

1847 Field *Life* 115. In 1847 he was a delegate to the Syracuse Convention, where the Democratic party was split in two over the question of the extension of slavery, and on that occasion he introduced the famous resolution, long afterward known as "The Corner-Stone"....

1852 *Scott Battery* 26 Oct. 2/4. Toleration is claimed by all politicians, and especially Democratic politicians, as the corner-stone of republics.

Blaine *Twenty Yrs.* 186. The principle of protecting the manufacturers and encouraging the navigation of America had been distinctly proclaimed in the first law enacted by the new government, and was thus made in a suggestive and emphatic sense the very corner-stone of the republican edifice which the patriots of the Revolution were aiming to construct.

corporal's guard.

A small group of supporters.

Since the corporal is the lowest ranking non-commissioned officer, the guard which he commands is a small one and not to be considered as a formidable line of defense. The sarcasm behind the political term is thus easily understood.

1836 *Ann. of Cleve.* No.808. State after State has gone against him [Van Buren], until, we fear, there will scarcely be left a corporal's guard to do him honor.

1848 in *Cong. Globe* 26 July App. 963/3. If it were known, believed, or suspected at the South that he would sanction that measure [Wilmot Proviso], he would not carry a corporal's guard in the approaching election.

1856 *Greenville* (Ohio) *Jrnl.* 16 July 2/2. The "wheel-horses" and fuglemen were busy thro'out all of Saturday in drumming up a corporal's guard of those who are still willing to lend themselves to its purposes, and contribute their share to the fastening of Slavery upon the National Territories.

1934 Carter *New Dealers* 86. If the New Deal succeeds he [Tugwell] will go down in history, along with Roosevelt and a corporal's guard of the other guiding minds of the Administration, as a man who saved capitalism.

The defection of President Tyler from Whig principles after the death of Harrison led to his being almost completely shunned by his party. The small group that remained with him were the objects of much abuse by the regular Whigs.

1844 *Niles' Reg.* LXVI.135/3. When John Tyler came into office he possessed the confidence of the whole party. He suddenly abandoned his principles; and did that party follow him? No, sir; with all the patronage of the government in his hands, he could not carry off a "corporal's guard."

1886 Poore *Rem.* I.280. The "Corporal's Guard" who sustained Mr. Tyler were all on hand and prominently seated to hear him abuse the Whigs.

cossack. [ ]

A general opprobrious term in the 19th century.

1830 *Niles' Reg.* 20 Feb. 429/2. "Cossacks." This is a new name *politely* given to the friends of domestic manufactures, in the New York Evening Post.

1844 *People's Press* 10 Oct. 2/1. Individuals whose vices have placed them beyond the pale of respectable society ... set themselves up as the censors of the good and great of the land! These Cossacks are found in the ranks of both parties.

1852 *Scott Battery* 27 July 4/3. Let the Russian Czar erect his rule upon the ruins of the Republic, and the servile

Hunkers would name Cossackdom a foundation on which to "go on and build."
1854 Parker *Additional Sp.* 374. No Russian despot has his sons as slaves to wait on him at table. You must come to America to find a Cossack President who could boast that honor!

Later it clearly refers to policemen.
1929 *N.Y. Herald-Trib.* 12 May 3/2. "Down with Walker's Cossacks."
1943 in Cross *Conn. Yankee* 355. "Did you receive my telegram last night demanding that you remove them Cossacks you sent down to Groton?"

cottonocracy.

A. Boston textile manufacturers.
1848 Bartlett *Americanisms* 94. Cottonocracy. A term applied to the Boston manufacturers, especially by the "Boston Whig" newspaper.
1848 in "Warrington" *Pen Portraits* 39. He [Robinson] turned this lance against his opponents "The Post" (organ of Milk Street) and the "lying Atlas" (organ of State Street). He bearded these lions in their dens, and defied the cottonocracy, and with untiring industry advocated the principles upon which his party was founded.

B. The South.
1861 in *Northern Editorials* II.834. Hence treason has been plotting rebellion, in the high courts of the "cottonocracy" for the last thirty or forty years.
1865 *U. S. Service Mag.* III.148. Nothing more was said on the subject of international exchanges by the representative of the Cottonocracy.

cotton ticket.

A ticket made up of pro-Southern Whigs. (See COTTON WHIG)
1850 *N. Y. Trib.* 24 Oct. 4/4. We are to have a Cotton Meeting and a Cotton Ticket in our City.
1850 *Ib.* 25 Oct. 4/3. No: this Cotton demonstration and the Cotton ticket which it is to indorse are both among the most potent elements of future agitation, heartburning and discord.

cotton Whig.

See Hoar quot.
1846 in G. F. Hoar *Autobio.* I.134. The Whig Party was already divided into two sections, one known as "Cotton Whigs" and the other as "Conscience Whigs." These names had been suggested in a debate in the State Senate in which Mr. Thomas G. Carey ... had deprecated some proposed anti-slavery resolutions by saying that they were likely to make an unfavorable impression in the South, and to be an injury to business interests; to which Mr. E. R. Hoar of Middlesex answered that "he thought it quite desirable that the Legislature should represent the conscience as well as the cotton of the Commonwealth."

The event alluded to is mentioned in the *Liberator* of 1846, where, however, the word *conscience* is not mentioned:
24 April 66. Mr. Hoar of Middlesex ... pointedly told Mr. Carey that it was as much our duty to pass resolutions in favor of the rights of Man as the interests of Cotton.

According to Wilson (*Slave Power,* II.117) Hoar's statement ran:
"It is as much the duty of Massachusetts to pass resolutions in favor of the rights of man as in the interests of cotton."

If Hoar's memory is correct then both *cotton whig* and *conscience whig* go back to the same incident; if, however, the contemporary accounts are accurate and complete records of the debate, then *conscience whig* must have arisen later in contrast to *cotton whig.* (See COTTON TICKET.)
1850 *N. Y. Trib.* 4 Nov. 4/3. Their object manifestly was to beat Washington Hunt by Cotton Whig votes in the city.

1851 *Ann. of Cleve.* No.1927. The New York election is over, and the "cotton Whigs" have defeated the regular Whig ticket.
1852 *Scott Battery* 27 July 1/2. It [the *Tribune*] makes its own Platforms and is denounced as heretical by Cotton Whiggery.

See CONSCIENCE WHIG.

counting house politician.

1806 Randolph in *Gt. Deb.* II.121. Britain is your rival in trade, and, governed as you are by counting-house politicians, you would sacrifice the paramount interests of your country to wound that rival.

courtesy of the Senate.

The custom in the Senate of considering the wishes of the senator or senators regarding appointments or legislative matters pertaining to his or their particular state. The phrase is found with a general meaning referring only to the etiquette of members on the floor of the Senate:

1852 in *Mangum Papers* V.725. I indicated, yesterday, a purpose to ask, by the courtesy of the Senate, that I might be permitted to speak on a matter which, I am aware, is not strictly in order this morning.
1867 *Cong. Globe* 17 Jan. 525/3. But it is not within the courtesy of the Senate to assault a person not present on the floor who cannot defend himself.

Only two days later, however, *courtesy* may be found in the same source with its specialized meaning:

1867 *Cong. Globe* 19 Jan. 586/1 ... it has always been customary to postpone any measure that affects a particular State if the Senator or Senators from that State are absent and it is known that he or they desire to be heard upon that subject.... I submit, therefore, whether, looking to the

courtesy which we observe toward each other, it is not better to let the matter stand until he shall be here.

The complete formula as it is now known appears a few years later:

1870 *Harper's W.* 210/4 ... Senator Fowler of Tennessee claimed the right which the courtesy of the Senate accords to every Senator of vetoing the appointment of any postmaster in the place of his residence who is not agreeable to him.
1878 Curtis *Works* II.122. The courtesy of the senate—a practice of modern introduction....
1879 *Harper's W.* 163/2. The Courtesy of the Senate. One of the significant and interesting facts in the recent action of the Senate upon the New York appointments was the rebuke of an abuse known as the courtesy of the Senate. This is a modern practice....
1880 *N. Y. World* 29 Dec. 2/3. The nominations that go to the committees of which Mr. Conkling is a member will, by what is known as the "courtesy of the Senate," be submitted to him.

Frequent references contained implied criticism of the practice:

1878 *Harper's W.* 7 Sept. 706/2. The effect of the Tenure-of-office Law and of "the courtesy of the Senate" has been to vest in the Senators almost absolute power over the livelihood of subordinate officers in their States, and the ambition of young men interested in politics.
1880 *Ib.* 6 March 146/3. "The courtesy of the Senate" is an exceedingly smooth phrase. It means control of patronage.

See SENATORIAL COURTESY.

courthouse gang.

Although generally associated with the Truman administration, there is evidence suggesting that the expression is much older. *Courthouse ring* is found in reference to 19th century county political groups.

c.1888 W. A. White *Autobio.* 149, 155. Those were the days when the ins of any local politics were called the Courthouse ring from one end of the United States to the other.

155. Perhaps he bought it because it had been abusing him and the Republican Courthouse Ring for a year or so.

1946 B. Smith in *Am. Mag.* May 110. Outside of Washington, the men he [Truman] knew and trusted were the OFFM's —the Old Friends From Missouri.... And this has led to talk of "government by crony," or of "that county-courthouse crowd around the President."

1955 Truman *Memoirs.* I.141. Fortunately for my prospects, however, I had become acquainted with all the county judges and county clerks in the state of Missouri and was familiar with the operations of the so-called "courthouse gangs" in all the country counties.

cowboy.

A. A Tory partisan in Westchester County, N.Y., during the Revolution.

1779 in *Geo. Clinton Papers* IV.502. Your whig Militia below have as great an Itch for plundering, as the Cow Boys.

1780 in Thacher *Mil. Jrnl.* 285. These shameless marauders have received the names of cow-boys and skinners.

1844 Goodrich *Am. Hist.* 309 ["Arnold's Treason"]. The eastern shore of the Hudson, between the British and American lines, was during the war infested by gangs of marauders who plundered the whole debatable territory. Those above called themselves "Skinners," and those below were denominated "Cow Boys."

1844 *Wash. D. Globe* 1 Aug. 727/4. A contrast.—The British Tories have imprisoned O'Connell but only for twelve months, and not at labor, or among felons. The American Whigs have imprisoned Gov. Dorr at hard labor, among thieves and burglars, and for life.... The bastard whigs of this country surpass the British tories in malignity as much as the cowboys of the revolution did the British regulars.

1868 Richardson *Grant* 81. Andre, trying to get back into the British lines at New York, fell into the hands of the "Cow Boys." This partisan organization existing on the neutral ground between the lines of the two armies, claimed to be British in sympathy, but was chiefly inspired by love of plunder.

B. According to Farmer, revived in New England during the Civil War.

1889 Farmer *Americanisms* 176. Now applied exclusively to Western herdsmen, but originally to the Tory partisans of Westchester County, New York, during the Revolution; and in 1861 to semi-secessionists in New England. In the latter sense *cowboyism* was used as indicative of the spirit and practices of these partisans whose treatment of opponents was barbarous and ruffianly.

1861 in *Northern Editorials* II.741. There is no neutral ground between high-handed treason, and the law, where the mere partisan may play the cow-boy of the revolution between his government and her enemies.

C. In the 1880's a faction in the Republican party. The quotations suggest that it was dominantly Western and similar to the migratory range cowboy in its moving from one candidate or group to another.

1880 *Cinc. d. Gazette* 28 May 4/4 [edit.]. There is in the Republican party a considerable number of "cowboys" who are ready to go from one camp to the other and trade with either party.

1880 *Ib.* 29 May 4/2 [edit.]. The driftwood of the party, which is ready to be drawn by any current, and which is liable to be carried off by a boom, and which poohs at such nice notions as the principle of limiting the use of patronage by Presidents to renominate themselves, is more like the "cowboys" of the revolution.

1884 *Boston Mng. Jrnl.* 10 June 2/1. It was the New York Evening Post which attrib-

uted the nomination of Mr. Blaine to the rude grangers of the west, and the New York Times which alluded to one of the controlling elements in the convention as "cowboys."
1884 *Nation* 3 July 2/1 . . . the Cowboy vote, because the Cowboys like magnetism.

cowdung club.

A Jacobin group in Massachusetts burlesquing the Black Cockade of Federalism. ¿
1798 *Columbian Centinel* in Warren *Jacobin and Junto* July 84. A certain Jacobin Quack Doctor, not five miles off, actually assumed an appropriate cockade on the 4th;—it was a piece of dried cow dung, four inches diameter. . . . This gang is to meet again the 10th August and 3d September, anniversaries famous for insurrection and assassination. They are to wear cockades of cowdung. A flag is to be displayed with the words "We are but dross and dung,"—and, in order to denote the humbleness of souls that will befit the expected and desired downfall of our "aristocratic government," the members are to assume the name of "The Cowdung Club."

crawfish.

To back out of a position or decision. The crawfish or crayfish moves backward when attacked.
1844 *Whig Battering Ram* 9 Aug. 4/1. Look out for such a specimen of crawfishing as the Locofocos alone can practice.
1850 *N. Y. Trib.* 16 Oct. 4/4 . . . Mr. Webster in his great crawfishing Speech.
1860 *Lebanon Western Star* 9 Feb. 2/1. The South Crawfishing [ed.].
1875 in *Cong. Record* 12 Jan. 397/1. No man is more anxious to escape peril than I am myself, but I cannot turn back in order to avoid it. I am not constructed upon the crawfish plan.
1879 *Puck* 21 May 163/2. He [Hayes] crawfished out of the African business, can't he scuttle back out of the one term statement?

1888 *The Voice* 5 July. The remark defeated him for Governor. He tried to crawfish out of it . . . but it didn't work.

creed.

See CHURCH.

creeping socialism.

An epithet labelling certain government activities which are held to be thinly disguised socialistic measures and thus but the beginning of full scale socialism.
1945 Hoover *Add. upon the Am. Road* 257. Today Communism and Creeping Socialism are sweeping over Europe. 260. While their [British Socialists'] program is a creeping socialism, their platform has been stated time and again.
1952 Stevenson *Major Camp. Sp.* 113. Now, of course, I suppose all of this government is what they call socialism—creeping or crawling. . . . But if I don't like what they call creeping socialism, there is something else I dislike just as much, and that is galloping reaction.
1953 *N. Y. Times* 18 June 1/2. President Eisenhower cited today [17 June press conference] the Tennessee Valley Authority . . . as an example of what he meant by "creeping socialism." . . . The President made his statements in reply to questions on his reference to "creeping socialism" in an off-the-cuff talk in South Dakota last Thursday night.
1953 *Ib.* 21 June iv.10/5. Big T.V.A. Area Can See No "Creeping Socialism." [head]
1953 *Ib.* 23 June 28/6 [letter to the editor]. It [the *Times* editorial] criticizes the President for his recent description of T.V.A. as "creeping socialism." It then goes on to prove his point, except that the editorial makes it leaping socialism. . . . The President was right. It is socialism, and it has been creeping, and creeping fast.

crossroads.

Speaking of the old Southern country stores, Thomas D. Clark says: "Like their post-bellum successors, they were found at the crossroads, at central points in the more populous and the older communities and along the rivers" (*Pills, Petticoats, and Plows* 29). The following quotations show that the political significance of the crossroad was by no means restricted to the South. Notice, too, the coupling of *crossroad* and *stump* in two of the early quotations:

c1803 Quincy *Josiah Quincy* 327. My father once asked him [Matthew Lyon] how he managed this matter. "By establishing myself at a crossroads by which everybody in the district passed from time to time, and abusing the sitting member."
1828 *Cong. Deb.* 6 Feb. 1416. Are you not converting this Hall into a mere "Court House yard"—"a crossroad"—"a stump" —from which to address electioneering harangues to your constituents?
1844 *Niles' Reg.* 8 June 236/3. This must forever dispel the charge, so loudly urged at the stump and the cross-roads, and at the cart-tail. . . .
1858 *Ohio Statesman* 16 Oct. 2/1. In the close, effective work at the school-houses and cross-roads, we had greatly the advantage.
1860 Stephens in Moore *Rebellion Record* I.225 . . . for the people in this country, whether at the crossroads or the groceries . . . are all equal, and they are the sovereigns in this country.
1869 Pollard *Secret Hist.* 164. Every candidate who was anxious to serve his country with braid on his shoulders, plied the men with the lowest arts of the crossroads politician.

The phrase *dirty work at the crossroads,* not mentioned in the dictionaries, is evidently based upon these conditions.

crusade.

The prevailing attitude that the Crusades were the products of heroic and self-sacrificing activities is apt to be challenged by writers of the Enlightenment who regarded them as the results of fanatical and intolerant folly.

17— Hume *Hist. of Engl.* V. (*OED*) The crusades . . . the most signal and durable monument of human folly that has yet appeared in any age or nation.

A. At first the unfavorable view prevails in American usage, although already in 1786 Jefferson says:

Works V.397. Preach, my dear Sir, a crusade against ignorance; establish and improve the law for educating the common people.

Among the questions which brought *crusade* into prominence are

1. The Bank:

1834 in *Reg. of Deb.* I.544/2. Honorable Senators, whose groans and lamentations for the sufferings of the people are accompanied by declamatory appeals against the bank, because it does not choose to help them in their crusade against that institution . . . must look for aid, in this holy warfare, in another direction.
1837 *New Yorker* 442/3. He [King of Ga.] condemned the crusade against the bank of the United States as the cause of all our woes. . . .

2. Slavery:

1820 Pinckney in *Gt. Deb.* IV.75. How, then, can that Constitution which expressly permits the importation of slaves authorize the national government to set on foot a crusade against slavery?
1860 Keitt in *Cong. Globe* 24 Jan. App. 93/3. We are now resisting, not an individual, but a party, a creed, a crusade.
1862 Christy *Pulpit Politics* 501. In addition to the productions of the political abolitionists, and the debates in Congress, we now turn to such of the leading incidents and opinions of individuals, or pub-

lic assemblies connected with this fanatical crusade. . . .

3. Oregon:

1846 *Ann. of Cleve.* No. 589. And when I say this [condemning Giddings], I know that John Quincy Adams led off in this crusade, avowing himself in favor of first taking possession of Oregon and then negotiating.

4. The liquor question:

1873 ? *Dayton Jrnl.* in Mother Stewart *Memories* 78. The lady to whom we refer is Mrs. Stewart, who is on a Temperance Crusade against liquor-selling.
1874 *Nation* 12 Feb. 99/2. Parts of Ohio, Indiana and West Virginia have become the theatre of an extraordinary but not unprecedented movement, which appears to be at present in the full tide of successful experiment. It is known as the temperance crusade. . . .
1874 *Cleve. Plain Dealer* 10 July 2/3. Mrs. Bolton, of Cleveland, a leader in the woman temperance movement, has written to the Chicago Advance that twenty-five thousand saloons have already been closed by the female crusaders of Ohio.
1875 *Cleve. Herald* 3 June 4/1. Dr. Dunn of Hillsboro sued the people who "crusaded" his place of business.

5. Others:

1816 Randolph in Sargent *Clay* 72. "What!" said he, "increase our standing army in time of peace, on the suggestion that we are to go on a crusade to South America?"
1941 Mencken *Newspaper Days* 37. It was a crusading time [c. 1900]. . . . I recall crusades against sweat-shops, against the shanghaiing of men for the Chesapeake oyster fleet, and against dance-halls that paid their female interns commissions on the drinks sold.
1952 Barkley *That Reminds Me* 245. I reminded the convention that the Republican presidential nominee, in his acceptance speech . . . had said he was going to lead a "great crusade." We Democrats, I asserted, were not beginning, but were

continuing, "a crusade that we began twenty years ago and more." . . . Not only a crusade to make our lives happier, fuller and freer, but likewise a crusade to increase peace and hope and cooperation among the nations of the world. . . .

crust-divider.

One who distributes political patronage.

1841 *Ann. of Cleve.* No. 1450. Mr. Van Buren proved a liberal "crust divider" as far as office spoils were concerned, for he not only distributed the rich loaves, but flung all the "small potatoes" he could get hold of among the greedy partisans following the camp.
See PIE.

Cuff Links Club (gang).

An unofficial group of friends and supporters of Franklin D. Roosevelt.
1934 Carter *New Dealers* 203 . . . the "White House Gang," the "Cuff-Links Club," the small group of men and women through whom the President functions, is in many ways the essence of the whole New Deal.
1936 *Time* 10 Feb. 11/1 . . . Louis Howe is the foremost member of the Cuff-Links Gang. This organization is composed of friends who helped Franklin Roosevelt run for Vice President in 1920 and to whom he gave sets of cuff links in remembrance of that unfortunate campaign.

cuttle fish.

To obscure an issue, so-called from the cuttle fish's power of emitting a black fluid to conceal itself from its enemies.
1853 *N. Y. Trib.* 14 Feb. 4/3 . . . he can talk of Social Phalanxes, Spiritual mediums, anti-Hanging, &c, &c, in such a manner as to "cuttle-fish" the whole business.
1853 *Ib.* 25 March 4/2. The game is to complicate and cuttle fish the whole mat-

ter [of city reform legislation] so that the Legislature may be induced to leave it unacted on, as too difficult a job to be perfected at the heel of the Session.
1868 *Harper's W.* 3 Oct. 626/1. The nakedness of the issue would undoubtedly have been avoided by some of the astuter men of the Democratic party. They favored a cuttle-fish policy. They desired to darken counsel.

czar.

Like other eastern titles (*sultan, mogul, pasha, bashaw*) *czar* is applied to public men of dictatorial tendencies. According to Lynch, (*An Epoch and a Man,* p. 358) Nicholas Biddle, director of the United States Bank, was known as "Czar Nicholas" in 1832.

The word also occurs in the long list of abusive synonyms that Petroleum V. Nasby uses against Andrew Johnson:
1866 *Swinging Round the Cirkle* 208. There wuz a immense crowd, but the Czar uv all the Amerikas didn't get orf his speech here.

The prominence of the word begins with the famous quorum decision of Speaker Thomas B. Reed (1890) :
W. A. Robinson *Thomas B. Reed* 231. The title of "Czar" which was conferred upon him in the early stages of the quorum contest, had no pleasant connotations in the early nineties. It conveyed no picture of benevolent despots who in our own days administer the affairs of the garment industry, the moving pictures, or professional baseball with firmness and righteousness. In 1890, it brought to the mind the Russian autocrat himself, together with George Kennan's description of the Cossacks, Siberia, and the knout.

Marion Mills Miller (in *Gt. Deb.* IX, 343) states that *czar* was applied to Reed on this occasion in preference to any of its synonyms from the necessity of finding a short word for a headline:
Julius Chambers, of the New York Times, wrote a graphic description of the arbitrary action of Speaker Reed. The copy editor of the paper used the word "autocrat" in the headline, and the composing office complained that it was too long. The matter being brought to Mr. Chamber's attention, he substituted the word "czar." This was at once adopted by the press of the country, and as "Czar" Reed the speaker was permanently enrolled in at least the parliamentary, if not also political, history of the country.

There are, however, indications that the statement in *Great Debates* is in need of confirmation. According to LaFollette (*Autobiography,* p. 97) *czar* was used on the floor of the House as soon as Reed had made his decision: "An angry roar went up; there were cries of 'Czar,' 'tyrant.' . . ."

Champ Clark (*Quarter Century,* I.278) , says that "Senator John Tyler Morgan, of Alabama, dubbed him [Reed] the 'great White Czar.' "

The influence of headline style is almost an unexplored chapter in the history of modern language. Whoever wants to investigate this interesting topic will find an authentic example in Al. G. Field, *Watch Yourself Go By.* The author's original name was Hatfield, which together with his first and middle names, Alexander Griffith, was too long for the handbills of his travelling show. It was therefore shortened to Al. G. Field.

D

Danite.

Partisan of James Buchanan.

A. A secret organization of the Mormons, taking its name from Genesis XLIX. 17: "Dan shall be a serpent by the way, an adder in the path that biteth the horseheels so that his rider shall fall backward" (see J. H. Beadle, *Life in Utah,* 1870, p. 46).

1838 *Rushville* (Ill.) *Test* 12 Dec. 3/4. There, Patton, one of the bloodiest of the Danites, directed two of his bands.

B. In a Springfield speech of June 12, 1857, Stephen A. Douglas stated:

That the Mormon government, with Brigham Young at its head, is now forming alliances with the Indian tribes of Utah and the adjoining territories—stimulating the Indians to acts of hostility—and organizing bands of his own followers, under the name of "Danites or Destroying Angels," to prosecute a system of robbery and murder upon American citizens, who support the authority of the United States, and denounce the infamous and disgusting practices and institutions of the Mormon government. [ ] ...

The fact that after the split between Buchanan and Douglas the former's partisans were nicknamed Danites must be connected with this speech in one way or another. There is the possibility that the first name of Dr. Daniel Brainard, a deserter from the Douglas to the Buchanan camp furnishes the connecting link.

1860 James W. Sheahan *Life of Stephen A. Douglas* 425. The next joint meeting was to be at Freeport, on Friday, the 27th, and during the interval a meeting of the Danite and Republican leaders was held at Chicago to prepare some trap for Douglas.

Ib. 432. The Hon. A. H. Stephens of Georgia was in Chicago during the summer, and an attempt was made by the Danites to use his name in approval of their proceedings.

dare to be free.

A slogan of the American Revolution.

Perhaps based upon Pope's "Who dared to love their country, and be poor" ("On his Grotto at Twickenham"), or going back still further, on Horace's *sapere aude!* (*Epistles,* I.240).

1766 in Davidson *Propaganda* 189.
With Loyalty, Liberty let us entwine,
Let us set an example, what all men should be,
And a toast give the world, *Here's to those* [who] *dare to be free.*

1768 in *Ib.* 190.
Come jolly Sons of Liberty—
Come All with Hearts United
Our Motto is "We Dare Be Free,"
Not easily affrighted!

dark horse.

A politician who with little or no advance notice suddenly is selected as a candidate.

A. The often repeated statement that James K. Polk was the first presidential dark horse must not be taken to mean that this term was applied to him by his contemporaries. It is quite probable that in his time *dark horse* (a horse about whose racing powers little is known) was a racing term that had not invaded the political vocabulary:

1831 Disraeli *Young Duke* ch. v. [*OED*] A dark horse, which had never been thought of ... rushed past the grandstand in sweeping triumph.

1831 *New Sporting Magazine* May I.23/1. Col. Wilson's colt, out of Black Daphne ... is whispered to be a miracle of stoutness and speed; but dark horses often lead their backers into the dark.

1834 *N. Y. Sporting Mag.* 170/2. With some qualification, our remarks will apply to other stables, or why were so many dark horses in the betting?

B. Our first political example dates from 1860 but seems to indicate that the term was already known in politics before this period:

1860 Fish in Nevins *Hamilton Fish* 79. We want a log-splitter, not a hair-splitter; a flat-boatman, not a flat-statesman; log-cabin, coonskin, hard cider, old Abe, and dark horse—hurrah!

C. We find the term in general use in and after 1876:

1876 *Lebanon Western Star* 1. June. Blaine is looming.... It begins to look as though he would be the "dark horse" at Cincinnati.

1876 *N. Y. Times* 11 June 1/1. It was conceded that with the two leading Western States casting eighty votes for Hayes, that his chances will be better than any other aspirant, and that he had ceased to be the *dark horse.*

1876 *Cleveland Leader* 23 June 4/5. Hon. Hugh J. Jewett of Ohio ... is looming up mildly as the "dark horse" who may win at St. Louis.

1877 *N. Y. Trib.* 19 Nov. 4/5. The "dark horse" [in Ohio], therefore, becomes of interest, and at present this mysterious factor bears a striking resemblance to William Allen.

1878 *Col. (Ohio) Democrat* 27 May 1/3. The Dark Hoss.... Another dark horse is being carefully groomed in the person of Judge M. F. Force.

1880 *N. Y. Trib.* 11 Feb. 4/5. A Western political prophet is sure that the dark horse who is bound to win the Republican prize at Chicago is named William

Windom. The prediction seems to be based on the principle that the darker the horse the better his chances.

1932 *Rev. of Rev.* LXXXV. 14/2. There continued to be much speculation about the potential dark horse candidates.

1948 *Time* 14 June 15/2. If the deadlock holds, the dark horses begin to pick up hope.... To prevent a dark-horse victory, the leaders dicker among themselves.

D. In 1880 *Harper's Weekly* (17 July 451/2) had a vignette dealing with a suggested origin of the phrase:

Once upon a time there lived in Tennessee an old chap named Sam Flynn, who traded in horses.... The best of his flyers was a coal-black stallion, named Dusky Pete.... Flynn was accustomed to saddle Pete when approaching a town, and ride him into it to give the impression that the animal was merely "a likely hoss" and not a flyer.... Just as the "flyers" were being saddled for a race, old Judge McMinamee, who was the turf oracle of that part of the State, arrived on the course, and was made one of the judges. As he took his place in the stand he was told how the betting ran, and of the folly of the owner of the strange entry in backing "plug" so heavily. Running his eye over the track, the judge instantly recognized Pete, and he said, "Gentlemen, there is a dark horse in this race that will make some of you smell h— before supper." The judge was right. Pete, the "dark horse," ... won the purse and Flynn's bets with the greatest ease.

We can not know whether the Judge intended a play on words similar to that in the *New Sporting Magazine* of 1831 (see above), or whether he was using a metaphor known to all at that time.

Dark Lantern.

A. A nickname of the Know Nothings, alluding to the secrecy that surrounded their order.

1855 *Hickory Flail* 19 Sept. 1/1. "Sam's Serenade."

Come all ye old foes of the Nation
Attend to the Know Nothing call;
Come haste on your country's damnation,
And roll on the dark-lantern ball.

1856 Washburn in Hamilton. *James G. Blaine* 114. Will the straight Whigs of Maine, who have opposed the dark lanterns so furiously, fall into the Fillmore ranks?

1865 Doesticks [Mortimer Thomson] *Plur-i-bus-tah* 238f.

(Liberty in Search of Yunga-Merrakah)
Then she went to the apartment
Of that strange and secret Order,
Of that mystic band of brothers,
Whose proceedings are so secret,
So profound and so mysterious;
And the brothers are so faithful,
That in spite of guard and watchman,
Spite of oaths and secret pass-words,
Fashioned to exclude Reporters,
Their proceedings, so mysterious,
And so mystical, are always
Published in next morning's Tribune.
  Here went Liberty to seek him,
To this room so dark and silent,
To the room of the Dark Lanterns.

In 1884 Blaine is called the "great Dark Lantern apostle" (*N. Y. World,* 1 Aug., 4/2). Since he was never affiliated with the Know Nothings, this probably refers to his alleged "jingoism."

The following quotation refers to the *Sag Nichts* order:

1855 *Ravenna Campaign Democrat* 20 Aug. 3/1. Gloom seemed to pervade this "dark lantern, midnight conspiracy."... Several "dark lantern" gentry drew their "pocket pistols" [flasks] and "discharged their contents."

Dark lantern conference, in the general sense of secret conference, is used as late as 1901.

1901 *St. Louis Star* in Cooper *Handwriting on the Wall* 71. It was for this reason that, as a result of a dark lantern confer-ence at the Southern Hotel, orders were issued to the police to keep the deputy sheriffs away from the polls.

dead beat (adj. and n.).

Completely beaten; a politician who has no chance of winning office or regaining his former power.

A. In watchmaking, a form of escapement that has no recoil. (See *OED*)

B. In metaphorical usage, anyone completely "beat."

1821 P. Egan *Tom and Jerry* 34. (*OED*). So dead-beat, as to be compelled to cry for quarter.

C. In American politics:

1856 *Statesman* in *Darke Co.* (Ohio) *Dem.* 25 June 2/2. It [Black Rep.'s] is a dead beat ticket, and never can raise to the dignity of a National Presidential canvass.

1872 in Ross *Lib. Rep. Movement* 77n. ...a gang of execrable dead-beats... called Labor Reformers.

1872 *Cinc. Enquirer* 3 Sept. 2. Such fossils as these only are mentioned because such political dead-beats only, it is well known, would accept.

dead duck.

One whose political effectiveness is gone.

A. The expression, based upon an old axiom, is found in political uses as early as 1829:

1829 *N. Y. Courier* 15 June 2/1. There is an old saying "never waste powder on a dead duck"; but we cannot avoid flashing away a few grains upon an old friend, Henry Clay.

1844 Jackson *Corr.* 7 May VI.283. Clay [is] a dead political duck.

B. Found occasionally later, the term was of particular interest in 1866 when President Johnson called John Forney a "dead duck."

1866 Johnson in *N. Y. Trib.* 24 Feb. 4/5. Some gentleman in the crowd says, "Give it to Forney." I have only just to say that I do not waste my ammunition upon dead ducks.
1866 *N. Y. Times* 26 Feb. 4/3. President Johnson's contemptuous allusion to Col. J. W. Forney as a "dead duck," has solved a problem which has sorely puzzled that conspicuous political acrobat for some months past.
1866 *Wash. Morning Chron.* 26 Feb. 2/5. To call a political opponent a "dead duck" may do very well for a bar-room, but is hardly graceful in the President.
1866 *Augusta Constitutionalist* 3 March 2/1. The President, not to be outdone by his doughty warrior, has subjected poor Forney to the excruciating rack of an epithetical epitaph. Hence forward he must be known as a "dead duck" ... Bottle Imp Butler and Dead Duck Forney—arcades ambo!
1866 *Boston Eve. Transcript* 3 Sept. 1/3. I don't think the fellydelfy talers are rite on the goose. They had better stick by the "ded duck" ef they want to fether their nest.
1868 *Harper's W.* 176. [Cartoon "A brace of Dead Ducks"—Forney and Andrew Johnson.]
1872 *Ann. of Cleve.* No.2442. All this because Palmer, who, in his lame attempt to persecute Sheridan for doing his duty at the Chicago fire, made a political dead duck of himself, and has chosen to ... follow the lead of the soreheads.
1954 Mockridge and Prall *The Big Fix* 235. Now, however, he decided that O'Dwyer was a dead duck politically, and that he never would be able to win another election.

dead issue.

A. Before the Civil War a means of brushing aside the slavery question. (See FINALITY)
1854 *Cleve. Plain Dealer* 5 July 4/5. We heard of many, who have never been Democrats, who disgusted with the restless attempts at agitating dead issues for the benefit of politicians, who have axes

to grind, are not slow in expressing their disapprobation of the [Fusion] movement.
1860 *Wash. Intelligencer* 1 Sept. 3/1. Discerning minds in both sections directed their energies to the task of securing for the fact such an acknowledgment as would have for its effect to rule this "dead issue" [slavery in the territories] out of the domain of our current politics.
1863 W. Phillips in Sandburg *The War Years* II.172. Matters of vexed dispute, of earnest doubt, the moment the bugle gave a certain sound, have passed into dead issues.

B. Later referring to other matters:
1872 in Adams *Emery A. Storrs* 104. The Alabama claims we propose to settle by arbitration. We shall thus settle them. Before the election has arrived they will be a "dead issue."
1899 *N. Y. Trib.* 21 Jan. 1/4. The 16-to-1 question is a dead issue.

Dead Rabbits.

See quot:
Werner. *Tammany Hall.* 63n. The Dead Rabbits got their name when a gang known as the Roach Guards, called after a prominent liquor dealer of the period, split into two factions. At one of their argumentative meetings some one threw a dead rabbit into the room, and one faction decided to assume that token.
1857 *Harper's Mag.* Aug. 402/1. A gang of thieves and desperadoes, known as the "Dead Rabbits," made an attack upon a few policemen on duty.
1876 *Cincinnati Daily Gazette* 24 June 2/1. If Mike Walsh could rise from the dead, he would be the man for the dead rabbits and short-boys.

debating club (society).

Humorous reference to Congress.
1842 *Bro. Jonathan* I.71/1. The House is engaged in "debating club," alias Committee of the Whole. ...
1860 *N. Y. Trib.* 2 Jan. 4/3 ... the remarks of both gentlemen in the Congressional

debating-club had been fairly reported. . . .
1863 in Pollard *Secret Hist.* 309. [Congress at Richmond] . . . the common bit of sarcasm in Richmond of "the college debating society" on Capitol Hill.

decapitation.

Removal from office for political reasons.

A later version of *guillotine* (q.v.).

1849 in Hamilton *Blaine* 95. You will find that about June and July and along there the heads will begin to come off pretty rapidly. I am looking for and hoping for a General Decapitation.
1858 Douglas in Sparks *Deb.* 337. You know that the axe of decapitation is suspended over every man in office in Illinois, and the terror of proscription is threatened every Democrat by the present Administration, unless he supports the Republican ticket in preference to my Democratic associates and myself.
1858 *Ann. of Cleve.* No.3008. The decapitated federal officer (ex-postmaster Gray) had the vanity to believe that the people would rebuke "Old Buck" (Buchanan) by endorsing him as a martyr to "Douglas and Popular Sovereignty."
1905 Phillips *Plum Tree* 144. He made a bitter fight against decapitation, and, as he was popular with the people of his district, we had some difficulty in defeating him.
1921 Depew *Memories* 120. Many of them were State Senators whose decapitation was assured if the old machine supported by federal patronage was revived.

decency party.

The Whig party, which often decried the roughness and vulgarity of the opposition.

1840 *Ohio Statesman* 1 May 2/2. I was surprised at the self-styled "decency party" for encouraging their new missionary in proclaiming at the top of his voice, such immodest language in the street.

defensive campaign.

Counterpart of *aggressive campaign*.

1888 *Nation* 5 July 1/1. No "defensive campaign" for Col. Ingersoll. . . . The "defensive campaign" upon which the Republicans have embarked.

demagogue.

A. Leader of the people originally in a neutral or even laudatory sense, the derogatory meaning is well developed in ancient Greece, but English authors of the 17th and 18th centuries occasionally used the word without bad connotations. (See *OED*) In American usage the opprobrious sense prevails from the very beginning:

1806 Fessenden *Democracy Unveil'd* 26n [also 84]. These wretches are generally demagogues, and the characters of most of them stained with vices.
1808 J. Adams *Works* VI.532. It is to no purpose to declaim against "demagogues." There are as many and as dangerous aristocratical demagogues as there are democratical. . . . and Milo was as much an agitator for the patricians as Clodius for the plebians; and Hamilton was as much a demagogue as Burr.
1837 in *Cong. Globe* App. 67/2. The cant phrases of "Goths," "Vandals," "Cormorants," "Destructives," "Loco-focos," "third-rate men in power," "slaves to Executive dictation," can be pronounced without either intellect or patriotism. A parrot could be taught to repeat them as well as a demagogue.
1852 *Scott Battery* 20 July 2/3. Now a more shameful, palpable, shallow and dishonest trick of demagogueism and hypocrisy was never before attempted to be palmed off on any party or any people.
1878 *Harper's W.* 5 Oct. 786/4. We shall probably know in detail the reason why the best men of both parties oppose him [Butler] as a dangerous demagogue, and

why his name has become the synonym of disreputable politics.

1911 Roosevelt in Lodge *Ltrs.* II.415. When there is a great unrest, partly reasoning and partly utterly unreasoning and unreasonable, it becomes extremely difficult to beat a loud-mouthed demagogue, especially if he is a demagogue of great wealth.

1931 Steffens *Autobiography* 474. I had begun to suspect that, whenever a man in public life was called a demagogue, there was something good in him, something dangerous to the system. And that since the plutogogues could not fasten any crime on him they fell back on the all-sufficient charge that he was a demagogue.

1954 Luthin *American Demagogues* ix. This book is concerned with the public careers of selected American demagogues of the present century—those "masters of the masses" who, in their aspirations for political place and power, pandered to the passions and prejudices, rather than the reason, of the populace, and performed all manner of crowd-captivating tricks, only to betray the people.

B. As a verb, to speak, usually with the sole object of impressing one's constituents:

1935 Helm *Truman* 73. Among his cronies, to demagogue meant simply to make a speech on the Senate floor. The word carried no sting, imputed nothing.

1938 Salter *American Politician* 157. "I [Maury Maverick] may demagogue," he observed, using the word as a verb after a fashion coming into vogue in Washington, "but never on a matter of importance."

democracy.

In the terminology of Greek political science, mainly a derogatory term meaning something like mobrule. A secondary current in the history of the word is its application to direct rule by the people as opposed to a representative government. When entering the vocabulary of modern languages, the word retains its unpleasant connotations (see, for instance, the discussion of various forms of government in Barton, *Argenis*, I.18). Leading colonists brought over these connotations to America:

1636 John Cotton in West *Source Book* 204. Democracy, I do not conceyve that ever God did ordeyne as a fitt government eyther for church or commonwealth. If the people be governors, who shall be governed?

Winthrop evidently considers democracy as highly undesirable:

1643 in *Ib.* 229 ... the true form of our government, and the unavoidable change into a democracy if the negative voice were taken away.

However, the change to a more favorable concept of democracy shows itself during the days of the English Commonwealth. Evidently *democracy* is a dignified word.

1659 Milton *The Ready and Easy Way to Establish a Free Commonwealth* [Everyman's Library, *Areopagitica*] 169. Neither are these diligent creatures hence concluded to live in lawless anarchy, or that commended; but are set the examples to imprudent and ungoverned men, of a frugal and self-governing democracy or commonwealth.

With the growing influence of the people, similar tendencies did not fail to develop in colonial speech. The following quotation seems to indicate that to the author democracy, the influence of the common people in political matters, is a legitimate supplement to aristocratic powers within the government.

1741 *Am. Mag.* Feb. 39/2. [Discussing the position of the governor of Md.] If it be asked where is the Democracy, or supreme Power of the people as the Ancients called it, we answer that it is also in the Governor; for he has the enacting Voice, and dernier Result on the Bills prepared for his Assent by the Delegates of the People.

A general tendency to smooth over rather than stress controversial points is probably responsible for the fact that Madison directs his criticism, not against democracy in general, but against pure democracy:

1787 *Federalist* 23 Nov. No.10 ... it may be concluded that a pure democracy, by which I mean a society consisting of a small number of citizens, who assemble and administer the government in person, can admit of no cure for the mischiefs of faction. A common passion or interest will, in almost every case, be felt by a majority of the whole; a communication and concert result from the form of government itself; and there is nothing to check the inducements to sacrifice the weaker party or an obnoxious individual. Hence it is that such democracies have ever been spectacles of turbulence and contention; have ever been found incompatible with personal security or the rights of property, and have in general been as short in their lives as they have been violent in their deaths.

During the following years, the history of *democracy* was determined by the back and forth exchange of influences between America and Europe. When during the political excitement in the Netherlands in the late 1780's, *democratic (al)* was for the first time used as a party label, the influence of American ideas was held to be the contributing cause.

1786 *Ann. Reg.* 48/2. The creed of America and the example of Ireland gave birth to the democracy of Holland.

A little later it seems that this use of the word was well established in England, at least as far as affairs in the Netherlands were concerned.

1787 *Ib.* 18–19. Notwithstanding this defeat, which took place about the close of the past, or the commencement of the present, year, the incessant efforts of the democratic party to overturn ... the established constitution and government, had since kept that city in a constant state of tumult and disorder.

The real turning point in the evaluation of democracy is, however, the French Revolution, which brought a new political terminology within which *democratie, democratique,* and the newly formed *democrat* have a prominent place (Brunot). With the victory of the new ideas, all these words became terms of honor and as such they were brought back to the United States and taken up as the watchwords of the Jeffersonian party to such an extent that the official designation, the Republican party, was almost superseded by the Democratic-Republican or simply Democratic party. It was probably Genet who acted as intermediary between France and America. According to Minnegarode, he suggested the name of Democratic Society to a pro-French club in Philadelphia, and further popularized the word by calling one of his privateering vessels La Petite Democrat. Evidence of the strength of this influence is provided by the fact that 13 of the 24 pro-French societies of these days have the word *democrat (ic)* in their names. (Luetscher, *Early Pol. Machinery,* 33n). However, up to and through the presidency of Jefferson, the official name of the party remained the Republican party. It was rather the exception to the rule if members of this party spoke of themselves as Democrats. William A. Robinson (*Jeff. Dem. in New Engl.* 62) quotes a letter dated Hartford, June 4, 1801, signed by 24 "Deserving Democrats" of Connecticut. On the other hand, *democrat* as an abusive word of the Federalists was in frequent use:

1800 J. Adams *Works* IX.87. Washington appointed a multitude of democrats and jacobins of the deepest die. I have been more cautious in this respect.

1806 Fessenden *Democracy Unveiled* 2, 7, 50.

And I'll unmask the Democrat,

Your sometimes this thing, sometimes that,

Whose life is one dishonest shuffle,

Lest he perchance the mob should ruffle;

. . . .

A mortal foe to fools and rogues,

Your Democrats and demagogues,

Who've sworn they will not leave us a brick,

Of freedom's blood cemented fabric.

. . . .

Some of their tenets we will trace,

Which one would think could ne'er have place

This side the Democratic club,

Whose President is Beelzebub.

In 1808 the Federalists of Connecticut formed a coalition with the "moderate democrats" (Robinson, 81). On the whole, Hammond (*Political History of New York*, I.585) sums up the situation correctly:

From the time of the adoption of the federal constitution, in 1787, till about the time of the election of Gen. Jackson,

in 1828, the party opposed to the federalists, was known as the Republican party. For a long time the word democrat or democratic, was used as a term of reproach. The republicans were by the federalists called democrats, as synonymous with the word Jacobin. And indeed it was intended to convey the idea that the republican party in principle and practice was nearly allied to the Jacobinic Clubs in France. On the other hand, the republicans, with a view to cast odium on their opponents, called the federalists aristocrats.

It is easily understood that the waning influence of the Federalists was a factor in the restoration of *democrat* to respectability. But the question why the word became so successful in its competition with *republican* remains open. Perhaps the answer ought to be solved along these lines: *republican* was not a term of absolute contra-distinction since Jefferson himself had said in his first inaugural address: "We are all Federalists; we are all Republicans" and had also written to Henry Knox:

1801 *Works* VIII.36. I was always satisfied that the great body of those called federalists were real republicans as well as federalists.

On the other hand, since the Federalists were being accused of being aristocrats, *democrat* offered itself as the natural counterpart of this term. Robinson, 133, quotes a Federalist preacher, Dr. Morse of Connecticut:

[The clergy of Connecticut were those who] numerous, able, harmonious, and very respectable as a body, have hitherto preserved a kind of aristocratical balance in the very democratical government of the state. This has happily operated as a check upon the overbearing spirit of democracy.

Robinson's comment, although undocumented, is probably correct: " 'Aristocracy' was a word which would stir the wrath of every Republican; to have the clergy openly so called by one of their own number was a challenge which was readily accepted." The decline of Federalism seems to have affected the development of the term *democrat* in more than one way. The party struggle having ended in their defeat, political allegiance became during the following years a matter of personalities rather than parties.
1829 *Niles' Reg.* 7 Nov. 165. It shews 32 "Jackson" in the senate and 15 "republican," ... (We wish some more certain definition of parties—and much dislike the calling of them after persons.)

When the Jacksonian campaigns brought a new alignment and a stricter party organization, the word *democrat,* having fallen into partial disuse, was available as a name that to every enemy of aristocracy must have had considerable attractions:
1838 *Cinc. Gazette* 4 Oct. 2/1. In the presidential struggles which had followed the second election of Mr. Munroe [sic], the name of "Democrat" or the "Democratic party" had fallen into disuse, the old Federal party having died out some years before, and the struggle between Crawford, Adams, Jackson, and Clay, having taken place between so many different portions of the Democratic party. The name then of Democrats happened to be lying in abeyance, and the friends of the administration caught it up, as a most lucky and convenient disguise, and such indeed have they found it.
1850 Kennedy *Wirt* II.224. The Jackson party was also compelled to seek new designations. In due course of time it became the Van Buren party; and as that was of a nature even more fleeting than the last, it was accounted a rare piece of good fortune when it stumbled upon the name of "The Democracy," which lay derelict by the way-side. [Kennedy's attribution of the word to the period of Van Buren is obviously incorrect.]

The Jackson men, however, did not have a monopoly on the word.
1828 *Weekly Democratic Press* (Phila.) 19 April 1/1. We have such entire confidence in the superiority of character, and well known principles of those put in nomination by the Democratic convention that we are desirous they should be compared with those who have been nominated by the Jackson Convention.

However, the new word did not have immediate and universal success, since to some people it still carried unpleasant connotations.
in Weed *Autobio.* 135. The name "Democrat" was not popular, and was in especial bad odor in the Slave States. As late as 1854, when Father Ritchie resumed temporary charge of the "Richmond Enquirer," he persisted in using "Republican" as the party designation, and the Regency sympathized with this early feeling. The name "Democrat," now in use by one of the great parties North and South, was originally a term of reproach, like that of Jacobin, and subsequently like that of Locofoco, and has been freely accepted at the South only since the Rebellion.

Even those who were not adverse to *democratic* found it useful to combine this word with *republican;* in fact, the official name of the Jackson party is Democratic Republican, and as late as October, 1837, the *Democratic Review* introduces itself to the public as a champion of "the principles of democratic republicanism." That the presence of *republican* in the name of both contending parties must have led to confusions and inconsistencies we would have guessed even had the clever satire of Seba Smith not made this perfectly clear. The feeling that both contending parties were only sections of one and the same led him to propose a new organization:

1830 *My Thirty Yrs. Out of the Senate* 98. And whereas, the Jacksonites and Adamsites, and Huntonites, and Smithites, have so multiplied in the land, and brought things to such a pass, . . . Resolved, That it is the highest and most sacred duty of every patriotic Democratic National Republican in the State to arouse himself and buckle on his political armor. . . .

The satire becomes still more pungent in the Downing letter of May 3, 1831, when he says of General Jackson that "he is not a Jacksonite, you know; he's as true a Republican as there is in Downingville." But at the same time, he speaks of Henry Clay as the "republican" candidate, of Calhoun as the "Republican" candidate for President, and winds up by saying that "in case General Jackson should be sick or anything, we must remember that Mr. Van Buren is the Republican candidate." An end to this confusion was achieved by the practical abandonment of *republican* by both parties. The Jackson wing seems to have done this by gradually dropping *republican* and *democratic republican* in favor of *democrat*. The Downing letter of August 12, 1833, for instance,

uses *democrat* and derivatives seven times, while *republican (ism)* occurs only five times.

On the opposite side, the name *National Republican* was officially abandoned by the adoption of *Whig* (q.v.) in 1834. Parallel to these developments goes a tendency of establishing *democracy* as a word of praise, not for any particular party, but for a universal ideal. In 1835 Alexis de Tocqueville published *Démocratie en Amérique*. Although by no means uncritical of the democratic system, Tocqueville makes it quite clear that democracy is inseparable from the American way of life and responsible for many of its best features:

I. 321. Democracy does not give the people the most skilful government, but it produces what the ablest governments are frequently unable to create; namely, an all-pervading and restless activity, a superabundant force, and an energy which is inseparable from it, and which may, however unfavorable circumstances may be, produce wonders. These are the true advantages of democracy.

II.240 Democracy, which destroys or obscures almost all the old conventional rules of society, and which prevents men from readily assenting to new ones, entirely effaces most of the feelings to which these conventional rules have given rise; but it only modifies some others, and frequently imparts to them a degree of energy and sweetness unknown before. Perhaps it is not impossible to condense into a single proposition the whole purport of this chapter, and of several others that preceded it. Democracy loosens social ties, but tightens natural ones; it brings kindred more closely together, whilst it throws citizens more apart.

This idealization of democracy in the abstract did not fail to carry advantages to the political party called "democrat." Particularly, European immigrants driven into exile for their advocacy of democratic ideas felt inclined to give their support to a party that seemed to express its adherence to these ideas in its name. The unwillingness of the Whigs to concede this terminological advantage to their opponents is probably a strong factor in the replacement of *democrat* by nicknames, one of the most common being *Loco Foco* (q.v. See also SHAM DEMOCRACY, COPPERHEAD), which according to Greeley ought to be the proper designation of a party whose right to the name *democrat,* in his view, had been forfeited by their abandoning of the principles of democracy.

1844 in Sanderson *Republican Landmarks* 167. They [Germans] have not; they are led by the word *democrat.*

1847 *N. Y. W. Trib.* 11 Oct. 3/1 [see also 18 Oct. 3/1]. As to "Democrat," "Democratic," and all that, we would always be courteous, but we cannot consent to trample on the Dictionary.... Right is Right, whether important or unimportant; and to be a Democrat and opposed to Equal Suffrage are plainly incompatible. We, therefore, use the term "Loco-Foco" not from choice but necessity.

1856 *Middletown* (N.Y.) *Banner of Liberty* 9 Jan. 13/4. By the way, the name Democrat has become so honorable that all sorts of isms and new-fangled parties claim the name.

The fact remains that from all these changes of meaning and connotations *democracy* finally emerged as the word that, perhaps, more than any other expresses the American ideal of statecraft. It

seems to be connected with two factors: 1. that *democracy* was defined as government of the people, by the people, and for the people (q.v.) ; 2. that this phrase was lent enormous prestige by Lincoln's Gettysburg Address. It must be stated that at an early period this favorable trend was opposed by criticism of democracy based on philosophical rather than political grounds.

democrat with a small d.

The confusion arising from the two meanings of *democrat,* an adherent to the principles of democracy and a member of the Democratic party, has led to various remedial attempts to arrive at a clear distinction (see *democracy*), the simplest being the spelling device of writing the party name with a capital D. On this basis the phrase "democrat with a small (or big) d" has been in use at least since 1936:

1936 Barry *Theme Song* 103. As he [Wallace] said over the air, this is the *democratic* way to do it, only his emphasis indicated the word should be spelled with a little "d," and the way it works out in everyday life "Democratic" is spelled with a big "D."

1946 Arnall *Shore Dimly Seen* 87, 89. Let me label myself, if I must have a label, as a democrat; with a small "d," please.... So let me close this parenthesis by saying that, for the time being, at least, I had rather be called a democrat, with a little "d," please, than to be called a liberal. It is a better label for a resident of Newnan.

1946 *Ib.* 134 ... though I do not think that I made any contribution to his recovery, which has resulted in his becoming a good Democrat, with a capital "D," and a man of substance in his community.

1946 *New Yorker* 30 Nov. 142/2. The author [Arnall], ducking the word "liberal," describes himself as a "democrat with a small d." Since he is also a Democrat with a big D, his book should be read by anyone interested in the future of the party he represents.

1947 *The Progressive* 25 Aug. 8. Jefferson often said that the conveying of information and ideas was basic to democracy. In that case, Fitzpatrick is a great democrat with a small "d."

1956 *Ib.* 6 April 8/1. The title of his talk was "The Big D and the Little D." He described the little D as an attitude taken by the politicians. The attitude of grass roots relationships within this country and in foreign relations. Dr. Lovenstein emphasized, however, that the little D is not only an attitude but a definite program, with the hopes and dreams of the people.

A similar device, that of introducing the "Democrat" party instead of the "Democratic" party, was made by Republican National Chairman Hall in 1955:

1955 *Ohio State U. Lantern* 7 Oct. 2. Lately Hall has tartly referred to the "Democrat" party rather than using the more common term, the "Democratic" party.... Hall says he dropped the "ic" from Democratic because "I think their (the Democrats') claims that they represent the great mass of the people, and we don't, is just a lot of bunk." ... Actually, a suspicious Republican could draw the conclusion that a democratic Democrat was the author of the definitions to be found there (*Webster's Dict.*)

Derringer policy.

Opposition term for Democratic intimidation in the South; the pistol substituting for the shotgun. See SHOTGUN GOVERNMENT.

1876 *Harper's W.* 2 Sept. 710/4. The "solid South" supports Tilden, or will if the Derringer policy prevails in South Carolina and Louisiana.

despotism.

A. One of the prominent terms of the Declaration of Independence: When a long train of abuses and usurpations, pursuing invariably the same object, evinces a design to reduce them under absolute despotism, it is their right, it is their duty, to throw off such government, and to provide new guards for their future security.

Jefferson, however, had used the term before:

1774 *Works* I.438. If the pulse of his [George III's] people shall beat calmly under this experiment, another and another will be tried, till the measure of despotism be filled up.

B. Other representative quotations:

1789 J. Adams *Works* VI.428. Governments are divided into despotisms, monarchies, and republics. A despotism is a government where the legislative and executive are invested in one man, but the judicial in other men.

1836 *Scioto Gazette* 27 April 1/6. We do not believe that any free people, since the establishment of civil society, ever made such rapid and fearful strides towards Absolute Despotism, as have been made by the people of this country within the last seven years.

1840 in Garrison *Garrison Story* 139. The State that cannot tolerate universal freedom must be despotic; and no valid reason can be given why despotism should not at once be hurled to the dust.

1840 Clay in Norton *Tippecanoe* 196. And one sole will predominates in, and animates the whole of this community. If this be not practical despotism I am incapable of conceiving or defining it.

1876 *Harper's W.* 22 Jan. 62/1. The founder of the Democratic party, as we know it, was Andrew Jackson; and Andrew Jackson was the author of the present despotically partisan civil service system, which has been always and every where enforced by the Democratic party.

1898 Hoar in *Gt. Deb.* III.258. We have heard of limited monarchies, constitutional monarchies, despotisms tempered by assassination; but the logic of the Senator from Connecticut makes a pure, unlimited, untempered despotism without any relief from assassins.

C. In phrases:

1864 Jones *Mirror of Democracy* 123. They saw established at the seat of Government, by the discipline of party, a despotism, the most perfect on earth—the *despotism of opinion!*
1874 Justice Miller in 20 *Wallace* 655. A government which recognized no such rights, which held the lives, the liberty, and the property of its citizens subject at all times to the absolute disposition and unlimited control of even the most democratic depository of power, is after all but a despotism. It is true, it is a despotism of the many, of the majority, if you choose to call it so, but it is none the less a despotism.

destructive, destructionist.

A. The political use of these words seems to have come over from England in the wake of *conservative* (q.v.). The *OED* gives the following early examples:

1832 *Examiner* 786/1. The Radicals (or Destructives as you are pleased to describe them).
1834 *Oxford Univ. Mag.* L.108. The two distinct lines of conservative and destructive policy.

B. The contrast: *destructive-conservative* persists even after the latter word had been adopted in America.

1837 *Ann. of Cleve.* No. 1740. Conservatives look out, the destructives are upon ye.
1839 Mayo *Sketches* ix...a general scramble between conservatives and destructives, federalists and republicans, whigs and loco focos.

Not always, however, is *destructive* used as an antonym of *conservative*. It can be applied to any "subversive" faction or tendency or even be employed as a general term of abuse: In 1836 Maryland Whigs applied it to the Van Buren men:

Washington Sun 24 Sept. 2/5. The Maryland Destructives.
...The mad and reckless course on which these Destructives have entered has already received the most emphatic condemnation from the free presses of the country.

In 1842 *destructive* was applied to the Dorrites in Rhode Island (*Wash. Nat. Intell.* 16 May 2/4) and in 1866 the *N. Y. Times,* 25 Aug. 4/2 has an editorial, "Plans and Purposes of the Destructives." From the text it becomes clear that *destructives* means the radical wing of the Republican party.

dictator.

A. In ancient Rome the word *dictator* applied to a magistrate appointed in order to avert a desparate situation and invested with the most extraordinary power. During the crisis of 1776 and later in 1781 attempts to create a legal dictatorship were defeated in the Virginia Assembly by narrow margins only.

Jefferson voices his objection to the idea in his *Notes on Virginia:* *Works* III.231f. In December, 1776, our circumstances being much distressed, it was proposed in the house of delegates to create a dictator,...and in June, 1781, again under calamity, the same proposition was repeated and wanted a few votes only of being passed. One who entered into this contest from a pure love of liberty...must stand confounded and dismayed. . . . Those who assume the right of giving away the reins of government in any case, must be sure that the herd, whom they hand on the rods and hatchet of the dictator, will lay their necks on the block when they shall nod to them.

B. The deterioration of the term, prefigured in Jefferson, continued in American politics, *dictator* becoming a term for a political boss or organization holding extra-legal power.

1823 *Cincinnati Nat. Rep.* 22 April 1/3. The New Hampshire Patriot—a paper which has been very incorrectly named, and which has exercised a supreme dictatorship over the state. . . .
1834 *N. Y. Courier and Enquirer,* 1 April 2/1. He [Jackson] is in fact, whatever he may be in name, A DICTATOR. His will is law.
1835 Crockett *Van Buren* 100. Crawford was as much the dictator of his own state as Van Buren was of New York.
1842 Clay in *Cong. Globe* 31 March 377/2. Mr. President, a recent epithet, (I do not know whether for the purpose of honor or of degradation,) has been applied to me; and I have been held up to the country as a dictator! Dictator!
1844 *Democratic Review* XV.326. Clay, with all the vehement and dictatorial pride of will. . . .
1854 Douglas in Nevins *Ordeal of the Union* II.113. I passed the Kansas-Nebraska Act myself. I had the authority and power of a dictator throughout the whole controversy in both houses.

[This is the only instance we have found in which a person boasted of his dictatorial powers.]

1878 *Harper's W.* 586. The absurdity of the talk about General Grant as an emperor and dictator. . . .
1895 Gail Hamilton *Blaine* 126. As Chairman of the State Committee, his organization was so thorough that . . . the other

party called him dictator. A dictator he was, but a dictator who believed that the reason and the conscience of the people was the true basis of popular government.

dimmicrat.
Humorous nickname for Democrat.

An attempt to suggest the rustic, uneducated, and probably Irish elements in the Democratic party by burlesquing its pronunciation. However, marginal connotations (see quot. 1842) also added to the force of the nickname.

1840 *Ohio Confederate* 4 June 2/1. Another glorious "dimmicratic" triumph—Don Quixote outdone!
1842 Byrdsall *Loco Foco* 50. No indeed, they [non-Loco-Foco-Democrats] stood by their darling monopoly system to the last, as long as it stood, and not until it came falling downward, did they fall away from it and condemn it. Such was the dimsighted dimocracy of these "dimmycrats."
1854 *Ohio St. Jrnl.* 21 Jan. 2/2. Only last week was the "Eighth of January"—and dimmicrats, and all sorts of crats congregated together at Columbus.
1865 in Julian *Sp.* 280. You may take the lowest specimen having the animal figure of a man, and you cannot make him vote anything but the *Dimocratic* ticket.
1912 *Cleve. Plain Dealer* 26 June 2/3. [cartoon] A Dimmycrat and for Harmony.

dinosaur.
A modern synonym for *fossil* (q.v.) .

1952 *N. Y. Times* 13 Oct. 27/1. Anybody who gets indignant [over corruption] is a hypocritical old dinosaur.
1952 Stevenson *Major Camp. Sp.* 248. Yet the same Republicans (the dinosaur-wing of that party) who object to service from our Government. . . .

dirt eater.

One of the opprobrious terms used chiefly in the South to stigmatize those who wanted to keep the Union together at all costs.

c1851 in Cole *Whig Party in the South* 189. The disunion men . . . tried to discredit the Union movement in the eyes of Democrats by applying to it such epithets as "Federalists," "Feds," "Submissionists," . . . "Dirt-eaters."
1855 *Ann. of Cleve.* No.2553. Let the dirt-eaters, and waxfaces unite their forces.
1858 *Toledo Blade* 14 Jan. 2/1. On Kansas affairs he [Buchanan] is with the "Fire Eaters," on Nicaragua affairs with the "Dirt-Eaters." Now he is with the "Higher Law" men; now with the "Lower Law" men.

The epithet was particularly distasteful since there was in the South a class of poor whites whose diet included dirt:

1840 Hoffman *Greyslaer* III.223. Even Bettys, little fastidious as he was, recoiled from the fare which these "Dirt Eaters," as the Indians called them, placed before them.

dirty linen.

A. Voltaire wrote to his niece, July 24, 1752: "Voilà le roi qui m'envoie son linge à blanchir" and to General Manstein: "The king [Frederick] has sent me some of his dirty linen to wash; I will wash yours another time." In each instance the "dirty linen" may be understood to refer to some private scandal or affair, which is best kept from public knowledge. Thus the popular proverb: "Wash your dirty linen at home."

B. In American politics the term has been used when certain mat-

ters, usually in intra-party disputes, are brought out in public debate:

1880 *Cleve. Plain Dealer* 3 June 2/4. The exhibition of dirty linen now on the lines at Chicago is, as Barnum would say, "The greatest show on earth."
1890 *N. Y. Times* 9 Feb. 16/3. More Washing of Republican Dirty Linen [head].

dirty shirt ticket. [ ]

1860 *Cleve. Herald* 29 May 2/1. A correspondent of the New York Herald says the ticket of Lincoln and Hamlin has already been christened "dirty shirt ticket" —from one of the candidates, well known for slovenliness.

Dismalcrat.

Nonce nickname for a Democrat, following a political defeat.

1840 *Ohio St. Jrnl.* 21 Oct. 1/6. A New Name for an Old Party—The Spoilsmen are now called DISMALCRATS. "The Dismalcrats can't open their mouths today," said an honest Farmer to his friend, the day after the election—"Dang 'em, we've licked them up like salt!"

disorganizer.

A. Like its counterpart *organiser, désorganiser* is an important word of the French Revolution. From Brunot, *Histoire* IX. pt.2.722 we take the following examples:

1789 *Arch. Parl.* Je ne crois pas qu'il soit prudent . . . d'inviter le peuple à désorganiser le corps politique.
1792 Wallon *Federal* I.61. Des "désorganisateurs," qui voudraient ramener le despotisme par l'anarchie.

B. The earliest English examples refer to French politics.

1793 Burke *Works* III.484. They published their ever-memorable decree of the 16th of December 1792, for disorganizing every country in Europe, into which they should on any occasion set their foot.

1793 *Ib.* 528. All is summed up in two points: "to create the French Republic, and to disorganize Europe; perhaps to purge it of its tyrants, by the eruption of the volcanic principle of equality."

C. In America the word like its synonyms, *Jacobin* and *sansculotte,* plays a part in the struggle between the Federalists and the Democratic party:

1798 Freneau in Leary *Freneau* 267. Men of Republican principles in this country are frequently denominated Jacobins by the leaders and printers of the aristocratic party. At other times they are stigmatized as desorganizers.
1800 Bishop *Conn. Republicanism* 48. Present him as a democrat, disorganizer, jacobin and satanist.
1801 *Federalism Triumphant* 6. A damn'd rascally set of Jacobins and disorganizers have got into office.

dissolution (ist).

Synonym of *disunion (ist)* (q.v.) .
The first quotation, however, suggests a sectional distinction:

1858 *Ann. of Cleve.* No.3155. The professed dissolutionists of the South are with the Administration Democracy . . . whereas the professed disunionists of the North are not with the Republican Party, but are opposed to it.
1862 Christy *Pulpit Politics* 493. The opinion of the elder Adams, in 1803—based upon the Louisiana question, then agitated—"that he saw no possibility of continuing the Union of the States, and that their dissolution must necessarily take place". . . .
1862 *Ib.* 488. This idea of "dissolution" was of early birth in New England. It broke forth from the classic lips of Mr. Quincy, of Boston, as early as 1811, in the Congress of the United States, when the admission of Louisiana was pending. His language . . . was clear and unequivocal, that its admission would virtually be a dissolution of the Union, as it would free the Northern States from their moral

obligations, and justify them in separating from the South, even by force, if necessary.

disunion (ist).

The cry of disunion and the charge that certain factions or sections are working toward the dissolution of the federal government, although found early in American politics:

1792 Washington *Writings* XII.204. Foreigners would . . . believe that inveterate political dissensions existed among us, and that we are on the very verge of disunion; but the fact is otherwise.

are prevalent mainly in critical periods of the North-South controversy over slavery, as for instance:

1. The South Carolina nullification debates:

1830 *New Engl. W. Rev.* 19 July 2/2. Disunion Doctrines. They [S. C. politicians] . . . cast in the teeth of our delegation the charges of "disunion" and "toryism."

2. The annexation of Texas:

1844 *Wash. Intell.* 15 Aug. 2/3. Rhett, McDuffie, and their Polkite strikers . . . have been crying out "Texas or Disunion."
. . . . "Disunion of '44, the American Rebellion of '76." [toast by Tillinghast]
1844 *Ib.* 30 Aug. 3/4. "Texas or Disunion" [edit.]

3. The Civil War period:

1856 Preston Brooks in Jones *Mirror* 206 . . . I have been a disunionist from the time I could think.
1859 *Harper's Mon.* XX.545. On the following day, Mr. Sherman withdrew his name saying that he should regard it as a national calamity that any supporter of the Administration, or anyone who had expressed disunion sentiments, should be chosen Speaker.
1860 in Nevins *Lincoln* II.130. The whole country is in a state of fearful agitation—

disunion! disunion! is the cry with our Southern friends, it is boldly spoken of by the fireside, in public, in all places it is the absorbing subject. The aggressions of the North and the insults to which we are subjected in their papers their treasonable acts how can it be otherwise if our rights as guaranteed by the Constitution are trampled under foot defiantly—disunion must follow.
1860 Helper *Impending Crisis* 226. [S.C.] is one vast hot-bed of disunion.
1860 *Century Mag.* I.289. Should we join hands with the disunionists and help on the storm....
1860 *N. Y. Trib.* 3 Jan. 2/6. It is remarkable how much the Disunion Democracy have cooled down their ardor since the call for the Nat. Rep. Convention. That call gave plain warning to the disunionists that after the approaching election of a Republican President, their treasonable conspiracy would be dealt with as it deserves.

By the end of the Reconstruction Period the term was no longer current.
1875 in *Cong. Rec.* App. III.63. Disunion has ceased to be a word in our language; it has dissolved, it has vanished, it has gone.

divan.

One of several Masonic terms adapted to the political vocabulary during the years when public attention was centered on the Morgan incident (q.v.) and the Masons in general.

In this instance it refers to a caucus:
1830 *Workingman's Advocate* 17 April 3/4. Of the 133 thus summoned, fifty-six attended the "close divan."

divvy, divy.

A dividing up of the spoils.

According to the *OED divvy* is a shortened form of *dividend*. It seems more likely, however, that it is an abbreviation of *division*. (See 1875 quot.)
1872 *San Diego Daily World* 22 Sept. 2/3. Orville Grant, the President's brother, proposed to Jussen, the collector of Internal Revenue of a Chicago district, to go snacks on a fraudulent "divy" with the runner of a distillery there.
1875 *Cinc. Enquirer* 10 Oct. 8/1. The Deacon ... would never have assisted in collecting money for so wicked a purpose, but when he found it collected he would see ... that the divvy was made according to long division, giving each of the boys his proper share.
1879 *Puck* 30 April 114/1. The primitive lobbyists of those days wooed their tympani with soft seductive hints of divvy-ful jobs or "bone"-bearing stock operations.
1880 *N. Y. World* 10 June 4/3. Congressman Kelley, who was with Garfield in the Credit Mobilier divvy....
1885 *Puck* 21 Oct. 114/2. They know what a Deal is, and what Divvy is, and what a Boodle is, and what Spoils are, generally.

Dixiecrat.

Southern Democrats who bolted from the national party.

The term was supposedly invented in 1948 by Bill Weismer, telegraph editor of the *Charlotte* (N.C.) *News,* who needed an abbreviated form for a headline to an article on the States Rights Democrats (*Am. N. & Q.* VIII:61).
1948 *Birmingham* (Ala.) *News* 22 May 5. Truman Finds Some Dixiecrats Supporting Him on A-Veto Stand [head].
1948 *Time* 5 July 20/3. Mississippi's John Rankin came out of the President's office and suggested that the secessionist Dixiecrats might stay hitched if the 1948 Democratic platform went no further on civil rights than the generalizations of the 1944 plank.

1948 *Cols. Citizen* 18 July 1. South Nominates Thurmond, Wright. Dixiecrats Acclaim Two Candidates [head].

Dixiegop.

A Southern Republican. See DIX-IECRAT.

1949 *Time* 28 March 20. Fearful Wayne Morse had plenty of company in Big Labor. The A.F.L.'s Political League called the Republicans "Northern Dixiecrats." A C.I.O. propagandist coined an angry name for the coalition: "Dixiegop," a nightmare animal with "the front legs and face of a donkey [and] the trunk and rear end of an elephant," which would haunt organized labor's dreams.

A possible forerunner of this hybrid name is suggested in a cartoon of 1909.

1909 *Harper's W.* 14 Aug. 27 [cartoon: donkey + elephant]. Can you suggest a name?

doctrinaire.

"The use of the term doctrinaire to designate a political opinion dates back to the winter 1816–17; the word had been invented by the ultra-royalists to designate a group of men of which at that time Royer-Collard was, so to speak, the chief."—Trans. from Block, *Dictionaire dePolitique*, 1863, I, 735/1.

According to Littré, a nickname invented by the satirical paper *Le Nain Jaune Refugie*, edited in Brussels.

The word was known in America relatively early—

1833 *Reg. of Deb.* I.48/1. He believed, however, that there were some who came under the classification of what the French termed "doctrinaires"—

but its use in American politics is surprisingly late:

1878 *N. Y. Trib.* 12 June 4/3. Senator Edmunds, of Vermont, has never been classed with the so-called doctrinaires in politics, and the staunchness of his Republicanism has never been called in question.

1884 Blaine *Twenty Years* 211. The advocates of actual free-trade according to the policy of England—taxing only those articles which are not produced at home —are few in number, and are principally confined to *doctrinaires*. The instincts of the masses of both parties are against them.

dollar diplomacy.

A derogatory reference to the foreign policy of the United States as set forth c. 1910 by Philander C. Knox (see quot. 23 April, 1910). The phrase follows the formula of the earlier *shirt sleeve diplomacy* (q.v.).

1910 *Harper's W.* 23 April 8. Our "Dollar Diplomacy" and Secretary Knox. An attempt is made, necessarily sketchy, to outline simply and clearly what is meant by the term "Dollar Diplomacy," as it has come to be commonly applied to certain of the activities of Secretary Knox as manifested in Honduras, in Liberia, and in negotiations now in progress looking to the participation of American capital in railway construction in the Far East.

1910 *Nation* 1 Sep. 179/3. "Whatever tends to increase commerce," will certainly not bring conciliation if the "whatever" comes in the shape of shotgun diplomacy and dollar diplomacy.

1913 Bryan in Baker *Wilson Life and Ltrs.* IV.437. It is pathetic to see Nicaragua struggling in the grasp of an oppressive financial agreement. . . . we see in these transactions a perfect picture of dollar diplomacy.

Dolly Varden.

Referring to the Liberal Republican party in 1872.

Dickens' description of Dolly

Varden, the little coquette of *Barnaby Rudge:* "in a smart little cherry-coloured mantle, with a hood of the same drawn over her head, and upon the top of that hood, a little straw hat trimmed with cherry-coloured ribbons."

A. 1. In 1872 Dolly Varden became the name for that year's high style:

1872 *Godey's* April 395/1. Dolly Varden costumes are now the rage for all styles of goods, but as the original Dolly Varden was more given to wearing "prints" than brocades, imported calicoes are now shown in great quantities in what are called Dolly Varden patterns. . . . The Dolly Varden is a polonaise, as our readers well know.

1872 *Harper's W.* 25 May 407/4. Was ever any new costume more criticized than the new "Dolly Varden"? If a lady wants to be noticed on the street, she has only to put on one of these bright-figured garments, and all eyes are directed toward her.

1872 *Godey's* Aug. 188/1. A Western writer describes a Dolly Varden dress as an animated old-fashioned window-curtain thrown over a red brick wall.

2. As a popular catchword for other products:

1872 *Godey's* July 96/1. A "Dolly Varden Cough Elixer" is announced, Dolly Varden horseshoe, Dolly Varden dog collar, Dolly Varden razor strops, and, running the thing in the ground, are Dolly Varden metallic coffins.

B. The application of the term to the political party is somewhat obscure, but a brief note in *Harper's W.* (13 July, 1872, 555/4), "The Original Dolly Varden—Joseph's Coat," suggests a similarity between the varied and perhaps piecemeal costume of Dolly and the heterogeneous composition of the Liberal Republican party.

1872 *Ann. of Cleve.* No.2460. Nothing is clearer than that the old-line Democrats are not to be caught by the Dolly Varden movement at Cincinnati.

1872 *Ib.* No. 2463. The great Dolly Varden May party at Cincinnati.

domestic concern.

A variation of *domestic institution* (q.v.).

1852 in Garrison *Garrison Story* III.349. He [Kossuth] has taken such a hold of people's hearts that they will hardly endure that our "domestic concern" should meddle with him.

1852 Kossuth in *Ib.* III.359. I claim the right for my people to regulate its domestic concerns.

domestic institution.

A. Like *peculiar institution* (q.v.) this phrase is used in defense of slavery, suggesting that any interference with it is an encroachment on the privacy of the individual state.

1831 S. J. May *Recoll.* 33 . . . the slave-holding aristocrats grew so bold as to demand that "this fanatical assault upon one of their domestic institutions should be quelled at once."

1836 in Beveridge *Lincoln* I.190. [Ky.], so long as she remains a sovereign member of this confederacy, can never permit another state to assail her local institutions, much less a combination of private individuals . . . [and will] declare to the world her determined resolution to maintain her domestic institution.

1836 Leggett *Writings* II.135. He [McDuffie] is for dissolving the Union, not when any measure, militating against "the domestic institutions of the south," is effected, but whenever it is proposed.

1836 Calhoun in Wiltse *Calhoun* II.371. [The government was obligated] to resist all attempts by one portion of the Union to use it as an instrument to attack the domestic institution of another.

1845 *Niles' Reg.* 1 Nov. 133/2. Was it part of Mr. Caleb Cushing's instructions to extend the "domestic institutions" of America in the Celestial Empire?

1845 in Jenkins *Polk* 151. It is a source of deep regret that, in some section of our country, misguided persons have occasionally indulged in schemes and agitations, whose object is the destruction of domestic institutions existing in other sections. . . .

1857 in Nevins *Emergence of Lincoln* I.248. Since the phrase "domestic institutions" had a meaning "limited to the family," wrote Buchanan, it embraced the relation of master and slave, but no other institution whatever.

That *domestic institution* had become almost entirely identified with slavery is shown by Stephen Douglas' explanation of what the phrase meant to him. During the debates on the Kansas-Nebraska Bill, which contained the provision: ". . . to leave the people thereof perfectly free to form and regulate their domestic institutions in their own way . . . " he said:

[Sheahan *Douglas* 316]. The Nebraska Bill said that the people would be left "perfectly free to form and regulate their domestic institutions in their own way"— not the Slavery question, not the Maine Liquor Law question, not the Banking question, not the School question, not the Railroad question, but "their domestic institutions," meaning each and all the questions which are local, not national—state not federal.

1858 *Marshall* (Mich.) *Statesman* 28 July 2/3. Mr. Douglas . . . tells Mr. Buchanan and the country, that by "domestic institutions" he meant Schools, Colleges, Banking and Tax laws, and everything pertaining to State policy. Mr. Buchanan still maintained his first position and contended that the "domestic institu-

tions" referred to in the Kansas-Nebraska Bill, related to Slavery alone.

B. Applied to other institutions:

1836 *Scioto Gazette* 6 Oct. 2/2 . . . at party bidding he bays like a terrier against a domestic institution [bank] of Pennsylvania.

do nothing sovereignty.

See SQUATTER SOVEREIGNTY.

don't change barrels.

A humorous variation of "don't change horses in the middle of the stream" (See SWAP HORSES)

1932 *New Republic* 22 June 141/1. The campaign will have been launched on the general philosophy of "don't change barrels while going over Niagara."

doodlebug.

Meaning not clear; perhaps a voter without fixed political convictions.

1884 J. F. Jameson in Donnan & Stock *An Historian's World* 37. We have had much animated and amusing discussion of politics at the table; there are one Bourbon, two Blaine men, eleven mugwumps, and one doodlebug.

1884 *N. Y. World* 14 Sep. 4/5. Statesmen arriving from abroad are more than a little puzzled over the meaning of "soaptails," "doodle-bugs," and "mugwumps" of American politics.

Dorrism.

A. The political philosophy of Dorr's Rebellion in Rhode Island, attacked, as was Dorr himself, by the Whig press throughout the country. (See also DORRITE.)

1844 *Whig Battering Ram* (Cols., Ohio) 4 Oct. 1/1 . . . the traitor Dorr—the fiend-bearded villain who seized a match, with his own unnatural hand, to cannonade the building in which his father and brother-in-law, in common with his neighbors and fellow-citizens, were assembled to defend the laws and Constitution of their country against the seditious movements of himself and his Locofoco myrmidons.

B. Applied to similar movements:

1844 *Henry Clay Bugle* 2 May 1/2. Let them come out from among them and fight under a leader, that they now in their hearts know to be as much superior to their own as Honor and Order is above Repudiation and Dorrism. **1848** Calhoun in *Cong. Globe* 20 Feb. 467. I hold that whenever the idea is a fixed one, that the mere numerical majority have a right to govern—that this right is holden by a sort of divine right—there is then no constitutional liberty. It is Dorrism.... It is bad enough when applied to a State; but when applied to the Union it is ruinous. **1848** *Old Zack* in *Cinc. Gazette* 26 Aug. 2/4. Progress of Dorrism. The Locofocos in Convention in this city, last Saturday, determined in favor of the Dorr Revolution—to disregard the apportionment law of last winter.

Dorrite.

A political follower of Thomas Dorr, of Rhode Island, who in 1842 led a rebellion directed toward the extension of the suffrage in that state. (See also DORRISM.)

1844 *Cong. Globe* 9 March App. 269/2. The Dorrites have gained a great deal of sympathy abroad by representing themselves as the exclusive advocates of the democratic doctrine of extended suffrage. **1846** *Niles' Reg.* 11 April 96/2. Elections. —Rhode Island. The contest has been conducted with renewed ardor between the "Law and Order" ticket and the Dorrites.... **1848** *Ohio St. W. Jrnl.* 10 May 2/7. The Dorrite traitor's convention assembled in this place [Trumbull County].

dough-face.

A Northern Congressman who did not oppose slavery in the South or its extension; a Northerner who favored the South during the Civil War Period.

Apparently introduced into politics by John Randolph:

1820 in (Prov.) *R. I. American* 17 March 2/5. Letters from Washington say that all the Southern members despise the miserable submission of those members from the North who voted with them in the Missouri Question.—They love the *treason*, but hate the *traitor*.—Randolph stung them even in debate, for their desertion. They writhed under the lash of the scorpion. He said, "They got scared. They saw their dough faces in the glass, and were frightened, and voted against restriction, and gave us (the Southern members) a majority of three."

A. The word had been used in folk-lore to designate masks made of dough used by pranksters:

1792 Wolcott (P. Pindar) *Works* III.81. The dough-faced Spectres crowded forth.

A vivid description of this costume is given in

1882 Eggleston *Hoosier School-Boy* 120. Two boys...agreed to furnish doughfaces for them all. Nothing more ghastly than masks of dough can well be imagined.

Although the *DAE* suggests that Randolph may have meant *doeface*, the fact that Randolph in 1809 used the word in exactly this meaning:—

1809 Randolph in HR 23 Feb. *Ann. of Cong.* 1509. The bill before the Committee [non-Intercourse] might bring on war, though it was not intended. Yes, sir, said he, it may bring us to fighting and to disgrace; it is something like dressing ourselves up in a dough-face and winding sheet to frighten others, who may blow our brains out at the moment we suppose them in the height of their terror.—

gives a definite clue to the understanding of his utterance of 1820; he meant that the Northerners were afraid of specters they themselves had created.

B. The word soon came into general use, but underwent a change of meaning in that it was taken to mean persons without a character who can be molded like dough.

1823 *Cinc. Nat. Rep.* 9 May 1/1 ... the curse of slavery, which was extended by the pusillanimous or corrupt conduct of the "dough-faced" representatives from the North. . . .

1823 *Ib.* 30 Sept. 2/1. His [J. Holmes'] *federalism* as late as 1810, and his *dough-facedness* in Congress, have furnished a proper clue to his character.

1824 *Delaware* (O.) *Patron* 22 July 3/1. The Southern politicians know very well how to manage the *dough faces* of the North. . . . The Editor of the Galaxy was at Washington during the last winter and returned home a thorough *"dough-face."*

1838 Clay in HR 11 Jan. *Cong. Globe* App.71/2. The two words [*dough (doe) faces*] with which that gentleman [Randolph] rated and taunted our Northern friends, did more injury than any two words I have ever known.

1846 Cooper *Redskins* 440 ... two-thirds of every meeting are nothing but dough-faces, that are moulded whichever way the skilful manager may choose.

1848 Webster *Works* II.439. I think that "dough faces" is an epithet not sufficiently reproachful. Such persons are dough faces, with dough heads, and dough hearts, and dough souls; they are *all* dough; the coarsest potter may mould them to vessels of honor or dishonor— most readily to vessels of *dis*honor.

1851 Rev. Wm. H. Furness in Garrison *Garrison Story* III.349. There is a simplicity and truth about him [Kossuth]

which go straight to the heart. I cannot believe there is an atom of dough on his face.

1854 *Ohio Statesman* 6 Oct. 2. " 'Dough-faces,' are we? If to be lovers of the Union and not selfish partialists, with souls as narrow as the edge of a sixpence, be dough-facing, we plead guilty to the charge."

1854 *N. Y. sw. Trib.* 7 Nov. 3/4. The genuine Doughface never alludes to the sad accident which deprived him of the use of his backbone.

1856 *Cleve. Plaindealer* 31 Oct. 2/1.
Who are the doughfaces?
The party who vote for a man claimed by them to be a South Carolinian, with a view of carrying out a strictly northern measure.
Who else are doughfaces?
Knows Nothings ... voting for a man for President, who is of doubtful nativity, or who like Topsy was born nowhere.
Who else are doughfaces?
Quakers voting for an open duelist for President.
Who else are doughfaces?
Sticklers for freedom of speech voting for a man for President who has denied it, and resisted it in blood in the halls of Congress.
· · · · · · · · · · · · · · · · ·
Who else are doughfaces?
Laboring men voting for a man for President who opposes the freedom of the gold mines.
· · · · · · · · · · · · · · · · ·
Who are "not" doughfaces?
American citizens voting for the tried statesman, patriot, James Buchanan on next Tuesday, for President of the United States.

1857 *Pontiac Gazette* 5 Dec. in Streeter *Pol. Parties* 281. Northern Democrats are called dough-faces but through their plastic dough they are showing a fearful array of tushes, which snap with savage emphasis.

1878 *N. Y. Trib.* 24 May 4/2. "Northern doughface" is out of date, but "Northern poodle led by a Southern Democrat" is decidedly contemporaneous.

down trodden.

A. The earliest American example yet encountered indicates clearly that the word is taken from the Bible:

1806 Littel, *Political Transactions in Kentucky* [Filson Club Publication, XXXI. 41]. Thus destitute of money, bereft of patrimony person and real, she [Ky.] acquired an independence beggarly and barren, a government of her own without means to support it, and the care of a people long devoted to destruction, "meted out and trodden down," plundered by foes, and despoiled by friends.

The phrase "meted out and trodden down" comes from Isaiah 18:2.

B. It would be more than a coincidence that so many of the following quotations are from the writings and speeches of Abolitionists:

1846 in Giddings *Speeches in Congress* 160. If those rights can be regained by the down-trodden sons of Africa in our Southern States, by quiet and peaceful means, I hope they will pursue such peaceful measures.

1852 in *Life of Henry Wilson* 100. The voice of freedom [in Europe] is heard only in the threatening murmurs of the down-trodden masses, or in the sad accents of their exiled leaders.

C. Applied to the working classes the word occurs in the *N. Y. Weekly Tribune,* 8 April, 1854, 6/5:

... impassioned appeals in behalf of the neglected and down-trodden classes of city population.

In 1875 Thurlow Weed writes to Vivus W. Smith:

Most prominent among the bad legacies bequeathed to the country by Mr. Greeley, is the homestead law. But I must do his memory justice by saying that, in his zealous and persistent advocacy of that law he believed that he was serving the "toiling millions," for whose prosperity and elevation he ever labored. And yet how few, how very few, of those "downtrodden millions" ever possessed themselves of what he regarded as their greatest boon and blessing.

These last two quotations suggest that more material might be found in the writings of Horace Greeley. For what it is worth we suggest that *down-trodden* may belong to a group of words which the feminists took over from the abolitionists.

In 1884 *Puck* (XV.213/1) speaks of "down-trodden womanhood."

dragnet.

A section of a bill in which logrolling or miscellaneous provisions are added; a rider (q.v.).

1842 Benton in *Cong. Globe* 5 July App. 661. These articles were caught in the omnibus, or drag-net section, which is placed in the rear of the bill.

Dred Scott (-ism, -ite).

The Supreme Court decision of 1857 which denied the status of citizenship to the Negro Dred Scott created great dissension within the Democratic party; thus *Dred Scottism* and *Dred Scottite* were frequently used terms for the principle behind the court's judgment and for its advocates.

1858 in Sparks *Deb.* 191. It was held to be a torchlight procession by a number of Dred Scottites.

1858 in *Ib.* 203. The champion of Dred Scottism had come to town.

1860 in Hollister *Colfax* 144. If beaten this year, Dred Scottism will be ratified and affirmed by the Executive and Legislative branches of the Government.

Also Dred Scott Democracy:

1857 *Ann. of Cleve.* No. 1480. Let every Republican remember that it is not in the power of the Dred Scott Democracy to beat us if each individual does his duty.

driftwood.

A. Floaters (q.v.).

1837 Weed *Autobio*. I.448. There was a large number of canal and river men always drifting about the poll of the fourth ward [in Albany], whose votes gave the ward to the party that succeeded in obtaining them ... the "driftwood" as it was called.

B. Factions within a party that obstruct its general policy.

1858 *Ann. of Cleve*. No.3043. The Washington Union, grown insolent, contemptuously calls the Douglas Democrats "driftwood." This kind of "drift wood," will dam the way of every Lecomptonite in the Free States.

drippings.

Corrupt gains.

1831 in Weed *Autobio*. I.383. Unclean drippings of venal legislation.
1872 *Harper's W*. 27 July 578/4. "It [nomination of Greeley] means no union," he adds, "for the spoils of office." How vociferously the Democrats must have cheered—they who despise "drippings" and "plunder."

drone.

The non-worker of society, in particular the politician who gets rich on the efforts of others.

1790 *N. Y. Advertiser* in Bowers, *Jefferson and Hamilton*, 59. A number of drones are brought into society and the industrious bee is forced to furnish them with all the honey of its search.
1792 Paine *Works* V.30. The aristocracy ... are the drones, a seraglio of males, who neither collect the honey nor form the hive, but exist only for lazy enjoyment.
1836 Hone *Diary* 212. [Striker's Handbill] ... laboring that drones may fatten on your lifeblood.

1837 in Byrdsall *LocoFoco* 111. Second. That we cease to confer political power on speculators and drones, or their tools and confederates.

drum and fife candidacy.

Minor candidates who enter an election with little hope of being victorious, their main purpose being to create interest either for a special cause or for their own advancement.

1854 *N. Y. W. Trib*. 25 Feb. 3/2. Fifty thousand majority was given to Jackson, twenty-five to Van Buren, and the only exceptions to a stolid presidential vote on her part have been drum and fife candidacies.

dyed in the wool.

Of the process of dyeing in the wool, the *OED* writes: To subject to the action of a colouring matter while the material is in the raw or primitive state; the effect of which is more thorough and lasting than when done after it is "made up."

Thus in politics the phrase is applied to a thorough-going, out-and-out partisan (see WHOLE HOG).

1830 *Mass. Spy* 10 Feb. In half an hour [he can] come out an original democrat, dyed in the wool.
1835 *Mich. Whig* 8 Jan. 3/1 ... several who are now pillars of the Jackson party, who have obtained absolution from the sin of federalism, and become original democrats dyed in the wool.
1835 *Ann. of Cleve*. No.312. After a few weeks of deliberation he places the name of Van Buren and Johnson on his forehead, and becomes a true Democrat, "dyed in the wool."
1835 Crockett *Van Buren* 72. He [Rufus King] was a federalist dyed in the wool, and a leader of the clan.
1884 *Ohio St. Jrnl*. 19 Aug. Williams, a prominent lawyer of the Western Reserve, who has been a life-long abolitionist—

as was his father before him—and a dyed-in-the-wool Republican.

dynasty.

The American use of this term is aimed at the monarchical tendencies of various ruling classes or factions.

Frequently used by Jackson Democrats.

1832 in Benton *Thirty Yrs.* I.219. The dynasty of '98 (the federalists) has the Bank of the United States in its interest. **1833** in Bigelow *Samuel J. Tilden* I.39. The capitalist class had banded together all over the world and organized the modern dynasty of associated wealth. **1834** in Byrdsall *Loco Foco* 16. It required both moral and physical courage to openly attack an established dynasty of monopolies. **1848** in *Mangum Papers* V.125. Some wretch who hoping thereby to secure favor with the New Dynasty has sold himself body and breeches.

E

earthquake.

A. A great political movement, especially that resulting in an election upset.

1829 in Garrison *Life* 49. But there is another evil [slavery]...a gangrene preying upon our vitals—an earthquake rumbling under our feet—a mine accumulating materials for a national catastrophe. **1834** *Mangum Papers* II.133. The earthquake voice of the people is beginning to be heard on all hands. **1836** *West. Hemisphere* 16 Nov. 2/4. Wanted Immediately.—Half a dozen pocket earthquakes, to celebrate a few federal township triumphs. **1840** in Norton *Tippecanoe* 310. The Democratic-Republican blood of the country was right up. You could hear the rumbling of the young earthquake clear from the District of Maine to Georgia. **1840** *Ann. of Cleve.* No.1660. The earthquake yesterday which swallowed up Locofocoism on the Reserve. **1848** Smith *Thirty Yrs.* 315. It all came out jest exactly as I told you 'twould in my last dispatch, a few days before the 'lection. The arthquakes and harrycanes was awful. Some of our friends was throwed up sky high, and haint been seen nor heard of since; some was swallowed up in the ground and buried alive; and all of us was ship-wrecked and splashed overboard, and left to the marcy of the wind and the tide.

B. A local semi-political (?) group.

1839 *Ohio St. Jrnl.* 2 July 2/1. Placards have been posted calling for a parade of the "Earthquakes" on the fourth. These Earthquakes, we take it, are what are familiarly called "Fantasticals"—humorous fellows, who rejoice in caricaturing the militia system.

eating crow.

A. The popular story behind the phrase is told in *Harper's W.* [1880, 419]. It is about a man who boasted he could eat anything and who being served boiled crow said, "I kin eat crow.... I've eaten crow.... But dang me if I hanker arter it."

As its source *Harper's* mentions the *Knickerbocker Magazine* "more than a quarter of a century ago." We have not found it in the latter magazine, but it turns up in a California paper of 1851 (see *DA*), and it was known during the Civil War (Sandburg, *War Years,* I.139).

B. In 1872 *eating (boiled) crow* was appropriately used to characterize the action of state Demo-

cratic conventions and of the Democratic convention in Baltimore, July 10, to accept Horace Greeley, the Liberal Republican nominee.
1872 *Nation* 11 July 17/1. Mr. Greeley appears to be "boiled crow" to more of his fellow-citizens than any other candidate for office in this or any other age of which we have record. The anti-Free-Trade Cincinnati men say he is boiled crow to them; the Free-Trade and Revenue-Reform Cincinnati men say he is boiled crow to them; boiled crow he is to his former Republican associates; and now the Democrats are saying in a curious way that to them also he is boiled crow.
1872 *Indianapolis Sentinel* 10 Aug. 4/1. Eating crow has become the synonym of late for accepting a leader of unsavory political antecedents.
1872 *San Diego Daily Union* 13 Sept. 1/1. The chief leader of the Democratic party of Rhode Island, Hon. Thomas Steever, who ran as the Democratic candidate for Governor last year, cannot and will not "Eat Crow." He prefers Grant to Greeley....
1872 *N. Y. World* 26 Sept. 6/5. Mr. Storey's Crow on Toast.... Mr. Storey is eating crow. He may consider it superior as a delicacy to woodcock on toast, he may publicly assert that it is woodcock....
1872 *Ann. of Cleve.* No.3193. There is a large Bourbon defection in that state [Ky.], a hopeful spirit among the Republicans, and a general feeling of disgust with "Crow diet" among the ones who have tasted it.
1876 *Cinc. Daily Gazette* 30 June 1/1. Boss Kelly swallows a whole crow in sight of all the delegates.
1876 *Ann. of Cleve.* No.2177. Old William Allen does not eat crow with any extraordinary relish. He says he will not take any decided stand in favor of Tilden.
1876 *N. Y. Trib.* 18 Sept. 4/6. The crow-sick Bourbon is to have his fill.
1880 *Cleve. Plain Dealer* 21 June 2/2. The current number of the Nation says: Not the least of the merits of General Garfield's nomination is that it will save the public from witnessing the "eating of

boiled crow," as the slang phrase is, by the editors who supported the candidature of Grant and Blaine.
1881 *N. Y. World* 7 Jan. 4/3. The "Tribune" has improved upon the delectable old story of the political sneak who, having been caught and convicted of slander and fed upon his own words, looked up pitiously from the unsavory meal and murmured: "I hev eat crow, and I kin eat crow, but I don't hanker arter crow."
1890 *N. Y. Times* 20 Feb. 1/7. A good deal of crow eaten in the Senate and Assembly by the wearers of Platt's collars.
1900 *Rev. of Rev.* XXII.525 [cartoon showing Schurz, Hill, and Olney eating "silver" crow]. "We can eat it, but—"

Ebenezer.

A German sectarian community established in Erie County, New York, in 1842.

The name is undoubtedly based upon the Biblical reference:
I Samuel, 7:12. Then Samuel took a stone, and set it between Mizpeh and Shen, and called the name of it Eben-ezer, saying, Hitherto hath the Lord helped us.

The society was considered to be one of the early communist organizations:
1854 *Washington Union* 24 Oct. 2/6. The Ebenezers are a communist or common-property association.

ebony.

A. In September, 1827, John Quincy Adams gave a toast in which he used "ebony and topaz" for black and white. He added that this was an allusion to Voltaire's *Le Blanc et Le Noir* in which Topaze and Eben are the names of a good and an evil genius. (See J. Q. Adams, *Diary*, VII and *Niles' Reg.*, 20 Oct., 1827, 113/2.) Even with this explanation the meaning of the toast was not clear. Adams' contemporaries refused to believe that this was merely a literary toast and guesses were made at whom among his opponents *ebony* was aimed.

1827 *Georgetown Castigator* 18 Dec. 4/1.

> O Johnny Q my Jo John,
>   It was a happy hit,
> (Yon Ebony and Topaz,)
>   Of Presidential wit.—

. . . .

> Those Jacksonites will say,
>   Your "Ebony" was meant for
> A hit at Henry Clay.

As a curiosity we add:

1828 *Niles' Reg.* 2 Feb. 372/1. "Ebony and Topaz." The following from the "Belvidera Apollo," is one of the happiest explanations of this toast that we have met with:

A subscriber wishes us to give him some information as to the meaning of these two words. Two of our patrons absconded last week without leaving the change due us—they are EBONY—and we received three subscribers this week who paid in advance—they are TOPAZ.

B. The Adams men themselves were nicknamed *ebonites* or *ebony boys.*

1828 *Georgetown Castigator* 19 Aug. 1/4. Any of the Ebony lads who are disposed to back their opinion of the issue of the ensuing Presidential election....

1828 *Cinc. Liberty Hall* 10 April 3/1. But vote the Jackson ticket ... and you will lay the Ebony Boys sprauling [sic] upon their backs.

1836 *Donaldson* (La.) *Creole* 18 Oct. 1/1. The friends of Jackson are cautioned against a trick which, it is understood, is to be the dernier resort of the Ebonites.

C. Later *ebony* becomes a synonym for negro. There may be a connection between this and its application to the negrophile Adams party.

1858 *Ohio Statesman* 7 Oct. 2/3. The Ebonies ... are confined in discussion to a mere weak negation of Democratic principles.

economic maturity. [ ]

1945 *Fortune* June 138/2. The Bogey of Economic Maturity.... It is not too misleading to call it an American theory.

1945 *American Mercury* July 56. We must acknowledge ... [Dr. Hansen] says, that we have reached "economic maturity."

economic royalists.

Franklin D. Roosevelt's term for those financiers and industrialists who opposed his public welfare policies.

1936 Acceptance Speech 27 June. The economic royalists complain that we seek to overthrow the institutions of America. What they really complain of is that we seek to take away their power.

eel. (long and short). ¿

c1850 in Ben Butler *Butler's Book* 94 It so happened that there were two vacancies in the United States Senate, one for the full term of six years, and the other for the remainder of the term to be made vacant on the fourth of March, 1851. These two senatorial terms were called in political parlance the "long eel" and "short eel." ...

eel skin. [ ]

1889 Farmer *Americanisms* 222. Of all the dark and devious ways of the ballot this was (for the practice is hardly possible now) perhaps the darkest and most "vain." An eel skin was a thin slip of gummed paper, on one side of which was printed a candidate's name, and employed to falsify the ballot, being secretly used to obliterate the name of an opponent. Bartlett cites New Englanders and New Yorkers as the chief sinners at this merry little game; possibly he knew.

egghead.

A. First cited in dictionaries in 1953 (see *ACD*), but from inquiries, we see that the word was fairly well known before.

1955 Survey by students at Ohio State Univ. "I heard this word when I was seven." "I first heard this word used when I was a child in grade school." "I heard it when I was a child (about 1938), but it was used descriptively then." "First saw it in a comic strip so-named around 1923." "First heard in 1947 while in the Air Force." "First heard it in 1948; the first American I met told me the day before Easter to tell another acquaintance 'Happy Easter, Egghead.'"

B. The sense is different from that of *egghead* as it now appears in politics. There is every indication that it is not a change of meaning but a new creation by somebody not acquainted with the older use. That somebody was John Alsop.

1952 Stewart Alsop in *Cleve. Plain Dealer* 27 Sept. 10/3. After Stevenson's serious and rather difficult atomic energy speech in Hartford, Conn., this reporter remarked to a rising young Connecticut Republican that a good many intelligent people, who would be considered normally Republican, obviously admired Stevenson. "Sure," was the reply, "all the eggheads love Stevenson. But how many eggheads do you think there are?" How many indeed, and how many people, not eggheads themselves, admire and would vote for such an obvious "egghead" as Adlai Stevenson?

1952 John Alsop to A. M. Schlesinger, Jr. 29 Dec. As far as I know, the term "egghead" is not local, nor is it my own invention (as I feel sure I have heard it somewhere), but its application to the nation's intellectuals is probably my responsibility. As he probably told you, Stewart happened to be in Connecticut with Mr. Stevenson during the early part of the campaign and he called me on the telephone to discuss the situation here. During the course of the conversation, he pointed out that certain intellectuals who

tended to support Eisenhower up to the Convention were deserting him. This made me rather angry because I knew that it was true, so I dredged up the derogatory term from my subconscious. [See *Partisan Review*, March–April, 1953; the above is from an exchange of letters between John Alsop and George Amick, a student at Ohio State.]

The subconscious element in John Alsop's mind may be the super-detective of the Poirot type—

1923 Agatha Christie *Murder on the Links* 11. Elsewhere, I have described Hercule Poirot. An extraordinary little man! Height, five feet four inches, egg-shaped head....

1948 Agatha Christie *There Is a Tide* 8. His eyes had traveled up from the patent-leather shoes—striped trousers—black coat—egg-shaped head and colossal mustaches.—

or the stereotyped professor:

1920 Warwick Deeping *Second Youth* in *Newsweek* 8 October 1956, p. 53. A little eggheaded pedant.

1937 Michael Innes *Seven Suspects* 222. He [Prof. Ransome] was a sandy egg-headed, prematurely bald young man... a very pretty specimen of the remote and temperamental scholar in the making.

C. The word caught on quickly, promoted by a desire to ridicule Stevenson's alleged highbrowism. A contributing factor may have been his baldness.

1952 *New Leader* 17 Nov. 2/2. "We lost the popularity contest," the machine men say, "and their words are being echoed by a strange assortment of "eggheads."

1953 *Ib.* 2 March 10/2. *Time* magazine, in a vicious attack on intellectuals, can now openly refer to them as "the eggheads." Such is the measure of their degradation.

1953 Crane Brinton *The Shaping of the Modern Mind* 16–17. "Egghead" has a nastiness (it seems indeed to have been derived from the Nazi *Eierkopf*) which neither "long-hair" nor the earlier "high-brow" had.

D. Though the examples are generally derogatory, a switch in connotations is described in *Newsweek*.

1956 *Newsweek* 8 Oct. 8–9. Both parties are treating a onetime figure of fun, if not downright contempt, with a new respect —namely the egghead.... Republicans who recognize the change in the status of the Democratic egghead have their own interpretation of it.... Such are some of the men—eggheads in good standing, all —who surround President Eisenhower these days. In Adlai Stevenson's opposing camp, the corresponding entourage is smaller but there is no mistaking the same shape to its head.

E. The popularity of the term has led to the creation of many witticisms.

1952? Stevenson [ ] "Via ovicipitum dura est." "Eggheads of the world unite; you have nothing to lose but your yolks."
1952 *New Leader* 17 Nov. 2/2. It's O.K. to be an "egghead" but it's not necessary to be a "scrambled egghead."
1955 James Thurber in *New Yorker* 28 May 30. "De-egghead," which would mean to disintellectualize or mentally emasculate—a crippling operation approved of by an alarming number of squash-heads in Washington and elsewhere.
1958 *Ohio State Lantern* 9 Jan. 2/2. Hard-Boiled Eggheads [head].

Egyptian Democracy.

The meaning is doubtful, but it probably refers to the slavery wing of the Democratic Party, a comparison with the slave-holding Egyptians of Biblical times. There is also the possibility of the influence of the name *Egypt* referring to the southern part of Illinois, a pro-slavery stronghold.

1857 *Ann. of Cleve.* No.1345. [*Harper's Weekly*] ... coming out in its initial number for the candidate of the Egyptian Democracy [Buchanan].

See *Bricks without straw* for a comparison frequently expressed in anti-slavery literature.

electioneer.

Already in the early history of American politics the term seems to suggest intrigue and propagandistic tricks.

1774 Gordon *Hist. Am. Rev.* I.252. Caucusing ... answers much to what we style parliamenteering or electioneering.
1798 Adams *Defence of Am. Const.* in *Gt. Deb.* VII.76. The whole judicial authority, as well as the executive, will be employed, perverted, and prostituted to the purposes of electioneering.
1800 Bishop *Conn. Republicanism* 58. Another electioneering delusion....
1807 *Weekly Inspector* 18 July 334 ... declared that any attempts to fortify or arm, or in any way prepare for possible cases of hostility, was an abominable, federal, aristocratic, electioneering manoeuvre, and calculated to destroy the liberties of our sovereign masters, the people.
1808 in Rush *Ltrs.* II.984. Our papers teem with electioneering scandal.
1809 in Cutler *Life of Ephraim Cutler* 278. ... he had been falsely charged with having, at an election in Ohio, engaged in electioneering, and spoken disrespectfully of the administration.
1811 Graydon *Memories of a Life* 359. The success of a good trick is only a theme for mirth among those who have talents for the business of electioneering.
1840 Duncan in *Cong. Globe* App. 434. Caricature, slander, and falsehood, were the means by which you electioneered against Thomas Jefferson; and they are the means by which you electioneer now, and have from that time to this.
1841 *Georgia Jrnl.* 17 Aug. 3/2. We know not whether the Governor is electioneering—and we do not charge him with it.

1859 in Congdon *Trib. Essays* 85 ... one well versed in the art which he denounces —the "electioneering legerdemain,"—the heartbreaking drudgery of franking cartloads of speeches and public documents.

1874 *N. Y. w. Trib.* 18 Nov. 1/1. Among the electioneering devices employed by the Republican leaders [was] the distribution of "overflow bacon." ... This bacon was appropriated by the Government for the relief of sufferers by the Mississippi overflow last Spring; and has been kept by the politicians for distribution during election week.

1879 *Nation* 17 July 34. It is intimated in Democratic circles that "Charley" Foster will devote himself to electioneering of the Colfax sort—a method said to consist in chucking babies under the chin and acquiring an encyclopaedic knowledge of voters' names.

1930 Cross *Conn. Yankee* 236. Though Roraback quit electioneering, the Republican High Command, taking a leaf out of his Red Top attack on me, proceeded to deflate my claims to qualifications. ...

electioneerer.

1824 *Cinc. Nat. Rep.* 2 Nov. 2/2. The most accomplished Electioneerer. ...

1834 *Morning Courier & N. Y. Enq.* 5 April 2/3. The Tories have been fairly caught offering $100 for a Whig of the 15th Ward to become a Tory electioneerer!

elephant.

The phrase *to see the elephant,* apparently the American equivalent of the older English *to see the lion* (see *OED*), was frequently found to describe an expedition or trip in which the new, or unusual was experienced; e.g., the Mexican War or the Gold Rush:

1846 *Frankfort Commonwealth* 1 Dec. 3/5. The only sovereign cure for Locofocoism now known is a peep at the Mexican war—the elephant, as the volunteers call it.

1849 *Nat. Intelligencer* 20 Nov. 1/3. It [story from Calif.] coincides with that of many others who have seen "the elephant."

Occasionally the phrase referred to political personages, either old or new celebrities.

1860 in Sparks *Men Who Made Nation* 398. Reporters in the governor's office in the State House described the crowds, which had come from Chicago "to see the elephant [Lincoln]."

1862 *Cols.* (Ohio) *Gazette* 11 July 2/2. He [Vallandigham] was made the "Elephant" of the convention, whom all were desirous of seeing and admiring.

The association of the animal with the Republican party may be found as early as 1860:

1860 *Railsplitter.* [Woodcut: elephant with boots; banner carried in trunk, "We Are Coming!" Announcing a big Lincoln demonstration.]

And again in 1872:

Ann. of Cleve. No.3280. In the procession was a huge elephant, made for the occasion, and placarded as follows: "Old Majority, captured twelve years ago in a Copperhead swamp. Can carry seven hundred thousand now and by 1876 will be good for a million. Epigoo cannot hurt Old Majority.

1872 *Harper's W.* 592. [Cartoon: Greeley on sham elephant—legs, "KKK" and "Tammany"; trunk, "State Rights"; covered with Confederate and U.S. flags.]

It was, however, a cartoon by Thomas Nast which made the first clear identification of the elephant with the Republican party.

1874 *Harper's W.* 7 Nov. [Nast cartoon showing elephant "The Republican Vote" about to plunge into pit of "Southern Claims Chaos." Other animals: donkey "N. Y. Herald" in lion's skin; giraffe "N. Y. Tribune"; ostrich "temperance"; etc.]

1879 *Puck* 7 May 130. We have again taken the liberty of utilizing Mr. Nast's elephant [for G.O.P.].

While both *donkey* and *rooster* have been used as synonyms for *Democrat*, we have found no instance in which *elephant* filled a similar rôle for *Republican*.

eleventh hour men.

Voters who change their party affiliation at the last moment before election.

1831 in Marquis James *Jackson* 491. The eleventh-hour men flocked around and they forced upon the President men like themselves by every artifice.

1834 *Niles' Reg.* XLVI.83/2. The "eleventh hour men" have gathered the "spoils of the victory" gained.

1841 *Cinc. Daily Gazette* 7 July 2/3. The 11th hour men, as usual, seem to get most of the offices, being almost always preferred to the original whigs.

embargoroon.

Supporter of the Embargo Act of 1807.

1808 *Mass. Spy* [*DA*]. The wretched dilemmas to which our Embargoroons are reduced in their attempts to prop the falling of their darling democracy.

1809 Fessenden *Pills Poetical* 20.

Yet the important aberrations
Are scarcely wilder speculations
Than those of our dod pated loons
By some y'clep'd embargoroons.

engine.

An early synonym for *machine,* which has now superseded it.

1794 Taylor *Principles and Tendency* 47. The funding system was intended to effect, what the bank was contrived to accelerate. . . . 2. A political moneyed engine.

1805 Dallas *Life* 219 . . . some men, who wore the legislative honors of their country, appeared at that time to undertake the direction of the revolutionary engine.

1823 *Cinc. Nat. Rep.* 9 May 1/2. In the mean time every engine to make converts was put in motion, and the legislative halls were thronged with lobby members.

1831 *Liberty Hall* 13 Oct. 2/5. The spirit of Anti-Masonry has diffused itself extensively over the middle and northern States. It has now erected itself into a formidable political engine, which may exert extraordinary powers over the affairs of the country.

1839 *Nat. Intelligencer* 28 Sept. 3/1. It [the Post Office] is truly a MIGHTY ENGINE. . . . But what we ask would be the consequence if, by the passage of the sub-Treasury bill, the whole of this "MIGHTY ENGINE" were placed under the immediate control of the President.

1840 *Rough-Hewer* 94/3. There is another enormous engine at work to mislead the people.

e pluribus unum.

"Out of many, one," the motto on the seal of the United States.

In an article in the *Classical Journal,* XVIII, 387–407, Deutsch believes that the phrase, which was first suggested by a Report on August 20, 1776, and officially adopted June 20, 1782, was based on the motto of the *Gentleman's Magazine,* first published in 1731. However, he traces the phrase still further to the *Gentleman's Journal,* edited by Motteux, which had *e pluribus unum* as its motto from 1692 to 1694. The ultimate origin Deutsch suggests to be "Quid te exempta levat spinis de pluribus una?" from Horace's *Epistles* II, 2.212.

The proposal of Du Simitiere (see Jefferson, *Papers,* I, 495–6) is apparently the one from which the committee received the idea for the motto; however, both Franklin and Jefferson are also identified with its adoption.

Equal Rights party.

The Anti-Monopolists of New York, a Democratic faction opposed to bank privileges, were frequently designated as the "Equal Rights party," a term favored by William Leggett, editor of the *New York Evening Post:*

1834 Leggett *Writings* I.91. What have the People, the Democracy, been struggling for in the last election? Was it merely to satisfy a personal predilection in favour of a few leaders, and to gratify a personal dislike to a few others; or was it for certain great principles, combined in the one great general term of Equal Rights?
1835 *Ib.* I.198. The grand principle which we aim to establish is the principle of equal rights.

In October, 1835, the term was poignantly used by Windt in a toast: "Equal Rights; no good Democrat will ask for more, and no true Democrat will be satisfied with less." (Byrdsall, *Locofoco*, p. 20)

The name was officially adopted at a convention in Utica, New York, on September 15, 1836:
in Byrdsall *LocoFoco* 68 ... the name of Equal Rights party, be, and the same is hereby adopted, as our political designation.

There is no doubt that the term got its popularity from the idea of equality as expressed in the Declaration of Independence:
1835 Leggett *Writings* II.76 ... we shall be found, nevertheless, always in the thickest of the fray, doing battle with all our soul and strength and understanding, under the democratic banner first unfurled by our fathers on the fourth of July 1776, the glorious motto of which is THE EQUAL RIGHTS OF MANKIND!

era of good feeling.

Introduced in connection with President Monroe's tour through the North by Benjamin Russell of the *Columbian Centinel.* [ ]
in Buckingham *Specimens* II.96. This union of old political enemies to honor the chief magistrate of the Union, was called, by the editor of the Centinel, the "Era of Good Feelings,"—a phrase, which passed into a by-word, and was frequently quoted as a word of reproach, by those who clung to the federal organization.
c1815 in Gillet *Democracy* 106. It was at this point that the Federalists declared that there existed an "era of good feeling," which should induce among Democrats a forgiveness of past Federal sins, by receiving them into full fellowship, like those who had spent their lives in defending and enforcing Democratic principles.
1817 *Western Spy* 6 Aug. 2/2. Era of Good Feelings [head. account of tour].
1817 *Niles' Reg.* XIII.166/2. The real or apparent moderation of party spirit, has caused the present to be called "the era of good-feelings."
1819 *Bucktail Bards* 36, 59.
Why should our honest Dick despair?
'Twas now the "era of good feeling,"
... So constantly called, in the *Columbian,* and the appointment of Messrs. Oakley and others given as proof. The phrase is certainly a good one, and its meaning, I trust, will soon be generally understood.

Revived during the Civil War in reference to the temporary arbitration of party lines in the North:
1863 Julian *Sp.* 205. Instead of winning them [Democrats] to our side, blotting out the lines of party, and inaugurating an "era of good feeling," it has breathed fresh life and vigor into the Democratic organization.

Later taken up by advocates of reconciliation with the South:

1868 Yates in *Cong. Globe* 11 June 352/2. It is the "era of good feelings" we want, such as existed in Monroe's administration, when all questions were settled, when all the States were in harmony each with the other.

1879 Calkins in *Cong. Globe* 10 June 1901/2. If abuses have crept into our judicial administration, it is to be hoped that in this era of peace and reconciliation, when we are all drawn so near together, when we are "shaking hands over the bloody chasm," and all that kind of things,—when you see here Confederate brigadiers and Union soldiers joining in the work of legislation—the "era of good feeling" will very soon enter the jury-box at the South.

Used by Franklin D. Roosevelt:

1928 in Gosnell *Champion Campaigner* 93. There is a period in our history known in all our school books as the "Era of Good Feeling." It is my hope that we stand on the threshold of another such era in this state.

erring brethren.

Euphemism for Southerners during and after the Civil War: [ ]

1865 Richardson *Secret Service* 170. Singularly enough—for a keen sense of humor was very rare among our "erring brethren"—Johnson appreciated the joke.

See LATE UNPLEASANTNESS, WAYWARD SISTERS.

escalator. [ ]

1928 Kent *Political Behavior* 55. At no time and on no occasion has he gone contrary to the organization. In Massachusetts they call it the escalator.

Essex junto.

Freely used by historians as a name for a group of politicians of which Cabot, Lowell, Pickering, Theophilus Parsons, Stephen Higginson, and Goodhue, all closely connected with Essex County,

Mass., were members. The origin of the phrase needs to be clarified.

1781 Lodge *Life of George Cabot* 17. It was at this time that Hancock is said to have bestowed on his opponents the title of the "Essex Junto," and this is the first appearance of the name in American politics.

1800 Hart, ed. *Hist. of Am. Nation* XI.288. Adams suspected them, and talked freely to his friends about the Massachusetts Hamiltonians, to whom he applied the term "Essex Junto," because a number of them lived in the county of that name. It was, however, an old term revived.

1801 *Mass. Spy* 16 Sept. If such an association existed, and was denominated by its enemies the Essex Junto, it has not retained that name because its members were thought to be confined to [that] county; but the name was extended.

1809 Adams *Works* IX.618. Upon my return from France in 1779, I found myself elected by my native town of Braintree a member of the Convention for forming a Constitution for the State of Massachusetts....I had at first no support but from the Essex junto, who had adopted my ideas in the letter to Mr. Wythe.

exodus.

Another Biblical allusion (see BRICKS WITHOUT STRAW, EGYPTIAN DEMOCRACY) based upon the similarity between the conditions of the Israelites and the American slaves.

1879 Williams, *Hayes Diary* III.553. The exodus of colored people from the South still attracts some attention.

1882 Cooper and Fenton *Am. Politics* I.240. During this summer [1879] political comment, long after adjournment, was kept active by a great negro exodus from the South to the Northwest, most of the emigrants going to Kansas.

expansion (-ist).

The policy advocating an enlarged paper currency; the advocate of that policy.

This is one of a group of terms which arose out of the conflicts on monetary questions in the 1830's and continued throughout the century.

1840 Davis in *Cong. Globe* App.157/3. But from that act of the President, which was the first movement to reform the currency, to this day, there has been what the Senator is pleased to call "expansion, contraction and explosion," in rapid and fearful succession; crisis upon crisis, pressure upon pressure, panic upon panic. ...the policy of the Administration... was the parent of the paper "expansion, contraction, and explosion," of which he has spoken in terms of just severity.
1865 Henderson in *Ib.* 532/2. I am no wild expansionist. I have been a hard-money man all my life. I am not in favor of a rag currency, as it is called.

See CONTRACTION AND RAG BABY.

extremist.

A fanatic; one who favors radical measures; during the anti-slavery conflicts the Southerners were generally alluded to as extremists.
1850 Webster *Sp.* 53. The extremists of both parts of the country are violent.
1852 in Wilson *Slave Power* II.369. Extremists always denounce all compromises.
Ib. II.285 [referring to 1850]. To add to the general bewilderment and demoralization that prevailed, the Southern extremists were abandoning their vaporing and abstractions, and were rapidly approaching, in words at least, toward open and avowed treason.
Blaine *Twenty Years* 275. He [Hunter of Virginia] was a sympathizer with the South Carolina extremists, and coalesced with the Whigs to defeat the regular Democrats who were sustaining the Administration of Mr. Van Buren.
Grinnell *Men and Events* 62. "Hangman Foote," of Mississippi had descended [in 1851] as an extremist to become a compromiser.

eyewash.

Something done, not for utility but for effect.

A. According to Partridge the term had its origin in English military slang: [ ]
1884 C. T. Buckland *Sketches of Social Life in India.* Most officers of any tact understand the meaning of eyewash.
1916 Bean *Ltrs. from France* 197. The ignorance which ... flies to the conclusion that everything written and spoken about the horrors of this war is humbug, and what the Army calls "eyewash."
1919 Ian Hay *Last Million* ch. ii. The greater the fuss a regiment made about its appearance—"eyewash," we called it—the better its work in the field.

B. The term recently has had a brief popularity in American politics as a result of President Truman's remarks concerning primary elections.
1952 *Cols. Citizen* 6 Feb. [Ed.]. Eyewash Isn't So Bad. ... Last week the President [Truman] said he would ask that his name be withdrawn. He said primaries in presidential years turned out to be so much eyewash by the time the party conventions got around to nominating a candidate.

F

fair deal.

A. When President Harry Truman in his "State of the Union" speech of January 4, 1949, said, "Every segment of our population and every individual has a right to expect from his government a fair deal," the press was quick to pick out the phrase "fair deal" as a label for the policies of the Truman Administration.

1949 *Cols. Citizen* 5 Jan. 1/7. He delivered his "Fair Deal" message in person.
1949 David Lawrence in *Cols. Dispatch* 11 Jan. President Truman took a bit of political risk when he promised in his State of the Union message a "fair deal" for everybody.... Already it is natural that questions should be asked seeking a definition of just what is meant by the "fair deal" offered by Mr. Truman.
1949 *Cols. Citizen* 1 March [ed.]. Watch Senate next week for clues to fate of President's Fair Deal legislative program.

B. Although it is obvious that the phrase as a label for an administration's policies is based upon the formula of the *square deal* and the *new deal* of the Roosevelts, *fair dealing,* a metaphor from the vocabulary of card playing, may be found much earlier in American politics.
1848 *Ann. of Cleve.* No.859. We like fair dealing. We like open, manly, honorable combat.
1879 *Puck* 5 March 3/1...either Mr. Hayes will have said VETO to any action of Congress which dishonored the national name for fair-dealing with other countries; or else Mr. Hayes will have allowed the bill to pass away without the Executive signature.
1880 *N. Y. World* 2 Nov. 4/2...an insult to every American who believes in honest elections, fair dealing and fair play.

fair shake.

An honest chance or bargain; the *deal* of card playing replaced by the *shake* of dice.
1871 *N. Y. Trib.* 23 Oct. 4. But they would not be asked to concede everything and receive nothing. There should be a "fair shake" and a just consideration of the claims and strength of all parties contributing to an anti-Ring triumph.

See FAIR DEAL, SQUARE DEAL, NEW DEAL.

fair weather politician.

Politicians who give only lukewarm support to their party.
1856 *Cleve. Plain Dealer* 3 Oct. 2/1. Just look at the news from Old Richland! Every hill and valley in Ohio is a blaze of Union loving Democracy! No "fair weather" politicians on our side.

false counter.

An election official who falsifies the election returns.
1879 Conkling in *Cong. Record* 24 April 805/2. Let repeaters, false-counters, and ruffians no longer be employed to carry elections.

farm bloc.

See BLOC.

fascist with a small "f."

See DEMOCRAT WITH A SMALL "D."
1946 Arnall *Shore Dimly Seen* 88. I have never met a Fascist that I liked; even an incipient fascist, with a little "f," busy with his thoughts of how a Third-Assistant-Vice-President might fare, come the managerial revolution, in the division of the surplus value contributed by manufacture. Most of the young fascists, with a little "f," seem to me to be as brittle as the young man who, quite likely, was a Communist; and both seem to be thinking about the same thing.

fat.

Lucrative, applied to offices or contracts usually offered for political support.

The term is very old in English clerical usage [see *OED, fat,* III,9b].

In American politics:
1824 *Cinc. Nat. Rep.* 22 Oct. 3/1...they [supporters of Clay] are all looking for something fat, from a Secretaryship down to an embassy to Barrateria.
1864 Carpenter *Logic of History* 296/2...

if they can get a fat contract or enjoy fat fees, they set themselves up as extra loyal!

Also the money to be gotten from these positions:

1880 *N. Y. Trib.* 7 Oct. 4/4 . . . but that mouthful will satisfy only that part of the faction which personally gets the little fat there is in these places.

fat cat.

According to Mencken (*Supplement* I, p. 282) "fat cat, a wealthy contributor to campaign funds, was coined by Frank R. Kent of the *Baltimore Sun,* and was first used in his book, *Political Behavior,* 1928" [p. 59]:

. . . these capitalists have what the organization needs—money to finance the campaign. Such men are known in political circles as "Fat Cats". . . .

This quotation itself suggests that Kent did not coin the phrase, and the historical facts add further evidence that he did not. The use of *fat* indicating *rich* is much older [see *fat*] and we have the *fat cat* formula in such instances as

1859 *Ann. of Cleve.* No.295. Griswold, formerly the "fat contributor" of Buffalo, will soon take charge of the local department of National Democrats in this city.

In 1883 the phrase occurs in an Opper cartoon in *Puck,* 5 September, p. 6, entitled "Hope Deferred Maketh the Heart Sick." Columbia is shown taking a fat cat from the pillow of office, while a Democrat standing in the doorway says, "Will she ever chuck out that fat Republican cat, and give me a show?" In this instance, however, the fat cat is an office holder, not a campaign contributor; thus the current meaning of the term ap-

parently derives from a generalized usage meaning any rich person, which was then again specialized to designate those who give substantial amounts to the party treasury.

Later example:

1932 Mencken *Making a President* 79. The falling away of such fat cats as John D. Rockefeller, Jr., Alfred P. Sloan, Jr. . . . is a good deal worse.

fat office.

A rich public office.

1830 *Liberty Hall* 2 Sept. 2/1. It was not known that he looked up to such a fat place [sheriffship].

1877 *Puck* 3 Oct. 4/1 . . . Ohio, who sniffed afar off up the stream of time the loaves and fishes of future fat offices, thought it expedient to have a finger in the Union pie.

1878 *N. Y. Trib.* 26 March 4/5. His [Nasby's] soul thirsts for conciliation by means of a fat office.

1879 *Puck* 21 May 163/1. Everybody is invited to chip in, biggest contributors to get the fattest offices.

favorite son.

A prospective candidate for national office who is strongly supported by the leaders of his own state or locality.

A. Although there are conflicting and erroneous accounts of the origin of the phrase—

1876 *Leslie's W.* 234. First applied to Van Buren after his nomination as minister to England had been rejected.

1923 in *N. Y. Times* 16 Dec. sec.10 8/1. Thus the favorite son who receives the vote of his State delegation at every Presidential convention bears the term first applied to Washington by the N. Y. Daily Gazette on the day following his inauguration in 1789.—

there is little doubt its first application was to Washington and

was without political significance:
1788 in Moss *Am. Metropolis* I.266 [banner inscription]. Freedom's favorite Son.

B. Later uses:

1793 in Leary *Freneau* 227. Sinbat, who steals fair freedom's holy name, The favorite sons of Freedom to defame—
1835 Crockett *Van Buren* 69 ... eulogize the life of a favourite son [Clinton] ... 198 ... the views and wishes of your "favourite son" [Van Buren]. ...
1835 in Hone *Diary* I.147. It would appear ... that the "greatest and best" and "New York's favorite son [Van Buren] do not consider it good policy to bestow unqualified praise upon the man whom they have heretofore united to pull down.
1839 Clark in *HR* 30 Jan. I should, however, do him justice to say, that he has not yet done entire execution on Virginia's favorite son, (Mr. Rives) the friend and eleve of Jefferson.
1840 *Dem. Rev.* Feb. 107 ... the Kentucky delegates may parade the magnanimous acquiescence of themselves and the gallant "favorite son" of their State ... [Clay].
1844 *Buckeye Eagle* 11 Sept. 2/2. We dislike this expression [favorite son], as it has been so often misapplied.
1878 *Nation* 26 Dec. 391. But the Democrats learn slowly and it will be some time before they discover how to baffle a sharp and unscrupulous adversary like Maine's "favorite son" [Blaine].
1888 in Roosevelt *Ltrs.* I.139. I presume the first ballot will be on all hands a "favorite son" affair.
1940 Stokes *Chip* 198. There was no mock nomination of "favorite sons" put forward to be traded off later in negotiations between leaders. There was only one "favorite" son [LaFollette] here. There were no state lines drawn, no state banners. This was a national movement for the people as a whole with no glorification of individual states to emphasize local prejudices.

C. The frequency with which favorite sons are brought forward with no possible chance to secure the nomination but only as a means of drawing attention to a state or its delegation leads to an occasional satirical usage.

1876 *Cinc. Comm.* 5 May 4/3. Poor Wheeler! He has the favorite sonny fever.
1880 *Cleve. Leader* 31 May 4/1. Had there been no stupid "favorite sonny" business in Ohio, the State would have been solid for Blaine, and that would have put an end to the third term question.
1889 Farmer *Americanism* 234. This phrase became so common, used in reference to local or State politicians, that the *Nation* at last made it the text for an editorial article so severely satirical that *favorite sons* have not been so numerous since its publication.

featherhead.

Another of the satirical epithets for the faction of the Republican party in New York who did not support the regular party machine. (See HALFBREED.)

1881 *N. Y. World* 9 Jan. 1/4. We could here have a group of Stalwarts; there a squad of "Half-breeds"; over in Sleepy Hollow might be packed a carefully selected assortment of "Featherheads". ...
1881 in Platt *Autobio.* 164. July 7, sixty two "Half-breeds" and "featherheads," as adherents of the Garfield administration had been characterized during the contest, called a caucus of the Republican legislators.

federal.

In the English social science of the 18th century *federal* means "pertaining to or of the nature of that form of government in which two or more states constitute a political unity while remaining more or less independent with regard to their internal affairs." (*OED*)

1707 Seton in *Parl. Hist.* VI App.142.

Sweden and Denmark were united by a federal compact under one monarch.

The earliest American use is the same:

1777 Robertson *Hist. America* II.197. The celebrated league that united the Five Nations in Canada into a federal republic.

Thus *federal* begins its career as a scientific rather than a political term (cf. DEMOCRACY). During the discussions leading to the formation of the union, *federal* is frequently coupled with *national.* To begin with, the two terms are different in stress rather than meaning in that national accentuates the "unum" idea, while federal stresses the "e pluribus." However, the growing unwillingness of the states righters to concede more than a minimum of power to the union sharpens the contrast between *federal* and *national.*

1788 Patrick Henry in Garland *Randolph* I.29. It is now confessed that the new government is national. There is not a single federal feature in it. It has been alleged within these walls, during the debates, to be national and federal, as it suited the arguments of gentlemen. But now when we have a definition of it, it is purely national.

At that early stage *federal* meant almost the opposite of what it does later. It applied to those who opposed, not those who favored, a strong "consolidated" central government (cf. CONSOLIDATION). The change of meaning seems to have its beginning in the tendency of the Hamilton circle toward hostility to the independence of the several states. Letter 39 in *The Federalist* is particularly significant. It

stresses repeatedly the federal features of the Constitution:

The act, therefore, establishing the Constitution, will not be a national, but a federal act.... In this relation, then, the new Constitution will, if established, be a federal, and not a national Constitution.... So far the government is federal, not national. The conclusion reached by the writer [Madison] is that if we try the Constitution by its last relation to the authority by which amendments are to be made, we find it neither wholly national nor wholly federal.... The proposed Constitution, therefore, is, in strictness, neither a national nor a federal Constitution, but a composition of both. In its foundation it is federal, not national; in the sources from which the ordinary powers of the government are drawn, it is partly federal and partly national; in the operation of these powers, it is national, not federal; in the extent of them, again, it is federal, not national; and, finally, in the authoritative mode of introducing amendments, it is neither wholly federal nor wholly national.

Perhaps the most important factor in the change of meaning is the decision of the authors to republish their work, originally called the "Publius" letters, under the title of *The Federalist,* thereby putting a still stronger accent on their denial of any hostility toward the states righters. By this device they succeeded in taking away the name of "federalist" from the latter party, who from then on as opponents to the bulk of ideas presented in the Federalist letters became known as anti-Federalists.

A new alignment of parties as well as party names, results from the rise of the Republican-Democratic party which brings about the state characteristic of the last years of the 18th and the early years of the 19th century, during which period the contrast between a central government and the states is overlaid by the struggle between the rights of the privileged classes and the people in general. (See DEMOCRAT and REPUBLICAN.)

Incidentally, the feud between Democrats and Federalists led to the first (?) use of party badges, in the form of tricolor and black cockades. (See BLACK COCKADE.) The alleged unpatriotic attitude of the Federalists (see BLUE-LIGHT FEDERALIST) and the activities culminating in the Hartford Convention further contributed to the decline of the word. In 1813 it was considered a libelous word in a trial in Franklin County, Indiana, in which the plaintiff was awarded damages of $10 when Nathaniel Herndon called him a "federalist." (Buley, *Old North-West,* II, 12n.) The disappearance of the party from the political scene did not put an end to the use of *federalist* as a term of abuse. In this rôle it ceased to be the monopoly of the Democrats but was used against them as well.

1840 *Springfield Register,* 2 Oct. in Lincoln *Uncoll. Works* I.570. Mr. Lincoln rose and told the people that if they would attend on the next day he would prove to their satisfaction that the Van Buren party was the old Federal party and that the Whigs were the old-fashioned Democrats.

The degeneration of the term was deplored by two contemporary writers:

1838 Price *Clement Falconer* II.126. My earliest political impressions were in opposition to Federalmen and Federal measures.... little did I expect to behold the degenerate off-spring of those gifted men asking forgiveness of their country; openly repudiating the name of Federalist, and consenting to bandy it as a bye-word and a reproach in the land.

1840 Hone *Diary* I.486. Federalism. It is strange that this term, by which was designated in former times, the purest, the wisest, and the most patriotic political party which ever existed, should continue to be a term of reproach and the means of exciting the bad feelings and prejudice of the people even now, when it has ceased to be a bond of union or badge of party.

Federo Americans.

Used by Jefferson after the War of Independence as a term for the citizens of the United States:

1786 Jefferson *Works* V.402 ... we can no longer be called Anglo-Americans.... I had applied that of Federo Americans to our citizens, as it would not be so decent for us to assume to ourselves the flattering appellation of free Americans.

feed trough.

Variant of *public crib* (q.v.).

1881 *N. Y. Trib.* 28 May 4/3. The Republican party is tired of Bossism, quarrels about patronage, slavery to the machine, and the statesmanship of the feed trough.

fellow-traveler.

A. Early quotations, mostly non-political, do not indicate an unbroken tradition leading up to our present use of the term.

1717 Wise *Vindication* 105. I therefore make bold to invite the said Testimony, to set out again with fresh Courage, and improve its Excellent Language, together with former acceptance it found with the Churches, to ingraciate and bespeak favour for this small Treatise, its new Allie and Fellow-Traveller.

1753 *The Stage-Coach: containing the*

Character of Mr. Manly, and the History of His Fellow-Travellers. [title]
1839 Clark in HR 30 Jan. Shall Conservatives travelling the high road of republican principle, turn aside, and madly rush down the precipice, because Whigs are fellow-travellers? No sir, Conservatives are pleased to act with Whigs when they go for the country, and I trust they will so continue to act.
1852 in *Amer. N. & Q.* III.191. In an 1852 issue of the *Lantern* (Vol. 2, p.114) is a cartoon bearing the caption "Fellow travelers," and below are two drunks, the one rich, the other poor.

B. Apparently a distinction made by Trotsky in 1925 between those who were devoutly dedicated to the Revolution and those who only professed an interest in it is responsible for the modern popularity of the expression. In its early stages, *fellow traveler* could be used in various contexts, but after World War II the term became narrowed in its meaning once again, applying only to those who were felt to be associated in interest if not in practice with Communism.
1925 in *Amer. N. & Q.* II.185. "The Fellow Travelers," so named by Trotsky, were a group of Russian authors who flourished in the twenties.... Trotsky said of this group (*Literature and Revolution,* N.Y., 1925) : They are not the artists of the proletarian revolution, but only its artistic fellow travelers.
1931 *Bus. Wk.* 27 May 48/1. Our fellow-travelers—bankers, labor, government—begin to indulge in back-seat driving and start quarreling.
1936 *Nation* 24 Oct. 471/1. The new phenomenon is the follow-traveler. The term has a Russian background and means someone who does not accept all your aims but has enough in common with you to accompany you in a comradely fashion part of the way.

1944 in Hoover *Add.* 246. With the blessing of the Attorney General, the Communists and the fellow-travelers are spending vast sums to reelect this regime.
1946 Arnall *Shore Dimly Seen* 87. Assailed on the one hand by these, and on the other by native reactionaries, scalawags and demagogues with vocabularies of invective of which "Communist," "traitor to Southern ideals," "fellow-traveller" and "nigger-lover" are the least opprobrious and only the beginning, most Southern liberals search for another tag to wear.
1947 Helm *Truman* 203. Dozens of these radical workers and their downtown kith and kin were carded in the files of the House Committee on Un-American Activities among thousands allied with Communist-front, fellow-traveler, and political-action groups.

fence, sitting on the.

While Congress at all times can contain men who in regard to the major parties occupy a borderline position, (see INDEPENDENTS) conditions in 1828 focussed attention on the one man in the Senate, Gardiner, who maintained a neutral attitude between the Adams and the Jackson men. The *Ohio State Journal* of January 23, 1828, gives the following summary of the situation:

Administration	22
Jackson	13
On the fence	1

The expression must have been at least relatively new:
1828 *Niles' Reg.* 2 Feb. 374/2. Two members, one in each house, are said to be "on the fence." A very significant term, but one that we have met with for the first time, we believe.
1830 *Ann. of Cleve.* No.316 ... we decree, that all fences in this town must here after be up, and all politicians on the

Fence must jump down, and that as the top-rails in this vicinity have been worn too round by a great number having sat upon them, the practice will no longer be permitted. Now all would-but-dare-not-be-politicians who insist in sitting on the fence, will be amerced a penalty for the same.

1832 in *Mangum Papers* I.445. I shall begin to think with Mr. Balche that the Post of honor is on the fence.

1835 *Frankfort Commonwealth* 16 May 3/2. Let poltroon desert to the strong party, and mercenary politicians slide down to the clover side, from the fence, on which they have long been stationed, in inglorious security, awaiting the fortune of the field.

1840 *Harrison Dem.* 26 May 4/2.

> Many too, who on the fence were
> Some time ago—
> Have jump'd into the field of old
> Tip-pe-canoe.

1840 (Milledgeville) *Georgia Jrnl.* 18 Feb. 3/3. Our advice to all politicians who have a hankering after the praise of all ... is to take a position near the fence, on the fence, or above the fence.

1846 *Cong. Globe* 30 March 571/1 ... the President intended to place himself on the fence, that he might fall on either side, as might be desirable ... he never went for either 49 or 54–40, but placed himself on the fence, ready to drop on either side, if necessary.

1856 *Ashland Times* 13 Nov. 2/4. Gov. Gary cannot disguise his real sentiments or sit on the fence any longer. That he is a pro-slavery man is well known.

While the connotations of the phrase are in the main derogatory, indicating a lack of principles, an attempt to rehabilitate it was made by Carl Schurz:

in Blaine *Twenty Years* II.440. He aspires to the title of "Independent," and has described his own position as that of a man sitting on a fence, with clean boots, watching carefully which way he may leap to keep out of the mud.

fenceman.

A politician who has not decided which candidate or party will gain his support.

1828 *Ohio St. Jrnl.* 30 Jan. 3/5. It would be well perhaps for him to inform the public as to their politics. How many neutrals, fencemen &c.

1832 *Georgetown Castigator* 2 Oct. 3/3. Much has been said of my being a fence man—a Clay man, a milk and cider Jackson man.

1848 *Groton Spirit of the Times* 28 July 2/5. Who does not contemn a fence man? —ay, a weathercock? The man on the fence is ever stretching his neck to ascertain on which side the strongest party and the majority lies.

fence politician.

Variant of *fenceman*.

1828 *Ohio St. Jrnl.* 30 Jan. 3/1 [from *Essex Register*].—That all the fence politicians will come over to their side.

fence straddler.

See FENCE, SITTING ON THE

1838 *Alexandria Western Messenger* 1 Aug. 1/3. By far the most important among political characters, is he who sits upon the fence.... To enjoy his full dignity, however, the fence straddler must know his own worth.

1877 *N. Y. Trib.* 17 April 4/6. This is an uncomfortable era for the constitutional fence-straddler.

fiat.

An order or law pronounced by a person in high political office, based on Genesis I,3: Fiat lux (Let there be light).

1824 in Weed *Autobio.* I.109. On the last day of the session, in persuance of a Regency fiat, John Bowman introduced a resolution....

1845 *Ann. of Cleve.* No.1512. The fiat has gone forth that the present tariff must be repealed.

1858 in Wilson *Slave Power* II.553. "I am content," he [Keitt] said, "impregnably to intrench the rights of the South behind the monuments which the hand of the Almighty has raised"; and he contended that "with the proclamation of the law was also uttered the fiat which sanctioned slavery and settled the relations between the master and the slave."
1896 *Nation* 5 March 188–9. They [international lawyers] were told by Mr. Olney last July that "our fiat is law" on the continent.... Your true "fiat" is self-executing. When the Creator said, "Fiat lux," there was no need for casting about for some means of producing light.... Fie on that [Olney's] kind of fiat!

fiat money.

Paper money not backed by specie but made legal tender only by government fiat.

The term was current during the Greenback controversies following the Civil War.
1874 Wells *Practical Econ.* 17. The generations of Texans who had had this experience of "fiat paper money" never again looked with favor upon any other currency than specie.
1878 *Harper's W.* 14 Sept. 726/2. The greenback is extolled as the money of the war, the gallant, glorious greenback that carried us through. But ... it is evident that it was not so for any of the reasons that are urged for its illimitable or irredeemable issue, or for the printing of an indefinite quantity of paper and calling it "fiat" or "absolute" money.
1890 in *Gt. Deb.* XIV.262. Senator Sherman said that Senator Ingall's theory was that of fiat money. Senator Ingalls.— "Fiat" money! Mr. President, there is no fiat money in this country that rests upon the credit of this Government when the capacity for redemption ... is lodged with the Secretary of the Treasury. No, sir!

The Biblical background of the phrase is still shown in several instances:

1876 Hoar *Autobio.* I.354. He [Butler] had said in explaining and defending his fiat money scheme that the word "fiat" means "let there be." God said "fiat lux," "let there be light," and there was light.
1878 *Harper's W.* 31 Aug. 87/2. The fiat dollar is to contain no promise to pay, but in its stead we are to have a fiat or proclamation. It would run in its simplest form thus; "This is a dollar," or if that formula is too brief, some decoration might be added, thus; "Hail, Columbia! this is a dollar," or "E Pluribus Unum! this is ten dollars." Or for the pious it might read; "In God we trust to make this a dollar," and the holder would mentally add, "For He only can."

fifth column.

The term originated in 1936 during the Spanish Civil War.
1936 *N. Y. Times* in *Am. Speech* XIX.47. Police last night began a house-to-house search for Rebels in Madrid.... Orders for these raids ... apparently were instigated by a recent broadcast over the Rebel radio station by General Emilio Mola. He stated he was counting on four columns of troops outside Madrid and another column of persons hiding within the city who would join the invaders as soon as they entered the capital.
1947 *Time* 8 Dec. 108/1. When, in 1936, General Emilio Mola announced that he would capture Madrid because he had four columns outside the city and a fifth column of sympathizers within, the world pounced on the phrase with the eagerness of a man who has been groping for an important word.

Referring to subversive organizations in America:
1940 *New Rep.* 7 Oct. 468/1. An interesting new pamphlet entitled "The Fifth Column in Washington" has turned up on newstands.... The *real* fifth column, it appears, is an insidious band of government employees ranging from Attorney General Jackson and Harold Ickes to....

See SIXTH COLUMN.

Fifty-four Forty or Fight.

A great many historical works are very positive in declaring this phrase a slogan of the campaign of 1844 and in attributing to it a decisive influence in the election of Polk.

A few characteristic quotations are:

McLaughlin and Hart *Cyclopedia of Am. Government* I.730. The Democratic rallying cry during the presidential campaign of 1844.

1922 E. I. McCormac *James K. Polk* 563. The candidate accepted the platform without reservation, while the rank and file voiced their approval by lusty shouts of "54° 40′ or fight."

1942 Carman, Kimmel & Walker *Historic Currents in Changing America* 206. During the campaign, however, the Democratic slogan was "fifty-four forty or fight." James K. Polk was elected President on this platform.

In not a few books William "Foghorn" Allen, U.S. Senator from Ohio, is named as the author of the phrase.

DAH. In a speech in the Senate in 1844, William Allen, of Ohio, used the phrase "Fifty-four Forty or Fight." A plank of the Democratic Platform of 1844 called for the reoccupation of Oregon, and the slogan ... became the battle cry of the expansionist Democrats.

Bartlett *Familiar Quotations* [12th ed]. The challenge of Senator Allen (of Ohio) became the slogan of the expansionists ...

In contrast to this widespread opinion, Thornton's *American Glossary* gives 1846 as the year of origin. This statement is based on a quotation from a speech in Congress by Senator Clayton of Delaware, June 15, 1854:

During the year 1846, the country went crazy for about six months in favor of the

Baltimore platform, "54° 40′ or fight." ... That same declaration was thundered here by the press, from day to day. It was very popular, and the canal-boat, and even some of the babies, it was said, were christened 54° 40′.

Earlier quotations in Thornton mention the boundary of 54 40, but do not offer the characteristic formula of 54 40 or fight.

Mathews' *DA* calls the slogan a "popular rallying cry used by the Democrats in the presidential campaign of 1844," but his first quotation is from 1846:

1846 [Philadelphia] *Dollar Newspaper* 8 April 3/3. Definitions ... P.P.P.P. Phifty-Phour Phorty or Phight.

We suspect that the idea of *54 40 or fight* as an inspiring slogan of the 1844 campaign is nothing but an unfounded, although amazingly stubborn legend. We have failed to find it in sources of that year, and we can state confidently that it was not used in Allen's senatorial speeches. Even when the Oregon question gained fresh importance by Polk's presidential message of December, 1845, the cry was not "54 40 or fight" but "the whole of Oregon or none"; or similar formulas:

1846 *Cong. Globe* 3 Jan. 133/1 ... to vindicate our title to the whole of Oregon— yes, sir, "the whole or none."

Ib. 3 Jan. 135/1. The cry is now, "The whole of Oregon or none."

Ib. 5 Jan. 144/2. I [Simms of Mo.] wish it to be distinctly understood what banner I fight under. It is "for Oregon, all or none, now or never."

It seems significant that the *ph* spelling is not restricted to the Philadelphia paper quoted above, but to begin with is the prevailing one:

1846 *Cleve. Plain Dealer* 10 April. An Iowa paper thinks we should go for Phyfty Phour Phorty or Phyght. Who's apheared!
Ib. 25 April 2/1. Phifty-Phour Phorty or Phight.... By G-d, I go for fifty-four forty or fight!

The reason for this orthographic vagary must be that the formula *fifty-four forty or fight* was used and, perhaps, originated as a humorous interpretation of the formula of the four p's. The Philadelphia *Dollar Newspaper* is not isolated in its reference to this combination. It turns up again:

1846 *Marion* (Ohio) *Buckeye Eagle* 5 Aug. 1/2. The Four P's. Democracy is never at a loss. It readily adapts itself to any change of circumstances. Even the old motto of the four P's is as appropriate as in the palmy days of 54 40. Then it meant Phifty Phour Phorty or Phight. Only the change of a single word is necessary. Now it is "Phifty Phour Phorty or Phlunk."

What the four p's really meant is not known, but a fair guess can be made on the basis of the following heading:

1846 *Buckeye Eagle* 3 July 2/4. Political Principles of J. K. Polk.

If this triad of P's was used in 1844, it would almost automatically be changed after the election into Political Principles of President Polk. However, the question will have to remain open until more material is discovered.

The theory that William Allen invented the slogan can be traced back at least to 1875:

1875 *Urbana* (Ohio) *Citizen and Gazette* 30 Sept. 2/3 [quoted from *Circleville Herald and Union*]. Allen, in the com-

mittee and on the floor of the Senate, swelled, strutted, and blustered around like a gobbler in a barnyard, protesting that he would never agree to a line below latitude 54 degrees and 40 minutes.—No! he would die first—"Fifty-four forty or fight!" was his ultimatum.

figurehead.

One who is placed in a position of prominence solely for his prestige value.

A. The popularity of the term in American politics may center around the incident which created such a furor in the 1830's. Jackson had suggested (?) that his likeness be made the figurehead for Old Ironsides.

1834 in *Mangum Papers* II.124. Figure Head—We learn that ... the cut-water of the U.S. Frigate Constitution ... is to be surmounted with a colossal figure of Andrew Jackson.
1835 in Ward *Jackson* 117. It is a fact that the old "Glory President," has issued his special orders for a Colossean Figure of his Royal Self in Roman Costume, to be placed as figurehead on Old Ironsides!!!

B. Later political uses:

1876 *Harper's W.* 27 May 419/1. The selection of a reformer as a party figurehead may be considered desirable as a stroke of Policy.
1876 *N. Y. Trib.* 3 Nov. 4/3. It appears that the Hon. Richard D. Hubbard, the Democratic candidate for Governor in that State [Conn.], is ... a mere figurehead for the party.
1876 *Cleve. Plain Dealer* 9 June 1/4. Blaine is the figure-head of republicanism.
1900 Roosevelt *Ltrs.* II.1161. But in the Vice-Presidency I could do nothing.... I do not like to be a figurehead.

file leader.

A leading politician.

Long an English military term,

used in American politics with derogatory connotations.

1803 Dwight in Goodrich *Recoll.* 577n
Old Deacon Bishop stands,
With well-be frizzled wig,
File-leader of the band,
To open with a jig—
1823 *Cinc. Nat. Rep.* 14 March 2/2. Most of the partisans engaged in this grand electioneering campaign appear to act on the presumption that the *people* who are in the ranks have very little to do, other than to follow certain drill sergeants and political file leaders.
1823 *Ib.* 22 Aug. 3/1. Come forward, thou file leader of the faction. . . .
1838 *New Yorker* 698/3. Mr. Calhoun, the grand file-leader of the Sub-Treasury party.
1839 Pickens in *Cong. Globe* App.42/1. What was my astonishment when I found my file leader wheeling to the right about, and voting *aye!*

That the military drill background of the metaphor could be forgotten is suggested by the following quotation:
1839 Underwood in *Ib.* App.376/1 . . . they follow their leader in Indian file, and make but one track in their march.

finality.

The opinion that the passage of the English Reform Bill of 1832 had led to a point where retrograde action was out of the question made *finality* an important word in British politics.
1833 Croker *Papers* II.200. The only important thing which occurred was Althorp's explanation as to the finality (a word which I coined, and which is now in great vogue) of the Bill.

Subsequent measures in the same direction kept the word alive, and brought Lord John Russell the nickname of Finality John. [See

Uno Philipson, *Political Slang, 1750–1850,* pp. 59, 208.]

The first known occurrence in American politics alludes to the British background of the word:
1849 *N. Y. W. Trib.,* 4 Aug. 5/5. Has American Democracy reached its "finality," like British Whigism?

After the passage of the compromise measures of 1850, *finality* became a favorite word of those who considered these measures a definite solution, while the Free Soilers and their sympathizers took a skeptical attitude:
1850 in Wilson *Slave Power* II.362. On the 20th of April, there was a Whig caucus, . . . motion being introduced indorsing the compromise measures as "a finality". . . .
1852 *Marion Buckeye Eagle* 20 May 2/3. The Compromise as a Finality [head].
Ib. 10 June 2/3. More About Finality [head] . . . the South would be the very first to desire to set aside the finality of the compromise measures.
in Stanwood *History of the Presidency* 254. [Free Soil Platform, August, 1854]. That the doctrine that any human law is a finality, and not subject to modification or repeal, is not in accordance with the creed of the founders of our government and is dangerous to the liberties of the people.

finality Whig.

1853 *Ann. of Cleve.* No.2472. "Union Whigs" and "finality Whigs" have been ingloriously beaten.

fire in the rear.

Opposition from supposedly friendly forces; fifth column (q.v.) activities.

A. The phrase was coined by General Winfield Scott during the Mexican War when he felt the administration in Washington was working against his prosecution of the war.

1846 Scott in C. W. Elliott *Winfield Scott* 427. My explicit meaning is—that I do not desire to place myself in the most perilous of all positions:—a fire upon my rear, from Washington, and the fire, in front, from the Mexicans.
1847 *Ashtabula Sentinel* 12 April 1/6. He would face the foe before him . . . rather than submit his motives to the eager censure of an enemy in the rear. That expression of Scott is destined yet to have a prophetic character.
1848 *Ohio St. Jrnl.* 9 May 2/4 [res. of Scott meeting]. Resolved, That the "fire in the rear". . . merits for its aiders and abettors, our pity and contempt.

B. In later political warfare.

1854 Parker *Additional Sp.* 372. Make a fire in the rear of your timid servants in Congress.
1861 *Detroit Free Press* in Greeley *Am. Conflict* 392n. If troops shall be raised in the North to march against the people of the South, a fire in the rear will be opened upon such troops, which will either stop their march altogether, or wonderfully accelerate it.
1864 Henry Conkling *Inside View of the Rebellion* 23. The blood of thousands of our brave and noble soldiers . . . cries for redress from the fire-in-the-rear party [anti-war Dems.].
1874 *Ann. of Cleve.* No. 2989. The remorseless election every second year for representatives in Congress, subjects our best worked public men to an unscrupulous fire in the rear as well as to the drudgery of public service in front.
1886 Logan *Gt. Conspiracy* ch.xxv. The "Fire in the Rear." [in 1864]
1902 *Nation* 19 June 480/1. A counter-cry was started, that those who accused Waller and Smith of barbarity were "attacking the army." They were starting "a fire in the rear" of our boys in blue.

fire the Southern heart.

To incite the passions of the Southern people.

A. Apparently coined by William Lowndes Yancey as a slogan to unite the South in its steps toward secession.

1858 in Du Bose *Yancey* I.376. We shall fire the Southern heart—instruct the Southern mind—give courage to each other, and at the proper moment, by one organized, concerted action, we can precipitate the cotton States into a revolution.
1858 Yancey *Cradle of Confederacy* 393. If we organize "committees of safety" all over the cotton States . . . we shall fire the Southern heart.

B. After the Civil War, referring to the Southern hatred of Northern Republicans.

1868 *Cinc. Campaign Gazette* 5 Nov. 4/7. The Republican party has by its oppressions fired the Southern heart and stirred up its just indignation.

C. Also *fire the Northern heart.*

1864 Carpenter *Causes of the War* 25. The wealth of the North was poured out, free as water, to set in motion a train of circumstances that should "fire the Northern heart."
1874 *N. Y. World* 28 Aug. 4/4. The comments of the Republican press, could be made to "fire the Northern heart" to a renewed support of the Republican candidates for office.

firebrand resolutions.

Calhoun's resolutions of 1847 dealing with slavery in the territories. [ ]

in Benton *Thirty Years View* II.697. When these resolutions were read, Mr. Benton rose in his place, and called them "firebrand.". . . These resolutions of 1847, called fire-brand at the time, were further characterized as nullification a few days afterwards. . . .

See INCENDIARY.

fire eaters.

A. Fanatical advocates of Southern rights.

1833 *Niles' Reg.* 19 Jan. 332/1 [from *Sumterville* (S.C.) *Whig*] . . . it is not the union men generally—the spiritless submissionists, as they have been scornfully termed—but chiefly the brave spirits, the pinks of chivalry, the fire and brimstone eaters, who have suddenly been enlightened as to the vast advantages of the western country.
1846 *Quincy Whig* 10 Jan. 2/3. Let Mr. Polk, father Richie, Judge Douglas, little Walker, and other fire-eaters, be obliged to do their share of the fighting, and who does not know that the matter would be more likely to be amicably arranged without an appeal to arms.
1854 *N. Y. Trib.* 21 June 1/5. Mr. Taber of the Charleston Mercury (the organ of the South Carolina fire eating clique) . . . .
1859 *Greenville* (Ohio) *Jrnl.* 3 Aug. 2/3. He is not one of the "fire-eaters," but as conservative in his opinions and in his actions as any man of the Southern Democracy.
1860 *Boston Transcript* 12 Oct. 2/2. The "Wendell Phillips of the South" [Yancey] —a genuine fire-eater—is to address the Democrats at Faneuil Hall tonight.
1861 Richardson *Secret Service* 88. The Fire-Eaters are intensely bitter upon the border States for refusing to plunge into the whirlpool of Secession.

B. The term is later used in its general meaning without reference to slavery or Southern rights:

1916 in Sullivan *Our Times* V.244. This policy may not satisfy . . . the fire-eater or the swashbuckler, but it does satisfy the mothers of the land. . . .

fireside chat.

On March 12, 1933, Franklin D. Roosevelt introduced to the public the type of radio report that came to be known by this name. Whether the term was used at that time is uncertain. In the volume of his *Public Papers* published in 1938, Roosevelt comments:

II.60n. The following is the first so-called fireside chat, which has been applied by the Press to the various radio reports I have made to the people of the Nation. It had been my custom as Governor. . . . The name "fireside chat" seems to be used by the Press even when the radio talk is delivered on a very hot mid-summer evening.

Evidently the word has an old tradition:

1821 *Niles' Reg.* XXI.196. It is now more than six months since I held a fire-side conversation with my numerous readers and friends, on things of deep interest to them and myself, as joint members of the government of the U. States.

Compare also:

1871 Lowell *My Study Window.* The simple confidence, the fireside plainness, with which Mr. Lincoln always addresses himself to the reason of the American people.

fireside policy.

Refers to an early feeling of isolationism in the House of Representatives. [ ]

John Randolph in *Gt. Deb.* II.260 . . . if there be not something behind this nothing which divides this House into two unequal parts, one the advocate of a splendid system of crusades, the other the friends of peace and harmony, the advocates of a *fireside policy;* for, as has truly been said, as long as all is right at the fireside, there cannot be much wrong elsewhere?

first flash in the pan.

A humorous counterpart of *first gun:* the gun that sparks but does not go off.

1850 *N. Y. Trib.* 28 Oct. 4/3. First Flash in the Pan. We understand that the candidate of the Bogus Committee declined the honor of being beaten for Assemblyman in the First District.

first gun.

The opening of a campaign; also the first election reports.

1838 *Ohio St. Jrnl.* 20 July 2/2. First Gun for a New Congress! [returns from Louisiana]

1840 *Rough-hewer* 48/1. First Gun from Illinois.

1876 Hayes *Diary* 4 Oct. III.364. The good omen of the day is that Colorado, the first State to elect electors (or rather a Legislature that will elect electors), has been carried by the Republicans. "First gun for Hayes," is the headline of the *Journal*.

1880 *Ib.* 11 June III.601. Oregon begins the campaign with a good first gun.

See BOOM, PRAIRIE ON FIRE.

fishing expedition.

A political trial venture, often for the primary purpose of testing public reaction.

1924 Stokes *Chip* 203 . . . many voters, undoubtedly, were willing to accept the Republican explanation that it [story of Harding scandal] was just "a political fishing expedition". . . .

1929? Lindley *Roosevelt* 265. He commented on the bill's "obvious lack of good faith," and pointed out that the power to undertake "any general fishing expedition" rested with the Legislature alone.

The fishing metaphor has long been popular in politics, especially in reference to the activities of a prominent figure who takes no active part in supporting his party during a campaign.

1876 *Cinc. Comm.* 2 July 2/2. There has been a great deal of inquiry as to whom Carl Schurz was going for in the Presidential campaign. Perhaps he is not going for anybody, but is going a-fishing.

Flannel-mouthed Bourbon. [ ]

1875 *N. Y. Trib.* 22 Oct. 5/1 "Flannel-mouthed Bourbon" is the last political title. The Washington Chronicle invented it as the proper description of Senator Bayard.

The origin of this phrase may be explained by the following:

Irvin S. Cobb's Own Recipe Book 15. Among the more advanced and cultured of that remote age, Flip sometimes was improved by breaking a raw goose egg into the dram before serving. It was then known as "A Yard of Flannel." People who couldn't afford a goose egg might use instead a hen's egg or, in emergency, even a wild pigeon's egg. Hence the familiar quotation: "The short and simple flannels of the poor."

floaters (floating population, floating vote).

The increase in number of immigrants together with the ease with which change of residence was effected created early difficulties, since the new arrivals tended to become an unstable element in politics. *Niles' Register* of 1835 refers to this situation:

27 June 289/1. We have several times seen an allusion made in the New York papers, to the remark of a distinguished politician of that state, made in the convention of 1822, as to the power of what he called the "Floating Population" over the result of elections. . . . And it is the "Floating population" that commands in many of our cities, and, by force, does what it pleases, through *combinations* which the fixed population cannot indulge in. . . . have always considered the gift of suffrage to the "floating population" alluded to, as a casting of "The Children's Bread unto Dogs". . . .

Somewhat later the expression *floating vote* makes its appearance:

1847 *Knickerbocker* April 328. There is yet a third and numerous class, who are destitute of the facilities for information, and who know but little of the principles which distinguish the two political parties of the country.... They are in the market, and the highest bidder is sure of their suffrages. Such constitute what in common parlance is called the "floating vote." 1856 *Cinc. Enquirer* 7 May 4/1. Fremont, having been a successful explorer and trapper, can discover and trap a great many floating votes. 1876 *Cinc. Daily Gazette* 27 June 1/1. Tilden's managers ... working hard to secure the floating vote. 1888 *Nation* 22 Nov. 412. Let us see how this "floating" vote was manipulated.

The short form *floater* appears almost as early as *floating vote:*
1847 *Knickerbocker* April 329. Early the next morning the "floaters" were marched in single file, with votes in hand, to the ballot box. 1888 *Nation* 22 Nov. 412. The number of "floaters," i.e., of marketable voters, in the entire state [Indiana] is said to be 30,000. ... It would seem that even the Hoosier floater cannot live by free whiskey alone. 1892 *Nation* 17 Nov. 368/2 ... so large a percentage of the money clings to the dirty fingers through which it must pass before it reaches the "floater" or other person whose vote it is to buy.

flop (per).

A change of support for an issue or a candidate; one who makes this sudden change.
1880 *Cleve. Leader* 8 June 1/7. On the twenty-fifth ballot the Florida flopper went to Sherman and the North Carolina chap to the financier. 1880 *N. Y. World* 22 Nov. 5/1. Mr. Skinner's apparent flop on the railroad question is injuring his chances in the Speakership struggle. 1881 *Ib.* 14 Jan. 1/6. Following the circumstantial evidence of the "flop" of the Wheeler men came numerous conferences. 1884 *Puck* 6 Aug. 359/1. The name of In-

dependents can change base without being "floppers." That's what's in a name. It is not the Independents who have "flopped" this time. It is the Republican Party that has "flopped" from honesty to dishonesty. 1892 *Ohio St. Jrnl.* 28 Oct. 4/3. The Fate of a Flopper [head].

flunky.

A hanger-on.

Apparently a Scottish word designating a manservant of the lower order, probably introduced in America through Burns' well-known poem "The Twa Dogs": His flunkies answer at the bell.

(See HODDEN GRAY)

Mostly applied to Northern supporters of Southern policies (See DOUGHFACE, LACKEY).
1850 *Julian Sp.* 44. The miserable flunkies of a God-forsaken Southern slave-hunter. 1854 *N. Y. W. Trib.* 25 Feb. 2/1. It is well-known that our Legations abroad have been nests of Flunkeyism. 1860 *Bobolink Songster* 55. Forward the Ninth! This was the watchword of the Flunkies (i.e., Seymour Democrats) during the last election in Connecticut. 1862 *Madison Co.* (Ohio) *Dem.* 20 Nov. 1/6. To thee [Lincoln] all office seekers cry aloud, "Flunkeydom," and all the powers therein.

fly the track.

To *bolt* (q.v.).
1840 *Ohio St. sw. Jrnl.* 17 June 1/3. Mr. W. G. Childress, a Van Buren candidate for Elector in Tennessee, has backed out, and declines to stand the canvass. This makes the fifth or sixth in that State that have flown the track. 1847 *Cong. Globe* 4 Feb. 322/2. I had been accused of flying the track on the creed of the Democratic party.

fly-up-the-creek.

Dialect name of the small American heron, used as a nickname of the Democrats during the campaign of 1844.

Another local name for the bird is *shite poke* with all possible variations, which was used for one of the innumerable puns on Polk's name (see POLKSTALK and other Polk puns).

1844 *Buckeye Eagle* 10 July 4/1.
The "fly-up-the-creek" a "Poke" we call,
That stretches its neck and tries to look tall
Its legs are long and its body is small
But this Tennessee "Polk's" no body at all.
. . . .
These Lokies at lying are certainly clever,
They swear a "Poke weed" was a Hickory ever;
Their shy "Polk" too is an Eagle forever,
As squawking it flies to the head of Salt River.

1844 *Ib.* 3 July 4/1. The Locos, we presume, will soon be at the head of the creek, as they have got a "fly-up-the-creek," for their leader!
1844 *Ib.* 26 June 2/1. What a sorry flock of owls, and buzzards, and carrion-crows was the Baltimore Convention, to select a "fly-up-the-creek" for their leader!
1844 *Ib.* 14 Aug. 3/2. Last Thursday, a fly-up-the-creek from the grand aerie at Columbus, with his head full of Pole-arity, brought in his lean beak. . . .
1844 *Frankfort Commonwealth* 25 June 2/2. The Louisville Journal makes merry over the ornithological synonym of the Loco nominee for the Presidency, having recently made some amusing references to the semi-aquatic bird, the poke. One of the common names of the bird is the "fly-up-the-creek"; . . . It is best known . . . by the very pretty common name of the "shite poke."
1846 *Ib.* 31 March 2/6. On the 4th of March after that of the year 1849, this delectable carterer [sic] for Locofoco palates will have a fine chance of displaying his divine skill in serving up dead fly-up-the-creeks for the lean stomachs of his Locofoco customers.

Forester.

A secret political society in New York. Coined, perhaps, as a pun upon the name of its leader, Fernando Wood.

1858 *N. Y. sw Trib.* 19 March 2/2. "The Foresters" is the name assumed by one of the last devised of these dark conspiracies against independence and popular freedom, of which the specific purpose is the recovery by Fernando Wood and his creatures of the control of Tammany Hall.

forgotten man.

The phrase allegedly used by Lord Byron (¿) was given currency by William Graham Sumner, who said in 1883:

The Forgotten Man and other Essays 491 Such is the Forgotten Man. . . . He is a commonplace man. He gives no trouble. He excites no admiration. He is not in any way a hero (like a popular orator); nor a problem (like tramps and outcasts); nor notorious (like criminals); nor an object of sentiment (like the poor and weak); nor a burden (like paupers and loafers); nor an object out of which social capital may be made (like the beneficiaries of church and state charities); nor an object for charitable protection (like animals treated with cruelty); nor the object of a job (like the ignorant and illiterate); nor one over whom sentimental economists and statesmen can parade their fine sentiments (like inefficient workmen and shiftless artisans). Therefore, he is forgotten. All the burdens fall on him, or on her, for it is time to remember that the Forgotten Man is not seldom a woman.

From this it is clear that by the *Forgotten Man* Sumner meant the quietly useful, unassuming citizen; however, Franklin D. Roosevelt proved that political capital, at least, could be made out of this type when he said on April 7, 1932:

These unhappy times call for the building of plans that rest upon the forgotten, the unorganized but indispensable units of economic power, for plans like those of 1917 that build from the bottom up, and not from the top down, that put their faith once more in the forgotten man.

From then on the phrase was often repeated and became more or less a synonym of *underprivileged* or *downtrodden* (q.v.) .

1945 Mencken *Supplement* I.303. The forgotten man of Sumner was the hardworking, self-supporting fellow who pays his own way in the world and asks for no favors from anyone. Roosevelt converted him, by a curious perversion, into a mendicant beneficiary of the New Deal doles.

forty thieves.

A group of politicians with control of the public finances and offices.

The political forty thieves may be actual plunderers like their Arabian Nights prototypes, or they may be only the targets of unfair epithets from the jealous opposition.

1820? in Van Buren *Autobio.* 104. Their [a group of Federalists'] demonstration against the Governor secured for them from his friends the less flattering sobriquet of "the forty thieves."
1832 Anti-Van Buren broadside in Lynch *Epoch and the Man* 357. The greatest robber, the best distributor of the spoils. Overture to the Forty Thieves.
1853 *N. Y. Trib.* 25 March 4/2. There are several earnest Reformers in our City Delegation ... but we fear the majority are Aldermen's men and will do anything to screen the Forty Thieves that they can do and not leave their track uncovered.
1870 *Nation* 31 March 200/2. No bill, however unobjectionable, could pass, it is said, unless it paid contribution to the "Forty Thieves"—an organized band [in S.C.], some of whom were white, some colored, some Democrats, and some Republicans.

fossil.

The background for the political use of the word is the splitting up of both major parties into conservative and progressive wings prior to the Civil War.

1853 "Warrington" *Pen Portraits* 201. Letter to the Whigs (Coalition) .... Set not your faces against everything that has an unwonted appearance. Be modern men, and not antique fossils.
1858 *Sandusky Comm. Reg.* 8 Nov. 2/2 ... Old Line Whigs—those fossils who still claim to be Whigs when no such party organization exists.
1859 Strong *Diary* II.473 ... the Old Line Whigs, the fossil remains of an extinct party.
1871 *Ann. of Cleve.* No.3600. While the fossil Democracy are rubbing their eyes in wonder at the political transformations which have taken place during their Rip Van Winkle slumber, the live and lively Republicans will carry off the laurels....

See DINOSAUR, ANTEDILUVIAN.

freebooter.

A variant of *filibusterer.*

1853 in *Ann. of Cleve.* No.157. An armed band of "Free-Booters" left San Francisco for Sonora. They landed at La Paz, lower California, seized the town, imprisoned its governor, and made a proclamation of the independence of the province! It is a deserted place, and far away from the thickly settled parts. This shows the prudence of the so called patriots. But even here they will be hunted out and beaten, for they have no strength and no means to maintain even that place. One thing will follow, we take it. Santa Anna will improve the golden opportunity to perfect his scheme. Whatever the fate of the "Free-Booters," Santa Anna will reap a harvest out of their action.
1853 *N. Y. Trib.* 25 March 4/3. A really just and wholesome (libel) act is most desirable, not for the restriction of honorable publishers, but for the control of the ephemeral and irresponsible, the free-

booters of ink and type, whose trade is slander and whose sustenance is wrung from black mail and mental prostitution.
1855 *San Diego Daily Union* 14 Dec. 2/6 ... that band of political freebooters who style themselves ... the republican party.

Free Democracy.

A party organized by Democrats opposed to slavery.

The Douglas quotations suggest that the name was occasionally used to disguise Republicans.
1848 *Ann. of Cleve.* No.1112. John Van Buren, this noble son of "Young" New York, who has recently been baptized in the name of "Free Democracy," spoke yesterday.
1849 *Hamilton Intelligencer* 26 July 2/2. "Free Democracy" is the new name for an old thing ... known during its brief existence by the names of Abolitionism, Libertyism, Free Soilism, and now "Free Democracy.". . . This newly renovated party styles itself the *Free* Democracy implying the existence of a Slave Democracy.
1849 in "Warrington" *Pen Portraits* 42. "The American" will be a political paper, advocating the principles, and supporting the organization, of the Free Democracy of the state and the nation.
1858 Douglas in Sparks *Deb.* 218. What is that name of "Free Democrats" put forth for, unless to deceive the people, and make them believe that Trumbull and his followers are not the same party as that which raises the black flag of Abolitionism in the northern part of this State, and makes war upon the Democratic party throughout the State? ...
341. The reason that Lincoln and his party adopted the name of "Free Democracy" down there was because Monroe County has always been an old-fashioned Democratic county, and hence it was necessary to make the people believe that they were Democrats.

free enterprise.

A. With words like *private enterprise* and *individual enterprise*

on the one hand and *free competition* on the other already common, it is natural that the formula *free enterprise* should be coined.
1913 Wilson in Heckscher *Politics of W. Wilson* 196f. It is absolutely imperative that we should give the business men of this country a banking and currency system by means of which they can make use of the freedom of enterprise and of individual initiative which we are about to bestow upon them.... This it can not be unless the resourceful business men who are to deal with the new circumstances are to have at hand and ready for use the instrumentalities and conveniences of free enterprise which independent men need when acting on their own initiative.

B. Since *laissez faire* had become a controversial word, *free enterprise* was often substituted for it in order to avoid invidious connotations, especially since 1938.
1932 *Readers' Guide* VIII.953/2. Free Enterprise. See LAISSEZ FAIRE.
1938 *Newsweek* 3 Oct. 37/3. Management leaders representing the world's democratic countries agreed that free enterprise, not government control, is the key to better times.
1939 in Nourse *Price Making* 48. The contribution that American industry can make to the national welfare depends upon the preservation of free enterprise and individual initiative.
1940 J. Howard Pew in Nourse *Price Making* 26. Our American system of free enterprise is far more than just a way of doing business. It is a system which at its best comprehends good sportsmanship; gives free play to the laws of supply and demand and of competition; produces an ever-improving standard of living; develops initiative, character, and discipline; and in many ways goes far toward improving the morale and bettering the lives of our people.... For a democratic government to destroy free enterprise, is for that government to destroy itself.
1943 *Fortune* Nov. 138. An excellent prec-

edent in cutting through this terminological porridge was recently established by Mr. Eric Johnston, President of the U.S. Chamber of Commerce, in calling for the supplanting of such mealymouthed phrases as the "free-enterprise system" and the "American way of life" by the precise scientific term "capitalism."

1944 Nourse *Price Making* 432. The free enterprise which the Founding Fathers of the American economic system sought under the emancipated conditions of a new land was democratic or individual free enterprise.

1944 Willkie *An Am. Program* 12. The American people believe in a life of enterprise and expansion by individual initiative. But all the talk today of a "return" to free enterprise and private initiative is merely an expression of feeling; not a solution of problems. . . . 29. Monopolies and monopolistic prices threaten the very existence of the free enterprise system.

1945 *Newsweek* 4 Jan. 54. Many times in the more than six years this column has been running, the term "individual enterprise" has been used to designate that economic organization which, along with our system of representative democracy, has made America. Other persons use such terms as "private enterprise," "free enterprise," "competitive enterprise," and so forth.

1953 Truman in Koenig *Truman Admin.* 254. Our economy has grown tremendously. Free enterprise has flourished as never before.

free soil.

In an economic rather than a strictly political sense *free soil* was early used to refer to farms free from mortgage:

1834 in Seward *Life* 239. Seward with Free Soil, or Marcy with Mortgage [campaign slogan].

One reference alludes to the neglected flats and overslaugh in the Hudson River, nicknamed "Marcy's Farm":

Those who have land like Marcy's farm
  Where naught but sloops take root,
May pawn it and sustain no harm—
But free soil brings forth fruit.

The use of *free soil* as a party name is presaged by a Democratic resolution of 1847, evidently influenced by Drake's poem (see below):

1847 *Ohio Statesman* 7 Jan. 2/3. Resolved, that the "democratic platform," is as broad and firm as the free soil protected by the stars and stripes of Columbia's flag; and as free for all to meet and stand upon, as the pure air that freemen breathe.

The stage for the further development of *free soil* into high politics was set by the Wilmot Proviso which forbade slavery in the territory acquired from Mexico. The first step is taken by D. D. Field at the Syracuse Convention of October, 1847; in which he quoted from Joseph Rodman Drake's poem "The American Flag":

1847 *N. Y. Trib.* 5 Oct. 2/3. Mr. Field paid a tribute to the gallantry of our army, and said they might carry their victorious standard to the isthmus of Darien, or plant it if they chose on the highest peak of the Polynesian Islands; but we must come out of the combat as we went in—

"With Freedom's soil beneath our feet
And Freedom's banner waving o'er us."

Another speaker—Brooks—contrasted free and slave soil at the same convention:

1847 *N. Y. Trib.* 9 Oct. 1/1. But we will not pour out the blood of our countrymen, if we can help it, to turn a Free into a Slave soil.

At the Herkimer Convention a month later *Free Soil* became one of the slogans of the party:

1847 *Ann. of Cleve.* 3 Nov. No. 981. They pledge the party to the Wilmot Proviso, and raise the banner of Free Trade, Free Soil, Free Labor and Free Speech.

In the following year a formal party was organized. L. E. Chittenden may be justified in saying that he and a group of friends were the first to suggest *Free Soil* as a party name:

in *Personal Reminiscences* 8. "I move," he [Field] read, "that we organize a new party to be called the 'Free Soil Party'...."

The formula consisting of the repetition of *free* set by the Herkimer Convention was reiterated with occasional variations:

1848 *Indianapolis St. Sentinel* 8 Jan. 2/3. The New York Evening Post, one of the organs of the "Barnburners," announces the following creed: "Free Trade, Free Soil, Free Labor and Free Speech."

1848 *Hamilton Intelligencer* 13 July 2/4 [Resolutions of Worcester Convention, June, 1848]. Massachusetts goes now, will ever go, for Free Soil and Free Men for Free Lips and a Free Press, for a Free Land [and] a Free World.

The slogan actually survived the party, for in 1856 Fremont, the Republican candidate, ran on the Free Soil slogan. In this instance, the presence of the syllable "free" in the candidate's name made *Fremont* a fitting addition to the established pattern:

1856 *Ann. of Cleve.* No.2329. Free Speech! Free States! Fremont!

1856 *Ib.* No.2371. Free Speech, Free Press, Free Soil, Free Men, Fremont and Victory!

A pun upon the name *Free Soil* was offered by Daniel Webster when Van Buren became one of the leaders of the new party:

1848 Webster *Works* II.434. That the leader of the Free Spoil party should so suddenly become the leader of the Free Soil party would be a joke to shake his sides and mine.

front porch campaign.

A. The McKinley campaign of 1900, which he conducted from the front porch of his home in Canton, Ohio.

1900 *Cleve. Leader* 26 June 7/1. "Front Porch Campaigns." "Front Porch campaign" stories have been coming from the East for months past, only to be denied the next day.

1921 Depew *Memories* 150. Mr. McKinley's front-porch campaign was a picturesque and captivating feature.

B. In 1920 the front porch also figured in the Harding campaign.

1920 *Nation* 25 Sept. 342/2. Front Porching With Harding [head].

to fry fat (out of).

To obtain money for campaign purposes by high pressure tactics.

Based upon the then well-known meaning of *fat* (q.v.), the metaphor was first used in the campaign of 1888:

in Sullivan *Our Times* I.294n. Hanna was called "the fat-fryer." Henry L. Stoddard writes me: "Hanna was *a* fat-fryer, but not *the* fat-fryer. *The* fat-fryer was John P. Forster, President of the League of Young Republican Clubs. It was in 1888 that he wrote a letter suggesting 'to fry the fat out of the manufacturers.' "

In a *Nation* editorial of the same year (26 July, p. 64) the same basic information is given; however the "famous confidential circular" it speaks of was written by James P. Foster, President of the Republican League of the United States. He wrote:

"If I had my way about it, I would put the manufacturers of Pennsylvania under the fire and fry all the fat out of them."

Later quotations comment upon this campaign of '88 and add further examples from subsequent presidential elections:

1890 *Cong. Record* 26 July 7790/1. I did not suppose there had been any authority of law for "frying the fat" out of the manufacturers in the last presidential campaign.
1892 Schurz *Writings* V.95. Republican leaders notified the protected manufacturers...that unless they permitted "fat to be fried out of them" for the benefit of the Republican party, they need not expect any further tariff favors.... The fat-frying process proceeded vigorously.
1904 *Nation* 28 April 321. His main qualification is admitted to be that of a good collector of funds. No one could, in the historic phrase, fry out more fat.

See FAT; FAT CAT; FAT OFFICE.

fugleman.

In the military sense, an especially expert and well-drilled soldier placed in front as a model for the other troops (from the German *flügelmann*) (*OED*).

In politics it is synonymous with *file leader* or *henchman*.

1835 *Frankfort Commonwealth* 1 Aug. 3/3. Adrian is a Frenchman, ... speaking always in French, which is translated by a fugleman on his left.
1838 *N. Y. Herald* 6 June 4/1. David Graham, Jr. was the file leader of the Whigs, and Alderman Tallmadge performed the part of fugleman to the loco focos in admirable style.
1840 Kennedy *Quodlibet* 218. Keep your eye upon Amos Kendall who has consented to act as fugleman.
1852 *Ohio St. Jrnl.* 14 Jan. 2. Prominent among the wire workers and fuglemen at the Eighth of January Convention was....
1860 *Cols. Gazette* 20 July 2/1. It is time

that fuglemen of this style were played out. It is time that the Augean Stables in this locality, filled as they are with filth and corruption, should be cleansed. It is time that the gump heads, mutton heads, blabbers, dogberrys, toadies, bloats, and other small beer politicians should be shuffed out.

This paper's remark that a certain type of fugleman should be taken out of the political scene may reflect the loss of popularity of the term and its replacement by other words such as *henchman*.

full dinner pail.

The slogan and symbol of the McKinley campaign of 1900.

The dinner pail as a visual symbol of full employment and good wages is found in a Thomas Nast cartoon of 1880 (*Harper's W.*, 16 Oct. 657), in which the contrast between Republican and Democratic promises is dramatized by the picture of two workers, one eating from a full dinner pail, the other protesting because his is empty. Again in W. H. Harvey's *Coin's Financial School* (21), published in 1894, the dinner pail is an important symbol of the difference between bimetallism and monometallism.

Apparently *full dinner pail* was a slogan within the labor movement already in 1894:

1894 Roosevelt *Ltrs.* I.399. I hear all around that the working men intend to vote "for the policy of a full dinner pail," as one of them in the village told my friend and coachman, Hall.

In the campaign of 1900.

1900 *Rev. of Rev.* XXII.543. Hurrah for a full ballot-box, a full dinner-pail, and continued prosperity!

1900 *Ib.* XXII.551 [Picture of huge dinner pail featured in parade in Youngstown, Ohio]. Four Years More of the Full Dinner Pail.

Later uses (see also FULL GARAGE) :
1908 Debs *Speeches* 316 ... the very party of "prosperity" which, on the strength of the "full dinner pail"....
1929 Alfred E. Smith *Up to Now* 408. Nevertheless the Republican party resorted to its old tactics and once more brought down from the garret the old full dinner pail, polished it up and pressed it into service.

full garage.
An elaboration of *full dinner pail.*
1928 Hoover in *Time* 29 Oct. 10/2. The slogan of progress is changing from the full dinner pail to the full garage.

fusion.
Disraeli tells us that in the 1840's *fusion* was a fashionable word in English politics:
Sybil 22. Political conciliation became the slang of the day, and the fusion of parties the babble of the clubs.

In the U.S. the new party alignment before and after 1850 leads to a great number of political coalitions to which, probably through British influence, the word *fusion* is frequently applied.

Similar tactics of an earlier date used to be designated as *coalition* or *combination:*
1855 *Hickory Flail and Fusion Thresher* 19. Sept. 1/1. One of the cardinal doctrines of the Fusion party in Ohio is to forget all antecedents. No matter what a man has been—no matter what he has done, provided that he will fuze now....
c1854 in Julian *Speeches* 130. Fusion was the magic sound that charmed all ears....

Thus was inaugurated our "Fusion" or "People's Party."
1878 in Hamilton *Blaine* 452. In Maine a Third party was in the field, known as the fusionists,—"greenback" or "fiat money" Republicans—ready, as the name suggests, to combine with the Democrats whenever it might seem desirable.

Like its predecessors, *coalition* and *combination, fusion* frequently is tainted by the connotation of sacrifice of principles. Characteristic in this respect is an anecdote of a railroad traveller who perceiving that the train had run over a skunk called out, "Conductor! Conductor! stop the train; we've run over a fusionist." (*Marshall* [Michigan] *Democratic Expounder,* 6 December, 1855, 2/5) .

G

gag (-bill, -law, etc.).
An act curbing the privilege of speech or writing.
A. Apparently first used in England:
1798 *Poetry of the Anti-Jacobin* 116.
But they deserve the worst of ills,
And all th' abuse of all our quills,
Who form'd of strong and *gagging Bills**
        A cross pair.
*These "Gagging Bills," of 1796, required that notice should be given to the magistrate of any public meeting to be held on political subjects; he was authorized to be present, and empowered to seize those guilty of sedition on the spot; and a second offence against the act was punishable with transportation. So exasperated were the Opposition with this measure that Mr. Fox and a large part of the minority withdrew altogether for a considerable time from the House.

B. Introduced into American politics to refer to the Sedition Act of 1798.

1798 *Aurora* 12 July in Smith *Freedom's Fetters* 110. May the friends of the Gag-bill sleep in oblivion until the angel Gabriel sounds his last trumpet.
1808 Adams *Works* IX.604. I would not repeal it, though it should raise a clamor as loud as my gag-law, or your grog-law, or Mr. Jefferson's embargo.
1824 *Cinc. Nat. Rep.* 18 June 2/4. Wonder if they mean the Alien or the Sedition Law? better known as the Gag-Law.
1864 Jones *Mirror of Modern Democracy* 34. The Sedition Act, especially, was held up to public opprobrium as the "gag law."

C. Later examples show that the name *gag law* was attached to any measure which was felt to be an unjust violation of the freedoms guaranteed by the Bill of Rights. Members of Congress considered it oppressive when debate was denied or limited, particularly on the May 26, 1836, House rule against petitions dealing with slavery.

1835 *Liberator* in Garrison *Garrison Story* App. 394. Cease your anathemas against the Vatican, and screw your courage up to resist the worse than papal bulls of Georgia, demanding, at the peril of your "bread and butter," the "Heads" of your citizens, and the passage of GAG-LAWS!
1841 Calhoun in Benton *Thirty Years' View* II.251. Did the senator from Kentucky [Clay] mean to apply to the Senate the gag law passed in the other branch of Congress? ... What is the difference, in principle, between his gag law and the alien and sedition law?
1874 *Cleve. Leader* 4 July 4/5. The great statesmen who engineered the press gag-law through Congress erred greatly if they hope to frighten the newspapers.
1880 *Cinc. Daily Gazette* 27 May 5/2. Gen. Grant is the only Republican candidate whose hope of nomination depends solely on the *gag law* and the unit rule.
1880 Brisbin *Garfield* 399. It had settled the Illinois district contestants at the expense of eighteen votes for Grant (this was a question of whether delegates elected by a gag-law convention or by the districts should be seated) .

D. Variations in form:

1803 *Old South Leaflets* 259. Their personal cowardice would be a sufficient "gag act" to check their insolence.
1876 *Cinc. Comm.* 4 Feb. 4/4. The *Times* speaks of "gagrule" in connection with the pressure of time in the Southern Railroad appropriation.
1876 *Cinc. Daily Gazette* 17 June 1/5. Will Cumback and Col. Thompson, of Indiana, supported Mr. Dutcher in his efforts to force the Chair to permit him to be heard, but failed in the general hubbub. Mr. Dutcher, getting excited, yelled, "A gag game is being played."
1880 *Harper's W.* 19 June 386/1. The attempt of the Grant interest in the Committee upon Rules to gag dissenting delegates with the unit rule.
1880 *Ib.* 3 July 418/2. The unit rule is merely a gag and suppression of the minority before the point has been reached which the majority must rightfully determine.
1935 Michael *Handout* 87. The bill was rushed through the House under a gag rule.

galvanized corpse.

One attempting a political comeback.

A. Following the first description by Galvanus in 1792 of the powers of galvanic action, there were apparently many attempts to revive the dead by this process. Although our first quotation is late, we may be sure it is indicative of a common practice.

1840 *Niles' Reg.* 11 Jan. 320/1. Galvinism. The Lancaster Intelligencer, after giving the particulars of the recent execution of Kobler at the jail of that place, publishes some details of the experiments which were afterwards made on the body with the galvanic battery, electrical machine, &c. After artificial breathing was established by means of a bellows, the galvanic battery was applied; upon this, Kobler moved his arms and legs, his left hand was raised from the box upon which he lay to his breast, and his fingers were opened and shut, as if to catch something, his features expressed every passion, his eyes were opened and closed rapidly, his jaws moved as if chewing, and he breathed with sufficient power to blow out a candle five times in succession.

1871 Calkins *Opium* 364. The case is as that of a dead man suddenly galvinized into full life again.

B. In politics:

1836 in *N. Y. Pub. Lib. Bul.* V.191, 195. A Galvanized Corpse [title of cartoon showing Francis Blair as corpse rising from coffin; a devil standing by says, "Lose him! No. But it's all for our gain that he should be galvanized."].

[Another cartoon of 1836, Loco Foco and Nullification Nuptials, has Blair saying, "Now we will see if Pikens (sic) dare say again that I am a 'galvanized Corps' (sic) &c.&c."]

1840 in Norton *Tippecanoe* App. 42.
And there lay Calhoun with his nostrils
    all wide,
And the "galvanized corpse" lay dark by
    his side.

1840 Kennedy *Quodlibet* 233. Ever since New Light Democracy and Nullification have shaken hands and sworn eternal friendship, or—in the poetical language of Theodore Fog, "ever since that Prodigy of Weathercocks, the great Nullifier, first endured, then pitied and then embraced the Galvanized Corpse," there has been a notable race set on foot over the Hard Money Course.

1856 *Middletown Banner of Liberty* 47/3. The people here [Sullivan Co., Ind.] are on their guard against Abolitionism, white-washed Democracy, and galvanized Whiggery, knowing that they consider our glorious Constitution of no more value than last year's almanac, that is, compared with their higher law.

1872 *At. Mon.* XXX.762. The nation breathes freer in the security of its delivery from Greeley and his galvanized Democracy.

1932 Carter *What We Are About to Receive* 192. The Republicans are striving desperately to galvanize the corpse of Coolidge prosperity into spasmodic knee-jerks, so that the voters may believe that the dead do rise again.

C. During the Civil War the term, *galvanized Yankee* was applied to those Southerners who joined the Northern armies or were sympathetic to the Northern cause.

1863 Heartsill *1491 Days* 101. There is [sic] several lively conversations going on between our men and "galvanized" Yankees.

1865 Bowles *Across the Continent* 11. They are known in the army as "white-washed rebs," or as they call themselves, "galvanized Yankees."

General Mum.

1840 in Gunderson *Log Cabin Campaign* 236.
Another gourd for General Mum,
Whose fame is like his fav'rite drum;
Which when most empty makes most
    noise,
Huzza for General Mum, my boys.

1840 Harrison in Norton *Tippecanoe* 247. Fellow-citizens, you have undoubtedly seen it oftentimes stated in a certain class of newspapers that I am a very decrepit old man, obliged to hobble about on crutches; that I was caged up, and that I could not speak loud enough to be heard more than four or five feet distant, in consequence of which last misfortune I am stigmatized with the cognomen of "General Mum."

See also MUM CANDIDATE.

ghost vote.

Votes cast in the name of no longer existing individuals:

1944 *Life* 21 Aug. 76. With the help of 50,000 "ghost" votes (names taken from tombstones) Pendergast got him [Truman] elected.

gift enterprise.

A business which offers free gifts to attract patrons or purchasers:

1855 Holbrook *Among the Mail Bags* 343. One of the Peter Funk "Gift Enterprise" firms in a large city, sent a package of tickets to a post master in Maine.

1868 *Harper's W.* 27 June 410/1. *Gambling*, we are happy to say, has been put down—utterly abolished—nowadays we only *speculate*. There is not at this time a single "gambling hell" in New York city; they are all "club houses." All the lotteries throughout the country have been "restrained" by legal "injunctions," and only "gift enterprises" are tolerated.

There is little doubt that gift enterprises flourished at this time. A book, *Secrets of the Great City,* published in 1868, has an entire chapter on "Gift Enterprises" in which the author, Edward Winslow Martin, discusses the various swindling operations then current.

It is evident that the element of fraud entered into most gift enterprises and it is in this relation that we find the phrase adopted into the political vocabulary. In attacking Grant and his administration, Charles Sumner said:

1872 *Cong. Globe* 31 May 4122/2. If he appoints relations to office and repays gifts by official patronage making his Presidency "a great Gift Enterprise," may not every officeholder do likewise. . . .

1864 *N. Am. Rev.* Jan. 240. They had come to consider the government as a kind of public Gift Enterprise conducted

by themselves, and whose profits were nominally to be shared among the holders of their tickets, though all the prizes had a trick of falling to the lot of the managers.

1872 in *Perley's Reminiscences* II.310. General Grant had been the recipient of many presents, and the epoch had been styled by Charles Sumner one of "gift enterprises."

1886 *Perley's Reminiscences* II.513. In the "gift enterprise" of seats, a New York Representative, Mr. Stahlnecker, drew the first prise and selected a seat in the third row from the front.

gladhand.

The cordial greeting or handshake which has become one of the prime requisites of the successful politician.

1896 Ade *Artie* 4. Say, she treated me out o' sight. She meets me at the door, puts out the glad hand and says: "Hang up your lid and come into the game."

1898 *Rev. of Rev.* XVII.158. [cartoon] Hanna (Disfigured) Gives His Friends the "Glad Hand."

1900 *Rev. of Rev.* XXI.131. [cartoon: Uncle Sam being welcomed by other nations into China] The Glad Hand and the Open Door.

gladhander.

1931 *Wash. Merry-Go-Round* 112. Stimson's failure as a gladhander, brought to light so glaringly during the New York gubernatorial campaign, has remained a handicap throughout his life.

1948 *Jim Farley's Story* 28. I was the official glad hander and stimulator of the party faithful.

1950 Allen and Shannon *Truman Merry-Go-Round* 48. They came in droves. High-school classmates and wartime buddies, provincial editors and obscure politicians, business failures and lame ducks, the alumni of Pendergast politics and the bootblacking profession, country bankers and county judges, broken-down bureaucrats and professional glad-handers.

gladhanding.

1939 Michie *Dixie Demagogues* 207. Early in July [1938], Happy [Chandler] was stumping the hinterlands, glad-handing, back-slapping, and singing. At a typical meeting in western Kentucky, he entered a small town with all the fanfare of a circus parade.... the crowd was treated to an artful blend of politics, Holy Rollerism, and autobiography.

glover.

A politician who uses the handshaking technique to win votes.

1854 *Cong. Globe* App.1220. I have always found [Pres. Pierce] a very kind and agreeable man—what the "rounders" in New York would term a "glover."

See HANDSHAKER.

gobbledygook.

Bureaucratic jargon.

Coined by Maury Maverick of Texas in March, 1944, as a protest against the stilted language used in official government orders and publications. (See *Am. Sp.*, XIX.237.) In the *New York Times*, 21 May, 1944, Maverick offered an explanation of the word's creation:

People ask me where I got gobbledygook. I do not know. It must have come in a vision. Perhaps I was thinking of the old bearded turkey gobbler back in Texas, who was always gobbledy-gobbling and strutting with ludicrous pomposity. At the end of this gobble there was a sort of gook. [See "Vigilans," *Chamber of Horrors*, p. 16.]

1944 *Time* 10 April 57/1. Maury Maverick ... railed against what he called Washington's "gobbledygook" language.

1945 *Tuscaloosa News* 7 Aug. 4/3. The trouble is that the explanations sound like gobbledegook [sic] to me.

God's (own) country.

In a speech delivered in the House of Representatives on December 15, 1859, Clement Vallandigham said:

in *Record of Hon. C. L. Vallandigham* 45–6. Then, sir, I am not a Northern man, nor yet a Southern man; ... Sir, I am of and from the West; ... Seat yourself, denizen of the sterile and narrow, but beautiful hills and valleys of New England, and you, too, of the great cities of the North, whose geography and travel are circumscribed by the limits of a street railroad; seat yourself upon the summit of the Alleghanies, and behold spread out before you a country stretching from the Alleghany to the Rocky Mountains—from the Gulf of Mexico to the Canada frontier—with limitless plains, boundless forests, fifteen States, a hundred rivers, ten thousand cities, towns, and villages, and twelve millions of people. Such a vision no man ever saw; no, not even Adam, when, in the newness and grandeur of God-made manhood, he stood upon the topmost hill of Paradise, and looked down upon a whole hemisphere of the yet unpeopled world. That, sir, is my country; if I may speak it without profanity, God's own country.

Here the phrase is used as a vehicle for sectional rather than national feeling. The same is true of its use in the following examples:

1865 R. H. Kellogg *Rebel Prisons* 118. I was willing to work hard, if I could only get out of that horrible den, into God's country once more.

1867 Goss *Soldier's Story* 171. In referring to the North, as distinguished from the South, it was often spoken of as 'God's country'....

1906 H. D. Pittman *Belle of the Blue Grass* 1. I entered 'God's Country,' as the natives call that portion of Kentucky which lies within a radius of thirty miles of Lexington.

1914 Atherton *Perch of the Devil* 43. They always come home talking about ...

God's Own Country, and the Big Western Heart.

The first quotation found in which *God's own country* refers to the United States as a whole is:

1904 O. Henry *Cabbages and Kings* 298. A man had better be in God's country living on free lunch than there.

That the phrase is much earlier than our first quotation is suggested by the following passage extolling the attributes of Kentucky:

1788 in Littell *Pol. Trans.* 105. Examine the luxuriant soil which those rivers traverse; then we ask, can the God of wisdom and nature have created that vast country in vain? Was it for nothing that he blest it with a fertility almost incredible? Did he not provide those great streams which empty into the Mississippi, and by it communicate with the Atlantic, that other nations and climes might enjoy with us the blessings of our fruitful soil? View the country, and you will answer for yourselves.

gold bug.

In the early quotations *gold bug* refers to the rich Eastern bankers, who would benefit by the law that interest must be paid in gold:

1878 *Harper's W.* 23 Feb. 156. [Nast cartoon] Bloated Bondholder. Gold Bug.

1878 *N. Y. Trib.* 15 Aug. 4/2. It is asserted that great mischief is done by a promise to pay gold at some fixed date, because the "gold bugs"—in the elegant language of Western statesmen—have the power to squeeze the debtor by making gold scarce at the time of payment.

1890 McRae in *Cong. Record* 28 Jan. 6090/2. The gold bugs of the East and the silver kings of the West have come to an understanding.

1893 Hendrix in *Ib.* 26 Aug. App. 986/1. The American banker ... is pictured here as a shark in Wall Street; a gold bug east of the Alleghanies.

In 1896 during the McKinley-Bryan campaign the gold bugs were the supporters of McKinley and the gold standard, and they were often identified by a small gold button in their lapel:

1896 *Cinc. Enquirer* 30 July 1/7. I had a gold bug on my coat. A farmer came up to me and took hold of my coat collar and held the gold button up to view.

1896 *Rev. of Rev.* XIV.264. [cartoon showing Bryan plowing up "gold bugs."]

Democrats who favored the gold standard were also given the epithet of *gold bug:*

1896 Bryan *First Battle* 127. In some of the Western states the gold bugs have insisted that silver Democrats should pledge themselves to support the nominee before taking part in the selection of delegates ...a doctrine which it has no power to enforce against the goldbug Democrats of the East?

goloid dollar.

A dollar based upon a mixture of gold and alloys (gol[d] + oid like) :

1878 *N. Y. Trib.* 30 July 4/5. He didn't administer a goloid dollar to him, but gave him "vivopathy"—quack medicine instead of quack finance.

good enough Morgan.

An issue or argument known to be spurious but kept alive until after the election.

On September 12, 1826, a man named William Morgan mysteriously disappeared from confinement at Fort Niagara. Since he had threatened to divulge Masonic secrets, he was widely believed to have been murdered by members of this order. Shortly before the election of 1827 a body found on the shores of Lake Ontario was identified by a jury as that of Morgan, while members of the Masonic order insisted that it was a different man. In his autobiography (p. 319), Thurlow Weed tells the story of how the phrase "good enough Morgan" developed from this incident:

While talking with him, Ebenezer Griffin, Esq., one of the counsel of the "kidnappers," ... observed, laughingly to me, "After we have proven that the body found at Oak Orchard is that of Timothy Munroe, what will you do for a Morgan?" I replied in the same spirit, "That is a good enough Morgan for us until you bring back the one you carried off." On the following day a paragraph appeared in the "Rochester Daily Advertiser," saying that in a conversation I had boasted that the body referred to, whatever might be proven to the contrary, was a "good enough Morgan until after the election."

1849 *Wilmington* (N.C.) *Comm.* 5 May 2/2. The *Standard* has got it up as a "very good Morgan" for political effect.
1858 *Ohio Statesman* 16 Sept. 2/2. As for Gurley, he ... would make as "good a Morgan" as any until after the election.
1870 *Harper's W.* 658. Gen. Blair used to tell us during the campaign of 1868 that if General Grant were elected he would gradually, or even suddenly, change the republic into an empire. The General's assertion was considered as "a good enough Morgan," but probably neither that gentleman nor any of his hearers seriously supposed that the government was in great danger of being imperialized.

Variants:

1832 *Am. R. R. Jrnl.* I.165/3. Let him be Morganized, and his work suppressed by burning.
1860 *Sandusky Comm. Reg.* 22 Feb. 3/2 ... a number [of papers] went gravely to work to prove that our surmise in regard to the Sons having Morganed him for telling their secrets, was incorrect.

good neighbor (policy).

The claim that the term was originated by Franklin D. Roosevelt must be abandoned since the phrase had been prominently used by Hoover on his tour to South America following the election of 1928:

Hoover *Memoirs* II.213. I would wish to symbolize the friendly visit of one good neighbor to another. In our daily life, good neighbors call upon each other as the evidence of solicitude for the common welfare.... We have a desire to maintain not only the cordial relations of governments with each other but the relations of good neighbors.

Roosevelt used the phrase in his first inaugural address:

1933 In the field of world policy I would dedicate this Nation to the policy of the good neighbor—the neighbor who resolutely respects himself and, because he does so, respects the rights of others—the neighbor who respects his obligations and respects the sanctity of his agreements in and with a world of neighbors.
1946 Arnall *Shore* 21. Much depends upon the diplomatic policies of the future and upon whether the relationship with South America associated with Hull's "good neighbor policy" is continued or is displaced by a proposed system of imperialism.

goody goody.

The advocates of Civil Service Reform (q.v.) and to some extent the spokesmen for a conciliatory policy toward the South were frequently ridiculed as well-meaning, but entirely impractical idealists. *Goody-goody* is one of the terms in which this criticism is condensed.
1878 *Harper's W.* 4 May 346/1 ... sneering at the President as a goody goody Sunday school superintendent.
1878 *Ib.* 27 July. These were all inventions

of the glory-to-God-regards-to-Babcock statesmen, who especially abhor goody-goody and Sunday-school politics, which is their name for whatever threatens their ascendency.

1880 *Ib.* 514/2. When the worst that can be said of a man or of a government is that it is "goody," it needs no other vindication.

In 1884 *goody-goody* is absorbed by the rich list of epithets used against the mugwumps.

See SUNDAY SCHOOL POLITICS, HOLIER THAN THOU.

goo goos.

Satirical nickname for members of the Good Government Clubs which were active in securing municipal reforms in the 1890's. Obviously, the expression depends much upon the connotations afforded by the older *goody-goody*.

1895 *Roosevelt Ltrs.* 14 July I.466. The Goo-Goos, and all the German leaders ... have attacked me.

1895 *Ib.* 3 Oct. I.483. The Republican machine men have been loudly demanding a straight ticket; and those prize idiots, the Goo-Goos, have just played into their hands by capering off and nominating an independent ticket of their own.

c1895 in Steffens *Autobio.* 255. For him [Wm. Strong] were the "honest Republicans," the fine old aristocratic Democrats, the reformers called goo-goos after their Good Government Clubs, the "decent" newspapers, and the good people generally.

Goosey-gander Revolution.

A satirical reference, based upon the nomenclature adopted by the French revolutionists, to a convention of Ohio Democrats who advocated a change in the constitution and government of their state.

1848 *Ohio St. w. Jrnl.* 17 May 3/1. From and after this date, we shall commence our calculation of time from the epoch of the Revolution; and in order that our friends may have the correct date from which to commence, we hereby inform them that this day, the 12th of May, O.S., corresponds to the 3 Ventose (windy) of the year 1, of the Goosey-gander Revolution.

G.O.P.

The Republican party.

This abbreviation seems to date back to the 1880's:

1884 *N. Y. Trib.* 15 Oct. 4/5. "The G.O.P. Doomed," shouted the *Boston Post*.... The Grand Old Party is in condition to inquire....

1884 *Puck* 26 Nov. 196/3. Q is the G.O.P.'s Quarrels, now come.

1888 *Cong. Record* 1 May 3598/1 ... the doings of the G.O.P.—the grand old party —the Republican party.

1960 *Detroit News* 16 Aug. 18B/1. It has been the Nixon influence in the national committee since 1956 which has sought to capitalize on the new appeal of the GOP.

The **1884** and **1888** quotations seem to bear out the generally accepted opinion that *G.O.P.* stands for *grand old party*. This is somewhat doubtful in view of the fact that the phrase *the gallant old party* already occurs in 1875:

Cong. Record 454/2. Is it true that this gallant old party, that this gallant old ship that has sailed through troubled seas before is going to be stranded now upon the rock of fury that has been set up by a clamor in this chamber and a few newspapers in the country?

On the other hand the formula *grand old party* (not the abbreviation) can be traced back almost as far:

1876 *Cinc. Comm.* in *Harper's W.* 1884 576/3. Grand Old **Party**.

1878 *Nation* 19 Sept. 172/1. A more sobering incident [defeat in Maine] or one better calculated to promote reflection, could not, in fact, have befallen "the grand old party."
1880 in Brisbin *Life of Garfield* 380. Each shall vie with the other in carrying our grand old party through the coming contest to victory.

Note that the original formula is not the exclusive property of the Republican party.

1879 *Cong. Record* 1913/1. We are for national parties now. We come back to the grand old party of the North that never went off after secession, that never went after the Baals of consolidation. If there are any men on the earth for whom I have a higher regard than others, they are the democrats of the North.

gospel of hate.

A policy charged by the Democrats in the Reconstruction Period to the Republicans who, it was claimed, kept the bitterness of the Civil War fresh in the minds of Northerners to further their own political supremacy:

1876 *Harper's W.* 26 Feb. 162/2. They would declare unreservedly that the Republican party was rotten with abuses; that it was daily overthrowing the Constitution; that corruption reeked in every corner of the Administration; that its platform was a gospel of hate, and its policy in the Southern states a cruel Oriental despotism.
1876 *Ib.* 22 April 322/4. Democratic organs and orators must devise some other policy upon the Southern question than the stale and stupid cry that the Republicans hope to carry the election by waving the bloody shirt and preaching a gospel of hate.

government by alphabet. [ ]

1936 *Am. Speech* XII.4. In urban centers the new host of government bureaus was ridiculed as alphabet soup, alphabetical what-nots, and government by alphabet.

government by assassination. [ ]

1881 William *Hayes* II.364. General Banks says what frightens the world is, that it is an attempt to administer government by assassination.

government by commission. [ ]

1878 *Harper's W.* 5 Oct. 787/1 General Butler arraigns the system of "government by commission." Mr. Endicott answers in a manner to open the eyes and the minds of honest voters. There are, he says, "fifteen commissions, of which the total cost to the State". . . .

government by crony. [ ]

1946 *Am. Mag.* May 110. [Applied to Truman's alleged practice of surrounding himself with personal friends as political advisers.] But the Missouri flavor is strong around the White House itself. . . . And this has led to talk of "government by crony."

government by plunder. [ ]

1878 *Harper's W.* 10 Aug. 626/3. One of the most amusing stupid but consistent touters of the practice of government by plunder steadily shouts that a man is a consummate ass or a hopeless lunatic who does not think that practice to be the flower of practical statesmanship.

government of the people, by . . ., for. . . .

Lamon's statement that the phrase goes back to Wyclyf is not authenticated and is in itself rather improbable. The earliest known use of a similar formula is Hamilton's.

1775 *Writings* I.85. No laws have any validity or binding force without the consent and approbation of the people, given in the persons of their representatives, periodically elected by themselves.

Barlow's *Advice to the Privileged Orders,* 1792, comes closer:

in *Notes & Queries* CLXXXIX. 59. It (French Revolution) was an operation designed for the benefit of the people; it originated in the people, and was conducted by the people.

Other early American parallels:

1794 Thomas Cooper *Some Information Respecting America* (quoted in *Rev. of Rev.* 1901, p. 196) . The government is the government of the people and for the people.

1824 in Ward *Jackson* 134. The destiny of holding up to a benighted and struggling world the great example of a government of the people by the people themselves.

In 1830 Daniel Webster anticipated Lincoln in saying:

Works III.321 (Second Speech on Foote's Resolution) . It is, Sir, the people's Constitution, the people's government, made for the people, made by the people, and answerable to the people.

While the expression has a long American tradition, its popularity has probably been increased by influences from Germany, where in 1848 similar phrases were widely used.

Valentin *Frankfurt u. d. Rev.* 368. Demokraten sind die jenigen, welche die Herrschaft der Volkssouveramitat wollen, das heisst, das alles im Staate für und durch das Volk geschehe. (quoted from *Frankfurter Volkesblatt,* 1848)

Bauernfeld *Republik der Thiere* 24. Ich bin aus dem Volke, für das Volk, durch das Volk.

Marcel Herwegh *Briefe* 154. Wir sind deutsche Demokraten, wollen Alles für das Volk, Alles durch das Volk! (see also pp. 183,212)

It is apparent that these German slogans are used as a definition of democracy just as a few years later

Theodore Parker uses their American counterpart:

1854 *Additional Sp.* 13 May II.25 (quoted in Walsh, *Lit. Cur.*) . . . the great Abolitionist spoke of democracy as "a government of all the people, by all the people, and for all the people."

The fact that Parker had used a similar phrase, "government of all, by all, and for all," in 1846 (See *Rev. of Rev.,* 1901, p. 336) does not necessarily contradict the assumption of German influence since it is extremely likely that similar phrases existed in Germany even before 1848.

The *New York World,* 26 September, 1880, 2/4, indicates that later Parker used exactly the wording made famous by Lincoln:

Mr. Lincoln has often been credited with the expressive phrase "of the people, by the people, for the people." It was not original with him, however. Theodore Parker first used it and often used it during the last decade of his life. A lady who was long a member of Mr. Parker's household and who assisted him in his intellectual work says that the idea did not spring at once to his mind in its perfect consciousness. He had expressed it again and again, with gradually lessening diffuseness, before he gave the address to the Anti-Slavery Society, May 13, 1854, where it appears thus: "Of all the people, by all the people and for all the people," as published in "Additional Speeches," vol. 2, p. 25. "But that," she adds, "was not quite pointed enough for the weapon he needed to use so often in criticizing the National action, to pierce and penetrate the mind of hearer and reader with the just idea of democracy, securing it there by much iteration; and I can distinctly recall his joyful look when he afterwards read it to me in his library, condensed into this gem: 'Of the people, by the people, for the people.' "

On more than one occasion Lincoln's famous phrase was parodied for critical and satirical purposes:

1879 Henry Adams *Democracy* 31. Democracy, rightly understood, is the government of the people, by the people, for the benefit of Senators.

1890 Hayes *Diary* IV.556. Lincoln was for a government of the people. The new tendency is "a government of the rich, by the rich, and for the rich."

1890 Mary Ellen Lease, in Josephson, *Politicos* 476 . . . government of Wall Street, for Wall Street.

grab bill.

The act passed by the 42nd Congress in 1873 to increase the salaries of many government officials.

The fact that it contained a retroactive provision granting the members of Congress $5,000 in back pay created much indignation throughout the country and resulted in this and other opprobrious names being applied to it.

1876 *Harper's W.* 6 May 363/3. The increase of salary, it will be remembered, was a part of the "grab bill," which was part of an appropriation bill. The grab was so called not because it raised the President's salary, but because it gave back pay to members of Congress as well as raised their salary.

grandstand.

Descriptive of spectacular political action which is aimed at attracting the public's attention.

A. Grandstands were common at both American and English race courses in the mid-19th century and later at other sporting fields. Many participants, particularly in horse racing, made their most determined efforts in front of the massed spectators in the grandstand.

1834 *N. Y. Sporting Mag.* Nov. 169/1 . . . Dangerous, who to all appearance was full of running as if he had just started. At the Grand Stand Chapple let him go, and he won by a length in a canter.

The figurative use of grandstand is attested:

1893 Post *Harvard Stories* 308. They all hold on to something or clasp their knees tightly—to faint or fall over would be a grand-stand play.

B. In politics:

1900 *Cinc. Enquirer* 23 June 1/9. [Kentucky will go for McKinley] if Teddy can only be secured to do some "Grand Standing."

1902 in Sullivan *Our Times* II.433. The operators were quoted by a New York Sun reporter as saying, after the conference, that they regarded the President's action as "a grand-stand play."

grandstander.

1914 White *Editor and People* 32. He is a four-flusher, a ring-tailed, rip-snorting hell-raiser, and a grandstander. He makes a big noise.

grapevine (telegraph).

Unconfirmed rumor.

The word may have its origin in an episode related by Shinn: *The Story of the Mine* 72. That curious and vivid Western phrase, "grapevine telegraph," originated in 1859. Colonel Bee constructed a telegraph line between Placerville and Virginia City, attaching the wire to the trees; their swaying stretched it until it lay in loops on the ground, resembling the trailing California wild grapevines. Frequent breaks occurred from falling trees and avalanches, till the line became almost useless, being sometimes beaten into Sacramento by the Pony Express. California and Nevada papers took it up, and whenever a journalist wished to cast doubts on the freshness of his opponent's news he forthwith accused him of running a grapevine telegraph.

We have no reason to doubt that the Colonel actually used the word and thereby contributed to its popularity, but he certainly is not its coiner, since it can be found as early as 1852.

1852 *Marion Buckeye Eagle* 24 June 2/4. By the Grape Vine Telegraph Line, in connection with the Virginia Fence and Mason & Dixon's Line, we have received the following. . . .

Late but apparently reliable reports indicate that the word originated among members of the Underground Railroad to whom it meant the secret code by which they exchanged information.

1888 H. F. Paden in *Firelands Pioneer*. The "Underground Railroad was simply a mythical name for an organized system of aiding slaves to reach Canada. The "Grapevine Telegraph" a similar mythical designation of the means whereby intelligence as to their movements, and the movements of pursuing parties, was carried from post to post.

This is confirmed by the statements of two old abolitionists cited in Siebert, *Underground Railroad,* 56n.

We suggest the following explanation: In pioneer days the grapevine was used as a substitute for a rope in many functions, for fastening a boat, for hanging, and also as a clothesline.

1843 Carlton *New Purchase* I.93. How getting to bed was managed could not be told, as Mrs. C. made an extemporary screen by hanging something—"what"—oh! a utility [petticoat?] on a rope or grape vine stretched near our quarters. . . . 1860 *Sandusky Reg.* 25 April 2/3 [fr. *Atlanta Southern Confederacy*]. We are opposed to hanging an abolitionist with a rope; we prefer something that is indigenous to the soil of the country. Hence we suggest a tough grapevine.

In view of this it seems very likely that the original grapevine of the abolitionists was a system of signals given by a prearranged way of hanging pieces of laundry on a clothesline—the same system that is described as the clothesline telegraph in Truesdale, *Blue Coats,* 133f.:

How he [Negro acting as Union intelligence spy] obtained his information remained for some time a puzzle to the Union officers. At length, upon much solicitation, he unfolded his marvellous secret to one of our officers.

Taking him to a point where a clear view could be obtained of Fredericsburg, he pointed out a little cabin in the suburbs near the river bank, and asked him if he saw that clothes-line with clothes hanging on it to dry. "Well," said he, "that clothes-line tells me in half an hour just what goes on at Lee's headquarters. You see my wife over there; she washes for the officers, and cooks, and waits around, and as soon as she hears about any movement going on, she comes down and moves the clothes on that line so I can understand it in a minute. That there gray shirt is Longstreet; and when she takes it off, it means he's gone down about Richmond. That white shirt means Hill; and when she moves it up to the west end of the line, Hill's corps has moved up stream. That red one is Stonewall. He's down on the right now, and if he moves, she will move that red shirt."

As long as the two armies lay watching each other on opposite banks of the stream, Dabney, with his clothes-line telegraph, continued to be one of the promptest and most reliable of General Hooker's scouts.

Civil War examples of the metaphor:

1863 in *Butler's Book* 510. [referring to an event of 1863] ... secret communications generally known as the "grapevine telegraph.". . . A despatch came from Richmond [to New Orleans] "via grapevine.". . .

1864 Wills *Army Life* 305. . . . "spring or grapevine" dispatch said ... I just thought I would give you a sample of the "grape cuttings" that accompany a march.

1865 *U. S. Service Mag.* Feb. III.180 ... the "Thousand and one" "Grape-vines," too, that we hear passing through camp daily, when we get cut loose from the outer world. . . .

grass in the streets. [ ]

A slogan designed to point out the financial disaster to be associated with the election of the opposition, the suggestion being that business will become so poor that there will not be enough traffic to wear down the tufts of grass sprouting in the streets.

1892 *Nation* 13 Oct. 272/3. This [argument for prot. tariff] is the old "howling wilderness" and "grass-in-the-streets" argument for protection.

1896 Bryan *First Battle* 205. Destroy our farms and the grass will grow in the streets of every city in the country.

grass roots.

The statement by Frank Vizetelly (see Mencken, *Suppl.* I,297n) that "to get down to grass roots" was in use in Ohio around 1885 is still unsupported. In 1912, however, the term was already in existence:

1912 *McClure's* July 324/1. From the Roosevelt standpoint, especially, it was a campaign from the "grass roots up." The voter was the thing.

Grass roots attained its greatest vogue in 1935 when a Republican conference was held in Springfield, Illinois, on June 10, with the purpose of unifying the party's forces and issues for the next presidential campaign:

1935 *Time* 17 June 15/3. At their "grass roots" conference, the grassrooters turned out to include Hanford MacNider (Hoover's Minister to Canada), Patrick Jay Hurley. . . .

1935 *Nation* 19 June 697/2. "No crisis so grave has confronted our people" since the Civil War, Mr. Lowden told the grassroots convention at Springfield.

1935 *New Rep.* 26 June 183. The Grass-Roots Conference.

1935 *Common Sense* July 24/1. Issues are hard to find, and the "Grass Roots" Convention in Springfield, Illinois, found itself stumped.

Later examples:

1936 William Allen White in Fowler *Alfred M. Landon* vii. Its [Landon boom] swift acceleration rising from the grass roots and sidewalks of America is a new phenomenon in American politics.

1953 *Cols. Citizen* 4 Nov. Sensenbrenner said he attributed his victory to a tireless "grass-roots campaign" in which he made more than 180 speeches during the last month.

1953 *Ib.* 22 Nov. Midwestern grassroots survey made by Rep. Richard Simpson . . . and William Warner. . . .

grease.

Money for political bribery; also, occasionally, other expedients of politicians:

1797 *Columbian Centinel* 15 April 3/2. Cash ... is a necessary article in their business, and without daily application of this specific grease their wheels must roll heavily on.

1801 *Ann. of Congress* 2 Sess. 721. When the American flag-staff comes down, it will take a great deal of grease [meaning money] to get it up again.

1837 Neal *Charcoal Sketches* 139. Talking is the grease for the wagon wheels of the body politic. . . .

1878 *Cinc. Enquirer* 29 Nov. 4/1. A few words from Mr. Ferguson about that "grease" used in the Ky. Legislature. . . .
1881 Myers *Bosses and Boodle* 181. At a meeting of the Democratic State Central Committee, at Columbus, in the Spring of 1881 . . . Mr. John G. Thompson . . . made a speech in which he said; "We must have grease to run a campaign."
1946 White *Autobio.* 132. The politics of the day [1890's] was full of intrigue, and the intrigue was greased more or less with corruption.

See FAT.

greasy mechanics.

A. The distinction between the worker and the aristocrat, between the man who earned his living by sweat and toil and him who enjoyed a life of idleness and ease was one of the *leitmotifs* of the Log Cabin campaign of 1840. However, the difference of classes had been emphasized earlier as is shown by the comments of J. H. Pleasants, editor of the *Richmond Whig,* and a well-born Virginia gentleman:

1836 *Cols. Western Hemisphere* 24 Aug. 3/3. *The Whig* is edited by J. H. Pleasants, the same man who wrote home to his friends, when in Europe, that his sufferings during his voyage had been intolerable, because he was on board of a vessel, filled with "FILTHY, GREASY MECHANICS."
1840 in Norton *Tippecanoe* 223. Insult To Mechanics. [head] . . . And this is done in this city of Baltimore, and in the face of a population consisting so largely of the mechanic classes!

The working man again came into his own, particularly during the campaign of 1860, when Honest Abe, the railsplitter, was his champion:

1856 *Ann. of Cleve.* No.2246. The small-fisted farmers and greasy mechanics must take care of themselves today. The Ballot is still theirs.
1860 Benedict *Wide Awake Poem* 10. He'll never fly into conniptions and panics/And call us his "mudsills" and "greasy mechanics!"

B. A later usage indicates a shifting of connotations based upon its relationship with *machine: mechanic* suggests *manipulator.*

1960 *Detroit News* 16 Aug. 18B/1. The President never liked the mechanics of politics. Even the phrases "ward politics" and "boss" were distasteful to him. He liked to praise the precinct worker, but left the job of dealing with him to the "mechanics."

See MUDSILL.

the great design.

Like *white plume* (see PLUMED KNIGHT) and *chicken in every pot* the phrase is connected with King Henry IV of France. It was introduced into America by a letter from a number of prominent Frenchmen, congratulating Theodore Roosevelt on his work on behalf of international arbitration and conciliation and pointing out that these endeavors were in direct continuation of the policies of Henry IV.

1906 Roosevelt *Autobio.* 531. They believe that the action of President Roosevelt, which has realized the most generous hopes to be found in history, should be classed as a continuance of similar illustrious attempts of former times, notably the project for international concord known under the name of the "Great Design of Henry IV" in the memoirs of his Prime Minister, the Duke de Sully.

Sully speaks of *Les Grands Desseins* in several places, sometimes in rather vague fashion, yet making it clear that the king's political system was largely defined by his wish to avert a terrible European war in the near future. (Sully, *Memoires,* London, 1745, VI.335) The phrase was taken up at the Teheran Conference and made the target for polemical remarks by Herbert Hoover at the Republican Convention of 1944:

in Hoover *Add. Sp.* 252–3. During the past month Forrest Davis has published a circumstantial account of the Teheran Conference. It is said to have been authorized. It has not been denied. It relates to President Roosevelt's new peace method, called by him, The Great Design. A peace method under this same name, the Great Design, was proposed by Henry the Fourth, a French monarch, some 350 years ago. It has some similarities to Mr. Roosevelt's idea.... The American people deserve a much fuller exposition of this Great Design.

great gun.

See BIG GUN.

great unknown.

A political *dark horse* (q.v.) ; based on the formula, the *Great Commoner, Great Pacificator, Great Unwashed,* etc.

1876 *N. Y. Trib.* 12 June 4/5. The prospects of the "Great Unknown" appear to be looking up.

1876 *Cinc. Daily Gazette* 14 June 2/1. Is the favorite son of a small part of Michigan the Great Unknown?

1876 in Hamilton *Blaine* 418. You may remember that Mr. Blaine has always prophesied the Great Unknown.

groans.

An expression of disapproval; the counterpart of the tiger cheer:

1823 *Cinc. Nat. Rep.* 9 May 1/22. The word was then given, three groans for Churchill....

1837 *New Yorker* 587/3. [Whig celebration in Wash.] The procession stopped at Mr. Kendall's when the performance commenced.... After an overture from the instruments, "Clear the kitchen" was sung by the whole strength of the company, intermingled with sundry distinct rounds of groans and invitations to the owner of the mansion to come out to them.

1845 *N. Y. Herald* 1 Nov. Three groans for Tilden was then called for and given.

grogshop politician.

1823 in James *Jackson* 370. The movements for Jackson have been made by the grog-shop politicians and the rabble....

1866 "Inside, a Chronicle of Secession" in *Harper's W.* 261/4 ... grog-shop politicians, bullies, and ruffians, the very sediment hitherto of society.

See BEERSHOP POLITICIAN.

groundswell.

In nautical terminology a groundswell is "a deep swell or heavy rolling of the sea, the result of a distant storm or seismic disturbance." (*OED*) The adoption of the term into the political vocabulary to apply to any popular movement or expression of feeling is still another example of the many metaphors that have been produced from the area of natural forces and phenomena. (See PRAIRIE FIRE, TIDAL WAVE, TORNADO, LANDSLIDE.)

1856 Buchanan *Works* X.95. A ground swell, however, in this State among a noble people who had sustained me for more than thirty years forced me reluctantly into the field.

1866 *Wash. Nat. Intelligencer* 1 Sept. 2/3. There is a great groundswell moving that will teach traitors in the North....

1884 in Stanwood *Blaine* 271. If it comes to you, it will come as the ground-swell of popular demand.

1888 Norton *Tippecanoe* 52. It [election of 1840] was a general ground-swell, an upheaval, that carried consternation into the ranks of the administration forces.

1921 Morgenthau *All in a Lifetime* 146. He [Clark] had better than a hundred more pledged delegates than Wilson, and the ground swell of the politicians in his favour.

guerrilla (warfare).

Irregular political procedures such as filibustering; a politician engaged in such activities:

1848 *Ann. of Cleve.* No.1091. The Taylor and Cass papers call the Free Soilers, the "Guerrillas."

1859 Brown in *Cong. Globe* 1363/2. They have been telling us for a week they have ten or fifteen, or twenty speeches to make, but when asked to make them they go off into a sort of guerrilla warfare, moving to postpone this bill and take up something else, and so on.

1880 *Puck* 20 Oct. 105/3. But the Republicans have had twenty years of practice, and they are able to discipline their bummers and guerillas [sic].

1880 *Harper's W.* 19 June 386/3. In nominating General Grant at Chicago, Mr. Conkling sneered at the independent voters, who give or withhold Republican majorities, and who left his candidate for Governor of New York in a minority of twenty thousand, as "tramps, jayhawkers, and guerrillas—men who deploy between the lines, and forage now on the one side, and then on the other."

1898 *McClure's* May 104/2 . . . this style of guerilla [sic] warfare as practiced by the insurgents. . . .

guillotine.

The act of removing officeholders from their positions.

The impression left by accounts of the French Revolution made

guillotine a dreaded name long after the events of the 1790's.

1839 John C. Clark in HR 30 Jan. Had he applied, as he undoubtedly would have applied, for the appointment of chief superintendent of the guillotine, he would have placed competition at defiance. He would have merited and secured their plaudits, and as a suitable reward for his zeal and devotion, would have been decorated with the fitting order of "Knight of the Lamp Post."

1841 *Ohio St. Jrnl.* 8 Sept. 3/2. The Guillotine in Motion [head].

1842 *N. Y. Am.* 5 Jan. 2/2. Look out, Locofoco office holders! They are screwing up "the guillotine" and I should not be surprised to see the heads fall in showers.

1844 in McGrane *Wm. Allen* 98. The true and brave portion of the Ohio delegation twenty in number stripped for the fight,—determined at least that if Van Buren could not be saved that the Jackson and Van Buren policy and its gallant body of supporters should not be offered upon the altar of corruption and proscription and that if Lewis Cass, by his friends, were determined that the guillotine should do its work *then,* that the . . . Cass cliques from one end of the Union to the other should be guillotined.

1845 *Ann. of Cleve.* No. 1498. While the broad axe is slowly striking off the full-fed necks, the small locomotive guillotines of the Departments are scouring the country for Tyler victims, and the race will soon become extinct.

1857 *Ib.* No. 1635. President Buchanan has set the guillotine in operation for the decapitation of the refractory of his own party.

1857 *Ib.* No. 2385. Who is the next candidate for the guillotine?

1866 Nasby *Swinging Round the Cirkle* 207. The President agreed with me that until after the trip the guillotine would stop [i.e., no office-holders would be removed].

1866 *Cleve. Leader* 27 April 2/1. The President's guillotine is in excellent running order.

1879 *N. Y. World* 21 June 4/4. We may look to see the "guillotine" and the "machine" set up as firmly in the Dominion as in the United States.

1886 *Perley's Reminiscences* 97. National politics was to them [clerks] a matter of profound indifference until, after the inauguration of General Jackson, hundreds of them found themselves decapitated by the Democratic guillotine, without qualifications for any other employment had the limited trade of Washington offered any.

gwibit. ¿

Mencken *Supplement I* 379. Gwibit, dedicated to the nation by Congressman Karl E. Mundt, of South Dakota in 1943 to designate "the guild of Washington incompetent bureaucratic idea throatcutters," seemed to meet a need, but it nevertheless died the death.

H

hack.

Short for *hackney horse,* in politics, a henchman, drudge, or petty officeholder.

In England the political use is attested since 1800, the metaphorical connotation probably being that the political hack is entirely under the domination of the "whip."

1820 *London Times* 8 March 3/5. These were engaged as hacks in the Parliamentary stable, and were ready to obey the Parliamentary whip.

In America where the word *whip,* party manager, is less well known the metaphorical connotations seem to be that the hack is an inferior horse and that it is for hire: **1801?** in Garland *Randolph* I.188. It was

further urged as an objection to the bill that it was merely designed to create sinecures and fortresses for broken-down political hacks.

1828 *N. Y. Enquirer* 16 Aug. 2/3. The Intelligencer calls the republican presses friendly to Gen. Jackson "political hacks."

1842 in Birney *Ltrs.* 699. I believe I [convinced?] him of the propriety of a firm and cordial support of our present candidate as the first thing, instead of wearying ourselves in a chase after worn out political hacks to make candidates of men who must be brought in and will then stand ready to be brought again.

1857 Julian *Sp.* Thousands . . . thought that political hacks and charlatans were to lose their occupation under the reign of the new order.

1875 DeForest *Playing the Mischief* 114. Any old political hack can beat him out of sight on this track.

1880 *Cleve. Plain Dealer* 1 June 2/2. The dark horse we have in mind for that important race on the Democratic side is no worn out, obsolete political hack, the continuous, favorite head of some faction or clique, but one fresh and untrammeled.

1950 Allen and Shannon *Truman Merry-Go-Round* 48. The gang there [White House, 1945–7] grew and grew and grew. But the recruits there were all alike, political stumblebums and weary, faceless hacks.

ha-ha speech.

A humorous campaign speech. [ ]

1840 in *Ohio St. Arch. & Hist. Qtrly.* LXI.270. A whole souled Tippecanoe mechanic [entertained Harrison meetings with some of] the most amusing, sideshaking, hearty ha-ha speeches ever listened to.

half-breed.

A dissenter or member of a faction split from the regular party organization.

A. The first entry of the term into politics that we have found is clearly an allusion to race.

1840 *Harrison Dem.* 17 March.
  Tecumseh's* half breeds to replace
  We'll vote for Tyler too, sir.
  The rights of States he will defend,
  And be a Tyler** true, Sir.
  * R. M. Johnson's children.
  ** a doorkeeper in Freemasonry.

B. Almost concurrently *half-breed* is used to designate any deviant from regular party discipline.

1846 *Quincy Whig* 27 Jan. 2/4. It seems that all the Jacks in the county, consisting of T. H. Owens . . . and a few "half breeds," were to assemble at Carthage on the day the Democratic County Convention was to be held.

1848 *Cinc. Campaigner* 30 Sept. 1/3 . . . a collection of mongrel Tylerites and half-breed rag-money political tricksters, styled Old Hunkers or Softs were also admitted.

1853 *Ann. of Cleve.* No. 2470. The 8th of January will afford a fine opportunity for the "Nationals" to bring the "half-breeds" up to the scratch. . . . We desire to see the Plain Dealer and its "half breed" backers, made to face the music.

1853 *Ib.* No. 2002. The result was that the strongest Whig hold in the State is now in the hands of the "half-breeds."

1858 *N. Y. Trib.* 17 May 6/1. Even the "Lecompton half-breeds," as they are called, see the ruin of any scheme connected with the Lecompton Constitution.

C. The warfare within the Republican party between those regulars who supported Grant for a third term in 1880 and those who favored a reform within the party led to the bolters' being characterized as *half-breeds* opposed to the regular *stalwarts*. The January 9 reference to "featherheads" and that of June 10, 1881 suggest that the Indian background of *half-breed* is still not forgotten.

1880? Stimpson *Politics* 275 [q. *N. Y. Daily News* after the election] A Cabinet of Half Breeds, as the party of Civil Service Reform are called.

1881 *Albany Eve. Jrnl.* in *N. Y. World* 8 Jan. 4/4. While the movements of the "machine" are thus clogged and strife and contention are rampant, the stigmatized "half-breeds" are as harmonious as they are confident.

1881 *Ib.* 9 Jan. 1/4 . . . we could here have a group of Stalwarts; there a squad of "Half-breeds"; over in "Sleepy Hollow might be packed a carefully-selected assortment of "Featherheads". . . .

1881 *Ib.* 18 Jan. 4/3. The Journal quotes with reprehension the assertion of the Buffalo Commercial Advertiser that that journal would rather have a Democrat for Senator than what it described as a "half-breed Republican". . . .

1881 *Ib.* 3 Feb. 1/6. The anti-machine or "half-breeds" are well satisfied with the present situation.

1881 *Harper's W.* 15 Jan. 34/1 . . . the assertion of the Troy Times that Mr. Conkling is a type of the faithful Republican party man is a challenge to contemplate his career as conspicuously illustrating party fidelity. He is praised for not being "half-and-half," but "steady and stalwart all the time."

1881 *Ib.* 5 Feb. 82/4 . . . it may have occurred to the "rebels" and "halfbreeds" of last spring . . . that they were in a position to dictate the terms not only of their return to fellowship, but of their promotion within the party.

1881 *Nation* 24 Feb. 121. According to the "Half-breeds" at Albany, General Garfield merely wished to "disarm" Mr. Conkling by offering him a place in the Cabinet.

1881 *N. Y. Times* 17 May 1/6. The Robertson Republicans, or the "halfbreeds," as they rather proudly call themselves, were at once delighted and frightened.

1881 *N. Y. Trib.* 10 June 4/4. Halfbreeds and Bucks. [Bucks among Indians are lazy and no good] If it is really obvious that the men who defend the President of the United States and the historic Republican party are Halfbreeds, it is at least obvious that the Bucks are not entirely unknown to American politics.

1882 Roosevelt *Ltrs.* II.1469 . . . the latter [Alvord] a rugged, white headed old countryman, a "half breed" or independent, but a bad old fellow.

1882 Cooper and Fenton *Am. Pol.* I.261. It has thus far been the effort of Pres. Arthur to allay whatever of factious bitterness remains in the Republican party. In his own State of New-York the terms of "Half-Breeds" and "Stalwarts" are passing into comparative disuse, as are the terms "Regulars" and "Independents" in Pennsylvania.

1883 Nye *Forty Liars* 271. Eng was a half-breed and Chang was a stalwart, and that made it bad about attending caucuses.

1883 Roosevelt *Ltrs.* I.63. I am a Republican, pure and simple, neither a "half-breed" nor a "stalwart". . . .

D. Recent evidence that the party distinction has again been lost:

1952 Stevenson *Sp.* 212. I'm a half-breed myself. My father was from an old, staunch Democratic family, and he was a Presbyterian. My mother was from an equally old and staunch Republican family and she was a Unitarian. And somehow, when I became conscious, I found that I was a member of her church and his political party.

half-horse, half-alligator.

A. There is a long tradition in tales of the frontier of describing the colorful figures in terms of three or more halves. In Kentucky and the Old Southwest, the horse, alligator, and snapping turtle were the characteristic animals and thus the chief ancestors in this fictional genealogy. There are, of course, many variations in the formula.

1809 Irving *Hist. of N. Y.* ch.3. It is an old remark that persons of Indian mixture are half civilized, half savage, and half devil—a third half being provided for their particular convenience. It is for similar reasons, and probably with equal truth, that the backwoodsmen of Kentucky are styled half man, half horse, and half alligator by the settlers on the Mississippi, and held accordingly in great respect and abhorrence.

1838 Drake *Tales and Sk.* 92. [fight at Ky. polls] Stones, clubs, and brickbats were hurled by the assailing party, and returned with equal violence; half horse half alligator encountered all Potowatomie; a Mississippi snag was loosed from its moorings by a full-grown snapping turtle; the yallar flower of the desert bruised the nose of Old Tecumseh.

B. The followers of Henry Clay of Kentucky and Clay himself were frequently described in this manner.

1824 *Cinc. Nat. Intell.* 1 Oct. 1/4 . . . and if Clay be his favorite, he is sure to be dubbed a half-horse-half-alligator sort of fellow, without a single leading card or trump in his hand.

1836 Hawes of Ky. in *Cong. Globe* App. 349. It has been said that we are divided into three parts, to wit: alligator, horse, and snapping turtle; and my colleague's candidate for the presidency should have recollected that, when the horse was removed, there still remained the alligator and the snapping turtle; one celebrated for holding on, and the other for destroying.

1844 Maurice and Cooper *19th Cent. in Caric.* 146. [cartoon: Clay riding half horse, half alligator; Calhoun on turtle, Van Buren on fox, etc.] The Great American Steeplechase for 1844.

C. Other variants:

1836 *West. Hemisphere* 10 Aug. 2/7. What does Gen. Harrison profess to be? Answer.—A whole hog Bank man—half nullifier, half abolitionist—half mason, half anti-mason, tipped off with a touch of New England blue-lightism, and a small sprinkling of a defeated heroine.

1849 (Akron) *Summit Beacon* 18 April 2/4. Fremont's Half Horse, Half Deer, and Half Camel.

1859 *Olympia Pioneer* 11 Feb.
> The Great Annihilator,
> Half Ass, half alligator,
> Hath made an offal speech.

halfway house.

A compromise position between two extremes.

1791 in Chinard *Jefferson* 279. I consider the establishment and success of their government [French] as necessary to stay up our own, and to prevent it from falling back to that kind of half-way house, the English constitution.

1841 Clay in *Gt. Deb.* XIII.169. I found him several years ago in the halfway house [pet bank system].

1844 *Wash. Daily Globe* 13 Jan. 47/3. [Rives] was patching up his paper-money scheme with Mr. Clay at the half-way house. . . . He, however, disclaimed having any scheme to advocate. He would not undertake to detain the Senate in the half-way house of the State Banks, far less in such a bawdy-house as the United States Bank of Philadelphia.

An interesting instance in which the first known metaphorical use of the expression antedates its earliest literal usage:

1793 in *Corr. Ld. Auckland* II.515. Yours will be an excellent half-way house, almost as good as the inn at Bromley.

handshaker.

An office seeker who solicits votes by appearing to be on intimate terms with all potential voters:

1879 *N. Y. Trib.* 2 April 4/6 . . . his [Bishop's of Ohio] winning ways as a handshaker.

See GLADHAND.

hard fisted.

Allusion to the laboring class, the "greasy mechanics," the "huge paws." (q.v.)

1835 *Ohio State Jrnl.* 14 Aug. 3/2 . . . the "real grit"—the "hard money" for the "hard-fisted boys," (who forgets the slang to catch the multitude?) . . . .

1835 *Ib.* 21 Aug. 3/2. The resolution speaks the voice of the Mechanics of this city—the silk-stocking mechanics of course, when assembled in a bona fide meeting, and freed from the presence of our worthy friends, the Lawyer-and-Post-master mechanics—the "hard fisted boys" with their "huge paws" and all that sort of thing, who figured at the former meeting.

1840 in *Log Cabin Song-Book* 29.
> But vote for the Farmer that's work'd the farm well!
> The hard-fisted Farmer,
> The honest old Farmer!
> We'll vote for the Farmer that's work'd the farm well!

hards and softs.

The following is largely based on Mamie Meredith's excellent article, " 'Hards' and 'Softs' in American Politics," *Am. Sp.* V.408–13.

A. Since the eighteenth century, the adjectives *hard* and *soft* have been used to distinguish coin from paper money.

1778 *Maryland Jrnl.* 8 Sept. [They] were going into the Indian country, loaded with hard money. . . .

1779 *N. J. Archives* 2 Ser. III.703. Each devoted racoon [is] to receive down forty soft or paper dollars.

1779 A. Adams in J. Q. Adams *Fam. Ltrs.* 365. Corn is sold at four dollars, hard money, per bushel.

B. This usage acquired political significance in connection with the bank conflict, especially when Jackson began the hard money policy laid down in the Specie Circular of July 11, 1836. From this time on the Democrats generally became the advocates of hard money, while the Whigs were more favorable to paper currency.

1816 Webster in *Gt. Deb.* XIII.56. There is no nation which has guarded its currency with more care; for the framers of the Constitution, and those who enacted the early statutes on this subject, were hard-money men; they had felt and therefore duly appreciated the evils of a paper medium....

1837 *Ann. of Cleve.* No.1626. And yet the bank makers—the hard money Vanjacks of Ohio—proclaim it . . . through their presses that the Whigs are the bank party.... No.1651. Col. Benton it is said has always been a hard money man since the bank notes were found in his cravat.

1839 *Ib.* 7 Dec. The governor's arguments on the banking situation are those of hard money men.

1840 *Ohio St. Jrnl.* 4 Jan. 1/3. They are the hard currency men, the Benton men, the "Perish Credit, Perish Commerce" men ... the "Red-dog, blue-backed, Locofocos."

C.1 When in 1842, the Latham Bill, aimed at the regulation of monetary matters in Ohio (Holt, *Party Pol. in Ohio,* chap. ii) , again brought the money question into the foreground, a faction within the Democracy had abandoned rigid hard money principles with the effect that at that time the party split into *hards* and *softs.*

1842 *Ann. of Cleve.* No. 171. We have at last found room for Mr. Hamer's third epistle to the head of the hard money faction in Ohio.

1843 *Ib.* No.1539. The candidates nominated made the pledge required, but it seems that even this pledge—equivalent to a declaration against all banks ... does not come up to the mark of the exclu-

sively hard money men of Old Hamilton.

1843 *Ib.* No. 1553. The Locofoco party in Old Hamilton are in a precious stew, and the hards and softs, after dealing each other all sorts of blows, have at last resorted to the keen weapons of wit! Ellwood Fisher is the hard candidate for senator and D. T. Disney the soft.

1843 *Ib.* No. 1629. The "hards" and the "softs" are at loggerheads in Old Hamilton.

1844 *Same Old Coon* 12 April 2/1.
For this man did the Locos shout,
The hards know well what 'twas about
They knew he was soft without a doubt
And so the Hards they brought him out.

1845 *Ann. of Cleve.* No. 1439. In Ohio the Hards and Softs constitute the two factions of Democracy, the former being dead bent on the destruction of all banks, and the others having like intentions, but decidedly less pronounced ones. In a word, the Hards are outspoken, and the Softs have two faces.

1846 *Ohio Statesman* 7 Jan. 2/3. Resolved, That it is the duty of every democrat in the state, to consign to the shades of oblivion, all personal bickerings ... and thereupon making a public sacrifice of such suicidal jealousies, local interests, and foolish hawkings of the terms "Hard and Soft"....

C.2 Similar conditions led to the use of *hard* and *soft* as party names in Missouri and Louisiana.

1844 *Wash. Nat. Intelligencer* 19 Aug. 3/3. The Locofoco party proper—which is distinguished in the nomenclature of that state as the "Hards," while the dissentients from it are denominated "Softs" —are certainly ... defeated.

1844 *N. Orleans Picayune* 26 Aug. 221/3. We don't know whether he runs on the hard or soft ticket; but we think ... he will give his opponents a hard run of it.

1846 *Niles' Reg.* 14 March 20/1. Hards and softs, as they are termed in Missouri.

C.3 There were also hard and soft Whigs:

1846 *Ohio Statesman* 20 Jan. 2/2. The "Hards and Softs."—These terms are now the trouble in the whig ranks: some are for keeping up in progress with the democracy, and others for keeping by the old rotten system of whig swindling. We understand that the hards of the whigs have progressed so far . . . that they are now willing to tax the bankers.

D. In the early '50's "hard" and "soft" are frequently applied to factions in the New York Democratic party. It is, however, unlikely that a direct connection exists between this and the earlier Western usage. The dividing line is no longer the money question but the slavery question. Besides, the frequent occurrence of "hardshell" for hard and "softshell" for soft (perhaps influenced by the longer forms as names of opposed groups in the Baptist Church; see Meredith's article, 412, and *DA*) makes it probable that in this later period, as far as New York is concerned, the longer forms are the original ones. A passage quoted by Meredith seems significant:

1854–5 Amelia Murray *Ltrs. from the U. S.* Upon some occasion, when the moderate Democrats were accused of yielding rather too much to the views of their opponents, a Whig during his address to a popular assembly said: "Now I think these politicians are blowing hot and cold; they are too much like crabs when in a state of transition between the soft and the hard-shell. I am a whole hog—I am a Hard-shell." And another said, "They are Pollywogs" (the Indian name for tadpoles) . . . .

1852 *N. Y. Trib.* 23 Aug. 1/4. The hard and softshelled Democracy.

1853 *Ib.* 2 April 3/6. The Hards embrace the Cass Hunkers of 1848 of the National School of politics, while the Softs are composed of the remnants of the Van Buren and Adams party of 1848, and such Hunkers as Secretary Marcy and Gov. Seymour.

1854 *Cong. Globe* 17 Jan. 191/3. What is the difference between the New York Hards and the New York Softs? [Walsh] The difference is the difference between an honest man and a rogue. (Great Laughter)

1860 *Stark County Republican* 12 July 1. The Soft Shells and the Hard Shells of New York are terribly distressed just now, on account of the bivalvular condition of their party.

1876 *Chic. Trib.* 6 July in Williams *Hayes* 1.467n. Tilden . . . generally reconciled the "soft shells" to his hard-money notions because of his loud proclamations.

hat in the ring.

A. As a variation of the challenging gesture of throwing down one's glove, the throwing down of the bonnet is mentioned in Holinshed. This gesture is not only a stereotypic but a necessary one, since a knight who has already engaged his hood must procure another one if he wants to utter a second challenge.

1577 Holinshed *Chron.* 40–1 . . . the said duke of aumarle said, that if the duke of Norfolke affirme it, he lied falselie, and that he would proue with his bodie; throwing downe an other hood which he had borowed.

Evidently as a modern adaptation of this use, boxers demonstrate their willingness to fight by throwing their hats into the ring:

1820 John Hamilton Reynolds *The Fancy*
Throw in his hat and with a spring
Get gallantly within the ring.

B. Political application of this usage:

1860 *Vanity Fair* I.309. The Northern Nipper shied his castor over the ropes first, and the Southern Secesher followed suit immediately.

1878 *Cinc. Enquirer* 12 Dec. 14/2. He [Blaine] shied his castor into the ring yesterday.

The phrase was made popular by Theodore Roosevelt, himself an amateur boxer, who announced his candidacy in 1912 by saying: "My hat's in the ring; the fight is on and I'm stripped to the buff." (Stimpson, *Book About American Politics* 353.)

1912 *Nation* 7 March 226/1. When Mr. Roosevelt threw his hat into the ring the other day, he gave the signal for a contest the like of which has not been seen before in this country.

1912 *Cleve. Plain Dealer* 26 June 6/5. [Song] "My Hat's in the Ring."

1960 *Time* 7 March 15/3. Lucia Cormier, 48, tossed her bonnet in the ring to oppose Maggie Smith's third-term bid.

have and have-not.

Ultimately the phrase seems to go back to Cervantes' *Don Quixote*, II, chap. xx, where Sancho remarks that there are just two families in the world, the Have (el tener) and the Have-Not (el no tener) (Dalziel's ed., 1868) : "There are but two lineages in the world, as my grandmother used to say: 'the Haves and the Have-Nots,' and she stuck to the Haves. . . . people are more inclined to feel the pulse of Have than of Know."

The phrase is international:

1836 Bulwer-Lytton *Athens, Its Rise and Fall* I.328. The division . . . of the Rich and the Poor—the Havenots and the Haves.

1871 Scherr *Michel* IV.35. Wie überall, löst sich dem nach hier der politische Gegensatz von Freiheit und Knechtschaft in den öconomischen von Haben und Nichthaben auf.

Referring to America:

1859 *At. Mon.* April 393 . . . the oldest contest that has divided society is that which has so long been waged between the House of Have and the House of Want.

1888 Bryce *Am. Commonwealth* II.iii.liii. 338[OED]. In the hostility of rich and poor, or of capital and labour, in the fears of the Haves and the desire of the Have-nots.

1898 Zola in *Rev. of Rev.* XVII.320. I told you when we spoke on this subject some weeks ago that the leaders of the movement with very wicked hypocrisy and deception have induced the people, the Have-Nots, to believe that the word Jew is synonymous with capitalist. . . .

1906 S. Fish in Bryan *The Commoner Condensed* VI.328. The contest is no longer between those who have and those who have not but between those on the one hand who have moderately . . . and on the other those who . . . seek by questionable practices to have excessively.

1918 Roosevelt *Writings* (Mem. ed.) XXI.381. And to oscillate between the sheer brutal greed of the haves and sheer brutal greed of the have-nots means to plumb the depths of degradation.

hayseed.

A. Grass seed recovered from hay and clinging to the clothing of a farmer has long been considered a symbol of his rustic manners and ideas.

1849 Melville *Redburn* 38. At this he laughed out with a great guffaw, and said there must be a hay-seed in my hair.

1862 Cook *Siege of Richmond* 13. Others were newly-appointed officials, with "hayseed still sticking to their collars," as the phrase goes.

B. The word gathered political importance during and through the Granger movement and finally became a synonym of *Populist.*

1874 *Ann. of Cleve.* No. 128. It [*Nation*] pretends to see nothing in the "hayseed" movement . . . and asserts that the movement never had any strength and that the press of the country treat the grangers as of no account whatever.

1874 *Cinc. Enquirer* 2 Sept. 2/4. I know him to be . . . a reputed granger, the seed of the hay filtering through his hirsute covering, and a huge ear of maize in his pantaloon pocket.

1890 *Farmers Alliance* 4 Oct. in Hicks *Pop. Revolt* 168. "The Hayseed"

And the ticket we vote next November
Will be made up of hayseeds like me.

19— in Clark *Qrt. Century* I.285. Next year . . . some hayseed delegate climbed on to a bench and bellowed: "Mr. Cheerman . . ."

headquarters.

A military term adopted into the American political vocabulary along with such other terms as *campaign, war horse* (q.v.).

1829 *N. Y. Mirror* 7 Nov. 137. A tavern . . . enjoys the honour of being the headquarters of a party.

1835 *Knickerbocker Mag.* VI.438–9 . . . transparencies shining from the headquarters of wards and parties, and glorious banners waving their stars and stripes in the gusty sky over the humming multitude.

1856 Cripper *Green Peas* 303. It is not as might be supposed, in these degenerate days, a political head-quarters. . . .

heckle.

A. Heckle as the name of the comb-like instrument with sharp teeth used in dressing flax and as the term for the process has long been metaphorically applied in Scotland to the questioning of candidates.

1808–25 Jamieson *Dict.* To heckle. (2.) To tease with questions, to examine severely.

B. According to one source *heckle* was first used in American politics in 1909:

1909 *Cols. Citizen* 11 Aug. 4/6. "Heckle" is the Latest Word in Local Politics. . . .

The heckle comes to this country from England, where it has long been a favorite method of drawing out candidates as to their position on public questions. Jerome first made use of the word.

There is no doubt that District Attorney William T. Jerome's conduct in the sensational Thaw murder trial accounted for the term's sudden popularity.

1909 *N. Y. Trib.* 26 July 4. Thaw Awaits Ordeal. His Counsel Prepares Him For Heckling By Jerome.

1909 *N. Y. Times* 30 July 1. Thaw . . . Frets Under The Heckling. [head]

Heckle had, however, been used several years earlier:

1900 Depew in Sullivan *Our Times* I.79. Now, if you nominate Governor Black and I am addressing a large audience . . . the heckler in the audience will arise and interrupt me. . . .

1906 *N. Y. Times* 31 Oct. 4. Hearst Is Heckled Into Talking Taxes [head].

hedge.

Although the English use of *hedge* meaning to shift or dodge is found in Shakespeare's plays (*Merry Wives,* II.ii.26; *Troilus,* III.iii.158) it appears that its present political meaning is American:

1858 *N. Y. W. Trib.* 27 July 1/2. There is an old and true proverb which says, "One man may steal a horse with impunity, while another will be hung for only looking over a hedge." The latest instance of this is the relative treatment of Northern and Southern Disunionists.

1871 *N. Y. Times* 5 Sept. 4. No sooner had they secured its passage, however, than they commenced "hedging," and even before the adjournment of the Legislature in 1870, it became evident that their professions and promises were a fraud.

1876 *Ib.* 9 June 4/2. The betting community are now engaged in staking their money on a variety of pure guesses, and

there probably never was an event in regard to which they have busied themselves that has given them more occasion for careful and elaborate "hedging."
1878 *Harper's W.* 12 Oct. 806/1. In his 7th of March speech Mr. Webster tried to "hedge" by insisting that nature had fixed limits to the spread of slavery.
1878 *Ib.* 19 Oct. 828/1. Some of the Republican papers, discrediting their party name, have shivered and hedged; but the press has been rather beyond than behind the party platforms.
1879 *Ib.* 14 June 463/2. Republicans have nothing to gain by silence or by hedging upon this subject.

heir apparent.

The vice president or other person who is expected to be the next president. Usually the term is a satirical jibe at the non-democratic procedure of the incumbent's selecting and grooming his successor.
1824 *Cinc. Nat. Rep.* 23 July 2/3. Such Conduct . . . may Comport with the "dignity" of the super-royal advocates of the "heir apparent" to the presidency.
1824 *Ib.* 20 Aug. 2/4. There has lately been established a *Royal Gazette,* through which are promulgated those *monarchical* principles . . . as are calculated to promote the elevation of his Royal Highness, John Q. Adams, to the dignity of his father and the throne of these United States. . . . This *Gazette, conducted* . . . by a numerous body of his Highness' most loyal, liege subjects . . . this official organ of the Heir Apparent.
1835 *Ohio St. Jrnl.* 24 July 2/3. The forty thousand household troops [officeholders] with all their satellites, are in motion . . . for the purpose of deciding the contest in favor of the heir apparent [Van Buren].
1900 *Rev. of Rev.* XXI. 6/1. Mr. Hay as "Heir Apparent."

hell bent for election.

A favorite slogan characterizing an all-out effort in a campaign for an overwhelming victory.

1840 in *Dialect Notes* VI.343.
Maine went
Hell-bent
For Governor Kent.
1888 Norton *Tippecanoe* 159. Edward Kent was nominated for Governor [in 1840], and the State went "hell bent" for him.
1935 Warburg *Hell Bent for Election* [title].

heroite.

A supporter of General Andrew Jackson.
1827 *Spirit of Seventy-Six* 29 March 3/2. From the best information I can gather, there is no chance of the Heroites between the Potomac and Delaware.
1828 *Ann. of Cleve.* No.355. That this visit was intended for political effect, there can be no doubt; and the partisans of the Hero at New Orleans had made their arrangements accordingly. But it seems that the legislature [in Louisiana] . . . would not "go the whole" with the Heroites.
1828 *Liberty Hall* 20 March 1/3. No real Heroite would do such a thing.
1828 *Ib.* 17 April 3/4. Heroite Literature [Head]

A country editor of the period voices his sentiments about this feature of hero-worshipping:
1835 *Niles' Reg.* 48.91/1. A country paper, speaking of the evil tendency of war, says that among other things, it "raises a crop of heroes to claim all the offices in the country for twenty years afterwards."

"He serves his party best. . . ."

Coined by President Hayes, who describes the creation of the epigram:
1880 in Williams *Hayes Diary* III.618. The sentence in my inaugural message which has been often quoted, viz., "He serves his party best who serves his country best," occurred to me as I was walking east on the north side of Broad Street in Columbus with a small party of friends

in February 1877.... "Serve your party by serving your country," "You will serve your party if you serve your country," "To serve one's country is the best way to serve one's party," are among the forms of statement that occurred to me. The best service of party is service to the country.

Hessian.

A. The hatred of the American Revolutionists for the hired mercenaries is clearly shown in the connotations of the epithet in the 19th century. The term stigmatizes anyone who is charged with selling his vote or his influence.

1776 *Norwich Packet* 8 July in Davidson *Propaganda* 371. [The Hessians] whose native ferosity, when heightened and whetted, by the influence and malice of the sceptered savage of Great-Britain, thirsting for the blood of his faithful American subjects, will exhibit such a scene of cruelty, death and devastation, as will fill those of us who survive the carnage, with indignation and horror; attended with poverty and wretchedness.
1840 *Ohio Statesman* 7 Aug. 3/3. One step more, and the rank and file of Whiggery will be as purely Hessian as Judge Heyl, or any of those hired by British money to fight against our fathers in the Revolution.
1842 *Albany Argus* 23 Sept. 2/3. Then [1838] were the "Hessians" imported from Philadelphia....
1860 Sheahan *Douglas* 396. Francis J. Grund, "the basest Hessian of them all," was dispatched to Chicago.
1890 Schurz *Works* V.78. His [Quay's] "matchless services" consisted merely in collecting an enormous campaign fund, or in enlisting pious men to do it for him, and in employing that money to "hire Hessians," to "purchase mercenaries," and to do various other things for his party.

B. During the Civil War Union soldiers were called Hessians by Southerners and Northern Democrats:

1862 Hunnicutt *Conspiracy* 231. "Hessians."—It was constantly affirmed by secessionists that old Abe Lincoln, Scott & Co. were coming down upon us.... On all occasions, the cry was, "The Hessians are coming!"
1866 *Cleve. Leader* 9 Oct. 1/4. Soldiers, remember that the Democratic party now asking for your votes called you "Hessians," "outlaws," "thieves" and "murderers," while you were periling your lives for the country.

hewers of wood.

The underprivileged.

A. The phrase occurs repeatedly in the Bible, as for example:
Joshua 9:23. Now therefore ye are cursed, and there shall none of you be freed from being bondmen, and hewers of wood and drawers of water for the house of my God.

B. Political:
1824 *Mangum Papers* I.116. The Yankees will make the Southerners hewers of wood and drawers of water for them.
1838 Price *Clem. Falconer* II.62. I will never consent that the South, those sons of chivalry and high honor ... shall be rendered mere hewers of wood and drawers of water, to the lordly manufacturers north of the Potomac.
185– in "Warrington" *Pen Portraits* 469. In Frederick Douglass and George Latimer the people of the North have a specimen of the serfs of the South—the hewers of wood and drawers of water for the chivalry par excellence of this republic.
1876 Usher *Greenback* 23. The day may come when this pendulum of National indebtedness shall swing the other way ... when instead of our being their hewers of wood and drawers of water, they will be ours.

hewgag.

A call for political action.
1850 *Ohio St. Jrnl.* 16 Feb. 2. General George W. Morgan has arrived in our

city. Can it be possible? Sound the Hewgag.

1854 *Ohio Statesman* 10 Jan. 2/2. Spread the news, then; bruit it abroad 'till it reaches every voter in the State. (Yes! Sound the hewgag!)

1889 *Voice* 21 Nov. When a leading paper ...sounds the hewgag, other papers take up the cry, and repeat it from one end of the country to the other.

Hickory (boy).

A supporter of General Jackson; a Democrat.

Walsh (*Literary Curiosities* 459) recounts two anecdotes which may be explanations of Jackson's sobriquet of Old Hickory; however, it is apparent that the nickname was very popular already in 1824 when Jackson was a leading contender for the presidency:

1824 *Cinc. Nat. Rep.* 19 Oct. 2/5. Hickory Boys, Turn Out! Every Jacksonian must be at his post.

1827 in Kennedy *Memoirs of William Wirt* II.207. So say the Hickory boys;— but the lads of Clay (instead of *wax*) tell a different tale.

1828 *Ann. of Cleve.* No.351. All those pliable Hickories...that now bend so lowly at his nod.

1832 Circular published at Cinc. 8 Feb. Let then the Democratic Party...assemble the hardy Hickories, and let the forests roar with indignant denunciation of their outraged feelings.

That *hickory* was still remembered in association with the Democratic Party is evident from the following:

1859 *Ohio Statesman* 8 May...Miami, Sambuck, Tite-bark, Loose-bark, and Shell-bark Douglas Lecompton-anti-Lecompton Buck Democrats....

Hickory cabinet.

1828 *Ohio St. Jrnl.* 31 Dec. 3/3. Who are to compose the Hickory Cabinet? and

who are to fill the minor offices within the gift of the Hero?

hide-bound.

Firm, unyielding, especially in regard to partisan matters.

A. Originally descriptive of a disease of cattle.

1559 Cooper *Thesaurus* [OED] Coriago, the sickenesse of cattall when they are clounge, that their skynnes dooe cleve fast to their bodies, hyde bounde.

B. The political usage follows a long tradition of metaphorical adaption, as indicated by the first quotation:

1724 R. Welton *Subst. Cr. Faith* 27. No narrow hide-bound mind that can only love and seek its own self.

1875? "Warrington" *Pen Portraits* 398. He can get an office under the rotten Republicans, or the hide-bound Democrats, —one just as easily as the other.

1923 *Rev. of Rev.* LXVIII.237. None of these men has about him any vestige whatever of hide-bound partisanship.

1932 Rogers *How We Elect* 137. The old "Hide Bound" Republicans still think the world is just on the verge of coming to an end.

higher law.

An antislavery slogan appealing to natural law rather than to manmade constitutions and ordinances.

Foreshadowed in classical and Biblical uses:

Cicero *De ReP.* III.22 ... one eternal and unchangeable law will be valid for all nations and all times, and there will be one master and ruler, that is, God, over us all, for he is the author of this law, its promulgator, and its enforcing judge.

Romans 7.25. I thank God through Jesus Christ our Lord. So then with the mind I myself serve the law of God; but with the flesh the law of sin.

and in early American political writings:

1774 in Miller *Origin of the Am. Revolution* 349. ... the great Law of Nature and Reason has possessed every Society with a Right to defend itself from Ruin, without having Recourse to Books or Statutes or recorded Customs.

1804 Channing *Works* I.321. A just man appeals from the laws of the land to the dictates of conscience.

1828 Calhoun *Works* VI.50. There is a higher power,—placed above all by the consent of all, —the creating and preserving power of the system,—to be exercised by three fourths of the States.

1839 Bushnell in Thayer *The Kansas Crusade* 84. The destruction of slavery will be accomplished, either with you or without you; or, if you make it necessary, in spite of you. There is a law in the cave above you and above us all. The river has been in motion for ages, with a deep, strong, broadsweeping current ... it will flow on in its predestined course, in the power and undiverted majesty of Him who bids it flow.

Channing later used the exact formula—

1842 Channing *Works* 874/1. On this point the Constitution, and a still higher law, that of nature and God, speak the same language; and we must insist that these high authorities shall be revered.

and Webster came very close to it on March 7, 1850:

Webster *Writings* V.350. I hold slavery to be excluded from those territories by a law even superior to that which admits and sanctions it in Texas. I mean the law of nature, of physical geography, the law of the formation of the earth.

It was, however, its use by Seward which gave the expression its popularity in pre-Civil-War debates.

1850 Seward in *Cong. Globe* 11 March App. 265. But there is a higher law than the Constitution, which regulates our au-thority over the domain, and devotes it to the same noble purposes. The territory is a part—no inconsiderable part—of the common heritage of mankind, bestowed upon them by the Creator of the universe.

1850 Giddings in *Ib.* 9 Dec. 15–16. Let no man tell me there is no higher law than this fugitive slave bill. We feel that there is a law of right, of justice, of freedom, implanted in the breast of every intelligent human being, that bids him look with scorn upon this libel on all that is called the law.

1850 *Ann. of Cleve.* 28 Dec. No.2318. The man who wrote the article in the Ohio State Journal, captioned "The Higher Law New Party Organization," did not know what he was talking about ... the "spirit of the age," which, as he hints, hovers about and dwells mostly in the hearts of the "Mad-dog-lunatic-higher-law-party."

1852 Webster in Wilson *Slave Power* II.361. And, when nothing else will answer, they invoke religion, and speak of a higher law. Gentlemen, this North Mountain is high, the Blue Ridge is higher still, the Alleghany higher than either; and yet this higher law ranges farther than an eagle's flight above the highest peaks of the Alleghany. No common vision can discern it; no conscience, not transcendental and ecstatic, can feel it; the hearing of common men never listens to its high behests; and, therefore, one should think it is not a safe law to be acted on in matters of the highest practical moment. It is the code, however, of the fanatical and factious Abolitionists of the North.

1852 Lincoln *Works* II.156. His [Seward's] supposed proclamation of a "higher law" is the only specific charge I have seen for a long time.

Later examples:

1863 Kelso *Stars and Bars* 27. This squeamishness comes of your higher law proclivities. I have sometimes observed that these higher-law men, all have tender-footed, weak-kneed consciences.

1892 in Page *Old South* 281. To the ac-

cusation [denying of franchise to Ne-
groes] it is replied, that the written law,
when subverted at all, is so subverted
only in obedience to a higher law
founded on the instinct of self-protection
and self-preservation.
1960 *New Rep.* 14 March 20/1. The values
of democracy while anchored in what
the Founding Fathers called the Higher
Law are for ever evolving and in the
process of becoming.

Although a German parallel of
an early date has been found, it is
unlikely that there is any connection, since the context is entirely different from the later
American uses.
1809 Adam Miller *Elemente der Staat-
skunst* III.226. Es muss...ein Gesetz
geben, das noch höher ist, als die Selb-
sterhaltung des individuellen Staates.

high finance.
A phrase of reproach during the
muckraking and trust busting days
of the early twentieth century.
1905 *McClure's* XXV.48. In other words,
we could eat our cake and have it, too—
which is one secret of high finance.
1908 Roosevelt *Autobio.* 456...the kind
of business which has tended to make the
term "high finance" a term of scandal....
1913 *Ib.* 456. It is this kind of business
which has tended to make the very name
"high finance" a term of scandal to which
all honest American men of business
should join in putting an end.

high minded (Federalist).
A Federalist opposed to DeWitt
Clinton.
in Van Buren *Autobio.* 104. In April,
1820, some forty gentlemen, of the federal
party, most of them young men of talent
and all occupying respectable positions in
society, came out with an address in
which they insisted that no "high-minded
Federalist" would support Clinton. The
use of this expression obtained for them

the designation of "the high-minded" in
the political nomenclature of the times,
while their demonstration against the
Governor secured for them from his
friends the less flattering sobriquet of
"the forty thieves."
1824 in Mackenzie *Van Buren* 169. It is
not very serviceable to talk much of Burrites, Lewisites, and the High minded.

hippogat.
A fanciful creation of W. B.
Stewart, cartoonist on the *Minne-
apolis Times.* It is a hippopotamus
labelled G.A.T.—Great American
Trust.
1899 *Rev. of Rev.* XIX.674. [Three repre-
sentative cartoons are reproduced, to-
gether with the following poem.]
Look out! look out! ye merchant-men
    all—
Look out for the HIPPOGAT,
Who eateth industries great and small
And waxeth so big and fat.
Cradles and coffins are babies' milk,
    Oil, sugar, refined and raw,
Newspaper print and the beldame's silk
All go to the monster's maw.

hireling (-ism).
A derogatory term for the laboring class, used especially by Southerners to counteract the charges
against the evils of slavery; also a
synonym for an unquestioning follower or party worker.
1851 *N. Y. Trib.* 12 June 4/3. Slavery and
Hirelingism [head]...one of these lucky
turns of language occurs in the report of
the Business Committee of the Southern
Rights Convention lately held in Georgia.
Instead of speaking of the Northern members of the Union as free, it calls them
Hireling States.
1858 Wilson *Slave Power* II.550. His
[Hammond's] characterization of Northern manual laborers as "hirelings," as essentially slaves, the "mudsills" of society
...became the ringing watchwords of
those replies and of subsequent conflicts
at the North.

1862 Heartsill *1491 Days* 58 ... march forth to meet the hireling hords of the North upon our borders.
1876 *Harper's W.* 5 Feb. 102/2. That Mr. Hill did not taunt the minority as Lincoln's hirelings and minions was probably an act of pure grace.

hoco poco.

A. A nickname of the Whigs, evidently coined on the part of the Democratic party to counteract the adverse effects of *Loco Foco*
1838 *Hickory Club* 6 Oct. 4/3. "Loco Foco" vs. "Hoco Poco." The federals, alias whigs, alias national republicans, alias antimasons, alias any name that can be devised, are now about assuming the name of Hoco Poco, derived from hocus pocus which means juggling, or schemes and tricks of darkness.... Loco Foco then, is light in the midst of darkness, Hoco Poco (or federal hoco pocus) is darkness in the midst of light.
1838 *Ohio Statesman* 6 Oct. 2/4. The "Hoco Pocos" seem to be a strange sort of politicians.
1838 *N. Y. Herald* 29 Oct. 2/1. Both parties—whigs and democrats—or, the hoco-pocos and the locofocos, as they call each other....

B. The Whigs, in turn, tried to destroy the effectiveness of their nickname.
1840 *Ohio Confederate* 5 Nov. 4/2. The Locos are supposed to have descended from Locus Focus a prince of a very hot country. Which name is supposed by Heraldic writers to be a corruption of Hocus Pocus, as these two words indicate the whole Policy of the Race.

hodden gray.

A. Characterizing the working class, gray hodden, a coarse undyed woolen fabric, associated with rusticity, is best known in its inverted form which Burns gave it in "For A' That and A' That":

What tho' on hamely fare we dine,
Wear hoddin gray and a' that....

That Burns was well known in the United States is obvious:
1842 Kirkland *Forest Life* I.227. With us it is emphatically true that "a man's a man"—and if he "wear hodden gray," he is none the worse, but the better.

B. In politics the phrase came to be associated with the working classes and later was one of the many symbols along with *log cabin* and *hard cider* in the campaign of 1840:
1830 *Workingman's Advocate* 8 May 1/2 ... whether they wear "Hodden Grey," or super super Blue; whether they have the odor of sweat or Cologne water; still have rights and as freemen mean to maintain them.
1840 in Norton *Tippecanoe* App. 8.
   No ruffled shirt, no silken hose
      No airs does Tip display;
   But like "the pith of worth," he goes
      In home-spun "hodden-gray."

See HOME-SPUN.

hold over.

An official who continues from one term of office to another.

Though the verb may be found earlier (*DA,* 1850) the popularity of the noun in the latter part of the century may be attributed to the use of *hold over* in regard to barnstorming (q.v.) theatrical troups.
1892 Roosevelt *Ltrs.* 15 Dec. I.300 ... the Democratic post office employees (the so-called "hold-overs") ought to contribute in the neighborhood of four hundred dollars....
1893 Chittenden *Reminiscences* 318. One of the auditors, a "hold-over" from some former administration, one day wished

to read me an opinion which he had just completed.

holier than thou.

Satirizing the pharisaical attitude of reformers and do-gooders.

The phrase may be found in Isaiah 65:5:

Which say, Stand by thyself, come not near to me; for I am holier than thou.

A. In general use in American politics:

1807? in Mayo *Clay* 288. His righteousness, his "stand by—I am holier than thou!" attitude, would have been ludicrous had it not been so dangerous.

1846 *Ohio Statesman* 6 Jan. 2/3. And these are papers which have said, "stand back! I am holier than thou!"

1854 Parton *Greeley* 353. These suggestions were listened to with respectful attention; but they did not elicit the "thunder of applause" which had greeted the "Stand-aside-for-I-am-holier-than-thou" oratory of the preceding speakers.

B. The independent Republicans of 1884.

1884 in Paine *Nast* 491. The Commercial Advertiser characterized them [Curtis, *et al*] as the "Holier than thou" Republicans, who had insisted on Edmunds or nothing.

1884 *Nation* 17 July 40. The only "charge" his [Blaine's] friends have yet made against his opponents is that they are not as good as they pretend to be, or that they are too good for this world. The "holier-than-thou" taunt really means that it is wrong to try to be better than the worst men of your party—just as cavalry take the pace of the slowest horse.

1884 *North Am. Rev.* CXXXIX.307. A cynical, carping spirit which says, stand aside, for I am holier than thou, a Pharisaic, self-righteous spirit, which thanks God that it is not as others are, may often put itself in the front rank of reformers, but it is not of such stuff that

high and lasting reforms are originated and consummated.

Later uses:

1908 in *Rev. of Rev.* XXXVIII.164. [Cartoon: stained glass design with William Jennings Bryan, hands folded in pious attitude, standing with one foot on the back of the prone Col. Guffey.] I am holier than thou [in Gothic letters].

1914 White *Editor and People* 3. There will be no bolting, no sulking, no "holier than thou" business about his politics....

1918 in Lindley *Roosevelt* 187 ... in the ensuing arguments, Roosevelt ridiculed "certain gold-laced gentlemen" and "the holier-than-thou" group at the Navy War College.

1932 Carter *What We Are* 80. Can the raging thirst of the beer belt be slaked without giving mortal offense to the self-righteous Kansas and holier-than-thou Idaho?

1946 Drew Pearson on ABC network 12 May. The Senate is now being called the holier-than-thou-club.

Holy (Unholy) Alliance.

In 1815 Czar Alexander I proposed an alliance of all Christian monarchs who were to pledge each other brotherly love, help, and support and to consider themselves as members of one and the same Christian nation. The idea was carried into effect, but even in Europe the "Holy Alliance," being used as a tool of reaction and despotism, soon came into disrepute (Ladendorf, 117f.)

In America the opposition to this coalition of monarchs was, of course, still stronger:

1824 in Jefferson *Works* (Ford ed.) X.298. With respect to the European combinations against the rights of man, I join an honest Irishman of my neighborhood in his Fourth of July toast: "The Holy Alliance,—to Hell the whole of them."

In U.S. politics the term was used ironically to designate political combinations of a doubtful character.

1821 Jefferson in Christy *Pulpit Politics* 531. Our anxieties in this quarter are all concentrated in the question, What does the holy alliance [the Federalists], in and out of Congress, mean to do with us on the Missouri question?

1832 *Globe* 9 May 3/5. The partizans of Messrs. Clay and Calhoun in the Senate, forming a coalition to be known by the name of the "Holy Alliance" . . . .

1843 Whittier *Writings* 110. They were just such democrats as the patricians of Rome and the aristocracy of Venice; lords over their own plantations, a sort of "holy alliance" of planters, admitting and defending each other's divine right of mastership.

Probably independent from Europe where *Unheilige Allianz* is attested from 1849 (Ladendorf, *loc. cit.*), *holy alliance* was changed to *unholy*.

1836 Matlack *Antislavery Struggles* 97. The Methodist Episcopal Church has an unholy alliance with slavery; she ought not, therefore, give herself any peace until she cleanses her skirts from blood-guiltiness.

1907 *Rev. of Rev.* XXXV.622/2. Because this control was threatened Murphy turned to Hearst; because of this coalition—"unholy alliance"—Jackson was elected. . . .

home rule.

The *OED* gives the term in a quotation from an Irish writer of 1860. By 1873, when a Federal Home Rule Platform was adopted at a conference in Dublin (James J. Clancy, *Land League Manual,* N.Y. 1881), it must have been in general use in Great Britain.

A. Very soon it was adopted in the U.S. by Southern anti-reconstructionists:

1878 *Cong. Record* III.App.37. The radical plan is to make slaves of ten million white men for the pretended good of four million blacks. Ours is to so shape the conduct of affairs that all, both white and black, may be happy and free. In a word, our principle is "home rule."

1878 *Harper's W.* 5 Oct. 787/3. Unless the Democrats repudiate "home rule" and "local self-government," they must concede the "regularity" of his [Butler's] nomination.

1880 in Adams *Emery A. Storrs* 215–6. What does the democratic party mean by "home-rule"? The evidences which they have furnished us of home rule in these states from which the one hundred and thirty-eight electoral votes are to be derived are not encouraging. From the practical evidences they have given us, home-rule means with them the right to fetter opinions, to stifle speech, to terrorize the voter and bully the courts at home.

B. In New York and other cities the term was later used in advocacy of relative independence of city government from the state.

1905 *N. Y. Sun* 6 June 6/2. In campaign season politicians of all stripes and kinds howl for "Home Rule!" Then they flood to Albany and ask the Legislature to tinker up what they consider imperfect in the city government.

1929 in Al Smith *Up to Now* 146. Employees of the cities of the state were opposed to the new constitution because of the home-rule amendment.

home-spun.

One of the terms associated with the farming and working classes, particularly in the campaign of 1840; on other occasions it is used as a symbol of domestic independence or of pride in humble origins.

1818 Birkbeck *Ltrs.* 63. Three years ago he made his appearance as a candidate for practice, in a home-spun coat, and probably without a dollar in his pocket. He was called "the home-spun lawyer." **1840** in Norton *Tippecanoe* 15 ... the days of substantial "home-spun and hodden gray"—of wool hats and linsey-woolsey—of innocence and integrity. **1860** Holmes *Elsie Venner* 4. Some of our most illustrious public men have come direct from the homespun-clad class. **186–** Ayers *Diary* 119. Home Spun Dress [poem].

The homespun Dress is plane I know
    my hats palmetto two
But then it shows what southern girls
    for southern writes will do.

See HODDEN GRAY.

honest money.

Money with a sound intrinsic value. A phrase popular during the monetary debates of the last quarter of the 19th century.
1876 *Harper's W.* 22 April 322/1. Mr. D. A. Wells was recently nominated for Congress by the Democrats in Connecticut, and he wrote a letter explaining his position. He said that he was for honest money, for progressive free trade, and for political reform. **1878** *Ib.* 5 Oct 786/2. Every Republican who hesitates or falters should be discarded as a candidate, and an honest-money Democrat preferred to a dishonest-money Republican. **1880** *Cinc. Gazette* 24 June 1/5. On the currency question it [Dem. platform] resolves in favor of *"honest-money"* and defines that term by specifications of gold, silver, and paper convertible into coin.

horn-stop campaign.

Cf. WHISTLE STOP, PROPELLER STOP.

1952 *Cleve. Plain Dealer* 16/2. Phil. G. Goulding of this newspaper's Washington bureau, who is now covering Gov. Stevenson's campaign, has introduced the readers of the Plain Dealer to a new bit of phraseology in the political handbook. It is "horn-stop campaigning." ... to refer to the peregrinations of a candidate as "whistle-stop campaigning" is an anachronism. Now that their railroads are largely Dieselized ... Diesel engine's horn.

horny-handed.

Descriptive of the working class. (See GREASY MECHANICS, HARD FISTED.)

Apparently coined by James Russell Lowell in a poem, "A Glance Behind the Curtain," first published in the *Democratic Review,* 1843:
... There is always work,
And tools to work withal, for those who will;
And blessed are the horny hands of toil.

According to *Notes and Queries,* 9th series, II.231, the phrase was popularized by Dennis Kearney on the sandlots of San Francisco. [   ] Later uses:
1884 *Nation* 17 July 41. Those horny-handed sons of toil, John Kelly and Benjamin F. Butler. ... **1884** *Cleve. Leader* 2 Oct. 1/4. Thousands of *Horny Handed Workmen* waved and shouted a welcome to the great champion of protection.

The influence of various German phrases using *schwielen* (callouses) ought to be investigated.

horse.

A leading politician or possible candidate; one of the many racing metaphors in the political vocabulary. See DARK HORSE.

1852 *Am. Whig Rev.* XVI.128. The Democratic suffrage is for the "horse" of the
Convention, and not for the candidate
and favorite of the people. It is not necessary that this "horse" should be a
"blood"; he is not expected to run; it is
the convention which runs.
1880 *Cleve. Leader* 1 June 1/5. One of
Bickham's peculiarities, it must be remembered, is a serene confidence that the
horse he backs is always sure to win the
race.
1880 *Ib.* 22 June 1/5. Bitter anti-Tilden
men cannot forgive Payne for his having
been preferred by the Gramercy Park
sage as his successor, and the dozen or
more horses in the field on account of
the prominence Payne assumed at the
outset has again assumed a violent form.

horse and buggy.

A. With the increasing popularity of the automobile and the
disappearance of horse drawn vehicles, the phrase *horse and buggy*
became a synonym for *old-fashioned.* Will Rogers comments
upon this change in American life:
1929 in Rogers' *Autobio.* 208. We drove a
horse and buggy and we don't drive one
now.

B. In politics the phrase
achieved a new vogue when President Franklin Roosevelt characterized a Supreme Court decision on
interstate commerce:
1935 *Public Papers and Add.* 209. The
whole tendency over these years has been
to view the interstate commerce clause in
the light of present day civilization. The
country was in the horse-and-buggy age
when that clause was written. 221. We
have been relegated to the horse-and-
buggy definition of interstate commerce.
1935 Warburg *Hell Bent for Election* 43.
Could any President who had not lost his
sense of proportion, have characterized
a unanimous decision of the United States

Supreme Court as putting the country
back "to the horse and buggy days"?
1937 in Sherwood *Roosevelt and Hopkins*
94. It was more than a year after Roosevelt had started to assail the "Nine Old
Men" for thinking in terms of the horse
and buggy era.

horse-shed.

1890 Locke *Demagogue* 275. They took
Democrats into horse-sheds, and explained the situation, took from them the
Democratic tickets with Stevens' name on
them, and gave them Democratic tickets
with Phelps' name for Congress; and
they did it so quietly that no one knew it.
Every Democrat was thus horse-shedded.

See BUTTON-HOLE.

huge paw.

Epithet for an unskilled laborer.
Daniel Webster is alleged to
have warned against untrained
laymen interfering with the law:
1842 *Nauvoo* (Ill.) *Wasp* 1 Oct. 2/1. Daniel Webster had stated that the farmer
ought not to put his Huge Paw on the
statute book.

Another Illinois paper uses the
same words four years earlier, but
does not mention Webster:
1838 *Quincy Argus* 1 Dec. 3/1. A farmer
with his Huge Paws on the statute book,
what can he do?

Since in 1840 Van Buren was frequently accused of aristocratic tendencies, and since the character of
the Log Cabin campaign caused
the Whigs to identify their cause
with that of the plain working
man and farmer, it was only natural that they should use *huge paw,*
as illustrated by the following examples:
1840 in Norton *Tippecanoe* App. 7.
What though the hero's hard "huge
paws,"

Were wont to plow and sow!
Does that disgrace our sacred cause!
   Does that degrade him? No!
1840 *Log-Cabin Song Book* 53. The Huge
Paw [title]

hunker (-dom, -ish, -ism, Whig; Young Hunker).

A member of the conservative
wing of the Democratic party.

A. No convincing etymology has
been offered. The often repeated
explanation that a hunker is one
who hankers for office (see, for instance, Alexander *Pol. Hist. N. Y.*
II.126) is unsatisfactory, but a variation offered by Lynch is at least
debatable:

in Lynch *An Epoch and a Man* 501. Van
Buren followers retaliated with "Hunkers," an epithet which stuck to the followers of Marcy. Our lexicographers have
erred in deriving *Hunker* from the Dutch
honk, a stake marking the terminus of a
racetrack; a goal, or home, used in the
children's game of tag. If they would visit,
even today, any of the old Dutch counties, they would find an occasional scholar
who would inform them that *Hunker*
is a corruption of *hunkerer*,—one who
desires, a selfish person. *Hunkerer* in
turn, is derived from *hunkeren*, the in-
finitive of "desire"; *ik hunker* is "I desire."

(Dutch *hunkeren*, "to desire eagerly," is well attested.)
The derivation from *honk*, a cry in
children's games meaning goal, is
mentioned by the *DAE*, but remains at best a vague possibility as
long as no supporting evidence is
available. It seems significant that
early and often the word appears in
the combination "Old Hunker."
This makes it hard to believe that
there is no connection between this

phrase and *Old Hunks*, a surly,
closefisted old man, attested in England from the 17th century and
well-known in America:

1829 T. Flint *Young Backwoodsman* 157.
The old hunks own half the county.
1831 in Kennedy *William Wirt* II.324. I
am unwilling to leave behind me the
character of having been a moping melancholy old hunks.

This in its turn seems to be connected with *on one*'s *hunkers*, in
a squatting position, (*OED*, since
1785):

1816 *Cinc. Western Spy* 19 July 1/5.
There, underneath the leaves umbrage-
ous,
Sniffing the mantling pool contagious,
Squat in his hunkers, solemn blinking,
An ancient Sachem sat him drinking.

B. If this is correct, then the
original meaning would be one
who sticks to his position (cf.
standpatter).

1843 in Weed *Autobio.* I.553. Let the
"Hunkers" and "Barnburners" contend.
1846 in Donovan *Barnburners* 82. Where
the "Hunkers" had the ascendancy ...
the opposite section of the party cast
their votes against the candidates. ...
1848 *Old Zack* 1 July 3/5. There are more
of the same sort [Democrats for Taylor]
in the city and county, than the Old
Hunker Locofocos can, or dare "shake a
stick at."
1848 *Ib.* 29 July 2/2. We have no knowledge of the primitive signification of the
phrase "Old Hunker," or of the manner
in which it came to be applied to designate a particular class of politicians. It
has, however, been in use for some time;
... it is employed to designate those individuals who look upon the emoluments
of office as the primary object for which
government is instituted.
1852 Parker *Additional Sp.* 111. The
Mother city of the Puritans is now the
metropolis of the Hunkers.

1854 *Ohio Statesman* 18 July 2. It is the old hunker, conservative federal Whiggery that speaks through the resolution.
1866 *Cinc. Comm. Campaign Special* 28 Sept. 39/5. [John Sherman] They say that I am a "hunker," a "conservative," and a "little backward"—and so I am, my friends, I don't deny it.

C. Other forms:
Hunkerdom.

1850 in Pike *First Blows* 70. If we were to follow the lead of the old Hunkerdom of Clay we should be led, as Byron says of the tide in the affairs of women, "God knows where."
1862 Christy *Pulpit Politics* 544. For the last ten years, yea, eleven, next seventeenth of March, the Hunkerdom of the North has been engaged in a constant effort to save the Union.

Hunkerish.

1856 in Pike *First Blows* 345 . . . Mr. McLean is the candidate of the slow and more hunkerish part of the Convention.

Hunkerism.

1848 Walt Whitman in (Brooklyn) *Freeman* 9 Sept. 2/4. But the words "Hunkers" and "Hunkerism" seem . . . to be in vogue as designating a certain class of politicians, and we shall use those words . . . not as terms of odium, but terms of description.
1849 in Streeter *Pol. Parties in Michigan* 97. It [Dem. Party] exhibited that hostility to old hunkerism, which even possessed the mass of the people.

Hunker Whig.

1855? in Dingley *Dingley* 40. While the privileged class are drawing to their support the name of the Democratic party, while Hunker Whigs are joining their aristocratic organization, let the friends of liberty, forgetting all past differences, buckle on the armor of freedom.
1880 Congdon *Reminiscences* 137. There was an equally unnatural coalition upon

the other side, of Hunker Whigs and Hunker Democrats.

Young Hunkers.

1846 *Ohio Statesman* 5 Feb. 2/2. The nomination of Mr. Bebb, the shinplaster and chicken tax candidate, is a complete triumph of what are called the "young hunkers."

hunters' lodges.

A euphemism which concealed the true purpose of the organizations which gathered stores of ammunition and arms along the north-east border in the late 1830's and early 40's preparing for a Canadian war of independence.
1842 in *Albany Argus* 15 Sept. 2/4. The Albany Argus insinuates that Gov. Seward either is or has been connected with the hunter's lodges, as the affiliated gangs of self-styled "patriots" along the Canada border, during the last three or four years, have called themselves. The organization of these insurrectionary lodges has been very extensive. Their designs are infamous. Col. Worth, when in command at Sockett's Harbor, obtained much information on the subject. . . . [Argus answers:] . . . the "insinuation" that Gov. Seward is or was a "paying member of a Hunter's Lodge," was repeatedly made through the Argus, during the last campaign, first in the shape of an interrogatory to the Eve. Journal, and afterwards in that of a distinct charge—the organ of the Junto scarcely venturing to notice the subject at all. . . .
1842 *Ib.* 22 Sept. 2/3. Now . . . we have an explicit denial through the governor's [Seward's] organ that he "is or has ever been a member of a hunter's lodge."
1846 Webster *Works* V.140. Why, it was the time [1842] when the "patriot societies" or "Hunters' Lodges" were in full operation, when companies were formed and officers appointed by secret associations, to carry on the war in Canada. . . .
1849 Wm. Brown *America* 51. When the Rebellion was raging in Canada, caused

mainly by the emissaries from the States, the sympathisers in the various cities bordering upon that country formed themselves into lodges, called Hunters' Lodges, of which there was one in Cleveland.

hurrah boys.

Noisily enthusiastic partisans.

The noise and enthusiasm of Jackson's supporters in 1828 and 1832 led to the coinage of this nickname.

1828 *Ohio St. Jrnl.* 19 June 2/1. When General Jackson was first brought before the public, his admirers...earned for their pains, the appropriate name of "hurra boys."
1828 *Western Cornet* (Xenia, Ohio) 15 Aug. 3/1. We are the hurra boys...and can, with empty bombast, gull the ignorant and ignoble part of the community.
1894 G. W. Curtis *Orations* II.25. This objection would probably have reminded Mr. Lincoln of a little story of the hot election of 1829. An anti-Jackson partisan fell into the water, and, when nearly drowned, was seized by the hand and drawn to the surface, while his excited rescuer, delighted to save him, expressed his joy in the familiar phrase, "Hurrah for Jackson!" "What d'you say?" asked the drowning man thickly, but not so far gone that he could not hear the obnoxious name—"what d' you say?" "Hurrah for Jackson!" replied the other. "No, I'll be darned if I'll be saved by a hurrah-for-Jackson man," said the first, shaking off his hand and sinking back into the water.

The first quotation seems to indicate that *hurrah boys* is connected with Jackson's first appearance in national politics, which would make the expression older than 1828. On the other hand, Edward Everett Hale states that in that year it was comparatively unknown, at least in New England.

Hale's remarks on the symptomatic significance of the phrase are so interesting that we quote them at length:

Hale *Memories of a Hundred Years* 271–3. It was on the third day of November in 1828 that I, who was then six years old, was led by the hand of Fullum as we four of us children returned, after dark, from a tea-party at Katharine Foster's in Avon Place. It was the night following the day when Massachusetts had given her vote for J. Q. Adams in 1828. As Fullum half dragged me and half lifted me across the "Main Street," a man's voice broke the silence of the evening by the cry "Hurrah for Jackson!" I think that such cries were then very unusual. I doubt whether the New Englanders were in the habit of expressing themselves in such ways. A counter cry from another direction immediately replied, "Hurrah for Adams!" But, alas! a third voice, evidently from a new interlocutor, replied at once with a second "Hurrah for Jackson!" I was but a child, but in one matter I saw the future of seventy years as well as I now see it in retrospect. Impossible not to observe that two men hurrahed for Jackson and only one for Adams! Impossible not to reflect that in the street neither my father, nor my uncles, nor any of the gentlemen whom I was used to see, would have hurrahed for anybody. And, at the same time, how clear, even to a child's observation, that there were many more men in the world of the kind who like to hurrah in the street than of the kind who do not like to! All that we children understood of the business was that General Jackson once hanged six militia-men, and that his election would be ruin for the country. Observe also that this was at the close of an election day in which Adams had four votes in Massachusetts for one given for Jackson. I believe this story about "Hurrah for Jackson!" is worth the precious three hundred words which it has cost, because it marks almost to a minute the period when the United States became a real democracy. It is as good a text as I shall have for saying a few words on the political change between the first third of the century and the last two-thirds.

1884 *Boston Daily Advertiser* 7 June 5/3. James G. Blaine has at length captured a presidential nomination from the Republican party. After having been rejected twice, he is now accepted at the demand of the "hurrah boys" of the west. . . .

1889 Hayes *Diary* IV.521. He [Gov. Foraker] is brilliant, witty, eloquent, and very popular with the hurrah boys, but the sober and conservative element of the party dislike his methods. [According to Beers, *Hanna*, 111, "hurrah boys" was a favorite expression of President Hayes.]

hurrah campaign.

One characterized by noisy demonstrations.

1884 *Harper's W.* 2 Feb. 70. "A Hurra Campaign." It is sometimes said that the Republicans should rely this year on a hurra campaign, or in other words . . . upon the personal popularity of the candidate.

hyena.

Although the most prominent use of this derogatory term is certainly more personal than political, we include the expression to show what it was possible to say in 19th century political debates.

A. A remark of S. S. Cox during a speech by Blaine concerning a pardon for Jefferson Davis.

1876 *Ann. of Cleve.* 15 Jan. No. 769. That Cox . . . should be caught saying, "O dry up, Blaine," and "talk on, hyena," in the midst of a serious debate is one of many things that should made Sam Cox blush for his record.

1876 *Ib.* 17 Jan. No.775. The Plain Dealer says: Cox made an important contribution to the congressional menagerie which needed replenishing after the departure of the "Butlerian rhinoceros." It is a very singular anomaly for those who defend or apologize for the deliberate starving to death of 18,000 union prisoners at Ander-

sonville to call Blaine a "hyena," merely because he denounced that atrocity.

1876 *Harper's W.* 5 Feb. 102/2. Mr. COX shouted to Mr. Blaine to "dry up," and called him the "honorable hyena from Maine."

1876 *Ib.* 18 March 222/3. There is no misapprehension, no ill-feeling, no "hate." Northern men and Republicans are not hyenas. They do not misapprehend the sincere wish of many intelligent Southerners to have done as soon as may be with the war and all that belongs to it.

B. Other political uses:

1858 in Sparks *Lincoln-Douglas Deb.* 27.
> We'll hunt the lion down,
> We jolly bold Hyenas.
>
> . . . . .
>
> Why can't he do like us—
> Stoop low for place and plunder?

1868 *Cong. Globe* 10 July 3910/2. A little while ago he spoke of the ticket at New York [Seymour and Blair] as a hyena ticket, for the reason, he said, its strongest part was behind. I have heard such a thing called before a Kangaroo ticket [q.v.], but never a hyena ticket, and what similitude my honorable friend can make out between that ticket and a hyena I do not know.

1906 *Nation* 10 May 377/1. The belated attack of the "hyena politicians" on Gov. Hoch of Kansas made it certain that he would be renominated by the Republicans. It used to be understood in the West that an attack on the private character of a candidate, in order to have any effect, must be made on the very day of the convention. Twenty-four hours of reflection was judged to be sufficient time for a reaction against the "slanderers" to set in.

I

illiberal (-ity).

Opposed to *liberal* (q.v.) :

1874 Foote *Casket of Reminiscences* 160 . . . though the envy of some, and the selfish illiberality of others, may for some time have succeeded in attaching some doubt as to the policy and propriety of this much-discussed measure. . . .

1946 *Time* 16 Nov. 23. Minnesota's Senator Joe Ball said he would introduce a bill to outlaw the closed shop, which he called "the most illiberal thing in our industrial picture."

I/me.

The allegation of fondness for the personal pronoun has been used as a reproach against many figures.

1830 Paulding *Chron. of Gotham* 185. This was the greatest triumph of eloquence ever witnessed in our state. I cannot go through the whole of my speech. It lasted eight hours and three quarters, and I should have made it nine, had not all the candles gone out, and left me and my subject in outer darkness. The reader may judge of its length from the fact, that it was ascertained by an industrious old person, who could not bear to be idle, that the word "Sir," occurred three hundred, and the monosyllable "I," five hundred times—the word "principle," six hundred and thirty, and the word "interest," not once. Can there be any higher proof of the purity of my motives?

Two of the better known political instances:

1858 *Burlington Gazette* 16 July in Sparks *Deb.* 549. We find that Lincoln made use of the personal pronoun "I" no less than 225 times! . . . And further, that he is known all over Suckerdom by the name of the "Perpendicular Pronoun."

Lincoln's use of the pronoun was defended by some:

1865 Lowell *Prose Works* V.208. He forgets himself so entirely in his object as to give his *I* the sympathetic and persuasive effect of *We* with the great body of his countrymen.

Applied to Andrew Johnson:

1866 *Cleve. Leader* 24 April 1/3. The

President, in his speech to the committee from the Philadelphia convention, says: "I am as much opposed to egotism as any one."

The following is proof of the number of times certain words occur in his speech: This humble individual, one; myself, two; me, nine; my, 28; I, 69. That's not much, only 109 allusions to himself in a 15 minute speech.

1866 *Ib.* 4 Sept. 2/4. It [Johnson's speech] made "seventy-nine" lines of ordinary print. It contained the personal pronouns "I, me and my" only "forty-four" times— or one for every other line, and something to carry. President Johnson is a my-ty man.

1866 *Ib.* 5 Sept. 2/5. The President read the following poem to the Albanians:

I, I, I, I, I, I, I,
Me, me, me, me, me, me, me,
I,me, I,me, I,me, I,
Me, I, me, I, me, I, me.

1866 *Ib.* 24 Sept. 2/4.

There was a man from Tennessee
    Considered wondrous wise
He jumped into a bramble bush
    And scratched out all his "I's."
And when he saw his I's were out,
    With all his might and main,
He jumped into a rebel bush
    And scratched them in again!

imperialist, imperialism.

A. In the 17th century *imperialist* meant primarily a soldier of the German emperor and occasionally of the Roman emperor, as in the oldest known American occurrence:

I. Mather *Preval. Prayer* 249 [OED]. The Emperour Marcus Aurelius going to war against the Quads, Vandals, Sarmats, and Germans . . . the Imperialists were so cooped up by their numerous Enemies.

Already during this period it can be applied to politics:

B. Harris *Parival's Iron Age* 119 [OED]. Favouring the factions of the Guelphs, against the Gibellins, or Imperialists.

B. The modern history of the word begins in France, where the followers of Napoleon are called "imperialists" even before he officially adopted the title of emperor: **1800** W. Taylor in *Monthly Mag.* VIII.599. These imperious imperialists are so effectually served as to bespeak at the same time a law against their antagonists in courts not allied. **1817** J. Scott *Paris Revis.* 315. People of all parties, royalists, imperialists, and republicans, affected . . . a fine indignant surprise at the bare suggestion.

In Europe the word was revived during the reign of Napoleon III, mostly as a critical word used by his enemies (see Ladendorf under *imperialismus*). This usage is reflected in American politics where it refers to U. S. Grant's alleged autocratic tendencies (see CAESARISM). **1874** *N. Y. Trib.* 22 May 4/6. Mr. Henry Watterson has returned to Louisville, but evidently has not left behind him his fear of a third term and possible imperialism. Along with this usage in which *imperialism* clearly is a derivation of *emperor* there is another that connects the word with *empire:* **1870** Senator Bayard in *Gt. Deb.* III.15 . . . it is proposed that we should embark the Government of the United States upon the vast and trackless sea of imperialism, to change it into an imperial government of outlying and distant dependencies. . . .

C. In the heyday of expansionism (q.v.), mainly in connection with the Spanish-American War, *imperialism* in this semantic variation becomes an important and much debated word. **1897** *Nation* 30 Dec. 511/3. It was at first known as "Jingoism" when it issued from the fertile brain of Disraeli, but it has been gradually getting rid of this somewhat vulgar appelation, and as "Imperialism," has become another name for a wide extent of territory, inhabited by divers races, speaking various languages, and kept in order by an immense apparatus of forts, native armies, and fleets. **1899** Schurz *Works* VI.29. The rest of the pleas for imperialism consist mostly of those high-sounding catchwords of which a free people when about to decide great questions, should be especially suspicious. **1900** Schurz *Ib.* VI.216. I consider the manner in which the imperialistic policy is being commended by some persons to popular approval, the hugest confidence game ever practiced upon a free people. **1900** in *Men and Issues of 1900* 86. If we adhere to these principles and aspire after these high ideals, the outcry to the alarmist, the shibboleth "imperialism" used by those who think it safe to sail by the light on the stern of the ship, can produce no terror in those who are not affrighted by the inviting prospect of our country's greatness. Imperialism is not incompatible with federalism. *Ib.* 96. Do the imperialists worship at no shrine except that of Mammon?

impracticable, impractical.

Epithet levelled against one whose positions or opinions are not always based upon political reality; specifically, against a reformer. **1836** *Richmond Enquirer* in *Ltrs. & Times of the Tylers* I.592. Every consideration was addressed to the "impractical Whigs to withdraw from their position." **1839** *Dem. Rev.* July 28 . . . his [Leggett's] uncompromising and "impracticable" boldness. **1841** *Cong. Globe* Sept. App. 295 . . . my colleague stood by my side, among a little band of impracticables. . . . **1878** *Harper's W.* 7 Sept. 706/1 . . . Senator CONKLING said that he did not understand belonging to a party a little. But it is those who belong to it a little who save us from the natural tendencies of party. Their "impracticability" is simply their refusal to lend their paws to the shrewd fellow with a taste for chestnuts.

1900 Roosevelt *Ltrs.* 2 Feb. II.1161 . . . a group of impracticables of the Godkin-Parkhurst type. . . .

in(un)alienable right.

The term *inalienable* belongs to the Middle Ages [See *Speculum* XXIX,488f.], during which period it applied to the privileges of king, church, etc. In its restricted sense *inalienable* and its derivatives are used in legal terminology [*OED* under *inalienable* and *inalienableness*]. In the 18th century the political philosophers of the Enlightenment attribute inalienable rights to the human individual regardless of rank. The preferred expression of this idea is, however, *imprescriptable rights,* the formula used by Rousseau in *La Contrat Social.* However, in a chapter discussing the question of whether a man can voluntarily become the slave of another, he comes very close to the idea that liberty is an inalienable right.

1761 I.iv. Si un particulier, dit Grotius, peut aliéner sa liberté et se rendre esclave d'un maître, pourquoi tout un peuple ne pourrait il pas aliéner la sienne et se rendre sujet d'un roi? . . . Aliéner c'est donner ou vendre. Or, un homme qui se fait esclave d'un autre ne se donne pas; il se vend, tout au moins pour sa subsistance.

The many competing synonyms are shown in English usages:

1764 Otis *Rights* 34. There are, thank God, natural, inherent and inseparable rights as men, and as citizens, that would remain.

1764 Gadsden in Gibbes *Doc. Hist.* 3. This privilege is due to us as British subjects . . . entitled to the inestimable rights of the same laws and customs.

1765 *Ib.* 8. Those natural and inherent rights that we all feel and know, as men and as descendants of English, we have a right to.

1765 Blackstone *Works* I.45. Those rights then which God and Nature have established, and are therefore called natural rights, such as life and liberty, need not the aid of human laws to be more effectually invested in every man than they are; neither do they receive any additional strength when declared by the municipal laws to be inviolable.

The phrase, of course, was fixed by its use in the Declaration of Independence: "certain unalienable rights." This usage by Jefferson was, however, adapted from the longer phrase he used in the Virginia Bill of Rights a month earlier.

in Hart *Sourcebook* 447. A majority of the community hath an indubitable, inalienable, and indefeasible right to reform, alter, or abolish it.

It seems clear that this passage is under the influence of John Adams since it varies only slightly from his formula "indisputable, unalienable, indefeasible." Unless it can be shown that Jefferson used a similar phrase prior to 1776, it must be assumed that the introduction of *unalienable* into the Declaration of Independence is due to Adams. The first draft has a compromise formula "inherent and unalienable."

1765 Adams, *Works,* III.456. [*Diss. on Canon and Feudal Law*] . . . but besides this [desire for knowledge], they have a right, an indisputable, unalienable, indefeasible, divine right to that most dreaded and envied kind of knowledge, I mean, of the characters and conduct of their rulers.

The influence that the phrase *inalienable rights* in its American sense exerted in European politics is, to say the least, very considerable. In England:

1780 Bentham *Works* III.554. That every commoner of this realm, excepting infants, persons of insane mind, and criminals incapacitated by law, hath a natural inalienable, and equal right to vote in the election of his representative in parliament.

1786 Sheridan, *Speeches,* I.230. How inconstitutional was the idea of purchasing with a bribe that which it had ever been contended no Englishman could sell or part with for money—his unalienable right of voting at an election.

But it is the 11th of June, 1789, that marks the decisive point in the European history of the word. On this day, Lafayette introduced in the French Assembly his famous Declaration de Loi de Land, a document closely patterned on the American Declaration of Independence.

in *L'Ancien Moniteur* I.148. Toute homme naît avec des droits inaliénables et imprescriptibles.

Later his declaration was used as an introductory chapter to the French constitution.

1791 in Block I.673. Les représentants du peuple français...ont résolu d' exposer, dans une déclaration solennelle, les droits naturels, inaliénables et sacrés de l'homme.

From France the word spreads to Germany, where *inalienable* after several other tries is translated by *unveraüserlich.*

1791 Forster, *Ansichter,* II.40. Alle so genannte Souverainitäts rechte, behaup-

ten die Demokraten ferner, sind ihrer Natur zufolge allen Menschen unveraüserlich eigen.

Sweden is reached at the latest in 1792:

Paine-Nordenschold *Människans Rattigheten* 119. Menniskans naturlija, oföranderlija och helija rattigheten.

In America since the writing of the Declaration, the phrase has been applied to countless situations, some serious, as abolition, and integration of the Negro; or the humorous, as the casting of a scratched ballot. A few quotations:

1788 in Mayo *Clay* 50. The first and greatest blessing of the Western Country ... the navigation of the Mississippi, our inalienable right.

1818 Adams *Works* X.357. The rights and duties are inherent, inalienable, indefeasible, indistructable, and immortal.

183– Channing *Writings* 689/1. Great truths, inalienable rights, everlasting duties, these will form the chief subjects of this discussion.

1851 "Warrington" 47. Impossible to aid by word or deed in remanding a fugitive slave to bondage without aiding to rob him of an inalienable right, and thus sinning against Christian light and against God.

1862 Christy *Pulpit Politics* 502. Interest, fashion, false religion, and tyranny may triumph for a while, and rob a man of his inalienable rights; but the people can not always be deceived, and will not always be oppressed.

1873 *Annals of Cleve.* No.2930. The inalienable right of scratching was exercised to an extent which drove the polling clerks to despair when it came to counting up returns.

1903 Mitchell *Org. Labor* 283. The inalienable right of a man to work will then be put upon a par with the inalienable right of a child to play truant.

1940 Helm *Truman* 136. We should recognize his [the Negro's] inalienable rights as specified in our Constitution.

incendiary.

A. The metaphorical use of *incendiary*, meaning a person who excites public passions, probably goes back to the religious dissensions in England in the 17th century, when church burning was not an uncommon practice:

1611 Speed *Hist. Gt. Brit.* [*OED*]. An incendiary outrage at Norwich, where the Citizens set on fire the Priorie Church.
1631 Gouge *God's Arrows* 356. Campion, and other Seminaries and Incendiaries were sent by the Pope.
1674–1710 Burnet *Serm. Royal Martyr* 5. Among the much-abused words of the late time were Incendiary and Incendiarism.

Also, in France during the Revolution castles were burned by incendiaries:

Blance *Histoire de la Revolution Française* II.477. Une brochure de l'époque, public sous ce titre: les Incendiaries des Dauphine ou les Ennemis des grands fait observer que les actes qui précéde ne furent en aucunne sorte le fruit de mêmees séditieuses.

B. Thus early uses in America of *incendiary* meaning a political agitator are easily found:

1793 in Leary *That Rascal Freneau* 236. Freneau ... is regarded here as a mere incendiary, or rather as the despicable tool of higher incendiaries....
1803 *Mass. Spy* 10 Aug. 2/4. He [Jefferson] paid Callender for ... calling Adams a hoary incendiary.

During the disturbances in Rhode Island we find the incendiaries again employing the practices of their English and French predecessors to gain their political objectives: [ ]

1842 Hone *Diary* II.597. The incendiaries ... swear that the State belongs to them and that they will govern it.

The main identification throughout the 19th century, however, was with the abolitionists:

1837 Leggett *Pol. Writings* II.274 ... to bait the abolitionists, by calling the latter all sorts of opprobrious names; ... as incendiaries, ready to burn to the ground the temple of freedom....
1842 in "Warrington" *Pen Portraits* 26. Not only is the man who burns buildings an incendiary in the estimation of some Southern people, but also he who dares to express his belief that one man has no right to hold another man as property, that slavery ought not to exist in free America, and that the respectful petitions of citizens of the North should have a respectful hearing by the representatives of the Union. If Mr. Torrey has done nothing more incendiary than to express these sentiments ... it is a burning shame that he should be imprisoned for it.
1850 Strong *Diary* II.19. Billy Seward and his gang of incendiaries....
1859 in Pike *First Blows* 452. The truth is, that to the South, ... all matter that is not carefully prepared with express reference to the institution of slavery is "incendiary."

independent

A. In the early 17th century *independent* was a word of church politics [*OED*]. It became a political word of the first order during the Cromwell revolution as the name of the Puritan party; however, there seems to be no unbroken connection between this use and that of the 18th century in England. During this period *in-*

dependent in itself is not a party name but occurs as an adjective characterizing factions in both the Whig and Tory parties:

1721 *Independent Whig* [title of London periodical].
1735 Bolingbroke *On Parties* 9. On this Foundation all the reasonable, independent Whigs and Tories unite.

Also in American usage the word to begin with is an adjective.

The American use of *independent* in the title of publications begins with the *Independent Reflector* [N.Y., 1753] and continues with the *Independent Citizen* [1787], *Independent Messenger* [1831], and the *Independent* [1848].

B. The adaptation of *independent* to party politics may have been retarded by the feeling that the word was not very distinctive since every American was supposed to be an independent. However, in 1817 and later we find an Independent Republican party in Pennsylvania:

1817 pamphlets printed by the Independent Republican party in Pennsylvania.
1818 Fearon *Sketches* 139. The moderate democrats [are] called by the several names of "Independent Republicans," "Democrats of the Revolution," and "Old Schoolmen."

Not as a party name but characterizing candidates running on the basis of their own merits rather than party affiliation, *independent* occurs in:

1828 Tracy to Weed in Barnes *Weed* 32. But what shall we do in the mean time? There's the rub. Are we strong enough for an independent ticket?
1840 Kennedy *Quodlibet* 136. Thus, when Theodore Fog first announced himself as the independent candidate,...

Mister Theodore Fog, of this Borough, an old practitioner at more than one bar, having waked up one morning with the idea that he was born to fill the measure of his country's glory, as well as he fills that of his own every night, has conceived the sublime project of running on an independent ticket, in the approaching election.

C. In 1848 we find the first (?) instance of *independent* used alone:

Chase 91. Two members of the caucus... had been elected as "Independents," or in opposition to the candidates of both the old parties.

It was first (?) applied to a political party in 1874, when the Grangers of Indiana chose the name of Independent for their newly formed organization:

1874 *Appleton's* 413/1. A resolution was adopted assuming the name of "Independent" for the party to be organized, "as an expression of the sentiment and purposes" of the delegates, and in order to "command due recognition."

D. As the reform movement directed against machine politics gained momentum in the Republican party the term *Independent* (*Republican*) acquires renewed importance:

1880 Curtis *Sp.* II.158... undoubtedly the independent Republican voters today hold the balance of power in this State [N.Y.] in the pending presidential election.
1882 in *Roosevelt Cyc.* 248/1. I now wish to speak for a moment to those Republicans who call themselves the Independents and work outside the party.
1884 *Ohio St. Jrnl.* 22 July. The Independents, however, cannot support a nomination which is the culmination of the tendency that they would correct.

1884 *N. Y. Trib.* 1 March. Only the man who can call himself an independent-indifferent-don't-care-whether-I-vote-or-not Republican, can properly demand that the terrible unlaundried garment, "bloody shirt," be kept out of sight.
1888 Lowell *Pol. Essays* 318. It has been proved, I think, that the old parties are not to be reformed from within. It is from without that the attempt must be made, and it is the Independents who must make it.

E. Independence gained fresh importance in the beginnings of our century. In 1905 William Randolph Hearst organized the Independence League in New York City which in 1908 was expanded into a national party by a convention at Chicago. The party was opposed to both the Democratic and Republican organizations and advocated a long list of reforms and progressive measures:
1908 *Nation* 30 July 83/2. In opening the first national convention of the Independence Party at Chicago on Monday, William Randolph Hearst....
Ib. 20 Aug. 153/1. Cannot the National Independence party make just enough headway in Ohio, Indiana, Kansas, and Nebraska to blast whatever hopes the Democracy may cherish?
1908 *Rev. of Rev.* XXXVIII.307/1. The Independence party ... is neither an accident nor an experiment.

F. The typical usage in the 20th century, however, follows the pattern of Wilson:
1915 *Public Papers* III.238. This country is guided and its policy is determined by the independent voter.

indomitables.
A Democratic faction in New York.
1839 Hone *Diary* I.443. In this appoint-

ment the President, it is said, has given mortal offence to the butt-enders and indomitables who form the elite of his party in New York.
1840 *Boston Transcript* 15 April 2/1. When the Registry Law was first spoken of, the tail of the Democratic party, the roarers, butt-enders, ringtails, O.K.'s (flat-burglary this latter title) and indomitables, talked strong about nullification and all that.
1851 in Wilson *Slave Power* II.349. But the great body of the Free-Soilers were firm, and, notwithstanding the fierce opposition arrayed against their candidate, the timidity of friends, the counsels of the governor, and the inflexibility of the "indomitables," as the twenty-three Democrats styled themselves, they still adhered to their candidate.

infected district.
A. Democratic epithet for the 8th District of western New York, where the Democrats could not gain a foothold because of the strong anti-Masonic feelings of that area.
1827 Hammond *Hist.* II.384. It is to be observed, that these remarks are to be deemed to be confined to the western counties, commonly called "the infected district," where anti-masonry had its origin.
1829 Jenkins *Hist. Pol. Parties in N. Y.* 364. They elected their Senators in all Districts, except the Eighth, which was the principal theatre of the Anti-Masonic excitement, and now began to be termed "the infected district."
1830 *Workingman's Adv.* 7 Aug. 1/4. Some may imagine that "speculative work" is more needed in the "infected district" than elsewhere.
1834 in Seward *Autobio.* 239.
Van came here to woo the folks,
Ha, ha, the wooing o't;
The "infected district" would not veer,
So back again Mat had to steer,
Ha, ha, the wooing o't.

B. Other districts which remained strongholds of the opposition.

1835 Sedgwick *Tales & Sk.* 23. The democrats for the most part occupied the hill. What an infected district it then seemed to me!

1846 *Hamilton Intelligencer* 19 Feb. 1/4. Tremendous Mass Meeting in the "Infected District." [downtown Cincinnati]

infidel (ticket).

A label placed upon the Workingman's Ticket in New York charging it with being under the influence of Frances Wright, who held radical ideas on religion and social institutions in general.

1829 *Workingman's Adv.* 7 Nov. 2/4. The most pitiful attempts were made to enlist religious prejudices in opposition to the ticket, by denouncing it as "infidel," &c. The cry of infidelity has ever been a fruitful theme and powerful auxiliary in the hands of aristocracy....

1829 *Ib.* 12 Dec. 1/1. Whereas, the Mechanics and Working Men of this city ... have been stigmatized as an "infidel party"....

1830 *Ib.* 9 Jan. 3/4. [from *Eastern Galaxy and Herald*] The Working Class in New York, ycleped, by the aristocratic, the "Infidel Class." [head] We are now satisfied that our suspicions of the incorrectness of the report concerning the "Infidel Ticket" lately supported in New York city, were correct.

1830 *Ib.* 23 Jan. 4/1. In New York, the "infidel ticket," so called, has been defeated by a small majority. This ticket was gotten up by Frances Wright and her infamous associates, under the specious title of the "working man's ticket"....

inflation, inflationist.

A. The metaphorical use of *inflation* to designate the policy of an expanded paper currency may be found in the American political vocabulary as early as the year 1837 during the conflict between the hard and soft money men, centering around the Specie Circular:

1837 in Bigelow *Tilden* I.64. If they are imprudent, prices, which have not fallen to a sound state, will rise, speculation revive, and a bubble will be inflated more disastrous in its explosion than the present one.

1838 *Sp. of D. Bernard* 195. The property pledge can have no tendency whatever to prevent an inflation of the currency.

1840 in *Cong. Globe* 13 Feb. App.739. He, to be sure, attributed it to the effects of inflated paper and credit; but did he not know that it was the late administration that had given impulse to and had been the hot-house of that inflation, if it existed?

B. Following the Civil War when money questions again became prominent topics for debate, *inflation* and *inflationist* were popular labels.

1870 *Nation* 3 March 129. The work of inflation by adding fifty million dollars to the currency ... is part of an arrangement between the Western inflationists, who want more greenbacks, and the Eastern tariff men, who are opposed to the reduction of duties.

1874 in *Cong. Record* 8 April 2931/1. I know that those of us who are in favor of a proper amount of currency are stigmatized by the name of "inflationists." We do not accept that designation at all.

1876 *Harper's W.* 8 Jan. 30/4. If you tell these facts [*re* evils of paper money] to an inflationist, he may denounce them vigorously, and scold you for remembering them, and say they have nothing to do with present questions....

See EXPANSION, CONTRACTION, RAG BABY.

initiative.

See 1899 quot.

1899 *Rev. of Rev.* XIX.515/2. It [San Francisco charter] also provides for what is known as the "initiative," a method by which a certain percentage of the voters may of their own accord, by signing a petition cause a given subject to be referred for decision to the popular vote. **1907** Lloyd *A Sovereign People* 62. The agitation for the initiative was thus coeval with that for the referendum [in Switzerland], and the "thinkers" of the movement, at any rate, saw and urged their linkage in the framework of democracy. But since it is more important to stop what you do not like than to secure what you do like, the logic of events gave priority to the referendum.... **1907** *Ib.* 246. This power of the people to effect constitutional changes has, through the "formulated initiative," developed into a practical power to initiate legislation which, though not complete, goes very far towards giving to the people a competency of legislation co-ordinate with, or, in case of conflict, superior to, that of the legislative assemblies.

innocuous desuetude.

Grover Cleveland's phrase characterizing the disuse into which the Tenure of Office Act had fallen. **1886** in *Public Papers of G. Cleveland* 65. After an existence of nearly twenty years of almost innocuous desuetude these laws are brought forth. **1887** Peck *Twenty Yrs.* 143...with the solid support of the Democratic Senators, the repeal was carried, as it was also in the House; and thus was blotted out a law which, as the President observed, had properly fallen into "innocuous desuetude." **1920** Clark *Qrt. Century* I.259. His [Cleveland's] most exquisite phrase, and entirely original, so far as I know, was "innocuous desuetude," still frequently quoted and perhaps to be quoted as long as our vernacular is spoken by the children of men. **1920** *Ib.* I.297. It was Henry Clay's habit [as Speaker] to participate in debate

whenever the spirit moved him, which was quite frequently. The custom, however, has fallen largely into "innocuous desuetude," to borrow Mr. Cleveland's famous phrase.

insolence of office.

This Shakespearean phrase has had frequent political usage, showing the perennial distrust of the man in office or power. *Hamlet* III.i
For who would bear the whips and scorns
  of time,
. . . .
The insolence of office and the spurns
That patient merit of the unworthy takes. **1765** Otis *Considerations* 28. The colonists, as they ever have been, would be in *general* better treated, less subjected to the insolence of office from Europeans, than from colonists. **1841** *Mangum Papers* III.145. Made up for excessive devotion to him [Harrison] by a slight exhibition of the "insolence of office" towards others. **1871** Morton in *Gt. Deb.* IX.298. They [English clerks] have one quality that our clerks have not got; that is, they have "the insolence of office" that results from a life tenure. **1871** Nye in *Ib.* IX.304. There is nothing that becomes so odious in every government as "the insolence of office," where the officers have life tenures.

the institution.

Slavery; a shortened form of *domestic institution* or *peculiar institution* (q. v.). The phrase illustrates the dominance of the slavery question in the political discussions of America's institutions. **1863** Jones *Mirror of Democracy* 234. Denouncing as "aggressors upon Southern rights," all who dare question the morality of "the institution." **1856** in H. Winter Davis *Sp.* 42. The Democrat is jealous of anything which impeaches the high duty of extending *the* *institution,* and is impatient of men who accept it as an existing institution, to be protected as any other industrial interest is to be protected.

instructed delegate.

A member of a convention who has been directed by his constituents to vote for a certain candidate or measure.

1844 *Niles' Reg.* 8 June 236/1. My position as an "instructed delegate" from this portion of the state to the democratic convention....

The practice of instructing representatives was common earlier in the United States:

1817 in Calhoun *Works* II.177. This doctrine of implied instruction ... is very different ... from the old doctrine that the constituents have a right to assemble and formally to instruct the representative.

insurgent.

A. Isolated uses of *insurgent* occur in party politics since the end of the 18th century:

1788 in Madison *Works* V.85. The antifederal party [in Mass.] is reinforced by the insurgents, and by the province of Mayne, which apprehends greater obstacles to the scheme of a separate Government from the new system than may be otherwise experienced.

B. The Cuban uprising against Spain gave the word increased popularity:

1897 *Rev. of Rev.* XVI. 6/2. The Cuban League of the United States, meanwhile, is making especial efforts to promote the cause of the insurgents.

1897 *Ib.* XVI. 647/1. From the very outset of the insurrection to the present time the insurgents have never had so good a reason for confidence as was given them by the recall of Weyler.

1898 *Ib.* XVII. 131/1. First, there is absolutely nothing whatever in the situation that justified the belief that the Cuban insurgents can be led to accept a political compromise.

C. Mencken suggests, doubtless correctly, that this vogue is behind the use of *insurgent* in politics during the beginning of our century and particularly around 1909, when a group of senators who opposed strict party rule became known by the name of "Insurgents."

1900 *Cinc. Enquirer* 25 June 2/4. Insurgents [head]. Ohio delegation to the National Convention of Republican Clubs ... appears to be made up very largely of the insurgent element.

1902 *McClure's* Sept. 390/2. There were nineteen Republican "insurgents" in the Senate....

Ib. 391/1 ... President Roosevelt spanked the beet-sugar insurgents.

1909 *Rev. of Rev.* XXXIX.653. It is by no means the object of these remarks to criticize the so-called "insurgents" in the Senate for having opinions of their own upon the problems of tariff and taxation.

1909 *Ib.* XL.138/1. The so-called "insurgent" Senators, a group of ten, will not have lost any credit with their constituents for having made an able and conscientious effort to secure a more thoroughgoing tariff reform.

1911 *Ib.* XLIII.263. The late Senator Dolliver ... made his witty definition of an "insurgent" as a man who insisted that a bill should at least be read before [being] finally voted upon.

1912 in LaFollette *Autobio.* 76. It is for this that the group of men called Insurgents have been fighting.

1916 White *The Old Order Changeth* ix. If the "Insurgents" of the first decade of this century could have read what has been done by the last congress in developing their ideas, they would have welcomed the rebuffs and defeats which they met in the early part of the century and would have regarded the game as worth the candle.

internal improvements.

While the question of the constitutionality of improvements paid for by the government is an old one, the formula seems to go back to 1807:

1807 in J. Q. Adams *Memoirs* 23 Feb. I.460. I moved that the bill, and an amendment proposed by General Smith of Maryland, should be postponed, for the purpose of considering a resolution directing the Secretary of the Treasury to report a general plan for internal improvements of this kind.

Adams himself in a later letter felt that this was the first instance of such a proposal:

1824 in *Niles' Reg.* XXVI.328. On the 23rd February, 1807, I offered to the senate of the United States, of which I was then a member, the first resolution, as I believe, that ever was presented to the congress contemplating a general system of internal improvement.

As the country expanded, the cry for the construction of roads and canals made internal improvements a popular subject on all political levels:

1817 in Madison *Works* VIII.386. Having considered the bill this day presented to me entitled "An act to set apart and pledge certain funds for internal improvements."...

1817 Paulding *Ltrs.* I.90 ... they ... look with a jealous eye on every internal improvement in roads or canals, that is exclusively advantageous to either.

1828 *Spirit of the Times* (Batavia, Ohio) 13 Sept. 3/2. Internal improvements will steadily and rapidly advance, extending their benefits to almost every section of the country.

As with other plans which originally had been begun to fill a definite need in the development of the country, politicians in order to advance their own popularity and wealth carried their internal improvement programs to extremes:

1836 in Byrdsall *LocoFoco* 63. Man alone sells his offspring to speculators and monopolists, and this by a gross desecration of terms is denominated by the demagogues of the day, "Internal Improvement."

1840 Kennedy *Quodlibet* 26. This verdict wrought a strange appetite in our county, amongst the landholders, to be ruined the same way; and I truly believe it was a chief cause of the unpopularity of internal improvements in this neighbourhood, that the commissioners were only able to destroy the farms on the lowlands....

interposition.

The action of intervention, particularly of a state in regard to an act of the federal government.

A. Long present in English usage, it refers among other things to geography, poetry, society, war, etc. (See *OED* for quotations.)

B. In the early history of the American government we frequently find this same general usage:

1774 in *Basic Writ. Jefferson* 14. Nay, the single interposition of an interested individual against a law was scarcely ever known to fail of success, though in the opposite scale, were placed the interests of a whole community.

1808 Madison in Dwight *Hartford Conv.* 74. To consider this evidence of the justice of his Britannic majesty as a pledge for an effectual interposition with respect to all the abuses against a recurrence of which the proclamation was meant to provide.

1810 Madison in *Ann. of Cong.* 5 Dec. 11. The Spanish authority was subverted and a situation produced exposing the country to ulterior events which might essentially affect the rights and welfare of the Union. In such a conjuncture I did not delay the interposition required for the occupancy of the territory west of the river Perdido.

C. The specific meaning of *interposition* (and *interpose*) develops after the adoption of the Constitution in instances in which a state or group of states attempts to circumvent an action of the federal government by asserting what it feels to be its constitutional rights as a state. Notable examples:

1. Alien and Sedition acts:

1798 *Va. Resolutions*... that in case of a deliberate, palpable, and dangerous exercise of other powers, not granted by the said compact, the states... have the right, and are in duty bound, to interpose....

2. War of 1812:

1815 Resol. of Conv. in Dwight *Hartford Conv.* 361. It is not only the right but the duty of such a state to interpose its authority for their protection, in the manner best calculated to secure that end.

3. Nullification controversy:

1828 Calhoun *Sp.* VI.54. To the States respectively—each in its sovereign capacity—is reserved the power, by its veto, or right of interposition, to arrest the encroachment.

1830 Hayne in Webster *Works* III.320. What he maintained was, that in case of a plain, palpable violation of the Constitution by the general government, a State may interpose; and that this interposition is constitutional.

1831 Calhoun *Sp.* VI.97. But it is no less clear that secession thus distinguished, is not only an act of interposition on the part of the State, but the very highest possible act of the kind,—and that it assumes principles which cover the whole ground of the State-rights doctrines.

1831 *Ib.* VI.61. This right of interposition, thus solemnly asserted by the State of Virginia, be it called what it may,—State-right, veto, nullification, or by any other name,—I conceive to be the fundamental principle of our system.

1833 *Ib.* II.256. It is only by this power of interposition that the reserved rights of the States can be peacefully and efficiently protected against the encroachments of the General Government.

1833 Webster *Works* III.481. The right of State interposition strikes at the very foundation of the legislative power of Congress. It possesses no effective legislative power, if such right of State interposition exists; because it can pass no law not subject to abrogation.

4. Civil War:

1861 in *North. Editorials* II.833. A great hoary wrong... surely calls on a righteous God and outraged man for effective interposition.

5. Supreme Court decision on segregation:

1956 *Cong. Record* 25 Jan. 1293. But the States have a remedy. It was first used by Georgia in the 1790's.... Jefferson, Madison, and Calhoun were its authors and originators. It was called the doctrine of interposition.

1956 *Ib.* 1295. Mr. Speaker, I have heard many say that they favor interposition, but are opposed to nullification. This is the same thing as saying that we favor the aiming and firing of our guns but we are against hitting the target.

1956 *Time* 30 Jan. 14/3. Last week in the Virginia Senate... Harry Carter Stuart, a great-nephew of General Jeb Stuart, introduced a resolution "Interposing the sovereignty of the State against the encroachment upon the reserved powers of this State."

invisible government.

Persons or organizations who are felt to control the decisions of government by their force and manipulations behind the scenes.

A. In England *invisible,* as applied to associations, was first used in theological discussions in which the dichotomy between the visible and the invisible church was carefully explained.

1638 Chillingworth *Relig. Prot. Ans.* iv.53 [*OED*]. The doctrine of Christ, the profession whereof constitutes the visible church, the belief and obedience the invisible.

Later in philosophical spheres:

1646-7 Boyle *Let. to Tallents* 20 Feb. [*OED*]. The corner-stones of the invisible, or (as they term themselves) the philosophical college, do now and then honour me with their company.

B. In American politics we find varied organizations characterized as *invisible,* particularly the invisible empire of the Ku Klux Klan.

1806 Randolph in Brant *Madison* IV.314. Not of an open declared Cabinet; but of an invisible, inscrutable, unconstitutional Cabinet, without responsibility. . . . I speak of back-stairs influence—of men who bring messages to this House.
1831 Kennedy *Wirt* II.315. Any secret society . . . is a political monster as fearful as the Invisible Tribunal of Germany, or the Inquisition of Spain.
1872 *Cong. Globe* 4026/1. The extent of the conspiracy from the Potomac to the Rio Grande justifies its real title, which is "The Invisible Empire of the South."
1879 Tourgée *A Fool's Errand and The Invisible Empire* [title].

C. The phrase *invisible government,* however, seems to have been a later coinage of Albert Beveridge, serving as temporary chairman of the Progressive Party convention of 1912.

1912 Beveridge in *Rev. of Rev.* XLVIII. 338. These special interests, which suck the people's substance, are bipartisan. They use both parties. They are the invisible government behind the visible government. . . . It is this invisible government which is the real danger to American institutions.

The expression was immediately exploited as a popular slogan:

1912 *Rev. of Rev.* XLVI.312/2. His phrase "the invisible government behind our visible government" was caught up and repeated by other speakers.
1913 *Ib.* XLVIII.334-8. "The Invisible Government" Under Searchlight [title].
1913 Roosevelt in *Century Mag.* Oct. The selfish opposition of the great corporation lawyers and of their clients is entirely intelligent; for these men alone are the beneficiaries of the present reign of hidden, of invisible government.
1915 Elihu Root in *Add. Govt. & Citizenship* 202. They call the system—I do not coin the phrase, I adopt it because it carries its own meaning—the system they call "invisible government."
1923 *Rev. of Rev.* LXVII.14/2. On November 19, Governor Parker of Lousiana appeared in Washington to consult with President Harding and the Department of Justice regarding an "invisible government" that was alleged to be interfering with the administration of justice in his own State and in other parts of the South.
1934 Carter *New Dealers* 396. The New Deal is, above all, a popular revolt against unsuccessful invisible government by vested interests.

An indication that the term is no longer current in the political vocabulary is the change to *secret government.*

1951 Jenner in Senate 11 April. Our only choice is to . . . find out who is the secret government which has so cleverly led our country down the road to destruction.

irreconcilables.

A. Originally the name of a French group opposed to Napoleon III.

1870 *Harper's W.* 12 Feb. 104. Napoleon III And The Irreconcilables. [head] . . . three of the most prominent members of the Opposition, who have earned for themselves the title of "Irreconcilables."

The word exactly describes their attitute toward the Imperial Government.... Under no circumstances will they be reconciled to any condition of affairs by which one man ... is placed in authority over his fellows.

B. On various occasions the word has been used in American politics:

1870 *N. Y. Times* 6 Jan. 4/2. There are few or no "irreconcilables" in American politics—few men who use their vote simply as a means of "testifying" against some enormity.

1870 *Ib.* 14 Jan. 1/1. The Georgia Irreconcilables And General Terry. [head]

1878 *Harper's W.* 26 Jan. 67/1. On the one hand would be the irreconcilable Republicans and the irreconcilable Democrats of the closing days of the last Congress. ...

1885 *Puck* 23 Sept. 56. The Opium-Joint of the Republican "Irreconcilables." [cartoon caption]

1919 in Longworth *Crowded Hours* 292. And by we, I mean the irreconcilables, who were against joining any League no matter how "safeguarded" with reservations.

itch.

A variant of *presidential bee* or *fever* (q.v.).

1871 in Hayes *Diary* I.422. If I thought there was the slightest danger of so obscure a personage as I being attacked with that wretched mania, an itching for the White House, I would beg for the prayers of your church for my deliverance.

J

Jack Mormon. [ ]

1845 *Niles' Reg.* 4 Oct. 70/1. Jack Mormon is the appellation by which the anti-Mormons designate every man that is suspected of taking sides with the Mormons against their lawless measures.

Jacobin.

A radical.

A. By reports from Paris the French party name became known in America almost as soon as it had been coined:

1792 G. Morris *Writings* II.154. The Jacobins, so called from their meeting at a convent or church of that name, were then the violent party. The others ... were those who termed themselves moderate men.

Inevitably it was taken up in abuse of the pro-French party by their opponents:

1793 Jefferson in Chinard *Thomas Jefferson* 273. The monocrats here still affect to disbelieve all this, while the republicans are rejoicing and taking to themselves the name of Jacobins which two months ago was fixed on them by way of stigma.

1795 in Leary *Freneau* 267. Republican principles in this country are frequently denominated Jacobins by the leaders and printers of the aristocratic party.

1801 in Fisher Ames *Works* 138. If the violent jacobins should have it in their power to do what they wish, there is not a shadow of a doubt, that they would make smooth work of all the most cherished system of the administrations of Washington and Adams.

Attempts were even made to make *Jacobin* a party nickname for the Jeffersonians:

1801 T. Dwight in Hart *Source Book* 197. Success having crowned the exertions of the party which ... assumes the role of Rupublican [sic]; but which, in more correct, and definite phraseology, is called jacobinical. ... In the meantime, let us profit by the lessons which the jacobins taught us.

In 1793 the Charleston (S.C.) Republican Society petitioned the

Paris Jacobin Club for admission into the Jacobin Order of France. (Luetscher, *Early Pol. Machinery*, p. 33.)

B. Later, *Jacobin* becomes synonymous with (*ultra*) *radical:*

1829 *Workingman's Adv.* 21 Nov. 2/3. Others have slandered them as a new Clay party; others, as Fanny Wright's party; others, as new Jacobins, aiming to establish atheism for religion, and a guillotine for law.

1832 C. R. Williams *Aristocracy* 74. The opprobrious epithet of Jacobin was afterwards indiscriminately applied to the whole Democratic party by the opposition.

18— in Garrison *Garrison Story* 91. There is something not only extremely unfair but positively slanderous in the naked charge, so frequently preferred against non-resistants, that they "deny the necessity of human governments" [as if they were] a band of Jacobins and anarchists, who took delight in shedding innocent blood, crying havoc, and letting slip the dogs of war.

1861 in Dennett *Hay* 26 Oct. 31. This evening the Jacobin club, represented by Trumbull, Chandler and Wade, came to worry the administration into a battle.... Then they talked about the Jacobins. Mr. C. said that Wade preferred an unsuccessful battle to delay.

1861 Brownlow *Sketches* 104 . . . the brawling Jacobin journals of a demoralized Southern Confederacy.

1866 Nasby *Swinging Round the Cirkle* 214. The infamous Jacobin Radical party that terms the President's party a "menajery."

1866 *Cong. Globe* Jan. I.425/1. "They are Rebels, and rebels have no rights but the right to be hung," cries the bloody-mouthed Jacobin.

1891 Grinnell *Men and Events* 62. Mr. Rhett . . . a Jacobin inviting a bloody conflict.

1908 in Pringle *Taft* I.366. The Wall Street Journal welcomes Mr. Taft's speech as evidence that he is neither reactionary

nor a revolutionist, neither a Bourbon nor a Jacobin.

janizary.

A. Originally a Turkish elite troop constituting the sultan's guard. Used in England in derision of Cromwell's soldiers:

1649 in *Leveller Tracts* 1647–1653 ed. Haller and Davies 446. To you, I say, in my present condition, as Shadrach, Meshach and Abdnego in their great distresse. . . . Be it known unto you, that for all your power and worldly greatnesse (with all your armed Jannisaries) that I fear you not. . . .

Jefferson uses the term to characterize a privileged naval caste:

1810 *Works* IV.153. The shipping interest, commercial interest, and their janizaries of the navy.

B. In 1826 the massacre of the janizaries in Constantinople occurred. This sensational event may account for the relative frequency of the word in later American politics, where it becomes a synonym of *henchman:*

1840 Clay in Norton *Tippecanoe* 282. But what is the contest now? Not between the hirelings of a foreign king and American troops, but between a miserable being engaged in stealing power by encroachments of the executive on the Constitution between an American king supported by his janissaries . . . and the people. . . .

1863 S. S. Cox *Eight Years* 325. Gentlemen know very well, if they know anything of the people of the border States north and south of the Ohio as represented in or out of the army, that they will never consent to the formation of this force of black janizaries for any purpose.

1941 *Time* 10 March 15/2. Justice Douglas still has a finger in all Janizariat pots, sees the President at least weekly. . . . The Janizariat generally believes that . . . Hughes . . . may retire.

jelly-fish.

Used in New York politics. [ ]

1881 *Nation* 16 June 415/2. The "Jelly-Fish" is a man who hesitates to vote decisively for or against the Machine.

Jim Crow.

The Negro, mainly as a victim of discrimination.

A. The ultimate origin of the phrase is an old plantation song quoted by Charles H. Day:

Fun in Black 6.

I went down to the creek, I went down a fishing,

I axed the old miller to gimmy chaw tobacker

To treat old Aunt Hanner.

Chorus:

First on the heel tap, den on de toe,

Ebery time I wheel about I jump Jim Crow.

I goes down to de branck to pester old miller,

I wants a little light wood;

I belongs to Capt. Hawkins, and don't care a d—n.

Chorus:

The primitive style and rhythm of this text seems to guarantee its age and authenticity and so does the lack of rhyme, since, according to T. Allston Brown in Day's *Fun in Black,* "the original verses of Jim Crow ran in this manner, without rhyme, as sung by the Negroes of Kentucky."

B. The song was first introduced on the stage by George Nichols, who, however, sang it in the costume of a clown, not as a Negro. (Hingston, *Genial Showman,* 57; *Fun in Black,* 5)

The classic form of the **Jim** Crow performance was introduced by Thomas Dartmouth Rice in Louisville in 1829, according to Hingston, whose authority claimed to be a personal friend of Rice.

Genial Showman 57–8. "Yes, sir-ree," said our informant, "it was in this city of Louisville, in 1829, that Daddy Rice first jumped Jim Crow.... I helped to black Daddy Rice's face the first night he sang; and if there had been no Daddy Rice whar would have been your Bryants and your Christys, and your Moores, and your Eph Horns, and your Morrises, and your Pells? ... He made Jim Crow as great a piece of acting in his way as Forrest makes anything in Shakespeare.

However, another anonymous writer who likewise claims to have first hand information insists that Rice's first appearance as Jim Crow took place in Pittsburgh (*Atlantic Monthly,* Nov. 1867, 609/1).

Because of Rice's success in the North and in England, *Jim Crow* became a synonym for Negro in general:

1837 *New Yorker* 610/2 ... the representative of the American Negro, Rice.... James Crow, Esq.

1838 *Bentley's Misc.* IV.582. Don't be standing there like the wooden Jim Crow at the blacking maker's store.

1840 *Knickerbocker.* Entering the theatre, we found it crammed from pit to dome, and the best representative of our American Negro that we ever saw was stretching every mouth in the house to its utmost tension.... It was *the* Negro par excellence. Long live James Crow, Esquire!

C. Rice himself prepared the soil for the political history of Jim Crow by flavoring his text with allusions to the questions of the day.

. . . .

Brown Univ. *Harris Coll.* No. 15.

> I told dem dare be Ole Nick,
>   Wat wants de bank renew;
> He gib me so much mony,
>   O lor, dey want it too.
> Weel about, and turn about,
>   And do jis so;
> Eb'ry time I weel about,
>   I jump Jim Crow.
>
> I den go to de Presiden,
>   He ax me wat I do;
> I put de veto on de boot,
>   And nullefy de shoe.
> Weel about [etc.]

However, during the '30's the refrain of the song, rather than the text of Rice's stanzas, is utilized in political slang. *Jumping Jim Crow* comes to mean changing one's political principles, bolting one's party.

1836 *Louisville Jrnl.* 16 Sept. A Mr. Collier of Virginia has "jumped Jim Crow."
1840 *Logansport Herald* 30 Sept. He [G. W. Ewing] has again "jumped Jim Crow."

D. About the same time the negro car on the Boston railroad was popularly known as the *Jim Crow*.

1841 *Liberator* 15 Oct. 4/4. The conductor ...ordered Douglass to leave, and to take his seat in the forward car; meaning the "Jim Crow," though he felt ashamed to call it by that name.
1882 *Life and Times of Frederick Douglass* 255 [describing same incident]. On that road as on many others, there was a mean, dirty, and uncomfortable car set apart for colored travelers, called the "Jim Crow" car.

E. Applied to other areas in which discrimination is found:

1933 Rogers *How We Elect* 145. Now all you Republican members of the Senate get over there in that Jim Crow corner of the ball room.

1952 *Nation* 18 Oct. 357/2. Washington in 1952 is still a Jim Crow town.

jingo, jingoism.

Excessive chauvinism.

A. "It is derived from the charms of a popular music-hall song of the time [1878]:

> 'We don't want to fight
> But by Jingo if we do,
> We've got the ships, we've
>   got the men,
> We've got the money too.' "

(Am. Sp. II.138/1) .

Almost immediately the word was used in America: to begin only with reference to English politics:
1878 *Harper's W.* 10 Aug. 627/2. "The Liberals and the Jingoes" [editorial].
Ib. 627/3. As the character and extent of the responsibilities which have been assumed (by Lord Beaconsfield) are gradually perceived and measured, and the character of the methods pursued is fairly apprehended, it will probably appear that English patriotism and principle are not monopolized by the "Jingoes."
Ib. 17 Aug. 647/3. It was a delightful stroke, and gives the noble earl a new claim upon the adoration of the "Jingoes."

B. In America the term was used against James G. Blaine in 1884, the accusation being based on his attitude in foreign policies and toward Chinese in America.
1884 in Gail Hamilton *Biography of James G. Blaine* 576. Mugwump convention in Boston, advocated "a government free from jobbery, free from jingoism."
1884 *N. Y. World* 7 June 3/4. [Blaine's nomination] augurs a jingo policy in our Foreign Relations.
1884 *N. Y. Tribune* 16 July 1/6. They say Mr. Blaine is a "Jingo." He is just as much a "Jingo" as was John Quincy Adams.

C. Later quotations:

1896 *Nation* 16 Jan. 46/2. The usual answer a Jingo makes to inquiry as to the cause of his desire to fight England is that she is "grabbing" and "insolent."

1938 P. S. Kern in Salter *The American Politician* 10. He [La Guardia] never yielded to postwar jingoism.

jobber, jobbery.

Long known in England (see *OED*).

1876 *Harper's W.* 18 March 222/1. Official jobbery is the most familiar fact in the political annals of England, for instance, from the purchase of place by bribes to the Duchess of Kendall, the mistress of George the First, and the frank corruption of Robert Walpole and the open sales under George the Third, to the securing of commissions by payments to the mistress of the Duke of York fifty years ago. Through English history jobbery of this kind has been gross and shameless.

The charges of jobber and jobbery became common in America in the latter decades of the nineteenth century during the exposure of the corruption connected with the "rings" and "machines."

1880 *N. Y. Trib.* 6 May 5/1 ... it [Republican party] wants a return of the old times when "bummers" were at the front and jobbery flourished.

1880 *Puck* 26 May 205/3. I will abolish Albany, and have no more legislative jobbery....

1881 *N. Y. World* 14 Jan. 1/6 ... the Speaker has placed the men known as jobbers in legislation on committees where they cannot ply their trade, and has thus shown a determination [on the part of Speaker Sharpe] ... to promote honest legislation.

1884 *Puck* 31 Dec. 274/1. And all this has been to gratify the sordid ambition of a man who wanted to establish the headquarters of jobbery and corruption in the capital at Washington.

1885 *Puck* 8 July 290/2. What jobbery

and ring-rule have done for politics, stock-gambling and monopoly have done for business.

John Brown Republicans.

One of the many terms aimed to bring discredit upon the party in its early days by associating it with radical or other unpopular causes or names.

1859 in Strong *Diary* II.467 ... the Black Republicans or (as the South would prefer to designate them) the John Brown Republicans.

See BLACK REPUBLICAN.

Jonah.

An issue fraught with disaster; a person proving a liability to his party.

1848 *Indianapolis St. Sentinel* 15 April 2/1 ... [The Indiana Journal] has thrown General Taylor overboard, as a political Jonah.

1874 *N. Y. Trib.* 18 Nov. 4/1. All the organs of public opinion blow one swelling strain in perfect harmony, the burden of which is, "Butler is the Jonah! Heave him overboard first and then we can talk."

1884 Blaine *Twenty Years* 380 Slavery, according to Mr. Lovejoy, was the Jonah on board the National ship, and the ship would founder unless Jonah were thrown overboard. "When Jonah was cast forth into the sea, the sea ceased from raging."

1890 *N. Y. Sun* 22 Nov. 6/4. [Cleveland a "Stuffed Jonah."]

juggernaut.

The huge car on which the idol of Krishna is dragged through the streets in Orissa.

In earlier days many Hindu devotees threw themselves under its wheels and were crushed to death. Thus in politics *juggernaut* refers to any overwhelming power which crushes an unsuspecting and trusting public:

1834 in Geary *Third Parties* 5. If it is your purpose, and the committee's to constitute yourself into a political car of Juggernaut! Roll on!

1840 *Ohio St. sw. Journal* 10 Feb. 2/3. The people are awakening from the slumber into which the Locofocos had lulled them, and disengaging themselves from the wheels of the Juggernaut.

1840 Kennedy *Quodlibet* 36 ... there is the glorious consummation of the war with the great money power, which, like Juggernaut, was crushing down the liberties of our republic.

1841 *Mangum Papers* V.642. He would incomparably rather adopt the Sub-Treasury than this monstrous Juggernaut, whose murderous car would make its way over the necks of a prostrate people.

During the campaign of 1912 the Taft steamroller (q.v.) was likened to the juggernaut. A cartoon reproduced in the *Review of Reviews*, July, 1912, p. 35, entitled "The Juggernaut" shows Taft steering the great steamroller, while figures pulling it fall before its crushing wheels.

juggler.

A politician who uses devious tactics to accomplish his plans and designs.

1800 Bishop *Connecticut Republicanism* 35 ... provided their learned, pious, juggling leaders. . . .

1806 Randolph in *History of Congress* 564. It is a mere juggle, played off for the benefit of those who put the mechanism into motion.

1823 *Cinc. Nat. Rep.* 25 Feb. 3/2 ... the ambitious schemes of a few political jugglers.

1828 *Sat. Eve. Chronicle* 17 May 1/4. A skilful politician is like a juggler. . . . When a political juggler tells you what you should keep your eye upon, watch him.

1829 in Crockett *Van Buren* 120 ... to frown indignantly upon all intriguers,

managers, political jugglers, and selfish politicians of every description, who are disposed to divide and conquer.

1839 *Cong. Globe* 16 Jan. App.374/3 ... but we shall come to it, unless the unprincipled career of political jugglers can be arrested.

Although throughout the long history of jugglers in Europe they have been usually associated with feats of magic and acrobatics, there are several instances of the term in American politics which suggest that there was also a connection between the juggler and the puppet show:

1820 *Ann. of Congress* 4 Feb. 1093/2 ... paving the way for some master juggler, behind the scene, to ride into the Chief Magistracy of the nation.

1823 *Cinc. Nat. Rep.* 24 June 2/3 ... we are taught to despise ... the grand operator, the chief juggler, who sits behind the scenes, and moves the wires.

1824 *Ib.* 1 Oct. 1/2. The whole course that has been pursued by the jugglers and principal managers behind the curtain, exhibits the strongest evidence of a deep-rooted conspiracy against the Democratic principles of our Republic.

See WIRE WORKER, MANAGER.

junket (-ing).

A political fence-mending tour or pleasure excursion disguised (because it is at public expense) as a factfinding trip necessary for the welfare of the people.

1843 in *Mangum Papers* III.468. Sir, have you forgotten what those junketings of his cost us in Ohio and Louisiana? They only waken up popular animosity and prejudice.

1876 *Cinc. Comm.* 7 July 4/3. President Grant has been fond of junketing in Philadelphia.

1877 *Puck* 26 Sept. 2/1...he [Hayes] would not go junketting round the country with his cabinet at this early stage in his administration....
1878 *N. Y. Trib.* 16 July 4/6. Look out now for the usual screams from the outs about the junketing at the public expense.
1895 Sherman *Recoll.* 590. Such trips are sometimes treated by the press as "junketing" at the public expense.
1956 Freidel *FDR the Triumph* 207. On June 29 [1931], Farley departed upon his junket, armed with names and detailed instructions.
1960 *Time* 7 March 16/1. Old politicos also resented his Eastern-style narrow-brim hat, his frequent out-of-state junkets, his preference for Scotch and soda over bourbon and branch water....

junto.

A group of men held together by common political purposes; a clique.

Already the first American (?) example gives the word a derogatory meaning, which usually attaches to it; however, there are many cases in which it carries no such meaning.

c1688 Mather *Magnalia* I.176...four or five persons had the absolute rule over a territory, the most considerable of any belonging to the crown....That this Junto made a law, which prohibited the inhabitants of any town to meet about their town affairs above once a year....
in Balch *Ltrs. and Papers* xxvi. The Junto was instituted by Dr. Franklin in 1727, for mutual information and the public good.
1775 Paine *Works* II.44. The removal of North, or the whole detestable junto, is a matter unworthy the millions we have expended.
1787 Hamilton in *Federalist* No. 22 14 Dec. But its real operation is to embarrass the administration, to destroy the energy of the government, and to substitute the pleasure, caprice, or artifices of an insignificant, turbulent, or corrupt junto, to the regular deliberations and decisions of a respectable majority.
1792 Leary *Freneau* 214. Three well-fed lads, in solemn junto met, Swore to destroy the National Gazette.
1794 Taylor *Principles and Tendency* 22. She [America] was too hard for her enemies, but a junto of false friends are too hard for her.
1799 Jefferson *Works* VII.18. There are large and populous districts in it [a county] without a justice....And there is no authority on earth which can break up this junto, short of a general convention.
1815 Davis *Mem. of Burr* II.434 [Burr to Alston, 20 Nov.]. A certain junto of actual and factitious Virginians, having had possession of the government for twenty-four years, consider the United States as their property.
1828 *Argus of America* 6 Feb. 2/2 [a toast]. By Daniel D. Brodhead, one of the Vice Presidents. The Junto Federalists—otherwise called the friends of the Administration.
1835 Crockett *Van Buren* 89...the little magician and his friends had a totally different object in their eye, which....ought to be known to the country, as a caution how they place its destinies in the hands of so dark and designing a junto as the Albany Regency.
1837 *N. Y. Herald* 1 Nov. 2/1. We understand that the whole Robinson junto throughout the city will be present.
1878 *Harper's W.* 16 Nov. 906/4. The entire business of the Convention is transacted by this self-appointed clique or junto.

justice shop.

A mildly derogatory reference to courts maintained by justices of the peace.

1904 *Weber's W.* 15 Oct. 4. The police [in Chicago] hate the "justice shop." It interferes with their "graft." With the State law "justice shop" out of the way, and mayor's justices in place of them, the police would be practically supreme. Much of the outcry against justice shops comes from the rotten police force.

K

kangaroo ticket.

See HYENA.

A. Satirical reference to a party's presidential nominations, in which the candidate for the vice-presidency is felt to be the better and stronger man.

1844 *Ann. of Cleve.* No.1657. When the news of the nomination of Silas Wright on the ticket with Polk for President reached the Capitol, a distinguished Tennessee Senator ... exclaimed, "A Kangaroo ticket, by G–d! strongest in the hind legs!"
1848 *Ib.* No.743. Intellectually this [Taylor and Webster] would be a real kangaroo ticket. We doubt some whether the hind legs would consent to bear the burden.
1879 *N. Y. Trib.* 6 June 4/6. The Ohio Democrats have a kangaroo ticket.

B. In some instances *kangaroo* seems to mean fusion.

1855 in Hambleton *Wise* 362. Some of the Antecedents of the Kangaroo [Know Nothing] Ticket.

kennel press.

Derisive name given by Jackson party men to a paper which supported the opposition.

One of the early metaphors arising out of the hunt (See STILL HUNT.)

1824 *Cinc. Nat. Rep.* 1 Oct. 2/1. Our opponents have become alarmed—their "kennel presses" (both Clayites and Adamsites in Ohio) are filled with the vilest falsehoods and most outrageous abuse of Gen. Jackson. . . .
1833 *Niles' Reg.* 23 March 51/1. But had this "affair" happened in one placed in office by president Adams ... what would the "kennel presses" have said of it.

keynote (-r).

A. Originally in American politics any act or agency which sets the dominant tone for public acts.

1837 W. Phillips *Sp.* 10. When Liberty is in danger, Faneuil Hall has the right, it is her duty, to strike the key-note for these United States.
1840 *Liberator* 29 May 85/1. The "grand organ" had struck the "key-note" for a general rally.
1863 Beecher *Patriotic Add.* 478. The keynote of Northern policy was No more Slave States—No more legislation in favor of slavery.

B. A definite statement to which a party attunes its campaign:

1842 in Birney *Ltrs.* 673. I am exceedingly rejoiced at the answer you have returned ... like the Letter of Acceptance to give us a good high key-note for our future movements.
1867 in Williams *Hayes* I.326. In every canvass you know there is a keynote. What was the keynote of that canvass? Who sounded it?
1875 *Ib.* I.398. At the Republican State Convention, he [Judge Taft] sounded the keynote to the canvass on this subject.
1878 *Chic. Trib.* 2 Sept. 3/1. Key-Notes. The Indiana Politicians Getting Down to Business. Benj. Harrison and Tom Hendricks as Key-Noters. [head]
1878 *Cleve. Plain Dealer* 15 Oct. 2/4. Thurman Talks A Key-Note for the Year 1880. [head]
1878 *Harper's W.* 21 Dec. 1007/1. The *Democrat* holds that the result was mainly due to the Republican press, which led the way and compelled the declaration of the Saratoga Convention in favor of honest money, and it thinks that Mr. Conkling not only did not sound the key-note, but "only came in at the end of the chorus."

C. A further narrowing is found in the 20th century when the keynote address becomes a regular feature of the party convention:

the speech which calls upon the party to accept the challenges for which it is so eminently suited.
1908 *Gt. Issues and Nat. Leaders* 54. He [Sen. Burrows] bowed his acknowledgments and began his "keynote" address at just 12.34 P.M. . . .
133. The "Keynote" Speech of Democracy. By Temporary Chairman Theodore A. Bell.
1928 Rogers *How We Elect* 66. The Convention opened with a Prayer. It was a Keynote prayer. . . . Then they brought on Simeon D. Fess. He delivered what is called the Keynote Speech. A Keynote Speech is Press notices of the Republican Party written by its own members.
1929 *Ib.* 83. Even the man that I had touted to all of you as being a world beater, Claude Bowers, the Democratic Keynoter, fell down on me.
1955 *Cols. Dispatch* 6 June [Raymond Moley]. They are contributions to that body of our folk literature known as "keynoting." Ed Lowry . . . thus defined that word in an essay on President Harding: "Keynoting implies the ability to make melodic noises and give the impression of passionately and torrentially moving onward and upward while warily standing still."

kicker.

One who deserts his party or revolts against party discipline on a particular issue or candidate.

A. The metaphorical background—the horse kicking in the traces—is apparent from an early political use of *kicking:*
1852 *Scott Battery* 10 Aug. 1/4. There's no use in kicking, and snorting, and tangling the traces.
1878 *Cleve. Plaindealer* 17 Aug. 1/2. We hear from Toledo that the friends of General Steedman are not going to be placed in the attitude of "kickers" and will vote for the regular candidate.
1881 *N. Y. World* 3 Jan. 1/1. Mr. Dennison informs your correspondent that the

"kickers," as he denominates the anti-machine faction, are playing a game of bluff with nothing in their hand worth betting a cent on.

B. A certain specialization of meaning developed in connection with the reform faction in the Republican party, and in 1884 *kicker* became practically synonymous with *mugwump:*
1880 *N. Y. World* 9 June 1/4. When the convention was assembling the twenty "kickers" learned of the action of the majority of the delegation and at first declared that they would not vote for Arthur.
1880 *Ib.* 2 Nov. 4/2. Finally we have a third class of independent Republicans who cherish "independence" as a cheap and simple article of barter for office. These are men whom the machinists know as "kickers."
1881 *Ib.* 1 May 4/1. Why should "kicking" and bolting be capital offences when a delegate commits them to the injury of a Boss, and become noble and meritorious action when a boss commits them to the injury of a President?
1884 *N. Y. Trib.* 25 June. But we will get more democratic votes, in my judgment, than the kickers will amount to, on the tariff question.
1884 *Cinc. Enquirer* 2 July 4/3. "By the way, what are your pa's politics? He is a Blaine man, isn't he?" "No, he's a kicker."
1884 *Ib.* 5 July 1/2. The Republican kickers get but little respect among any faction. . . . The Republican kickers are so far overboard that they will vote for any Democrat.

See BOLTER, MUGWUMP.

kick upstairs.

A. It can not be ascertained whether the "noted instance" to which Foote refers in 1874 is that alluded to by Lord Halifax (1661–1715) :

c1697 Burnet *Orig. Mem.* 145 [*OED*]. He [Halifax] had said he had known many kicked down stairs, but he never knew any kicked up stairs before.

1874 Foote *Casket of Reminiscences* 233. Mr. Benjamin's renomination by Mr. Davis for the Department of War was defeated in the Confederate Senate, but this, as it chanced to turn out, was only equivalent to "kicking him up stairs," as is known to have been the case in a certain noted instance in English history.

It is nevertheless quite clear that the phrase was known early in American politics:

1775 S. Adams in *Warren-Adams Ltrs.* 94. I find that two of the former Boston Members are left out [of the House of Representatives]. C [Cushing] is kicked up Stairs [to the Council].

B. Perhaps the most notable instance in recent politics occurred prior to the election of 1900, when Theodore Roosevelt strenuously opposed his selection as the vice-presidential candidate:

1900 in *Roosevelt Ltrs.* 9 April II.1253. In default of any other way, they would like to kick me up stairs.

1900 *Nation* 28 June 488/2. Platt now makes little effort to conceal the animus against Roosevelt which led the New York boss to work strenuously to kick the Governor up-stairs into the Vice-Presidency.

See SIDETRACK.

kid glove.

Characterizing a soft or non-aggressive policy, kid glove being a frequently used symbol of the elegant gentleman.

1859 Strong *Diary* 20 Dec. II.479. Roughs preponderated, and I heard frequent denunciations of "my" ticket as having "too much kid glove on it, by God!"

1864 Schurz *Writings* I.230. You remember the results of that period of kid-glove

policy, which the South found so very gentlemanly. . . .

? 1924 in Stokes *Chip* 203. The subsequent Davis speechmaking campaign, which Fraser followed, was described by him, very aptly I thought, as a "kid-glove campaign." The Democratic nominee, he said, "just won't take off his gloves and take down his back hair and go after 'em."

kids.

A Democratic faction in Ohio in 1884–5.

1884 in *Gt. Deb.* IX.339. The young reform element, known as the "Kids," endeavored to reelect Senator Pendleton.

1884 *Ohio St. Jrnl.* 12 July 1/1. The "kids" are celebrating it [Cleveland's nomination] with parades while the "mossbacks" are hanging their heads.

1884 *Cleve. Leader* 5 Oct. 2/5. Durbin Ward is classed among the mossbacks by the kids.

See MOSSBACK.

King Alcohol.

A personification prominent during the temperance crusades.

1842 *Wabash Gazette* (Logansport, Ind.) 24 Nov. 3/2. The Teetallers in Indianapolis have opened the winter campaign against King Alcohol.

1842 *Bro. Jonathan* I.245/1. The first one declared war against King Alcohol.

1919 F. C. Iglehart *King Alcohol Dethroned* [title].

King Caucus.

Satirical allusion to the power of the congressional caucus, based upon the formula established by *King Log* and *King Mob* in England.

1823 *Louisville Public Advertiser* 3 Dec. 5/1. Some little opposition was manifested by the adherents to Crawford, and slaves of "King Caucus."

1824 *Niles' Reg.* 28 Feb. 402/2. They will not be dictated to by "King Caucus," or King Nick.

1824 *Cinc. Nat. Rep.* 18 May 2/3. This, however, appears to be a very trifling objection, when put in opposition to the immense benefits which would inevitably flow from the reign of King Caucus.
1824 *Ib.* 15 June 1/2. The minions of King Caucus will fail in their attempts to destroy such a man.
1824 *Ib.* 5 Nov. 2/2. What is the chief duty of republicans? To obey the decrees of King Caucus.
1824 in Parton *Andrew Jackson* III.21. General Jackson's great personal popularity contributed greatly, doubtless, to the overthrow of that renounced personage, "King Caucus," as it was then derisively called.

Thomas Nast revived the figure of King Caucus in 1879 in a cartoon (*Harper's W.*, 31 May, 436) aimed against the efforts of a small group of Republicans to force the nomination of Grant upon the party as a whole. The cartoon shows a figure weighed down by a huge crown labelled "King Caucus." A later issue of the magazine (14 June, 462/2) comments upon this drawing:
This kind of attempted party despotism is well satirized in Mr. Nast's recent sketch of King Caucus. It is bad enough when a caucus or a convention assumes to crush the expression of individual opinion or to bind individual responsibility; but when, before any authorized action whatever is taken, there is a kind of tacit conspiracy to compel an appearance of uniformity of sentiment, the crown becomes altogether intolerable.

King Cong.

A derisive term for the Continental Congress:
1877 in Garfield *Works* II.472. Jealousy of its power was manifested in a thousand ways; and the epithet "King Cong" was a byword of reproach during the latter half of the war.

King Cotton.

The phrase *cotton is king* was introduced in 1855 by David Christy in a book bearing that title. A quotation from the text (p. 11) indicates his use of the metaphor:
... now, after nearly a "thirty years' war," we may say, emphatically, COTTON IS KING, and his enemies are vanquished.

With already existing terms such as *King Cong* and *King Caucus* (q.v.) as formulas, it was probably inevitable that Christy should carry his metaphor to its ultimate end—*King Cotton*. Thus we have:
p. 186. King Cotton cares not whether he employs slaves or freemen.... His majesty, King Cotton, therefore, is forced to continue the employment of his slaves; and, by their toil, is riding on, conquering and to conquer!

During the Civil War period the identification of *King Cotton* with the slave-holding aristocracy was very common:
1860 *At. Mon.* VI.494/1. Mr. Hammond has proclaimed the accession of King Cotton, but he seems to have forgotten that history is not without examples of kings who have lost their crowns through the folly and false security of their ministers.
1861 *Phila. Press* 25 Jan. in *Northern Editorials* II.580. Their war cry is something like that of the Mohammedans, "Great is Allah, and Mohammed is his prophet!" Their version being "Great is King Cotton—we are his apostles—let no man dare to oppose us."
1861 *Phila. Inq.* 11 Feb. in *Ib.* II.867. Cotton shall not only be king, but if these councils of ruin shall prevail, Cotton shall be tyrant. The negro is the liegeman of Cotton, and of Cotton only.
c 1861 in Binkley *Am. Pol. Parties* 243 [refrain of popular song].
Old King Cotton's dead and buried;
Brave Young Corn is King.

1862 Pollard *First Year of the War* 212 . . . the power of "King Cotton."

Occasional later uses:

1900 *Cinc. Enquirer* 4 June 5/2. Cotton again King. [head]
1946 *Time* 28 Oct. 89. U.S. Commodity prices, which have risen sky-high in the last six years, cracked last week. Down with a resounding crash tumbled King Cotton.

kiss joke ticket.

Kiss, kiss joke, or *sugar kiss ticket* as terms for a technique of ballot box stuffing are allusions based upon the comparison between the thin paper upon which the ballot was printed and the tissue paper mottoes with which candy kisses were wrapped.

1876 *Cong. Record* 25 July 4873/2. The Conservatives of Portsmouth [Va.] . . . had printed tickets of the smallest possible size, on the thinnest paper, and by folding several in a large ticket and presenting it as their vote they succeeded in filling the ballot-boxes with over a thousand of these small tickets—sugar kiss tickets as they are called.
1878 *Cinc. Enquirer* 11 Dec. 4/8. The tissue "kiss tickets" . . . were introduced by them [Republicans] in South Carolina and Florida in 1876. . . .
1879 *Cong. Record* 24 April 843/1. In many States . . . ballot-stuffing, kiss-joking, bulldozing, and murder have been . . . unrestrained.
1880 *Ib.* 26 May 3809/2. There were in the box 135 kiss-joke tickets. . . . When they came to count the ballots, there were 164 straight republican, 388 kiss-jokes, and 47 large democratic tickets [in South Carolina].

kitchen.

Short for *kitchen cabinet.* (q.v.)
1834 *Niles' Reg.* 4 Jan. 307/1. He has ascended the tripod, surrounded by "sul-

phureous" vapors from below, even from the "kitchen" of foul cookeries and stinking things, where "roasted monkeys, stuffed with lizards," are prepared to feed the morbid appetites of servile conductors of the press.
1834 in *Mangum Papers* II.233. Martin Van Buren and the Kitchen are not spared. . . .
1840 in Norton *Tippecanoe* App. 62.
There was mounting and tramping of
    Cabinet clan,
And the kitchen concern, some rode and
    some ran;
There was racing and chasing o'er Capital
    lea,
But the little Magician no more could
    they see!

kitchen cabinet.

Nickname of a group of Andrew Jackson's personal friends who served as an unofficial advisory cabinet. (See BACKSTAIRS INFLUENCE.)

1832 in Cole *Whig Party* 13 n. W. S. Archer, a Virginia Jackson supporter, wrote to Crittenden, July 8, 1832, that there was only one consideration which would induce him to take the mission to England: "If there be no other mode of preventing its being given to the most despicable of all the Proteges of the Kitchen Cabinet."
1833 *Cols. Sentinel* 3 Oct. 3/3. Our fair-quoting neighbor of the *Monitor* will have the goodness to confine his cant phrase of the "Kitchen Cabinet" to his own columns. It is one which never had a place in the columns of the *Sentinel.*
1833 Biddle in James *Jackson* 650. When we begin, we shall crush the Kitchen Cabinet at once.
1834 *Niles' Reg.* 83/2 . . . there is not, in what is called the "kitchen cabinet," more than one "original" friend of the general!
1834 C. A. Davis *Downing Ltrs.* 205. That attempts should be made by the Kitchen Cabinet, to thwart him in his disinterested efforts to promote the public welfare . . . is not to be wondered at.

1834 Crockett *Life* 107. I might easily have been mistaken for one of the Kitchen Cabinet, I looked so much like a ghost.
1838 *Wash. Globe* 30 Jan. He [Jackson] brought about him men fresh from the ranks of the people, acquainted with their wants and understanding the current of their opinions. He consulted those men; and for that cause alone, his opponents charged him with being under the influence of a "Kitchen Cabinet."

B. Applied to groups in later administrations.

1844 in *Mangum Papers* IV.238. Mrs. Tyler, who it is thought will still retain some influence with the new Kitchen Cabinet.
1844 *Wash. Globe* 13 Jan. 47/4. This is but the opening of a long speech in which Mr. Clay puts Mr. Rives out of the pale of his party, and endeavors to identify him with the excommunicated President—nay worse, to degrade him to the kitchen cabinet!
1845 *Ann. of Cleve.* No. 1489. It is very evident that John Jones at least has not been transferred from the "kitchen cabinet" of John Tyler to the "kitchen cabinet" of James K. Polk.
1878 *Harper's W.* 2 Nov. 866/2. Had he [Tilden] become President, his most trusted friends and personal associates would have accompanied him to the White House, and what some of the most intimate of them are is now fully shown. They would have been the kitchen cabinet of his "reform" administration, and they would have always held over him the threat of disclosure.
1880 *N. Y. Times* 18 March 4/1. It is somewhat unfortunate for the influence of Gov. Cornell that he should this early in his official career have given ground for derisive allusions to his "kitchen cabinet."

klandidate.

A candidate supported by the Ku Klux Klan:
1924 in Luthin *Am. Demagogues* 169. Although he [Pa Ferguson] scorchingly assailed Robertson as the "Klandidate," Pa

was privately not too much opposed to the principles of the white-hooded order.

Already in the earlier Klan there is evidence of a sort of worship of the letter *K:*
1877 Beard *K.K.K. Sketches* 36 . . . and on the right, left, and middle, at top, the mystic "K."
Ib. 95. [Description of drill formation] It may be imitated by arranging two letters K with their backs to each other, and doubtless originated from this device.
Ib. 100. [alleged speech of Negro preacher] Let us taik de consummant k, which is de indecks letter, and pints to what follers. Duz dis letter have any siggerfication . . . ? I beleevs dat de intellumgence of every pusson in dis orgunce, . . . will bar me out dat it duz.
Ib. 181 . . . Karl Konstant Kain, the last of the K's. . . .
1872 Horn *Invisible Empire* intro. [adv. from *Harper's W.*]. Kommon Kerosene Kills.
1880 *Nation* 30 Sept. 230/1. The "Cuclux clan" is reported also to be revived in North Carolina, with the spelling slightly changed. . . .

In the revived Ku Klux Klan of the 1920's, the older form of letter mysticism is taken up in a different form in that the combination *Kl* plays a dominant part in the terminology of the order. *Cavern* becomes *Klavern; convocation Klonvokation,* etc. Indeed this usage is so common that Frost is justified in wondering why the constitution did not become the Klonstiklution (p. 43) .

More examples of this curious word-formation: Frost, *Challenge of the Klan,* 262; Simmons, *Klan Unmasked,* 103, 225; Booth, *The Mad Mullah,* 91 ff.
1946 Arnall *Shore* 308. Then in 1945, the Klaverns began again to function. . . . The

suckers began paying their Klatockens to the Kligrapp for distribution to the Kleagle and Titan and Dragon.

knife.

To defeat in a treacherous manner:

1881 *N. Y. Trib.* 14 May 4/4. If the President proposes to knife us by giving Mahone the patronage . . . it is none of our affair to aid him in his present dilemma.
1884 *N. Y. World* 8 March 4/3. If Arthur should be the Republican nominee for President the Ohio Republicans would "knife" him.
1884 *Nation* 17 July 41. The O'Brien machine leaders are going about chuckling that "it is all arranged with Tammany to knife Cleveland in the city."

Know Nothing.

A member of a political party later known as the American Party. The organization apparently was known by a number of different names, such as Grand Council of the United States of America, The Supreme Order of the Star Spangled Banner, [Hambleton *Wise*, pp. 47, 54.], and The Sons of '76 [Farmer, 335].

A. The name *Know Nothing* was given in reference to the extreme secrecy of the party.

1854 *N. Y. Trib.* 25 March 6. The "signs" and "passwords" for admission into the lodge are simple enough. . . . Rap at the outer door several times in quick succession. As the doorkeeper peeps through the wicket, ask him, "What meets here tonight?" He will answer "I don't know." Reply "I am one," and he will open the door. Rap four times slowly and distinctly at the second door. On its being opened, whisper to the conductor, "Thirteen" and pass in.
1854 *Cleve. w. Plain Dealer* 30 Aug. 5/1. The token of recognition has finally been discovered by a close observer. When one

Know Nothing wishes to recognize another, he closes one eye, makes an O with his thumb and forefinger, and places his nose through it, which interpreted, reads —"Eye-nose-O" "I-knows-Nothing."
1855 in Lee *American Party* 210. The know nothings originally assumed their denomination as a disguise to conceal their identity with the former self-denominated native American party.

Although there is evidence that the party may have been organized in 1852 or '53 [Barnes, *Weed*, p. 134; Farmer, p. 335], its high point of popularity was in 1854–55.

1854 *Ohio Statesman* 20 June 2/1. How do you stand on the "Know Nothing" alias Native American question? . . . No one who watches the signs of the times can have failed to mark the mysterious advent of a new, unheralded, but powerful organization in the country under the sobriquet of "Know Nothings."
1854 *N. Y. w. Trib.* 24 June 2/2. The "Know-Nothings." [edit.] Know-Nothingism is an epidemic, having its causes in past errors and vices like other epidemics.
1854 *Lancaster* (Ohio) *Eagle* 6 July 2/2. Know Nothing Intolerance [edit.]
1854 *Ohio St. Jrnl.* 8 July 2. The Statesman has made several attempts of late to identify us with the mysterious body of men known as the "Know Nothings." The object of this is transparent: the design is by so doing to excite the political jealousy of the foreign population against the True Democracy of the country, and attach it sympathetically to the Slave Democracy.
1854 *N. Y. sw Trib.* 5 Sept. 3/2. A pic-nic gathering of Know-Nothings to the number of 4,000 or 5,000 was held in Georgetown yesterday.
1855 *Yankee Notions* IV.54. These Know Nothings were very much down on the Dutchmen and one of the most rabid said he would not like any better fun than gunning after the Greeks, by which classic name the Irish are sometimes called.
IV.61. Motto of the Know Nothings:

"When ignorance is bliss, 'tis folly to be wise."

Frequently referred to by its initials, which led to more satirical designations:

1854 *N. Y. sw Trib.* 19 Sept. 3/3. The K.Ns. will do a glorious work if they are instrumental in sweeping away all this mass of ignorance and roguery.

1855 *Annals of Cleve.* No.2466. The "Cayenne" as the *Dispatch* calls the Know Nothings.

B. Although Farmer states the party "did not altogether disappear from national politics until 1860," it is evident that the term enjoyed later use.

1875 *M'Connellsville* (Ohio) *Dem.* 30 July 4/2. A new Know Nothing movement has been set on foot. It is called the American League and was organized in 1871.

1875 *Marietta Times* 7 Oct. 2/5. Certain office holders and government pensioners of this city have formed a secret lodge, with grips, pass words, etc.... The Republican "ring" of office holders and pensioners control this Know Nothing lodge.

1884 *Cinc. Enquirer* 5 July 1/1. Tammany has great unpopularity among the intense Know-Nothing kind of native Americans.

1952 *Nation* 5 April 317/1. Know-Nothing Republicanism.

Know Something.

An anti-slavery political organization of the 1850's.

The name is obviously intended as an antonym for the Know Nothing party. The Know Somethings favored the ideas which the Know Nothings held in low esteem. Apparently the faction enjoyed only a short life.

1854 in Wilson *Slave Power* II.416. The "Know Somethings," an antislavery organization which had held a national convention in Cleveland....

1855 *Cleve. Leader* in *Cleve. Herald* 9 Feb 2/3. You [Herald] are very much mistaken in one important particular. The platform you publish is that of the seceding or bolting Know Nothings who supported W. H. Seward. It is very similar to the platform of the Ohio and Mass. Know Somethings, and differs radically from that of the old Know Nothing order, which is based on Nativism alone. The secessionists are open anti-slavery, anti-Papal, and anti-Rum, and have no communion in the councils of the "Hindoos."

1903 Hoar *Autobio.* I.31...a meeting or conference was held [1855] representing the American or Know-Nothing party, the Know-Somethings, an antislavery organization which held a National Convention at Cleveland in June, and the Chapman Hall convention.

L

lackey.

A hanger-on.

Used to describe the same class as flunky (q.v.).

1856 *Greenville* (Ohio) *Jrnl.* 1 Oct. 2/4. The party were represented fully, by the leaders, and the rank and file from the "wheel horse" down to the second-hand "lackeys" who do the "small work" on all occasions.

1864 *Harper's W.* 2 Jan. 2. But when the Pennsylvania election came and the rebel papers prayed for the success of Woodward, and Lee moved to support his chances, and the lackeys of slavery and rebel partisans strained every nerve for Woodward, and every loyal Union man in the land knew that his election would be equivalent to a victory over the Army of the Potomac....

1876 *Ib.* 29 Jan. 82/2. In these views [Southern feelings on secession] they

were encouraged by their Northern lackeys.

lame duck.

A. In financial circles the use of
lame duck for a bankrupt financier
dates back to the 18th century in
England:

1771 Garrick *Prologue to Foote's Maid
of B.* Change Alley bankrupts waddle out
lame ducks!

This use is known in America as
well:

1833 *Niles' Reg.* 30 Nov. 209/1. We are
sorry to observe that the terms "bulls"
and "bears" are becoming familiar at New
York. . . . A person is called a *lame duck*
when not making prompt payment of the
loss sustained by his contracts about
stocks.
1839 Morris *The Little Frenchman* 142.
His lots, building and water reverted to
their original owners; and Mr. Beverly
Lee, was . . . obliged to "waddle" out of
Wall Street as "lame a duck" as was ever
hatched in that nest of disappointment
and speculation.

B. Not later than 1836 when
General Harrison visited Wall
Street did the term enter the po-
litical vocabulary:

1836 *Ohio St. Jrnl.* 21 Oct. "What is a
lame duck?" "Why," said another member,
"if Dallas should not be able to deliver
the State of Pennsylvania, and Van Buren
not have a department at his disposal,
they are both called lame ducks, being
unable to settle the difference or borrow
from a neighbor.
1840 *Ohio State Jrnl.* 17 June 1/3. Another Lame Duck.—Mr. W. G. Childress,
a Van Buren candidate for Elector in
Tennessee, has backed out and declined
to stand the canvass. This makes the fifth
or sixth in that State that have flown the
track.
1861 *Ib.* 1 Jan. 2/3. A Lame Duck. The
canard that the Chicago Republicans in-

tended to seize the St. Louis Arsenal for
the benefit of Captain Montgomery.

C. In the following decades the
special meaning of a defeated politician emerges:

1863 *Cong. Globe* 14 Jan. 307/1. In no
event . . . could it [Court of Claims] be
justly obnoxious to the charge of being a
receptacle of "lame ducks" or broken
down politicians.
1865 N. Brooks in Sandburg *War Years*
IV.107 . . . party men who had lost at the
last election, each "like a lame duck, to be
nursed into something else."
1876 *Cinc. Daily Gazette* 24 June. Hendricks regarded as a Lame Duck.
1910 *Nation* 15 Dec. 570/3. The Washington correspondents have had a good deal
of fun over "Lame Duck." This is the
name they have given to a screened-off
corridor in the White House offices, where
statesmen who went down in the recent
electoral combat may meet to display
their wounds. . . . They are "Lame Ducks"
in the sense that they have been winged,
but hope to preen their plumage again.

D. In 1922 and the years following *lame duck* came into particular prominence when Senator
George Norris initiated his proposal for a "lame duck amendment" (finally ratified Feb. 6,
1933) which would avoid the situation in which defeated members
of Congress sat in the short session
following the election.

1922 *N. Y. Times* 6 Dec. 18/2. So Senator
Norris is all for the plan "to have the
convening of Congress moved up to avoid
lame-duck Congresses."
1923 *Cong. Record* 12 Feb. 3501/1. Ani-
madversions have been made upon the
present system of permitting hold-over
or lame-duck Members of Congress to
make laws.
1923 *N. Y. Times* 3 March 1/6. The time
has come, declared Senator Norris, for
Congress to take cognizance of the Presi-

dential practice of caring for "lame ducks." 1923 *Nation* 14 March 284/1. The act which would have most become the final days of a lame-duck Congress failed. Senator Norris's proposed constitutional amendment convening a new Congress in the January after its election instead of December passed the Senate but died in the House.

landslide.

Although it is possible to state that *landslide* follows the pattern of *tidal wave* [q.v.], we have not been able to find evidence which would give its etymology the precision of the latter's.

A. It is known, however, that *landslide* was used by geologists as early as 1838 and that it competed with *slide, landslip,* and *avalanche.* [See *DA* and *OED.*]

B. On a number of occasions there is a close chronological relationship between the geologic term and its metaphorical use in politics:

1843 *Ohio Statesman* 24 Feb. 3/3. Great Land Slide at Troy, Forty Lives Lost, Several Buildings Destroyed. [head]
1844 *Hamilton Intell.* 29 Aug. 2/5. Another Land Slide!—Polk and Texas Too Strong a Dose For the New Yorkers. [head]
1878 *N.Y.Trib.* 11 March 1/6. In Peru another landslide occurred on the Transandine line, on the evening of the 14th inst., just when the line had been cleared preparatory to the resumption of traffic.
1878 *Ib.* 13 March 4/6. If Mr. D. A. Wells can start that belated Free Trade Landslide he ought to send it to the immediate relief of Mr. Wood.
1885 *Science* 31 July 84. The Recent Land-Slide in the White Mountains. [head]
1888 *N.Y.Trib.* 1 Oct. 2/3. It seems to me there is a regular landslide in Indiana, and if we can prevent boodleism the State is ours.

C. 1888 seems to be the critical year, for it is then that *landslide* becomes firmly fixed in political terminology, eventually becoming the primary metaphor designating an election in which the winner secures an overwhelming majority of votes.

There was an October landslide in Italy:

1888 *N.Y.Trib.* 22 Oct. 1/1. Scores Buried Beneath a Landslide. [head]
1888 *N.Y.Times* 22 Oct. 1/1. A dispatch from Potezza says that 10 cars of a train crowded with people returning from Naples fetes were crushed in a remote portion of that district by a landslide consisting of about 50 meters of rock.

and the election which followed was for some a political disaster.

1888 *N.Y.Times* 4 Nov. 5/1 . . . a veritable landslide in Mr. Hewitt's favor.
1888 *N.Y.Trib.* 6 Nov. "It looks like a landslide," said the silent Senator Quay, whose management throughout the campaign has been distinguished by the absence of empty boasting.
1888 *Harper's W.* 17 Nov.866. There has been no "cyclone," no "landslide."

In the following years and later:

1890 *Cleve. Plain Dealer* 5 Nov. 1/1. A Democratic Landslide Sweeps the Entire Country. [head]
1890 *N.Y.Sun* 5 Nov. 1/6. A tremendous vote was polled all over the States [Mass.]. The first intimation of the landslide came when the vote of Boston was declared.
1892 in *Roosevelt Ltrs.* 11 Oct. I.292. The movement among the Lutheran and Catholic German against us is most formidable; and it means a landslide, unless the latent Americanism in native Democrats is awakened.
1896 in *Cabinet Diary of William L. Wilson* 162. The papers this morning fully confirm the news of the great landslide.
1954 *Time* 15 Feb. 21/1. A post-election day "correction" of the southeast Texas vote gave Johnson a margin of 87 out of

almost a million Texas votes and the nickname "landslide Lyndon."

last ditch (to die in the).

A. The saying attributed to William of Orange, later William III of England, that he would not survive the ruin of his country but would die in the last ditch was taken up by American patriots even before the outbreak of the Revolution and later repeated on many more or less appropriate occasions.

1774 in Koch and Peden *Writings J. Q. Adams* 37 ... and, like the Prince of Orange, are resolved never to see its entire subjection to arbitrary power, but rather to die fighting against it in the last ditch.
1800 *Aurora* 8 Dec. [This] is now the last ditch of argument in which the federals take refuge.
1806 in Jackson *Corr.* 12 Nov. I.153. I would delight to see Mexico reduced, but I will die in the last Ditch before I would yield a foot to the Dons or see the Union disunited.
1840 in Norton *Tippecanoe* 34. There are considerations in Missouri that make the name of General Harrison a tower of strength. He is rich in the affections of his countrymen, and the Whigs of Missouri will do their best—will die in the last ditch.

B. Taken up in the South during the Civil War, the phrase became the target of much Northern ridicule.

1861 in Frank Moore *Personal Ballads* 293.
"Hear me, great Jeff! Today I'll dig
    A ditch both deep and wide,
And then I'll gird my sabre on,
    Which is both true and tried.

"And ere I run from that 'last ditch,'*
    Along Sewanee's shore,

One hundred thousand Yankee hearts
    Shall fill it with their gore.
    * The Nashville newspapers of 1861, passim. [ed. note]
1862 *Cinc. Comm.* 9 April 2/1. Only six thousands of those fellows who proposed to "die in the last ditch," ...
1863 Newell *Kerr Papers* 268. It was noticed, however, that, as he was being carried into the wood, he asked a gentleman in remarkable tatters, to take him to the last ditch.
1864 *U. S. Service Mag.* II.80. "The last dollar" is reached, if not "the last man." How is it about "the last ditch?"
1864 Post *Soldiers' Ltrs.* 344. I find these Southern nabobs, yes, and nabobesses, who were going to die in the last ditch, are quite willing to swear any amount of oaths in order to taste the sweets of Uncle Sam's pantry.

After the war *last ditcher* became an epithet for the unreconstructed:
1874 *Cong. Record* 8 June 4696/2. The political parties in Louisiana as they crystallized after the "war of the factions," under Warmoth and Carter, were the national republican, last-ditch democracy, reformers, and liberal republicans.
1876 *Cinc. Comm.* 12 May 2/1 [affairs in La]. The attempted assassination ... was the beginning, it is believed, of another effort on the part of the "Last Ditchers" to secure control of affairs.
1875 *Harper's W.* 6 March 204 [cartoon]. The "Last Ditchers" in their proper place.

late unpleasantness.

Euphemism for the *Civil War;* attributed to Petroleum V. Nasby:
1867 in Williams *Hayes* 20 July I.306 The war, whose burdens, cost, and carnage they had been so fond of exaggerating, suddenly sank into what the Reverend Petroleum V. Nasby calls "the late unpleasantness"....
1867 *Harper's W.* 7 Sept. 563/1. These [war memories] forbid ... the horrible pretense that the war was but a difference, "an unpleasantness."
1871 *Cong. Globe* 3 March 2008/2 ... cer-

tain property ... destroyed in a bombardment of that city [Charleston] which took place during what my friends from South Carolina and his southern friends, I suppose, would call the "late unpleasantness"....

1872 *Harper's W.* 31 Aug. 666/2. Beauregard, Semmes, Vance—all the peculiarly unpleasant participants in the late unpleasantness—fell into step.

law and order incumbent. [ ]

1844 *Niles' Reg.* 1 June 210/1. The official canvass of the votes cast at the recent state election in Rhode Island shows the election of all the "Law and Order" incumbent without opposition.

leg treasurer.

Humorous term for officials who abscond with public money; prominent in the political vocabulary after the embezzling of Swartwout (q.v.). The early quotations show the basis of the term in the expressions: *to take legs; to run;* and *leg bail.*

1838 *Cong. Globe* 21 Dec. App. 387/1 ... this very leg-treasury, Swartwout, at New York, was in default $336,718.

1839 Lincoln *Uncoll. Works* I.632. Resolved ... that it [Sub-Treasury] will fasten a swarm of Sub-treasuries as leeches on the public monies, whose security to the Government after they are glutted will be like that of Price and Swartwout— leg-bail in a foreign land.

1839 *Ohio Confederate* 6 April 1/4. The banks have no legs and cannot run off! 2/1. But what ... are bank cashiers but men, and men, too, who, so far as my knowledge goes, "have legs."

1840 *Mercantile Jrnl.* 12 March 2/2. The weather last week was "just the thing" for the sap, and the way it ran was a caution to buckets and leg-treasurers.

1840 *Little Magician* 17 June 2/1. The Swartwouts and other federal whig leg treasurers.

1840 in Norton *Tippecanoe* App. 41.

And the eyes of the Vanites grew deadly and chill,
And Sub-Treasurers' legs forever grew still.

1840 *Ib.* App. 19. See the spoilsmen and leg treasurers, treas, treas,
All in a stew,
For well they know they stand no chance With Tippecanoe....

1846 in *Prenticeana* 137. The "Journal," with legs more numerous than a milliped's, and longer than a leg-treasurer's, kicks all manner of blackguards at all manner of distances.

leper, leprosy.

One of the abolitionist terms for slavery:

1818 Birkbeck *Ltrs.* 71. It [slavery] is the leprosy of the United States.

1850 in Foner *Douglass* II.133. The first spot poisoned by its [slavery's] leprous presence, was a small plantation in Virginia.

1854 in Pike *First Blows* 197. Slavery is an Ishmael.... It is the leper of modern civilization, but a leper whom no cry of "unclean" will keep from intrusion into uninfected company.

1884 Morgan *Yazoo* 431 ... the infections which that foul leper had scattered abroad in the social and political body were being rapidly expelled.

let the Union slide.

In a much heralded speech at Portland, Maine, in 1855, Nathaniel P. Banks used the phrase:

in Harrington *Fighting Politician* 26. I am not one of that class of men who cry for the perpetuation of the Union. I am willing in a certain set of circumstances to "let it slide."

This was quickly picked up to be used against Banks and other radical abolitionists:

1855 in Christy *Pulpit Politics* 527. The gentleman from Massachusetts has announced to the world that, in certain contingencies, he is willing to "let the Union slide."

1856 *Middletown* (N.Y.) *Banner of Liberty* 100/1. As a result of the noxious teachings of Garrison, and others of the same clique, the highest place in the legislative department of the government of the United States is occupied by a Nigger Worshipper, who said that, under circumstances, he would "let the Union slide."

1858 *Ohio Statesman* 28 Sept. 2/1 . . . like Banks, "in a certain contingency," he would "let the Union slide."

1864 Greeley *Am. Conflict* I.372/2. Strange as it must now seem, this assertion of the radical impotence of the Government, this avowal of a fixed purpose to "let the Union slide," on the part of the President and his legal adviser, were received in Congress with general and concerted taciturnity on the part of the upholders, and with a bounteous display of indignation on that of the banded assailants, of the National life.

The pattern of the phrase had been used much earlier:

1846 Nason *Life of Henry Wilson* 77. At all events, I am for liberty; and if dissolution of the Union must be the result of the abolition of slavery, or of lawful and constitutional action, why, then, let that dissolution come. Let the Union go; the sooner, the better.

let us alone.

Slogan identified with a policy of non-interference in what are considered purely local matters.

The origin of the phrase is probably Biblical:

Mark I.23–4. And there was in the synagogue a man with an unclean spirit; and he cried out

Saying, Let *us* alone; what have we to do with thee, thou Jesus of Nazareth?

A. Early applied in American politics to general subjects:

1824 *Niles' Reg.* 10 April 83/1. "Let all alone," or protect all. We acknowledge no privileged classes.

1832 *Ib.* 20 Oct. 113/1. Such is the difference between doing and talking—thinking and bawling: the Pennsylvania *forward*-policy, and the Virginia *let-us-alone*-policy.

1834 Leggett *Pol. Writings* I.116 . . . the old notions of government bounty, protection, prohibition and coercion in matters of trade, are totally exploded by the wisest men and deepest thinkers of the age,—that mankind have discovered at last that they are governed too much;—and that the true democratic principle, and the true principle of political economy, is "Let us alone."

1856 *Middletown* (N.Y.) *Banner of Liberty* 2 Jan. 7/4. We as a nation must return to the "old platform" as laid down in the Constitution . . . : 'To think and let think,' or in other words, 'let alone and be let alone,' in our domestic capacities.

B. During the periods of anti-slavery agitation, specifically associated with the attitude of the South.

184– Channing *Works* 783. Our friends, as well as foes, have said, "Be quiet; let the South alone; it will find for itself the way of emancipation. . . ."

1859 *N. Y. Trib.* 30 Dec. in Pike *First Blows* 457. The Richmond Whig indorses the sentiment of the Memphis Avalanche that all the South wants is "to be let alone." But how "let alone?" This phrase covers a very comprehensive meaning, or may be made to do so. The burglar may say all he wants is "to be let alone."

1861 Lowell *Pol. Essays* 88. The little Bopeep policy of

"Let them alone, and they'll come home
 Wagging their tails behind them"

was certainly tried long enough with Conspirators who had shown unmistakably that they desired nothing so much as the continuance of peace, especially when it was all on one side, and who would never have given the Government the great advantage of being attacked in

Fort Sumter, had they not supposed they were dealing with men who could not be cuffed into resistance.

1861 in *Northern Editorials* II.610. The one asks peace and to be let alone. The other threatens coercion and war.

1874 *Cinc. Comm.* 19 Sept. 2/1. All the negroes ask is to be let alone.

1875 in Hayes *Diary* 27 July III.286. As to Southern affairs "the let-alone policy" seems now to be the true course. . . .

1879 *Harper's W.* 26 April 821 [Nast cartoon]. He (the Solid South) Will Soon Be "Let Alone."

C. Later uses show the phrase to have become again a non-restrictive one.

1903 Mitchell *Organized Labor* 33 . . . "The Wealth of Nations," in which the doctrine of "let-alone," or "no interference," was propounded as the correct relation of government to industry.

1924 Will Rogers *How We Elect* 26 June 32. He is the first President to discover that what the American people want is to be let alone.

leveller (levelling).

Originally, an English political party during the reign of Charles I.

1647 *Newsletter* 1 Nov. [*OED*]. They have given themselves a new name viz. Levellers, for they intend to set all things straight, and rayse a parity and community in the kingdom.

In the 18th century it became the name of an Irish secret society, which apparently employed tactics that justified its use of the term on a practical basis:

1763 *Brit. Mag.* IV.162 [*OED*]. The mischiefs committed by those people called Levellers, in the county of Tipperary; by levelling park walls, breaking down fences, &c.

In America we find *leveller* a more or less opprobrious term, ranging between the poles of liberalism and jacobinism:

1787 Madison in *Fed. Conv.* 26 June 243. No agrarian attempts have yet been made in this country; but symptoms of a levelling spirit . . . have sufficiently appeared.

1814 Adams *Works* VI.459. Will Mr. Taylor profess himself a downright leveller? Will he vote for a community of property?

1830 *Workingman's Adv.* 27 March 2/5. I remember the time when all democrats were denounced as jacobins, disorganizers, levellers, enemies to all religion, order, and regular government, atheists, deists, and a whole catalogue of all that was abject and vile.

1837 Martineau *Society* I.11. I heard from so many tongues of the desolations of the "levelling spirit," and the approaching ruin of political institutions.

1840 *Cong. Globe* 12 Feb. App. 739 . . . the doctrine for which the opponents of this levelling destructive policy contend. . . .

1840 in Norton *Tippecanoe* App. 71. Subtreasurers, Levellers, and all The spoilers of the land.

1853 in *Gt. Deb.* X.24. I am not one of those levelers that wish to pull down elevated men.

Applied to Americans in general:

1832 Butler *Jrnl.* I.64 . . . a my Lord, or my Lady, are just as precious in the eyes of these levellers, as in those of Lord and Lady-loving John Bull himself.

liberal.

During most of the 18th century *liberal* meant generous or broadminded. Toward the end of this period it showed an occasional tendency to enter the province of politics:

1761 Churchill, *Night* 50.
And Reason to herself alone is law;
That freedom she enjoys with liberal mind,
Which she as freely grants to all mankind.

1781 Gibbon *Decline and Fall* III.142. A Grecian philosopher . . . published his liberal opinions concerning the duties of kings.

1791 Mackintosh *Essays* 427. The commercial or monied interest has in all nations . . . been less prejudiced, more liberal, and more intelligent than the landed gentry . . . liberalizing the modern world.

1798 W. Godwin *Memoirs of the Author of a Vindication of the Rights of Woman* 76. Burke had been warmly loved by the most liberal and enlightened friends of freedom, and they were proportionably inflamed and disgusted by the fury of his assault, upon what they deemed to be its sacred cause.

An important point in the history of the word is the beginning of Napoleon's dictatorship. In his first pronunciamento, it occurs repeatedly; for instance:

18 Brumaire quoted in Brunot IX.661 . . . les idées conservatrices tutélaires, "liberales," sont rentrées leur droit.

As a party name the word appears first in Spain, where *liberales* and *serviles* became the names of opposing parties (see Ladendorf). From there the word came into French and later English politics. It is significant that "early in the 19th century the substantive occurs chiefly as applied by opponents to the advanced section of the Whig party: sometimes in Spanish or French form, apparently with intention of suggesting that the principles of those politicians were unEnglish, or akin to those of the revolutionaries of the Continent. As, however, the adjective was already English in a laudatory sense, the advocates of reform were not reluctant to adopt the foreign term as descriptive of themselves." . . .

1786 *Annual Reg.* XXVIII.33. The liberal disposition to improvement, at present prevalent in the court of Madrid, is not, however, confined to rural and domestic matters.

1816 *Quarterly Rev.* XV.69. These are the personages for whose sake the continuance of the Alien Bill has been opposed by the British Liberals.

1826 Scott *Journals* 19 Nov. Canning, Huskisson, and a mitigated party of Liberaux.

Later *liberal* became the official designation of the progressive party, largely replacing *Whigs:*

1850 Leigh Hunt *Autobio.* I.248. Its [*The Examiner's*] great object was a reform in Parliament, . . . which had lately been suffered to fall entirely into the hands of those newer and more thorough-going Whigs, which were known by the name of Radicals, and have since been called Whig-Radicals, and Liberals.

In America the word never acquired the prominence it had in Europe. It was, however, adopted by several local parties:

1839 *New Yorker* 20 April 2/2. Liberal Ticket [of third party in Rhode Island]. [head]

1840 *Rough Hewer* 292/2. What Irishman . . . can refuse to vote for the candidates of the "liberal party," Martin Van Buren and Richard M. Johnson?

1854 *N. Y. Trib.* 22 April 5/5. The "Liberals" of Maine have called a "State Democratic Mass Convention" at Portland.

1854 *Ib.* 24 June 4/6. A mass Covention of individuals styling themselves "Liberal Democrats" was held at Portland, Maine, on the 15th inst.

Of greater importance is the formation of a Liberal Republican party in Missouri. The choice of the name may be due to Carl Schurz, to whom the word must have been well-known from his European background:

1869 Schurz *Writings* I.474 . . . my election to the Senate . . . is an evidence of the liberal and progressive spirit moving the people of Missouri.

1870 *Cong. Globe* App. 5/1. He [Schurz] and his friends organize a "Liberal Party," so called; and by way of vindication its irresisble [sic] claim to liberality, its first act is to pronounce its separation from its party associates for a mere difference of opinion on a point of policy.

1870 *Annual Cyc.* 518/1 . . . the organizers of the liberal movement did not abandon their plans, and the Republican party of the State was rapidly becoming divided into two widely-separated wings, known as the liberal and the radical.

1871 *Ib.* 531 . . . to call a State Convention of Liberal Republicans. . . .

1871 *Cinc. Commercial* 14 Nov. 4/5. I [J. Jonson] propose a People's National Convention, to be held in this city early next year, to be composed of all the elements of opposition to Grant's administration . . . that may unite Democrats and Republicans upon a sound Liberal policy.

1872 *Ib.* 776/1 . . . the achievements and purposes of the "Liberal Movement," and calling a mass meeting, to be held at Jefferson City, on January 24, 1872. . . . It closed its proceedings by issuing a call for a National Convention, to be held at Cincinnati, on the first Monday of May. . . .

Notice that in this and later quotations *Liberal* and *Liberal Republican* are used indiscriminantly.

The Missouri call for a national convention was realized in 1872, when Horace Greeley was nominated in Cincinnati as the Liberal Republican candidate.

1872 Schurz *Writings* II.315. You are certainly right in saying that the same principles which the Liberal Republicans of Missouri inscribed upon their banner in 1870 are now in issue on the larger field of National politics.

1872 Hayes *Diary* III.202. The city [Cincinnati] is filling up with Liberals.

1872 Durbin Ward *Sp.* 252. Through the columns of the Cincinnati Commercial, over an assumed signature, I urged, in November of last year, the calling of a National Convention at Cincinnati, of all opposed to Grant's administration, and the formation of a "Liberal" party to accomplish that end. This was the earliest suggestion of the Cincinnati Convention, except one made in the New Orleans Bee.

The claim for priority of Ward and the New Orleans paper is challenged by the very paper in which Ward is supposed to have made his call:

1875 *Cinc. Comm.* 6 May 2/1. They [Fenton *et al.*] invented the title of "Liberals," and it is perhaps because they liked it so much that it is now thrown overboard. The new party is henceforth to be called the "Independent Voters." It is rather an unhandy name but perhaps this is of no great consequence.

In modern times *liberal* is hardly used as a party name proper, but is a designation of progressive groups within either of the major parties:

1939 Vogan *Mod. Hudibras* 55.
Because it helps the game a lot
To keep our slogans new and hot,
Of late we tested out a few,
And hoped that "Liberal" would do;
But then so many people cried—
They thought Miss Liberty had died.

1940 in Seldes *Witch Hunt* XI. *Liberal* has been a word of confusion. Everybody who was not a Conservative became a Liberal or Radical or Red, whichever came first to the mind. In the newspapers, it was often a matter of headline convenience.

1952 *Reporter* 19 Aug. Will Republican leaders awaken to the fact that Eisenhower must be free to further his chances of appealing to the vote of liberal Republicans and independents?

1953 *Dem. Digest* Nov. 26/1. One day he

[Eisenhower] makes a pronouncement that appeals to the Republican liberals. **1958** *New Rep.* 1 Dec. 2/3. Paul Douglas and Hubert Humphrey, it appears, are "advanced liberals" (presumably Lyndon Johnson is just a "liberal") .

Liberty party.

A short-lived party dedicated to the abolition of slavery.

1842 Birney *Ltrs.* 690n. I gave it in my opinion, that the strenuous effort which some of the advocates of the Liberty party movement in Ohio were making to separate themselves from the abolitionists ... would be injurious to the whole cause.
1843 Stanwood *Hist. of the Presidency* 216. Resolved, That the Liberty Party, placing itself upon this broad principle, will demand the absolute and unqualified divorce of the general government from slavery, and also the restoration of equality among men, in every State where the party exists or may exist.
1845 Weed in Barnes *Weed* 230. I know how the Whigs of Madison County have been oppressed by the falsely-styled "Liberty" party, and I respect the indignant sentiments entertained there by Whig friends.... Demagogues of the "Liberty" faction have beguiled ten or twelve thousand honest men and true Whigs from allegiance to the country.
1847 Webster *Works* V.260. The party in the North which calls itself, by way of distinction and eminence, the "Liberty Party," opposed with all its force the election of the Whig candidate in 1844....

lily white.

A Republican faction, principally in Texas, desirous of excluding negroes from the party.

1898 Stanwood *History of the Presidency* 516. An independent electoral ticket, by the so-called "Lily White" faction of the Republican party of Texas, received 3,969 votes.
1903 *N. Y. Times* 23 Sept. [*DA*]. The report that the President was seeking reconciliation with the "Lilywhite" faction, which eliminated the negro from the last State Convention.
1932 Lewinson *Race, Class, and Party* 110. The term seems to have been coined in Texas in 1888, after riots between white and Negro Republicans struggling for the control of a convention.... 170 ... coined in 1888 in Texas by the Negro Republican leader Norris Wright Cuney....
1932 Mencken *Making a President* 38. His agents are trying to throw them [colored delegates] out and seat lilywhites in their places.

Little Band. [ ]

?**1802** Van Buren *Autobio.* 109. Thus disappeared from the political stage a party which, though small in numbers produced nearly or quite as great an impression as its predecessors and counterpart, the Burrites—in their days distinguished by the name of the "Little Band."

loafer.

The word entered the American vocabulary in the 1830's. The suggestion that it was first used in 1791 (see 1839) has no evidence to support it. [ ]

1835 *Knickerbocker* VI.63. Ben was a metropolitan loafer and a phenomenon. He was the ruling luminary of a whole shoal of shag tailed comets that used to shoot madly about the terrestrial firmament of New York.
1836 *Cinc. Republican* 26 July 2/4. The Battery ... the fashionables have altogether abandoned to the "loafers," a new word by the way, which we find in use here without knowing the exact meaning of it.
1839 *Cong. Globe* App. 39/3. [Petrikin of Pa.] ... taking the money from the many and industrious part of the people, to put into the pockets of the few idlers, speculators, and loafers.
1839 *Am. Weekly Messenger* 22 May 3/1. The word "loafer" was employed as long ago as 1791, in a work on banking by John Taylor, of Philadelphia. It used to signify what we term "blackleg."

Despite an occasional denial or quasi-serious etymology, it seems probable that *loafer*, is derived from *loaves and fishes*. We find many early examples associating the idler or beggar with the loaf of bread.

1823 *Delaware* (Ohio) *Patron* 25 June 3/3. I would sooner support an acknowledged federalist, than a man who deserted their ranks for the purpose of sharing the "loafs and fishes."

1828 Paulding *New Mirror* 176. But it was never yet known that either men or geese were content with half a loaf when they could get the whole.

1836 *Scioto Gazette* 14 Sept. 1/2. The Boston Transcript is wrong in imputing to the New York Express the first true etymology ever published of the word *Loafer*. The Star, if there is any merit in a derivation so obvious, has it. Low-Fellow comes Lo-fellow—Lo-fell'r—Lo-fer. The same as a small cucumber termed Gerkin, comes from Jeremiah King—Jerry-king—Jer-king—Gerkin.

1837 *Am. Weekly Messenger* 12 July 2/6. Loafer.—Instead of a vulgarism, why not regard Loafer as a classic compound of English and Latin? Loaf, bread—Fur, a thief. Bread-thief. This would be appropriate.

1837 *Ohio St. Jrnl.* 26 Aug. 1/1. Their cognomen is not derived from loaf.

1846 *Frankfort Commonwealth* 21 July 2/7. ... he was accosted by a tatterdemalion boy, who begged piteously for a sixpence to buy a loaf of bread for his dying mother.... "I'll pitch with any on you now, for I've got the brass."... "Oh I cum de bread act on a green un," was the reply.

1859 Jones *Wild Southern Scenes* 75 [describing rioters]. Women were with them in great numbers, some on foot, bearing loaves of bread on poles, and others drawn in open carriages, covered with fantastic decorations.

1871 *Prenticeana* 247. An Arkansas editor complains that his town, for some time past, has been "filled with fishermen and loafers," and wonders "what they are after." After loaves and fishes no doubt.

Although mostly referring to social standing, *loafer* occasionally was given political application.

1840 *Cong. Globe* App.50/2. Sir, with many honorable exceptions, our streets are crowded with blacklegs, political jugglers, hungry expectants, lounging, lean lazaroni loafers, bank vassals, and Federal minions, congregated from all parts of the Union.

1840 *Ib.* 17 Oct. 2/4.... the disappointed Loafers sneaking up the back alleys in the direction of their "Headquarters," better known as "Jake's Doggery."

1840 *Straightout Harrisonian* 17 Oct. 1/3. ...tools of the aforesaid leaders, and whose names I have forgotten. Some of them keep doggeries, and the balance are generally seen loafing about such establishments.

1840 *Cong. Globe* App.376/3. [Watterson of Tenn.] In that living, moving, ranting band [of Whigs], the boys, negroes, loafers, and a new species of the same animal, familiarly known in the city of New York as soap-locks, took the lead....

1874 *Leslie's* 28 March 34/1. There was a struggle between Grant's loafers ... and the respectable people of the country.

applied to Canadian politics. [ ]
1838 *Hamilton Intelligencer* 1 March 2/5. Canada Loafers [head]

1839 Hone *Diary*, I.391. General Scott has returned from his last excursion to the northern frontier, where he was sent to set matters to rights between the loafer loyalists of Canada and the loafer patriots of the United States.

loaves and fishes.

The phrase goes back to the Biblical story:

John 6:9. There is a lad here which hath five barley loaves, and two small fishes: but what are they among so many?

A. Used facetiously as early as the 17th century to refer to the perquisites of ecclesiastical office.

1614 Hall *Recoll. Treat.* 954 [*OED*]. If it were not for the loaves and fishes, the traine of Christ would bee lesse.

B. In European politics:

c1761 in Lascelles *Fox* 15 ... the House of Commons, where according to Fox, the Government must rely upon "the Tories, the Scotch, and the loaves and fishes."

1791 Paine *Works* VI.84 (Patriot's ed.). The French Constitution says, That to preserve the national representation from being corrupt, no member of the National Assembly shall be an officer of the government, a place-man, or a pensioner. What will Mr. Burke place against this? I will whisper the answer: *Loaves* and *Fishes*. Ah! This government of loaves and fishes has more mischief in it than people have yet reflected on.

1792 Morris *Writings* II.237. They aver that those, whom they call the Brissotines, had no wish to overturn the monarchy, but only to get the loaves and fishes for themselves and their friends.

1795 *Rolliad & Pol. Misc.* 229.
Come, Brunswick, come, great king of loaves and fishes,
Be bounteous still to grant us all our wishes!

C. In American politics:

1800 Bishop *Conn. Republicanism* 50 ... when you look around for federalists, you will not see men as trees walking. Separate those who follow for the loaves and fishes, with those who habitually follow the multitude....

1805 Fessenden *Democracy Unveiled* 77. Gives foreigners our loaves and fishes, To bend our counsels to his wishes.

1816 *Cinc. Western Spy* 23 Aug. 2/4.
There was Clay the scold,
And Johnson the bold,
Who did not shoot Tecumseh, O!
And Ormsby and Lowndes,
As eager as hounds,
On the scent of the loaves and fishes O!

1824 *Cinc. Nat. Rep.* 22 June 1/3 ... his [Jackson's] decision of character and manly firmness, are not calculated to recommend him to those who are in quest of the loaves and fishes.

1832 *N. Y. Mirror* 394/2. The *many* have run away with the "loaves and fishes," while we have been left to the proud but beggarly consolation of having done our duty.

D. Referring to the benefits to be found deriving from the spoils system.

1835 *Lebanon* (Ohio) *Western Star* 3 April 3/3. Now-a-days Democracy means "loaves and fishes," spoils of victory, "good fat offices."

1836 *Ib.* 25 Nov. 3/2. The whole object of that party seems to be the preservation of the "loaves and fishes" won under the banner of the Hero of New Orleans.

The joke was given new point by attributing the five loaves and two fishes to the seven principles of the Democratic party, based perhaps upon a quip of John Randolph (see 1840, 1844):

1835 *Mich. Argus* 2 July 3/2. What a commentary this upon the declaration made by one of their papers in this territory, that the Whigs of Michigan did not want office, but acted from principle. Surely they have seven principles, viz: "Five loaves and two fishes."

1840 in Norton *Tippecanoe* 185. The men of office and party, who are governed by the principles of John Randolph, to wit: the five loaves and two fishes, seem to have their ears constantly directed to the bell at headquarters, to indicate how the little ones shall ring.

1840 *Straightout Harrisonian* 1 May 1/2. The Locos have but one principle, which is, love of the loaves and fishes.

1840 *Ohio St. Jrnl.* 10 June 1/1 ... 7 dark principles of "the loaves and fishes."

1842 *N. Y. w. Trib.* 17 Sept. 6/5. They [office seekers] had seven good reasons for their doings, to wit, five loaves and two fishes.

1844 *Niles' Reg.* 20 April 122/2. This party is governed by seven principles—as John Randolph is reported to have said of Thomas Ritchie—the five loaves and the two fishes.

1844 *Wash. Nat. Intelligencer* 23 Aug. 3/4. There was no common bond of union upon the broad platform of principle. In fact, the only principle he could perceive which bound them [Dems] together were the seven, viz., the five loaves and two fishes.

1860 in Foner *Douglass* II.510. Instead of the five loaves and two fishes—the usual number of political principles—we have five parties and no principles in the present canvass.

lobby.

A. The earliest examples of *lobby* in American politics suggest that it was first used to designate an entrance hall used in lieu of a gallery from which the public might watch the proceedings of their congress.

1765 Jefferson in Wirt *Patrick Henry* 79. I was then a student, and stood at the door of communication between the house and the lobby (for as yet there was no gallery) during the whole debate and vote....

18—*Annals 10th Cong. I sess.* II.1536. If we move to Philadelphia we shall have a commanding lobby; we shall learn the sentiments of the population!

B. In England the lobby, a large entrance hall to the House of Commons, open to the public, had long been used for interviews between members and persons not belonging to the House.

1640 *Rushw. Hist. Coll.* III.I.1 [*OED*]. The outward Room of the Commons House, called the Lobby ... where the Cryer of the Chancery first made Proclamation in the King's name.

C. We may assume that this practice of meeting the public in

the lobby was also popular in the United States and resulted in the asking of favors and other implications which led to the later meaning of the term. In 1819 we find the modern meaning emerging with the association of lobbying and corruption.

1819 in Lynch *Epoch and the Man* 239. Corruption has erected her court on the heights of the Hudson, in the avenues of Albany, in the lobby of the legislature.... Her throne was the lobby.

1822 King *Corr.* VI.467 ... all the old Bank members backed by the Lobby agents and speculators....

1823 *Cinc. Nat. Rep.* 9 May 1/2. Several of those who are here [Ill.] called lobby members....

1828 Paulding *New Mirror* 174. They are called by way of honourable distinction Lobby-members because they form a sort of third estate, or legislative chamber in the lobby.

1832 Seward *Life* 213. The lobby are becoming corrupt and impudent.

1837 *Ann. of Cleve.* No.1839. He spent a great deal of time last winter in Columbus, lobbying to procure the establishment of a bank in Ohio City.

1844 in *Mangum Papers* IV.105. You will meet with many "lobby members" of the Conventions from N.Y. and some actual ones.

1854 Bungay *Off-Hand Takings* 321. It was the first time that ever a Governor of the State of New York was found in a Convention, lobbying and bargaining with its members, and I believe it will be the last.

1869 *N. Y. Trib.* 12 Jan. ... that higher legislative body the Lobby.

1877 Hamilton *Blaine* 439. The Senator talks of a lobby being here. That is always the cry when anything comes up, "There is a lobby."

1886 *Perley's Rem.* 513. The lobby is a quiet but efficient part of Congressional machinery. Scores of bills are considered and passed during every session, each involving thousands of dollars, and those having them in charge do not feel like turning a deaf ear to any one who can promise support.

lobbygog.

A ward heeler (lobby + [dema] gog[ue]).

1946 *Time* 21 Oct. 19. An apologetic First Ward lobbygog (Chicagoese for ward heeler) explained: "He was retired too long. If you don't go to other people's funerals they won't go to yours.

local sovereignty. (self-government)

A variation of *popular sovereignty* (q.v.).

1850 *Cong. Globe* App. 64/1. Admit that they [Congress] may organize a government which shall protect the lands purchased, and provide for the administration of justice among the settlers, it does by no means follow that they may establish slavery. This is a relation which must be created by local sovereignty.... 1872 in Stanwood *History of the Presidency* 343. [platform of Liberal-Republican party] 4. Local self-government, with impartial suffrage, will guard the rights of all citizens more securely than any centralized power.

1872 Adams *Pol. Oratory of Storrs* 127. Enough of money and enough of lives have already been wasted on the settlement of that question (centralization of government); and no such thin disguise as "local self-government" will ever seduce us into the re-opening of that subject.

Loco Foco.

Originally the name of a self-igniting match or cigar promoted by John Marck, whom Bartlett considers the coiner of the word:

The mode of getting at the name is obvious. The word "locomotive" was then rather new as applied to an engine on a railroad, and the common notion was, that it meant self-moving; hence as these cigars were self-firing, this queer name was coined. So Mr. John Marck has the

honor of inventing the name. His patent for "self-igniting cigars" bears the date April 16, 1834.

A new, political meaning developed almost overnight after a stormy meeting in Tammany Hall (October 29, 1835), when an attempt by regular Democrats to secure the adoption of their ticket was foiled by the Anti-Monopolists (q.v.):

1835 *Richmond Whig* 3 Nov. 2/6. Shortly after the meeting had been organized, the lights were extinguished, and in the hubbub, the meeting was again called to order, a new Chairman appointed, and the conspirators drawing candles from their pockets, ignited them with loco foco matches, throwing a new light upon the aspect of affairs.

For more detailed accounts see Byrdsall; *Niles' Reg.,* 7 Nov. 1835, 163–5.

Consequently the nickname *loco foco* was attached to the Anti-Monopolists, according to Byrdsall (p. 29) by the *New York Enquirer and Courier,* while the *New Yorker* (December 9, 1837) attributes it to the *Daily Advertiser.* Within a very short time the name was very widely adopted.

1835 *Ohio St. Jrnl.* 8 Dec. 1/3. The Tammanies and the Loco-focus [sic] divide the great Republican party there [Boston] as well as elsewhere, as we find by a notice in the Boston Courier, of a very amusing row, which took place between them at Faneuil Hall, where the melo-dramatic performances first gotten up by the New York troupe were repeated with great success. The putting out of the lights, and the re-illumination by means of the loco-foco (becoming more popular than hocus pocus) process, were exceedingly well done, and elicited much applause.

1836 *Indiana Palladium* 30 Jan. 1/4.
Rejoice! because in Tamm'ny Hall,
In recent loco-foco brawl
Of partisans so very many
Were served like Cats of fam'd Kil-
kenny. . . .
1837 *Phila. W. Messenger* 13 Sept. 2/2.
What is a Loco Foco. A Loco Foco in the
present acceptation of the term is a man
not satisfied with anything as it exists;
but in favor of an equal distribution of
property, an uprooting of the institutions
of the country, and substitution of some
monstrous and impracticable fancy of his
own in their stead.
1837 *N. Y. Herald* 1 Nov. 2/1. In short,
Fanny Wright is a vulgar locofoco—
Rosina Townsend a dashing whig conservative.
1838 *Ib.* 2 Nov. 2/1. By urging the credit
system beyond its natural limits, the Pari-
sian locofocos of 1792 broke down paper
credit and paper money in France.
1839 *Dem. Rev.* July 27. [Reform party]
to which was at first attached in derision
the name, now recognized as a badge of
honor in all parts of the Union, of *Locofocoism.*
1839 *Cong. Globe* 13 Feb. App. 176/3.
This word Loco Foco is one of those caba-
listic terms which a certain class of politicians use to conjure up any accusation
it may suit their convenience to fasten
upon their adversaries. Its acknowledged
unintelligibility relieves them from all ob-
ligation to explain, and it fixes a sort of
undefined odium upon whomsoever or
whatsoever they choose to denounce. . . .
At one time it is Agrarianism; at another,
a general community of every thing, unregulated by law.

While these examples show that
the notion of *loco foco* was that of
an ultra-radical, other uses from
the same years indicate that the
term was used indiscriminately by
the Whigs as a name for all Democrats, with varying effect; a development furthered by the fact that
in 1837 shortly before the election

a large number of the loco foco
wing rejoined the regular party:
Byrdsall chap. xiii (see in particular 188).
Gradually, the Loco-Focos of both sections became merged in the Democratic
Republican party, and they brought not
only their "new fangled notions" with
them, but also their significant designation as a party.
1837 *N. Y. Mirror* 27 May 383/3. "Locofocoism," for instance, has already become
a good Colonic word, meaning ultra-
political-economy. . . .
1838 *Democratic Rev.* Jan. A use was made
of the unfortunate word "Loco-foco" . . .
alone sufficient to frighten fifty thousand
very worthy and honest people from the
ballot boxes.
1838 Hone *Diary* 5 Nov. The Locofoco
have triumphed throughout the State;
there will be a majority for them of two
in the Senate, and in the Assembly there
will only be 20 or 30 Whigs.
1838 *Ib.* 7 Dec. The breaking up of the
Loco-foco forces in different parts of the
country produces every day some new
development of party atrocity.
1840 in Norton *Tippecanoe* App. 16.
    Then let us vote for Harrison,
    And turn out scheming Van;
    Capsize his kitchen cabinet,
    And rout the loco clan.
c1841 in Kendall *Autobio.* 454. Some
Democrats, we perceive, are accommodating enough to adopt the name "Locofoco"
prescribed by their adversaries.
1848 *Free Soil Banner* 4 Sept. 4. The Loco
Foco party of Michigan seems to be
crumbling to atoms. . . .
1853 *N. Y. Trib.* 18 Jan. 4/3. The proceedings of the late Ohio Loco-Foco State
Convention are very significant.
c1846 in Buley *The Old Northwest* II.213.
Governor Thomas Ford, writing ten years
later, said that the name "[loco foco]
had no effect whatever on elections" and
that no squeamish man ran away from or
became disgusted with a party "having
this uncouth name."

In 1863, Williams (*Model Republic,* 278–9) gives a late but plausi-

ble reason for the rapid progress in the spread of *loco foco:*
They [Whigs] peremptorily refused to designate their opponents any longer by their ancient title of "democrats." They said it was too sober, too grave—the very sound made them melancholy; and they never applied the word "democrat" to their adversaries again. They called them "Loco-focos"—said there was something light as well as sulphurous about that name which pleased them; and ever afterwards they refused to recognize their adversaries by any other title. Their coat of arms was a log cabin, with the string of the doorlatch upon the outside, a jug of hard cider, a "coon rampant," regarding with a sardonic grin a "loco-foco" couchant.

A witty attempt to counteract the force of *loco foco* is told by Congdon:
c1852 *Reminiscences* 61. I heard him once [D. Brownson] raise a mighty roar of applause by defining a loco foco "as a man always carrying his own light."

log cabin.
One of the symbols used in the Harrison campaign of 1840.

All evidence points to the Loco Focos for the origin of the story about Harrison and the log cabin; there are, however, many conflicting reports as to the exact source. Since the Whig convention was held at Harrisburg, the following suggestion is at least plausible. (Compare, Norton, *Tippecanoe,* 11; Barnes, *T. Weed,* 80; *Georgia Jrnl.* 12 May, 1840, 3/4.)
1840 *La. Advertiser* 25 April. The origin of "Log Cabin and Hard Cider!" words now in the mouths of all the agriculturalists from Maine to Missouri, is traced to the Harrisburg Correspondent of the Baltimore Republican, a loco foco print: immediately after the nomination he

wrote:—that upon his [Harrison's] receiving a pension of two thousand dollars, and a Barrel of Hard Cider, he would no doubt consent to withdraw his pretensions, and spend his days in a Log Cabin, on the banks of the Ohio.
1840 Webster *Works* II.29. But it is to be remembered, that this matter of the log cabin originated, not with the friends of the Whig candidate, but with his enemies. Soon after his nomination at Harrisburg, a writer for one of the leading administration papers spoke of his "log cabin," and his use of "hard cider," by way of sneer and reproach. As might have been expected, (for pretenders are apt to be thrown off their guard,) this taunt at humble life proceeded from the party which claims a monopoly of the purest democracy. The whole party appeared to enjoy it, or, at least, they countenanced it by silent acquiescence; for I do not know that, to this day, any eminent individual or any leading newspaper attached to the administration has rebuked this scornful jeering at the supposed humble condition or circumstances in life, past or present, of a worthy man and a war-worn soldier. But it touched a tender point in the public feeling. It naturally roused indignation. What was intended as reproach was immediately seized on as merit. "Be it so! Be it so!" was the instant burst of the public voice. "Let him be the log cabin candidate. What you say in scorn, we will shout with all our lungs. From this day forward, we have our cry of rally; and we shall see whether he who has dwelt in one of the rude abodes of the West may not become the best house in the country!"

During the campaign of 1840:
1840 *Rough-hewer* 26 March 45/1. The supporters of Harrison have staked their existence as a party, upon the fact that their candidate resides in a log cabin, and that he is therefore, a log cabin candidate.
1840 Hone *Diary* 10 April I.472. Processions parade the streets at night with music, torches, and banners; the prevailing device for the latter is the log-cabin;

and hard cider has become the fountain of Whig inspiration. In an evil hour the Loco-focos taunted the Harrison men with having elected a candidate who lived in a log cabin, and drank hard cider, which the Whigs, with more adroitness than they usually display, appropriated to their own use. . . .

1840 Duncan in *Cong. Globe* 10 April App. 434/2. Tens of thousands and hundreds of thousands of these vile panders of falsehood and slander have been franked by Whig members . . . to advance the cause of the "log cabin candidate" for the presidency.

1840 *Ann. of Cleve.* No.1734. Little did the Locofoco simpleton who proposed pensioning Harrison with a log cabin and hard cider dream when penning it, that his taunt would raise such a tornado about the ears of his party.

1840 Jackson *Corr.* VI.68 . . . the inclosures, which I retain to refute the vagrant falsehoods of our noisy worshippers of Hard cider, logg Cabins and Coons. . . .

A later allusion:

1841 *Sketches of Mike Walsh* 24. I shall not, however, endeavor by any low artifice to raise a thoughtless laugh, nor shall I insult your understandings by re-echoing the long, stale, worn out, cant and clap trap phrases of "log cabin," "hard cider," "stuffed owls," "coon skins," "two dollars a day and roast beef". . . .

log cabin bill.

Satirical name for the preemption act of 1841. Opponents of the bill felt that the introduction of the phrase *log cabin* was a mere delusion to win support.

1841 in *Mangum Papers* V.620. But this is a log cabin bill. In its title it purports to be especially for the tenants of log cabins.

Ib. V.629. But this is really a log cabin bill—a bill for the poor man. I could not but regret to hear these party "catchwords" introduced into this Chamber.

Ib. V.631. This log cabin movement is no more like the little feverish excitements

got up by party trick and machinery and bribery, than mimic theatrical thunder is like the resistless bolt that leaps from the cloud.

logrolling.

The prevailing idea that *logrolling* means the rolling of logs to the site where a cabin is to be built is in need of some adjustment. The word is also, and perhaps primarily, used in connection with the work of clearing woodlands, the logs of the felled trees being collected in one place for burning:

1843 Carlton *New Purchase* I.240 f. Now, it is to a clearing the log-rolling, or, for brevity's sake, "a rolin," pertains. . . . When the logs are all cut or niggered, they are then rolled, but often dragged together, in different parts of the clearing. . . .

Also the process of building itself necessitates some logrolling as seen from Horace B. Riddle's *American Boyhood* (1876), 38:

Whene'er the walls were up so high
  They could not reach the top,
They put up poles, peeled, smooth and
  dry,
  To form a gentle slope;
Then laid the logs on longer skids,
  And pushed them up with forks;
And many were the dangerous slides,
  The slips, and sudden jerks.

It is immaterial which aspect of logrolling is behind the metaphorical use of this word in politics; the main point being that in all its semantic variations the idea of co-operation is very clear. In political usage it occurs first in 1809:

Chillicothe Supporter 26 Jan. 3/1. Now Preparing, and shortly will be put to press, A New Work! to be entitled The Legislative Log Roller. By Timothy Tickler, Esquire.

This work will contain a brief history of the rise, progress and beneficial effects of this useful art. Its origin will be traced to that celebrated junto, who, in November, 1802, entered into a solemn league to divide all the officers of state among themselves. . . . It will also contain biographical sketches of several great log rolling captains. . . . The whole will be calculated to demonstrate the manner in which private ambition and self interest may cover itself under the veil of patriotism. . . .

The derogatory nature of the metaphor seems to be clear from the beginning:

1819 in Cutler *Life of Ephraim Cutler* 120.
Resolved, To instruct our Trimble and Ruggles
To aid by log-rolling, and speeches, and struggles
. . . .
That thus we may all be elected again.

1820 T. Flint in *Thwaits Western Travels* IX.215. Combinations are formed for effecting particular purposes. These are called log rolling; a very significant metaphor, borrowed from the practice of several farmers uniting in rolling together large timber to be burnt.

1823 *Cinc. Nat. Rep.* 2 May 1/1. The Metaphor [log rolling] . . . is . . . borrowed from the customs of backwoodsmen. "Do you help me roll my logs, and I'll help you roll yours." This is the literal sense. "Do you vote for my measure, and I'll vote for yours." This is the metaphorical sense. This is legislative log-rolling; and in this manner are various acts . . . all rolled together in the statute books.

1827 *Georgetown* (Ohio) *Castigator* 1 May 3/3 . . . by log rolling to use a common phrase a member accomplished in the legislature, what he might just as well have done at home without the farce of legislative interference.

1830 *Workingman's Adv.* 5 June 1/4. There is a system of "log rolling" practiced in every county in this state, at al-most every election; that by associating several men, and of course their influence, upon one ticket, gives it the strength of which, intrinsically, it is not worthy.

1834 *Reg. of Deb.* III.300 . . . it resulted from that kind of system pretty generally understood under the term of "log-rolling," a system in which the various interests were combined, and made to harmonize with each other, to their especial profit.

1854 Bungay *Off-Hand Takings* 84. No electioneering tricks, no flattering nominations, no log rolling, no wire pulling, no efforts of friends, no party considerations; nothing contained in the exchequer, could cause him to swerve a single hair.

1871 *N. Y. Times* 17 Oct. 6. Faithless Republicans have dishonored their party and disgraced themselves by corrupt alliances with the enemy in the way of 'log-rolling' legislation, and sometimes by the downright sale of their votes for money.

long hair.

Before the Civil War long hair was considered characteristic of Southern "chivalry." Whether this continues the tradition of Charles I's Cavaliers as opposed to the Roundheads is an open question. It is likewise uncertain that this is behind the present use of long hair as characteristic of the unrealistic intellectual or the extravagant aesthete. In any case an element to be strongly considered is the influence of German immigrants. Some of the '48ers carried on the tradition of long hair and beard from the days "when the lice had a fine time, while the barbers were afraid of starvation" (Heine, *Die Hartsreise*), and satirical remarks on this subject are by no means rare in American politics.

1856 *Cleve. Plain Dealer* 11 Oct. 2/1. Look out for the Hair-Lipped Germans! **1861** *Peoria Daily Transcript* 8 May. This long-haired model of good breeding and honor [the Southerner] has been held up before us on all occasions.... They even denied that there was any evidence of true manliness or superior culture in the long-haired, loose-jointed, strangely-clad person with pea-green gloves and superabundant watchchain, who wrote his name on hotel registers or college records as a native of the Sunny South. **1864** *Cinc. Comm.* 13 May 2/3. A National Convention of the long-haired Tartars of Northern radicalism has been called, to be held in the city of Cleveland on Tuesday, the 31st of May.... Emil Praetorious, a Long-haired impracticable from St. Louis.... *Ib.* 26 May 3/6 ... the Cleveland gathering of the long-haired was scarcely mentioned. **1872** *Nation* 18 July 40/1. The Southern element was, of course, more prominent ... the long hair; the eccentric dress.... **1875** *Ib.* 6 May. The long-haired school of journalists and lecturers, the doctrinaires and the political schemers generally were fully represented. **1881** *Ib.* 14 July 28/3. An aesthete is a person ... who declines to have his hair cut by a barber because it is "part of himself".... **1918** Brissenden *I.W.W.* 376. "The Preacher and the Slave."

Long-haired preachers come out every night,
Try to tell you what's wrong and what's right.

1931 *Wash. Merry-Go-Round* 226. In a few minutes a long-haired, wild-eyed professor came rushing into the barn to acknowledge the parentage of the little child he called "Oleo." **1931** Allen *Only Yesterday* 17 ... short-haired women, like long-haired men, are associated with radicalism, if not with free love. **1953** *Cols. Dispatch* 16 Nov. [edit.] Before Attorney General Brownell stated the facts of Harry Dexter White's association with the Truman administration there had been a lot of long-haired talk (and some not so long haired) about the recent special elections....

long pull.

Though popularized by Churchill, the phrase "a long pull, a strong pull, a pull (al) together," has long been used in America, both politically and nonpolitically:

1801 *Columbian Centinel* 7 Jan. 2/2. The Federalists of New Jersey have taken a long and strong pull to Federalize their Members of Congress.... **1818** Fearon *Sketches* 144. Huzza for William Findlay, and no bribery.—A long pull, a strong pull, and a pull altogether. **1835** Haliburton *Clockm.* 319. Who's for a pull of grog? suppose we have a pull, gentlemen—a good pull, and a strong pull, and a pull altogether, eh! **1836** *Ohio St. Jrnl.* 28 Oct. 3/2. It is yet possible to rescue the country from the death-like grasp of the "spoilers." "A long pull, a strong pull, and a pull together," will effect it. **1838** *Ohio Statesman* 2 Oct. 2/2. We are ready, sir, in short, to make one long pull, strong pull, and pull altogether, for the potential redemption of dishonored, disgraced, and deluded Ohio!

The origin of the expression may be in naval terminology as the following examples suggest; or it may be a more general, concerted effort of pulling.

1799 in *Ann. Reg.* 302/2. In the marine language of Admiral Mitchel, they pulled heartily together. **1840** *Ann. of Cleve.* No. 1548 ... a few more pulls at the oar will give full and complete success to the Whig party.

long Tom.

See BIG GUN.

lords of the lash, lords of the loom.

Alliterative reference to the slave owners of the South and the textile manufacturers of the North.

1848 in Shotwell *Sumner* 206. The statement in Sumner's speech at the organization of the Free-Soil party in Worcester in 1848, that Taylor's nomination had been the result of a conspiracy between the lords of the lash of Louisiana and the lords of the loom of New England. . . .

1862 in Congdon *Trib. Essays* 301. No; it is not the tint of my epidermis that my Lord of the Lash will care for when he has brought the Middle Age back to Virginia.

Possibly a variant of an earlier poetical or rhetorical phrase such as: [ ]

1827 Cooper in *Niles' Reg.* XXXIII.31. Lords of the spinning jenny and peers of the power-loom.

lost cause.

Ultimately the phrase is due to the business instinct of a New York publisher, E. B. Treat, who objected to the original title of a "history of the war" offered to him by E. A. Pollard. The story is told by this author in *Appleton's Journal:*

[1867] "Could not some title be found more unique and captivating, and not quite so heavy?" The writer promised to think of such a title. The next day he presented himself to the publisher and said, "I have thought of a name for the work I design: it is *The Lost Cause.* . . . I think there is something of proper dignity in the word *Cause;* then *The Lost Cause* is an advertisement of something valuable that is gone; besides, the associations of the title are tender and reverential,— there is a strain of mourning in it. How do you like it?" "Exceedingly well," replied the publisher, "it is just the thing." The title proved an instant success, and

has since become *monumental.* The words "The Lost Cause" have been incorporated into the common popular language of the South; and the universality of their reception implies a significance that is itself interesting.

The phrase was not invented by Pollard. Its last root may be Lucan's often quoted verse:

Victrix causa diis placuit, sed victa Catoni. [*Pharsalia,* I, 128]

And it was used in American politics before the Civil War. [ ]

1851 Wilson *Slave Power* II.349. Indeed, Mr. Cushing took occasion to say that Mr. Sumner's cause was "a lost cause."

After the publication of Pollard's work, *The Lost Cause,* New York, 1867, and undoubtedly influenced by it:

1867 Durbin Ward *Sp.* 105. It [downfall of the South] was the grave of the "lost cause."

1868 *Trial of Johnson* II.461. They are understood by the common, plain people as the utterances of an expiring rebellion in the aid of the lost cause.

1876 Rev. Taylor Martin in Garfield *Works* II.372. The South is to-day ruled over by the miserable thrall of Yankeedom; but they cannot muzzle our chivalry and patriotic devotion to the "lost cause."

Lotophagi.

Visionaries.

The lotus eaters of ancient Greek legend lived in a state of dreamy forgetfulness and unreality.

1923 *N. Y. Times* 16 Dec. sec. X. 8/1. United States Senator Medill McCormick recently [October] set news-paper readers to searching their dictionaries when he referred to those who advocated the entry of the United States into the League of Nations as "Lotophagi."

lower law.

The counterpart of *higher law;* thus applied to a rigid adherence to the letter of the Constitution in matters pertaining to slavery.

1853 *N. Y. Trib.* 26 Jan. 4/3. Mr. Everett is no fanatic, no radical, but a leading devotee and magnifier of the lower law, who has proclaimed on the floor of Congress his readiness to shoulder a musket in bloody resistance to any slave insurrection.

lower law men.

Opposition term for those who, during the slavery controversy, scoffed at the idea of a higher law than the Constitution.

Daniel Webster was one of the leaders of the "lower law" group.

1852 Parker *Additional Sp.* I.239. Where were the men of the "lower law," who made a denial of God the first principle of their politics? Where were they who in Faneuil Hall scoffed and jeered at the "Higher Law".... The "lower law" men and the kidnappers strained themselves to the utmost.

1858 *Toledo Blade* 14 Jan. 2/1. On Kansas affairs he [Buchanan] is with the "Fire Eaters," on Nicaragua affairs with the "Dirt-Eaters." Now he is with the "Higher Law" men; now with the "Lower Law" men.

lunatic fringe.

A derogatory term characterizing those whose zealous support of a cause or movement is felt to be neither rational nor practical.

Fringe became an important term in late 19th century psychological terminology:

1890 James *Prin. of Psych.* I.258. Let us use the words psychic overtone, suffusion, or fringe, to designate the influence of a faint brain-process upon our thought, as it makes it aware of relations and objects but dimly perceived.

Also in the geo-political sphere to designate an isolated or marginal group:

1902 D. G. Hogarth *Nearer East* 181. It is necessary to detach the Arabs, who are found in the Arabian and Mesopotamian Fringe, from the central Semitic group. [also 162, 185, 221]

The phrase *lunatic fringe* is attributed to Theodore Roosevelt, who frequently used *lunatic* and *lunatic fringe* to apply to overzealous reformers:

1899 Roosevelt *Ltrs.* 12 April II.987. I explained in Chicago that the greatest help I got was from the genuine reformers, but that when you came to the lunatic type, they did a great deal more harm than good.

1913 Roosevelt *Works* (Mem. ed.) XXIV. 207. I am always having to fight the silly reactionaries and the inert, fatuous creatures who will not think seriously; and on the other hand to try to exercise some control over the lunatic fringe among the reformers.

1913 *Ib.* XIV.406 ... and yet we have to face the fact that there is apt to be a lunatic fringe among the votaries of any forward movement.

1913 Roosevelt in Lodge *Ltrs.* 27 Feb. II. 434. The various admirable movements in which I have been engaged, have always developed among their members a large lunatic fringe. . . .

Later uses:

1945 *Texas Outlook* May 18 ... the Boston Globe spoke of the "lunatic fringe" as having produced "its phenomena of political patent medicine men."

1946 White *Autobio.* 521. We Kansans came to Chicago [in 1916] with what might be called a high-grade delegation. It was not rag, tag, and bobtail. It was anything but the lunatic fringe.

lynch (law).

While there is no doubt that the word is derived from the proper name Lynch, there is a lack of agreement on the particular person who originated the practice of Lynch Law. (See Cutler, *Lynch Law*; Albert Matthews, *Mass. Col. Soc. Trans.* XXVII, 256 f; also *Niles' Register,* 8 Aug. 1835, see below.)

At first the word has a sectional character, being relatively unknown wherever the method so designated was not practiced.

1820 Hall *Ltrs. from the West* 291f. No commentator has taken any notice of Linch's law, which was once the lex loci of the frontiers.

1829 Dow *Omnifarious Law Exemplified* 23. In the "Whig and Tory" days of the South, when no man's person or property were safe, . . . a man by the name of Col. Lynch formed an association, to expel suspicious characters from the neighborhood;—and chastizing them at discretion —which practice is continued in some parts of the South and West to the present day. . . .

1834 Simms *Guy Rivers* I.63. Sometimes they give him Lynch's Law, after old Nick Lynch, who invented it in Virginny. [More examples in Cutler, pp. 77f.]

The purge by which Vicksburg rid itself of gamblers in 1835 is clearly the event that made the word nationally known. Its relative novelty in the North appears from the following quotations, especially the one of August 8:

Hone *Diary* I.167. A terrific system prevails in some of the southern and western States of late, which consists in the people taking the law in their own hands and inflicting a summary punishment upon persons who have made themselves obnoxious to their high mightiness; beating, tarring and feathering, and in some cases hanging the unhappy objects of their vengeance, and this is quaintly called Lynch's law.

Niles' Reg. 1 Aug. 381/2 [dated Vicksburg, July 9th]. Consequently it was determined to take him into the woods and Lynch him—which is a mode of punishment provided for such as become obnoxious in a manner which the law cannot reach.

Ib. 8 Aug. 402/1. As "Lynch law" has recently become almost as general as it is proverbial, and as the question is asked a hundred times a day "what is Lynch's law?" it may be well to relate the following anecdote, which may serve as an answer. [Account of farmer in Wash. County, Pennsylvania.]

Ib. 22 Aug. 436/2 . . . Mr. Damewood's back bears evident marks of the supremacy of Lynch's law.

Leggett *Pol. Writings.* II.51. But this Judge Lynch, with the proneness to usurpation which characterizes all possessors of ill-defined power, has lately extended most fearfully the prescriptive boundaries of his authority. All places are now within the limits of his jurisdiction. . . .

Scioto Gazette 30 Sep. 1/3. Lynch law is not merely a practice, but a theory; the Constitution is *Lynched.*

Niles' Reg. 3 Oct. 74/1. On the cross bar [of a gallows erected in front of Garrison's home] was an inscription, Judge Lynch's law.

In those days condemnation of these methods is rare, although already it begins to take shape (see the quotation from Leggett) .

Although lynching seems to be associated in some instances with hanging, Cutler seems to be justified in saying that "previous to 1840 the verb (lynch) was occasionally used to include capital punishment, but the common and general use was to indicate a personal castigation of some sort" (p. 116) . This is borne out by Lovejoy:

1835 *Memoir* 2 Nov. 156. I expect that I shall be Lynched, or tarred and feathered, or it may be, hung up.

Later, opposition to lynch proceedings became more frequent:

1874 *N. Y. World* 23 Aug. 4/2. Now trial by Lynch, in cases of violent crimes, is the exact analogue of "trial by newspaper," which the Nation has justly and inconsistently denounced in cases of character.

1893 *Forum* XVI.300. Lynching is barbaric, anarchic and wrong *per se*. It belongs to the darker and deeper of the two classes of criminal conduct into which human wickedness has been divided; it is not merely *malum prohibitum,* it is *malum in se.*

1900 *Roosevelt Cyc.* 321. One of the greatest blots on American civilization is lynch law.

lynchism.

1835 Leggett *Pol. Writings* II.51f. There is one little doubt which sometimes obtrudes itself into our minds to prevent us from being wholly proselyted to the faith of Lynchism; namely, whether after all, the best mode of correcting error of opinion is to destroy the freedom of speech.

lynchite.

1835 Lovejoy *Memoir* 159. We are getting quiet again. The Lynchites are getting ashamed of their doings.

M

machine (machinery).

Metaphors comparing the mechanism of government with a machine are found in European authors at least as early as the 18th century:

Fielding *Tom Jones* vi, ii [*OED*]. The great state wheels in all the political machines of Europe. . . .

Gibbon *Decline and Fall* v, 12 [*OED*]. The nice and artificial machinery of government was out of joint.

Similar passages occur in American writers:

1823 *Cinc. Nat. Rep.* 16 May 1/4 [translated from The Constitutionel]. Happy land! . . . where every wheel in the political machine moves without noise and without expense.

1829 in Garland *Randolph* II.327. I am much opposed, except in great emergency —and then the legislative machine is always sure to work with sufficient rapidity —to this "dispatch of business."

1835 *West. Mon. Mag.* IV.4. The machine of government must be framed, and its wheels put in motion, before matters of lesser importance can receive due attention.

Perhaps the Jeffersonian tendency of considering a strong government a necessary evil rather than a beneficial force is responsible for the early deterioration of the word.

1782 Jefferson *Basic Writings* 138 . . . the bungling machinery of county committees.

179– Jefferson in Dwight *Hartford Convention* 16. Hamilton's financial system had then passed. It had two objects: 1. As a puzzle to exclude popular understanding and inquiry; 2. As a machine for the corruption of the legislature.

1824 *Cinc. Nat. Rep.* 30 March 2/2. Her citizens equally despise and disregard the corrupt machinery of Legislative dictation, and the unhallowed principles of Congressional usurpation.

The first known application to party politics occurs in 1830:

N. Y. Sentinel 23 June 3/3 . . . so complete has been the operation of the machinery of the party, that every office in their gift has been disposed of before the ballot-boxes were opened.

In a similar sense Wirt uses *engine* in 1831:

Kennedy *Wirt* II.306. Thinking thus of it [Free-Masonry], nothing has more surprised me than to see it blown into consequence, in the Northern and Eastern States, as a political engine, and the whole community excited against it as an affair of serious importance.

This last quotation brings us to the now prevalent use of *machine:* a local organization dominated by a boss. This narrowing of meaning seems to be connected with the fact that around 1850 a new metaphorical element enters the history of the word. There are indications that at this period *machine* was understood to mean fire engine. A passage in Thompson's (Doestick's) *Pluri-bus-tah* (1856) describes the search for missing Yunga-Merrakah, son of Pluri-bustah, who found him:

Found him coming, in his shirt sleeves,
With an engine from the Bowery,
From a fire up in the bowery.

The running title for the pages on which this episode is described is "Yunga-Merrakah Runs With The Machine" (pp. 158–9). When in the early days of Boss Tweed, his fire company became an important factor in his political organization the phrase *running with the machine* came to mean following a political leader:

1860 Burlingame to Banks in Luthin *Lincoln's Campaigns* 110. Our old policy of "running with the Seward machine" is the true one.

That this expression was felt as a living metaphor even as late as 1876 is shown by a Nast cartoon (*Harper's W.*, 20 May, 404) representing Tilden as a fire-chief standing in front of a fire machine with the Tammany tiger emblem, but carrying the tag "This is not a 'machine'; it is the spirit of reform." In the background is the door to the White House with a picture of the Republican "machine" inscribed "This machine has put out many a fire." Under the cartoon are the words "He will *run* the 'Machine' (raised 'out of the gutter') to St. Louis 'as a Unit,' then to the 'White House,' and the People who doubt it are 'Idiots or Knaves.'"

Later uses:

1871 Tilden in Hart *Source Book* 352. The very definition of a ring is that it encircles enough influential men in the organization of each party to control the action of both party machines....

1878 *Harper's W.* 7 Sept. 706/2. "The Machine" is the system of using the patronage of office to carry out the will of a few persons in a state, and especially of the head of the system, who is the Senator.

1878 *N. Y. Trib.* 15 Jan. 4/3. Machine partisans have long been a common pest. Of late machine reformers have reached the same plane.

1880 *San Diego Daily Union* 22 June 1/3. It would be a curious development in the manipulation of machine politics to show how the California delegation, elected by a Convention in which on a test vote Field's name was only greeted with one friendly voice, had been induced to present a solid front for the aspiring Supreme Court Justice.

1888 *Overland Mon.* XII.553. In most cities the nominating conventions are pretty thoroughly controlled by the party machines, and pervaded by all sorts of questionable influences.

Theodore Roosevelt attempted to rescue *machine* from this almost universal condemnation:

1886 *Century* Nov. On the contrary, the machine is often a very powerful instrument for good; and a machine politician really desirous of doing honest work on behalf of the community is fifty times as useful an ally as is the average philanthropic outsider.

malcontent.

A dissatisfied person or faction.

The popularity of the term in the early days of the government may be attributed to the amorphous quality of parties, so that a more or less neutral term was needed to distinguish groups with a common ground of opposition.

1791 Paine *Works* II.347. The mal-contents had by this time concerted their measures with the court....

1805 in Dallas *Life* 215. But it early occurred to the malcontents that this system of denunciation could not be supported by the mere weight of their own authority.

1805 *Ib.* 216. The malcontents have arbitrarily enrolled as a *Quid* or a *Federalist,* a *traitor* or a *Tory;* involving them all at last ... in a comprehensive proscription of "the Constitutional Republican."

1872 McMichael in Blaine *Twenty Yrs.* II.526. The malcontents who recently met at Cincinnati were without a constituency.

1878 *N. Y. Times* 6 Aug. 4/7. What the Baltimore *American* calls the "malcontents" are said to be about to make an effort to "reorganize the Republican party in that city."

1912 *Rev. of Rev.* XLVI.311. Nor was it the motley crew of malcontents that gathered with David in the cave of Adullam. [ref. to Prog. Conv.]

man and brother.

A. See quot.

1768 in *Horizon* 1959 May 96. One of Wedgwood's best-known medallions (ill.) was commissioned from William Mackwood in 1768 and became the seal of the Slave Emancipation Society. [Kneeling Negro, with motto: "Am I not a man and brother?"]

B. Man and brother became an occasional synonym for negro:

1865 *At. Mon.* 68/1. "Halt!" exclaimed this dusky man and brother, bringing down his bayonet,—"de countersign not correck."

managed masses.

See quot.

The odium seen to be associated with *manage* (r) (q.v.) is still dominant in this alliterative phrase.

1956 *Cols. Dispatch* 20 Feb. 4/2. In his Lincoln Day address in New York, Vice President Nixon used a phrase which has the possibility of wide use in the coming national campaign and in subsequent politico-economic controversy. He referred to the "managed masses" philosophy of the Democratic Party, as influenced by the ADA and other leftist elements within the party.... Mr. Nixon's use of the expression "managed masses" perhaps has more appeal than "welfare state" and some of the other phrases which have been tried out as labels for the socialistic designs of the Democratic Party leftists who more often than not control the Democratic Party nowadays. "Managed masses" is a picture phrase.

manager.

A politician who directs his party's campaigns and strategy.

A. The verb *to manage,* originally "to handle, train or direct (a horse) in his paces" (*OED*), is found early in English politics:

a 1609 Sir T. Smith *Commw. Eng.* I.xxiv. 34 [*OED*]. To speake of the Commonwealth, or policy of England, it is governed, administered, and managed by three sorts of persons.

Also the noun:

1710 *Managers Pro. & Con.* 4 [*OED*]. To Him and to Me, He and the Council seem'd to be the Managers for the Pretender.

B. In America, however, probably because of early associations with bargain and corruption, secret caucus, etc., *manage, manager,* and *management* have had definitely derogatory connotations.

1824 *Cinc. Nat. Rep.* 15 June 2/5. The calling of Mr. Ruggles to the chair, was acknowledged to be a master-piece of management; but how signally have they been defeated. 1828 *Balt. Rep.* 12 Feb. 2/4. It has been the habit with certain little narrow-minded politicians ... to present Mr. Van Buren as a mere *electioneerer, an intriguer, a manager.* 1835 Crockett *Van Buren* 87. Will any one pretend to say, after this, that the terms "New York tactics," "Albany regency," "Manager," and "Little Magician" are untruly ... applied to Van Buren? 1838 *Ohio St. Jrnl.* 7 Nov. 3/5. The elections which have been recently held in several States—the manner in which they have been *managed* by our political opponents.... 1884 *Puck* 20 Aug. 386/1 ... he [Blaine] has not placed himself passively in the hands of his "managers."

man Friday.

In politics, a righthand man.

The allusion is, of course, to Robinson Crusoe's servant, and carries satirical connotations.

1832 J. Randolph in Jackson *Corr.* IV. 414. As to Mr. V. P. he and his man Friday the grand and lofty tumbler of the lower House.... 1846 *Tax-killer* 20 June 2/3. Kelley's man Friday is making the most ridiculous blunders, in his stupid attempts to bolster up the infamous federal tax law. 1860 *Lebanon* (Ohio) *West. Star* 22 March 1/5. The "man Friday" who clings to the broken fortunes of his master is Pugh.

1872 *Harper's W.* 313 [cartoon]. Will Robinson Crusoe [Sumner] Forsake His Man Friday [the Negro]? 1879 *Harper's W.* 811 [cartoon]. Cetwayo (Man Friday) Submits to British Robinson Crusoe. 1954 Mockridge and Prall *Big Fix* 244. But the appointment that really took the prize was the one that O'Dwyer gave to his Man Friday—James J. Moran.

Manhattan Club.

A Democratic club in New York City. [ ]

1865 *Harper's W.* 2 Dec. 755/2. There is a new club just established upon the Fifth Avenue. It is called the "Manhattan," and its object is "the dissemination of Democratic principles." 1868 Strong *Diary* IV.223. July 10. Western Democrats are much disgusted by it [nom. of Seymour], and think themselves out-manoeuvred and swindled by the Manhattan Club and by New Yorkers generally.

manhood suffrage.

Attested in the *OED* for 1873, *manhood suffrage* turns up several years earlier in American politics: 1866 Henry Wilson in *Gt. Deb.* VII.25–6. I am against this qualification of reading and writing.... There was a time when I would have taken it, because I did not know that we could get anything more in this contest, but I think the great victory of manhood suffrage is about achieved in this country.

manifest destiny.

The idea that by some sort of pre-ordination the Anglo-Saxon race has the task and therefore the duty to extend its rule over the whole of the North American continent is criticized by William Channing: 1837 *Works* 776. I have alluded to the want of wisdom with which we are accustomed to speak of our destiny as a people. We are *destined* (that is the word) to overspread North America; and intoxicated with the idea, it matters little to us how we accomplish our fate. To spread, to supplant others, to cover a boundless space this seems our ambition, no matter what influence we spread with us. Why cannot we rise to noble conceptions of our destiny?

Since the term is used in the Bible (John IX.3) and is frequently associated with religious writings, it is probable that in the beginning *manifest destiny* carried a religious tinge.

1824 in Ward *Jackson* 133. A country manifestly called by the Almighty to a destiny which Greece and Rome, in the days of their pride, might have envied.

1838 *Hamilton Intell.* 5 April 3/3 ... one country, one Constitution and one destiny are ours.

1848 *Niles' Reg.* 22 Jan. 336/1 [Gen. Shields]. If ever there could be a nation of destiny, we were such a nation, created and controlled by destiny, to carry out the will of destiny, but as he trusted not to be crushed by destiny as that great man, the child of destiny, Napoleon, was crushed.

In 1845 Sullivan found the formula that helped to propagate the idea of ordained territorial expansion, *manifest destiny* [see Weinberg, *Manifest Destiny* and *Am. Hist. Rev.*, XXXII]:

Democratic Rev. .... [other nations have tried to intrude themselves] between us and the proper parties to the case, in a spirit of hostile interference against us, for the avowed object of thwarting our policy and hampering our power, limiting our greatness and checking the fulfillment of our manifest destiny to overspread the continent allotted by Providence for the free development of our yearly multiplying millions.

1845 *N. Y. Morning News* 27 Dec. Our legal title to Oregon, so far as law exists for such rights, is perfect. There is no

doubt of this. Mr. Calhoun and Mr. Buchanan have settled that question, once and for all. Flaw or break in the triple chain of that title, there is none. Not a foot of ground is left for England to stand upon, in any fair argument to maintain her pretensions. . . .

And yet after all, unanswerable as is the demonstration of our legal title to Oregon —the whole of Oregon, if a rood!—we have a still better title than any that can ever be constructed out of all these antiquated materials of old black-letter international law. Away, away with all these cobweb tissues of rights of discovery, exploration, settlement, continuity, etc. To state the truth at once in its neglected simplicity, we are free to say that were the respective cases and arguments of the two parties, as to all these points of history and law reversed—had England all ours, and we nothing but hers—our claim to Oregon would still be best and strongest. And that claim is by the right our manifest destiny to overspread and to possess the whole of the continent which Providence has given us for the development of the great experiment of liberty and federated government entrusted to us.

During the succeeding years the idea was treated with an almost religious fervor by its adherents and criticized vigorously by its opponents:

1852 Senator Cass in *Cong. Globe* 23 Dec. 141/3. And let us fulfill our manifest destiny in no spirit of aggrandizement or of propagandism, but fearlessly and rightfully. And I have been much pleased to see that recently the assaults of the British press have been met in a proper spirit by our own ...

1853 in *Cong. Globe* 3 Jan. 190/2. Manifest Destiny—our power of expansion, and our duty to propagate free principles —demands so extended a theater as this whole continent and the islands adjacent thereto.

1853 *N. Y. Trib.* 21 Jan. 4/3. We should think the Manifest Destiny statesmen would get tired of hearing themselves talk.

... Will not the Manifest Destiny statesmen die to oblige us? ... Mr. Cass has had
his day. Let him retire. We shall be rid of
at least one of the Manifest Destiny statesmen, a leading characteristic of all of
whom is that they love to dwell upon the
vague and uncertain things of the future,
rather than devote themselves to the discharge of the vital, practical duties of today.
1853 *Ib.* 17 Feb. 4/3. The big balloon of
Manifest Destiny collapsed ...
1858 in Hollister *Colfax* 135. I don't think
I shall speak at this session, but if I do, it
will be to rebuke and condemn this thiev-
ing aggrandizing "manifest destiny" tendency to steal land—coveting Cuba, Mexico, Central America, etc.
1859 Lincoln *Works* V.100. As Plato had
for the immortality of the soul, so Young
America has "a pleasing hope, a fond desire—a longing after" territory. He has a
great passion—a perfect rage—for the
"new"; particularly new men for office,
and the new earth mentioned in the
Revelations, in which, being no sea, there
must be about three times as much land
as in the present. ... He knows all that
can possibly be known; inclines to believe
in spiritual rappings, and is the unquestioned inventor of "Manifest Destiny."

At this time there is evidence that
the slogan of *manifest destiny* is
overworked and must be replaced:
1859 in *Gt. Deb.* III.95. I see that "manifest destiny" has been ridden to death; we
have got rid of it, and now succeed to
"manifest destiny," "political necessity."
1882 *Harper's W.* 7 Jan. 2/3. The bump-
tious school of "manifest destiny" has
dropped into merited discredit. There was
never less occasion for "serving notice
upon all mankind" that America is for
Americans.

A revival of the expression is
found in connection with the imperialist movement at the end of
the 19th century:
1898 *Gt. Deb.* III.207f. We hear much of
"manifest destiny." That is a charming

phrase. It tickles the ears of men; it
panders to human vanity; it feeds the
lurid flames of our ambition; it whets the
sword of conquest; it is an anodyne for
the troubled conscience, but it lureth to
destruction. At the last it biteth like a
serpent and stingeth like an adder. It is,
however, no new doctrine. It is as old as
the hills, "rock-ribbed and ancient as the
sun." Years and years ago, stripped of all
disguises and adornments, it was formulated by that eminent annexationist, Rob
Roy, in this plain, blunt language:
The good old rule, the simple plan,
That they should take who have the
power,
And they should keep who can.
1899 in Sullivan *Our Times* I.50. Only
Anglo-Saxons can govern themselves. The
Cubans will need a despotic government
for many years to restrain anarchy until
Cuba is filled. ... It is the Anglo-Saxon's
manifest destiny to go forth as a world
conqueror.
1916 H. M. Chittenden in *At. Mon.*
CXVII.48. "Manifest Destiny" has long
been a favorite catchphrase with political
rhapsodists in the United States, and a
rare Fourth-of-July orator is he who
feels that he can add nothing to his resources in eloquence. ... It is neither fatal-
ism nor determinism, but an assumed
natural tendency of events.

man in the street.
The average man, who in politics
becomes representative of the desires and opinions of the general
electorate.
A. First attested in English usage
in 1831 (*OED*), the phrase was apparently introduced into America
by Emerson in a number of his essays. For instance:
1841 Emerson *Self-Reliance* 62. The man
in the street, finding no worth in himself
which corresponds to the force which
built a tower or sculptured a marble god,
feels poor when he looks on these.
B. Political use:

1900 Roosevelt *Ltrs.* II.1214. But the man in the street naturally does not look as far ahead as this.

C. Lord Bryce's statement that the common phrase in America is "man in the cars" (*Am. Com.* III.*IV*.lxxvi.7) has not been substantiated by contemporary quotations.

man of straw.

Weak or secondary politician who acts only in accordance with the dictates of stronger, more influential men.

1832 *Niles' Reg.* 1 Dec. 215/1. The inference is, that many of them [independents in South Carolina] were men of straw—made for the occasion.
1833 *Cols. Sentinel* 26 Sept. 3/3 ... the "men of straw" ... are but mere puppets to move as the strings are pulled.
1858 *Ohio St. Jrnl.* 22 Oct. 2/2. This Mr. Ellis turns out to be no man of straw.

See PUPPET.

man on horseback.

The *DAE* cites it as a nickname originally applied to U. S. Grant:
1879 *Cong. Record* 23 June 2324/2. An Army under President Hayes, or "the man on horseback," if he should come back into power.
1880 *Ib.* 10 May 3200/1. The "man on horseback" is the battle cry ... of the most dangerous element of the Republican party.

Another passage given by the *DAE* is interesting because it shows that the phrase was known in England in a slightly different form and that it was known to be of American origin.

1887 *Pall Mall Gaz.* 21 July 1/1. The man on the horse ... to use the picturesque

American phrase, is not now Lord Salisbury.

It can be shown, however, that in American politics "the man on horseback" was known several years before Grant became nationally prominent, and eight years before he played any role in politics. In 1860 Caleb Cushing wrote a widely noticed letter to a meeting of Maine Democrats assembled at Bangor on January 11 of that year in which he gave expression to his fear of an impending civil war and what might follow it in the following words:

in Fuess *Life of C. Cushing* II.243. Why, all history is there to tell us what then; social convulsions, hostile combats in the town streets, predatory guerilla bands roving up and down the country, shootings and hangings, in a word, that which we have not yet had, but which all other nations have,—cruel war, *war at home;* and, in the perspective distance, a man on horseback with a drawn sword in his hand, some Atlantic Caesar, or Cromwell, or Napoleon, to secure to the weary world a respite from the dissonant din of the raving ideologies of the hour, and the fratricidal rage they engender....

During the presidential campaign of 1860 the phrase must have been used by the parties opposed to Lincoln in order to impress the voters with the dangers anticipated in the event of his election. Of this, we have at the present time no direct evidence, but on October 11 the *Boston Eve. Transcript* commenting on the attitude of financial circles after the Republican victory in several state elections writes as follows:

Contrary to the ridiculous fears of the alarmists, the huge Republican majorities

261 man on horseback

in the States which voted on Tuesday, enhanced the price of stocks, instead of diminishing their value. Caleb Cushing's man on "horseback" is not feared by either the stockholders or capitalists.

A few days before the election the same organ satirizes those who had been too much impressed by the slogans with which politicians tried to scare the public. Among others, "the man on horseback" comes in for its share of the ridicule.

1860 *Boston Eve. Transcript* 31 Oct. 2/1. But our readers must not be alarmed.... The "man on horseback" is not coming in reality—that was only a figure of speech borrowed for the occasion from James the novelist. The pony and rider, after the fifth of November, will retire to the realms of fiction.

That the *Transcript* was not alone in the opinion that Cushing had taken the phrase from James the novelist becomes clear from an article by J. R. Lowell in the *At. Mon.,* October, 1860 [VI. 2/1]. General Cushing, infringing the patent-right of the late Mr. James the novelist, has seen a solitary horseman on the edge of the horizon. The exegesis of the vision has been various, some thinking that it means a Military Despot,—though in that case the force of cavalry would seem to be inadequate,—and others the Pony Express. If it had been one rider on two horses, the application would have been more general and less obscure.

The probability that Lowell was right in his assumption that it was the work of G. P. R. James which gave Cushing the idea of the man on horseback is supported by the following facts. First, this now-forgotten author was so popular during the period in question that

Justin McCarthy could say about him:

Hist. of Our Own Times I.558. Many of us can remember, without being too much ashamed of the fact, that there were early days when Mr. James and his cavaliers and his chivalric adventures gave nearly as much delight as Walter Scott could have given to the youth of a preceding generation. But Walter Scott is with us still, young and old, and poor James is gone. His once famous solitary horseman has ridden away into actual solitude.

Second, according to S. M. Ellis, whose biography of James is characteristically called *The Solitary Horseman* (Kensington, 1927):

James wrote fifty-seven works which may be classified as romances, and in only seventeen of these horsemen—single, or in pairs, or parties—make an early appearance. In six books "a solitary horseman" appears in the first chapter and in two others he delays his arrival until the second....

Third, the sobriquet of "solitary horseman" was fixed on James by no less an author than Thackeray, who parodied James's style in his burlesque *Barbazure, by G. P. R. Jeames, Esq.* Taking all this together, we seem to be justified in assuming that not only Lowell and the writer in the *Boston Transcript,* but the American reading public in general, must have been led to think of James's horseman when Caleb Cushing introduced the "man on horseback" into American politics.

Later uses:

1904 *Courier-Jrnl.* 21 July 4. It is Parker, the Jurist and Patriot, against Roosevelt, the would-be man on horseback.

1946 Arnall *Shore* 275. The man-on-horseback has never been popular in the United States as a political leader.

man owners.

The southern slave-holding aristocracy, so-called by abolitionists.

1862 Congdon *Tribune Essays* 281. We understand in a measure, why the Man-Owners are fighting—it is for caste, aristocracy, political power—but why are the Poor Whites fighting?

man stealer.

Man stealer occurs in Timothy I.1,10 and in Exodus 21.16. It is evident that it refers to one who enslaves another:

For whoremongers, for them that defile themselves with mankind, for menstealers, for liars. . . .
And he that stealeth a man, and selleth him, or if he be found in his hand, he shall surely be put to death.

In American politics it was used by the abolitionists against the Southern slave holders:

1835 Leggett *Pol. Writings* I.207 . . . the abettors and supporters of Garrison, and other itinerant orators who go about stigmatizing the people of the south as "men stealers," are not the organs or instruments of the democracy of the north, but of the aristocracy. . . .

marrow fat fraud. [ ]

1903 A. B. Hart *Actual Government* 75. The "marrow-fat" fraud consists in a voter's putting in more than one ballot, while the clerk puts down fictitious names to cover the extra ballots.

mass meeting.

A great political gathering.

Although it is probable that this type of democratic political activity, characterized by speechmaking and mass electioneering occurred much before 1840, there is little doubt that the Log Cabin campaign then gave it its greatest popularity.

1840 *Cinc. D. Chron.* 5 Sept. 2/2. Morals of Politics. The Great Mass Meetings. The Administration party . . . have taken a strong dislike to Log Cabins, to popular songs, to mass meetings, to exciting harangues, and to all the moods by which the people show their irrepressible feelings.

1840 *Rough-Hewer* 253. The Great Mass Meeting at Saratoga [edit.]

1842 in *Mangum Papers* III.292. I have strongly urged them to decline that [legislative caucus], & to follow our nominations by "Mass Meetings" as they call them.

1863 Russell *My Diary North and South* 266. If these high physical, metaphysical, moral and religious reasonings do not satisfy you, and you are bold enough to venture still to be unconvinced and to say so, then I advise you not to come within reach of a mass meeting of our citizens, who may be able to find a rope and a tree in the neighborhood.

1889 Farmer *Americanisms* 360. This term, for a large meeting of citizens for any purpose whatsoever, was first used in the electoral contest of 1840—the hard cider campaign as it was called, when General Harrison and Mr. Tyler were candidates for the Presidency. Mass Meeting has now passed into general use not only in England and America, but also in France and Germany.

1923 Alexander *Four Famous New Yorkers* 207. Other journals and several great mass meetings spoke as plainly.

masterly inactivity.

Behind the phrase are reminiscences of the Roman general Quintus Fabius Maximus, whose dilatory strategy turned the trend of the second Punic War in favor of Rome. (See below, Hannegan, 1846). The opinion that the phrase was introduced into English politics by Lord Chatham (be-

low, same) is unconfirmed. In 1792 Mackintosh used it in reference to French politics in 1789.
1792 Mackintosh *Misc. Works* 411/2. The Commons, faithful to their system, remained in a wise and masterly inactivity....

The expression was launched on its American career by John Randolph, who toward the end of the John Quincy Adams administration advised the incoming Democratic party against premature action:
1828 *Cong. Deb.* 25 Jan. 1170. We ought to observe that practice which is the hardest of all—especially for young physicians—we ought to throw in no medicine at all—to abstain—to observe a wise and masterly inactivity.

During the nullification crisis the slogan was taken up by Calhoun; and again in 1843 during the Oregon controversy:
1831 Calhoun *Works* V.143 ... if the Government should be taught thereby, that the highest wisdom of a State is, "a wise and masterly inactivity,"—an invaluable blessing will be conferred....
1843 Calhoun *Works* IV.245. There is often, in the affairs of government, more efficiency and wisdom in non-action than in action. All we want, to effect our object in this case, is "a wise and masterly inactivity."
1846 Calhoun *Works* IV.285. On the contrary, secure peace, and time, under the guidance of a sagacious and cautious policy, "a wise and masterly inactivity," will speedily accomplish the whole. I venture to say "a wise and masterly inactivity," in despite of the attempt to cast ridicule upon the expression. Those who have made the attempt would seem to confound such inactivity with mere inaction. Nothing can be more unlike.... He who does not understand the difference between such inactivity and mere inac-

tion—the doing of nothing—is still in the horn-book of politics, without a glimpse of those higher elements of statesmanship by which a country is elevated to greatness and prosperity.

The phrase was found useful by those who did not want the Oregon crisis to interfere with the annexation of Texas.
1846 Hannegan in *Niles' Reg.* 3 Jan. 279/3. I am sorry to see that a portion of the press of the country have iterated and reiterated ... that beautiful expression embodying the Fabian policy, and used, I believe, by Lord Chatham, "A wise and masterly inactivity."
1846 Giddings *Sp.* 5 Jan. 153. Southern gentlemen, whose voices at the last session were heard, loud and long, in favor of Texas and the *whole of Oregon* now see "a lion in the way" ... a year ago their motto was, *now or never;* at this time, *"a masterly inactivity"* is their maxim.
1846 *Niles' Reg.* 14 March 17/1 ... the "masterly inactivity" party have evidently concluded that procrastination is no longer available.
1846 Starkweather in *Cong. Globe* App. 389/2. I would rather yield Oregon to the imperious demands of England than be guilty of stealing it by masterly inactivity.

From then on, the phrase was used inside and outside of politics as an excuse for avoiding decisive action.
1850 Strong *Diary* II.13. I shall advise a masterly inactivity, for if the measure be pressed, it must fail.
1860 *Cleve. D. Herald* 5 Nov. 2/2. Masterly Inactivity Course of the Bell-Everett Men.
1861 *N. Y. Times* 21 March in Perkins *North. Ed.* I,366. The true policy of the Government is unquestionably that of *masterly inactivity.*

An early attempt to counteract the charge by varying the formula:
1836 in *Mangum Papers* V.611. The State Department may safely rest its hopes of immortality upon its masterly diplomacy

in the late negotiation with France. Besides enduring fame in lexicography which it has achieved for our country, it has well nigh got us into a war. . . .

maturism. [ ]

1944 *Life* 19 June 106. Again and again he [Eric Johnston] accused the Roosevelt administration of spreading "defeatism" with its philosophy of "maturism." By "maturism" he meant the theory that our era of capital expansion had suddenly come to a dead end with no new business possibilities in sight.

See ECONOMIC MATURITY.

measures not men.

A slogan extolling the high principles of a party.

A. Attributed to Lord Chesterfield in a letter of March 6, 1742. (Bartlett) .
Further popularized by Goldsmith and Burke:

1768 *The Good-Natured Man* II. Measures, not men, have always been my mark.
1773 *Present Discontents* I.531. Of this stamp is the cant of, Not men but measures.

B. In American politics:

1834 Leggett *Pol. Writings* I.55. Of this stamp is the cant of *Not Men but measures;* a sort of charm by which many people get loose from every honourable engagement.
1848 Hammond *Wright* 143 . . . the maxim of "measures—not men," which we have said generally controlled his [Wright's] political actions, ceased at this moment to influence him.
1874 *N. Y. World* 18 Sept. 4/3. There is danger in the blind following of *Canning's* maxim, "Measures, not men."

medicine ball cabinet. [ ]

Allusion to personal friends of President Hoover.

1932 *More Merry-Go-Round* 103. As a member of the medicine-ball Cabinet which exercises with the President before breakfast each morning in the rear of the White House, Stone has no illusions about Hoover's ability.

medicine show.

Satirical reference to the crowd-pleasing techniques of some candidates. The medicine show usually featured some entertainment and much hokum:

1932 in Luthin *American Demagogues* 176. The Fort Worth Star-Telegram said: "Texas has been made a laughing stock of the States." It appealed to Texans not to swallow Ferguson's tonic again: "Refuse to be fooled twice by the same medicine show staged by the same performer."

merchant prince.

A political word only in the sense that it belongs to the terminology developing around the monetary problems. Probably based on Isaiah 23:8:

Who hath taken this counsel against Tyre, the crowning city, whose merchants are princes, whose traffickers are the honourable of the earth?

1841 Mrs. Child *Ltrs. from N. Y.* 52–3. In view of these things, I sometimes ask whether the age of Commerce is better than the age of War? Whether our "merchant princes" are a great advance upon feudal chieftans?
1842 Byrdsall *Locofoco* 108 . . . to show his public spirit . . . and an opportunity to please the merchant princes, or at least the presses they subsidized. . . . He in the summer following went to Washington in behalf of the merchant princes.

The earliest English example is from 1847 (*OED*) :
Leigh Hunt *Jar Honey* 13. A noble-hearted merchant prince.

mermaid ticket.

One which includes members of more than one party or faction.

In the 1840's P. T. Barnum and other museum directors created considerable attention throughout the country with their exhibitions of made-up monsters which they called "mermaids." The most famous was Barnum's "Fejee Mermaid."

1923 Werner *Barnum* 56. The greatest of Barnum's early curiosities, if we are to judge from the controversy caused by its exhibition, was the Fejee Mermaid.

In 1855 in Virginia the Know Nothing party attempted to win Whig votes by including a few Whigs on its ticket. The opposition called this hybrid the *mermaid ticket.*

1855 *Lynchburg Republican* in Hambleton *Wise* 166. Since the publication of the Know Nothing ticket, we have been vexing our curiosity to find some prototype to it in the physical, animal, or mineral kingdom. We have found one after much agony of brain. It is the mermaid. This animal has a doubtful existence. So has the Know Nothing ticket—its paternity being a matter of speculation. The mermaid is a sea animal, represented to have the head and body of a woman with the tail of a fish. This Know Nothing ticket has the head of a Whig, while its tail is certainly composed of *fishy* Democrats. Nor does the analogy cease here. The mermaid is associated with that public imposter and general circulator of impositions, Phineas T. Barnum. This mermaid ticket is presented to the world under the auspices of a set of politicians whose experiments upon popular curiosity and credulity have been as numerous as those of Barnum. It is like the mermaid in another light. One of the amusements of this half woman and half fish is to . . . feed upon the bodies of deluded victims. So it is with this political mermaid ticket. It too sings songs of American melody, but

woe to the deluded wretch who listens to their treacherous music.

See also MONGREL, PIEBALD.

me too.

In his *Autobiography* Thomas Platt claims that the spectacular resignation of Roscoe Conkling and himself from the United States Senate was at his initiative. However, the editorial writers and cartoonists assumed that the more dominant Conkling was responsible for the action and fixed the "me too" label on Platt:

Platt *Autobio.* 159. The next day [16 May, 1881], the Garfield organs flayed Conkling and myself. . . . in editorial and cartoon I was pictured as a small boy sticking out of Conkling's pocket, with a card labeled "Me, too!" tied to one of my hands. ¿

This must refer to earlier cartoons than those published in *Puck* and *Judge* long after 1881.

1884 *Puck* 26 March 56–57. [Cartoon picturing Platt as a young frog on Conkling's back. "Me too" label.]

189– *Judge* [reprinted in *Cartoon History of Roosevelt,* p. 47]. Platt is shown using a "me too" drum stick to support the homecoming of TR.

The phrase was revived and frequently used in recent campaigns beginning with 1936:

1936 in Stokes *Chip* 441. The scene was well laid for this drama of beneficence, what I termed at the time Landon's "Me, too," act.

1940 in Black *Dem. Publicity* 133 . . . the New York News dubbed the G.O.P. nominee "Me, Too" Willkie, adding: "Instead of a knockdown and dragout political fight, this is getting to be a love feast."

1948 *Cols. Citizen* 6 Nov. (edit.) The defeat of Gov. Thomas E. Dewey probably was not as great a blow to the Tribune as to other staunchly Republican newspapers. The Tribune had labelled Dewey a "me-too" candidate.... The Tribune said: "For the third time, a Republican convention fell under vicious influences and nominated a "me-too" candidate who conducted a "Me-too" campaign.

Mexicanize.

To nullify the efficiency of government by constant threats to overthrow it or to ignore its laws.

The metaphor is based upon the almost incessant dissension and revolt in Mexico in the 19th century.
1866 Sen. Davis in *Gt. Deb.* VIII.16. It [the South] shall become so much Mexicanized as to be incapable of self-government, and its government by the North become a necessity.
1878 *N. Y. World* 21 May 4/3. The Republican newspapers charge that the course adopted by the Democrats in Congress will tend to Mexicanize the Government by weakening the Administration, making it disreputable and eventually overthrowing it.
1878 *Nation* 13 June 383. "Mexicanization." [head] There was much not unnatural alarm before the last election about the "Mexicanization" of our Government, apropos of the Southern practice of carrying elections by intimidation.... True "Mexicanization" consists in the spread among the voters of both parties of the belief that the Government can only be carried on by one party, and that if the other party gets into power it ought to be resisted as a foreign invader and driven out by force of arms if necessary.... Mexicanism is not civil war; it is not any overt act whatever; it is a state of mind....

Mexican Whig.

Epithet designating those Whigs who opposed the war with Mexico (1846).
1847 *Cleve. Herald* in *Ann. of Cleve.* 5 May No. 997. The Cleveland Times says: "A Whig artist of New York City has sent General Santa Anna a new cork leg.

Hurrah for Mexican Whiggery." And a Loco President has sent Gen. Santa Anna a new "Pass." Hurrah for Mexican Polkery.
1848 Webster *Works* V.275. And here, I dare say, I shall be called by some a "Mexican Whig." The man who can stand up here and say that he hopes that what the administration projects, and the further prosecution of the war with Mexico requires, may not be carried into effect, must be an enemy to his country.... He is a Mexican.
1848 *Ohio Statesman* 3 May 2/2. The name of Mexican Whig will be as odious as that of *tory* in 1776, or *Hartford Convention Federalist* in 1814.
1849 Jay *Rev. of Mex. War* 253. Such members as voted against granting further supplies, were stigmatized as Mexican Whigs.

middle of the road.

Characterizes those members of the Populist party who opposed joining with the Democrats.

According to McKee (*National Conventions and Platforms...*) the phrase "is taken from the adjuration of Milton Park, of Texas, who led the bolt, to 'Keep in the middle of the road' " at the Populist convention in St. Louis in 1896. However, the term must have been in use earlier than 1896. Its probable source is a Populist campaign song of 1892 (in Haynes, *James Baird Weaver*, p. 468):

Side tracks are rough, and they're hard to walk,
Keep in the middle of the road;
Though we haven't got time to stop and talk
We keep in the middle of the road.
Turn your backs on the goldbug men,
And yell for silver now and then;
If you want to beat Grover, also Ben,
Just stick to the middle of the road.

In a speech of 1894 at Des Moines, Weaver said (Haynes, p. 357) :

I am a middle-of-the-road man, but I don't propose to lie down across it so no one can get over me. Nothing grows in the middle of the road.

From his way of using it, it is apparent that at that time *middle-of-the-road man* must have been a well-known term.

In modern politics *middle of the road* means not extreme:

1953 *Progressive* June 6/3 ... in general agreement with what Eisenhower considers his own "middle of the road" approach to problems.

1953 *Ib.* June 7/1. He would naturally not consider Cole ... anything other than a "middle of the roader."

1953 *Cols. Citizen* 24 Sept. ADA Rates Vorys Middle-of-Roader. . . .

millionaires' club.

The growing interest of big business in politics and the increasing number of wealthy men who were elected to the Senate is satirized in the following:

1888 *Nation* 2 Aug. 83/1. A millionaire named Palmer from Michigan, who joined "the pleasantest club in the country," otherwise known as the United States Senate, has surprised everybody by the announcement that he is going to let his membership lapse, although it is universally conceded that he could retain his place by simply meeting his regular dues.

The exact formula occurs in a pun of 1896 and later quotations clearly identify the millionaires' club with the Senate:

1896 *Literary Digest* 26 Sept. 681/2. Mark Hanna proposes to beat Mr. Bryan with a millionaire's club.

1907 *Rev. of Rev.* XXXV.340. The United States Senate is no longer renowned for its scholarship, but for its wealth. Statesmen have gone and millionaires now fill their places. The "millionaires' club" is a facetious but truthful alias for our Upper House.

1928 *Ib.* LXXVII.151. Who is so young that he cannot remember when the Senate of the United States was characterized as the Millionaires' Club. . . ?

minion.

A favorite; a fawning party hack.

Even in its original sphere (love), *minion* early suffered a degeneration from lover to mistress. In politics the same procedure occurred: from favorite to servile follower.

A few examples from American politics illustrate the overwhelming popularity of the term's opprobrious connotations:

1775 in Moore *Ballads of Revolution* 81. Lead on thou paid Captain! tramp on thou proud minions!

177– in Stevenson *Poems* 143. Mass. Song of Liberty.

Ye Minions, ye Placemen, Pimps, Pensioners, all. . . .

1829 in Jackson *Corr.* IV.15. Clay and his minions.

1862 Christy *Pulpit Politics* 507 [fr. *Political Text-Book* 27]. Yes, with freedom and Fremont and Dayton emblazoned on the ample folds of our national banner, we will drive the base minions of slavery from their control of the Government. . . .

miscegenation.

A mixture or fusion.

A. The term was coined by the anonymous writers of a pamphlet, *Miscegenation: The Theory of the Blending of the Races, Applied to the American White Man and Negro,* copyrighted in 1863. Under a heading "New Words Used in This Book" we find:

Miscegenation—from the Latin *Miscere,* to mix, and *Genus,* race, is used to denote the abstract idea of the mixture of two or more races. . . . Reasons for coining these words— (1) There is, as yet, no word in the language which expresses exactly the idea they embody. (2) Amalgamation is a poor word, since it properly refers to the union of metals with quicksilver, and was, in fact, only borrowed for an emergency, and should now be returned to its proper signification.

P. T. Barnum in *Humbugs of the World* (1866, ch.23) calls the "miscegenation hoax . . . one of the most successful of known literary hoaxes." He further identifies the writers to be D. G. Croly, George Wakeman, and E. C. Howell.

B. In politics the word became generally synonymous with *amalgamation.*

1864 *Ann. of Cleve.* No.1518. Miscegenation is a new name given by the radicals to amalgamation.
1864 *N. Y. Day-Book* 16 April in *Jrnl. Negro Hist.* xxxiv.305.
Beautiful word, and more beautiful thought!
None but the wise have its origin sought; . . .
Fill with mulattoes and mongrels the nation,
This Is The Meaning Of Miscegenation.
1891 Grinnell *Men and Events* 142. It was a cold and unfeeling part which he [S. S. Cox] played on the Freedmen's Bureaus Bill, and after the war naming Republicans miscegenationists, as more offensive to the "groundlings" than that of Abolitionists.

C. Also designating fusions of various party factions.

1866 *Cleve. Leader* 9 Aug. 1/3. The miscegenation between the Copperheads and the so-called Johnson Republicans is daily becoming more brazen and bold.
1866 *Ib.* The meeting of a little squad of "Johnsonites" and Copperheads . . . deserves notice only as the first overt miscegenation of the Senter clique with the Democracy.

Modoc.

In 1873 the Modoc War created a great sensation (*Harper's W.,* 26 April, p. 339 *et passim*). *Modoc* turns up as the name of an anti-negro organization in Mississippi:

1873 in Ames *Chron. from the Nineteenth Century* I.476. There are two wings on our party in this county, or rather city [Natchez] as you doubtless know. The Lynch side is named the "Warm Spring Indians" and the other the "Modocs." The "New South" is controlled by the "Modocs.". . . I have from the first looked upon the "Modocs" as Modocs. They are "Bolters," naturally, seeking to destroy what they cannot control.
1875 in Raum *Existing Conflict* 313 . . . the widow of Senator Caldwell . . . testified. . . . "After the bodies were brought to my house, Professors Hillman and Martin stayed until one o'clock, and then at one o'clock the train came from Vicksburg with the 'Modocs.'. . . and they carried on there like a parcel of wild Indians over those dead bodies, these Vicksburg 'Modocs.' "

mogul.

A politician of high rank or prestige.

The Great Mogul was the common designation of the East Indian emperor at Delhi. The appearance of the term in American politics in the late 1850's is undoubtedly related to the events in India surrounding the dethronement of the Great Mogul in 1857.

1856 *Middletown* (N.Y.) *Banner of Liberty* 103/2. Has it come to this that the people no longer possess the ability to govern themselves, and that in lieu thereof they have vested the power in these gangs of rowdies and midnight con-

spirators, whose grand Mogul, the acknowledged head and front of the clan, claims and receives the homage and obeisance of each subaltern!
1858 *Ohio St. Jrnl.* 5 Oct. 2/1 ... the great Mogul who sits in the White House.
1884 *N. Y. World* 8 March 8/1 ... the bankers, merchants and the big moguls will not attend the next meeting.

See BASHAW.

Mohawk.

According to Miller (*Origins of the American Revolution,* p. 347) a name adopted by the patriots who staged the Boston Tea Party⸴ A similar group was active in New York:
Becker *New York Parties 1760–1776* 109. "The Mohawks," we are told, "were prepared to do their duty at a proper hour," the people were too impatient, and at 8 o'clock a number of men boarded the ship and dumped the tea into the harbor.

mongrel.

A derogatory term indicating a mixture, whether of politicians or of political principles.
1798 in *Gt. Deb.* II.72. He knew only of two states: a state of neutrality and a state of war; he knew of no mongrel state between them.
1824 in Klein *Penn. Politics* 168. We remonstrated against amalgamation meetings, mongrel meetings, and all sorts of meetings except general meetings of the democratic party.
1844 *Niles' Reg.* 1 June 217/2. It was true, he said, that a firebrand [Texas question] had been thrown into their camp by the "Mongrel administration in Washington"....
1854 *Ohio Statesman* 3 July 2/2. The mongrels are already in trouble in old Columbiana.
1871 *Ann. of Cleve.* No. 3683. Will the Democratic Ring managers keep faith with their Republican complots and be able to deliver the votes for the mongrel ticket for which they have contracted?
1879 in Chamberlain *No Truce* 113. "Mr. Osborne is a splendid young fellow," it [*Auburn Daily Advertiser*] had said after characterizing the Democratic slate as a mongrel ticket, "and outside of politics the *Advertiser* has always liked him immensely."
1956 *Nation* 28 April 361. In the October issue of *The White Sentinel,* racist organ of his association, Hamilton ... warned his readers that "when you purchase Falstaff beer ... you are aiding the integration and mongrelization of America." Mongrelization is a favorite word of Hamilton's.

See also MERMAID TICKET, PIEBALD.

monocrat.

A favorite term of Jefferson to designate those who favored the monarchy of England rather than the democracy of France.
1792 Jefferson *Writings* VIII.440 ... Samuel Adams, and Mr. Ames, the colossus of the monocrats and paper men, will either be left out or hard run.
1792 *Ib.* VI.147. The monocrats here [Penn.] still affect to believe all this, while the republicans are rejoicing and taking to themselves the name of Jacobins....
1793 *Ib.* VI.193. The death of the king of France has not produced as open condemnations from the Monocrats as I expected.
1794 *Ib.* IX.293. The denunciation of the democratic societies is one of the extraordinary acts of boldness of which we have seen so many from the faction of monocrats.
1799 *Ib.* X.124. The Anglomen and monocrats had so artfully confounded the cause of France with that of Freedom, that both went down in the same scale.

monopoly (monopolist).

Already well established in 18th-century-English economic thought:

1776 Smith *Wealth of Nations* 473. We must carefully distinguish between the effects of the colony trade and those of the monopoly of that trade. The former are always and necessarily beneficial; the latter always and necessarily hurtful.

As the following quotations suggest, the use in America was mainly concerned with the preponderance of British carriers in Anglo-American trade:

1775 Jefferson *Writings* I.457. The monopoly of our trade . . . brings greater loss to us and benefit to them than the amount of our proportional contributions to the common defense.
1775 *Ib*. I.479. It is not just that the Colonies should be required to oblige themselves to other contributions while Great Britain possesses a monopoly of their trade.
1797 *Ib*. VII.121. The British have wished a monopoly of commerce . . . with us, and they have in fact obtained it.

The word came into prominence in American national politics during the debates over the United States Bank, which led to the formation of an Anti-Monopoly party (q.v.) :

1819 *Niles' Reg.* 20 March 65. The opinion [Sup. Ct. on bank] before us establishes the broad principle that congress may grant monopolies, almost at discretion . . . .
1830 *Workingman's Adv.* 16 Jan. 1/3. All this is for the benefit of some dozen auctioneers and monopolists.
1830 *Ib*. 3 April 3/4 . . . this and other abuses naturally arise from their being a licensed monied monopoly.
1830 *Ib*. 17 April 1/3. You find in that council, the iron handed though licensed monopolist, and incorporated swindler, who year after year fill their coffers, by draining the pockets of the honest and industrious.
1830 *Ib*. 29 May 1/4. It must be gratifying to every friend of liberty, to notice the many risings of the people, to wrest the privileges, of right belonging to *them*,

from the hands of a monopolizing aristocracy.
1832 *Ib*. 30 Aug. 2/4. The Mammoth Monopoly [bank].
1833 in Nevins *Pol. Cartoons* 41. The Downfall of Mother Bank. "Major Jack Downing I must act on this case with energy and decision. You see the downfall of the party engine and corrupt monopoly!!"
1840 *Cong. Globe* 5 June App.775/2. If he [Van Buren] does not mean this, why crowd every message with denunciation upon denunciation, . . . resorting to the low demagogue cant, such as "monopolies," "irresponsible corporations," "dangers of associated wealth". . . .

With the rise of big business and the trusts, attention was once again focused on monopoly from many different political points of view:

1881 *Daily St. Jrnl.* (Lincoln, Neb.) 26 March 3/2. Republican papers, who will not bow down to the Janus of Nebraska politics . . . are hooted at . . . as a "railroad copper" or a monopoly hireling.
1882 in Nevins *Cartoons* 141. [Uncle Sam chained to a rock "Monopoly," his liver being eaten by "Monopolists."]
1884 *Nation* 30 Oct. 369/1. It [veto of 5 cent fare bill] was a blow aimed at a monopoly whose controlling spirits are the most unpopular capitalists in America.
1889 W. S. Morgan in Taylor *Farmers' Movement* 286. Laboring men of America! . . . Strike from the face of the land the monopolies and combinations that are eating out the heart of the Nation.
1889 in Nevins *Cartoons* 163. The Senate of the United States of the Monopolists by the Monopolists for the Monopolists!
1903 *Boston Daily Globe* 13 March. Public Monopoly, He [H. D. Lloyd] Says, Provides Only Escape from Evils of Private Monopoly. [head]
1913 Roosevelt *Works* XXII.492. The true way of dealing with monopoly is to prevent it by administrative action before it grows so powerful that even when courts condemn it they shrink from destroying it.

monster.

The many-headed Hydra, a terrible and insatiable monster, served as a popular metaphor to call attention to the destructive qualities of certain public institutions, particularly the U.S. Bank.

1762 Otis *Vindication* 51. Supply the treasury, again, tax the many headed monster* once more.
* An approbrious Name by some given to the People.

1815 Adams *Works* X.123. The monsters, paper money, tender law, and regulation of prices, all stalked in horrors before me. . . .

1831 J. Randolph in *Jackson Corr.* IV.386 . . . if you were a friend to the chestnut street monster as you were its bitter enemy.

1834 *Reg. of Deb.* III.6/1. The bank, created by the Congress and President Madison, was a "monstrous golden calf," and President Jackson (as a modern Moses) has produced a new monster, a huge many-headed serpent, to swallow the golden calf.

1834 *Ib.* III.448. It [bank] has been called a "monster." The name is arbitrary; and any thing else can be called so if the user of the term be skilled on the low and vulgar abuse of the day.

1834 in *Mangum Papers* V.580. But all this violence on the part of power, and this distress in the country, are to be borne, to put down the "monster."

1834 *Ib.* V.593. The Senator [Benton] has strangled the monster, more fearful than the fabled Lernaian hydra, or, rather, he has cut off its head; but I fear he has not skilfully cauterized the wound.

1841 *Ib.* V.629. Who has not heard the euphonious sounds of Bank! Bank! Monster! Monster! rung and rung again, throughout the whole gamut?

1853 *N. Y. Trib.* 4 Feb. 4/1. Mr. Brodhead's substitute for the Pacific Railroad bill was then brought (before the Senate) upon the tapis, and the point argued whether it created a monster corporation worse than the United States Bank or not.

Moses.

The term is another in the group comparing the slavery of the Negro with that of the Israelite. A leader who was dedicated to the emancipation of the slave could be called a "Moses." However, an early quotation indicates that the term was also applied to any leader:

1834 *Reg. of Deb.* III.6/1. The bank, created by the Congress and President Madison, was a "monstrous golden calf," and President Jackson (as a modern Moses) has produced a new monster, a huge many-headed serpent, to swallow the golden calf.

1837 Garrison *Garrison Story* II.126. Tremendous applause was given when an ex-slave, a native of Africa, after reciting some horrible tales, from his experience, turned suddenly to Mr. G. with—"Dat man is de Moses raised up for our deliverance."

The word became associated with Andrew Johnson after a campaign speech which he made in 1864 to a colored group in Nashville. Johnson said, ". . . I am almost induced to wish that, as in the days of old, a Moses might arise who should lead them safely to their promised land of freedom and happiness." When the crowd shouted "You are our Moses," he continued, ". . . I will indeed be your Moses, and lead you through the Red Sea of war and bondage to a fairer future of liberty and peace." (Frank Moore, *Speeches of Andrew Johnson,* xl.) When Johnson became President, Petroleum V. Nasby revived the term to mock him:

1866 *Swinging Round the Cirkle* 74. I hev had hopes uv Androo Johnson. . . . He wuz the Moses wich I spected wood lead the Democrisy out uv the desolate Egypt. . . .

Ib. 121 . . . and Androo feelin a call to continue in the Moses bizness. . . .

Other writers repeated the jibe:

1866 *Wash. Morning Chronicle* 24 Feb. . . . thousands of liberated slaves who were looking up to him as their volunteer Moses.

See BRICKS WITHOUT STRAW, EGYPTIAN DEMOCRACY.

mossback.

Originally a fish so old that it has moss or seaweed growing on its back; later a backward or reactionary human being:

1850 Lewis *Swamp Doctor* 181. Here you sit, like a knot in a tree, with the moss commencing to grow on your back.

Certain primitive Southern types and those who fled to the swamps to escape conscription:

1869 *Notes and Queries* 30 May 1.507. A Mossyback is a man who secreted himself in the woods or swamps to escape the conscription for the Southern army, where he is said to have remained hidden until the moss grew on his back.
1889 Hinman *Si Klegg* 366. [Picture of a Southern "Mossback."]

In post-Civil War politics the term becomes some sort of Northern counterpart to *Bourbon* (q.v.), especially in Ohio.

1879 *Cols. Dem.* 22 April 3/3. The mossbacks and haw-eaters of the Hocking hills held a meeting in the editorial rooms of the Sentinel office. . . .
1880 *N. Y. Trib.* 30 Aug. 4/5. Imagine a moss-backed Bourbon sipping the usual Sabbath-school refreshment of watery lemonade.
1884 *Ohio St. Jrnl.* 12 July 1/1. The "kids" are celebrating it [Cleveland's nomination] with parades, while the "mossbacks" are hanging their heads.

1884 *Cleve. Leader* 19 July 1/6. The Mossbacks and Thurman fail to materialize and paralyze the machine.
Ib. 3 Oct. 1/4. Durbin Ward is classed among the mossbacks by the kids.
Ib. 6 Oct. 4/3. Leckey Harper, the mossback selected by Locke as his Original for Petroleum Nasby.
8/5. One of the old-time genuine mossback Democrats.

Later examples:

1929 W. Rogers *How we Elect* 94 . . . but they prefer 'em to the Democrats' old-fashioned ideas. Now, taken out from under the influence of a lot of these old Mossbacks, you are a pretty progressive fellow, Al, and with you and this Fellow Roosevelt as a kind of nucleus, I think we can, with the help of some Progressive young Democratic governors and senators and congressmen, make this thing into a Party, instead of a Memory.
1938 Salter *Am. Politician* 228–9 . . . he [Farley] . . . could gossip about crop prospects responsively, even with the G.O.P. Mossbacks from undiluted farm districts.
1948 *Nation* 9 Oct. 396/2. He talked about the "bunch of old mossbacks" in the Republican Party.

mucker.

A fanatical reformer.

1876 *Cinc. Daily Gazette* 19 June 1/4. He [Hayes] has on his side all the muckers, temperance fanatics, and Know-Nothings.
1891 *Cyc. of Temperance* 269/1. The saloon-keepers then resolved to make "the muckers take their own medicine," and insisted that the Mayor enforce the Sunday law against "common labor."

muckrake(-r).

The man with the muckrake is one of the allegorical figures in Bunyan's *Pilgrim's Progress:*

(World's Classics ed.) 196 . . . his muckrake doth shew his carnal mind. And whereas thou seest him rather give heed to rake up straws and sticks, and the dust of the floor, than to what He says that calls to him from above. . . .

Then said Christiana, Oh, deliver me from this muck-rake!

In American politics a muck-rake was first known as an office-seeker:
1871 DeVere *Americanisms* 618. Muck-rakes, a slang term in politics for persons who "fish in troubled waters," from the idea of their raking muck to see what valuable waifs and strays they may find in it.
1872 "Warrington" *Pen Portraits* 479. He [Grant] nominated a New York muck-rake for secretary of the treasury.
1889 Farmer *Americanisms* 376. Muck-rakers. A slang political epithet for those who seek the "small change" of office—place-mongers, as they are otherwise called.

As a word designating those journalists who made sensational exposures of the corruption on various political levels in the early 1900's, *muckraker* was given widespread attention after its use by Theodore Roosevelt. According to Sullivan (*Our Times*, III.94) Roosevelt first alluded to the muckraker in a Gridiron Club speech on March 17, 1906, and "in the amount of comment he heard he realized the potentiality in the chance inspiration that had led him to revive Bunyan's generally forgotten figure of speech." At the laying of the cornerstone of the House of Representatives Office Building, April 14, 1906, the figure was brought before the public:
Roosevelt *Works* XVI.415f. Now, it is very necessary that we should not flinch from seeing what is vile and debasing. There is filth on the floor, and it must be scraped up with the muck-rake; and there are times and places where this service is the most needed of all the services that can be performed. But the man who never does anything else, who never thinks or speaks or writes, save of his feats with the muck-rake, speedily becomes, not a help to society, not an incitement to good, but one of the most potent forces of evil.

The word took hold immediately:
in Ray Stannard Baker *Am. Chronicle* 201. I remember one day that spring (1906) meeting a friend on the street. "Hello, Muckraker," he bantered me. I did not at first know what my friend meant, but I speedily found out.

Many of those classified as muckrakers objected to the name:
Ib. 201. He had attached a name of odium to all the writers engaged in exposing corruption regardless of whether they deserved it or not.... The more I heard of the President's proposed address, the more anxious and indignant I became, the more fearful that such an attack might greatly injure the work which we were trying honestly to do.
Steffens *Autobio.* 357. I did not intend to be a muckraker; I did not know that I was one till President Roosevelt picked the name out of Bunyan's *Pilgrim's Progress* and pinned it on us; and even then he said that he did not mean me.

And despite these initial objections of some:
in Sullivan *Our Times* III.97. With equal promptness, and equal glee—and with a good deal of generosity, considering the circumstances—all the writers of exposure accepted the epithet that was meant for some of them, and in the eyes of most of the public "muckraker" became a term of approval.
1911 Roosevelt *Works* XIII.668. Muckrakers who rake up much that ought to be raked up deserve well of the community.... The type of magazine which I condemn is what may be called the Ananias muck-raker type.

mud.

Slander or defamation.

1872 *Harper's W.* 5 Oct. 763/1. Mud As An Argument [head]. We speak elsewhere of the slanders of this campaign. There is a storm of the most reckless falsehoods, incessantly repeated after the most constant exposure.

1876 *N. Y. Trib.* 13 April 4/6. Mud doesn't stick to Mr. Blaine any better than it does to Mr. Bristow. The slander peddlers are having a bad season.

1877 *Puck* 11 May 1. Mud for Defacing Reputations. [cartoon: label on pail which Dana is using to daub over Hayes' face.]

1877 *Ib.* 4 July 4/1. Metaphorically, Peleg, while on the platform, still rolls in the gutter, and then throws the mud at the "rummies."

As the last quotation suggests (see MUD THROWING) the metaphor was often extended or made humorous by euphemistic language:

1878 *N. Y. Trib.* 25 June 4/2. More Louisiana Mud [head]...dredging machine was set at work again yesterday, and brought up a small load of sediment from the dirty stream of Louisiana politics.

mud batteries.

1876 *N. Y. Times* 19 June 1/1. As far as regarded his own name in the canvass, Mr. Wheeler had no fears that the mud batteries of the enemy would effect anything.

mud hunt.

An investigation of the mud-throwing type:

1880 *Puck* 30 June 298/2. Even the most industrious mud-hunt will probably fail to bring to light a hidden murder or a long-concealed "crooked" financial operation.

mud machine.

Agency for political mud-throwing (q.v.).

1806 *Balance* V.162/3. The Mayor and Corporation of the city of New York will man their mud-machine.

1827 *Spirit of Seventy Six* 14 June 3/2. From the extensive circulation of this "Mud Machine," and the total disregard to truth...we had apprehended that it was to have some influence in our Presidential contest.

1848 *Xenia* (Ohio) *Torchlight* 30 March 2/7...it is no marvel that he should make his paper a mud-machine.

1876 *Cong. Record* 11 Aug. 5464/2. I do not know what the gentleman means by a mud-machine. I have endeavored to keep myself above mud-machines.

1880 *Cinc. Daily Gazette* 14 June 1/1... and we can advise the mud machine, called partisan papers, that attempts at blackmailing Garfield's character will be signal failures.

In one instance an actual dredging machine figured in the political campaign:

1884 *Ann. of Cleve.* No.1346. The "mud machine" has raised more dust (in politics) than was ever dreamed of by its inventors....We expect, at the next election, to see it adopted as a banner by the victorious party, and supported in future contests with "three horse power."

mudsill.

On March 4, 1858, J. H. Hammond of South Carolina spoke in defense of the doctrine that slavery existed in the North as well as in the South (see WHITE SLAVES) and that in fact slavery under one name or another was necessary in every organized society:

Cong. Globe App. 71. In all social systems there must be a class to do the menial duties, to perform the drudgery of life. That is, a class requiring but a low order of intellect and but little skill. Its requisites are vigor, docility, fidelity. Such a class you must have, or you would not have that other class which leads progress, civilization, and refinement. It constitutes the very mudsill of society and of political government; and you might as well attempt to build a house in the air, as to build either the one or the other, except on this mudsill.

According to Beveridge (*Lincoln*, IV.317) the mudsill metaphor had been suggested to Hammond by the fact that his new-built residence stood on marshy ground that made it necessary to employ a mudsill (the lowest sill of a structure, usually embedded in the soil). However, Hammond had already used the term as early as 1854 in a letter to a friend:

1854 in *Johns Hopkins Studies* XLI.119. I do believe that a proper appreciation of money and the exaction of strict punctuality in all pecuniary transactions is the very cornerstone or perhaps I should say the mud-sill on which the fabric of human happiness in this life rests.

In the congressional debate of 1858 Hannibal Hamlin criticized the comparison:

in Wilson *Slave Power* II.550. "Sir," he added, "I can tell that Senator that they [Northern laborers] are the "mudsills" of our community. They are the men who clear away our forests. They are the men who make the green hillside blossom. They are the men who build our ships and who navigate them. They are the men who build our towns and who inhabit them. They are the men who constitute the great mass of our community. Sir, they are not only pillars which support our government, but they are the capitals that adorn the very pillars."

However, the general reaction in the North was different. Exactly like *greasy mechanics* (q.v.) with which *mudsill* is frequently coupled, the word was largely accepted as an appropriate means to satirize the overbearing spirit of the Southern chivalry (q.v.), and was used locally by Democrats as well as Republicans.

1858 *Mt. Vernon Republican* 3 Aug. 2/6. Being one of the conclomerate [sic] mass of "greasy mechanics," two fisted farmers, workies generally, and "mudsills" in particular, I would announce my name ... for nomination to the office of auditor.

1858 *Ib.* 27 July 3/1. Mudsill Clubs are being organized in California. Some of the Douglas-Broderick men there say they will organize political clubs under that name all over the State.

1858 in Sparks *Debates* 375. [Banner used at Galesburg, 9 October.] Small-fisted Farmers, Mudsills of Society, Greasy Mechanics, for A. Lincoln.

1859 Lincoln *Works* V.251. According to that [the Mudsill] theory, a blind horse upon a tread-mill is a perfect illustration of what a laborer should be—all the better for being blind, that he could not kick understandingly. According to that theory, the education of laborers is not only useless, but pernicious and dangerous. In fact, it is, in some sort, deemed a misfortune that laborers should have heads at all. Those same heads are regarded as explosive materials, only to be safely kept in damp places, as far as possible from that peculiar sort of fire which ignites them. A Yankee who could invent a strong-handed man without a head would receive the everlasting gratitude of the "mud-sill" advocates.

1860 *Xenia* (Ohio) *Torchlight* 2 May 1/3. Next to Senator Hammond, of "greasy mechanic and mudsill" notoriety, he is the most insulting and senseless member from the South.

mud throwing (slinging).

Using billingsgate, especially of a slanderous type.

1876 *N. Y. Trib.* 16 March. The Democratic party must understand by this time ... that it is not going to carry the Presidential election by throwing mud. ... Mud-throwing is not reform.

1876 *Harper's W.* 29 April 342/1. The consequence is that they denounce as mud-throwing every assertion that there is anything wrong.

1876 *Ib.* 20 May 402/3. He [Conkling] has been of the Republican school that thought investigations of Republican abuses were mud-throwing, and exposures of offences discredits to the party, which should be left to the Democrats.

1878 *Ib.* 20 July 566/2. That is the purpose of the Potter inquiry. It is part of the campaign of mud-throwing.... The Democrats wish to establish fraud. General Butler wishes to smirch the administration.

1880 *N. Y. Trib.* 22 May 4/1. Another experimenter in mud-slinging has found out that Mr. Blaine is an unprofitable target.

1954 *Cols. Citizen* 10 Jan. Crack of the week at the State House: "During the next governor's campaign, Jimmy Rhodes is going to sling so much mud that even Frank Lausche's tears won't be able to wash it all away."

mugwump.

A bolter, especially a Republican who bolted the party in 1884.

From the Algonquian *mugquomp,* a chief, the term was used following the tendency to surround political and secret organizations with Indian terminology (see, e.g., BUCK-TAIL, SACHEM, WISKINKI), particularly in Masonic orders to signify a leader or high official:

1832 in *Nation* LII.414/3. [*DA*] The secret bulletin ... has extensively circulated among the Knights of Kadosh, and the Most Worshipful Mug-Wumps of the Cabletow.

[The coupling of *mug-wump* and *cabletow* indicates the Masonic character of this quotation.

1828 *Anti-Masonic Rev.* I.257 ... they are both rarest in the masonic cable-tow, and readiest to sever it.]

1835 Thompson *Adv. T. Peacock* 6. This village, I beg leave to introduce to the reader under the significant appellation of Mugwump, a word which being duly interpreted means ... much the same as Mah-hah-bone—which last ... I have fortunately discovered to signify nothing in particular, though, at the same time, I am perfectly aware that both these terms are used at the present day, vulgarly and masonically, as synonymous with greatness and strength.

1877 *N. Y. Trib.* 16 Feb. 4/4 in *Saturday Rev.* 22 Nov. 1884 659/1. John A. Logan is the Head Center, the Hub, the Kingpin, the Main Spring, Mogul and Mugwump of the final plot by which partisanship was installed in the commission.

1884 *N. Y. Sun* 23 March 1. The Hon. D. O. Bradley, who served his country in the Assembly in 1879 and 1880, and who has always been looked upon as the Republican mugwump of Dobbs Ferry.... The Hon. Edward Fitch intimated that being a mugwump, Mr. Bradley ought to know that under the new laws governing the Republican State Organization the election would not be legal unless ballot boxes were used.

1884 *Ib.* 15 April 2/3 [reply to reader's query]. Mugwump is an ancient New England term and smacks of the language of the red man. It is used to signify when gravely spoken, a man of importance, but more commonly a man who thinks himself important. Gov. Walker of Conn. is responsible for the renewed and widened interest in the word, it having been discovered in some recently published letters of his. A leader such as Gov. Walker is in Conn. or an authority like Lindley Murray is a mugwump. A synonym for the word in its other sense is the New York term Big Bug, or the Washington expression Swellhead. Brewster, Attorney General, is sometimes called a mugwump.

The turning point in the history of the word was the Republican convention of June, 1884, at which a group of reformers opposed the nomination of Blaine. The ridicule heaped on this group found expression in the term the *little mugwumps,* meaning the little big men:

N. Y. Sun 5 June 3/1. How the Little Mugwumps took It [head. of convention report making fun of reformers]

Puck 1 Oct. 66/2. Why, there was not ... a little local mugwump in the Chicago convention who could not have made an easier fight for the Presidency than this.

Later in the campaign the *little* was dropped, and the bolters became known as *mugwumps:*

N. Y. Trib. 26 June. A choice collection of eccentric words will doubtless be added to the political dictionary this year. The returns already include such fanciful specimens as "mugwump," "pachyderm," "kids," and "moss-backs."

Harper's W. 5 July 429 [Nast cartoon]. Have we Democrats got to nominate a ticket to suit them Republican "Pharisees" and Mugwumps?

N. Y. Trib. 11 July [letter of Rufus Choate, 1 July]. The "Mugwumps" because of their chagrin, now want to vote the Democratic ticket.... The party is not composed of "Archangels" nor of "Mugwumps."

Nation 24 July 61/2. A large meeting of anti-Blaine Republicans was held in Concord, Mass.... We presume they can be partially disposed of by calling them "free-traders"—all educated men are free-traders, it seems—and if any of them hold out after that they can call them mugwumps.

Roosevelt *Ltrs.* I.80. I get so angry with the "mugwumps," and get to have such scorn and contempt for them....

N. Y. World 14 Sept. 4/5. Statesmen from abroad are more than a little puzzled over the meaning of "soap-tails," "doodlebugs," and "mugwumps" of American politics.

1935 Chamberlain *No Truce* 131. This sounds like a paraphrase of Horace Porter's *bon mot* in the Cleveland-Blaine campaign of 1884. "A Mugwump," defined Porter, "is a person educated beyond his intellect." And yet [... this definition is]

kinder than the modern version describing a mugwump as a sort of bird that sits on a fence with his mug on one side and his wump on the other.

mugwumpery.

1885 *Boston Jrnl.* 25 April 2/2. Has he [Cleveland] thrown his bombshell into the very citadel of Mugwumpery?

1890 Bryce in Roosevelt *Ltrs.* I.230. "I won't let myself be captured by excessive mugwumpery after your warnings."

mulatto candidate.

A derogatory reference to a candidate whose views and principles are not held to be consistent.

1848 *N. Y. Herald* 7 July 2/2. All the candidates, including Mr. Van Buren, who is a sort of stump, half-tinted, Wilmot proviso, or rather mulatto candidate, are in the same fix.

(See HALF BREED, MONGREL, MERMAID TICKET.)

mulatto democracy.

A Republican counter-epithet to *Black Republican* (q.v.).

1858 *Ohio St. Jrnl.* 5 March 2. [The Ohio Statesman] the organ of the Mulatto Democracy.

See BLACK DEMOCRACY.

mule riding.

A Mississippi variant of *stumping* (q.v.).

1873 in Ames *Chron. from the Nineteenth Century* I.468. "Mule riding" means an active canvass of each county by the local politicians, who make their way over the county on mules or horses.

mum candidate.

An opposition nickname for General Harrison. [ ]

1844 *N. Y. Trib.* 26 Oct. 6/2. The Orators and the Press of the opposite party stigmatized him as "the man in the cage," "The mum candidate"....

A letter from Jackson is quoted in the same article:

That man deserves to be a slave who would vote for a mum candidate.

mushroom (politician, aristocrat).

A man who has come into sudden prominence.

1827 Randolph in Slaughter *Reminiscences* 191. He warned them against the danger of tinkering with the constitution ... reminded them that change was not always improvement, that the change then sought began in the west for sectional power, that it was the work of "mushroom politicians"....
1839 *Alexanders Western Messenger* 11 Sept. 1/7. What a glorious satire could be made ... to be entitled "the Rise and Progress of Mushroom Aristocracy."
1847 Temple *Notable Men* 225. He [Andrew Johnson] had denounced the venerable John Blair, ... and the Jonesboro Democratic leaders, as mushroom aristocrats.

muzzle.

A gag, specifically referring to the unit rule:

1880 *Harper's W.* 22 May 322/4. The Muzzle in Politics [head]. The progress of the discussion of the "unit rule" reveals the deep and strong popular opposition to it as a muzzle and gag unworthy of honorable men.
1880 *Ib.* 29 May 338/2. Unmuzzling [head]. We deny altogether, as we denied in our comments upon the action of the Convention at the time, its right, upon any sound theory of instructions, to muzzle district delegates.

myrmidon.

Both the popularity and the derogatory implications of the term may be explained by the various accounts of Achilles and the Myrmidons. (See Shakespeare, *Troilus and Cressida*, V.)

1834 *Mangum Papers* II.214. But she [New England] will rush it, if she can get such Myrmidons as those of Gen. J. to do the fighting.
1835 Peleg Sprague in *Garrison Story* App. 416. He, that slaveholder (pointing to the full length portrait of Washington) who from this canvass smiles upon you, his children, with parental benignity, came with other slaveholders to drive the British myrmidons from this city and this hall.
1839 Hone *Diary* I.447 ... in a few months the whole policy of the country will be changed, and the general government (or rather the President and his myrmidons) become the masters of the people, and the regulators of their private as well as public affairs.
1840 in Norton *Tippecanoe* App. 16.
For there's no luck at the White House,
There will be noe at a'
Till Martin and his myrmidons,
Are driven far awa'.
1837 Byrdsall *Loco Foco* 136 ... when they boldly advanced against the myrmidons of injustice, leaving the bloody tracks of their unclad feet upon the frozen ground.

Mystic Red. [ ]

1860 Wigfall in *Gt. Deb.* V.353. An association called "The Mystic Red" was entered into by members of the Methodist Church North and the John Brown men; and their purpose was to carry out the irrepressible conflict, to burn our towns, burn up the stores of our merchants, burn up the mills, to bring free-soil Northern capital in, and thus get possession of Texas, and make it a free State.

N

national (-ist, -ism).

Among the many shades of meaning, the following seem to be most significant:

A. In the 18th century *national* was used in reference to the whole country as against special and party interests.

Bolingbroke *Works* II.13 *(OED)*. A prince can scarce become irreconcilable with his people, and be reduced, for want of national strength, to support his power and dignity by the force of faction.... But faction has no regard to national interest.

This usage is also to be found in American writers:

1801 Adams *Works* IX.585... the commencement of it [Jefferson's administration] is too strongly infected with the spirit of party, to give much encouragement to men who are merely national.

B. Toward the end of the 18th century the contrast *national/federal* becomes predominant. This phase is treated under *federal.* To the material given there add:

1847 Calhoun *Writings* IV.357... it is attempted to subvert the federal government, plainly established under it [Const.], and rear in its place a great national consolidated government—to expunge the word "Union" and insert in its place that of "Nation."

1867 Sumner *Works* XVI.8. Pardon me, if I confess that I have never reconciled myself to the use of the word "Federal" instead of "National." To my mind, our government is not Federal, but National; our Constitution is not Federal but National....

1876 *Harper's W.* 8 Jan. 22/1. They denied that they were rebels, upon the ground that the Union was not national, but a simple partnership of sovereign States.... Nationality like belligerence, is a fact, not a theory.

After the Civil War, *nation* and *national* as implicit denials of the states rights theory were odious words:

1875 *N. Y. Trib.* 13 Aug. 4/4. Are We A Nation? Mr. Beck, the sturdy Kentucky Congressman, recently said: Yes, gentlemen, there is that contemptible word *Nation*—a word which no good Democrat uses, when he can find any other, and when forced to use it, utters in disgust. This is no nation. We are free and independent States.

1876 in *Cong. Record* 11 Feb. 1025. If I may use the word "national"—and not offend the Senator from Connecticut.

C. In the decades before the Civil War the contrast between the South and the North and, occasionally, between the East and the West caused a new alignment that brought *national* into contradistinction to *sectional.* This distinction is probably inferred in the earlier division which resulted in the National Republican party (q.v.).

1824 *Cinc. Literary Gazette* 15 May in *Miss. Valley Hist. Rev.* XXXV.413. Next ... to cherishing a national feeling, we would cherish a Western feeling.

1831 *Nat. Intelligencer* 5 March 3/1. There remains, to the friends of the constitution, to stay the progress of the administration, and to save the country from the effects of its measures, but one course. ... They are National Republicans; they are friends of Union; they are the great party of free Americans.

1848 *Old Zack* 19 Aug. 2/1 ... the morals of a great people have been treated with derision by permitting negroes to participate in the deliberations ... of a Sectional Convention—sectional we style it, for National it was not.

1850 in Streeter *Pol. Parties in Michigan* 118. This sectionalism claims on one side everything for the North, and on the other everything for the South.... We must cultivate a national, instead of a sectional patriotism.

An epoch in the *sectional/national* contrast was marked by a speech of

Sumner in the Senate, August 26, 1852. Sumner's remarks were widely reproduced in newspapers and pamphlets, translated into German, and echoed throughout the country.

Works III.266, 274. Painfully convinced of the unutterable wrong and woe of Slavery, —profoundly believing, that, according to the true spirit of the Constitution and the sentiments of the Fathers, it can find no place under our National Government,— that it is in every respect sectional, and in no respect national . . . p. 274. According to a curious tradition of the French language, Louis the Fourteenth . . . changed the gender of a noun. But Slavery does more. It changes word for word. It teaches men to say *national* instead of *sectional,* and *sectional* instead of *national.* . . . According to the true spirit of the Constitution, and the sentiments of the Fathers, *Slavery,* and not Freedom, is *sectional,* while *Freedom,* and not Slavery, is *national.*

1856 in Christy *Pulpit Politics* 527. The great boasting idea of that party is, that freedom is national, and slavery is sectional.

1856 in *Ib.* 528. You cheat yourself with the delusion that your platform makes you national. . . . To justify so absurd a position, you love to employ the specious phrase that "freedom is national, and slavery sectional."

1878 *Harper's W.* 10 Aug. 626/4. They tend to unite the North in a policy of distrust of the South, because they are supposed to represent not only the general but the natural Southern feeling. Yet the Republican leaders will fall into a fatal mistake if they count upon making this sectional jealousy the reliance of the national campaign.

1936 Barry *Theme Song* 51. He preaches the doctrine that the purpose behind the middle western states is not sectional, but national.

D. While the early American development of *national* bears out

Henry Steele Commager's views, that American and European nationalism are essentially different ("The Nature of American Nationalism," in *The World of History,* 1954), a certain adaptation cannot be overlooked. The European brand stresses the right and frequently assumes the superiority of one's nation in regard to other nations. To begin with, this tendency is most clearly marked in countries that are struggling for their national existence.

1873 *Spectator* 23 Aug. 1059/1. Prince Bismarck also observed that concession would encourage the Polish nationalists.

1885 *Sat. Rev.* 11 April 463/1. It is to them that the portentous development of American-Irish Nationalism is due.

1919 C. Nagel *Sp.* II.209. A strong nationalism is better calculated than a weak internationalism to guarantee the essential conditions of self-respecting world peace.

National Democracy.

A. A name adopted by those Democrats who emphasized the national rather than the local or sectional role of the party:

1854 *Cong. Globe* 17 Jan. 191/1. There was never a more sublime spectacle presented to the world than that presented by the National Democracy in 1848, when . . . they stood up to defend the integrity of the Constitution against those who . . . were endeavoring to create a sectional feeling.

1857 *Atchison Squatter Sovereign* 3 Feb. 2/2. One Party—The National Democracy.

1858 Lincoln in Sparks *Debates* 347. In the contest of 1856 his [Douglas'] party delighted to call themselves together as the "National Democracy"; but now, if there should be a notice put up anywhere for a meeting of the "National Democracy," Judge Douglas and friends would not come.... They would not suppose themselves invited.

1858 *Ohio State Jrnl.* 16 Sept. 1/4. "You were once an old Whig ... Mr. Stephens?" "Yes, sir, but now I am a National Democrat!" "National in reputation only, Mr. Stephens, not in principles. Your principles are sectional."

1860 *Wash. Intelligencer* 6 July 3/1. Each member of "the party" is now called to ... risk his own choosing between the candidates of two competing organizations, which both alike claim to represent the "National Democracy."

B. Characterizing those Democrats who favored the gold standard against the dominant silver faction of the party:

1896 *Rev. of Rev.* XIV.434. The Rise of the "National Democracy." The Movement For Sound Money And The Indianapolis Convention.

1896 *Ib.* XIV.553 ... the old-fashioned Democrats, who believed in a gold standard and had been read out of the party at Chicago.... Mr. Bryan himself admitted that these "National Democrats" were well generalled, though he believed that they lacked the support of rank and file.

1896 Osborne in Chamberlain *No Truce* 124. "I see the National Democrats have done themselves the honor of nominating you," he wrote a fellow Democrat. "I might have been in the same boat had I not sternly repressed the enthusiasm of my supporters." Of the state convention he had remarked: "We shall nominate a good Democrat—if I have to run myself."

National Reformer.

The National Reform Association was organized in 1844 (?) "with the aim of saving the public domain for small farmers and incidentally emancipating the exploited wage-earners of the industrial centers of the East" (Christman, *Tin Horns and Calico,* p. 69) and was characteristic of the general feeling of the time concerning the agrarian problem. (See AGRARIANISM, ANTI-RENT.)

1848 Hammond *Silas Wright* 674. There was an attempt made to organize still another party in the city of New York, known by the name of "National Reformers." It consisted of philosophical and speculative men, who established a weekly newspaper, called "Young America," which was conducted by Mr. George H. Evans, an able but rather visionary writer.

National Republican.

in Blaine *Twenty Years* 106. Modern political designations had their origin in the Presidential election of 1824. The candidates all belonged to the party of Jefferson, which had been called Democratic-Republicans. In the new divisions, the followers of Jackson took the name of Democrats; the supporters of Adams called themselves National Republicans.

This account of the origin of the name, also cited by more recent historians (for instance, see Lynch, *Epoch and the Man,* p. 321) seems in need of some adjustment. Although *National Republican* was used occasionally in 1828—

Address to Electors of Middlesex County (Conn.) [pamphlet] [Signed by] Committee on behalf of the National Republicans of the town of Middletown.

—the word became popular between the presidential elections and became the official party name in the Jackson-Clay contest of 1832.

1830 Webster *Works* III.259. I am a unionist, and, in this sense, a national republican.

1831 in *Memoir of Bennett* 26. ... the organization which is attempted under the name of "National Republicans" is intended not only to overthrow the Republican Party, but even to crush the Anti-Masonic party.

1831 *Wash. Nat. Intelligencer* 22 Feb. 3/2.

National Republican is an excellent designation for a national party in our republican Union. Let it be adopted every where, by all who would uphold the Federal Constitution; secure the independence and continuance of the Supreme Court; preserve a sound currency; possess a substantive and enlightened President of the United States; prevent offices from becoming the booty of mere partisans and parasites; and obtain a truly responsible and visible government.

1832 *Niles' Reg.* 12 May 206/1. National Republican Convention of Young Men.

1832 Spencer in Barnes *Weed* 43. I begged him to abstain from all comments, for he might do mischief when he does not intend it. I hinted that their Jackson friends in Boston might be very willing to embroil us with the National Republicans of the State, but that I trusted our anti-Masonic friends there would not be accessory to any such design.

1832 Baltimore [pamphlet]. *An Address to the People of Maryland from Their Delegates in the late National Republican Convention made in obedience to a resolution of that body.*

1834 Hone *Diary* I.118. The municipal election in Utica has gone in favor of the National Republican candidate by 800 majority.

The name was later superseded by *Whig* (q.v.).

Naylorizing. [ ]

1840 *Cinc. Daily Gazette* 28 Sept. 2/1. Naylorizing ... new term, meaning "depositing votes in the ballot boxes before the opening of the poll." ... This, then, is the way in which the Advertiser would have its readers suppose it believes Mr. Naylor obtained his election over Mr. Ingersoll, in the Third District, Philadelphia, at the last election.

Nebrascal.

Satirical name for those who supported the Kansas-Nebraska Bill.

The portmanteau development is obvious:

1854 Pike in Isely *Horace Greeley* 15 May. Give the boys aid and comfort in the House. We'll give the Neb. rascals hell in the Tribune.

1854 *Cleve. Leader* 6 Oct. 3/2. The Nebrascals are secretly running a man named Spayth for coroner.

negative (noun and verb).

Defined by *veto* (q.v.).

In the early 18th century, to reject a person considered for a position:

1706 Sewall *Diary* II.162. In stead of the Negativ'd were chosen B. Brown, 55, Ephr. Hunt, 42.

Negative with the meaning of to forbid or veto an act was used by Jefferson in the Declaration of Independence—

Determined to keep open a market where Men should be bought and sold, he has prostituted his negative for suppressing every legislative attempt to prohibit or to restrain this execrable commerce.

—and was the favored word throughout the first decades of the Republic:

1792 Jefferson *Works* IX.115. A few of the hottest friends of the bill expressed passion but the majority were satisfied and both in and out of doors it gave pleasure to have at length an instance of the negative being exercised.

1821 Adams *Works* X.397. While the Senate of the United States have a negative on all appointments to office, we can never have a national President.

1832 Webster *Works* III.423. It [Congress] has acted, and its act has been negatived by the President.

1834 in *Reg. of Deb.* I.792/1. His power of veto is not a legislative power—it ought to be as it is, a mere negative.

negrophilist.

Epithet applied to abolitionists by Southerners; later to Republicans:

1842 in Longfellow *Life* I.449. When the Eastern negrophilists are prepared to pay a tax, they will. . . .

1848 Theodore Parker *Works* II.79. [letter from slaveholder] . . . we can only be so informed by such infinatessimal [sic] atoms of vanity and mental rascality as you Negrophilists.

1848 *John Donkey* 232 . . . to be ridiculed by a woolly-hearted negrophilist. . . .

1858 *At. Mon.* II.753. Mr. Cushing knows very well that the multitude have nothing but a secondary office in the making of Presidents, and addresses to them only his words, while the initiated alone know what meaning to put on them. If, for example, when he says *servant* he means *slave,* when he says *Negrophilist* he means *Republican,* and when he says *false philanthropy* he means *the fairest instincts of the human heart,* we have a right to suspect that there is also an esoteric significance in the phrases, *Loyalty to the Union, Nationality,* and *Conservatism.*

negro supremacy.

A counter-charge to *negro equality,* designed to sway those who were luke-warm in favor of negro equality by forcing them to choose between the two extremes, supremacy or inferiority.

1867 S. Carolina Conv. in *Appleton's* 700/1. What do these Reconstruction Acts propose? Not negro equality, merely, but negro supremacy. In the name, then, of humanity to both races—in the name of citizenship under the Constitution—in the name of a common history in the past—in the name of the civilization of the nineteenth century—in the name of magnanimity and the noble instincts of manhood—in the name of God and Nature, we protest against these Acts, as destructive to the peace of society, the prosperity of the country, and the greatness and grandeur of our common future.

1867 *Harper's W.* 9 Nov. 707/1. Is it to be forever idiotically roaring about the inferiority and barbarism of "niggers," and "nigger equality," and "nigger supremacy". . . .

1868 *Ib.* 22 Feb. 115/2. The Convention now sitting in Richmond is regarded as a body which means to subject the State to negro supremacy.

1868 *Ib.* 19 Sept. 595/1. General Longstreet says . . . that the whites of the South know that the talk about "negro supremacy" is gammon.

1875 *Cong. Record* 43 Cong. III.65. App. The South never looked to anarchy or chaos as their desperate deliverance from negro supremacy.

negro thieves.

1832 *Liberator* 29 Sept. 154/2. The English themselves declare that no people treat their slaves so cruelly as the English and the Americans, and of all negro-thieves and kidnappers, certain it is, that none are so inconsistent and so guilty as American slaveholders.

See MAN STEALER.

nepotism.

Originally the practice of appointing nephews (*nepotes*) and other relatives of the Pope to influential positions.

Popularized by Sumner, who in 1872 berated Grant for favoritism shown to his family:

1872 *Cong. Globe* 4111/3. Here the details are ample; showing how from the beginning this exalted trust has dropped to be a personal indulgence . . . how the presidential office has been used to advance his own family on a scale of nepotism dwarfing everything of the kind in our history. . . .

1872 *Harper's W.* 13 July 546/2. Nepotism. . . . The word nepotism has played an imposing part in the arraignment of the President. . . . Mr. Sumner solemnly appeals to history, cites the terrible example of popes, conjures the image of a monster, and then denounces the President as a nepotist.

The derogatory connotations are still clearly evident in Bierce's satirical definition:

1906 Bierce *Devil's Dictionary* 126. Nepotism—appointing your grandmother to office for the good of the party.

nest egg.

A financial reserve set aside for a period of depression.

Long used in England in its figurative sense, *nest egg* was originally applied to an egg or facsimile which was placed in the nest in order to attract the hen to lay eggs there.

1932 F. D. Roosevelt in *Time* 24 Oct. 15/2. It would be advisable for governments of all kinds to set up in times of prosperity what might be called a nest egg to be used for public works in times of depression.

new deal.

A modern slogan with a very old tradition. Soon after the introduction of playing cards, a wealth of metaphors connected with them turns up in European literature. We are interested in those that allude to the distribution of wealth and power within the state and in international relations. In his famous poem "Ich hab's gewagt" (1521) Ulrich von Hutten (Kürschnar, *Deutsche Nat.-Litt.* XVII.ii, 270) says—

Nun ist oft diser gleichen
Geschehen auch hie vor,
Dass ainer von den reichen
Ain gutes spil verlor....
Wil mengen bass die karten.
[I will shuffle the cards in a better way.]
1651 Hobbes *Leviathan* 53. On the contrary, needy men and hardy ... are inclined to continue the causes of war; and to stir up trouble and sedition, for there is

no honour military but by war, nor any such hope to mend an ill game, as by causing a new shuffle.

In American politics of the Jackson period, metaphors of this type occur frequently, probably favored by Henry Clay's alleged gambling activities.

1824 *Cinc. Nat. Rep.* 22 Oct. 2/2. A New Finesse—In Cards! By Henry Clay [head]. A friend of Mr. Clay in New York ... has very wisely published a very patriotic pamphlet, in which he very disinterestedly proposes what may be termed a new finesse in cards, that he who has all the honors and all the trumps shall throw up his hand, and give the stakes to him who holds but one knave, and is playing for the odd trick!

1834 Davis *Downing Ltrs.* 177. Some of you say, the owners of this Bank hain't got no right to a recharter—they have had it long enuf—and its time now to have a new shuffle and cut....

Ib. 180. I won't shuffle and cut with you after that fashion; for make what I might by a new shuffle, I would be asham'd to look one of these innocent foreigners in the face—to say nothin of this long list of widows, and orphans, and trustees of estates, and old folks....

New *Deal* first turns up in an 1834 letter to Biddle—

1834 in James *Jackson* 671 ... a new bank and a New Deal.

—and off and on between this date and the Civil War:

1856 *Cleve. Campaign Dealer* 31 Oct. 3/3. It [Herald] has been shuffling the cards so long in the Kansas game of deception, that it thinks it can make a new deal advantageous to the Buchanan party.

1858 *Toledo Blade* 22 Jan. 2/1. The action of the eighth of January Convention has satisfied nobody, and the people insist on a new deal.

1865 Noah Brooks in Sandburg *War Years* IV.102. The President considers that as the people have voted to keep him in another term because the public good could best be served, he ought to make no changes in office which the public good does not demand; but politicians will not see it in that light, and will avail themselves of the excuse of a new term to have a new deal.

During the Reconstruction Period *new deal* appears quite frequently, sometimes in connection with the spoils system, but more often in utterances that stress the necessity of reorientation in regard to the South:

1866 Nasby *Swinging Round the Cirkle* 109. Wilkes Booth's gost came in, and wanted to know what he wuz to hev in the new deal, "for," sed he, "ef't hadn't bin for me, where'd yoo all hev bin?"
1871 Schurz in *Gt. Deb.* IX.316. There the spoils ahead, with the prospect of "a new deal."
1872 Watterson *Editorials* 40. What we should strive for is moral enfranchisement . . . and this can only be obtained by a new "cut, shuffle and deal" all around.
1874 *Dayton Jrnl.* 17 Sept. 2/2. A "new deal" is just what is needed now, and the people without distinction of party should insist upon it by voting in favor of new men.
1876 Schurz *Writings* III.296 . . . how 60 or 70 or 80 thousand officers are dismissed . . . to make room for a "new deal."
1877 *Puck* 21 Nov. 2/2. He [Bell of Ga.] was of the opinion that in a few millions of years, when all mankind had evolved into a higher order of animal, and there had been a new deal all round, that resumption might be practicable. . . .
1878 *N. Y. Trib.* 31 Aug. 4/2. No more convincing proof of the emptiness of the Democratic claims to the Presidency could be offered than this proposition for "a new deal."

At various times the cry for a new deal was raised by independents:

1882 *Nation* 25 May 433. The languid interest now felt in them is due to the strong suspicion that they originate in a desire for a "new deal."
1893 *N. Y. Trib.* in Funk *Merry-Go-Round* 106. Millions are in distress because hundreds of thousands were misled by an irrational inclination to take a chance of "a new deal."
1908 *Rev. of Rev.* XXXVIII.309/2. The cry of the times is for the square deal. But the Independence party answers, There is no square deal without a new deal.
1924 La Follette *Autobio.* 1117. We [Com. of 100] believe that the time has come for a new deal. . . .

Franklin D. Roosevelt introduced the term in his acceptance speech, July 2, 1932:

Public Papers I.659. I pledge you, I pledge myself, to a new deal for the American people. Let us all here assembled constitute ourselves prophets of a new order of competence and of courage.
1932 Freidel *FDR the Triumph* 315. No one noticed when several hours before on that very day [July 2] in that same hall, John McDuffie of Alabama, in nominating Garner, had intoned: "There is a demand for a new deal in the management of the affairs of the American people."

Roosevelt claimed his source to be Mark Twain:

1945 *Colliers* 1 Dec. The source of the term "New Deal" used by the Roosevelt Administration is still controversial, despite the fact that it was disclosed by the late President himself in a letter which he wrote to the International Mark Twain Society on December 8, 1933. In this letter, F.D.R. stated that he took it "from that passage in the book, *A Connecticut Yankee at King Arthur's Court,* in which the Yankee declares that, in a country where only six people out of a thousand have any voice in the government, what the 994 dupes need is a new deal."

New deal was immediately parodied by such terms as *new dole, raw deal, new delights, jew deal* (see *Am. Speech,* XIV.10) and by attempts to employ other card metaphors:

1932 in *Am. Speech* VIII.20. His promise of a new deal was matched late in the campaign when Hoover described it, rather, as a new shuffle.

new departure.

Both *departure* and *new departure* are well established nautical terms, at least since the 17th century.

1669 Sturmy *Mariner's Mag.* IV.158 [*OED*]. Retain the observed Difference of Latitude . . . and thereby find the observed Departure from the Meridian.

1699 Hacke *Coll. Voy.* I.42 [*OED*]. Next day we took a new Departure from thence.

The first known use of the phrase in political language is clearly a metaphorical adaptation of naval terminology.

1837 in Horton *Buchanan* 223. We are left, at this moment, entirely free to decide what is best to be done with the public money. To use the language of the Senator from South Carolina (Mr. Calhoun), we have reached a point from whence we are about to take a new departure. But three courses have been, or, in the nature of things, can be presented for our selection.

1839 Calhoun *Works* III.399. My aim is fixed, to take a fresh start, a new departure on the States Rights Republican tack.

After the Civil War, when both major parties felt the need of a revision of their principles and policies, *new departure* offered itself as a catching slogan to the advocates of these tendencies. Henry Wilson ("New Departure of the Republican Party," *At. Mon.*, Jan., 1871) said:

. . . That fearful upheaving of everything political and pecuniary, social and religious, the fierce strifes of the field and of the forum, the unexpected though legitimate, results of a disturbance so deep and wide, the new under-currents in the popular mind and heart which have received motion and direction from those great events, have driven and drifted the ship of state from its former course, and rendered necessary new observations, new calculations, and a new departure.

Wilson is still conscious of the connections of the term with nautical speech; he not only uses *ship of state,* but begins with a quotation from Webster's speech of 1830, which is full of naval metaphors:

"Mr. President," said Mr. Webster as he rose in the Senate of the United States to reply to Mr. Hayne of South Carolina, in what is still remembered as the great debate of 1830, "when the mariner has been tossed for many days in thick weather and on an unknown sea, he naturally avails himself of the first pause in the storm, the earliest glimpse of the sun, to take his latitude, and ascertain how far the elements have driven him out of his course. Let us imitate his prudence, and before we float farther on the wave of this debate, refer to the point from which we departed, that we may at least be able to conjecture where we now are. I ask for the reading of the resolution before the Senate."

On the Democratic side the word was used even earlier:

1870 *Ann. of Cleve.* No.3276. Their [Democrats] "new departure" seems to consist not in taking up new men, but in adopting the soured members of all the parties and principles which they have hitherto opposed.

However, what gave the expression its real vogue was speeches by Vallandigham at Dayton and Columbus in May, 1871, advocating a reorientation of his party (*Life of Vallandigham,* 444) :

It is not a New Departure, but a Return; the restoration of the Democratic party once more to the ancient platform of *Progress and Reform.*

In direct contrast to Vallandigham's statement, the reaction to the speech was that *new departure* became the name of the very policy which he had refused to consider a new departure.

1871 Hayes in Williams *Hayes* I.355. The change of principles which a majority of the late Democratic State Convention at Columbus decided to make, commonly called "the new Departure," lends to the pending political contest in Ohio its chief interest.

1872 Durbin Ward *Sp.* 252. Next year [1871] Vallandigham popularized the idea under the name of the "New Departure" and procured adoption by the State Convention.

1874 Foote *Casket* 455. The celebrated New Departure of Mr. Vallandigham.

The nautical background of the metaphor is still evident in 1874:

1874 *N. Y. Trib.* 24 April 3/2. The President has again saved the country. If we may be permitted to use a worn-out figure—the Ship of State, which has been for months floundering about dangerously near the breakers, its sails filled alternately by the opposing blasts of windy debate, or flapping idly, has felt the touch of the Captain's hand at the helm, and has been righted about, on its new departure toward safer seas.

New Idea Republican.

An insurgent Republican; a term that apparently never became well-known outside New Jersey.

1912 Wilson in Davidson *Crossroads of Freedom* 90. I have known the insurgent Republicans a long time. They first began to crop up in that supposedly backward state of New Jersey a great many years ago. There we called them the "New Idea" Republicans, when the idea [that] what the Republicans were doing at Washington was wrong was a new idea— a new idea among Republicans.

1912 *Ib.* 126. They were called at first in New Jersey "New Idea" Republicans, when it was a new idea that a Republican could do wrong. Later in other states they came to be called "insurgent Republicans."

1912 *Ib.* 260. We saw the day in New Jersey when there arose a little group of Republicans who called themselves the "New Idea" Republicans; when the idea of serving the whole people was a new idea with the Republican party.

New Freedom.

The title of a collection of Woodrow Wilson's campaign speeches which became synonymous with the policies of his administration. (See SQUARE DEAL, NEW DEAL, FAIR DEAL.) The collection, announced in the December, 1912, issue of *World's Work,* appeared in that publication from January to July, 1913. The title is taken from the last chapter:

1913 *World's Work* XIV. 309. And the day is at hand when it shall be realized on this consecrated soil—a New Freedom—a Liberty widened and deepened to match the broadened life of man in America. . . .

Theodore Roosevelt was quick to recognize the potency of such a slogan and to voice his opinion of its meaning:

1913 *Works* (Mem. ed.) XIX.519. The "New Freedom" is nothing whatever but the right of the strong to prey on the weak. . . . The "New Freedom" when practically applied turns out to be that old kind of dreadful freedom which leaves the unscrupulous and powerful to make slaves of the feeble.

1913 *Ib.* XIX.541. A patient and sincere effort to find out what Mr. Wilson means by the "New Freedom" leaves me in some doubt whether it has any meaning at all. ... the phrase "New Freedom" must stand as any empty flourish of rhetoric, having no greater and no smaller value than all the similar flourishes invented by clever phrase-makers whose concern is with diction and not action. **1925** Coan *Red Web* 47. How the reds, the pinks, and the putty-colored protagonists of "the new freedom" hated Palmer, and Judge Anderson, and Judge Landis!

new light (Democrat).

Attested since 1743 as a term for a member of various groups in sympathy with the revival of religious zeal and in particular with seceders from the regular Presbyterian church (See *DA, new light*), *new light* also became a name for a faction of the Democratic party. The nickname was probably influenced by the loco foco incident (q.v.). One of the accounts of the struggle within Tammany Hall refers to the new faction as "new lights" in a way in which it is apparent that the lighting of the loco foco matches was a factor in the choice of words:

1835 *Niles' Reg.* 7 Nov. 153/1. The veteran political hucksters and their satellites were turned out of doors by the new lights, whom last year they themselves fell down and worshipped. **1840** Kennedy *Quodlibet* 107, 126. This thing is certain, that the New Light Democracy will undoubtedly go with the government. . . . 126. I am an old, tried and trusty, unflinching and unterrified Quodlibetarian New Light Democrat. . . . **1842** *Cinc. Giraffe* 10 Sept. 2/1. Locofocos. It is high time the Democratic party was purified by casting out the New Light Democrats, the Radicals and the Destructives.

1848 *Old Zack* 1 July 2/1. Mr. Tappan ... gave the meeting to understand that he was opposed to the old hunker democracy, and should go with the New-York barnburners, or new light democrats, who have set themselves up in opposition to the Cass wing of the party.

nigger broker.

A slave trader.

1857 Congdon *Trib. Essays* 11. He is no mere "nigger" broker, although with commendable modesty he so writes himself upon his business card.

nigger in the woodpile.

A hidden difficulty or trap.

A. Apparently a reminiscence from the days of the Underground Railroad, whose members used specially constructed woodpiles in which to conceal fugitives:

in Siebert *Underground Railroad* 63. A station-keeper at Plainfield, Illinois, had a woodpile with a room in the centre for a hiding place. **1947** *Ohio Arch. & Hist. Qrtly.* July 272. The rear basement of the chapel [of Methodist preacher Jason Bull]was piled high with hickory wood for the winter's use. That wood was so arranged that it walled in a number of small rooms for concealing fugitives. [Information furnished by W. H. Siebert.]

B. In metaphorical uses:

1846 *Ohio Statesman* 8 July 3/2. Cannot the Whigs trust their "democratic laws" with the people? Ah! no.—They smell a "rat." They talk as though there was a "nigger in the woodpile.". . . **1848** *Ann. of Cleve.* No.913. . . . now we ask any man of common sense, if it is not strange that General Taylor should have refused those letters? . . . Perhaps "There is a nigger in the woodpile" somewhere and perhaps there aint. **1866** Wilson *Slave Power* III.652. So afraid, in the slang parlance employed on the occasion were they of the "nigger in the woodpile."

1876 *Cong. Record* 5153/1. If some one should say that my motives were mysteriously concealed, that there was some "nigger in the wood-pile," some "cat in the bag," some motives to actuate me.

C. Attempts were occasionally made to lessen the vulgarity of the phrase (as in the case of *whole hog,* q.v.) :

1858 Lincoln *Works* II.445. They begin to think there is a "negro in the fence,"—that Douglas really wants to have a fuss with the President....

1865 *Cairo Daily Dem.* 4 Oct. 4/3. The house filled, the audience became anxious for a little gushing melody, but not a gush was heard, and it was soon evident that a "free American of African descent" had become secreted in the woodpile.

1866 Dye *Hist. of the Plots and Crimes of the Gt. Conspiracy* 25. One man in the Senate and one in the House had sagacity enough to see the black man in the fence.

1947 *Chic. Sun* 20 Oct. 54/1. The fact that he [Eisenhower] is supported by some people who believe in the United Nations is evidence [according to Chic. Trib.] that he must be a "new Willkie in the Republican woodpile."

nigger worshipper.

Disparaging term applied to those who sought to improve the status of the Negro, particularly to members of the Republican party before the Civil War:

1856 *Cinc. Daily Enquirer* 7 May 4/1. The Nigger worshippers, or Black Republicans, will meet in Philadelphia to make nominations on the 17th of June.

1856 *Marshall* (Michigan) *Statesman* 13 Aug. 2/3. "Nigger Worshipers." This choice epithet has been generally applied to the Republican Party, by their opponents.... Let it not be forgotten, that three slaves out of every five make one vote for the slave holder. This is the god that slaveholders ... are kneeling down to and worshipping ... [Northern Democrats were compelled] to bow down in

the dust, and become humble and servile "negro worshipers." Douglas is the great High Priest of "negro worshipers."

Despite this attempt to shift the term to the opposition, it is obvious that *negro worshipping* remained associated with the Republican anti-slavery advocates:

1874 DeForest *Honest John Vane* 29. Don't go into the war memories and the nigger worshipping; all those sentimental dodges are played out. Go into finance.

noble experiment.

A satirical synonym for *prohibition* based upon a statement of Herbert Hoover's:

1928 Hoover in Mencken *Am. Language.* Suppl. I.303n ... a great social and economic experiment, noble in motive.

1928 Will Rogers *Autobio.* 184. He [Hoover] said prohibition was a "noble experiment," and he believed in noble things, even if they were only experiments.

1932 *New Rep.* 22 June 141/2. He once called prohibition an experiment noble in purpose—which sounds well, means nothing and commits him to no stand.

1932 *Ib.* 13 July 232/2. The noble experiment had been put on the spot four hours back [at Democrat Convention] and everybody was hep.

1932 Mencken *Making a President* 7.... not a few delegates and alternates had to be taken to spas when the Apostle of the Noble Experiment was finally nominated.

The phrase has been used earlier in American politics:

1861 in *Northern Editorials* II.946. Here ... where political freedom is conducting her noblest experiment among men.

no face.

1852 *Am. Whig Rev.* 128. Northern politicians with a Southern policy have received the name of "dough-faces" from the facility, we suppose, with which they receive impressions.... Now, since the

Virginian delegation were the nominators of the "horse" of the Convention, we shall have to call the Northern men of that Convention, not dough-faces, but no-faces . . . there is no face at all.

See DOUGH-FACE.

nominal candidate. [ ]
1888 *Nation* 23 Aug. 141/1. The Nominal Candidate must have enjoyed reading the accounts of the scene at Portland, Wednesday week, when the Real Candidate "struck the keynote of the campaign."

non-interference.
Synonymous with *non-interven-tion* (q.v.) ; used in Polk's Annual Message of 1848:
in *Gt. Deb.* IV.167. If Congress, instead of observing the course of non-interference, leaving the adoption of their own domestic institutions to the people who may inhabit these Territories. . . .
1860 Douglas in *Gt. Deb.* V.235. So long as the people of a Territory want slavery, and say so in their legislation, the advocates of the caucus platform are willing to let them have it, and to act upon the principle that Congress shall not interfere. They are for non-interference so long as the people want slavery, so as they will provide by law for its introduction and protection. . . .

non-intervention.
A prominent word in the vocabulary of post-Napoleonic reaction in Europe. In the U.S. it originally designated the principle of letting slavery alone:
1849 in Schucker *Life of Chase* 102. For what will be the cost to the Democracy of the alliance with the slaveholders in a presidential campaign? . . . It is non-intervention upon the subject of slavery. That is, Northern men may think and act at home as they choose, and Southern men likewise; but when Northern men and

Southern men meet at Washington either in executive or legislative capacities, they must not take any action against slavery, but leave the slaveholders at liberty to introduce slaveholding wherever they can.

From a speech by Douglas in 1860, it appears possible that the phrase had been used [as early as 1848] by Yancey of Alabama (*Gt. Deb.*, V.231).

From Schucker's [p. 120] account (see below) of the debates of 1850 it appears that the application to the territorial question is due to Jefferson Davis.
in *Cong. Globe* 31 Cong. 1 sess. 261. We ask you to give us our rights by Non-Intervention; if you refuse, I am for taking them by Armed Occupation.
1854 *Washington Union* [20 Jan.] in Schucker 138. To repeal the Missouri Compromise might, and according to our view, would clear the principle of congressional non-intervention of all embarrassment. . . .
1855 *Marshall* (Mich.) *Democratic Expounder* 25 Oct. 2/3. It is evident that the next presidential campaign will turn upon the direct issue of intervention or non-intervention, by Congress, in the domestic affairs of the territories . . . the principle of non-intervention will triumph.

In commenting on Jefferson Davis' attitude, Schucker makes the following remark (p. 120) :
This amendment covered the doctrine of "non-intervention," as Mr. Davis said, though at the same time he alleged that by the adoption of it the Senate would recognize—by strong implication at least— the existence of slavery in the Territories; that at any rate it would recognize the constitutional right of slaveholders to carry their slaves into the Territories and hold them there, and enjoy the fruits of their labor; rather a remarkable kind of non-intervention.

This inherent dishonesty of the word, reminiscent of Talleyrand's definition (in Guedalla *Wellington*, p. 391) —

"un mot metaphysique et politique qui signifie à peu près la même chose qu'intervention"

—may have been the reason why it was largely replaced by *popular sovereignty, squatter sovereignty* and *self-government*.

The interest in competition between these terms is illustrated in a speech by Douglas of May 15, 1860:

in *Gt. Deb.* V.228. The facts stated in the speech of the Senator from Mississippi conclusively show that the doctrine of squatter sovereignty, or popular sovereignty, or non-intervention, as the Senator has indifferently styled it in different parts of his speech, did not originate with me in its application to the Territories of the United States. . . .

Later used with special reference to the right of the territories to make their own laws in regard to slavery.

normalcy.

Introduced into the political vocabulary by Warren G. Harding in 1920 in a pre-convention speech in Boston:

in Allen *Only Yesterday* 41. America's present need is not heroics but healing; not nostrums but normalcy; not revolution but restoration; . . . not surgery but serenity.

The phrase *return to normalcy* became the key word of the post-war era, degenerating quickly into a term of ridicule and abuse.

1920 letter to Harding in *Selected Ltrs. of William A. White* 10 July 206. My mail is full of cantankerous letters. . . . They

don't like this "back to normal" business. **1920** *Nation* 13 Oct. 394/1. At Marion they are busy building a super-cabinet to function around a "normal" President. **1920** *Emporia Gazette* 3 Nov. Here's hoping he [Harding] will face forward and forget old "normalcy." **1930** Richberg *Tents of the Mighty* 103. The Spoils of Normalcy [head].

The satire of the phrase was made even more pointed in a White editorial "Back to Abnormalcy" (*Emporia Gazette*, 1 Aug., 1922).

In later uses *normalcy* became synonymous with reaction and extreme conservatism:

1936 *Rev. of Rev.* XCIV 26. Unquestionably the pressure is on now, not for a return to "normalcy," but for a return to balance; not for extreme reaction, but for reasonable moderation. **1943** Cross *Conn. Yankee* 346. It became clear that Republican policies in prime essentials aimed at "a return to normalcy" though that phrase could not be safely used, for normalcy now had come to mean Herbert Hoover. **1948** *Time* 28 June 12/1. The Republican Party . . . is composed of two factions: responsible progressives and conservative standpatters who hanker for "normalcy."

Northern man with Southern principles.

Apparently coined by Ogle in an anti-Van Buren speech during the campaign of 1840.

1840 in Lynch *Epoch* 447. And where was Van Buren in the War of 1812? Opposed to Madison and the war along with the Federalists and the Peace party who supported DeWitt Clinton for President. Ogle appealed to the prejudices of the South by recalling that one of the reasons advanced by Clinton's friend for their opposition to Madison in 1812 was that Madison "is devoted to the Southern policy." Continued Ogle, "Was it a crime then to be 'a *Northern* man with *Southern* principles?'

...." Ogle played with the phrase "*a Northern man with Southern principles.*" What would the Southerners think of a Southern man with Northern principles? **1840** in Norton *Tippecanoe* 316. In conclusion, said Governor Call, what is the great argument that Mr. Van Buren addresses to the South? He is a Northern man with Southern principles. **1840** *Niles' Reg.* 18 April LVIII.103/2.... to support the re-election of Mr. Van Buren because he is "a northern man with southern principles!" **1841** *Ib.* 17 July 309/1. I would as soon have a "northern man with southern principles," as a southern man with exclusive southern spirit. **1848** *Cleve. Herald* 26 May 2/1. Gen. Cass has received the nomination of the Democratic National Convention as the "Northern man with Southern principles." **1864** *Mirror of Democracy* 247. The speech of this "Northern man with Southern principles" [Seymour].

Evidence that we may expect to find the phrase or its reversal earlier in American politics:

1836 Mrs. Child *An Appeal* 120 . . . on all occasions, some little support has been given to Northern principles in Maryland, Virginia and South Carolina; because in portions of those States there is a considerable commercial interest. . . .

nose of wax.

A thing or person easily moulded to one's liking.

The Latin *cereus nasus* is attested in Alain of Lille (c 1203).

A. Found as early as the 16th century in England to refer to interpretations of the Scriptures, This theological use is probably connected with the German usage represented in such writers as Luther. (See Grimm, *DWB*, *wächsern*.)

1532 Tindale *Expos. Matt.* vi.23 [*OED*]. If the Scripture be contrary, then make it a nose of wax and wrest it this way and that way till it agree. **1589** Cooper *Admon.* 58 [*OED*]. Affirming . . . that the Scriptures are darke . . . because they may bee wrested every way, like a nose of waxe, or like a leaden Rule.

B. The influence of the Scriptural allusions is clearly seen in the early American political usages.

1824 *Cinc. Nat. Rep.* 15 Oct. 3/1. He [Clay] has thus . . . endeavored to make of the constitution a mere *nose of wax,* and *by construction,* destroying all our *past notions, that we have any constitution.* **1827** *Liberty Hall* 19 July 2/4. [Gen. Jackson] seems pretty much a nose of wax in the hands of his flatterers. **1835** Leggett *Pol. Writings* I.187. But the Constitution, in the Attorney General's plastic hand, is a mere nose of wax, and is moulded into what shape he pleases. **1855** *Ann. of Cleve.* No.2586. The waxnoses of Cincinnati boast loudly of the "great Trimble" meeting held in Cleveland. **1855** *Ib.* No.2900. The pro-slavery Democracy . . . have united . . . with the waxnoses in its county nominations. **1863** Kelso *Stars and Bars* 72. Oh, we must bend a little to the wind; wear a nose of wax for convenience,—incline it toward the South; put on a make-believe face,—and talk secesh.

nullification (nullify, nullifier).

In the Kentucky Resolutions of 1798 the doctrine of nullification was first formulated:

. . . but, where powers are assumed which have not been delegated, a nullification of the act is the rightful remedy: that every State has a natural right in cases not within the compact, (*casus non foederis,*) to nullify of their own authority all assumptions of power by others within their limits. . . .

The connection between the terminology of the Kentucky Resolutions and that of the Nullification controversy of the Jackson period is apparent from Calhoun's South Carolina Exposition in which he specifically mentions the Kentucky and Virginia Resolutions. His use of *nullify* in the Exposition (*Works* VI.38) —

... thus giving to that high tribunal the right of final interpretation, and the power, in reality, of nullifying the acts of the State Legislatures. . . .

—in its reference to the Supreme Court is not directly associated with the States Rights movement with which *nullification* soon after became identified:

1830 *Cinc. Liberty Hall* 24 June 1/2. The Nullifiers of the South are in raptures.
1830 L. Williams in *Mangum Papers* I.372. I am opposed totally to the doctrine of nullification and deny to any State either in convention or the ordinary legislature, the right to secede from the Union unless she proceeds upon the revolutionary principle.
1830 Jackson *Corr.* IV.155. This Tariff excitement is the very thing for Calhoun and Clay, bating a little for the nullifying doctrine.
1831 *Wash. Intelligencer* 2 April 1/1. Mr. Crawford charges Mr. Calhoun with being a nullifier, and neither Mr. Calhoun nor any of his adherents . . . have denied it.
1831 Calhoun *Works* VI.61. This right of interposition, thus solemnly asserted by the State of Virginia, be it called what it may,—State-right, veto, nullification, or by any other name. . . .
1833 *Niles' Reg.* 19 Jan. 332/1. The Winchester Republican defines the difference between nullification and secession to be this: "Come out here, McCarty"—"McCarty, come out here."

Later uses:
1840 Norton *Tippecanoe* App.19. To nullify subs that so long have annoyed us And have fattened themselves from the treasury spoils.
1840 Clay in *Ib.* 206. The practical effect is to nullify the agency of the Senate.
1854 *Liberator* 14 July 110/2. We can nullify the Fugitive Slave Bill. . . . Try a little nullification on our side.
1923 Vizetelly *Padding Pol. Vocabulary.* Nullification, best beloved term of the Anti-Saloon Leaguers in characterizing opposition to the Prohibition Enforcement act. . . .

O

October states.

Those states which held their general elections in October.
1884 *Nation* 16 Oct. 319/1. Efforts are made to carry the October States out of all proportion to their numerical or electoral importance.
1888 *Ib.* 9 Aug. 101/1. This year, for the first time, there are no "October States"—that is to say, none that count, for Georgia, which still elects her Governor in that month, is too one-sided to carry any weight. Pennsylvania held its last October election in a Presidential year in 1872, Indiana in 1880, and Ohio in 1884.

octopus.

Popular stories about a giant cephalopod were revived by fiction writers, the best-known passage, perhaps, being that in Victor Hugo's *Toilers of the Sea,* quoted in *Harper's W.,* 22 April, 1876, "The Devil-Fish."

Applied to big business organizations:
1878 in Tarbell *Hist. Standard Oil* I.182. One refiner after another . . . fell shiver-

ing with dislike into the embrace of this commercial octopus.

1898 H. Demorest Lloyd *Labor Copartnership* 117 ... the English Co-operative Wholesale, which has something of the reputation of an octopus.

1900 *Puck* 27 Jan. 7/1. If Trusts can be platformed to death, the friends of the Octopus would do well to gather at his bedside.

1900 *Rev. of Rev.* XXII.330/1. William T. Wardwell was ... treasurer of the Standard Oil Company, and his connection with the "octopus" had no little to do in engendering the discontent that led to the split in the party in 1896.

1901 Norris *The Octopus* [title].

off horse.

A party malcontent.

1879 *Harper's W.* 682. There is often within the party itself a troublesome body of "off-horses," which is roundly cursed as impracticable and "sore-headed," but which, nevertheless, must be considered.

See BOLTERS.

off year.

A year in which there is no presidential election, usually characterized by a scarcity both of issues and of voters.

1873 *Garfield-Hinsdale Ltrs.* 247. Almost one half is lost because it is the "off year" in politics. ...

1876 *N. Y. Trib.* 17 Oct. 4/2. We are told that Mr. Tilden ran in an "off year," when the full strength of parties was not polled.

1877 *Ib.* 19 Nov. 4/5. The Republican party can stand an off-year, provided there is an extra session of Congress thrown in.

1882 *Cong. Record* 277/2. It is true this was in the off year, and not the Presidential year.

Ohio idea.

A. The common idea that the word originated in Ohio in 1867 is,

so far as we can see, entirely without foundation.

DAH "Ohio idea" refers to the proposal to redeem the five-twenty bonds in greenbacks instead of coin (1867–68). Launched as an inflationary measure by the Cincinnati Enquirer, its popularity forced both political parties in the Middle West to endorse it, although neither committed itself outright to inflation.

DAB "Pendleton." If he did not originate the "Ohio Idea" of paying the 5–20 bonds in greenbacks instead of coin, he, at all events, early in 1867 sponsored the proposal.

In 1865, when the formula is first attested, it does not refer to money questions but to the distribution of representation for the Southern states on the basis of actual voters rather than of population.

1865 Williams *Hayes* I.278. [The caucus] adopted, on a test vote the Ohio idea.

B. In 1875 and the following years the description of monetary policies in Ohio give rise to the phrases *Ohio doctrine, -platform, -programme, -heresy, -folly,* all referring to plans along the lines advocated by the Greenback Party.

1875 Williams *Hayes* I.393. This Ohio doctrine inculcates the abandonment of gold and silver as a standard value. ... The only currency of the people is to be paper money.

1875 *Ohio St. Jrnl.* 23 June 1/1. "The Ohio folly" is what the Democratic New York World calls the rag money platform of the Ohio Democracy.

1875 *Ib.* 1 July 2/1 ... this Ohio programme is a serious drawback.

1875 *Ib.* 6 July 1/2. Now it [*N. Y. World*] saves itself from a pitfall of its own digging by arguing that the influence of the Ohio platform will be mainly local.

1876 *Cinc. Enquirer* 29 May 4/3. It does appear that the Ohio doctrine is not without strength in the Southern States.

1876 *Ib.* 29 May 4/4. Nowhere in the South has the Ohio heresy taken so deep roots as in Tennessee.

1876 *Ib.* 1 July 4/2. Two years ago this greenback, currency reform idea was as a little cloud out of the sea. . . . No longer ago than last October Stewart L. Woodford taunted General Ewing in that joint debate with the statement that the Ohio doctrine had in all the land only succeeded in capturing a scanty majority fraction of an adjoining State. . . . what he called the Ohio "heresy."

The phrase *Ohio idea* itself emerges in 1878 and from then on gains the upper hand over its earlier synonyms.

1878 *Cinc. Enquirer* 6 June 4/2. Ten years ago the Republicans of Indiana and Ohio, and of half a dozen States in the North-west, adopted the Ohio Democratic idea, and repudiated it when in power.

1878 *Ib.* 25 June 4/2. Thousands outside of Ohio are anxious to see if, as the "Ohio idea" is marching steadily to victory in all the States, the Ohio Dem. Conv. will falter in affirming the Ohio Democratic belief.

1878 *Ib.* 1 July 4/1. The "Ohio idea" is a phrase found in every newspaper in the land.

1878 *Ib.* 16 July 4/2. The green back idea, the Ohio doctrine, stands now in the political discussions of the country as the name of the various phases of currency reform that are popularly and clamorously demanded. The remedies needed group about this phrase and this idea. . . . In two of the New England States the Democratic party has adopted the Ohio idea.

1878 *N. Y. Trib.* 22 July 4/5. There is no doubt that The Cincinnati Enquirer is right in claiming that the National Democratic party is virtually unanimous to-day in favoring the "Ohio-idea," which was born, nurtured, and reared in The Enquirer office.

1878 *Ib.* 10 Aug. 4/5. The "Ohio idea" is simply the rag baby galvanized into life again and rechristened.

1878 *Harper's W.* 2 Nov. 866/1. The Republicans had not expected so large a majority even if they carried the popular vote, and the Democrats did not believe the Republicans could prevail against the "Ohio idee."

1879 *Council Bluffs Nonpareil* in *N. Y. Trib.* 7 Jan. 5/1. Any list of the illustrious dead of 1878 is manifestly incomplete which does not include "The Ohio Idee."

1881 *N. Y. Trib.* 28 May 4/3. Garfield . . . made Ohio the grave-yard of "the Ohio idea."

C. Also used in a wider sense, sometimes facetiously.

1878 *Wilkesbarre Spirit* in *Cinc. Enquirer* 5 Dec. 4/8. The "Ohio idea" is to get all the offices you can and hold on to all you can get.

1879 *Harper's W.* 14 June 472. [Nast] Columbus, Ohio. June 4th. Democratic Convention. The Ohio Idea. That the road to the White House is through the Gubernatorial Chair.

1886 Poore *Rem.* II.349. Mrs. Hayes brought with her from her rural home what was known as "the Ohio idea" of total abstinence from intoxicating drinks, and she enforced it at the White House.

1903 *Rev. of Rev.* XXVIII.161. [Cartoon: TR straddling two bucking horses] "The Ohio Idea. Hands off the tariff." "The Iowa Idea. Tariff Revision Policy."

O. K.

A. The numerous earlier theories about the origin of *O. K.* surveyed in Mencken (*Suppl.*) have all been superseded by Read's article "The Evidence on 'O.K.'" (*Sat. Rev. of Lit.*, 19 July, 1941). His findings show that the letters had definitely from their first appearance a political meaning. Among the numerous Democratic clubs of New York there was one that adopted the abbreviation of *Old*

Kinderhook, a well known nickname of Martin Van Buren, whose birthplace was Kinderhook, N.Y. The first public appearance is an invitation to a meeting scheduled for March 24, 1840.

A few days later the letters appear at the head of an advertisement evidently directed to the members of the O.K. Club and advising them to be present at a Whig meeting.

B. If the intention was to cause disturbances, it was certainly fulfilled, since the meeting ended in a veritable riot—a riot that naturally attracted much attention and caused the letters *O.K.* to be widely known. During the following campaign the abbreviation spread over the whole country—to begin with, as a caption that announced Democratic successes. Later the Whigs followed the Democratic practice by using *O.K.* as a symbol for victory.

B. 1. Used in Democratic papers:
1840 *Ohio Statesman* 21 April 3/1. Democracy Triumphant! O.K. The British Whigs defeated. K.O.
1840 *Ib.* 2 Oct. 2/6. Democrats O.K. in Delaware.
1840 *Ib.* 24 Oct. 4/1. All Hail Pennsylvania! The Old Keystone O.K.

B. 2. In Whig papers:
1840 *Rough-Hewer* 253/1 [inscription on banner]. We rise to conquer—O.K.
1840 *Ib.* 14 July 4/1. O.K. Sickness.—head it O.K., and we'll say in November The State of Ohio for Martin will go.
1840 *Log Cabin* in *Ohio Confederate* 23 Dec. 1/5. Spirit of the Loco Foco Press. Blarney before election: Dear People! nobody but us can imagine how pure, patriotic, shrewd and sagacious you are.... You are always as right as a book, and

nobody can gum you. In short you are O.K.

B. 3. Used satirically in Whig papers:
1840 *Harrison Dem.* 2 July 3/1. O.K. The Ohio interpretation of this cypher is Oll for Korwin.
1840 *Ib.* 14 July 4/1. O.K. Sickness.—Benj. S. Tuleg, the locofoco candidate for Lieut. Governor of Indiana has declined the honor of being beaten. "Bad health" is the alleged cause of his declining.
1840 *Straight-out Harrisonian* 9 Oct. 3/3. An exchange paper gives the following definition of "OK:" "OK—Ohio Koming—Ohio Korrect—Orful Katastrophe—and in a few days we may say, Ohio for Korwin." The Whig definition of O.K. is— Oll Koming. Locofoco definition—Orful Katastrophe.
1840 *Ohio Confederate* 5 Nov. 3/3. O.K.K. Orful Konspiracy Krushed.
1840 *Tornado* 19 Oct. 1/3. New Definition.—The Wheeling Times, noticing the result of the Ohio election, heads an article in this wise—O.K. over kalculation.
1840 *Ib.* 21 Oct. 1/2. Still Another.—O.K. —Since the Maine election, Amos Kendall's children are O.K. (Oll krying.)
1844 *Ohio St. Jrnl.* 3 Sept. 3/2. Old Knox oll for Klay [head].
1854 *Ann. of Cleve.* No. 1706. When the Plain Dealer pronounced New Hampshire "O.K.," we presume its editor meant "Oil [sic] Kaved."

C. Already in 1840 we find *O.K.* in its general, modern usage.
1840 *Ohio St. Jrnl.* 7 Aug. 3/2. He looks at it, and if it is O.K. he draws two checks on the Bank of America.
1840 *Richmond Whig* 13 Nov. 3/4. O.K. Cure Your Colds. Call and buy some of J. Pease & Son's clarified Essence of Hoarhound Candy.
1840 *Raleigh Reg.* 1 Dec. Go to it tulips! you, at least are O.K.

D. There are indications that as late as the Civil War O.K. was still considered a slang expression not to be used by educated persons.

1891 Kirkland *Company K.* 103. "I guess Aleck will come out all O.K.," said Aleck. "All right? Of course he will. . . ."

While nothing is known [has come out] to connect Jackson with the use of O.K., his misspelling of such words as *congress* and *Cuyahoga* offers a plausible background.

1828 *Ohio St. Jrnl.* 24 April 3/5. The Jackson Telegraph acknowledges the gross ignorance of Gen. Jackson, and thinks it rather a recommendation than a disqualification for the office of Chief Magistrate.—"We care not," say the editors of the Telegraph, "if he spell Congress with a K."
1828 *Ann. of Cleve.* No.410. He has mistaken, too, the orthography of Cuyahoga; but we are not surprised at that. Old Hickory and George Kremer would probably spell it with a K.

A cartoon, "Loco foco Consternation or the Orful Kat-Ass-Trophe," that contains the inscription "K.O. that means Kustom Ouse," is of importance to the *O.K.* question only if it is correctly dated to 1836 or 1838, which Weitenkampf considers doubtful. It may very well be from 1840 (*N. Y. Pub. Lib. Bul.* LVI.221).

However, a cartoon bearing the imprint 1838 and representing Van Buren saying "Oh! Kendall." must be given more attention than it has received till now (*Ib.* 225).

old fogy.
A conservative, a hunker (q.v.).
A. The word *fogy,* originally Scottish, was used by Thackeray in *The Book of Snobs,* first published in *Punch,* 1846–7. Probably from

there it found its way into *John Donkey,* which is an imitation of *Punch,* both in style and typographical make-up.

1847 *Punch* 2 June XII.8. ["Snobs of England," xliv] . . . the honest rosy old fogies, the mouldy old dandies, the waistbelts and glossy wigs and tight cravats of those most vacuous and respectable men.
1848 *John Donkey* 22 Jan. I.51. A correspondent asks us what is an old Fogy, and what is the object of old Fogyism. The description of an old Fogy he will find elsewhere in our journal; but the object of old Fogyism is the old Fogy himself—and a very miserable object it is.

Later (5 Feb.) the *John Donkey* transfers the name from the social to the political sphere in an article "The Political Old Fogy."

B. In answer to George N. Saunders, who in the January and February 1852 issues of the *Democratic Review* advocates the infusion of new blood into the Democratic party, John C. Breckinridge says:
1825 in *Cong. Globe* 4 March. App. 302/1. . . . their principles are denounced in the cant language of the day as "old fogyism," and themselves as "old fogies"; and the public is assured that their age, their experience, and the fatality of their birth, make them wholly incompetent to fathom the ideas or control the policy of this generation.

In his rebuttal Saunders says:
1852 in *Dem. Rev.* March. Such have been the antecedents of the young fogy [Breckinridge], who . . . dares to become the advocate of the antiquated gentlemen of moderate capacities and sensitive feeling, against the progress of history and republicanism . . . old fogydom generally, or its youthfully distinguished representative. . . .

C. During the following years the word meant mostly "conserva-

tive Democrat" in contradistinction to "Young America"; occasionally, however, it referred to
conservatives in other parties.

1852 Seba Smith *Thirty Yrs.* 381. The
Douglas team was made up mostly of
young steers.... But it wasn't equal to
the Old Fogies for a heavy pull.
1852 in Hayes *Ltrs.* I.422. The progressive
Whig is nearer in sentiment to the radical
Democrat than the radical Democrat is to
the "fogy" of his own party.
1852 "Warrington" *Pen-Portraits* 55. We
beat the Whigs and fogy Democrats....
1853 *N. Y. Trib.* 17 Feb. 4/4. The old
ones [Young America leaders] are getting quite too old fogyish. Turn 'em out
and try some new ones.
1853 "Warrington" *Pen-Portraits* 205.
[One of the reasons for the defeat of the
new const. in Mass.] The opposition of
the old-fogy Whigs.
1854 *N. Y. sw. Trib.* 5 Dec. 4/1. Wise's
nomination is a staggering blow to the
Old Fogies who have ruled Virginia
despotically for a number of years.
1855 *Boston Eve. Trans.* 7 Feb. 2/4. It is
quite too late for "old fogy" politicians to
cry "keep cool!"

old guard.

The legend that in the battle of
Waterloo General Cambronne refused surrender with the words "la
garde meurt, et ne se rend pas" has
often been debunked (Hertslet,
*Der Treppenwitz der Weltge-
schichte,* 7th ed., Berlin, 1909, p.
389), which, of course, did not
prohibit politicians in the U.S. and
elsewhere to speak of the diehards
of their party as the *old guard,*
sometimes with an unmistakable
allusion to Waterloo:

1844 *Ohio St. Jrnl.* 19 Nov. 3/2. "The
Old Guard knows how to die; but the
Old Guard does not know how to surrender." So said Napoleon on a celebrated
occasion. So will all the Whigs say, on the

present occasion, the country over ... we
have gallant Whig champions and a
glorious cause: "The Old Guard will
never surrender!"
1848 *Reserve Battery* 31 Aug. 2/3. There
was quite a number of the "Old Guard"
of the Whig party, who were rather sitting on the fence awaiting the results of
their [free soil] deliberations.
1849 *Wash. Union* 24 March 3/3. The old
Democratic Guard not dead. [editorial]
1855 in Hambleton *Wise* 92. If the good
old flag ship of Democracy is to go down,
let it be with colors flying ... is token that
the Old Guard may die, but cannot surrender.
1877 in Platt *Autobio.* 86. I may not deserve the distinction of representing that
Old Guard of the Republican hosts.

In 1880 the expression had a new
vogue, being applied to the advocates of a third term for Grant:

1880 in Adams *Storrs* 212. Assailing no
competitor, the rank and file, the Old
Guard, declare that they are for Grant,
because again and again they have
marched under his banners, but never to
defeat,—and every battlefield over which
his flag ever floated was a field of victory.
Ib. 215 [during the Convention, but before the nominating speeches] ... take the
old tried hero,—let us take him if we can
get him; and then I believe, with the old
guard behind him, who have never kept
step in this world to any music but the
music of the Union....
1880 *Cinc. Gazette* 16 June 4/2. And we
may say this for the "old guard" that
stood by Grant in the convention, with
their column not even shaken, that they
do not belong to the class that sulk in the
tent when the battle is on.
1880 in Chidsey *Gentleman from N. Y.*
293. Three hundred and six of them stood
on the burning deck [supported Grant]
whence all but them had fled.... One,
Chauncey I. Filley, went so far as to have
306 Grant medals struck, and he distributed these: they bore not only the
much publicized number, but also the
words "The Old Guard," and thereby

gave Republican reactionaries, when the term Stalwart was outworn, a new title.

Reference to reactionary Republicans in general:

1921 Tumulty *Woodrow Wilson As I Knew Him* 17. All the Old Guard moving with Prussian precision to the nomination of the man who was to destroy for a time the machine rule in New Jersey and inaugurate a new national era in political liberalism.

1931 *Merry-Go-Round* 89. To the social Old Guard of Washington, Charley and Dolly may be a riotous joke.

1960 *Detroit News* 16 Aug. 18B/1. This failure by the Old Guard mentality was, he believed, one reason why the number of registered Democrats outnumber the Republicans.

old line Whig.

Probably the word *line* in this expression derives from the military use of the word. The fact that this use is not documented for the U.S. before 1865 (*OED*) is probably deceptive. It ought to be much older. We base this assumption on passages like—

in Perley *Reminiscences* 116. When Mr. Webster went to the Senate Chamber to reply to General Hayne, on Tuesday, January 20th, 1830, he felt himself master of the situation. Always careful about his personal appearance when he was to address an audience, he wore on that day the Whig uniform, which had been copied by the Revolutionary heroes—a blue dress-coat with bright buttons, a buff waistcoat, and a high, white cravat.

1848 *Reserve Battery* 28 Sept. 2/3 ... the buff and the blue of the old Whig line.

Evidence that the Revolutionary forces of '76, not satisfied with calling themselves Whigs, even adopted the English Whig cos-

tume (see *OED*) is scarce; however, the buff and blue along with other color combinations turn up among the Revolutionary uniforms (Ward, *War of the Revolution, passim*).

Originally *old line whig* must have been an honorary designation.

1856 *Middletown* (N.Y.) *Banner of Liberty* 53. Honor, then everlasting honor, to the wise heads and noble hearts of "old line" Whiggery!

However, frequently the expression is used derisively:

1854 *Chapman's Chanticleer* 28 Sept. 2/7. It should be remembered that most of the big guns in the so called, old line party, were a short time since, the dirtiest kind of whigs.

1856 Strong *Diary* II.293. Mr. Ruggles has been vice-presidenting the Old Line Whig convention at Baltimore.... It looks like a Historical Society or Congress of Antiquarian Associations, rather than a practical political assemblage, for the Whig party is dead, decomposed, and disintegrated.

1858 *Sandusky* (Ohio) *Comm. Reg.* 8 Nov. 2/2 ... Old Line Whigs—those fossils who still claim to be Whigs when no such party organization exists.

1859 Strong *Diary* II.473. ... the Old Line Whigs, the fossil remains of an extinct party.

1877 *N. Y. Trib.* 19 Nov. 1/5. "What about the Old Line Whigs?" "They are all dead."

Also *old line democracy:*

1854 *Chapman's Chanticleer* 14 Sept. 2/5. You can vote the negroes in if you please; and you may call it "old line" democracy....

See also WHIG, FOSSIL, SILVER GREYS, OLD FOGY, OLD GUARD.

omnibus (bill, committee).

Very soon after the popular vehicle named *omnibus* had made its appearance in London and New York (1829, 1830) its name was used in political metaphors.

Irving *Life and Ltrs.* II.455. The great reform omnibus [the Reform Bill] moves but slowly.

In 1842 Thomas Hart Benton came very close to using the term *omnibus bill* when he described a bill containing disparate material:

Cong. Globe App.66. These articles were caught in the omnibus, or drag-net section, which is placed in the rear of the bill.

When Henry Clay in 1850 introduced the famous compromise bill containing eight different and only loosely connected sections, Benton opposed this procedure by calling it "a conglomerate bill" (Benton *Thirty Years,* II.759) and an "unmanageable mass of incongruous bills" (II.765).

On May 6 and later the committee in charge of the bill was called the "omnibus committee":

1850 *Ann. of Cleve.* 6 May No.2348. The omnibus committee of 13 will help in this work.

Ib. 14 May No.2349. At an early hour of the Senate's session to-day, Mr. Clay presented his report of the Omnibus committee.

On May 8 the term *omnibus bill* itself appeared:

Cong. Globe App.524/1. I am opposed to any scheme for qualifying or coupling it [adm. of Calif.] with other arrangements. I am opposed to all omnibus bills, and all amalgamation projects.

From then on the term is used frequently, occasionally shortened to *the omnibus.*

1850 *Cong. Globe* App.913. The hon. Senator says this is an omnibus bill, and that there are three passengers on board legitimately.

1850 *Ann. of Cleve.* No.2393. The bill was announced to the house.... "Long John" rising to his full height, exclaimed, "Give way, gentlemen, for the Omnibus!"

1850 *Cong. Globe* App.1697. I do not desire to see this omnibus coopered up again.

An old tradition ascribes *omnibus bill* to President Zachary Taylor. It seems certain that he used it, but in view of the preceding material quite improbable that he coined it.

1850 Taylor in Barnes *Weed* 178. "Mr. Hamlin," said he, "what are you doing in the Senate with the omnibus bill?" (so-called) then before the Senate. My reply was prompt: "Mr. President, I believe the bill wrong in principle, and I am doing what I can to defeat it."

1850 Clay in Nevins *Ordeal* I.310. He thanked Pres. Taylor for giving the omnibus bill its appellation. "The omnibus is the vehicle of the people, of the mass of the people."

Ency. Brit. 11th ed. XXVI.475 ... his [Taylor's] contemptuous reference to the territorial portion of Clay's compromise measures as the "Omnibus Bill."

Applied to later legislative measures:

1872 Ames *Chron. of 19th Cent.* I.362. The "omnibus bill," so-called, came on last evening, and ... was susceptible of political amendments. They were added and of course a political struggle resulted.

1877 *Puck* April 5/1. The "Omnibus" bill seemed to afford all the amusement the [N.Y.] Senators required.

1888 *Cong. Record* 3793/1. It is very evident that a majority of the members of this House have been tenderly cared for by the committee in the preparation of this omnibus bill.... Wise and sagacious committee!

one and inseparable. [ ]

1830 Webster *Works* III.342. Everywhere, spread all over in characters of living light, blazing on all its ample folds, as they float over the sea and over the land, and in every wind under the whole heavens, that other sentiment, dear to every true American heart,—Liberty *and* Union, now and for ever, one and inseparable!

Whether Webster's phrase is based upon the slogan of the French Revolution, *une et indivisible* (see Desmoulins, *Le Vieux Cordelier, passim*) has still to be investigated.

100 percent American.

A. Mencken (*Am. Lang. Suppl.* I.302) includes the phrase in a list of words coined or revived by Theodore Roosevelt. Higham (*Strangers in the Land*) doubts this, saying that he has not found the word in TR's writings. However, in 1917 Roosevelt used a term that suggests it:

Newer Roosevelt Messages 867. There can be no such thing as a fifty-fifty allegiance here. If the man is not an American, and nothing else, he should be sent out of this country.

100 percent American (*ism*) itself occurs in a speech of July 18, 1918.
Ib. 946 There can be no fifty-fifty Americanism in this country. There is room here only for 100 per cent. Americanism, only for those who are Americans and nothing else.... No man who is not 100 per cent. American is entitled to the support of any party which is itself entitled to be considered an American party.

B. 100-percenters—the name of a short-lived anti-radical group.
1935 *Common Sense* June 24/2. The Hollywood Hussars, Gary Cooper's little private army of 100-percenters, is only one of several groups of "storm-troopers" to bait all radicals.... "Hundred-percenters" like Hearst are all strong on preparing for war.

one idea.

Whether Schouler in speaking of the Anti-Masons as "the first of our moral-idea or one-idea parties" uses the language of his own period or of the time when Anti-Masonism was a living issue cannot be decided at the present time:
1889 Schouler *Hist. of the U. S. of A.* IV.81. This was the first of our moral-idea or one-idea parties, such as leaves the business of government alone.

Already in 1849 J. P. Kennedy applied the term to the Anti-Masons:
Kennedy in *William Wirt* II.301. The most intractable of all men are those whose minds are engrossed with one idea.

But this was probably written after the campaigns of 1844 and 1848, during which the Liberty Party and the Free Soilers had been frequently accused of "one idea-ism."
1844 Hammond *Life & Times of Silas Wright* 478. This [Liberty] party had one article in their creed which they regarded as paramount to all others. Indeed, some of their presses claimed that it was a party of *"one idea."*
1848 *Old Zack* (Columbus, Ohio) 15 July 2/1.... the one idea party or the self-styled exclusive friends of Free Soil.
1848 *Reserve Battery* 12 Oct. 4/4... standing upon a narrow, odious one idea "platform"—a ricketty tripod of abolitionists and bolting whigs and democrats.
1849 *Wash. Nat. Era* 28 June 2/4. The Richmond Whig does not speak intelligibly when it sneers at the One Ideaism of the Free Soil Party.
1854 *Sp. by Gerrit Smith* 377. Assuming, as they did, that I was but a "one-idea abolitionist," they further and very naturally, assumed that I stood up to make

that speech with nothing, but slavery and slaveholders, in my eye.

Later the term was used against the Republican party:

1858 in "Warrington" *Pen Portraits* 232. No: the Republican party's title to support does not consist in its intention to see fair play between slaveholder and non-slaveholder. It consists, in the language of Mr. Seward, in "that very characteristic, which, in the mouth of scoffers, constitutes its great and lasting imbecility and reproach. It lies in the fact that it is a party of but one idea; but that idea is a noble one. . . .

one man power.

A typical expression of American hostility to an excessive assumption of power by any one individual.

Although the earliest quotation is from 1842, the expression probably arose during the Jackson era, along with such other terms as *dictator, King Andrew,* etc.

1842 *Cong. Globe* App.812. Those whose clamors are so unceasing against what they are pleased to call the "one-man power."
1848 Polk in *Pres. Mess. and Papers* IV. 663. The executive veto is a "one man power," despotic in its character.
1848 *The Battery* 28 Sept. 198/1. The Will of the People vs. the One-Man Power.
1875 *Harper's W.* 9 Oct. 828. [Nast cartoon, showing Tilden pulling strings of "N. Y. Democratic Party" puppet] A One Man Power—Pulling The Strings.
1878 *Ib.* 9 Nov. 887/2. The union of all the opponents of Tammany Hall in the city of New York to defeat "the one-man power" of Mr. John Kelly is a very powerful and very promising combination.
1896 *Nation* 16 Jan. 47/3. "One-Man Power" in America [edit. on Venezuelan controversy].
1925 Bryan *Memoirs* 245. We want no one-man power.

open door.

As a symbol for free access to salvation, *open door (gate)* is found in the Bible:

1526 Tyndale *Revel.* iii.8. Beholde I have set before the an open doore and no man can shutt hit.
Isaiah 60.11. Therefore thy gates shall be open continually.
Acts 14.27. And when they were come, and had gathered the church together, they rehearsed all that God had done with them, and how he had opened the door of faith unto the gentiles.

In 1856 Emerson applied the symbol to free trade:

English Traits II.134. England keeps open doors, as a trading country must, to all nations.

When in 1898 it was suggested that China be divided into "spheres of influence," *open door* became the slogan of the English opponents of this idea.

1898 *London Daily News* 25 Jan. 4/7. Why should Russia object to the policy of the open door which has been proclaimed . . . as the essence of British policy?
1898 in *Parl. Deb.* LVI.178. Very precise statements have been made as to the policy which Her Majesty's Government considered to be the true and sound policy as regards the interests of this country. That policy has been generally known as the "policy of the open door."
1898 in *Ib.* LXIV.799. Where is the open door closed?
1898 in *Ib.* LXIV.808. When we talk of the open door we do not mean the planks composing the door, but the room into which the door leads. If the room is occupied you will have accomplished nothing in having the door open.
1898 in *Ib.* LXIV.827. That is the open door of which he [?] spoke when he used that famous phrase which has been quoted and requoted almost *ad nauseum.* I maintain that so far as the open door—

in the only true legitimate sense—is concerned it has never been shut.

1898 *Westminster Gazette* 25 July 1/2. There is no necessary opposition between the sphere of influence policy and the "open-door" policy.

1898 Lord Heresford in Bemis *Am. Sec. of State and Their Diplomacy* IX.137. As America has got over 50% of the import trade into the North of China, it is imperative for American interests as well as our own, that the policy of the "Open Door" should be maintained.

1898 Nation 1 Dec. 408/2. To those who think of what Epictetus meant by "an open door" that expression is now ominously suggestive, as national suicide is not unknown in history, and we may reach it quickly in our land-grabbing designs in the Philippines and the Carolines and Borrioboola Gha.

1899 *Rev. of Rev.* XIX.85. The United States will help the mother country in an open-door policy, but not in a policy of spheres of influence. . . .

The document that gave the term general currency was John Hay's note to the interested powers of September 6, 1899, published on January 2, 1900, in which he adopted the English phrase:

1899 Hay in *For. Relations of U. S. 1899* 132. While concluding by formal agreements . . . the possession of "spheres of influence or interest" in China . . . Her Britannic Majesty's Government has therefore sought to maintain at the same time what is called the "open door" policy.

1900 *Nation* 4 Jan. 1/1. The reported success of Secretary Hay's efforts to obtain a joint international guarantee of the "open door" in China will constitute, if real, a great diplomatic achievement.

1900 *Rev. of Rev.* XXI.39. His great achievement will appear in history as the maintenance of the "open door" in China. . . .

1901 Roosevelt *Works* (Mem. ed.) XVII. 159. [Annual Message] We advocate the "open door" with all that it implies. . . .

1910 T. Roosevelt in Dulles *Forty Years of Am. Jap. Relations* 87. The Open Door policy in China was an excellent thing, and I hope it will be a good thing for the future. . . .

1910 *Lit. Digest* 5 Feb. 214/2. Slamming the Open Door.

The importance of Hay's letter was so considerable that later he was considered the coiner of the phrase. (See Büchman, *Geflügelte Worte*, p.528, who, however, attributes the letter to 1889.)

Later example:

1953 Mockridge and Prall *Big Fix* 333. "I have heard," Silver told Special Sessions Justice Irwin Davidson, "that bookies and policy operators think there's going to be an open-door policy as a result of the new administration at City Hall."

organ.

The international use of *organ* designating a newspaper supporting a particular man or party is first attested in America in 1807:

1807 *Weekly Inspector* 223. But let us hear this mouth-piece [*Nat. Intell.*] of the president, this organ of Presidential will!

1836 *Ohio St. Jrnl.* 28 Oct. 3/1 . . . the Globe, the "official organ" of the "Spoilers."

1848 Hammond *Silas Wright* 346. The journal printed by the state printer was always looked upon as the organ of the administration, and was looked upon with jealousy by the people at large.

1853 *N. Y. Trib.* 17 Feb. 4/4. We do not wonder that their organ is advertised for sale—stock and fluke. But who will buy *The Democratic Review* after all this collapsing of the Young American Leaders. . . .

1860 *N. Y. Trib.* 21 Nov. 4/5. Mr. Lincoln's Organ. [Ref. to new paper in Wash.]

1871 *N. Y. Times* 15 Oct. 4/2. One of the Ring organs sneers at Deputy Controller Green's circular to the City employees under his control. . . .

In 1872 and later the phrase "this is not an organ" was used satirically against the *New York Tribune* after Greeley, the Democratic candidate for President, withdrew as editor.

1872 *N. Y. Trib.* 15 May 4/1. The Tribune has ceased to be a party organ.... The Tribune is not and will nevermore be a party organ.

1872 *Harper's W.* 25 May 416. [Nast cartoon showing Greeley holding horn "N. Y. Trombone."] Whoever calls this an "organ" is "a liar, a villain, and a scoundrel."

1872 *Ib.* 8 June 448. [Nast cartoon showing Whitelaw Reid as organ-grinder with Greeley as his monkey begging votes. Sign on organ, "This is not an organ."] "The New Organ-(we beg the Tribune's pardon) -ization on its 'New Departure.' "

1875 *Ib.* 20 Nov. 937. [Nast cartoon with Reid carrying organ and monkey (Tilden this time). On organ, "This is Not an Organ."]

1874 *Cinc. Comm.* 1 Aug. 4/2. The Boston *Traveller,* the organ of the New England prohibitionists, confesses that liquor is sold freely in Boston and Portland....

organ-grinder (-editor).

The editor of a party newspaper.

In addition to the Nast cartoons (see ORGAN), we have the following editorial examples:

1871 *N. Y. Times* 14 July 4. An Organ-grinder's Grievance. [Reference to Manton Marble, editor of the *World*.]

1871 *N. Y. Trib.* 30 Sept. 4. The platform which Mr. Ellis H. Roberts, Mr. Conkling's organ-editor and Congressman, gave the Convention is about the clumsiest, most spiritless, and tedious piece of platform literature we have encountered.

outrage business (outrage mill).

Exploitation for political purposes of wrongs done to the Negro. (Cf. BLOODY SHIRT.)

1874 *N. Y. World* 20 Aug. 4/6. The fact is, the outrage mill has been started in every Republican newspaper office about the middle of summer every year since the party was formed. The outrage is an indispensable part of the campaign stock in trade.

1875 *Cong. Record* App.2/1. But men can be murdered, American citizens... but it is not exactly right to speak about it in the Senate of the United States; or, if you do, you are engaged in "the outrage business." ... the existence of Ku Klux in the South was denied steadily and bitterly upon this floor. It was called "the outrage business" then as now.

1875 *Ib.* 373/2. Shall we be told that we are talking about the "outrage business" when we mention these things?

1878 *Nation* 26 Dec. 391/1. There are several other gentlemen in Congress who wish to be nominated in 1880, and they have no idea that Mr. Blaine shall run the "outrage mill" as if he had property rights in it. "Outrages" are no man's property, but are a common fund upon which all prominent party men have a right to draw.

outside voter.

A voter brought into a district to help win an election for a particular party or candidate.

1858 *Cong. Globe* 537/2. The evidence conclusively points to John C. Hudelson, clerk of Henry circuit court, as treasurer and principal contractor to furnish "outside" voters for Rush county.

See FLOATING POPULATION, BLOCKS OF FIVE.

P

palace (troops, guard).

During the early decades of the 19th century, the White House was occasionally referred to as the Palace:

1833 *Md. Hist. Mag.* XIII.280. There are other lions in the city—especially the "roaring Lion" up in the Palace, as they call the President's House here.

William Leggett strenuously objected to the usage:

1837 Leggett *Writings* II.189. The above paragraph [from the *Nat. Intelligencer,* in which Palace is used instead of White House] is meant as a serious and plain announcement of a fact in which it was thought the public would take an interest. The word *palace,* therefore, as applied to the President's house is entirely out of place. . . . We have no palaces in this country, as we have no princes.

This use of the word is behind the various phrases referring to supporters of the President as—

Palace troops:

1809 Quincy *Life of J. Quincy* 174. The result [of the voting] was astonishing to Campbell and the leaders of the Palace troops.

Palace guard:

1948 *Jim Farley's Story* 232. Housing Administrator Nathan Straus brought me word that the White House "palace guard" realized the anti-Catholic campaign against me had failed. . . .
1952 *Progressive* Sept. 5/1. The palace guard in the White House had blocked his plans for a genuine housing program.

See also PRETORIAN BAND.

Pan-American (ism).

In its earliest use the term refers to the states of the United States and later to the countries of North, Latin, and South America.

1865 Lieber *Misc. Writings* II.160. Grote, the historian, correctly observes that the distinguished men or states of ancient Greece were always greatest, or truly great, when they were Pan-Hellenic. It

was so in our revolution, and has been ever since so in our history. Has there ever been a great American that was not Pan-American, that is, National-American, or who was not great because he was National-American?
1915 Woodrow Wilson *Public Papers* III. 409. This is Pan-Americanism. It has none of the spirit of empire in it. It is the embodiment, the effectual embodiment, of the spirit of law and independence and liberty and mutual service.

panic session.

Applied to the first session of the 23rd Congress, 1833–4, so named because of financial troubles of the time.

1840 Steenrod in *Cong. Globe* App.402/3. I now, sir, invite the consideration of the House to the operations of the bank, as developed in this report, during the memorable and distinguished years of 1833 and 1834; the period that is known in the history of this body as the panic session of Congress.
1854 Benton *Thirty Years View* I.369/2. On the second day of Dec., 1833, commenced the 1st session of the 23rd Congress, commonly called the Panic Session.

pap.

A term meaning the soft or liquid food upon which babies are nourished, *pap* was adapted to the political vocabulary as a satirical and mocking synonym for *government funds* received either by easy jobs or by graft. It also means a woman's breasts, but in the following quotations, we have made no attempt to separate the two meanings since the context makes the referent obvious. It was early applied to financial matters without application to any individual:

1794 Taylor *Principles and Tendency* 44. It [funding system] is the pap of paper, upon which the child was to subsist, until it was old enough to be weaned.

However, when the government became a lucrative source of income and one which all had an opportunity to share, the "treasury pap" became the sole subsistence of many politicians:

1825 *Delaware* (Ohio) *Patron* 10 Feb. 3/2. An irresistible desire . . . to serve the state, and to taste a little of the "Treasury Pap," impelled us towards the capital. . . .

1828 *Liberty Hall* (Cinc.) 3 April 2/1. Verily friend Kendall has shown that he has procured a portion of the Treasury pap.

1840 *Cong. Globe* App.370. Born of wealthy parentage, he never knew what want was. And why should he? Ever since he left his paternal roof, he has been sucking at the Treasury pap—has been an office holder—and has pocketed from the General Government between seventy and eighty thousand dollars!

Many of the uses of the metaphor were even more barbed and suggested that these office-holders were little more than human parasites, or less:

1829 Jackson *Corr.* IV.20. These are the men who cry out principle, but who are on the scent of Treasury pap. And if I had a tit for every one of these pigs to suck at, they would still be my friends.

1852 Webber *Southern Border* 73. That august official [President of Texas] had far too many hungry pap-seekers clinging to the lean bosom of the home-Treasury to spare one generous drop even for the nourishment of this distant frontier.

1862 in Ranck *Brown* 217. Young, strong men . . . were feeding on government pap whilst wounded soldiers . . . were in a state of positive want.

pariah.

The untouchable caste of India, a word used as an epithet for the slave class and later for lower class in general:

1833 Whittier *Writings* 68. Compelled to perform the despised offices of the slave, they can hardly rise above his level. They become the pariahs of society.

1877 Dacus *Gt. Strikes* iv. In the large cities the cause of the strikers was espoused by a nondescript class of the idle, the vicious, the visionary and the whole rabble of the Pariahs of society.

parlor Bolshevist.

See PARLOR SOCIALIST.

parlor radicalism.

1922 White *Editor and His People* 332. He never will be a pink pioneer in the ranks of parlor radicalism.

parlor socialist.

A term applied around 1906 to the socialites who felt it to be the fashionable thing to hold socialistic ideas:

1906 Sullivan *Our Times* III.428. Wealthy young gentlemen and ladies taking up Socialism, Socialism as an incident of pink teas, current prevalence of a type later denominated by Roosevelt "parlor Socialists". . . .

Another writer, Gilbert (*Lost Chords,* p. 286) attributes the term to Woodrow Wilson; however, no documentation is offered. Although there is no evidence for the use of *parlor socialist* in 1906, the frequency of other synonymous terms indicates that the concept was a popular one at that time.

1906 *Nation* 8 March 192/2 . . . at the sight of dilettante writers and inheritors of great fortunes going to discuss Socialism at dainty breakfasts. . . .

Ib. 19 April 312/3. "Comic" is the only word to apply to the surprise and pain of our own rosewater and angel-cake Socialists. . . .

The popularity of *parlor social-ism* may have been influenced by the German *Kathedersozialisten,* whose battles in 1875 attracted much attention in America:

1875 *Nation* 4 Nov. 296/1. The name "Kathedersozialisten," given to them as a nickname by their opponents, has been adopted by them in a fit of student-like humor. *Ib.* Treitschke calls the quarrel between the Manchesterians and the "Kathedersozialisten" a windmill-fight. . . .

A variant of the phrase, *parlor Bolshevist,* was used by T. Roosevelt in 1918 in an article in the *Metropolitan Magazine:*

in *Life and Messages* III.1043. Prominent, although not always powerful, among the latter are the professional intellectuals, who vary from the softhanded, noisily self-assertive frequenters of frowsy restaurants to the sissy socialists, the pink tea and parlor Bolshevists. . . .

1922 Daugherty *Harding Tragedy* 133 [quoted from memory in 1932]. Ten of these directors constituting the cone of the conspiracy appear both in the radical as well as "Liberal" groups and at the same time among the "Civil Liberties," "Parlor Bolshevik" and "Intelligentsia" groups.

party line.

In political battles the opposing forces are divided by issues and policies along lines which a devout partisan would never presume to cross. *Party line* may refer either to the principles of the party or to the party itself.

1834? Benton *Thirty Years View* I.431. Look to the memorials, resolutions, and petitions, sent in here to criminate the President, so clearly marked by a party line. . . . Look at the vote in the Senate, . . . also as clearly defined by a party line

as any party question can ever be expected to be.

1843 *Cleve. Herald* 8 Feb. 2/1. The votes on this bill broke down party lines.

1875 in Mayes *Lucius Q. C. Lamar* 148n. I pity the man who in a great crisis says to himself: "I can't go there, because there is the old Whig line; nor there, because that is the Republican line; nor there because I will be compelled to cross the Democratic line." It sometimes happens that a man gets himself into such a condition of mental delusion that old party lines or names are like running water to a witch. Under some mysterious law or eccentric antipathy he can't cross them.

See OLD LINE WHIGS, COLOR LINE.

party orthodoxy.

Rigid adherence to the policies and practices of the party, an acceptance similar to religious belief.

1839 *Cong. Globe* 30 Jan. By this time it had become the test—the touchstone of party orthodoxy. The terrors of denunciation were threatened against every man who would not surrender his independence, his conviction of right, at the feet of the Executive.

1878 *Harper's W.* 5 Oct. 787/2. Democrats were brought into the meetings, their party orthodoxy was attested by the machine-runners, and they supported the machine candidates.

The formula is also varied to *political orthodoxy.*

1858 in Sparks *Deb.* 334. Now, the question arises, What was that English bill which certain men are now attempting to make a test of political orthodoxy in this country?

paster.

See 1885 quot.

1870 *Cong. Globe* 2659/3. There were ten tickets . . . which were scratched and had pasters with the name of Caleb N. Taylor. **1880** *N. Y. World* 3 Nov. 2/1. "Pasters" for W. W. Astor for congress, for Horace Russell for Judge, for Isaacs, for Rollins, and for Hess, abounded on all sides. **1885** *Mag. Am. Hist.* 297/2. Narrow slips of paper gummed on the back and bearing printed names of candidates . . . are distributed by local political leaders prior to or during an election, so that voters may readily re-arrange ballots to suit their own individual preferences. Pasters . . . reduce "scratching" . . . to a system.

See SCRATCHING.

paternalism.

Long a mildly derogatory term for what was held to be the over-concern of the government for the welfare of the people.

1858 *At. Mon.* I. 114/1. Such was the genius of the Lecompton Constitution, and such the nursing it had received at the hands of the paternal government at Washington. **1881** *Chic. Times* 11 June. There is nothing in the proposal that looks in the direction of paternalism, or the ownership and administration of industrial enterprises by the government. **1888** *Overland Mon.* XII.218. A certain trend, in the successive opposing parties toward paternalism and centralization, is unmistakable. **1893** *N. Y. Eve. Post* in W. Funk *Merry-Go-Round* 126. The demand for an appropriation by Congress for the relief of distress caused wholly by unwise laws is the most flagrant form of paternalism. **1897** *Cong. Rec.* 623/1. The "bogy man" of the Government ownership of railroads has seemingly been conjured up . . . to frighten timid legislators, and every time it is mentioned there are loud cries of "Paternalism!" **1897** Depew *Sp.* III.39. Under such conditions [in West. agric.] it is not the workingman who becomes a socialist and a believer in every form of paternalism, but it is the man of small property. **1921** in Crowther *Presidency vs. Hoover*

143. That independence and ability of action amongst our own people which saves our Government from that ultimate paternalism that would undermine our whole political system.

patriot (ism).

The long tradition of public approval of the patriot and patriotism is easily demonstrated:

1644 Milton *Tract. on Educ.* [*OED*]. Enflamed with the study of learning and the admiration of virtue; stirred up with high hopes of living to be brave men and worthy patriots, dear to God, and famous to all ages. **1917** Roosevelt *Works* [Nat. ed.] XIX.181. Patriotism is an affair of deeds, and patriotic words are good only in so far as they result in deeds. . . . Patriotism means service to the nation, and only those who render such service are fit to enjoy the privilege of citizenship.

However, it is equally evident that in all periods we may find those who, following the statement of Dr. Johnson (see 1898 quote), were as strongly critical of the word.

1763 in Adams *Works* II.143. Recipe to Make a Patriot. Take of the several species of malevolence, as revenge, malice, envy, equal quantities; of servility, fear, fury, vanity, profaneness, and ingratitude, equal quantities; and infuse this composition into the brains of an ugly, surly, brutal mortal, and you have the desideratum. **1791** Morris *Works* II.151. As to the state of things here, I would convey it to you as fully as propriety will admit; but I know not yet by what opportunity this letter will go. . . . Every letter I receive bears evident marks of *patriotic* curiosity. **1836** Lydia M. Child *An Appeal* 115. The Southern States have even gone so far on this subject, as to assume the designation of "patriot States," in contra-distinction to their Northern neighbors. . . . It certainly was a pleasant idea to exchange the appellation of *slave* States for that of *patriot* States.

1838 Drake *Tales and Sketches* 91. One of that race of immaculate patriots, whose "constitutional scruples" wouldn't permit them to cross the line, in the late war to whip the British.

1851 *N. Y. Trib.* 2 May 4/3. Thus it is we entertain no doubt that the question of resistance to this [Fugitive Slave] law, now so rife, and so distressing to all manner of cattle who feed at the troughs of trade and the Treasury, so alarming to aldermanic sensibilities and quilted velvet patriotism in general.

1898 Schurz *Sp.* V.464. Disreputable politicians who discover in the general disturbance a new chance for themselves, and who expect the loudest kind of war patriotism to lift them into popular favor and public place, trusting that everything will be forgiven to the "patriot" who is most vociferous in denouncing the enemy. ... This is the class of "patriots" well fitted by old Dr. Samuel Johnson's robust saying, that "patriotism is the last refuge of a scoundrel."

1943 Carlson *Under Cover* 132–3. The Pied Pipers of "Patriotism" [chap. head]. ... My experience convinced me that under the slogans of "patriotism" they were inoculating innocent Americans with the virus of hate, undermining confidence in our leaders, promoting doubt and suspicion.

patronage.

The power over appointments and privileges associated with public services.

A. 1 Originally in England, "the protection and defence of the rights of the Church." (*OED*)

1412 in *Laing Charters* 24 [*OED*]. He ... sal noth iniure na disese the place throuch na titil of patronage bot as it is granttit ... in this indenture.

A. 2 Later applied to powers of the nobility:

1553 T. Wilson *Rhet.* [*OED*] I therefore commende to youre Lordeschyppes tuition and patronage this traictise of Rhethorique.

B. The abuse of this practice and the derogatory connotations which developed with it, carried over into the American political use. Thus, in most instances, *patronage* is a word belonging to the group of such terms as *spoils* and *plunder.*

1792 Morris in Sparks *Life & Writ.* II.259. The ministers possess more patronage than any monarch since Louis the Fourteenth.

1826 in *Covode Rep.* 2. The power of patronage, unless checked by the vigorous interposition of Congress, must go on increasing until federal influence in many parts of this confederation will predominate in elections as completely as British influence predominates in the elections of Scotland and Ireland.

1834 Leggett *Pol. Writings* I.46. We have no objection that the Democratic Committee should glorify that paper, and recommend it to "patronage" (a most undemocratic word, by the way) ....

1877 *N. Y. Trib.* 19 Nov. 4/2. But if the patronage is to be taken away from the Senate only in order that the President and one or two of his Cabinet officers may exercise it in the old way. ...

pay as you go.

Probably based upon a proverbial warning against incurring large debts in taverns.

1855 in Stevenson *Home Book of Proverbs.* Pay as you go and keep from small score.

1879 Williams *Hayes* II.278. One [of Franklin's proverbs] is, "Never live beyond your means"; and the other is like unto it, namely—"Pay as you go."

The political slogan is found in connection with many different financial issues.

1839 in Weed *Autobio.* 458. The Democracy proclaimed itself in favor of the "pay as you go" policy [ref. to Erie Canal].

1847 *N. Y. w. Trib.* 23 Oct. 3/3. "Mr. President," said John Randolph of Roanoke, breaking off abruptly in the midst of one of his Congressional harangues, "I have found the Philosopher's Stone! It is contained in four words: *Pay-as-you-go!*"

1856? in Hollister *Colfax* 116. He opposed the issue of Treasury notes without corresponding levies to meet them. Pay as you go, and collect as you pay, he held to be a sounder policy.

1871 in Williams *Hayes* I.342. The rule "pay as you go" leads to economy in public as well as in private affairs.

1874 in *Cong. Record* App. 147/1. This is the road to financial and commercial independence. The people will then be prepared to appreciate the appropriateness of the remark of John Randolph upon the floor of Congress, when he exclaimed that he had discovered the philosopher's stone, which was simply "pay as you go."

1949 *Sat. Eve. Post* 5 March 34/1. Now, thanks to the pay-as-you-go policy [of income tax], there are many who find they owe the government nothing, and millions find themselves in the pleasant role of creditors.

1960 *Time* 11 April 29/1. But even as popular Newcomer Rockefeller got what he wanted in the way of tax increases and a pay-as-you-go budget....

peace Democrat (democracy).

An epithet levelled against Northern Democrats during the Civil War. The satiric label apparently grew out of such statements as:

1860 in *Vallandigham's Record* 239. That Constitution was made in peace; it has, for now more than seventy years, been preserved by the policy of peace at home, and it can alone be maintained for our children, and their children after them, by that same peace policy.

1862 *Ann. of Cleve.* No.3723. It is strange that the peace Democrats will still insist that the triumph of the Democratic party at the polls is a voice in favor of the government and against the Rebels.

1862. *Ib.* No.3600. A strong opposition party is organizing all over the country. It takes various names. Its leaders are democrats, "peace" democrats, and "conservatives."

1862 *Ib.* No.3468. The Peace Democrats stayed at home to vote.

1864 *Ib.* No.1590. The New York News contains a letter signed "Peace Democrat" favoring the nomination of Fremont.

1864 in Winter Davis *Sp.* 433 ... these are the men who are supporting him [F. Wood]; ... these are the men who represent the great mass and body of the so-called Peace Democracy; and if there be any thing but a Peace Democracy any where that is not now supporting Abraham Lincoln, I do not know who the man is, or where he is.

1877 Wilson *Slave Power* III.556. For not only did the Rebels and peace Democrats make the most of it by stigmatizing him as averse to peace, except on degrading conditions, but it greatly alarmed some of the Republican leaders....

peanut politics.

Petty or unimportant politics.

1887 *N. Y. Mail* 27 May. If the Governor would consent not to play peanut politics.

1895 Myers *Bosses and Boodle* 130. His [Blue Jeans Williams'] efforts at economy were met with ridicule by the Republicans as a "peanut" policy.

1909 *N. Y. Eve. Post* 4 Feb. They used to talk about "peanut politics" at Albany, but a peanut is too large and respectable an object to yield a comparison for yesterday's action of the State Senate.

194– Salter *Am. Politicians* 161 ... he [Maverick] regards the mixing of secret societies and politics, i.e., peanut politics, as not worth the trouble involved.

While most of the quotations are clearly metaphorical (peanut = unimportant or insignificant) the Al. G. Field account of the consumption of peanuts by Columbus (Ohio) politicians suggests a connection not based upon metaphor.

1880 in Al. G. Field *Watch Yourself Go By* 428. Those from the West Side chewed tobacco. All ate peanuts. Special appropriations were requested by John Ward, city hall janitor, to remove the peanut hulls after each talk fest. And thus it was that peanut politics and peanut politicians came to be known in Columbus. Peanut politics like all infections spread until the whole political system became affected.

See SMALL POTATO.

peculiar institution.

A euphemism for slavery.

A. The opinion often expressed by Southern statesmen that the North had no right to interfere with slavery because it did not understand its true character must be considered the ideological background of this phrase. Foreshadowed by Clay, it was first used by Calhoun in the "South Carolina Exposition":

1823 Clay *Works* IV.81. I would not ... give to the peculiar interests of great sections all the protection which they would probably receive if those sections constituted separate and independent States.
1828 Calhoun *Works* VI.59. Finally, because South Carolina, from her climate, situation, and peculiar institutions, is, and must ever continue to be wholly dependent upon agriculture and commerce....
1836 Child *An Appeal* 113. A Southern governor has dignified duelling with the name of an "institution," and the planters generally seem to regard it as among those which they have denominated their "peculiar institutions."
1842 Buckingham *Slave States* 216. Slavery is usually called here "our peculiar institution."
1844 *Wash. Daily Globe* 15 Jan. 51/1. Mr.

Calhoun [stands surrounded] in the South by peculiar interests, feelings, and institutions.

In the North the expression is, of course, used critically and sometimes ironically.

1842 Garrison in *Garrison Story* 50 ... the Democratic party is openly and avowedly the defender and upholder of the "peculiar institution" of slavery.
1847 *Wash. Nat. Era* 8 July 1/2 ... the men who demand that the freemen of the free States should quietly submit to the spread of their "peculiar institution."
1863 Jones *Mirror of Democracy* 261. She [the South] will wonder at her folly in having clung with such tenacity to her "peculiar institution"....

B. The term is found in further developments:

B. 1. applied to institutions characteristic of the North, often humorously:

1852 *N. Y. Trib.* 23 Oct. 6/6. We spent a week among the Mormons, had a very fair opportunity of forming an opinion of them and their (peculiar) institution.
1853 *Harper's Mag.* April 621/1. Pratt, the great expounder of their [Mormon] doctrines, boldly advocates this practice, at the same time explaining the various guards which they profess are thrown around the "peculiar institution" to prevent immoral results.
1855 *Yale Lit. Mag.* XX.278. Yankees do have a weakness for patent medicine. It is one of their peculiar institutions.
1860 Cameron in *Cong. Globe* 15 June. While you, gentlemen of the South, are protecting your peculiar institutions, you ought, at least, not to forget that we of the North have a peculiar institution to protect and encourage—our free white labor.
18— E. Stone *Life of J. Howland* 282. Judge Branch ... welcomed the guests to all the enjoyments of a Rhode Island "peculiar institution" [a clambake].

B. 2. applied to slaves.

1860 *Charleston* (S.C.) *Merc.* 11 Dec. 1/5. I met ... the "peculiar institution" carrying lightwood up the back steps and sweeping the gravel walks. **1861** *Richmond Enquirer* 20 July 3/2. Several "peculiar institutions" were ordered to be punished for various offenses.

C. Occasionally the word *peculiar* in itself takes the sense "connected with slavery."

1862 *Cleve. Herald* 8 Nov. 2/2. A "Peculiar" Case [head].

peeled stick convention. [ ]

1880 in *Cong. Record* 1708/2. Did they not meet in Cleveland in the "peeled stick" convention, all armed and ready to resist the authority of the U.S.?

People's party.

A. To begin with, *People's party* was used not as a party name proper but as a designation of persons who regardless of party affiliations had the common interest of the people as a whole at heart.

1811 *Niles' Reg.* I.9/2. I will attach myself, as an editor, to no party but the People's Party, whose wish is "peace, liberty and safety."

Repeatedly the phrase was used as a clear party name. The following list is probably very incomplete:

1823 Van Buren *Autobio.* 144. The people's party—a temporary faction generated by the refusal of our friends to pass the Electoral law. **1854** *Ohio Statesmen* 10 June. The Cleveland Herald says that at this forthcoming Convention will be "inaugurated the Party of the People".... What is the object, the practical end, of this People's Party? **1856** Julian *Recoll.* 155. In my own state the opposition to the Democracy repudiated over the name Republican and entered the field as "the People's party."

1874 *N. Y. World* 11 Aug. 1/6. The People's Party Movement [head]. *Ib.* 5 Sept. 2/3. There is an attempt to organize a third party, to be called the "People's party"....

B. In 1891 the term acquired national significance by the action of a convention held in Cincinnati, May 19, that adopted it officially as the name of an organization opposed to money power, railroads, trusts, etc.

Cincinnati Platform in Hicks. *The Populist Revolt* 433 ... we believe that the time has arrived for a crystalization of the political reform forces of our country and the formation of what should be known as the People's party of the United States of America.

Almost from the beginning the use of *people's party* was restricted by the competition of *Populist Party* (q.v.) .

people's ticket.

A slate of candidates sponsored by no traditional party organization. It is interesting to note that in 1856, in its first national election, the Republican party was so designated.

1823 *Cinc. Nat. Rep.* 21 Nov. 2/2 ... the *People's Ticket,* in opposition to the *Caucus Nomination,* has succeeded [in N.Y.] by more than 500 majority.... **1824** in *Mangum Papers* I.134 ... they have got him, as I understand, on the people's Ticket, in his country. **1828** in Simms *Whigs in Va.* 31. The Jackson ticket was called by the opposition "The caucus, Military Ticket," while they called their own ticket, i.e., the Adams ticket, "The People's Ticket." **1842** Neal *Bro. Jonathan* II.3 ... the eloquent Livingston, the corner stone of the "stump," or as the placards had it, "The People's Ticket." **1856** Hollister *Colfax* 75. Many Democratic papers [in Indiana] declared for the "People's ticket."

1874 *N. Y. W. Trib.* 7 Oct. 1/6. New Orleans, Oct. 2.—One of the best results of the late revolution is the impetus given to movements looking to a better understanding politically, between the white and colored races. The Terrebonne plan, which involves a people's ticket, giving each race a fair share of candidates, seems to be growing in favor in every parish.

People's Union.

A. The name of an ephemeral party aimed at the fusion of the Know-Nothing and Republican parties:

1856 "Warrington" *Pen Portraits* 219. The "People's Union" is the name of a new secret order, which is designed to bring together, if possible, the Americans and the Republicans.

At the beginning of the Civil War, the People's Union party offered "a local ticket or list of candidates pledged to support the government despite politics as distinguished from those supporting the government as partisans." (*DA*) **1861** (Richmond, Va.) *Daily Dispatch* 31 May 3/2. The only tickets in the field are known as the People's Union ticket and the Republican Union ticket.

B. As an earlier party name. [ ] **1828** *Niles' Reg.* 18 Oct. 116/1. At Charleston, S.C. a legislative ticket called *"the people's union ticket"* has been published —in opposition to the anti-unionists; but without reference to political preferences of persons for the presidency.

pepper and salt.

Applicable to a ticket or convention composed of both Negroes and whites.

Used only rarely in the post-Civil War period.

1867 Strong *Diary* IV.173 . . . some stories of black voters putting their ballots into the post office are quite enough to make these pepper and salt conventions ridiculous in the eyes of Copperheads.
1892 in Hicks *Pop. Rev.* 247. In Edgecomb County a "pepper and salt ticket" was named—i.e., a negro was nominated along with whites.

persimmon.

An earlier version of *plum* (q.v.).

1844 *Buckeye Eagle* 28 Aug. 2/2. David Tod should go there and repeat that original remark of his about the longest pole knocking down the persimmons.
1848 *Xenia* (Ohio) *Torchlight* 17 Aug. 1/5.

Tho' Cass has lived all his six lives
In office for the trimmings
Yet Old Zack carries the longest pole
And he'll knock all the " 'cimmons."

1888 *Lebanon* (Ohio) *West. Star* 10 April 5/2. Hon. H. L. Morey Gathers the Political Persimmons.
1900 Dennett *Hay* 340. The Vice Presidency is, at this date, anybody's persimmon.

personal government.

1876 *Harper's W.* 1 Jan. 2/2. Then let every Republican paper which knows that a renomination would not represent the real preference of the party, and could be procured only by the triumph of executive patronage, which would be the triumph of a purely personal government under constitutional forms, declare at once and plainly, that it is opposed to a third term. . . .
1876 *Ib.* 8 Jan. 23/2. [Caesarism] is the advocacy of personal government in a country of laws. It is the assertion that in a republic some one person is essential to the national safety.

Peter Funk.

Characterizing deceiving or presumably dishonest politicians or policies.

A. Barnum may be correct in attributing the origin to the founder of mock auctions. At any rate, the term is early associated with swindling operations on Pearl Street, New York.

1834 Greene *Perils of Pearl St.* 51. Peter Funk . . . is the very imp of deception; . . . his name is sometimes used figuratively to signify any thing which is employed for the purpose of deception.
1866 Barnum *Humbugs of the World* 172. The name, Peter Funk, is said to have been that of the founder of their system [of mock auctions]; but I know nothing more of his career.

B. In politics.

1854 *Ohio St. Jrnl.* 13 March 2/1. The *Empire,* the *Statesman,* and other few papers who have shown so much agility in adjusting their principles to the precise gauge prescribed to them from Washington, are a fair type of the Peter Funk democracy of the times.
1854 Mike Walsh in *Cong. Globe* 1230/3. It [opp. to Dem. policies] comes from men whose object is to revolutionize the land. I know them—a set of peanut agitators and Peter Funk philanthropists.

petticoat.

Descriptive of government by weak male politicians or by women who were held to have forgotten their proper role in society.

A. During the reign of Queen Anne, petticoat politics was commonly discussed in England with apparently not the strong satirical emphasis found in later American usage.

1702 *The Prerogative of the Breeches: an answer to Petticoat-Government, written by a True-born English Man.* [title] [*OED*]
1702 J. Dunton *Petticoat-Government* 70 [*OED*]. By Petticoat-Government, I mean when Good Women Ascend the Throne,

and Rule according to Law, as is the Case of the present Queen.
1784? in Trumbull *M'Fingal* 173. Somebody had the boldness, at the beginning of George's [III] reign, to place a large placard on the Royal Exchange, with the words "No Petticoat Government—No Scotch Ministers."

B. American politics:

1836 in McGrane *William Allen* 51. Allen referred to the fact that "while a sword was in preparation in Chillicothe for the victorious Croghan, a petticoat was contemplated to be presented to General Harrison."
1836 *West. Hemisphere* 3 Aug. 1/7. Chivalrous Knight of the Red Petticoats. [head]
1837 *Alexander's West. Messenger* 5 July 2/3. Her [H. Martineau's] Abolitionism, her petticoat politics . . . afford ample room and verge enough for criticism.
1856 *Cleve. Plaindealer* 12 July 2/1. We expect that, should Colonel Fremont be elected, he would travel under the title of Mrs. President Fremont and J. C., her husband! Better keep the petticoats out of the political ring, or there'll be a smashing of "hoops."
1864 *Cinc. Gazette* in Sandburg *War Yrs.* II.574. As to Miss Dickinson's nomination of Mr. Lincoln for the next Presidency [ref. to her speech in Congress, 16 Jan.], I object to it as the inauguration of an era of petticoat government for which we are not prepared at present.

Pewter Mug.

A tavern located on Frankfort Street, New York, the headquarters of a Tammany faction.

1828 Halleck *Poems* 169.
   On others, at the heart's delight,
   The Pewter Mug in Frankfort Street;
Ib. 377n: The "Pewter Mug."—The sign conspicuous over the door of a tavern in Frankfort Street, in the rear of Tammany Hall, the frequent resort of politicians in general, and of the Tammany-Hall party in particular.
1829 *Workingman's Adv.* 7 Nov. 2/5. The

morning papers say the Pewter Mug ticket is elected, which is probably the fact. This ticket was nominated by a fragment of the Tammany Hall party and is the same as the Tammany ticket with the exception of three names.
1830 *Ib.* 29 May 3/3. The Evening Journal may now be considered . . . the organ of the St. John's Hall or Pewter Mug faction, which is a "split" from old Tammany. . . .
1835 *Knickerbocker* V.420 . . . Tammanymen and Pewter-muggers. . . .
1842 *N. Y. Trib.* 4 June 5/2. Eight of its [election jury's] members . . . were taken from the Pewter Mug groggery, under the wing of Tammany Hall.

phalanx.

A solidly united group.

One of the many Greek allusions adapted to the political vocabulary. See TROJAN HORSE, MYRMIDONS, SPARTAN BAND.
1845 Lyon *Gov. of the United States* 76. There is no difference of opinion allowed to exist in the democratic party, all are gathered in, and are taught to either have no private opinions or yield them up to party. They are drilled and whipped in until they form a unit, a solid phalanx—can count before hand votes, and calculate their strength mathematically.
1871 *Every Saturday* 18 March 243/1. Unfortunately for them [Democrats in Ill.] a group of less than a dozen were determined on having a Free-Soiler; they rallied around Judge Trumbull, and neither threats nor persuasion could break or intimidate the little phalanx.
1880 *Cinc. Daily Gazette* 18 June 1/4. "How does the California delegation stand?" "Almost a phalanx for Field."
1880 *Cleve. Plain Dealer* 5 June 1/1. If the Grant phalanx should break it might happen that the Minnesota Senator would profit by it, but as it will be a long time before the phalanx breaks, if it breaks at all, the chance is not worth considering.

The popularity of this expression in America in the 1840's may be attributed to interest in Fourierism, in which this was one of the prominent terms.
1840 Brisbane *Social Destiny of Man* xiii Phalanx—The body of persons, or the inhabitants composing an Association.

pharisee (pharisaical).

The Pharisees, members of that sect of ancient Jews which held to strict observance of traditional law and felt itself to be the model of sanctity, were the objects of many attacks by Jesus.
Matt. 23:27. Woe unto you, scribes and Pharisees, hypocrites! for ye are like unto whited sepulchres, which indeed appear beautiful outward, but are within full of dead men's bones, and of all uncleanness.

A. A general derogatory term in American politics for a reformer or any other individual whose actions are held to be hypocritical or overly sanctimonious.
1835 in Garrison *Garrison Story* 154. It is unjust and pharisaical for one portion of the country to say to another, "Stand by, for I am holier than thou."
1844 *Frankfort Commonwealth* 17 Sept. 3/2. He [Clay] and they have been repeatedly denounced as blue-nosed Presbyterians, Methodistical, Maw-worms, sanctimonious Pharisees, &c, &c.
1865 Strong *Diary* IV.21. One would think it most desirable to get the South into good order again without delay. But our Chinese conservatives protest against any step that way, unless chapter and verse of the Constitution can be cited for it. They are political Pharisees, who would let government perish (government being not in the hands of "our party") , rather than see it saved "on the Sabbath Day."
1876 Morton in *Cong. Record* 498/2. Those who make daily outcry about frauds . . . but turn a deaf ear to the cries of murdered men . . . are pharisees and hypocrites of the basest sort.

B. The Liberal Republicans of 1872:

1872 *Cinc. Times* & *Chron.* 3 July 2/2. The battle had scarcely opened before I saw that Greeley's Pharisees and Tweed's followers had bargained.

C. The "mugwumps" of 1884:

1884 *Ohio St. Jrnl.* 9 Aug. 4/2. The "fainting pharisees," otherwise known as "Independents."

1884 *Harper's W.* 21 June 390/3. Phariseeism. It is a derision of "Pharisees" and "holier-than-thou-men," and an assertion that "the remnant" is no better than other people.... In our present partisan lingo the demand for honesty in public life is Phariseeism.

Later:

1920 W. A. White *Sel. Ltrs.* 208. The Pharisees are running the temple and bossing the religion and handling the caucuses and the people are getting the worst of it.

picket.

Long a military term, the labor union use of picket is attested in the *OED* from 1867. Occasionally the word is found in a strictly political sense:

1876 *Cinc. Comm.* 7 Sept. 4/4. Watterson's pickets are so thick along the Kentucky-Indiana front, that from the river the shore resembles an inverted cross-cut saw. ...Watterson has pickets two feet apart all along the Kentucky-Indiana front, to prevent the colonization of voters in Indiana.... There is not a picket along the Kentucky-Indiana front who would not lay down his life rather than allow a Kentucky patriot to cross over and give Blue Jeans Williams a lift with his vote.

1925 Coan *Red Web* 73. The pamphlet referred to, extensively circulated by the General Defense Committee, which also staged a number of demonstrations in Washington and brought delegates of "pickets" to do duty at the gates of the White House....

pick (the) flint.

To prepare for a renewed effort; usually as an expression of continued support for a candidate.

c1816 in Sargent *Henry Clay* 68–9. During the canvass, Mr. Clay encountered an old hunter, who had always before been his warm friend, but now was opposed to his election on account of the compensation bill. "Have you a good rifle, my friend?" asked Mr. Clay.—"Yes." "Does it never flash?"—"Once only," he replied.—"What did you do with it—throw it away?"—"No, I picked the flint, tried it again, and brought down the game."—"Have I ever flashed but upon the compensation bill?"—"No."—"Will you throw me away?"—"No, no!" exclaimed the hunter, with enthusiasm, nearly overpowered by his feelings; "I will pick the flint, and try you again!"

1841 in *Mangum Papers* III.172. I have voted for him [Clay] every time he has been a Candidate for President & that I wish to pick the flint & try it again.

1842 *Frankfort Commonwealth* 11 Oct. 2/3.

The Whig Rifle.

. . . .

Harry Clay of Kentuck is our leader!—
  Come, rally from mountain and plain!
Think no more on the thing that betrayed
    us;
  But pick flint and try it again:
But pick flint and try it again,
But pick flint and try it again,
    Think no more on the thing that betrayed us,
But pick flint and try it again.

pickings and stealings.

Humorous reference to swindling and stealing by government employees.

1861 Lowell *Pol. Essays* 75. The Pickens-And-Stealin's Rebellion. [title]

1874 Nichols *Am. Life* 51. A place under Government was said to be worth a certain amount, including "pickings and stealings." The Government was plundered remorselessly in contracts, in smuggling, in every possible way. There was a lax notion that a man was only taking his own, or taking money out of one pocket to put it in the other.

1878 *Puck* 3 July 8. Political Pickings and Stealings [Label on moneybag in Keppler cartoon].

See PLUNDER, PUBLIC CRIB.

pie.

A metaphor based upon the desire of politicians to share in the spoils of the government, whether by patronage or by graft.

1879 *Puck* 9 July 273 [Keppler cartoon] The Rapid Transit Pie. And now Mr. Vanderbilt wants to have a few fingers in it.

1913 Roosevelt *Autobio.* 74. These papers reported the introduction of the bill, and said that "all the hungry legislators were clamoring for their share of the pie"; and they accepted as certain the fact that there was going to be a division of "pie."

1931 *Wash. Merry-Go-Round* 219. "But if other States are going to get it, I'm going to have my slice of pie as well."

E. C. Smith in his *Dictionary of American Politics,* p. 317, offers an unsupported story as to the origin of the term:

The term arose from the story of a Texas editor who offered a public official a chicken pie in addition to a money bribe for securing a contract.

See PUBLIC CRIB, PAP.

piebald.

See also MERMAID TICKET, MONGREL.

1875 *Nation* 270/1. The Democratic State ticket has no claims to confidence and is "piebald," while the Republican ticket contains the names of pure and good men only.

pie counter.

The source of political grants or graft.

1903 *N. Y. Times* 16 Dec. 3. When his constituents asked him why he could not secure more routes the only reply he could make was that he could not get up to the "pie counter."

1915 *Emporia Gazette* 23 April. A lot of the others ... are going to do nothing that will alienate them from the pie counter.

pie foundry.

Synonym of *pie counter.*

1922 White *Editor and His People* 325 ... Elmer Dover, Senator Hanna's private secretary twenty years ago, who was appointed last year to restore normalcy to the pie foundry in Washington. His resignation came because he could not get jobs for the hungry in the department of internal revenue.

pillar.

Biblical and literary metaphors:

Galatians 2:9. And when James, Cephas, and John, who seemed to be pillars....

Revelations 3:12. Him that overcometh will I make a pillar in the temple of my God....

Shakespeare *Henry VI* pt 2, I.i [Duke of Gloster]. Brave peers of England, pillars of the state....

Milton *Paradise Lost* II.300.

> ... with grave
> Aspect he [Beelzebub] rose, and in his
>   rising seemed
> A pillar of state.

Its frequent and early use in America may have been inspired by Otis's use or by a well-known passage in Pitt's speech on the Right of Taxing America; however, Franklin had used the metaphor several years earlier than either of these.

1737 Franklin *Works* II.285. Freedom of speech is a principal pillar of a free government; when this support is taken away, the constitution of a free society is dissolved, and tyranny is erected on its ruins.

1764 Otis *Rights* 33. And upon those grand pillars of liberty shall my defence be rested.

1766 Pitt in *Brit. Eloquence* 107. America, if she fell, would fall like the strong man; she would embrace the pillars of the state, and pull down the Constitution along with her.

A specific American application of the metaphor is *pillars of the Constitution* for those states that had ratified:

1788 Madison *Works* V.100. There seems to be no question that the issue there [N.H.] will add a seventh pillar, as the phrase now is, to the federal temple.

In a different sense the word was used by Fox:

1797 in *Brit. Eloquence* 519 . . . to try if we can to effect a reform without touching the main pillars of the Constitution. . . .

In other phrases:

1778 in Thornton *Pulpit in Am. Rev.* 333. Violent and opposing parties, shaking the pillars of the State, may arise under the best forms of government.

1799 Fisher Ames *Works* 102. Then they [Democrats] are let alone to undermine the pillars of the publick order.

1801 *Federalism Triumphant* 8 . . . these turnpike companies established on the immoveable pillars of an Energetic Government will be more productive and infinitely more certain.

1880 Adams *Emery A. Storrs* 228. Have you seen any trouble with the pillars of the government? The trouble was not with the pillars of the government: they did not rock; the trouble was with the gentlemen who were looking at the pillars of the government.

pincher.

See Farmer quot. ¿

1889 Farmer *Americanisms* 421. A term of political origin and usage, and applied to

a legislative measure calculated to secure a pecuniary regard to those who are interested in its defeat.

pitiless publicity.

Coined by Emerson in a non-political context, the expression was revived by Woodrow Wilson and later used by Franklin D. Roosevelt.

1860 Emerson *Conduct of Life* VI. As gaslight is found to be the best nocturnal police, so the universe protects itself by pitiless publicity.

1910 Wilson in Tumulty *Woodrow Wilson* 41. I would propose to abolish it [govt. of privilege] by the reforms suggested in the Democratic platform, by the election to office of men who will refuse to submit to it, and who will lend all their energies to break it up, and by pitiless publicity.

1910 *Nation* 15 Dec. 571/2. Woodrow Wilson promised the New Jersey voters that, if elected, he would go upon the plan of "pitiless publicity," in all that related to the interests of the State.

1920 *Ib.* 21 Aug. 203/1. The hurried departure of Charles Huszar, ex-Premier of Hungary . . . marks the climax of a campaign of "pitiless publicity," waged without funds, without deliberate attempt at coordination, with the sheer force of truth for its only motive force.

1931 Lindley *F. D. R.* 245. The preliminary skirmishing had begun early in the session when Roosevelt found the legislative leaders had drafted bills detailing methods of handling the budget inconsistent in his opinion with the intent of the amendment to compel, as he termed it, "pitiless publicity."

pivotal (state).

A state whose electoral vote may be considered a decisive factor in the election:

1834 Hone *Diary* I.139. This [N.Y.] might be called the pivotal State.

1840 in *Ohio Arch. Qrtly.* L.136. Ohio is

the pivot on which the next presidential election must turn.

1876 Hayes *Diary* III.356. Indiana is a Democratic State.... Until within a fortnight I have seen a small chance of carrying it. The chances are still greatly against us. The true pivot is New York.

1885 *Nation* 15 Jan. 44/2. Governor Hoadley, of Ohio, recommends in his message that the State cease to be "pivotal," or in other words that the State elections should cease to be held in October.

Pivot was an important term in the vocabulary of the Fourierists, during their short-lived vogue in the 1830's and '40's.

1840 Albert Brisbane *Social Destiny of Man: or, Association and Reorganization of Industry* xii. Pivot signifies the principal part or member of a system, mechanism, or species. The sun, for example, is the pivot of the solar system. White is the pivotal color; mercury is a pivotal metal. The lion is the pivot of the feline species. The thumb is the pivot of the hand with the four fingers. Bread is a pivotal food, because it amalgamates with every other kind. The general and his staff are the pivot of an army. With these examples, the reader will see what we understand by pivot and pivotal.

plank.

The vogue that in 1848 brought *platform* into general use could not fail to create secondary metaphors, among which *plank* is probably the best known. It is well attested during the later days of the presidential campaign, usually in a way that makes it quite clear that its metaphorical character is still strongly felt.

1848 Lowell *Biglow Papers* 214.
Truth is, the cutest leadin' Wigs, ever
  sence fust they found
Wich side the bread gut buttered on, hev
  kep' a edgin' round;

They kin' o' slipt the planks frum out th'
  old platform one by one
An' made it gradooally noo, 'fore folks
  know'd wut wuz done....

1848 *Cong. Globe* App. 1082. [They] have admitted that the principal plank of the Cass platform had fallen to the ground, and precipitated him and them with it.

1848 *Ohio St. Jrnl.* 4 Oct. 1/4. Here are two planks from the Buffalo platform, on which Mr. Van Buren and Mr. C. F. Adams are striving hard to stand side by side.

1848 (Hamilton, Ohio) *Free Soil Banner* 10 Oct. 4/1. Two Planks of the Platform. The composition of that patchwork bit of joinery, the Buffalo Platform, is a sore puzzle to a great many honest men, who are unable to find out what sort of timber was used in the building of it.

1850 *Ann. of Cleve.* Aug. Old Zack knocked out plank after plank of their [Dem.] platform, until the sensible and reasonable portion of the Freesoilers had come to look to the honest patriot as the impassable bulwark against slavery extension....

1863 Williams *Rise and Fall of the Model Republic* 69. It is necessary that he and they should go before the country upon a platform. The putting together of the "planks" in such a manner as will satisfy all the factions is a most difficult, delicate and dangerous duty.

A factor that certainly contributed to keeping the image alive is the use of plank in political cartoons. On the other hand, there are early signs that a process of mechanization had set in as indicated by such verbs as *to read, to strike out:*

1852 *Scott Battery* 27 July 3/3. The first plank of the Democratic platform reads as follows....

1856 *Cong. Globe* 1127. That plank in the platform was stricken out by the convention.

Another sign of mechanization is an occasional mixing of metaphors. The plank that goes into the building of the platform is confused with the plank on which the shipwrecked floats to safety.

1876 Wilson *Slave Power* II.298 [quoting Dawson in the House]. It might be ... an emanation of disappointed political ambition—mere effort to hold on to one plank in the wreck of a recently established political platform and to save a sinking party.

Incidentally the metaphorical use of the "saving plank" is attested as early as 1836:

1836 (Ohio) *People's Press* 22 June 3/1. The Last Plank! ... deprecating the resort to an election by the House. 'Tis their last plank, and if they reach not the shore on that, farewell to the Chief of Spoils and the clansmen of the Kitchen!

platform.

Originally meaning a representation (of a building) on the flat, a ground plan (*OED*), has branched out into a great variety of meanings, of which two seem to be of importance to its development as a political term.

A. It means a plan or draft of church government or discipline; a scheme of principles and doctrines made by or on behalf of a religious party, church, or sect (*OED, platform* 4b). In this sense the word was already used by Cotton in America through the Cambridge Platform and the Saybrook Platform, 1708.

B. (*OED* 9) A temporary or sometimes permanent piece of raised floor ... from which a speaker addresses his audience and on which the promoters of a meeting sit. ... Also the body of sup-

porters who appear on a platform.

According to *OED* the modern political use of platform, "declaration of principles and policy," has no direct connection with sense 1 but is "associated directly with the material platform on which persons meet and publicly speak." In support of this opinion the *OED* quotes the metaphorical use of *plank* and the phrase, *to stand on a platform,* in the sense of to plant oneself on the principles of one's party. It cannot be denied that these phrases are in frequent use even before 1848, when *plank* turns up for the first time.

To the examples in *OED* add:

1830 *Niles' Reg.* XXXIX.18 ... it is highly important that his opinions, on great national subjects, should be fully understood; and this speech was manifestly designed to proclaim them. We suppose that it may be called the "platform" on which he stands.

1838 *Liberator* 15 Dec. For ourselves, we care not who is found upon this broad platform of our common nature.

1839 Garrison *Garrison Story* II.294. I suppose the platform of the Society to be broad enough to sustain all.

1840 *Rough-hewer* 134/3. We say ... that every freeman shall stand on the broad platform of liberty and equality.

1840 *Liberator* 5 June 89/4. Resolved, That the Old Anti-Slavery Organization furnishes this platform, where humanity can stand and battle for those rights.

1841 in *Mangum Papers* III.154 ... he will cut the Webster clique and fall back on the old Democratic platform where he can be seen and can be felt.

1841 *Ib.* III.183. The only alternative, in my opinion, was for the Cabinet to have brought the President to the broad Whig platform, or to have handed in the seals of office.

1846 *Cleve. Herald* 27 Jan. 3/2 ... we shall

stand upon the sound platform of the Constitution.

1846 Colton *Clay* I.193 ... to determine the relative right of the states in respect to slavery, as defined in the federal constitution, and to plant his foot on that platform, to stand while it stands, and to fall only when that must fall.

However, the idea that the modern use of *platform* could have developed from such phrases exclusively and without the influence of the theological use of the word is not convincing. In the first place, it has to be considered that this use was by no means forgotten even among laymen around 1840:

1837 *New Yorker* 599/3. The Rev. Royal Robbins ... seems to have confined himself to a particular persuasion, and hardly to have stepped off the Saybrook platform.

It is hard to believe that at that time and even earlier the word *platform,* applying to a document, could have been used without bringing to mind connotations of a religious character. We may assume that this applied to an article in the *Massachusetts Spy* of 1803: "The Platform of Federalism." There is no doubt that the religious platform was in the minds of politicians who said:

1844 *Niles' Reg.* LXV.408/1. These are our doctrines—this the broad platform on which we stand. Here is our confession of faith ... old as the constitution—old as the days of our fathers.

1848 Webster *Works* II.455 ... and I believe, with all respect, that that Buffalo platform was constructed of such slight materials, that, while it would not bear a very heavy tread, it would sustain the fox-like footsteps of Mr. Van Buren. The creed was drawn up and made such as he could sign.

Furthermore, it seems that among the abolitionists with whom religious influence was particularly strong *platform* was in frequent use before the word had acquired its present political sense. An article by Garrison stating the principles of the society has the title "The Anti-Slavery Platform" (in *Selections from the Speeches and Writings of William Lloyd Garrison,* Boston, 1852.) This document is not dated, but since it refers to the defection of a number of clergymen at the New England Convention of 1838, as an event of "the last year" it must have been written in 1839. In 1840 another New England Anti-Slavery Convention adopted a set of resolutions in which *platform* occurs in several prominent places:

Liberator 5 June 89/4. Resolved ... we must, if possible, unite an equally wide diversity of interests by some common bond,—upon a platform broad enough to contain the whole human family. ...

Resolved, That the Old Anti-Slavery Organization furnishes this platform, where humanity can stand and battle for those rights ...

Resolved, That all attempts to narrow down or destroy our noble platform. ...

Resolved ... the broad platform of genuine anti-slavery. ...

Other early examples from the Garrison circle:

1839 *Liberator* 6 Dec. 195/1. Having abandoned the good old anti-slavery platform, it is not to be expected that Richard will be "himself again," until he plant his feet where they stood of yore.

1840 *Ib.* 12 June 95/1. The "platform" of an independent journal ... is one thing; the "platform" of an anti-slavery society, ... is another thing.

1841 *Ib.* 26 Feb. 39/1. A new organization

having been effected in the anti-slavery society of this town, the friends of the "old platform" have formed another, with the original constitution. . . .

The approach to the modern meaning was probably helped along by the often used phrase *to stand on the platform of the Constitution.*

To the examples already quoted add:

1848 *Marshall* (Mich.) *Statesman* 25 July 2/6 . . . it is the broad platform of the constitution.

1848 *Marshall* (Mich.) *Expounder* 23 June 2/4 . . . seven resolutions were adopted, but not one of them asserts a principle except that the whig party stands "on the broad and firm platform of the constitution, braced up by all its inviolable and sacred guarantees and compromises."

1850 Webster *Works* V.437. I mean to stand upon the Constitution. I need no other platform.

Another factor to be considered is the usefulness of the platform metaphor in stressing the necessity of concerted party action. Phrases of the type "a platform broad enough for all to stand on" are quite frequent. To those already quoted add:

1840 *Wash. Globe* 7 May 3/1. What are the principles on which we stand? . . . every freeman shall stand on the broad platform of liberty and equality.

1846 *Ohio Statesman* (Columbus) 7 Jan 2/3. Resolved, That the "democratic platform" is as broad and firm as the free soil protected by the stars and stripes of Columbia's flag; and as free for all to meet and stand upon.

1846 *Ib.* 4 Feb. 2/3 . . . the resolutions adopted by the Convention at Columbus, on the 8th inst., are of the right stamp— the platform which they set up is one on which the whole party can stand.

While the preceding analysis of the complicated early history of *platform* is necessarily a tentative one, the question at what time *platform* acquired the specific sense of declaration of principles and intents, issued by a convention, can be answered with more confidence. Occasional phrases of this type occur as early as 1844:

1844 *Niles' Reg.* LXV.404/3. His [Van Buren's] friends in 1840 prepared the resolutions—his friends submitted them for revision. . . . His friends made the platform. We stand upon it. . . . We invite— we urge—we demand, that they shall make it the ground of the party.

1844 in Bigger *Gibson* 7 July 175. I am a Whig from education and by opinion, and can subscribe to all the platform of the Baltimore convention.

But these occurrences do not represent common usage which becomes clear from the fact that newspapers discussing the resolutions of the Democratic and Whig conventions of that year do not call them *platforms*. Between '44 and '48 this meaning of *platform* seems to gain ground: (see above quotations from the *Ohio Statesman,* 1846) .

The event that finally brought the word *platform* into common use and gave it its unquestioned standing in the terminology of the Presidential convention was the election of 1848. In this year the word is in everybody's mouth, but we have ample evidence that many people considered it a word of recent origin.

1848 Lincoln *Works* 20 June I.480. The late democratic convention which sat at Baltimore . . . adopted a set of resolutions, now called the democratic platform. . . .

1848 Toombs in *Cong. Globe* 1 July. This business of making "party platforms" for Presidential candidates is a modern innovation. It was unknown in the better days of the Republic.

1848 in Dyers *Free Soil Convention* 18. ... we now plant ourselves upon the National Platform of Freedom in opposition to the Sectional Platform of Slavery.

1848 Webster *Works* 1 Sept. II.431. I see that one part of what is called the Platform of the Buffalo Convention says that the candidates before the public are nominated under the dictation of the slave power.

1848 Cass *Ltr. of Acceptance.* [Oct] I have carefully read the resolutions of the Democratic National Convention, laying down the platform of our political faith.

1848 *John Donkey* 24 Jan. ... while they may be regarded as the Whig platform in the coming campaign, present at a glance all the opinions of General Taylor.

1848 *Old Zack* 1 July 2/1. We shall wait with breathless anxiety for the advent of that "platform" [Free Soil].

1848 Groton *Spirit of the Times* 28 July 2/4. "Whig Platform—The Whigs have laid down no creed—have erected no platform!"

1848 *Ann. of Cleve.* No.694 [*Daily True Democrat*]. Our platform is before the world.

The sudden popularity of the word causes a number of popular jokes:

1848 *John Donkey* 22 Jan. He [Calhoun] will stand on the Tariff platform, and by a single flip-flop alight on the Free Trade sawdust. ... and tickled by the whip of Mr. Clay, the ringmaster, will alight on the "no-war-for-the-sake-of-territory" platform.

1848 *Old Zack* 12 Aug. 2/2. As he mounted the rostrum, or rather, the old rickety one-legged abolition platform, a thrill of horror ran thro' the mixed crowd.

Ib. 19 Aug. 1/3. The one-legged platform of the Buffalo Convention People, and that leg a side leg of the table, won't do to

stand a party upon, no more than Native Americanism.

1848 *Xenia* (Ohio) *Torchlight* 19 Oct. 1/7. "Pa, hasn't boards riz?" "No child, what made you think they had?" "'Cause I see that all the big men are making platforms."

The excessive use of the term leads to a mixing of metaphors:

1848 *Battery* 21 Sept. 186/2. It then goes on "to nail the old Whig platform to the mast"—a very awkward place for a platform by the way.

1856 *Greenville* (Ohio) *Jrnl.* 14 May 2/2. The Platform will be cooked up by the politicians of Virginia, South Carolina and Mississippi, and the Northern Democracy will gulp it down with scarcely a contortion of countenance.

John Donkey Oct. II.100. Political Platforms. [Includes cartoons of the various platforms] We hear a great deal of talk concerning political platforms; and in order to give our readers some idea of the various platforms on which the parties execute flip-flaps, we shall resort to the pen and graver combined.

In the first place, then we have THE WHIG PLATFORM. The conception and execution of this is so bold, so expressive, and yet so delicate, as to give great satisfaction to the connoisseurs—at least to all who understand what it is all about. It is drawn on the same principle used by the little boy in drawing the pig behind the house, where, nobody could see it.

Then we have THE DEMOCRATIC PLATFORM. Its very broad outline of surface, and its extreme flexibility and mobility on its pivot, as well as capability of being presented to all points of the compass at once, specially recommend it.

The third is THE NATIVE PLATFORM. This is distinguished by the severity of its truth, as appears in its blown up and broken condition.

The last we shall present, is THE VAN BUREN PLATFORM: which, as the party has no bottom whatever, is always up side down.

plebiscite.

Used in France and Italy during the 1870's, the word is occasionally used in America as a synonym for *direct vote*.

1874 *Nation* 19 March 181/1. The *plébiscite* has in fact become the Bonapartist fetish. . . . 187. The only government which will deserve his [Prince Napoleon's] support will be a government founded upon the direct vote of the people, upon a *plébiscite*.
1898 Schurz *Writings* V.530. I know, such a plebiscite [on Annex.] would be a new thing. . . . And it seems to me that an act providing for the taking of such a plebiscite might be so formed as to avoid all Constitutional difficulties.
1900 Oberholtzer *Referendum in America* 400. The next step seems to be the referendum or plebiscite. . . . The name plebiscite in French and Italian history is at once suggestive of the plebiscites of the Napoleons, and of Victor Emmanuel during the reconstruction days in Italy.
1910 J. L. Heaton *Cobb of "The World"* 51. Accordingly it prints a coupon which its readers are urged to fill out and send to the office of the periodical. . . . The "plebiscite" covers nearly every political question before the country. . . . Even a decade ago such a "plebiscite" would have been greeted with derision. Now it is treated soberly and earnestly, not to say reverently.
1919 Heckscher *Politics of W. Wilson* 364. If the Peace Conference itself was to be the end of coöperative authority . . . properly safeguarded plebiscites could not be provided for where populations were at some future date to make a choice what sovereignty they would live under. . . .

plum.

An office or other advantage obtained by political pull.

The term became well-known in politics as a result of a phrase reputed to have been originated by Matt Quay, "shake the plum tree."¿

1882 Wilkins *Cleverdale Mystery* 22. You millionaires think newspaper men can scoop in all the plums.
1884 *Boston Jrnl.* 7 Oct. 2/6. A Plum for Hubert O. Thompson.
1885–7 Quay in Stimpson *Handbook of Politics* 258. Buy and carry a thousand Met for me, and I will shake the plum tree.
1887 *Louisville Courier Jrnl.* 13 Jan. 3/4. Senator Beck gets the credit for most of the Federal appointments in Mason County. . . . The boys enjoying the plums will support anybody who is for him and them.
1901 Bigger *Gibson* 192 . . . defeat [in Dem. Conv. 1848] came to Levi Woodbury and James Buchanan, who were expecting respectively, a luscious plum to fall their way from the convention tree.
1908 *Rev. of Rev.* XXXVII.546. Under the Democratic Plum Tree. [cartoon: Judson Harman sitting beside "Democracy" tree looking longingly at "Presidential Plum."]
1905 Phillips *The Plum Tree* 24. I mentally called the roll—wealth, respectability, honor, all on their knees before Dominick, each with his eye upon the branch of the plum tree that bore the kind of fruit he fancied.

plumed knight.

The white plume of Henry IV of France, proverbial in French where *panache* has become a synonym for *pluck,* must have been known to any reader of English poetry through Macaulay's "Ivry":
1824 *Speeches and Poems* 245.
Press where ye see my white plume shine, amidst the ranks of war,
And be your oriflamme today the helmet of Navarre.

Bret Harte's "John Burns of Gettysburg" must have contributed considerably to this knowledge:
Complete Works 62.
And some of the soldiers since declare
That the gleam of his old white hat afar,

Like the crested plume of the brave Navarre,
That day was their oriflamme of war.

Already in 1861 *white plume* was used in political writing by Wendell Phillips:
Sp. 406. "Under the Flag." The Tribune, whose unflinching fidelity and matchless ability make it in this fight "the white plume of Navarre."

Thus the soil was well prepared for Ingersoll's famous nomination of James G. Blaine at the Cincinnati Convention of June 15, 1876:
Cinc. Gazette 16 June 3/1. Like an armed warrior, like a plumed knight, James G. Blaine marched down the halls of the American Congress and threw his shining lance full and fair against the brazen forehead of every defamer of this country and maligner of its honor.

The white plume slogan was received with great enthusiasm and was alluded to innumerable times:
1879 *Cong. Record* 225/2. The "plumed knight" from Maine and the distinguished gladiator from Georgia were the central figures in the discussion in Congress.
1880 *Cleve. Plain Dealer* 18 May 2/2. When the third termers and the followers of the plumed knight meet in mortal combat....
1880 *Cinc. Gazette* 25 May 1/6. For himself, a Blaine man, he stood by "the plumed knight of Maine."

Attempts to capitalize on the slogan in favor of Democratic candidates proved unsuccessful:
1880 *Cinc. Gazette* 24 June 3/4. [Vorhees nominating Hendricks] And Indiana? Has she faltered? Sometimes borne down but often triumphant, and always with the plume of Thomas A. Hendricks in the front.
Ib. 24 June 9/1 [Hubbard seconding nomination of Hancock]. Here is a soldier that

bore down even upon us like the brigade at Balaclava, like a plumed knight to the front....

It is characteristic of Blaine's shrewdness that he himself did not countenance this sobriquet, being apprehensive that it might be turned into ridicule:
Ltrs. of Mrs. James G. Blaine I.129n. It is interesting to note that Mr. Blaine himself never liked this appellation, thinking that it suggested "white feather" as much as "helmet of Navarre."

His apprehensions proved correct when Thomas Nast took hold of the subject in 1884 when Blaine was running against Cleveland. A few representative cartoons in *Harpers W.*:
21 June 395 "Plumed Crow," 30 Aug. 569 "The Knight of The Moneybag," 20 Sept. 623. "Another Feather in His Cap; or, 'Dodged, By Gosh!'" 4 Oct. 661 "The Brazen Knight of the White Feather on His Round Trip for Votes."

The same line is followed in
1884 *Puck* 18 June 242/2.
No matter if Mulligan knows his plume
Is only a feather white.
1884 *N. Y. World* 10 Aug. 4/4. It was Infidel Ingersoll's poetic fancy that fashioned the politician in the rat-trap to a prancing knight with a chicken feather in his pot-metal hat.

plump.

To vote plump is to cast all votes unanimously or without qualification.

1776 Adams *Works* X.398 "New Jersey has dethroned Franklin, and in a letter, which is just come to my hand from indisputable authority, I am told that the delegates from that colony 'will vote plump!'"

In *Ib.* III.55 [15 June]. "We are passing the Rubicon, and our delegates in Congress, on the first of July, will vote plump."

1880 *N. Y. Trib.* 2 April 4/6. One of the English election phrases for which there is no equivalent in the United States is "plumping." Whenever a constituency returns two members, each voter can give one vote each to any two candidates but he cannot give his two votes to any one candidate. If he chooses he can give one vote to only one candidate, and this is termed "plumping."

1904 *Weber's W.* 24 Sept. 1. The practice of casting three votes for one candidate [in legislative elections where a representative may have many votes] has come to be known as "plumping." By "plumping" the minority may concentrate its votes.

plumper.

A vote given entirely to one candidate.

A. Long used in English politics:

1813 W. Taylor in *Monthly Mag.* XXXV. 427. C, who splits none of his votes, will have seven supporters. The majority falls to the lot of the candidate whose adherents give plumpers.

B. In American use: [ ]

1878 *Cinc. Enquirer* 8 Oct. 4/1. Many mild Republicans and "Independent" voters have agreed to cast "plumpers" today for Fayette Smith....

plunder.

The spoils of government.

Like *spoils* (q.v.), long a military term, probably introduced into English during the Thirty Years War.

A. Also used in England in a political sense:

1672 South *Sermons* V.vi.243 [*OED*]. Those Reforming Harpies, who, by Plunders and Sequestrations, had scraped together three or four Thousand a Year.

1790 Burke *Works* V.224 [*OED*]. They would not hear of transferring the whole plunder of the kingdom to the stockholders in Paris.

B. American political uses:

1787 Mercer in Madison *Fed. Conv.* 421. The executive has not *force:* deprive him of *influence*...and he becomes a mere phantom of authority. The aristocratic party will not even let him in for a share of the plunder.

1800 Hamilton in Parton *Burr* 267. Burr was "bankrupt beyond redemption, except by the plunder of his country."

1802 Fessenden *Dem. Unveiled* 135 ...the Aurora...published a number of articles, with the title of "Public Plunder," which contributed not a little to the election of Mr. Jefferson....

1805 J. Randolph in *Hist. of Cong.* 1016. The United States are not the property of an hereditary despot, or the rich prize of a military adventurer, whose favorites and followers may batten on the spoil of plundered provinces....

c 1828 Swartwout in Lynch *Epoch* 326. Whether or not I shall get anything in the great scramble for plunder remains to be proven.

1840 in Norton *Tippecanoe* App. 24.
And we'll remember each blunder,
While he's flying with plunder
Of the wily magician caught napping at last,
Long after the spoilers from pow'r are cast.

1846 Bowlin in *Cong. Globe* 516/2. The gentleman [Woodward] had talked about the "public plunder" in relation to the Mississippi River, and of which the West was the recipient.

1867 Nasby *Swinging Round the Cirkle* 109. Thurlow Weed sed nothin, but looked on with a sardonic smile, knowin perfeckly well that whoever took the biggest part uv the plunder, he'd control it, anyway.

1876 *Harper's W.* 3 June 443/2. All parties and politicians are willing to say that the offices should be filled only by the honest and capable. But they are careful to add that they hope there are honest and capable men enough in their own party to fill them. That is merely to say that the outs are as good as the ins; and the election thus becomes a fierce struggle for plunder.

pocket veto.

The right of the President to invalidate a bill passed by Congress less than ten days before its adjournment by simply withholding his signature was used by the early Presidents in very rare cases. Not before the days of Jackson did it become a political factor of importance.

1886 Blaine *Twenty Years in Congress* II. 306. Seven of these vetoes were of the kind which, during his [Jackson's] Presidency, received the name of "pocket-veto."

This statement cannot be accepted without some reservation. To begin with, this procedure was not called the "pocket veto" but the "silent veto" or the "silent negative," although there is an early statement that suggests the practice was used by legislators:

1828 in *Cong. Deb.* 11 Feb. If such a doctrine were to prevail, a committee might put documents in their pockets and keep them there until the end of the session.
1832 Webster *Works* I.267. The silent veto is, I believe, the exclusive adoption of the present administration. I think, indeed, that some years ago, a bill, by inadverture or accident, failed to receive the President's signature, and so did not become a law.... In an internal improvement bill of a former session, and in the State interest bill, we have had the silent veto, or refusal without reasons.
Ib. I.268. This seasonable presentment rescued the [Bank] bill from the power of the silent negative.

Speakers and writers less imbued with Senatorial dignity, soon found a more drastic way of describing this form of veto by using phrases centering around the word (verb or noun) *pocket.*

1837 *Ann. of Cleve.* No. 1671. Now, if a bill sanctioned by four-fifths of both branches of our national legislature is to be pocketed....
1840 Hamilton (Ohio) *Harrison Democrat* 18 Feb. 3/1. We...assert...that during this period every great measure originating with the people's representatives in Congress, has been either vetoed or pocketed by the Executive except the bill... which was passed too soon in the Session to be pocketed and by too great a majority to be successfully vetoed.
1840 J. P. Kennedy *Quodlibet* 146 [cf. 53–4]. What between specy circulars, antimasons, pocketing of bills (Lord knows what that means), vetoes, distribution, fortifications, abolition, running down Indians, running up accounts, politics has got into a jumble that a Philadelphy lawyer couldn't steer through them.

As seen from these quotations pocketing a bill was not generally considered a form of the veto. This may be the reason why *pocket veto* is found only at a relatively late date.

1842 *Ohio Statesman* 19 Dec. 3/1. The Pocket Vetoes. [head]
1848 *Ohio St. Jrnl.* 21 Oct. 3/6. In more than half of these instances, the "pocket" veto, that contrivance of tyranny to crush with inevitable death its object—was shamelessly resorted to. The direct Veto was used eleven and the pocket veto twelve times.

point with pride.

To call public attention to the good works of an administration or party program.

Usually associated with *view*

with alarm (q.v.). Frequently used ironically as indicated by quotation marks.

1878 *Nation* 8 Aug. 75/1. Besides "pointing with pride," the remainder of the platform approves of "temperance among the people" and of the navigation laws, and exposes the evil designs of the Democrats, including the payment of $100,000,000 of suspended war claims. **1890** *Nation* 51.144/2. This policy was to result ... in the demonstration to the business community that the Republican party was the only party which could carry on the work of legislation "with neatness and despatch," so that Congress might adjourn early in the summer with a record to which the majority could "point with pride" during the fall campaign. **1892** *Ib.* 4 Aug. 78/2. The Republican Convention in the Portland (Me.) district ... adopted a platform which "points with pride" to the McKinley Law.... **1921** Tumulty *Woodrow Wilson* 12. In view of my subsequent intimacy with Mr. Wilson ..., I cannot now point with pride to the speech I then made attacking him.

political capital.

As in the financial world material goods and property are the financier's capital with which he adds to his wealth by profitable investments, so, too, fortunate advantages and influence are the political capital with which the politician secures advancement and position.

1842 *Ohio Statesman* 30 Jan. 2/4 ... the attempt of the whigs ... to make "political capital," as was avowed by whig members, fizzles out.... **1843** Vanzandt in Tyler *The Tylers* III. 129. If the President concludes he can make capital by the move or can secure the ratification, he will make the treaty as early as he can afterwards.... **1856** *Ohio Statesman* 10 Oct. 2/2. They have their instructions to make political capital in the states for the Black Republicans. **1876** *Harper's W.* 22 Jan. 62/3. And all this service has been performed, as we said, unostentatious, without the least self-seeking or attempt to make political capital.

political general.

An officer who exerts his political influence to secure a commission, which could in peace time be turned again into political advantage.

1863 Russell *My Diary North and South* 389. As an officer of the regular army he [McDowell] has a thorough contempt for what he calls "political generals"—the men who use their influence with President and Congress to obtain military rank, which in time of war places them before the public in the front of events, and gives them an appearance of leading in the greatest of all political movements. **1864** Fremantle *Three Months in the Southern States* 152. [Grenfell] spoke to me in high terms of Bragg, Polk, Hardee, and Cleburne; but he described some of the others as "political" generals, and others as good fighters, but illiterate and somewhat addicted to liquor. He deplored the effects of politics upon military officers.

political necessity.

An early synonym for *imperialism,* emphasizing the inevitability of a certain act or course.

1859 in *Gt. Deb.* III.95 ... but I see that manifest destiny has been ridden to death; we have got rid of it, and now succeeds to "manifest destiny," "political necessity." ... I do not know but what it is necessary that this should come under the auspices of "political necessity"; because I believe the doctors who taught in the school of "manifest destiny" only contend that manifest destiny extended over the whole continent, and now we are to leave the continent and go to sea; we must have a new era and we are to take "political necessity."

See MANIFEST DESTINY.

political orthodoxy.

See PARTY ORTHODOXY.

politician.

While *politician* (with its cognates) is an international word and frequently used in a derogatory sense in many languages, it seems this sense is also strongly prevalent in American usage.

1776 Paine *Works* II.152. Such a thought's unworthy a man of honor, and is the true characteristic of a narrow heart and a pidling politician.

1807 Adams *Works* IX.591. You ask me, if I do not sometimes imprecate evils on the day on which I became a politician.... I do not curse the day when I engaged in public affairs. I do not say when I became a politician, for that I never was.

1839 *Buckeye Whig* 9 Aug. 4/5. I cannot look upon him [Van Buren] in any other light than as a mere party politician.

1852 *Scott Battery* 13 July 2/2. We wish to be understood by *politicians,* those who make their politics a stock in trade, and set themselves up to the highest bidders.

1863 Halpine *Miles O'Reilly* 93 ... to be now called a politician is almost equivalent to be called a rogue.

1864 *Ann. of Cleve.* No. 1628. Some men believe that the profession of politics is a mean and unworthy one. They may admit that the calling of a politician or statesman, and in the higher sense these are synonymous, is an able or useful one, but believe that the affairs of state have gotten into such a condition that honest men cannot afford to be associated with politics or politicians.

1864 Storrs in Adams *Emery A. Storrs* 46. So thoroughly chronic have scoundrelism and base selfishness become with some of those who have hitherto disgraced the name of politics by calling themselves politicians, that I fear the disease is alto-

gether ineradicable in them. What I do mean to say is this: that the people have always appreciated the greatness of our nation and its value infinitely better than politicians as a class have done; that had its salvation been entrusted to politicians alone it would have miserably perished the first year of the rebellion.

1876 *Harper's W.* 22 April 323/1. In general, by active politicians we mean that class of our fellow-citizens who regard the government as a system of offices which they either hold or would like to hold, and which they consider to be the proper possession of those who have worked for the party.

1935 Pollard *A Connotary* 47. Politician— (a) One who thinks of the next election; whereas the statesman thinks of the next generation. (b) The only animal who can sit on the fence and keep both ears to the ground.

1947 in *Time* 6 Jan. 27/1. That showed me he was a loyal man—but also, which is perhaps better—that he was a damn smart politician. Politician is a word which has got a bad connotation in many parts of the world.... I sometimes think what the world needs is more smart politicians— especially if they are loyal men too.

See BAR ROOM POLITICIAN, BEER SHOP POLITICIAN, COFFEE-HOUSE POLITICIAN, GROG SHOP POLITICIAN, POT HOUSE POLITICIAN, SMALL POTATO.

Polk stalk (and other Polk puns).

During the campaign of 1844 the stalk of the pokeberry was often used as a Democratic symbol:

1844 *St. Louis Reveille* 9 June 2/1. When a Polk procession shall come to march through the streets, with a tall poke stalk, as their standard, and gaunt poke fluttering on its top [see FLY-UP-THE-CREEK], what a tremendous enthusiasm they will create!

1844 *Buckeye Eagle* 11 June 2/6. He would have found that the coon is an animal of too much sense ever to touch a

Polkberry. He would have learned, more-over, that the Polk is a good-for-nothing, poisonous, stinking weed...and that about the last of October and first of No-vember, a succession of heavy frosts comes on, which invariably KILLS the Polk-stalks down to the very root....

But after Polk's veto of the River and Harbor bill, the snags in the Mississippi River became known as "Polk stalks":

1846 *Frankfort Commonwealth* 22 Sept. 2/6. It will be seen that snags are now dubbed "Polk Stalks"—a very appropriate name as all will agree.
1848 *Xenia* (Ohio) *Torchlight* 22 June 2/4. Polk-Stalking. His boat ran foul of a "Polk-Stalk"....
1852 *Scott Battery* 27 July 1/4. We were called "Polk stalks" after our former friend vetoed the River and Harbor Bill....

Other puns:

pork.

1845 (Logansport, Ind.) *Logan Chief* 1 March 2/6. No doubt they would vote for the daily arrival of "Pork and Dol-lars." [Polk and Vice-President Dallas]

Polka.

1846 *Cleve. Herald* 2 Jan. 3/2. The way the nation danced the Polka....

Polkat.

1844 *Wash. Intelligencer* 23 Aug. 3/3. A Chance for the Polkats [head].
1844 *The Coon Hunter* (Ann Arbor) 13 July 3/2. The real Polkats also now for ...selling....
1844 *Frankfort Commonwealth* 13 Aug. 2/4. Polk-at Infidelity.

Polkocracy.

1844 *Whig Battering-Ram* 16 Aug. 2/3. The Statesman...again omitted to record its lists of wonderful changes in favor of Polkocracy!

Polko-foco.

1844 *Buckeye Eagle* 16 Oct. 3/3. A Polko-foco Pleasure Excursion [head].

to poke.

1844 *Buckeye Eagle* 19 June 4/2.
O, annexation was the yoke
That fixed Van like a "pig in a poke."
They poked it to the cunning elf
By poking Jimmy Polk himself.
Ib. 1/5.
  Let Freedom's sons all faithful be,
    And surely they'll be lucky;
  And poke out Polk of Tennessee,
    And poke in Old Kentucky.
1852 *Scott Battery* 27 July 1/4.
The Whigs were Polked in forty-four,
We'll Pierce them in fifty-two.

pony convention.

Probably referring to a minority or rump convention. The *DA* lists one meaning of *pony* as "some-thing small of its kind." [ ]
1844 *Niles' Reg.* 14 Sept. 21/1. The third —General Drew—was put up by a sort of poney [sic] convention at Little Rock.

poor man's candidate.

1835 *Scioto Gazette* 23 Sept. 2/1...they wished that the time would arrive when they have a poor man's candidate, an honest and an able man, yet the poor man's candidate.

popular sovereignty.

Cass' letter to Nicholson of De-cember 30, 1847, while stating the theory that the inhabitants of the territories ought to be granted the right to make their own laws, does not use *popular sovereignty,* which term at that time was syn-onymous with *sovereignty of the people* with no special reference to the territories. However, this ex-pression would inevitably turn up in the lively discussion about this theory.

Our earliest example is from 1832:

Edmund Pendleton *The Crisis* 33 [pamphlet]...whose [Jackson's] usurpations have inflicted deep wounds on the Constitution; whose tyranny has gone far to discredit the whole system of popular sovereignty....

The more the term became connected with the slavery problem the more it assumed the character of an exciting catchword.

1849 in *Cong. Globe* 30 Cong. 2nd sess. 191/2. According to the theory of our Government, the creation of a state is an act of popular sovereignty, not of ordinary legislation....

1854 *Ann. of Cleve.* No. 556. "Popular Sovereignty" is one of the catch phrases of the demagogues.

1855 *Marshall* (Mich.) *Expounder* 18 Oct. 2/1. The principle of popular sovereignty in Kansas is now undergoing a fiery ordeal....The final triumph of popular sovereignty in Kansas is only a question of time.

1856 Phillips *Kansas* 410. The term "popular sovereignty" was made the foundation-stone of American despotism.

During the Lincoln-Douglas controversies, the term achieved renewed prominence. We quote only one example:

1856 Lincoln in *Lincoln Cyc.* The essence of squatter or popular sovereignty—I don't care how you call it—is that if one man chooses to make a slave of another, no third man shall be allowed to object.

See SOVEREIGNTY, SQUATTER SOVEREIGNTY.

Populist (Populite) party.

Early in the history of the People's party the need for a convenient appellation for a member of this party made itself felt. John D. Hicks in *The Populist Revolt* (238n.) gives the following report on a contemporary discussion of this matter, naming as his source John W. Breidenthal, a Kansas leader of the new party:

At a conference of Democratic and People's party leaders to discuss fusion plans the late W. F. Rightmire complained about the difficulty he had in using the name "People's party" in ordinary conversation. For example, he could easily refer to a man as a Republican, or a Democrat, or a Prohibitionist, but he could not call him a People's. He had to use a whole sentence in referring to a member of the People's party.

"We need a shorter name for everyday use," said Rightmire. Then turning to Overmyer, one of the Democratic leaders, he said: "Dave, you are long on words—give us a nickname for our party."

Overmyer scratched his head and brought forth from his recollection of Latin the word Populist.

"I'm afraid of that, because the newspapers would be calling us Pops within a week," said the judge.

"So much the better," Overmyer replied. "You want a short name. You can't find one much shorter than 'Pops.'"

According to Stewart (*Ind. Mag. of Hist.*, XIV.361) *Populist* does not occur before the summer of 1892.

[Similar considerations seem to have led to the adoption of Fenian as a party name.]

See PEOPLE'S PARTY.

pork, pork barrel.

Chap. I of E. E. Hale's story "The Children of the Public" (*Frank Leslie's Illustrated Newspaper*, 24 Jan. 1863; reprinted in *If, Yes, and Perhaps*, Boston, 1868) is called "The Pork Barrel." Hale explains that by this expression he means the public's interest in his work that furnishes him with a living:

We have found that this sovereign, in a reckless and unconscious way, is, all the time, making the most profuse provision for all the citizens. We have found that those who are not too grand to trust him fare as well as they deserve. We have found, on the other hand, that those who lick his feet or flatter his follies fare worst of living men. We find that those who work honestly, and only seek a man's fair average of life, or a woman's, get that average, though sometimes by the most singular experiences in the long run. And thus we find that, when an extraordinary contingency arises in life, as just now in ours, we have only to go to our pork-barrel, and the fish rises to our hook or spear.

This comes very close to the later political use of the word, but since as a political expression *pork barrel* has not been found before 1909, we cannot confidently assume a connection. However, the use of *pork* may help to bridge the chronological gap.

1879 *Cong. Record* 2131/1. I will say that those who concocted the idea wished to enlarge the number that would have a part of the "pork." We know how "pork" makes men "holler." Saint Louis is going to have some of the "pork" indirectly....
1888 *Ib.* 3793/1. It is gravely suspected that where there are no votes there is no "pork."
1888 *Ib.* 3793/1. Has the "pork" been so cunningly divided amongst the members of the House in this bill that its final passage is assured notwithstanding its unreasonable and needless appropriations?

Of particular interest are the headlines:

1890 *N. Y. Times* 7 March 1/2. Landed from the Barrel/Result of the first day's fishing for Pork.

It is hardly a coincidence that the three theme words of Hale's story, *pork, barrel,* and *fishing,* recur in such close connection.

The same combination occurs in *Time,* 21 June, 1948, 26/2:

...he [Peter J. McGuinness] fished in Tammany's pork barrel for 28 years to bring improvement to "me people."

In 1909 the pork barrel must have been generally known, since otherwise the cartoons in *Review of Reviews,* September, p. 294 ("The Census Appointments Pork Barrel"), December, p. 674 ("President Taft Kicking out the Pork Barrel") would not have been understandable.

In the following year Beard, *American Government,* p. 271, writes:

...astute wire-pullers, whose tenure of position and standing with their constituents depend...upon the success with which they may secure appropriations for selfish local interests—to use the congressional phrase, "get pork out of the public pork-barrel."

In *National Municipal Review,* VIII (1919). 69, C. C. Maxey gives an interesting although undocumented interpretation of the word:

On the southern plantations in slavery days, there was a custom of periodically distributing rations of salt pork among the slaves. As the pork was usually packed in large barrels, the method of distribution was to knock the head out of the barrel and require each slave to come to the barrel and receive his portion. Oftentimes the eagerness of the slaves would result in a rush upon the pork barrel, in which each would strive to grab as much as possible for himself. Members of congress in the stampede to get their local appropriation items into the omnibus river and harbor bills behaved so much like negro slaves rushing the pork barrel, that these bills were facetiously styled "pork-barrel" bills, and the system which originated them has thus become known as the pork-barrel system.

See BARREL, PUBLIC CRIB.

possum.

The possum's well-known act of playing dead becomes in political metaphor a subterfuge for winning elections or promoting policy. In the 1840's the possum was one of the many animals in the political zoo, which at this time was dominated by the coon, the favorite symbol of the Whig party.

1843 *Lima* (Ohio) *Porcupine* 7 Oct. 3/3. To all public appearances, they are acting the "possum" but privately they are cooning it still. . . . These sly humbug coons thought by "possuming" it, that they might catch the democrats asleep.

1843 *Wm. Ballaert's Texas* 276. Since his Vice-Presidency under La Mar, he has only been playing "possum" in the woods and now comes out with this strange epistle—hoping that he may find supporters.

1844 *Nat. Clay Minstrel* 19.
Oh habe you heard dat possum's case
How he got beat in de 'lection race
De licking he got from dat old coon
While we all sing dis jam up tune.—
    Oh see de possum's treed
    Oh see de possum's treed
    We'll do a little more
    In forty four.
So let 'em now take warning
Heigh ho! another such blow
And de possums all dead in Ohio.

1848 *Marshall* (Mich.) *Democratic Expounder* 22 Sept. 2/5. We understand he is now playing possum with both sides of the house.

In 1872 the possum policy played an important part in the nomination of Greeley:

1872 *Ann. of Cleve.* No. 2533. As it now stands, he [Greeley] is playing possum by pretending he is dead as editor of the Tribune.

1872 *Cleve. Leader* 23 Oct. 2/1. We have wondered . . . what "possum" game the Liberal Democrats were at, that everything should be so quiet all round the political horizon on the side of their camp.

in Chamberlain *Struggle of '72* 322. It [the Missouri Policy] was otherwise designated as the Passive Policy, or "Possum Policy" —the latter phrase referring aptly to the habit of the oppossum to play dead.

in Champ Clark *Quarter Century* I.21. The name of "Possum Policy" was given to that great political movement in Missouri headed by Gen. Frank P. Blair . . . which overthrew the Republican party in Missouri and eventuated in the "Liberal Republican" upheaval and the nomination of Horace Greeley for President in 1872.

postal card platform. [ ]

1908 *Candidates and Issues* 137. A declaration of principles for their 1908 campaign, which will be known in the history of the Prohibition party as their "postal card platform" was adopted by a viva voce vote. . . . it would be a postal card platform of just 321 words.

pot-house politician.

1809 *Knickerbocker* IV.6. He was distracted by petitions of numerous and respectable meetings, consisting of some half a dozen scurvy pot-house politicians.

1834 Frelinghuysen in *Reg. of Deb.* I.817. Of the whole, I will say, Mr. President, that these are no *"pot-house politicians"*. . . .

1875 in *Gt. Deb.* VIII.219 . . . the unprincipled "carpet-bagger," "scalawag," and "pot-house" politician.

1880 *Cleve. Plain Dealer* 5 June 2/2. Instead of a convention of statesmen it is a roaring mob of pot-house politicians.

See POLITICIAN.

power behind the throne.

On March 2, 1770, William Pitt the elder said in the House of Lords,

A long train of these practices has at length unwillingly convinced me that there is something behind the throne greater than the King himself.

This evidently is the source of the phrase *power behind the throne* frequently used in American politics to designate extralegal influences on the President or other high officials. The connection with Pitt's speech becomes clear from those of the following quotations that speak of the power behind the throne greater than the throne itself.

1834 *Mangum Papers* V.580. But the power behind the throne, greater than the throne itself, will begin to find that it has been a little too bold....

1847 Seba Smith *Thirty Years* 248 ... he called your paper a "powerful journal," and then the thought struck me that I had read somewhere that "there's a power behind the throne greater than the throne itself." Well, thinks I, that Ingersoll is a cunning feller, but he ain't agoin' to get ahead of me. If he writes to the power behind the throne I will, too.

1863 Gurowski *Diary* II.73. I read in the paper that ... he, Sumner, is a power behind the throne.

1863 F. Douglass in Sandburg *War Years* II.417. But we are not to be saved by the captain, at this time, but by the crew. We are not to be saved by Abraham Lincoln, but by the power behind the throne, greater than the throne itself. You and I and all of us have this matter in hand.

1864 Kirke *Down in Tennessee* 194.

Woman, in this century, is everywhere that "power behind the throne" which is mightier than the throne itself.

pow wow.

A political meeting, usually characterized by noisy demonstrations.

The term's popularity in the political vocabulary was undoubtedly dependent upon the frequent use of other Indian words, such as *sachem, wigwam* (q.v.).

1840 in *Cong. Globe* App.376/3 ... if we are to judge its population by those who composed the Whig "Pow-Wows" not long since....

1876 *Cleve. Plain Dealer* 13 June 1. The great Republican pow wow at Cincinnati....

1880 *Cinc. D. Gazette* 19 June 1. Hon. Clay Sexton, the Chief of the St. Louis Fire Department, will be the guest of Chief Bunker during the pow-wow.

1947 W. A. White *Ltrs.* 436 ... the Republican pow wow at Topeka.

prairie fire.

Political enthusiasm similar to the rapid and widespread fires on the Western prairies.

The appropriateness of the political extension of the metaphor —similar to the bandwagon or the boom—is suggested in the following quotation:

1846 *Mangum Papers* IV.489. In our State, it is a finable offence, to set fire to the prairie; and yet ... it is usual for all our people, when at a distance they see the devouring flames rage towards them ... they at once go to "firing against fire" and so, save their own premises.

Political uses:

1838 *Mangum Papers* II.528. It [Whig victory] will spread, like a prairie fire, over the Van Buren districts.

1840 *Frankfort Commonwealth* 21 April 3/3. Old Hudson this morning rolled

down upon us a spring-tide of Whig victories obtained at the town meetings in the interior. We have been talking of the Harrison fires blazing upon the prairies of the West.... How are the fires of liberty kindling upon our own mountains—the Catskills are illuminated, and the crests of the Shawangunk mountains of old Ulster are burnished with gold.
1840 *Rough-hewer* 48/1. First Gun from Illinois. "The Prairie on Fire!"
1858 *N. Y. Eve. Post* in Sparks *Deb.* 319. "The prairies are on fire" and all parties partake of the general enthusiasm.
1872 *Nation* 11 July 17. After the hush before Baltimore is over, and the loud bawling after Baltimore has subsided a little, we shall be able to see whether there is any "prairie fire" sweeping all before it, or whether there is to be an excessively tiresome fight.
1872 *Ib.* 18 July 34/1. On the whole, if the Governor [Blair of Mich.] is as good a prophet as he is an historian and observer, he will sweep the Northwest like a prairie fire, and Greeley and Brown will be elected long before November.
1876 in Garfield *Works* II.374. We had our revenge, though, in taking which we inaugurated the policy of the canvass in spite of him which carried the State like a prairie on fire.

A variant of the usual formula:
1838 Strong *Diary* I.93. Speech from Philip Hone and another from Reynolds. Neither were much more than sufficient to set the North River on fire.

predatory wealth.

An epithet for big business coined by Theodore Roosevelt.

His first formula was apparently *predatory capitalist.*
1907 Roosevelt *Works* XVI.81. This is the view announced from time to time... now by a group of predatory capitalists.
1907 in White *Autobio.* 393. In 1907 Theodore Roosevelt was fighting this consolidation, or what he called "predatory wealth."

1908 Roosevelt *Works* XV.495. It is not at all infrequent to read in the same speech a denunciation of predatory wealth fostered by special privilege and defiant of both the public welfare and law of the land.
c 1910 in Luthin *Am. Demagoguery* 49. When Bilbo's mentor Vardeman rattled the saber at "predatory wealth," it was an indication that there existed a direct connection between the Populism of the 1890's, the "progressivism" of the pre-World War I decade, and the later southern demagoguery.

presidential bee.

Comparisons between the aspirations to become President and the irritating sting of a bee seem to be older than the actual expression *presidential bee.* In speaking of Grant as a possible candidate, Lincoln is reported to have said:
1864 in Whipple *Story-Life of Lincoln* 587. I was afraid of Grant, because we are all human; although I would rather be beaten by him than by any living man. When the Presidential grub gets inside of a man it hides itself and burrows deep. That basilisk is sure to kill.

When it was suggested that Salmon P. Chase's ambitions made him unfit for a cabinet post, Lincoln countered with a story about a weak, old horse bothered by a chin fly. The driver protested that the insect should not be driven away because it was the only thing that made the horse go.
in Whipple 588. Now, if Mr. Chase has a Presidential "chin fly" biting him, I'm not going to knock it off, if it will only make his Department go.

The presidential bee seems to be a cross between these insects and the proverbial bee in the bonnet. It is first found in 1878.

Ohio St. Jrnl. 15 Aug. 2/4 ... Thurman with the Presidential bee buzzing in his ears.

1896 *Puck* 19 Feb. [cartoon]. The Presidential Bee. Hear the merry hum of the Presidential bees as they flit from flower to flower in the political garden.

1900 Roosevelt *Ltrs.* II.1446 ... it seems to me there can be no more awful fate than for a man to get a Presidential bee in his bonnet.

The *Puck* cartoon is not the only use of this motif. In *Rev. of Rev.* (1907, XXXVI.163) Bryan is shown having been stung so hard by the bee that he seemed to be put out of consideration for the nomination in the following year.

presidential fever.

A desire prevalent among many political leaders to become President of the United States.

1858 Parker *Life and Corr.* II.222. The Land Fever is more contagious than the Presidential Fever, and equally fatal to the moral powers.

1874 *Urbana* (Ohio) *Citizen and Gazette* 10 Sept. 2/3. The "old man eloquent" [Allen] evidently has the Presidential fever....

1879 Sherman *Recoll.* II.730. I am not now, and do not intend to get, infected with the presidential fever.

1879 *N. Y. Trib.* 29 May 4/5. The Presidential fever is raging fearfully now.

President maker.

A. Probably based upon *king-maker,* the epithet applied to the Earl of Warwick during the reigns of Henry VI and Edward IV:

1599 Daniel *Civ. Wars* [*OED*]. That great King-maker Warwick, so far growne In grace with Fortune, that he gouverns it, And Monarchs makes.

B. The term *president-making,* however, is older than *president-maker* in American politics:

1830 *Argus of W. America* (Frankfort, Ky.) 1 Sept. 2/3. This new mode of President making invented by Mr. Clay, whatever may be its results, excites some curiosity.

1832 *Mangum Papers* V.532 ... our modern President-making American System.

1835 *Cinc. Gazette* 14 March 2/1. President Making.... The constitution has reserved to the people the privilege of making their President....

1846 *Cong. Globe* 388/3. App. The gentleman from South Carolina tells us that this notice is a war measure, and that rumor says that it is a scheme for President-making.

1859 Wilmer *Press Gang* 216. Mr. Forney, president-maker and editor of the Philadelphia Press, is already on his side.

1880 Brisbin *Life of Garfield* 374. The Alabama delegation was first to file in as a body, and its two rows of President-makers nestled down in front of the stage....

pretorian band.

Established as an imperial bodyguard under Augustus, the Roman praetorian guard came into bad repute under the later emperors because of its excessive assumption of power.

In American politics the term *pretorian guard* (or *band*) was applied to those groups who attempted to dominate the affairs of government, their leader usually being characterized as a Caesar.

1791 Madison *Writings* 8 Aug. VI.58. The stock-jobbers will become the pretorian band of the Government, at once its tool and its tyrant.

1836 *Scioto Gazette* 27 April 1/6 ... our American Caesar [Jackson] ... designates his successor, and calls upon his Praetorian Cohorts to confirm the selection.

1840 Clay in Norton *Tippecanoe* 281.
There is yet another class, which, in the
administration of State justice, should not
be unnoticed. I mean the boisterous office-
holders, the Praetorian guard, I was going
to say, of Mr. Van Buren.

1869 Curtis *Orations* II.28. The rings, the
demagogues, the Swartwouts, the pretorian guards, all the minions of prejudice,
passion, and selfish interest, will cry to
heaven.

1874 Foote *Casket* 147. So terrific had Mr.
Davis and his Pretorian bands become....

See PALACE (TROOPS, GUARD).

principles not men.

American variant of *measures
not men* (q.v.).

1793 *Nat. Gazette* in Leary *Freneau* 236.
Principles and not men, ought ever to be
the objects of republican attachment.

1828 *Ann. of Cleve.* No. 427. The motto of
Mr. Niles has ever been, "principles and
not men," and he does not now directly
avow any preference for either of the opposing candidates for the presidency.

1834 Leggett *Pol. Writings* I.52. Among
the catchwords on which they [Whigs]
seem most to rely for success, are the
shouts which they are forever bawling in
our ears, of "Constitution and Laws!" and
"Principles, not men!"

1834 *Ib.* I.54. Among the vague and ambiguous sentiments by which they profess
to be governed, is the stale and unmean-
ing phrase, of "Principles not Men." This
is one of those puzzling maxims with
which sordid and selfish politicians have
ever attempted to cheat mankind.

progressive.

From an ideological point of
view the history of progress has
been treated by Ekirch (*The Idea
of Progress in America, 1815–1860*,
1944). From his rich material it
becomes clear that leading American thinkers of the first part of the
nineteenth century firmly believed

in the progressive tendency of human culture, i.e., a general development from worse to better. We
supplement Ekirch's ideological
findings by quotations illustrating
the use of *progressive* in politics
where the advocates of reform frequently used it because it recommended proposed changes as lying
in the natural path of evolution.
The first introduction of *progressive* into the field of party politics
occurred in 1844:

Ohio St. Jrnl. 20 Aug. 2/2. Some time ago,
that prominent Jacobinical sheet, the Cincinnati Enquirer, gave ... an exposition of
the aims and character of *Modern* or
"Progressive Democracy.".... this "Progressive" faith. We consider it identical
with the ultra-federalism of 1800—and of
1807–08.

From the *Buckeye Eagle* it appears
that the "progressive" Democrats
were identified with free trade and
direct taxation:

19 June 1/4. Jackson Democracy in 1828
vs "Progressive Democracy" in '44. [Head
of article.]

Already at this time there were
objections from the Democrats to
the term:

Democratic Mon. Mag. I.129. It has lately
become the wont of the enemies of Democracy in this country, to characterize it
as "Progressive Democracy.".... the term
progressive, as applied to the Democratic
party, is intended to cast reproach and
odium.

In 1846 a group called the "progressives" is mentioned in connection with the election of judges in
New York (*Frankfort Commonwealth*, 15 September, 1/5).
Between 1850 and the end of the
century the word turns up here

and there, partly as a mere political term and partly with a distinct philosophical background.

1851 *N. Y. Trib.* 12 June 4/1. The truer way of testing institutions is to enquire whether they are progressive, whether they tend to the improvement of the masses, and to their own reform and amelioration, not what accidental evils may attend them.

1852 *Garrison Story* III.372 . . . the women are claiming entire equality of rights with men—the right to be ministers, doctors, lawyers, and even legislators! Really, the age is "progressive"—and, beyond all cavil, "the world moves."

1852 *Am. Whig Rev.* XVI.8. It [Dem. platform] is so directly hostile to that liberality and progressiveness of spirit which is the peculiar boast of at least some portions of the "Democracy," that we should wonder at the air of satisfaction with which it has been bolted by the "progressionists," did we not know how much the Locofoco idea of "Democratic progression" is really worth.

1853 *Ann. of Cleve.* No.2421 . . . the Whig party is broken down and the progressives must form a new party.

1853 *Ib.* No.2464. The pro-slavery element [in the Democratic party] is sloughing off and joining the hard shells. The remainder are the liberal progressives.

1859 G. F. Train *Spread-Eagleism* xii. Egypt gave Industry, Greece Liberty . . . leaving America to combine the whole and represent the Progressive Idea.

1863 Forney in Dennett *Hay* 146. Lincoln is the most truly progressive man of the age, because he always moves in conjunction with propitious circumstances, not waiting to be dragged by the force of events, or wasting strength in premature struggles with them.

1870 *Harper's W.* 27 Aug. "Progressive Democracy" [head of editorial dealing with movement within the party to handle the intransigent elements, particularly in the South].

1884 *Century* XXVIII.143. Wanted. A Party of Progress. [head]

In 1886 we find a local party in New York calling themselves the Progressive Labor party. (*Cyc. of Am. Govt.*)

The rise of *stand pat* (q.v.) in the first years of the new century gave a fresh impulse to the word *progressive;* the contrast between *standpatism* and its synonyms on one side and *progressive* and its synonyms on the other is stressed:

1910 *Rev. of Rev.* XLII. 4/2. He [Taft] has made the mistake of treating these men as if their fundamental attitude was "insurgent" rather than "progressive."

1911 *Ib.* XLIII. 337/2. It is a mistake to say that the progressive movement sprang into being at the beginning of the present Congress. The struggle between the progressives and reactionaries went on while Roosevelt was President.

1912 *Rev. of Rev.* XLVI. 195/1. There was a sharp line of cleavage between Progressives and Standpatters.

1911 marks a short period during which *progressive* was the name of a nation-wide party:

1911 *Rev. of Rev.* XLIII. 273/1. Senator Bourne of Oregon is the president of a National Progressive Republican League, the object of which is announced to be "the promotion of popular government and progressive legislation."

1911 *Ib.* XLIV. 535/1. The first national conference of "Progressive" Republicans was held at Chicago on October 16.

1912 *Ib.* XLVI. 397/1. It is purely a matter of guesswork whether in the long run the Progressive Republicans of the West will keep the name "Republican" or let it drop. . . . the formation of the new Progressive party has seemed to be the only means by which people could this year act together who desired to oppose the machines of both of the old parties.

During this same period *progressive* continued to be used as a term applying to a general political attitude:

1913 Wilson *Public Papers* III.27. Therefore I shall not be acting in a partisan spirit when I nominate progressives—and only progressives.
1915 *Ib.* III.238... you would have to admit that only about one-third of the Republican party is progressive, and you would also have to admit that about two-thirds of the Democratic party is progressive. Therefore the independent progressive voter finds a great deal more company in the Democratic than in the Republican ranks.

propaganda.

A. An abbreviation of *Congregatio de propaganda fide,* an institution for the propagation of the Catholic religion, officially organized in 1622. According to Feldman (*Zeitschrift für deutsche Wortforschung,* XIII.275) its history as a term of secular politics goes back to France and the year 1790, when reactionary papers hinted at the existence of a club *de la propagand,* a secret organization aiming at the dissemination of revolutionary ideas in the neighboring countries. This may have been a hoax, but it was generally believed and both German and English writers uttered warnings against the subterranean work of the French propaganda:

1800 *Der Politische Thierkreis* 202... indem sich die Fürsten bestrebten den Thron eines Einzigen zu befestigen, erschütterten sie die Throne Aller. Ihre Gespensterfurcht vermehrte sich dadurch und einige Unsinnige liessen sie überall die Fackel der Propagande erblicken, wo manchmal kaum ein Oellämpchen zu sehen war. Die Propaganda, diese berühmte Chimäre unserer Zeit, das Schrecken der Grossen, die Belustigung der Vernünftigen, glich jenen fabelhaften Ungethümen der Vorzeit, denen jedes Jahrhundert eine Kralle mehr andichtete; unsre Kindeskinder werden noch von ihr singen und die Furcht jener Allmächtigen spotten.

B. Both the French Revolutionary *propaganda* and the Catholic *propaganda,* the knowledge of the latter probably being kept alive by political agitators of the Know Nothing type, are behind the earlier American uses:

1792 *Nat. Gazette* in Bowers *Jefferson and Hamilton* 168... a vile sycophant, who ... finds his interest in attempting to poison the minds of the people by propaganda and by disseminating principles and sentiments utterly subversive of the true republican interest of the country.
1807 *Weekly Inspector* (N.Y.) 75. We have ever been disposed to attribute the wonderful success of the French, since their revolutionary era, to Propagandism or, in other words, to the poison of their principles, circulated by their emissaries; and corrupting the mind of the nations they proposed to attack.
1836 *Scioto Gazette* 23 March 4/2. A report became very prevalent in a contiguous county, that Van Buren was a Roman Catholic, and ardently engaged in advancing his Holiness' last Bull of Propagandafide.
1857 *Leslie's Ill. Newspaper* 3 June 415. The Propaganda—The Christian Advocate and Journal condenses from the North British Review certain interesting statistics of the great Romish "Society for propagating the Faith"....

C. In the same internal American politics, the word *propaganda* became a slogan after the Mexican war in connection with the efforts of pro-slavery men to carry the "domestic institution" into the newly acquired territory. That these efforts were felt to be similar in spirit to the Catholic *propaganda* becomes clear from Seward's words:

1858 in *Gt. Deb.* V.174. To expect the Democratic party to resist slavery and favor freedom is as unreasonable as to look for Protestant missionaries to the Catholic Propaganda of Rome.

However, Seward was by no means first to characterize pro-slavery tendencies as *propaganda:*

1850 in Going *David Wilmot, Free-Soiler* 373. Forney and his particular friends, a knot of ultra slave propagandists, did not want that any democrat other than Forney should be elected.

1850 in *Ib.* 375. The resolutions of our last county convention ... declare that any attempt to impose upon us Slavery propagandism as a test, would be regarded as an invasion of our rights.

1854 in *Ib.* 458. He expressed his determination to vote for no man who ... joined hands with the slavery propaganda.

1856 *Ann. of Cleve.* No.2339. The cowardly need not remind us of the power and union and shrewdness of the slavery propaganda.

It is worth noticing that while in American usage *propaganda* still is a derogatory word, it has sunk down to "harmless generalities" (Feldman, 275) in the European languages. Braun, *Lily,* I.248: "Er machte propaganda für eine Schlittenfahrt."

The reason must be that in Europe the word was never closely connected with any excited group in conflict after the days of the French Revolution, while in America it has not had time to get rid of the connotations caused by its connection with the slavery conflict.

1929 Seldes *You Can't Print That* 427. The term propaganda has not the sinister meaning in Europe which it has acquired in America (due, no doubt, to its conjunction with the adjective "German") .... in European business offices the word means advertizing or boosting generally.

propeller stop.

A modernization of *whistle stop* (q.v.) :

1954 *Cols. Citizen* 31 Oct. Republican National Chairman Leonard W. Hall in Washington, today denounced Democrats who criticized Friday's four-state "propeller-stop" election campaign by President Eisenhower....

protection.

Very early in the history of the United States there arose a cry for the protection of young American industries and manufacturers against the overwhelming European competition:

1789 R. W. Thompson *Hist. of Protective Tariff Laws* 38 [petition from tradesmen, laborers, etc. of Baltimore] ... your petitioners rejoice at the prospect this affords them, that America, freed from the commercial shackles which have so long bound her, will see and pursue her true interest, becoming independent in fact as well as in name; and they confidently hope that the encouragement and protection of American manufactures will claim the earliest attention of the Supreme Legislature of the nation....

The preamble to the first tariff law, presumably written by Madison, repeated their phrase:

Ib. 47. Whereas, it is necessary for the support of the Government, the discharge of the debts of the United States, and the encouragement and protection of manufactures, that duties be laid on goods, wares and merchandise imported.

The divergent economic interests of the North and the South produced a controversy over the value of the protective tariff until the term *protectionist* became almost a party name. While in 1816 John Calhoun had advocated a protective tariff—

in *Gt. Deb.* XII.23. Should the National Government not afford the American manufacturers protection, the dangers which invest and threaten them will destroy all their hopes, and will close their prospects of utility to their country.—

by 1828 the growth of sectionalism had changed his opinion as to its merits and need:

Calhoun *Works* VI.2 . . . is a unanimous opinion that the act of Congress of the last session, with the whole system of legislation imposing duties on imports,—not for revenue, but the protection of one branch of industry at the expense of others,—is unconstitutional, unequal, and oppressive, and calculated to corrupt the public virtue and destroy the liberty of the country. . . .

Other Southerners voiced similar objections:

Claiborne in *Gt. Deb.* XII.50. There is no necessity for the Government to resort to a hot-bed system of legislation, to force into premature existence a number of sickly manufacturing establishments that will want constant aid from the Government. When the population advances to that point, Government has only to afford protection to all. . . .

public crib.

A. The financial resources of the federal government, from which all may share.

Our earliest quotation clearly shows the agricultural background of the phrase:

1824 *Cinc. Nat. Rep.* 13 April 1/3 . . . he [Randolph] thought it was time that every member who did not intend to rely on the public crib, but to feed out of his own corn-house, should go home and plant his corn.

B. As the spoils system (q.v.) became an accepted policy and the quest for patronage the sole aim of many office holders, the metaphor developed more satirical connotations, and those who fed at the public crib were the objects of scorn and ridicule.

1834 *Niles' Reg.* 8 Nov. 147/2. The desire to feed at the "public crib" is excessive. It is truly astonishing with what eagerness offices are sought that yield a less annual amount, than a respectable mechanic earns by his daily labor.

1844 *Nat. Clay Minstrel* 46.

Our little Mat from Kinderhook, no
  friend to country quarters,
Resolved to rule a second time, or dangle
  in his garters;
Though Lindenwald grow cabbages, he
  got but little of it:
"Twixt *Public* crib and *private* crib,
  there's a difference in the profit.

1857 Benton *Thirty Yrs. View* I.49. They have no other view . . . than to get one elected who will enable them to eat out of the public crib.

See PORK BARREL.

public debt a public blessing.

The widespread opinion that this axiom was authored by Hamilton must be modified. It is true that in 1781 he wrote to Robert Morris:

1781 Hamilton *Works* III.387. A national debt, if it is not excessive, will be to us a national blessing. It will be a powerful cement of our Union.

But this is really not meant to proclaim an economic theory; evidently what Hamilton meant to say was that anything that tended to create interests common to all the States was bound to prove beneficial even though it might be bad in itself.

When he took up a similar phrase in 1790, he made it quite clear that any generalization of this original meaning was foreign to his intention:

1790 Hamilton *Works* II.283. Persuaded, as the Secretary is, that the proper funding of the present debt will render it a national blessing, yet he is so far from acceding to the position, in the latitude in which it is sometimes laid down, that "public debts are public benefits"... that he ardently wishes to see it incorporated as a fundamental maxim in the system of public credit of the United States, that the creation of debt should always be accompanied with the means of extinguishment.

1792 *Ib.* III.40. Much declamation has been indulged against certain characters, who are charged with advocating the pernicious doctrine, that "public debts are public blessings," and with being friends to a perpetuation of the public debt of the country.... That officer [Hamilton], it is very certain, explicitly maintained, that the funding of the existing debt of the United States would render it a national blessing.... But whether right or wrong, it is quite a different thing from maintaining, as a general proposition, that a public debt is a public blessing.

To judge from frequent later criticisms it appears that the phrase was used in justification of irresponsible financial propositions:

1790 in Link *Democratic Societies* 51.

Tax on tax, young Balever cries,
More imports, and a new excise,
A public debt's, a public blessing,
Which 'tis of course a crime to lessen.

1794 Taylor *Principles and Tendency* 21. A dishonest policy comprises its principles in its motto. It exclaims "A national debt is a national blessing," and it filches all it can get.

1795 Freneau *Suppl. to N. Jersey Chron.* 2 May. With some people "national debts are national blessings"! a system borrowed from the wretched policy of Great Britain.

1803 *Mass. Spy* 10 Aug. 3/1. "A public Debt is a public Curse"—say the Jacobins.

1813 Jefferson *Works* IX.411. At the time we were funding our national debt, we heard much about "a public debt being a public blessing".... This paradox was well adapted to the minds of believers in dreams, and the gulls of that size entered *bona fide* into it.

1830 Webster *Works* 26 Jan. III.303. The gentleman has not seen how to reply to this, otherwise than by supposing me to have advanced the doctrine that a national debt is a national blessing.

public office a public trust.

A slogan generally attributed to Grover Cleveland.

However, the slogan and variants are found much earlier in American politics:

1778 Payson in Thornton *Pulpit in Am. Revolution* 343. Power being a delegation, and all delegated power being in its nature subordinate and limited, hence rulers are but trustees, and government a trust....

1835 Calhoun in *Covode Report* 6 Jan. 4. So long as offices were considered as public trusts, to be conferred on the honest, the faithful, and capable, for the common good, and not for the benefit or gain of the incumbent or his party....

1844 Briggs in *Mass. Acts* 363. Public offices are public trusts, created for the benefit of the whole people, and not for the benefit of those who may fill them.

1872 Durbin Ward *Speeches* 266. Has he [Grant] ever treated the great office you gave him as a public trust?

1872 Sumner in *Cong. Globe* 31 May. The phrase, "public office is a public trust," has of late become common property.

1880 in Forney *Lives of Hancock and English* 390. Public office is a trust, not a bounty bestowed upon the holder.

The phrase reached the peak of its popularity in the campaign of 1884, when it became the dominant slogan of the Democratic party. W. C. Hudson gives his account of what he considered its original coinage: as a title for a political document:

Random Recoll. of an Old Pol. Reporter 180. I went at the making of one, much after the manner of the headline writer in a newspaper office.... "Public Office Is a Public Trust" was the result. That was what the platform of 1876 had said and what Cleveland had said on every occasion that was proper. It was the dogmatic form of what he had expressed with greater elucidation.

A proof of the amended page was required, and, when it was received, I took it to the Governor for his inspection. His eye at once went to the top line and, pointing to it, he asked: "Where the deuce did I say that?"

You've said it a dozen times publicly but not in those few words," I replied.

Hudson later (p. 182) acknowledges the presence of earlier usages of the slogan, but insists that he had never been aware of them.

public opinion.

The concept of public opinion as a force to be considered and respected by the rulers is, of course, international, and much older than the United States. In France it is attested as early as the 18th century:

1775 Voltaire *Don Pédre* I.ii. L'opinion publique est une arme puissante....

Utterances both praising the power of public opinion and criticizing it are quite common in American political literature.

1791 *Nat. Gazette* in Bowers *Jefferson and Hamilton* 163. Public opinion sets the bounds to every government, and is the real sovereign of every free one.

1791 Jefferson *Works* V.282. Government being founded on opinion, the opinion of the public, even when it is wrong, ought to be respected to a certain degree.

1799 Fisher Ames *Works* 99. It must be remembered too, that publick opinion is the great auxilliary of good government.

1811 Monroe in Mayo *Clay* 391. The President does indeed hold the rudder of the Ship of State; he guides, but it is public opinion which makes the vessel move.

1816 Jefferson *Works* VI.524. Public opinion is a censor before which the most exalted tremble for their future as well as present time.

1835 in Garrison *Life of Garrison* App. 391. In every direction I see the minority prostrate before the majority; who ... perpetuate every enormity in the name of "public opinion." "Public opinion" is at this hour, the demon of oppression.

1852 Phillips "Public Opinion" in *Sp. and Lectures* 52. All hail, Public Opinion! To be sure, it is a dangerous thing under which to live. It rules to-day in the desire to obey all kinds of laws, and takes your life.

1856 Lincoln *Works* II.310 [Chicago speech]. Our government rests in public opinion.

1874 in *Appleton's Encyc.* 161/1. Public Opinion! what sacrifices has it not commanded....

Occasionally the phrase is *public sentiment:*

1845 in *Cong. Globe* 9 Jan. Another gentleman (Mr. Ingersoll) advanced a similar doctrine. He said "that public sentiment was the great law of this and every free country, and is much better than written law."

1858 Lincoln *Works* III.252. In this [Ottawa] and like communities, public sentiment is everything. With public sentiment nothing can fail; without it, nothing can succeed.

pull.

Pull meaning "political influence" is one of that group of metaphors centering around puppet, wire-pulling, etc., but there is a possibility that *long pull* was also a factor in its development.

1887 *N. Y. Herald* 21 Feb. 3/3. He can't be put in jail because he has a pull.
1888 *N. Y. Trib.* 29 Oct. 3/1. The Democratic Committee has a strong "pull" here.
1899 *Rev. of Rev.* XIX. 136/1 ... they have somehow got the notion that everything yields to the political "pull."
1901 Flynt *World of Graft* 32. It is comparatively easy to make a "spring" out of the clutches of the law when there is sufficient money to hand around to the various persons with "pull."
1904 Riis *Roosevelt* 106 ... the man who was determined that the fellow with no pull should have an even chance with his rival who came backed.

pump priming.

1882 Ogilvie (*OED prime*). To prime a pump, to pour water down the tube with the view of saturating the sucker, so causing it to swell, and act effectually in bringing up water.

Though the term *pump priming* (or *to prime the pump*) is probably much older in American politics, it became very popular during the administration of Franklin D. Roosevelt when the vast expenditures for public works (PWA and WPA) were characterized as only means to bring the nation back to a firm economic status.

1722 *New-England Courant* 7–14 May 3/1. And when Men (covetous Men especially) endeavour to advance themselves by Gifts, it is strong proof that they design to pay themselves by an unjust Improvement of their Places tho' at the Expence of those who have promoted them. No covetous Person will use more Water to fetch the Pump, than he designs to pump out again.
1937 Burns *Roosevelt* 322. The things we had done, which at that time [1935] were largely a monetary and pump-priming policy for two years and a half, had brought the expected result, perfectly definitely.
1938 in *Public Papers of Roosevelt* VII.192. Mr. Ray Bills. "The first thing that we would like to ask you is, while it has been deemed necessary to do a lot of direct pump priming, we would like to know ... what other methods there are. ..." The President. "... I do not look at this just from the point of view of priming the 1938 pump.
1938 *Jim Farley's Story* 131. The solution to be offered Congress was five billion dollars of pump priming in cash and credits, including $1,250,000,000 for the Works Progress Administration. ...

puppet.

Applied to those members of the public who are easily manipulated by more dominant figures; servile party members.

1775 in John Adams *Selected Writings* 40 ... we should be little better than puppets, danced on the wires of the cabinets of Europe.
1807 *Weekly Inspector* 390. But men who happen to possess a little more intellect than these wooden headed puppets of the dominant party. ...
1823 *Cinc. Nat. Rep.* 24 June 2/3. The puppets which they send upon the stage. ... It is not the automaton, nerveless and senseless, we are taught to despise, but the grand operator, the chief juggler, who sits behind the scenes, and moves the wires.
1824 *Ib.* 8 Oct. 2/4. It is the intriguing politician, who sits behind the scenes and moves the wires, while his puppets perform the deception, that is dangerous to a free people.
1838 Hone *Diary* 365 ... the puppet who thought it "honor enough to follow in the footsteps of his illustrious predecessor."
1858 T. Parker in *N. Y. Antislavery St* 27

Feb. 1/6. His [Douglas'] head is familiar with the strings that move the puppets of the party.

See WIRE WORKER.

purge.
Ezekiel 20:38. And I will purge out from among you the rebels, and them that transgress against me. . . .

There is every indication that this word entered politics through its use in church disputes, as, for example, "Pride's Purge" of December 6, 1648, when Colonel Pride excluded all members of the Long Parliament who were suspected of Presbyterian and Royalist leanings (see *OED*).
Early American uses:
1842 in Birney *Ltrs.* II.665. To be and do so, it [our country] must be purged and purified, I know. . . .
1862 *Ann. of Cleve.* No.3035. Ruffians have recently taken it upon themselves to assault colored men. Cincinnati needs some purging.
1872 *N. Y. Trib.* 3 Oct. 4/4. "The Baltimore amalgamation" is fated to be dissolved, and when that happens, then is to come a new party under the old name, "purged" (to use his own beautiful language) "from baser incrustations."

While these early uses are rather sporadic, the word gained importance in 1935 when the purges in Russia were followed soon after by discussions in the United States on the pro and cons of party loyalty:
1935 *Common Sense* March 4/2. Several of the more intelligently radical Brain Trusters . . . were recently removed or transferred in what was called a "purge" by correspondents.
1935 Michael *Handout* 26. "Mr. President, how about that so-called 'purge' down in the Department of Agriculture?" a re-porter asks. "Purge?" smiles back the President [FDR]. "I didn't know they had a purge down there. . . . I guess you mean those changes in officials they had down there, eh? Well, that's just one of those things. I wouldn't call it a purge. We're just going ahead on the trial and error system, you know. . . ."

Puritan.
The term apparently first applied to those 16th century dissenters in the Anglican Church by their opponents (See D. J. McGinn, *The Admonition Controversy* and *OED*).
We have found no evidence that the early settlers of America ever applied the name "Puritans" to themselves. Very likely the derogatory use prevailing in England was also dominant in America:
1630 John Smith in West *Source Book* 164. If it over-glad me to see Industry her selfe adventure now to make use of my aged endevours, not by such (I hope) as rumour doth report, a many of discontented Brounists, Anabaptists, Papists, Puritans, Separatists, and such factious Humorists. . . .

The rehabilitation of the word which led to the meaning now common in historical writings where *Puritan* is a term of praise rather than of obloquy is probably due to the influence of English historians: Neal's *History of the Puritans,* in which he states his purpose to be "to preserve the memory of those great and good men among the Reformers, . . ." was reprinted in 1793; Macaulay in an essay of 1825 called them "the most remarkable body of men, perhaps, which the world has ever produced." (*OED*)

1804 in *Mass. Col. Soc. Publ.* XVII.341 [toast]. The New England Minority— Like true Puritans, not intimidated though involved in the "sin and danger of Non-conformity."
1836 Leonard Withington *The Puritan* I.168. No class of people ever came nearer to consistency in the views they adopted concerning the religious part of these questions, than the ancient Puritans. [On p. 182 he points directly to Macaulay.]
1853 Sumner *Works* IV.75. Few persons in history have suffered more from contemporary misrepresentation, abuse, and persecution, than the English Puritans.
1868 Curtis *Orations* III.6. The larger and generous Puritanism of America inspired the Revolution. They were Puritan guns whose echo is endless upon Bunker Hill. It was the Puritan spirit that spoke in the Declaration of Independence. It was the Puritan will that shook the glittering hand of the Cavalier Burgoyne from the Hudson. It was to the Puritan idea that Cornwallis surrendered at Yorktown; and, eighty-three years later, it was the Cavalier who again surrendered to the Puritan under the Appomattox apple-tree.

The older meaning of *Puritan* as a narrow-minded, fanatical religious and social reformer still prevails, especially in the Civil War period:
1863 S. S. Cox *Eight Years* 282. Puritanism is the reptile which has been boring into the mound, which is the Constitution, and this civil war comes in like the devouring sea! . . . they [the West] detest the idea of Puritan politics, that sins should be reformed by the State.
1863 Lydia Post, *Soldiers' Ltrs.* 203. They [rebels] think they like us, Western men, pretty well, and they don't like to fight us; but when they speak of the "Puritanic Yankees," they can hardly find words to express their hatred and contempt.
1876 in Garfield *Works* II.373. We are to-day united to the Puritanical host by an artificial tie. . . .
1919 Watterson *Marse Henry* I.141. There was never a more absurd theory than

that, begot of sectional aims and the sectional spirit, which proposed a geographical alignment of Cavalier and Puritan.

The fluctuations in the value of the term give some justification to an otherwise debatable suggestion by G. L. Kittredge:
1914 in *Mass. Col. Soc. Publ.* XVII.393 . . . he [Kittredge] wished that the term Puritan could be eliminated from scientific historical use, inasmuch as it never had a settled meaning such as attaches to "Congregationalist" or "Roman Catholic". . . .

purse-proud.
A derogatory epithet applied to the rich aristocracy; particularly common in the Jackson era as a countercharge to *greasy mechanic, hornyhanded,* etc. (q.v.) .
A. Found in England already in the 18th century.
1745 DeFoe *Eng. Tradesman* II.149 [*OED*]. I think a purseproud tradesman one of the most troublesome and intolerable of all Men.

B. American uses.
1838 Price *Clem. Falconer* II.65. I have no idea that the suffering people of the south are to be ridden down roughshod by the purseproud lordlings of the north.
1840 in Norton *Tippecanoe* 224. It is in such things that the arrogance of the purse-proud office-holder shows itself, and the hypocrisy of those who would use the mechanics is manifested.
1840 *Ib.* App. 21.
We've tried your purse-proud lords, who love
In palaces to shine;
But we'll have a plowman President
Of the Cincinnatus line.
1844 *Wash. D. Globe* 6 Jan. 23/2. Resolved, That each Democrat of Russell [County, Ky.] be appointed a committee . . . to dissuade their neighbors from that influence which has brought ruin on the

laboring classes, and enriched the few purse-proud aristocrats who care nothing for the poor.

1860 in Brownlow *Sketches* 50. The purse-proud aristocrats of the Cotton States.

purse-strings.

Federal spending power. [ ]

The quotation suggests that this particular usage may be American in origin, since the *OED*'s first reference is to 1849.

1833 *Niles' Reg.* XLV. 66/1. It is congress, and not the executive, which holds the purse-strings of the nation.

pussyfoot.

To wage a campaign quietly and without aggressive or positive action.

Apparently first used in the vocabulary of prohibition to designate the stealthy methods of certain agents.

1907 in F. A. McKenzie *"Pussyfoot" Johnson* 86f. It was shortly after this that his famous *sobriquet* first came into use. I find in the Muskogee *Democrat* for December, 1907, two little notes: "The Booze Department of the United States Government under the able direction of 'Demon-fighting' Johnson has saved many a man from swearing off this New Year's Day. . . . Special Agent Johnson, he of the 'Panther' tread, has resented the action of the peddlers of bogus beer and had them all indicted by the Grand Jury. It is evidently *lese majeste* to sue a velvet-shod emissary of Uncle Sam's Booze Department.

1916 Wilson *Somewhere in Red Gap* 63. Kind of like him Wilbur was, talking subdued and cat-footing round very solemn and professional.

1922 *New Rep.* 12 July 173. Pussy Footing on the Railroad Strike [head].

1925 Coan *Red Web* 29. Usually such occasions were followed by a yielding to the counsels of his [Wilson's] pink and pussy-footing advisers.

1927 *Sat. Eve. Post* 24 Dec. 9/1. A good politician is a natural-born pussy-footer.

1932 in Farley *Behind the Ballots* 113. We Democrats must meet the issue fairly, without any pussy-footing.

1944 Willkie in W. A. White *Autobio.* 646. I'm getting pretty sick of the pussyfooters who try to catch the WPA and the National Association of Manufacturers with the same kind of talk.

1950 J. Fidler in *Indianapolis News* 28 April 5/2. Offhand, I don't remember just which politician it was who coined that word, "pussy-footing," but it strikes me as an ideal description for the current "cleanup" campaign of the Motion Picture Association.

Q

quadroon.

A Democratic faction in Philadelphia; refers to the mixed nature of the group. [ ]

1809 Rush *Ltrs.* II.996 . . . he is said to be under the influence of a new sect of Democrats, called "Quadroons." A Mr. Binns, an active and intelligent printer, is at the head of them.

R

radical (reform).

Derived from Latin *radix,* "root," the word means originally "connected with the root," "from the roots up," "thorough." It is used metaphorically in many different ways, of which the one used in medical terminology is most closely connected with its later political use:

1674 R. Godfrey *Inj. & Ab. Physic Pref.* [*OED*]. How to cure a cut Finger radically.

With reference to the ailments of the body politic it occurs in 1735: Bolingbroke *On Parties* xviii.220 [*OED*]. Such a Remedy might have wrought a radical Cure of the Evil, that threatens our Constitution.

The stubborn debates on the English electoral system divided the advocates of its revision into those who thought that a gradual and partial reform would do and those who advocated a "radical reform." 1783 Fox in Goodrich *Brit. Eloquence* 476/1 ... a fact which strikes at the great bulwark of our liberties, and goes to an absolute annihilation, not only of our chartered rights, but of those radical and fundamental ones which are paramount to all charters, which were consigned to our care by the sovereign disposition of Nature, which we can not relinquish without violating the most sacred of all obligations; to which we are entitled, not as members of society, but as individuals and as men; the rights of adhering steadily and uniformly to the great and supreme laws of conscience and duty; of prefering, at all hazards, and without equivocation, those general and substantial interests which we have sworn to prefer; of acquitting ourselves honorably to our constituents, to our friends, to our own minds, and to that public whose trustees we are and for whom we act. 1791 Mackintosh *Defence of the French Revolution* 421. If radical reform is not, at such a moment, procured, all partial changes are evaded and defeated in the tranquillity which succeeds. The gradual reform that arises from the presiding principle exhibited in the specious theory of Mr. Burke, is belied by the experience of all ages.

Up to the days of the French Revolution there is no sign that the friends of radical reform, whose ranks included prime ministers and dukes, were considered as less respectable. At this time, however, a downward trend set in, due to the fact that many of the radical reformers did not conceal their sympathy with French extremists: 1794 Erskine *Sp.* II.204 ... whether the late alleged and unheard of persecutions and sentences shall ... excite us to pursue a radical reform with an ardour proportioned to the magnitude of the object. 1798 *Anti-Jacobin Rev.* 5 March. At Bowood trill his wood-notes wild— How these and more (a phrenzied choir) Sweep with bold hand Confusion's lyre, Till madding crowds around them storm "For one Grand Radical Reform!" *Anti-Jacobin* I.598.

Thus reconcil'd, fond, and delighted,
 Together we'll ride in the storm,
While Jacobin Clubs, all united,
 Make a radical, perfect Reform.

The *OED*'s first example of the shortened *radical* (instead of *radical reformer*) reads: 1802 *Spirit Pub. Jrnls.* VI.4. The sagacious only could have foreseen that he should have become a r-c-l.

By that time the shortened form must have been in general use, since otherwise the abbreviation would not have been understood. We may also deduce that, at least in some quarters, the word was in bad odor, which seems clearly indicated by the choice of the abbreviation r-c-l, instead of the natural r-d-l; it is fairly obvious that the reader was offered a choice of interpreting as either *radical* or *rascal*. And the opprobrium attached to *radical* is put beyond doubt by 1819 Scott 16 Oct. in *OED*. Radical is a word in very bad odour here, being used to denote a set of blackguards.

Referring to the same period:

Robert Dale Owen *Threading My Way* 164. At home we found our father doing well in business, but, as a radical reformer, having lost much in public estimation.

In spite of this devaluation, the word was accepted as a party name by the progressives themselves:

1809 Bentham *Catechism for Radicals* [title].

Early American examples usually refer to English politics:

1817 John Quincy Adams *Memoirs* III.535 ... the Whigs, or, as they style themselves, the Moderate Reformers in Parliament, who, he observed, were utterly disavowed and contemned by the Radical Reformers without-doors.

1828 James Hall *Ltrs. from the West.* If he [the English immigrant] happen to be a ... radical, he disgusts his hearers by his utter disregard of order, law, decency and virtue.

1838 *Wash. Nat. Intelligencer* 24 Jan. 1/1. The mass of the Infidels in this city [NY] are English radicals, well-dressed, strong-minded men but as ignorant of this Government as men in the moon....

In American politics *radical* is is from the beginning a double-edged word. On the one hand its unpleasant connotations are taken over from England, hence *radical* to many people means a disturber of the peace. On the other hand, the idea of radical reform clearly appealed to reform-minded people in various states, hence in this camp *radical* comes to mean something like *progressive*. Both tendencies continue through the later history of the word. How far the adoption of the word by reformers within the Methodist church influ-

enced and perhaps preceded the political use remains to be determined.—[ ] (*Cyclopedia of Methodism*, p. 742)

In 1814 H. G. Otis proposed in a committee report preceding the Hartford Convention:

Hammond *Pol. Hist.* I.384. To enable the delegates from those states, should they deem it expedient, to lay the foundation for a radical reform of the national compact.

In 1822 we find *radical* for the first time (?) as a party name:

1822 *Liberty Hall* 21 Sept. 3/1. They [Tammany followers] now, forsooth, assume the appellation of Reformists, and the people's friends," but are more fitly designated by the appropriate term of Radicals.

In the following year, *radical* appears as the accepted name of the Crawford section and for a short time assumes some degree of national importance. The connection between the Southern party and the New York radicals is clearly indicated in the quotations to follow:

1823 *Cinc. Nat. Rep.* 3 June 2/2. William H. Crawford and the Radical faction of which he is the life blood, are spoken of in terms only of reprobation and contempt.

1824 McDuffie *Internal Improvements* 8. In the same spirit the radicals of New York have defrauded the people out of their right to choose electors of President....

1824 *Albany Argus* 24 Aug. Mr. Crawford is the head and chief of the Radical party whose object it is to beat down and destroy all the most useful institutions of the Federal Government.

1824 Clay *Works* IV.98. But strange—the ultras [Feds] will join the radicals—the extremes meet.

1830 Webster *Works* III.299. Names being regarded as things in such controversies, they bestowed on the anti-improvement gentlemen the appellation of Radicals. Yes, Sir, the appellation of Radicals, as a term of distinction applicable and applied to those who denied the liberal doctrines of internal improvement, originated, according to the best of my recollection, somewhere between North Carolina and Georgia.

In the 1830's the development of *radical* seems to center again in New York where the contrast between "moderate" and "ultra" elements in the Democratic party culminated in the rise of the Loco Focos. (q.v.)

For some time the words *ultra, Loco Foco, agrarian,* and *radical* seem to be almost synonymous.

1830 *N. Y. Sentinel* 26 June 2/1. Quite an Agrarian farce was played last evening in the Eighth Ward, by a few of the real stamp of foreign radicals.

1837 *Madisonian* 16 Sept. 1/6. It is a striking fact that the Locofocos or radicals—a faction that has been known in our country but a year or two—in repeated instances have coalesced with the opposition in order to defeat the regular democratic party.

1838 *Ohio Statesman* 26 Feb. 2/2. If a Democrat had uttered such sentiments [Webster's in 1832], the Federal press ... would have bawled out locofocoism, radicalism, etc. ... Let a man this day express the opinion advanced in the following extract ... and he is immediately denounced as a disorganizer—a radical—an agrarian.

1838 *N. Y. Evening Star* in Thornton *Am. Gloss.* I.302. In a city of 300,000 inhabitants, 2000 radicals, agrarians, Fanny-Wright men, and loco focos can be found.

1840 *Cinc. Gazette* 13 July 2/3 ... it is from these Radical Reformers of Democracy,—the little band in the city of New York—the Fanny Wright, Robert Dale Owen, Tom Skidmore, Imported Democ-

racy, that he [Van Buren] has derived his "Title."

The last example shows that at that time the idea of radical reform is not forgotten, but on the whole it is clear that *radical* is widely used to describe the extreme left rather than the advocates of any particular reform. More and more, *radical* is a term describing the political attitude which is the opposite of *conservative.* (q.v.)

In many of the following examples, the contrast *radical-conservative* is apparent. While in general the attitude of the writers is decidedly a hostile one, we find occasional utterances more or less favorable to radicalism:

1835 *Knickerbocker* V.92 ... the tendency of Americans, instead of being aristocratic, is decidedly radical.

1840 *New Yorker* 25 Jan. 297/1. It has been remarked with some justice as well as smartness that "every man who thinks is naturally a radical." ... But it might with at least equal truth be remarked that every man who thinks deeply ... is a conservative also.

While the preceding examples show that *radical* was applied mainly to Democratic factions, a readjustment took place during the 40's and 50's with the result that at the end of this period the word most frequently refers to Republicans. This was at least partly caused by the development that carried numbers of left-wing Democrats (see BARNBURNER), first into the Free Soil then into the new Republican party. This connection is illustrated by:

1847 *N. Y. Trib.* 27 Oct. 1/6. The Mass Convention of the Radical Democracy assembled at Herkimer today.... They of course reaffirm and stand fast by the principle of the Wilmot Proviso.

1851 Dix *Memoirs* I.263. I gave my views at large as to the course our Free-Soil Democrats should take ... that we must either run a Radical Free Soil Democrat and nail our flag to the mast ... or take some man who can break up the Hunker coalition.

1854 *N. Y. Times* 12 Sept 3/1 ... radical or Barnburner portion of the Democracy, as contradistinguished from the "Soft" or patronage Hunkers.

An important factor was that the reproach of radicalism was frequently used against the abolitionists in general, many of whom likewise merged with the Republicans.

1845 in Elias Nason *Life and Public Services of Henry Wilson* 50. It was more popular to keep along with the current of prejudice, than, by resisting it, to be denounced as a "radical or abolitionist."

1855 *Nat. Antislavery Standard* 8 Sept. Radical Abolitionists ... believers in Spooner's doctrine of the unconstitutionality of slavery, and in the right of Congress to abolish it in the states.

1860 *Ashland* (Ohio) *Times* 12 April 2/2. The oligarchy were aiming at me [Cassius Clay] in the expulsion of the Bereans from their homes, being in hopes that I would forcibly defend them, "the radicals".... The proslavery affairs of Kentucky are not content with driving out what are called "radical Bereans"....

1860 *Louisville Jrnl.* 4 April. Mr. Clay has separated himself from the Radical Abolitionists, whose nefarious sentiments provoked the recent lamentable, though perhaps necessary, proceedings in Madison county....

Already before the war, *radical* and *republican* are used together as in:

1857 "Warrington" *Pen Portraits* 83 ... on the other hand, he [Gov. Gardner]

had too little faith in the political ideas and machinery of the radical Republicans to suit them.

This use by which the radicals are known as a Republican section continues through the war:

1861 *Cols. Crisis* 3 Sept. 4/3 ... the more radical of the Republicans in and out of Congress have abandoned all expectation of restoring the Government.

1863 Phillips *Sp.* 524. The Sixteenth Ward of New York, the banner ward for radical Republicanism....

But through these years there is also the tendency to use *radical* as a party name almost synonymous with *Republican*. To begin with, this tendency seems to be local, for instance, in Missouri:

1863 in Dennett *Hay* 29 Sept. 95. I told him the impression derived from talking with people from there was that there were two great parties in Missouri, the secession-sympathizing Democrats and the Radicals....

This tendency gained momentum during the conflict between Andrew Johnson and Congress. Since the opposition to the President comprised practically all the Republican party, the identification of *radical* with *Republican* becomes almost complete:

1866 *Cleve. Leader* 11 Oct. 2/1. "Radical to the core" and "radical to the backbone" are mottoes conspicuous and frequent in every Republican political procession throughout the North and West. An epithet applied as a stigma to opponents of the policy which would restore the rebels to power has been joyfully accepted and is proudly worn.

1866 Welles *Papers* II.633 ... the radical, or as they now call it, the Republican, caucus.

Due to this tendency and to the increasing sharpness of the conflict, *radical* becomes more than ever a bi-polar word. To some radicalism is something to be proud of; others speak of it with the deepest contempt.

1864 *N. Am. Rev.* XCVIII. 258. Radicalism may be a very dangerous thing, and so is calomel, but not when it is the only means of saving the life of the patient. **1865** Josh Billings in *Springfield* (Ohio) *D. News* 4 Jan. 1/2. I argy in this way, if a man is right he kant be tu radikal, if he is rong, he kant be tu consarvatiff. **1866** Benjamin Wade in *Cinc. Comm.* Special Campaign Edition 11 Sept. I thank God I am a Radical. You know the word was once Abolitionist. You don't hear that now. That term has become good and honorable. Every man has become an Abolitionist. . . . But it was necessary to coin another word and make that odious. It is "Radical." **1866** *Cleve. Leader* 17 Sept. 2/2 [Spaulding speech at Sandusky, Ohio]. Every hair on my head is radical. **1868** *Nation* VII.324. He [Butler] is being cried up as a genuine "Radical," and his opponent as a mere "Conservative.". . . There is no magic in the term "Radical." . . . There are times when it is good to be a "Radical"—that is, a tearer up by the roots; and there are times when it is good to be a Conservative—that is, an advocate of preservation or construction. . . . Moreover, it is high time that those who are fond of using the word "Radical" as a spell should explain to the public what they *now* mean by it. They clearly cannot mean what they meant three years ago. Three years ago, a "Radical" was a person who held that conditions ought to be imposed on the South. . . . In the mouths of a great many of those who now call themselves "Radical" and put the name forward as their great title to confidence, it has ceased to mean anything either good or useful. They have made it a synonym for violence, for extravagance, for perturbation and disorder, for scorn of the human understanding. . . . **1868** *Cols. Crisis* 8 July 3/1.

> The Radical
> Of all the men I e'er have known
>   One only wholly bad I call
> The Puritanic, Jacobinic,
>   Raving, roaring Radical,
>   The nasty, ugly Radical—
>   The Heaven-detested Radical—
> The ranting, canting, tearing, swearing,
>   picture-stealing Radical.

rag baby.

A symbol for the inflationary policy of the Democrats, centered primarily on their support of the issuance of greenback paper currency.

A. Although there is a possibility that *rag baby* was used as early as 1862—

1875 *Cinc. Enquirer* 25 Oct. 4/1. By the "rag baby" it means the child brought into the world by the Republican party in 1862. . . . The *Commercial* adopted and accepted the "rag baby" as its standard. With a little "rag baby" doll, stamped five cents and branded "U.S.," any person could have the delightful privilege of perusing the columns of the Cincinnati *Commercial,* and if the "rag baby" was worth more than five cents the Cincinnati *Commercial* handed over the difference in lawful money.—

it seems more probable that the expression had its origin in another rag doll episode in 1875:

Ann. of Cleve. No. 2571. This evening's meeting was chosen . . . to present a ragdoll to Foran, Stowe, and the crowd of rag-money men. [at *Plaindealer* office]

A few weeks after this incident in the *Plain Dealer* office, the term *rag baby* is found in frequent and elaborate metaphors dealing with the Ohio Democracy.

1875 *Ohio St. Jrnl.* 18 June 1/1. After a painful and dangerous labor of about seven hours duration, the Democratic Party of Ohio was yesterday delivered of a

Rag Baby, when the patient immediately relapsed into puerperal convulsions. Dr. Thomas Ewing, and other distinguished *accoucheurs,* assisted on the interesting occasion, with Beer and Godfrey's Cordial. **1875** *Ib.* 22 June 1/1. The Democratic press from Maine to Georgia is engaged now chiefly in cuffing the Rag Baby of the Ohio Democracy. The New York World knocked the stuffing out of it and tossed it to the St. Louis Republican; the Republican kicked it over to the Chicago Times; the Times belted it under the ear and knocked it clear back to the New York Tribune; the Tribune dropped it out of the tower like a hot shot, and the poor baby don't know where to go. It hasn't had time to draw a drop of sustenance from the maternal fount in the Enquirer office since the poor thing was born.
1875 *Cleve. Herald* 26 June 4/1. A touching sight—"Pot-metal Bill Allen" nursing the Democratic Rag Baby.
1875 *Cleve. Plain Dealer* 29 June 2/2. If a Democrat in 1863 had spoken of a greenback as a "rag baby"—the name now given that currency by the Republicans— the lamp-post patriots would have been after him and indicated their patriotism by attempting to mob him.

B. The great impetus which made *rag baby* a popular and nationally known term was undoubtedly the creation by Thomas Nast of an inane looking doll which he christened "rag baby." Its first appearance was in *Harper's Weekly* of Sept. 7, 1875, in one of the most impressive cartoons Nast ever drew. Allan G. Thurman of Ohio is shown standing on his doorstep gazing down at a grinning rag baby in a basket. The caption reads, "That Irredeemable Rag Baby. This is a nice position for a 'Hard Money' bachelor to be placed in!" The cartoon may have been inspired by an earlier editorial which first appeared in the *N. Y. World:*
1875 *Cleve. Herald* 26 June 4/2. The Democratic New York *World* speaks of the Ohio Democratic Rag Baby as a bastard left on the doorstep of Governor Allen by some merciless enemy, "basketed in the Ohio undemocratic platform."

That Nast's creation was responsible for the great popularity of the symbol is indicated by an early notice of the first cartoon (which incidentally shows that *Harper's* appeared about two weeks before the date of issue), by Nast's continued use of rag-baby cartoons throughout 1875 and later and by its numerous imitations.
1875 *Cinc. Comm.* 27 Aug. 4/5. Nast's cartoon touching the Ohio campaign, this week, represents Senator Thurman in a state of profound perplexity over a ragbaby deposited on his door-step.
1875 *Harper's W.* 9 Oct. 813 [Nast cartoon]. Holy Murder!!! Governor Tilden and the Ohio Rag Baby.
1876 *Ib.* 12 Feb. 136 [Nast cartoon]. Hush-a-bye (Rag) Baby, Be Still!
1876 *Ib.* 8 April 288 [Nast cartoon]. The Haunted House; or, The "Murdered" Rag Baby Will not be still. Shake its gory locks at them until they make it vanish.
1876 *Ib.* 26 Aug. 689 [Nast cartoon]. A Hard Summer for the Soft Rag Baby.
1879 *Ib.* 26 April 336 [Nast cartoon]. The Baby of Many "Lives" and "Deaths."
1880 *Ib.* 17 July 449. [Nast cartoon: little girl talking to her rag doll] Baby Politics.
1884 *Ib.* 13 Sept. 591. [Nast cartoon: Butler in bonnet, dress, apron, holding "rag baby" and spoon]
1876 *Ib.* 22 April 336. [Colt cartoon: rag baby being hauled from river by men on " (Inflation) Bridge of (Sighs) Size."]
> Take her up tenderly,
> Lift her with care!
> Fashioned so slenderly,
> Young and so fair!

1876 *Ib.* 8 July 560. [Colt cartoon: "Reform Rag Baby" led by "Reform Brute," "Reform" Priest, "Reform Tammany," and "Reform KKK."] Goin' to St. Louis.
1876 *Ib.* 29 July 624 [Alexander cartoon: Rag baby in arms of clown]. Grand Re-Opening. The Rag Baby Pantomime Again.
1876 *Ib.* 12 Aug. 659. [Frost cartoon: Rag baby on desk peering into Tilden's face; other gnomes—"Hard Money," "War Record," "Tweedism," "Ring Record," "Repudiation"] Uncle Sammy trying to write that Letter of Acceptance.—A few little things that would come up!
1876 *Ib.* 26 Aug. 699. [Colt cartoon: cart with "Reform Rag Baby," "Rag Money," "Rags," and sign: "Democratic Reform (?) Rag Cart, Tilden & Hendricks Proprietors. 'We denounce the resemption clause of the act of 1875, and we hereby demand its repeal.' St. Louis Platform."] Rags! Rags! Rags!
1876 *Ib.* 9 Sept. 748. [Bellew cartoon series entitled "The Democratic Frankenstein"]
(1) The great Western experimental Money-Doctor, after infinite pains and study, succeeds in making a Rag-Baby. He breathes into it the breath of life.
(2) Bless its dear little heart, it is as good as Gold! [baby with "$"]
(3) But the little pet grows rapidly, and becomes too heavy to carry. [baby bigger than creator.]
(4) So he drops it at a neighbor's door, and flies. [at Republicans' door]
(5) But the creature he has created arises and pursues its parent, and—[baby chasing creator]
(6) Finis. [baby sitting on top choking creator]
1875 *Cinc. Comm.* 25 Aug. 4/2. The "Rag Baby" and the "Red Woman" together are worse than the "twin relics of barbarism"....
1875 *Ohio St. Jrnl.* 14 Oct. 1/2.
Dear Rag Baby, thou hast petered,
  B'lallen wind did make thee howel—
The people just sat down on thee,
  And busted thy inflated bowel,
Gone to meet the Southern Confederacy.

1878 *Cinc. Enquirer* 29 June 4/2 ... the "rag baby" has done pretty well. It has survived all the attacks peculiar to babyhood. It is possessed of a sound constitution, and its life is insured for a large number of years.
1878 *Ohio St. Jrnl.* 10 Aug. 2/4.
  Blow, blow, trumpets blow,
  Set the wild echoes flying.
  Blow, blow, oh Tommy, blow,
  For the babe of rags is dying!

rainbow chaser.

A political pollyanna; a visionary.

1892 *Ohio St. Jrnl.* 12 Nov. 1/3. Rainbow Chasers. [head] ... I believe our defeat is due to the rainbow chasing of the Republican National committee.
1923 Alexander *Pol. Hist. N. Y.* IV.172. Calvin Brice, admittedly the wittiest and cleverist member of the Senate [in 1892] was a fascinating "rainbow chaser," radiating charm without inspiring trust.

rain maker.

A politician, particularly in the Mid-West, whose appeal for votes is based upon extravagant promises. [ ]

1893 in Taylor *The Farmers' Movement* 288. Thus was produced that clamoring brood of Peffers, Simpsons, Kems and McKeighans and the hundred other political rain-makers who proclaimed their virtue on the Western prairies in 1890.

rally.

The *OED* gives no example of the phrase *rallying round the flag* as a military term. In America the expression is reported to have been used by Andrew Jackson in a speech before the Battle of New Orleans (*Anti-Slavery Standard*, New York, 23 January, 1858). It came into common use as a metaphor when another military man,

William H. Harrison, became a presidential candidate.

1835 *Scioto Gazette* 14 Jan. 2/2. If Pennsylvania shall adopt him as her candidate, the west will rally around the Old Pioneer.
1840 in Norton *Tippecanoe*. The Federal party took ground against that war, and as a party there never existed a purer band of patriots, for when the note of strife was sounded, they rallied under the banner of their country.
Ib. App.80. Around liberty's standard, we'll rally, we'll rally.
Ib. 60.

Love ye not, love ye not, O, my brave
  Buckeye boys,
To the rally with Tippecanoe.

These examples seem to indicate that the phrase was predominantly a Whig phrase, but if so it was not allowed to remain a monopoly of that party. Very soon it was adopted by both the Democrats and the Liberty party.

1840 Kennedy *Quodlibet* 94. Then our course is plain. Poor men, one and all, rally round our Democratic banner.
1844 Phillips in *Liberator* XIV.82 . . . until slavery be abolished, the watchword, the rallying-cry, the motto on the banner of the American Anti-Slavery Society shall be "No Union With Slave Holders!"

rank and file.

Long used in English military language to designate the common soldier; in politics, the lower party worker.

1872 Adams *Emery A. Storrs* 107 . . . and the rank and file of the party never followed one single step after the leadership of any man, where that man, essaying to be its leader, did not go in the direction which the Republican party desired to go.
1878 *Harper's W.* 7 Sept. 706/1. These few thousand, this minority, are the important factor. The "rank and file," as they are offensively called, will follow the bell-

wether over any wall and into any pasture, but the independent sheep will not.
1888 *Forum* V.237 . . . a general and overpowering demand for the one man capable of exciting genuine enthusiasm among the rank and file of the Republican Party.
1912 TR in *Harper's W.* 29 June 8/3. We have got—we, you here, we here—represent the rank and file of the Republican party; and our opponents represent nothing but a partly successful effort to strangle the sentiment of the rank and file of the Republican party.
1923 *Rev. of Rev.* LXVIII.229. He [McKinley] had gained the good-will of the party's rank and file, gathered from all sections.

rascal.

An often repeated epithet in American politics.

1804 in Shipp *Life & Times of Crawford* 56. Do you not recollect that you said of him, that he was a damned corrupt, partial rascal . . . ?
1854 Pike *First Blows* 201. The Rascals at Washington [head. fr. *N. Y. Trib.* 26 Jan.]
1871 *Every Sat.* 25 Feb. 171/3. The several combatants [in Mich.] speak of their opponents as "rascals," "scoundrels," "thieves," "heads of corrupt rings," "right bowers of venality," "cold-blooded villains," "dishonest fellows," "unblushing intriguants," "gratuitouscalumniators," "venomous little souls," "weak-brained men," "egotistical spirits," "luxuriating in slander and vituperation," "professors of craft and malignity," "biters of files," "credulous idiots," [etc.]
1876 Cox *Why We Laugh* 310. John P. Hale . . . once remarked: "I never said that all the Democrats were rascals; only that all the rascals were Democrats."
1884 *N. Y. Times* 9 May [ltr.]. Let the Times take the lead in the reform and defeat the rascals.

Also, to rascal.

1835 Crockett *Life* 247. I have no doubt that I was completely rascalled out of my election, and I do regret that duty to myself and to my country compels me to expose such villainy.

rascalocracy:

1842 *Wash. Intell.* 8 April 3/2. The following articles in the Rochester Democrat show that the rascalocracy of the frontier...stand this side to kidnap kindred Canadian spirits that come over.

raw head and bloody bones.

Expressions based upon superstitions and popular beliefs are not too prominent in American politics; however, a group of words—*bugaboo, bugbear, raw head and bloody bones,* and *doughface*—certainly belongs to this sphere.

Raw head and bloody bones, a nursery demon known in England at least since the sixteenth century, must have been equally popular in Colonial America. Frank Moore, *Songs and Ballads of the American Revolution,* (342) has a song, "New Year's Day, 1781," to be sung to the tune "Get you gone, raw head and bloody bones." Also, **1807** Irving *Works* V.29. I have sometimes particularly noticed a hungry-looking Gaul, who torments a huge bassviol, and who is, doubtless, the original of the famous "Raw-head-and-bloody-bones" so potent in frightening naughty children.

Metaphorically, but with no reference to politics:

1799 Jefferson *Works* X.78. And I am for encouraging the progress of science in all its branches; and not for raising a hue and cry against the sacred name of philosophy; for awing the human mind by stories of raw-head and bloody bones to a distrust of its own vision, and to repose implicitly on that of others. . . .

1823 *Cinc. Nat. Rep.* 8 April 4/1. Raw-head-and-bloody-bones or bug-a-boo
    Was to my wildered fancy less terrific
        [than a Yankee pedlar].

Such comparisons serve as the connecting link between the folklore tales and the first political uses of the term.

1835 *Lebanon* (Ohio) *Western Star* 2 Oct. 2/3. The Kitchen Cooks of the Baltimore office-holding humbug are in a bad way, for the want of a good and sufficient RAW HEAD AND BLOODY BONES with which to frighten "THE PARTY" in to regular obedience.

1841 *Georgia Jrnl.* 15 June 3/2...all the fuss which has been kicked up about Mr. Damson's Anti Central Bank candidacy...like a raw head and bloody bones affair, will fail to alarm those who have been long enough from the nursery to entitle them to the privilege of voting.

1855 *Ravenna* (Ohio) *Campaign Dem.* 6 Aug. 2/3. But the "raw head and bloody bones" of Know-Nothingism is dragged in to arouse the prejudice and the opposition of our adopted citizens.

During the Reconstruction Period the word seems to have received a revived popularity: (cf. bloody shirt)

1874 *N. Y. World* 9 Sept. 4/6. The Northern people...are not going to have their attention diverted again by the regularly "put up" display of raw head and bloody bones.

1874 *Cinc. Enquirer* 16 Sept. 4/1. Ben Butler has opened his canvass...with a raw-head and bloody bones speech, having "Southern outrages" for a basis.

Ib. 19 Sept. 4/1. Mr. Morton, who is a sort of Raw head and bloody bones, is trying to convert the troubles of the South into an invigorating tonic for the dilapidated Republican party of Indiana.

reaction (reactionary).

Before becoming a political word, *reaction* had long been in use in religious terminology (1771, Wesley, *Works* V.232. A continual action of God upon the Soul, and a re-action of the Soul upon God) as well as in science (1644, Digby, *Nat. Bodies,* xvi.139. Of reaction ... in locall motion, that each agent must suffer in acting and acte in suffering). The word was introduced into politics in pre-Revolutionary French writings:

1772 Rousseau *Gouvernement de Pol.* xii. Tout l'art humain ne samrait empêcher l'action brusque, du fort contre le faible, mais il peut se ménager des ressorts pour la "réaction." ... Apres chacune des crises qui ont en lies depuis la Révolution, une "réaction" s'est fait sentir.

During the Revolution itself it was used to characterize actions of the more conservative elements against the ultra-Revolutionist (Brunot, *Histoire* ... IX. pt 2. 843). Evidently it was the policy of the restored Bourbons that settled the modern slant of the word, bringing it into direct contrast with *progressive* and its synonyms. It is noticeable that in 1816 English writers still considered *reaction* a French word:

1816 *Edinburgh Rev.* Dec. XXVII.480. Napoleon sought men of talents from every party, and employed them in the public service. All men dreaded what the French call a *reaction.* Napoleon checked every symptom of reaction. ...

A few years later it turns up in American discussions of European politics:

1823 Holcombe *Life of Thomas A. Hendricks* 31. The action and reaction of tyranny throughout the world must ever produce a corresponding vibration in the hearts of free men.

Seemingly, *reaction* and *reactionary* became active words in American politics not before the end of the Civil War when they were applied to Southern politicians and their Northern allies:

1868 *Harper's W.* 25 Jan. 51/2. The fruit of the "Great Reaction" is rapidly ripening. The Ohio Democratic Convention nominated for the Presidency ... Pendleton. ... The resuscitation of every notorious Copperhead to control the Government ... is the beautiful plum which the "Great Reaction" offers the country.

1868 *Ib.* 8 Feb. 82/1. Amidst the loud shout of reactionary and partisan exultation which saluted the success of last November. ...

1868 *Ib.* 22 Feb. 114/2. Those who truly comprehended the position of affairs felt that he [Grant] had succeeded Mr. Stanton as the representative of the anti-reactionary spirit in the Cabinet. ...

1868 *Ib.* 21 March 179/2. We know nothing of Consul Cushman. He may be as much of a reactionaire as his official superior in the State Department.

1876 *Ib.* 24 June 510/3. Republicanism ruled for a few years at the South, and its traces are seen in lines of railways that have opened up vast districts to agriculture and trade, and a scheme of universal education that still lingers amidst the barbarous reaction.

1880 Schurz *Writings* IV.2. It [letter of acceptance] is universally accepted ... as a reactionary movement in the direction of the worst of old abuses.

1908 Pringle *Taft* I.366. The Wall Street Journal welcomes Mr. Taft's speech as evidence that he is neither reactionary nor a revolutionist, neither a Bourbon nor a Jacobin.

1908 *Nation* 1 Oct. 302/2. Part of Wall Street will vote for Taft because it believes him at heart a "reactionary," or, at least, the less of two evils.

Harding *Pol. Campaign of 1912* 33.

> R's for reactionary,
> He wants to turn back.
> But believe the progressive,
> He's on the wrong track.

1913 Roosevelt *Autobio.* 351. This had ... tended to throw the party into the hand not merely of the conservatives but of the reactionaries.

1919 *Ltrs. of William A. White* 199 ... don't ever think you can elect anybody who is an incrusted old reactionary.

1945 Hoover *Add. Upon the Am. Road* 260. If it be "reactionary" to be for free men then I shall be proud of that title for my remaining days.

1953 *Cols. Citizen* 12 Aug. [editorial]. Over the last couple of decades of rapid political change in this country, reactionary has been a term of derision on the tongues of the self-proclaimed "more enlightened," especially those who hail all movement as improvement, all change as progress. Hardly anybody now is willing to admit he is a reactionary.

See BOURBON.

readjuster.

A member of a faction of the Democratic party in post-war Virginia which favored the repudiation of the state's debt.

1882 *Century Mag.* April 945. The movement of the Virginia Re-adjusters has been watched at the North with much distrust, owing to the fact that readjustment appeared, at first, to be merely a new name for repudiation.

To avoid the stigma associated with the term *repudiators* they adopted the euphemism:

1878 *Cyc. of Pol. Sci.* III.611. By this time the issue was fairly before the people, and the state divided into "debt payers" and "readjusters"—a euphemism for repudiators.

1879 *Nation* 13 Nov. 317/2. Further news from Virginia indicates that the Repudiators, or Readjusters, as they call themselves, have elected a majority of the General Assembly.

Organized by General William Mahone at a convention in February, 1879, the readjusters achieved a short-lived majority in Virginia politics, but failed in the general election of 1880, when the national Democratic party, fearful of the growing power of such a group, asked for support of the regular Democrats.

1881 in Cooper and Fenton *Am. Pol.* III. 212 [in the Senate]. Mahone. ... I was elected as a readjuster. Do you know what they are? (Laughter and applause) Hill. I understand there are in Virginia what are called readjuster democrats and debt-paying democrats, or something of that kind, but as I understand they are all democrats.

read out of the party.

To be expelled from a political party.

A. In the discipline of the Methodist and other churches:

1830–1 Mrs. Trollope in Buley *The Old Northwest* II.488. Having thus declared yourself, your next submission must be that of unqualified obedience to the will and pleasure of your elected pastor, or you will run a great risk of being "passed out of the church." This was a phrase that I perpetually heard, and upon enquiry I found that it did not mean being passed neck and heels out of the building at the discretion of the sexton, but a sort of congregational excommunication which infallibly betides those who venture to do any thing that their pastor and master disapproves.

1836 Dunlap *Mem. Water Drinker* I.201. By the death of his parents, he was left in possession of some property, which he dissipated even before he "was read out of meeting."

1855 Osmon C. Baker *Guide-book in the Administration of the Discipline of the Methodist Episcopal Church* 161. It is made the duty of the "official minister or preacher," at every quarterly meeting to read the names of those who have been excluded from the Church during the preceding quarter.... When persons are thus read out of the society by the official minister....

B. The religious background of the phrase is clearly shown in several of the political quotations:

1840 *Logansport Herald* 15 April 3/4. If their candidates in expectancy are guilty of the unpardonable sin of telling the truth . . . they are immediately read out of the party.

1841 *Cong. Globe* 133. Mr. Alford of Georgia warned the "tariff bugs" of the South that, instead of their reading him out of church, if they did not mind, he would read them out of church.

1846 Jeff. Davis in *Cong. Globe* 320. A good deal had been said about reading out of the Democratic church members of the Democratic party.

1857–8 Douglas in Sheahan *Douglas* 345. It [*Wash. Union*] has read me out of the Democratic party every other day, at least, for two or three months, and keeps reading me out (laughter) ; and, as if it had not succeeded, still continues to read me out, using such terms as "traitor," "renegade," "deserter," and other kind and polite epithets of that nature.

1870 Ben Butler in *Cong. Globe* 717/2. I have never threatened to read Mr. Bingham out of the Republican party.

1889 Farmer *Americanisms* 453. A man is read out of a party when denounced as a deserter from its ranks.

re-annexation.

To the material found under *annexation* (q.v.) must be added the following:

1838 in Wiltse *Calhoun* II.387. Calhoun's State Rights resolutions were still being debated when on January 4 Preston introduced a resolution calling for annexation. With diabolical ingenuity he called it "re-annexation," and based his case on the allegation that the Rio Grande was the true boundary of the United States. . . .

1844 *Ib.* 152 [memoranda of R. J. Walker]. [They] would take my bill with the following amendments. . . . 3rd, Strike out re-annexation and insert annexation. Mr. Calhoun is vehement on this subject and says it is an implied censure of Mr.

Monroe and all his cabinet in relation to the Florida Treaty. . . . As approved by the historical records. . . . Texas was once ours under the Treaty of 1803; to get Texas again then is clearly re-annexation.

1844 *Dem. Rev.* 425 . . . the reason assigned in 1825, 1827, 1829, 1833 and 1835 for the re-annexation of Texas.

1844 E. Blair Lee to Walker in Tyler *The Tylers* 135. My father desires me to say . . . he will earnestly advocate the reannexation of Texas.

1844 in Blaine *Twenty Yrs.* 34. The convention which nominated Mr. Polk took bold ground for the immediate re-annexation of Texas and re-occupation of Oregon. This peculiar form of expression was used to indicate that Texas had already belonged to us under the Louisiana purchase, and that Oregon had been wholly ours prior to the treaty of joint occupancy with Great Britain.

1844 in Logan *Gt. Conspiracy* 36. Polk . . . stood upon a platform declaring for the "re-occupation of Oregon and the re-annexation of Texas at the earliest practicable moment"—as if the prefix "re" legitimatized the claim in either case.

rebel(-dom, brigadier, democracy).

A. Colonist during the Revolutionary period.

1775 "Reflections on Gage's Letter" in Leary *Freneau* 58. "Rebels you are," the hopeful Gen'ral cries, Truth stand thou forth and tell the wretch he lies.

. . . .

If to protest against a tyrant's laws,
And arm for battle in a righteous cause
Be deem'd rebellion—'tis a harmless thing,
This bug-bear name, like death has lost
   its sting.

1766 "Book of America" in Thornton *Pulpit in Am. Revolution* 116.

28 And they would establish themselves as a people, and suffer us to have no power over them.

29 Behold, they have opposed the *edict,* and they are become as *rebels.*

30 Wherefore then go we not forth with a strong hand, and force them unto obedience to us?

1776 Paine *Writings* II.167. While we profess ourselves the subjects of Britain, we must, in the eyes of foreign nations, be considered as Rebels.

1841 Rev. P. S. Cleland in Curti *Probing* 106. If slavery is right . . . the American Revolution was but a successful rebellion; and our fathers should be regarded as a band of rebels. . . .

1856 *N. Y. Trib.* 26 Jan. in Pike *First Blows* 304. The Richmond Enquirer already talks in a lordly strain of the "rebellion in Kansas," which it declares must be put down, with a confidence as marked and a tone as resolute as characterized the edicts of the British government during our revolution. . . . He [Lord North], too, called the people who chose not to be imposed upon "rebels," and said the "rebellion" must be crushed.

B. Southerner during the Civil War.

The first quotation indicates that in the few years preceding the outbreak of the war the term was generally used in both the North and the South. Later quotations (1861, 1867) indicate the efforts of Southerners to avoid what they considered an opprobrious and inexact epithet.

1861 *Mng. Courier & N. Y. Enq.* 8 Jan. in *Northern Editorials* II.931. Why then, should we try to find for those who have plotted treason, and are now in open rebellion against the Government of the country, any other than the true and significant appellations of *Traitors* and *Rebels?*

1861 *Cong. Globe* 15 Jan. 391/3. Why, sir, to hear the taunts that are made to the South; to hear the epithets of "treason," "rebellion," "revolt,". . . one would think that the people of the South were a reckless, wayward people, seeking only to do wrong.

1861 Lincoln *Works* VI.312. It might seem at first thought to be of little difference whether the present movement at the South be called "secession" or "rebellion."

. . . With rebellion thus sugar-coated they have been drugging the public mind of their section for more than 30 years. . . .

1861 *N. Y. Trib.* in Wright *The Prospect* 16. Fernando Wood at Volks Garden the other night, by his bold secession speech, avowed himself a rebel.

1862 *Ib.* 5. Our perils are less from the rebellion than from political corruption.

1864 *Harper's W.* 2 Jan. 2. There are times in which every man's vote is strictly scrutinized to see whether he prefers the unconditional surrenders of the rebels or of the government. There is no middle ground.

1867 Nasby *Struggles* 474 . . . The President perceeded:—"Here, upon this spot, the armed hosts of rebellion were met and hurled back by—" Governor Swann sejested that that be omitted. The word "rebellion," when applied to a brave people, who wuz strugglin for wat they deemed their rites, wuz, to say the least, too harsh.

1862 *Ashland Times* 21 Aug. 2/3. The Sufferings of Rebeldom. [head]

1878 *Harper's W.* 13 April 286. But Republicans were scornfully indignant that . . . the President was betraying the Republican party by gross leniency to "rebels," joined hands heartily with "rebel brigadiers" to smirch the honor of the United States.

1874 *N. Y. W. Trib.* 25 Nov. 4/1. A few weeks ago Republican newspapers and speakers from Maine to Oregon menaced the country with a general massacre of the negroes if the Rebel Democracy should succeed in the November elections.

recall.

1903 *Cyc. of Am. Govt.* III.157. This modern recall first found place in American law in an amendment to the Los Angeles charter, 1903, introducing a process of removal, the model for which seems to have been taken from the cantonal law long in force in Schaffhausen, Switzerland.

1911 in *Gt. Deb.* IX.530. The right to recall is simply a matter of advising a man that he is not an acceptable public servant. The man who is defeated in a recall goes from his office without any necessary disgrace and without any deep stigma.

1911 in *Ib.* IX.533. The power to recall a judge who renders an unpopular judgment is to my mind so utterly subversive of the principles of good government that I can never get my own consent to withhold my condemnation and disapproval of it.... The recall puts into the scale, upon one side or the other, in every case where strong public feeling exists, the artifically induced anxiety of the judge for the retention of his place.

1912 in White *Autobio.* 456. He [T. R.] made a speech in Columbus [on Feb. 21], a most radical and indefensible speech, advocating the recall of judicial decisions.... it hurt him; probably it crippled him more than any other one thing that he did in his life. For the speech shocked millions of his countrymen whom he had gathered about him as followers, and it attracted only the radicals who are never dependable to follow in any man's train nor to pursue any consistent course. I tried to explain that he meant by recall of judicial decisions only the legislative enactments needed to amend the statutes upon which the decisions were made.... But the phrase "recall of judicial decisions" set the key of the marching song in the political combat that made the year such a time of clamor and alarm.

reconciliation.

A post Civil War slogan of the Democrats, who favored a more friendly reconstruction policy for the South than the Republicans proposed.

1868 *Harper's W.* 26 Sept. 610/1. Conciliation. [head] Mr. Pendleton and the other Democratic orators continually preach conciliation.

1872 *Ib.* 24 Aug. 650/2. Of course the Democrats all say that they want "reconciliation," as they did in 1868. They want "reconciliation" now precisely as they wanted "peace" during the war—that is to say, they wish to return to power under the most plausible pretext.

1872 *Ib.* 9 Nov. 866/1. The sacred names of reconciliation and reform have been invoked as the cry of one of the most absurd coalitions ever proposed....

1876 *Ib.* 29 Jan. 82/3. Mr. Tilden is a Democrat highly favored as a Presidential candidate by many friends of "conciliation." ... We do not expect a man who has been beaten to say that he likes it. But if he can be "conciliated" only by having his own way after all, conciliation must evidently be postponed.

1876 in Hayes *Diary* III.329. But I do favor a policy of reconciliation, based on the observance of all parts of the Constitution....

1877 *Harper's W.* 27 Oct. 838/2. In the light of recent events, the Democratic cry of "Tilden and Reform" in 1876 seems to have been as hollow as that of "Greeley and Reconciliation" in 1872.

The term may also have been a slogan during and after the Revolution:

1776 Paine *Works* II.130f. I challenge the warmest advocate for reconciliation to show a single advantage that this continent can reap by being connected with Great Britain.... Reconciliation is *now* a fallacious dream.

reconstruction.

The program for a reorganization of the government of the United States following the Civil War had its origin in the South even before the outbreak of hostilities. In opposition to the Southern "fire eaters" (q.v.) many conservatives felt that the Union could be saved by compromise and cooperation. The radicals attacked their proposed reconstruction.

in White *Rhett* 186. "Reconstruction" was soon [late 1860] to be the fiercest and most hated word in the Mercury's vocabulary.

1861 in Wilson *Slave Power* III.42. It is

useless to talk about reconstruction. This Federal government is dead.

Northern observers also commented upon this plan:

1861 Olmstead *Cotton Kingdom* 4 ... the purpose of the more prudent and conservative men, now engaged in the attempt to establish a new government in the South, was for a long time simply to obtain an advantage for what was talked of as "reconstruction"; namely, a process of change in the form and rules of our government that would disqualify us of the Free States from offering any resistance to whatever was demanded of our government, for the end in view of the extension and eternal maintenance of slavery.

1861 in *Appleton's Annual Cyc.* 177 ... no such reconstruction is practicable, and therefore, to the maintenance of the existing Union and Constitution should be directed all the energies of all the departments of the Government, and the efforts of all good citizens.

1861 Lowell *Works* VI.96. Doubtless the aim of the political managers in these states was to keep the North amused with the schemes of arbitration, reconstruction, and whatever other fine words would serve the purpose of hiding the real issue.

During the war the discussion continued both North and South on the possibilities of reconstruction:

1861 in *Mangum Papers* V.385. I am a Strong Separate State actionist and bitterly opposed to reconstruction.

1862 *Leslie's Ill. Newspaper* 8 Feb. 178/3. No Reconstruction. There must be a considerable party favorable to the Union in the South, or else the leaders of the rebellion would not feel called upon to protest against "the reconstruction of the Union."

1863 in *Lincoln Encyc.* 11 Sept. 272. The reinauguration must not be such as to give control of the state and its representation in Congress to the enemies of the

Union.... Let the reconstruction be the work of such men only as can be trusted for the Union.

1863 in Lincoln *Works* VII.52. Saying that reconstruction will be accepted if presented in a specified way, it is not said it will never be accepted in any other way.

When the outcome of the war became apparent and the relationship of the seceded states a problem of increasing concern, as is shown by the Lincoln quotations above, the term *reconstruction* was expanded to mean not only a reorganization of the government but the restoration of the Southern states to the Federal Union and their due punishment.

1866 *Harper's W.* 6 Jan. Mr. Stevens sees that the end we must seek is sure rather than swift reconstruction.

1868 *Cong. Globe* App.2631/3. But neither Washington nor Madison nor Jackson nor Tyler thought of inflicting the pains and penalties, the confiscations and disfranchisements which follow in the train of modern reconstruction.

1867 *Fredericksburg News* 12 July 2/2. The new Reconstruction bill ... sets aside the Southern State Governments, and puts them under complete subjection to the military authority.

1868 *Democratic Convention Proc.* 60. We regard the reconstruction acts, so called of Congress, as ... an usurpation.

Following the official end of the reconstruction governments in 1877, the term has continued to be an anathema in the South to the present day, as an incident reported in *Newsweek*, November 16, 1953, p. 52, reveals:

Surrender. New Orleans officials, who had inspired noble Confederate wrath by placing a "Reconstruction" sign at the site where a Robert E. Lee monument was being repaired, beat a complete retreat last week. The objectionable word was removed and the unoffensive "Rebuilding" substituted.

Although the following can not be directly related to the events of the 1860's, *reconstruction* may be found in association with slavery much earlier than the actual separation of governments.

1837 Leggett *Pol. Writings* II.293. It is by discussion alone that those who are opposed to slavery seek to effect a reconstruction of southern society.

red herring.

A red (smoked) herring is used in training dogs for their track but, also, in order to divert them from the proper trail. (See *OED*) Hence *red herring* means a side issue brought up in order to draw attention from a particular problem. In this sense it is used by Kent: (*Without Gloves,* 1933, p. 78), "Three Red Herrings" being the title of a chapter dealing with side issues.

1935 *Nation* 12 June 679/1. Together these records tell the story of a nauseous attempt to drag a red herring across the trail of the Salt Creek oil frauds by besmirching Walsh, the man chiefly responsible for the exposures.

1940 Seldes *Witch Hunt* 204. Merchants of Red Herrings. When a slaughter of workingmen takes place ... the dead and the wounded are denounced at the coroner's inquest as agitators, aliens, reds, or the victims of radical leadership. . . .

On August 3, 1948, at the hearings of a Congressional Investigating Committee, John Abt said:

in Liebling, *Mink and Red Herring* 183. It is evident ... that the Thomas committee has once again disinterred an old, particularly malodorous red herring which

it is endeavoring to warm up and serve as a substitute for price control. . . .

On the following day a reporter asked President Truman if the action of the Un-American Activities Committee "was not in the form of a red herring to cover up what the Republican Administration in the 80th Congress had not done." (*Col. Cit.* 8 Jan., 1954)

The phrase was immediately taken up by the Republican press and the red herring became a symbol of negligence and laxity in dealing with Communism.

1948 *Time* 16 August 17/2. The Republicans, said Harry Truman firmly, are using the congressional spy investigations as a "red herring to keep from doing what they ought to do."

Having been used by numerous persons who were unfamiliar with the origin of the phrase, its hunting background has almost been lost.

red hunt (menace, scare).

A search for and rounding up of Communists, usually in political positions.

Based upon the formula *witch hunt.* (q.v.)

1925 Coan *Red Web* 6. It is time, right now, to get down to cases about this thing we hear called "the red menace."

1931 *Wash. Merry-Go-Round* 118. The dread Count Karolyi, whom the nervous Frank B. Kellogg had barred from the United States as a red menace.

1931 *Ib.* 78. He [Chas. Curtis] never went Red hunting.

1932 Carter *What We Are About To Receive* 204. But once the election is over ... we shall quietly lay aside our witch hunting, put the Red Menace in cold storage. . . ,

1932 *Ib.* 195. Unfortunately for the cause of political liberalism and social progress in America, we face another "Red Scare"....

1953 *Cols. Citizen* 22 Nov. 2. Red Hunt To Go 'Full Speed Ahead' Despite Hopes Of The President. [head]

red patch.

Designating the working man; apparently the expression originated as a nickname for one who did not want to identify himself with the laboring class.

1844 *Whig Battering-Ram* 13 Sept. 2/4. One whom people know as "Red Patch Stone!"

1844 *Ib.* 27 Sept. 2/2. Did you [A. P. Stone] not also declare ... that the mechanic should have a *red patch* attached to his posteriors, so as to distinguish him from a gentleman?

red mouth and speckled back party. [ ]

1833 *Boston Evening Trans.* 17 Sept. A new political party has sprung up in Cumberland County, Pennsylvania. It is denominated "Red mouth and speckled back."

Red Republican.

During the revolution of 1848 radical advocates of the republican form of government were known in France as *republicains rouge* and in Germany as *rote Republikaner.*

Early American usage usually refers to European conditions:

1849 *Wash. Nat. Intelligencer* 12 July 1/1. The Letters of Mr. Walsh ... are exceedingly instructive just now on the subjects of the Revolutionary, Socialist, and Red Republicanism of France and Germany.

Other early examples refer to Americans of German origin among whom radicalism was rampant:

1856 *Cleve. Plain Dealer* 16 July 3/3. They [Germans] call themselves "Red Republicans," indicating by that name their bloody and revolutionary purposes. They have found congenial spirits in a party in this country called "Black Republicans."

1856 *Ib.* 23 July 3/1. [Edit.] Hair-lipped Germans alias Red Republicans.

1864 in Dennett *Hay* 222. Some of the transcendental, Red Republican Germans were honest enough in their moonstruck theorizing.

Almost as soon as the term became known in America *red republicanism* developed the tendency of becoming a synonym of *radicalism* of the most extreme description:

1849 *Augusta Chron.* in Shyrock 202. The Democratic journals, led by the Washington Union, were "hotbeds of Red Republicanism" and of "rank Dorrism."

1851 *Boston Pilot* 7 June. As a general thing, wherever you find a free-soiler, you find an anti-hanging man, woman's rights man, an infidel frequently, bigoted Protestant always, a socialist, a red republican, a fanatical teetotaller, a believer in mesmerism, Rochester rappings, and in every devil but the one who will catch him.

1852 Stowe *Uncle Tom's Cabin* ch. xxiii. "I tell you," said Augustine, "if there is anything that is revealed with the strength of a divine law in our times, it is that the masses are to rise, and the under class become the upper one." "That's one of your red republican humbugs, Augustine!"

1852 *Am. Whig Rev.* 135. Soon after [Mexican War] there was revived on the other side a faction calling itself republican, but which was in truth Jacobinical, since known as the "Red (or bloody) Republican."

1856 *Richmond Examiner* in *N. Y. Nat. Antislavery Standard* 11 Oct. The Union was not founded on the Red Republican principle of the equality of all men....

There are strong indications that *red republican* furnished the pattern for *black republican* (q.v.) .

reform is necessary.

A. A Democratic slogan of 1876, taken from their national platform:

1876 *Harper's W.* 22 July 590/4. The Democratic party proposes a campaign of reform.... We quote its [platform] upon this subject: "Reform is necessary in the civil service...."

B. Nast adapted the slogan in his attack upon Tilden by supplying new endings to the basic phrase. A few examples from his cartoons:

1876 *Harper's W.* 22 July 589. "Reform is necessary" in Betting. "Reform is necessary" in Gamblers. "Reform is necessary" in Sham Reformers. "Reform is necessary" in Humbug. "Reform is necessary" in Political Tricksters. "Reform is necessary" in Red Tape. "Reform is necessary" in the Rag Baby.

1876 *Ib.* 12 Aug. 652. Reform is Necessary in nigger killing.

1876 *Ib.* 23 Sept. 773. "Reform is Necessary" in the "Reform" Campaign.

reform within the party.

A. The Republican counter-slogan to the Democratic "Tilden and Reform" and "a reform is necessary" in the campaign of 1876.

1876 *Harper's W.* 18 March 222/2. The Connecticut Republicans are plainly of the opinion that reform is practicable "within the party," and that it is not necessary to call upon Mr. Ben Hill and Mr. Landers to give us loyal and honest government.

1876 *Ib.* 8 April 282/1 ... every honest Republican in the country must see that reform is practicable within the party, and that the election of this year need not be a mere choice of evils.

1876 *Ib.* 28 Oct. 866/3. Reform Within The Party [head].... Unlike the Democrats, if the Massachusetts Republicans wish to prove that they believe in reform, they do not go out of their party to find a candidate, but they nominate one of the truest and most resolute of Republicans.

In later campaigns:

1881 *Nation* 20 Jan. 35/1. A better illustration of the difficulties of "reform within the party" could hardly be afforded.

B. The expression, however, had been used earlier in the political vocabulary but did not achieve the status and popularity of a slogan.

1838 in *Cong. Globe* 384/1. I have no hope of reform in the party in power; my only hope is that the people ... will hurl them from the high places they have so long disgraced.

regency.

Originally short form of *Albany Regency;* later any inside group or clique.

1830 *Workingman's Adv.* 13 Nov. 1/2. To put down what, in the slang of the day, is termed "the Regency" (by which is meant the Ins or officeholders) ....

1956 *New Rep.* 9 Jan. 2/3. There's some evidence the Administration "Regency" is using Ike's absence to even old scores.

regulator.

English uses:

1687 Hallam *Const. Hist.* Chap. XIV.290. [James II] appointed certain regulators to inspect the conduct of several borough towns, to correct abuses where it was practicable, and where not, by forfeiting their charters, to turn out such rotten members as infected the rest. But in this, as in most other cases, the king had the fortune to choose persons not too well qualified for such an employment, and extremely disagreeable to the people....

1734 North *Lives* II.16. [*OED*] There was an itinerant crew of the worst of men.... These were termed regulators.

The unfavorable connotations attaching to the name from its earliest beginnings frequently continued effective when various American organizations either adopted the name of "regulators" or were termed so by their opponents. A non-political organization existed in New Jersey in 1752–53, and later groups in the Carolinas also adopted the name:

1767 Gregg *Hist. Old Cheraws* 136. Those licentious spirits that have so lately appeared in the distant parts of the Province [S.C.] ... assuming the name of Regulators, have ... illegally tried, condemned, and punished many persons.
1768 *Boston Evening Post* 17 Oct. A letter from Pine Tree (S.C.) contains the following intelligence, viz: The Regulators have fixed upon the 5th of next month to have a meeting here to draw up their grievances.
1769 *Boston W. News-Letter* 4 May. We learn from North-Carolina that the People in that Province, who stile themselves Regulators, tied the Sheriff of Orange County to a tree, and gave him 500 lashes. ...
1770 *Ib.* 12 Nov. [from Newbern, S.C.]. A violent insurrection in Orange County, among a sett of men who call themselves Regulators, and who for some years past have given infinite disturbance to the civil government of this province, but now have sapped the whole foundation.

Later organizations of the same name were active in many places and at various periods:

1832 Paulding *Westward Ho!* I.96. Such a state of existence at once entails the necessity of an association among the honest portion of the community for the defence of their rights and the punishment of aggression. Hence originated the institution called the Regulators.
1839 C. F. Hoffman *Wild Scenes* II.61. A disbanded regulator of the Georgia guard, with a Lynch-ing corn-cracker from that

state [Ky.] ... had scented the contents of my master's saddle bags. ...
1860 *Sandusky* (Ohio) *Comm. Reg.* 28 July. Cleveland Regulators. [men disguised as negroes clean out brothels]
1879 *Nation* 21 Aug. 119. It is worthy of note, too, that the Yazoo (Yazoo County, Miss.) regulators think it necessary to defend themselves before the public.

reign of terror.

While *Jacobin, sans culotte,* and similar French terms were Americanized as useful slogans against sympathizers with the French Revolution, *reign of terror* seems to have been used by these very men in their attack against Federalists and their measures, in particular John Adams and the Alien and Sedition law.

1801 in *Mt. Vernon* (Ohio) *Republican* 9 Nov. 1858. [from the song "Jefferson and Liberty]
The reign of terror now is o'er.
1811 Graydon *Memoirs of a Life* 361. It [rebellion in Pa.] gave occasion too, for a useful nickname on the administration of Mr. Adams, which ... was, by the recent shouters for the mountain party of Robespierre denominated. A reign of terror now become a truly odious thing.
1824 *Cinc. Nat. Rep.* 12 Oct. 3/1. Every American ... must remember with horror and detestation, the eventful period, from 1798 to 1800, justly called "the Reign of Terror."
1840 *Rough-hewer* 91/3. Gen. Harrison and the Reign of Terror [head] 92/1 ... that period [of Alien & Sedition laws] in our country's history acquired the appropriate name of "the reign of Terror."

Alleged terrorist attacks like the abduction of William Morgan led to the application of *reign of terror* to the Freemasons:

1831 letter in Kennedy *Wirt* II.305 ... any secret society which, by the force of mysterious oaths and obligations, and by the extent of its combination, seeks to disturb the action of those laws ... and to establish a reign of terror over the initiated and uninitiated, is a political monster as fearful as the Invisible Tribunal of Germany, or the Inquisition of Spain. ...

repeater.

One who votes, or attempts to vote, more than once in an election. (See ROUNDER.)

Although Mencken in *American Language,* p. 148, says, "There were primaries in New York City in 1827, and hundreds of repeaters voted," there is no evidence that the word was in use at that time. The first known quotation is from 1861:

Newell *Orpheus C. Kerr* I.244. This morning ... I discovered six Repeaters among my men. Each of them voted six times last election day.

Later examples:

1868 *Harper's W.* 10 Oct. 647/4. First Democratic Repeater. [head] "Mr. President, this is Mike M'Ginnis; wants to join our Club. He's got lots of naturalization papers, and is going to vote 'em in every ward—he is."
1876 *N. Y. Trib.* 28 Oct. 7/1. Would that be worse than to pack New York and Brooklyn full of repeaters?

republican.

Since the Constitution guarantees to every state a republican form of government (Art. IV, sec. 4), it would seem that *republican* from the beginning had every chance of becoming a unifying not a partisan word. That this became not the case is due to two main reasons:

1. In many quarters the term *republican* met criticism on the ground of its being too vague.

1790 John Adams *Works* VI.415. It is a fixed principle with me, that all good government is and must be republican. But, at the same time, you can or will agree with me, that there is not in lexicography a more fraudulent word. ... Are we not, my friend, in danger of rendering the word republican unpopular in this country by an indiscreet, indeterminate, and equivocal use of it?
1816 Jefferson *Works* X.31. On this view of the import of the term republic, instead of saying, as has been said, "that it may mean anything or nothing," we may say with truth and meaning, that governments are more or less republican as they have more or less of the element of popular election and control in their composition. ...

2. More important is the well-known fact that many influential Americans of the Washington era did not consider the republic as a permanent form of American government but advocated, or at least expected its replacement by, some form of monarchy. We quote Jefferson's description of the state of affairs in 1790:

1818 *Works* I.159. I returned from the mission [in France] in the first year of the new government ... and proceeded to New York to enter on the office of Secretary of State. Here, certainly, I found a state of things which, of all I had ever contemplated, I the least expected. ... Politics was the chief topic, and a preference of kingly, over republican, government was evidently the favorite sentiment. An apostate I could not be, nor yet a hypocrite; and I found myself, for the most part the only advocate on the republican side of the question. ...

In view of this contrast, it became quite natural that when the democratic forces formed a political organization its name became *the*

Republican Party. In spite of the early competition of *democrat* (q.v.), this remained the official designation to Jefferson and many of his followers.

1793 Jefferson *Works* VI.326. The war between France and England has brought forward the republicans and monocrats in every State so openly, that their relative numbers are perfectly visible.

1809 *Ib.* VII.47. Two parties ... exist within the United States. ... The anti-republicans consist of. ... The republican part of our Union comprehends. ...

1793 *Ib.* I.257. Without knowing the views of what is called the republican party here [Phila.], ... I could undertake to assure him [Washington] from my intimacy with that party in the late Congress, that there was not a view in the republican party as spread over the United States, which went to the frame of the government. ...

1796 in Brant *Madison* III.439. Such have been the exertions and influence of Aristocracy, Anglicism and Mercantilism, in that quarter, that Republicanism is perfectly overbalanced, even in the town of Boston.

It has been pointed out under *democracy* that during the Jackson period *republican* lost a great deal of its usefulness because both major parties adopted it as part of their name and was accordingly dropped by the Democratic-Republicans, who preferred to call themselves "Democrats," and by the National-Republicans, who adopted the name "Whigs."

For almost twenty years *republican* was used only infrequently although it never dropped out entirely. In some circles the old aversion against *democrat* kept *republican* alive (see DEMOCRACY, quotation from Thurlow Weed).

1840 *Cong. Globe* App.401/3 [Steenrod of Va., HR]. Is it the policy of the Republican party which causes the alternate distress and prosperity to which this country is so often subject?

Ib. 402/2. Mr. Steenrod congratulated his colleague on his conversion to those principles, and pronounced them the principles of the Republican party, and informed Mr. W. where he could find the speech referred to.

In others it was synonymous with *democrat*.

1840 *Straight-out Harrisonian* 14 Aug. 4/2. We frequently hear the words Federalist and Democrat used by almost every person at the present day. ... Hence the word Democrat is synonimous [sic] with that of Republican.

1840 in Norton *Tippecanoe* 214. There were two meetings held, and, as the processions were passing, a "Harrison" banner was unfurled in the Democratic line by one who spoke to them and then marched out with sixty others into the Republican crowd.

However, these remnants of an earlier usage cannot be considered characteristic of the general usage of the early forties. Evidently to many, *republican* had ceased to be an active part of their political vocabulary and could, therefore, be revived by new parties who were equally dissatisfied with the Whigs and the Democrats. A Native American paper of 1843 writes:

Am. Citizen (N.Y.) 18 July 3/1. Our friends will understand us as cutting adrift from both the political parties of the day—that we are neither Whigs nor Democrats, but Republicans.

A similar attempt was made during the Taylor campaign:

1848 *Phila. North Am.* The Republican Party. ... A new and mighty party is rearing its gigantic form before the world. It is not merely the Whig party, nor the

Democratic party—not the Native party nor the slavery party—it is the great TAYLOR REPUBLICAN PARTY.

But also the anti-Taylor whigs made use of *republican* to emphasize their disagreement with the regulars of the party:

1848 "Warrington" *Pen Portraits* 39. In August, the paper [*The Whig*] was enlarged; and its name was changed to "Republican," because the name "Whig" had been appropriated by the new Taylor party....

Under these conditions the men who finally succeeded in reviving "republican" as the name of the party so designated since 1854 cannot be said to have been altogether original, but they succeeded where the sporadic efforts of their predecessors had failed. The name seems to have been suggested privately as early as 1852, two years before the actual party came into existence.

1854 A. E. Bovay letter to Greeley in Flowers *Hist. of Rep. Party* 160. Urge them to forget previous political names and organization, and to band together under the name I suggested to you at Lovejoy's Hotel in 1852, while Scott was being nominated. I mean the name *Republican.*

According to a later source, the name was suggested publicly in the same year:

1872 *Ann. of Cleve.* No.3305. After the presidential election of 1852 the Cleveland Leader, then called the Forest City Democrat, came out in favor of the union of the Whig and the Free Soil parties under the name of the Republican party. The Forest City Democrat was the first paper in the country to advocate such a union. [?]

Two years later the word was in the air and suggestions along the same lines came in quick succession

from various parts of the country.

1854 Washburn in Flowers *Hist. of Rep. Party* 168. Do you remember that impromptu meeting of anti-Missouri Compromise Repeal Democrats and Whigs at the rooms of Congressmen Eliot and Dickinson, of Massachusetts, at Crutchett's on Sixth street, on the morning after the compromise bill passed the House, [May 21, 1854 see Wilson, II.410] at which ... we discussed the necessity of forming a new party from anti-slavery extension Whigs and Democrats, and the name of Republican was suggested? [See also Kleeberg, *Formation of Republican Party,* 14]

1884 *N. Y. Trib.* Oct. 2/1 [A. N. Cole referring to a letter to Greeley written in April, 1854]. I said: You seem to think the time has come to organize our long anticipated party of freedom. Tell me, will you, what name you would give it? His answer came quickly, saying: "Call it Republican,— no prefix, no suffix, but plain Republican." I published Mr. Greeley's letter in my paper, The Genesee Valley Free Press.

The decisive event was, of course, the meeting at Jackson, Michigan, that organized the party and officially adopted the name "republican."

1854 *Zachariah Chandler by contributors to Detroit Post and Tribune* 112. Resolved, that ... we will cooperate and be known as Republicans until the contest be terminated.

The name was in general hailed by the anti-slavery press as a fortunate choice:

1854 *Ohio St. Jrnl.* 11 July 2. The name of "Republicans" which they have chosen is significant. In opposition to the Slave Democracy of the free States, this new combination of true Republicans is bound to sweep all before them.

1854 *N. Y. Trib.* 15 July 4/3. The name under which the [Michigan] opponents of the Nebraska iniquity have enlisted

for the war is simply Republican, and this, we think, will be generally adopted. 1854 *Kennebec Jrnl.* in Muzzey *Blaine* 26 and Stanwood *Hist. of Presidency* 41. [Since neither Muzzey nor Stanwood give dates for this quotation, it may very well postdate the Jackson meeting.]
The term Republican has come to have a self-defined meaning and informs everyone that the person thus designated sympathizes with and belongs to the new fusion movement or People's party that is springing up throughout the free States to resist the encroachments of Slavery and maintain the rights of the North.

That the name met with local criticism is clear:
1857 in "Warrington" *Pen Portraits* 224. [from Banks paper friendly to a coalition of the new party with the Know Nothings] I am glad that you have, since the election, plucked up courage enough to resume the use of the word "Republican." You remind me of the henpecked man, who, after being driven under the bed by his wife, at last ventured to look out, and, in reply to a threatening shake of the broomstick, valiantly said, "As long as I have the spirit of a man, I will peek!" This is a good sign. Before the election, the unlucky wight who had dared to intimate that the Banks party was Republican would have had his hat knocked over his eyes.
1859 *Ib.* 233. All over the United States, from Passamaquoddy to Key West, from Galveston to Fraser River, the opposition to the Democratic party is known as the "Republican party."...What a bother it is, when you are accosted by some New Yorker or Illinoisian, and are asked if you are a Republican, to be obliged to say, "I belong, sir, to the party which is opposed to the present corrupt National Administration and the aggressions of the slave-power, and is in favor of the general policy of the present State Administration"!...though the word "Republican" is in common conversational use, we can't use it in conventions and committees and official documents just yet.

It goes without saying that the Democrats found fault with the propriety of the new name:
1854 *Cleve. Plain Dealer* 19 July 2/2. They [Michigan Fusionists] even went so far as to christen the party by the name "Republican."
1854 *Ib.* 2 Aug. 4/1. The Whigs are horribly bothered about their mongrel ticket. They don't know what to call it. The Herald, after much cogitation, has settled upon the word "People's," while the State Journal selects the equally insidious phrase "Republican."
1860 *Xenia Fairchild* 25 Jan. 1. Disabuse the North of this delusion, do it fairly, truly, and the Republican party will shrink at once to the comparatively insignificant faction of radical Abolitionists upon whom it was originally based.

The tendency appearing in these weak protests comes out much clearer in the coining of a great variety of nicknames like "Black Republican," "woolly head," "niggerlover," "radical."

Recently it has been suggested that "republican" as a party name be dropped in favor of "conservative":
1946 *Ohio State Lantern* 26 Feb. 4/1. A change of name for the Republican Party has been advocated by Clarence Budington Kelland, who besides being an author is also Republican Committeeman for Arizona. He proposes that the name be changed to the "Conservative Party" to oppose the Democratic Party or "Radical Party."

Mr. Kelland has more imagination than knowledge of politics, or so it would appear from this proposal. No matter how conservative certain segments of the Republican Party may be, the connotations of the word "Conservative" would be crippling politically. "Conservative" implies "backward" and "unprogressive" to many people.

restrictionist.

One opposed to the extension of slavery into the territories.

1820 *Niles' Reg.* XVIII.258/2. We undertake to say that there is not a single *confessed* restrictionist elected throughout the whole territory.
1836 *Ohio St. Jrnl.* 6 Sept. 3/4. Then, [c.1820] a Restrictionist was as odious in the South, as an Abolitionist is Now.
1849 in Stephens *War Between the States* II.179. Besides the Southern Whigs, who had thus separated themselves from their former Party organization, there were fourteen extreme Restrictionists from the North, composed partly of Whigs and partly of Democrats, who refused to support either of these nominees.

retrenchment and reform.

As an alliterative slogan intended to fasten the attention of the voters upon the wastefulness and rascality of the party in power, and on the good intentions of their own party, politicians used this phrase throughout the 19th century following its introduction in England during the reign of William IV. In a cartoon by H. B. published in 1830, the following conversation is given:
William IV: Your conditions?
Earl Grey: Retrenchment, Reform, and Peace.
William: Done!
[See *Notes and Queries,* 9th series, XII.333]

The first evidence of the slogan in America is from the Michigan elections of 1839:
in Streeter' *Pol. Parties in Michigan* 21. Though the conservative Democrats gained the upper hand and nominated one of their number as the candidate for Governor, the party was defeated and the Whigs rode into office on the promise of "retrenchment and reform."

Given national currency the following year, it became a standard cry for economy:

1840 Kennedy *Quodlibet* 146. "Retrenchment and reform!" says every big fellow there at Washington; and the same words are bawled all the way down amongst us, even to Theodore Fog. . . .
1841 J. A. Meriwether in *Georgia Jrnl.* 3 Aug. 1/2. He tells us that last year he heard nothing but the cry of "retrenchment and reform". . . .
1853 *Cong. Globe* 195/2. I trust that a spirit of conservatism will characterize the incoming Administration; and that economy, retrenchment and reform, will be its watchword. . . .
1874 *Cong. Record* 1089/1. The flag under which political victories will be won, in the immediate future, is the flag upon which is inscribed "Retrenchment and reform". . . .
1875 *Ohio St. Jrnl.* 18 June 2/5 [Platform of Democratic State Convention]. Retrenchment and reform in every department of government—Federal, State and local.
1881 Ridpath *Garfield* 404. The county and state organizations have their treasuries . . . and their cries of robbery, reform, and retrenchment.

revenue reformer.

A Republican who favored changes in the financial policies of the party.

1870 *Nation* 28 April 263/2. A meeting of revenue reformers . . . was held in Washington, last week, for the purpose of talking over the financial situation.
1870 *Every Sat.* 3 Dec. 775/1 . . . in Missouri where Hon. B. Gratz Brown was elected Governor by the combined votes of Democrat and Revenue reformers.
1871 *Ib.* 14 Jan. 26/4. The Revenue Reformers [head] . . . Some taxes they would reduce, others—like the offensive, unrepublican income tax—they would abolish altogether. They would shift the general burden of taxation from articles of

necessity and utility to articles of luxury, like tobacco and spirits.

1871 Scott in *Cong. Globe* 3 March 2006/1. I say, if it is understood that the declared policy of the Republican party,... is to be abandoned for the purpose of an attack upon one of the industrial interests [coal] of the country, and if that attack is to be led by the gentleman who is put forward as the head of the new revenue reform party....

rich man's war; poor man's fight.

The phrase is a characteristic expression of the feeling in the South during the Civil War that the poorer classes, although doing most of the fighting, had no real stake in the outcome of the conflict.

1862? Kirkland *Company K* 326... for I do perceive that it is to be the rich man's war, but the poor man's fight; that those will get rich who do not fight; and those who do fight will not get rich—no, never.

1863 in Sandburg *War Years* II.418... General Magruder in Louisiana warning Confederate troops against demagogues who had told them it was a rich man's war and a poor man's fight.

1864 in Hayes *Diary* 27 Sept. II.516. Rebel prisoners—the common soldiers—all talk one way. "Tired of the rich man's war"....

rich richer; poor poorer.

The phrase *to make the rich richer and the poor poorer* has been a popular political expression used against any measure that seemed to favor the moneyed aristocracy. Thus we find early examples referring to Hamilton's financial schemes, the bank in particular:

1794 J. Taylor *Principles and Tendency* 15. Its [the Bank's] chief design was to make the rich, richer; and the poor, poorer.

Examples of legislative acts:

1828 *Argus of Western America* 6 Feb. 1/2. That bill [the Woolens Bill] was calculated to make "the rich, richer, and the poor, poorer."

1840 in *Cong. Globe* App.739... the doctrine for which the opponents of this levelling destructive policy contend is, that the object and effect is to reduce the price of free labor and produce, for the benefit of the capitalists of the nation; or, in other words, to make the rich richer, and the poor poorer.

In addition to being a slogan against certain bills, it was also used to sway public opinion against rival groups or parties:

1829 *Workingman's Adv.* 28 Nov. 1/4. In the city and county of Philadelphia the working men have remonstrated against the increase of banking institutions, as having a tendency to make the rich man richer, and the poor man poorer—to make a nation of nabobs and slaves.

1838 in *Cong. Globe* 14 May. It is alleged that these charted rights cramp and fetter the energies, and have a tendency to make the rich richer, and the poor poorer.

1840 Kennedy *Quodlibet* 168. The Whigs are for making the poor poorer, and the rich richer—and I say any man who goes against the Sub Treasury can't have no respect for dimmicratic principles.

rider.

A clause or amendment added to a bill.

Usually the "rider," which could probably not become enacted on its own merits, is assured of passage by its being appended to a popular measure.

A. The original word in English usage is *rider-roll.*

1669 Noy *Rep. & Cases* 84 [*OED*]. That which is certified shall be annexed to the Record, and is called a Rider-roll.

B. Many quotations suggest that neither the term nor the practice gained sudden popularity in the United States.

1817 M. Carey *Olive Branch* 54 ... a rider was annexed to it by the former [Brit. Commissioners].

1835 *Jrnl. of House of Representatives* (Ohio) 207. It was amended by way of ryder, the amendment engrossed, again read, and the bill passed.

1837 *Nat. Intell.* 6 March. It would have been at least more respectful to the new President ... to have published his address independently, and not as a sort of *rider,* merely, to the Address of the Ex-President.

1842 *Ohio Statesman* 21 Dec. 2/5. Mr. McNulty moved to amend the bill by way of a ryder, by adding the following. ...

1867 Greeley *Conflict* I.208. The bill organizing the territory of New Mexico was added as an amendment or "rider" to the bill defining the Northern boundary of Texas.

1879 in Williams *Hayes* II.203n. Another bill for the marshals, with the objectionable rider attached, will also be sent to me.

1879 *N. Y. World* 10 April 4/3 ... it would ... leave the Democrats no option whatever but to adopt the "rider" tactics.

1880 *N. Y. Trib.* 4 Feb. 5/3. During the debate on the report of the Rules of the House yesterday, Speaker Randall, Mr. Cox and Mr. Whitthorne stated that they are opposed to political "riders" on appropriation bills.

ridiculosity.

1870 *N. Y. Times* 12 Jan. 1/2. A New Word. Senator Sumner gave the Senate and the dictionary makers a new word to-day. In the Debate in Virginia he said that the rescinding by a State of a vote on a constitutional amendment was utterly null and void, and was merely a constitutional ridiculosity.

1870 *Harper's W.* 139/3. Senator Sumner has the credit of coining the last new word, "ridiculosity." Some poetic genius thus relieves his mind in regard to it:
Slowly rolled forth the novel sound—
    "Ridiculosity,"
From out of the classic mouth of great
    "Preponderosity";
And through the Senatorial hall,
    With great velocity,
Echoed from mouth to mouth the word
    "Ridiculosity!"
Sure Worcester never dared to write
    "Ridiculosity;"
Nor Webster either, murmured they,
    With grim ferocity.
Is there of terms gigantic then
    So great a paucity,
That we must coin this fearful one,
    "Ridiculosity?"

right to work.

A. As an inherent right of every man, *droit au travail* was propounded by Fourier in his *Théorie des quatre mouvements:*

1808 in Ladendorf *Schlagwörterbuch* 261. Wir können also, was die Menschenrechte anlangt, die Philosophie und die Zivilisazion ersuchen, uns der Hülfsquelle nicht zu berauben, die uns Gott für den schlimmsten Fall und als Züchtigung gelassen hat, und uns mindestens das Recht zu Arbeit, für die wir erzogen worden sind, zu garantiren.

B. American followers of Fourier adopted this principle, and the "right to work" became one of the chief slogans associated with the development of trade unionism and the betterment of the position of the workingman in society.

1840 Brisbane *Association* 111. But its [industrial servitude] falseness does not end here; to it is added the violation of the fundamental right of man, The Right To Labor.

1846 Greeley in Sotheran *Horace Greeley* 201 [essay "The Right to Labor"] ... But the Right to Labor—that is, to constant Employment with a just and full

Recompense—cannot be guaranteed to all without a radical change in our Social Economy.

1897 *Rev. of Rev.* XVI.13/2. The old-fashioned economists have hated nothing so much as the doctrine of the "right to work."

1903 *Am. Fed.* April 258/2. If the capitalist methods of industry at once produce and require as a condition of continued exploitation an army of unemployed laborers—what hypocrisy is it to prate of the "right to work"?

1903 Mitchell *Org. Labor* 283. The inalienable right of man to work will then [after compulsory union membership] be put upon a par with the inalienable right of a child to play truant, and the compulsion exercised by the trade union will be likened to that of a state.

C. As unions became more powerful, however, the "right to work" became a cry of non-union laborers against the exclusive organization of the closed shop.

1870 *Workingman's Adv.* in Commons *Labor* IX.250. The exclusion of colored men, and apprentices from the right to labor in any department of industry or workshops . . . by what is known as "trade unions," is an insult to God, injury to us, and disgrace to humanity.

1922 Harding in Vandenberg *If Hamilton* 179. Liberty is gone in America when anybody is denied by anybody the right to work and live by that work.

1955 *Nation* 8 Jan. 24/1. A party organization which governs fourteen states out of a total of seventeen which have adopted union-busting "right-to-work" laws.

1957 *Time* 11 March 20/1. Some 7,500 wrought-up Indianians marched into the Statehouse in Indianapolis last week to protest a "right-to-work" bill passed.

D. When strikes and walkouts became techniques of a highly organized labor group, it is, perhaps, inevitable that we find *right to cease work.*

1922 Gompers in Vandenberg *If Hamilton* 180. The right to cease work at will is one of a small group of rights upon which our whole civilization and our whole future progress must rest.

ring.

The opinion that the political use of *ring* goes back to the Tweed organization in New York can be accepted only in so far as this organization certainly is an important factor in the history of the word. However, it occurs as early as 1825:

William Patchell to Jackson in Weston *Election of 1828* 50. The aristocratic Ring will be dethroaned [sic].

Even in New York *ring* seems to have been used before the days of the Tweed regime. The generally well-informed Parton testifies to its existence around 1850:

Topics of the Times 384. It was then that . . . "Rings" were first formed.

A new era begins with the formation of the Board of Supervisors of which Tweed was a member, but not, to begin with, the boss. Tilden gives a definition of what is understood by a ring:

1871 Tilden *Iniquities of the Tweed Ring* in Hart *Source Book* 352. The Ring had its origin in the Board of Supervisors. That body was created by an Act passed in 1857. . . . The very definition of a Ring is that it encircles enough influential men in the organization of each party to control the action of both party machines,—men who in public push to extremes the abstract ideas of their respective parties, while they secretly join their hands in schemes for personal power and profit.

The following quotations refer to the Board of Supervisors.

1860 *N. Y. Trib.* 2 Aug. It is to this Ring that we owe the shameful Battery swindle.... Confirming contracts is a good business for the Ring.

1862 *N. Y. Times* 26 April 2/5. The *Leader* then denounced the Aldermanic "Ring"....

However, at that time, this body was not *the* ring but, as indicated from the following quotations, was one of several rings:

1862 *Independent* 13 Feb. 4/4. [Parties] are more responsible in regard to the character of those they nominate than are those ... profligate rings that are so apt to take control of a merely local election.

Probably already at that period the word was known outside of New York. DeForest mentions a cotton ring operating in Louisiana during the war:

1867 DeForest *Miss Ravenel's Conversion* 371. At New Orleans there were greedy capitalists, who had not been lucky enough to get into the Ring [organization for smuggling cotton].

During the heyday of the Tweed Ring the word was, of course, in everybody's mouth. We give only a few quotations from a less well-known source:

c. 1868 Halpine *Poetical Works* 261.
Look at Twee—holy Father! Bill Tweedie
   —look at him;
   Did you ever see feedin' like that in
   your life?
Like a Suffolkshire pig when you stuff
   him and fat him—
   An' I guess—like the pig—he's just fit
   for the knife.
Musha Tweedie, ahagur! 'tis you have
   soft weather,
   It was we tuned your pipes and we
   taught you to sing;
Do you mind o' the time we wor "bunk-
   ers" together,
   Before you grew rich, fat, and proud in
   the "Ring?"

. . . .

The "Ring" goes down—we'll clear the
   town
Of all the brood o' Brennans;
An', faix! Charley Cornell, an' Tweed
   as well,
   Shall fly before our pennons.

The history of *ring* does not end with the fall of the Tweed Ring; on the contrary, it is used abundantly as a designation of organizations more or less following the same methods. Between October 2, 1872 and October 14, the *New York Tribune* mentions the following rings:

2 Oct.	1/1	Treasury ring
2 Oct.	1/2	Pennsylvania ring
3 Oct.	1/4	Grant-Cameron ring
3 Oct.	4/5	Hartranft ring
9 Oct.	2/3	Bumstead ring
12 Oct.	6/3	Erie ring
14 Oct.	5/1	Clayton ring

Indicative of the influence of American slang on European politics—an influence not yet properly investigated, but certainly important enough to deserve a thorough treatment—is an incident in the German Reichstag in 1881. In a parliamentary debate of that year, Bismarck said:

in Ladendorf 273. Ich glaube, es ist eine weltbekannte Sache, dass in Berlin der Fortschritt regiert, ein fortschrittlicher Ring die Stadt beherrscht, der gar nicht zu durchbrechen ist.

In view of the many ways in which *ring* has been used metaphorically it is hard to determine in what field of ideas it was at home before it entered politics. The occasional use of *ringmaster* for *boss* might suggest that the word originally belonged to the sphere of the circus. (See STRADDLE, SIDESHOW.)

1868 *Harper's W.* 23 May 323. The ascendency of the Democratic party in the State [N.Y.] means the control of its government by certain well-known "ringmasters."

But these examples are too rare and too late to make this explanation plausible. Another vague possibility is suggested by indications that the word may have been used in Masonic terminology as a synonym of circle. (See George Gray, *The Mystic Circle,* 1867. The circle represents that boundary or line within which our every thought, word, and action should be circumscribed.)

It seems not improbable that the song "Come, Brothers, Join the Mystic Ring," mentioned by Halpine, *Private Miles O'Reilly,* p. 124, in a satire on ring politics is of Masonic origin.

It should not be overlooked that *ring* also formed a part of the spiritualistic terminology. Just at the time when *ring* came into frequent political use, the Rochester ghost rappings and similar spiritualistic manifestations had created a furor to which even such prominent men as Horace Greeley contributed their share (Greeley, *Recollections of a Busy Life*).

1851 *Carpetbag* I.4/1. Rapology.... As de time ob conservation wid der spirits hab come, I must request de sembly to mix demselves into two distinct circles round dis pine wood table, de "belebers in der spirits" to consumate de inside ring, and de speptics, non-belebers and incomwincibles to make de oudside ring....

A connection between the inside ring of the rapologists and the po-

litical ring may be indicated by the fact that Miles O'Reilly too speaks of an inside ring:

116. "Inside rings" will then have to be formed, having for their object a further "consolidation" of plunder.

128. There were other clauses providing for the formation of "inside rings" to cheat each other....

ring-tailed roarer.

As the name of a mythical animal the ring-tailed roarer turns up in many variations in the boatmen's vocabulary (see SALT RIVER). Like other words of this formula it acquired a place in political language, mainly as a name of political clubs.

1842 *Vincennes Western Star* 3 Sept. 1/4. They [Whigs at Bunker Hill Celebration] were distinguished by the political epithet of "whig ring tailed roarers of the legitimate hard cider and coon skin order."

1844 *Wash. Globe* 18 Oct. 995/1. We read enough [handbills] to perceive that this new litter just emerged from the coon's hole, have all the marks of the best upon them. They are all "ringtailed roarers" or Roorbacks.

ripper bill.

1914 *Cyc. Am. Government* III.229/1. Ripper Bills. A term applied to acts of state legislatures for the reorganization of city governments, intended to turn incumbents out of office, and to put in a new set of officials.

1895 *Cols. Dispatch* 1 April 4/2. The Merryman ripper bill looks very much as if the Republicans of this city were going to the legislature for offices.

1907 J. C. Cooper *Handwriting* 85. It was in this way that the ripper bill was passed.

1929 Al Smith *Up to Now* 114. Some of the warmest arguments in the legislature in these days occurred over what were called "ripper" bills. The party in power would legislate their political opponents out of office.

The ripper is a form of cutting tool or saw. (see *OED*)

rock ribbed.

Uncompromising. (See also ROCK ROOTED.) Seems to go back to Bryant's "Thanatopsis":—
The hills,
Rock-ribbed and ancient as the sun, the vales
. . . .
Are but the solemn declarations all of the great tomb of man—

although it is attested in England as early as 1776 (*OED*). The popularity of the quotation is attested by the fact that a portion of Ohio is known as the rock-ribbed region (see *Marietta Intelligencer,* 4 October, 1859, 2/3 and *Cincinnati Gazette,* 25 June, 1880, 3/1) and by Andrew Johnson's use of the term:
1861 in Pollard *Secret History* 79 . . . we stand immovable upon our basis, as on our own native mountains—presenting their craggy brows, their unexplored caverns, their summits, "rock-ribbed and ancient as the sun"—we stand speaking peace, association and concert to a distracted Republic.

Transferred from nature to man and his political behavior:
1923 *Rev. of Rev.* LXVIII.265. In a rock-ribbed open shop town, where anti-unionism was a gospel among most employers, Publisher Harding not only permitted but actively promoted the unionization of all the crafts represented in his business.
1934 Carter *New Dealers* 123. He [Sprague] was in sympathy with the objectives of the New Deal and, far from being the rock-ribbed conservative which the Old Gang strove to make him, saw no

necessity for balancing the budget in time of depression.
1960 *Time* 7 March 16/1. In a state (Maine) that was long a fortress of rock-ribbed conservatism. . . .

rock rooted.

Variation of *rock ribbed.*
1878 *Cinc. Gazette* 30 Sept. 4/1 . . . will vote the full Democratic ticket on election day, and no questions asked. Such are the habits of the rock rooted.

Roorback.

In 1844 the *Ithaca* (N.Y.) *Chronicle* published an account of a trip through the South in 1836 in which the author, Roorback, claimed that he saw slaves branded with the initials J.K.P. This attack against the Democratic presidential candidate James K. Polk was almost immediately denounced as a forgery:
1844 *Albany Argus* in *Wash. Globe* 23 Sept. 907/5. Roorback is a fictitious name . . . Don't undertake to palm off upon us . . . your "Roorbacks" and strawmen that nobody can know.
1844 *Spirit of the Times* 3 Oct. The Roorback Forgery has been traced to a Mr. Linn of Ithaca, N.Y., a violent abolitionist and an intemperate man.

After it was evident that the whole story was a forgery, Whig papers tried to absolve themselves by branding it as a Locofoco trick:
1844 *N. Y. Trib.* 5 Oct. 4/3. The Roorback Forger Discovered. [editorial calling the Roorback a Locofoco forgery] (See also *Harper's W.,* 29 Jan., 1881, 67/3.)

Roorback became the label tagged to any campaign story which seemed to have little authenticity or which was an out and out fabrication:

1852 in *Cong. Globe* 327. Let me raise my warning voice, and say to my Southern friends, beware of these Birney Roorbacks. **1856** *Ohio St. Jrnl.* 27 Oct. 2/2. But we doubt the statement of a paper which invented the "Roorback" in regard to Col. Fremont's birthplace. **1860** *Ashland Times* 7 Oct. 2. Look out for the Roorbacks. As the day of election draws near it will be well for Republicans to be on the look-out for all manner of false reports having no foundation. **1876** in Hayes *Diary* III.358. You can denounce all charges of [my] hostility to foreigners as voters and officeholders as utterly unfounded. They are the merest roorbacks.

rooster party.
Humorous reference to the Democratic Party.
1844 *Whig Battering Ram* 13 Sept. 2/4.
How I make the feathers fly
From the Rooster Party.
1852? *Prenticeana,* 189. The "Cincinnati Enquirer" calls the Whigs "the foul party." We think it must be the fowl party that elects Mr. Henn to Congress in Iowa, and adopts a rooster as its emblem.

root and branch.
A Biblical expression (Malachi 4:1 . . . and the day that cometh shall burn them up, saith the Lord of Hosts, that it shall leave them neither root nor branch) that assumed political importance through the London *Petition* of December 11, 1640:
That the said government, with all its dependencies, roots, and branches, be abolished.

As Macaulay points out (*Hist. of England,* I.96) —the root and branch men of the Cromwellian period are, politically and etymologically, the predecessors of radicals of later days. Through the

18th and 19th centuries words like *root and branch -party, -bill, -reformer,* are current in England (see *OED,* I.1053 and Philipson, *Political Slang*).
American repercussions of the English usage:
1802 Chester *Federalism Triumphant* 5. I'll let all the rascally Democrats know what it is to be a governor and quell at once all this mutinous behavior of the Jacobins—whirl 'em at once into the old whirlpool of extermination, root and branch. **1837** Jackson *Corr.* V.516. Mr. Bancroft . . . a root and branch Democrat. **1863** in Logan *Conspiracy* 525. I want a vote on my Bill for the destruction of Slavery, root and branch. Van Buren *Autobio.* 126. He was . . . a root and branch Democrat, clear headed, honest hearted, and always able and ready to defend the right regardless of personal consequences.

root, hog, or die.
A drastic warning to office holders who did not show enough zeal in supporting the party in power; probably an application of an old proverb. [ ]
1829? in Poore *Perley's Reminiscences* 97. Many of them [clerks after Jackson's inauguration] were left in a pitiable condition, but when the Telegraph was asked what these men could do to ward off starvation, the insolent reply was, "Root, hog, or die!" **1836** *Calumet and War Club* 17 Aug. 2/2. Root, hog, or die,—work for your office, or leave it—support the party, right or wrong—are the terms of the agreement [of the Jackson administration]. **1882** *Judge* 18 March 10/3.
And he strode up ahead as the path he made
For the Stalwart Three Hundred, with the watchword
"root hog or die."

rotation (in office.)

A regular succession in public offices; succession as spoils to the victorious party.

A. From the earlier astronomical meaning we find the metaphor in English political usage already in the 17th century.

1656 Harrington *Oceana* 54 [*OED*]. Equal Rotation is equal vicissitude in Government, or succession to Magistracy confer'd for such convenient terms . . . as take in the whole body by parts.

1721 Sheffield *Works* II.180 [*OED*]. This is no small advantage in Republicks, where a sort of rotation is necessary, by which men are seen under several capacities.

B. In America this concept of a periodic change of officials was strongly advocated by the early political theorists such as Adams and Jefferson and continued to be regarded by many as one of the most significant features of our democratic government.

1774 Adams *Works* 25 June IX.339. I think the arduous duties of the times ought to be discharged in rotation, and I never will engage more in politics but upon this system.

1776 *Ib.* IV.197. A rotation of all offices, as well as of representatives and counsellors, has many advocates and is contended for with many plausible arguments.

1787 Jefferson in Dwight *Hartford Conv.* 12. They [newspapers] have abandoned rotation in office; and particularly their president may be reelected from four years to four years, for life, so as to render him a king for life, like a king of Poland.

1819 in Barnes *Weed* 11. When, in July, 1819, Thomas J. Oakley, by a revolution in politics, succeeded Martin Van Buren as Attorney-General of New York, this step was sustained by the young editor at Norwich, as warranted by the strictest principles of republican justice, and in-

deed imperiously called for as a means of protection to the administration. "Rotation in office," he wrote, "is the most striking and brilliant feature of excellence in our benign form of government. . . ."

C. However, with the adoption of the doctrine "to the victor belongs the spoils," *rotation in office* developed a secondary meaning— the turning out of office of those who were members of the opposition party. Thus also *rotator:*

1832 *Address to the People of Md.* 17. [pamphlet] "Rotation in office" was defined by its practice, to be an expulsion of the president's opponents, in favor of his party friends.

1836 *Voice of the People* & *Albany Whig* 25 Oct. 3/1. The New Jersey Tories at their recent Congressional Convention made an entirely new ticket, which has given mortal offense to the old *Rotators,* who wished to *rotate* for a couple of years longer.

1838 *Ohio Statesman* 5 June 2/3. The General [Murphy] admitted that they [Democrats] were in favor of "rotation in office"—but it was always a *rotation upwards!*

1839 Underwood of Ky. in *Cong. Globe* App.376/1. Why, sir, the party in power preach the doctrine of rotation in office. I know they practise upon it by occasionally rolling the incumbent from one fat office to a fatter, and then to the fattest. . . .

1842 *Bro. Jonathan* II.3 . . . immaculate principles of rotation in office. . . .

1843 Birney *Ltrs.* 746. Rotation in Office is now their watchword.

1849 in Barnes *Weed* 176. But, if the country is to be benefited by our services, it seems to me that you and I ought to remember those to whose zeal, activity, and influence we are indebted for our places. There are plenty of Whigs just as capable and honest, and quite as deserving of office, as the Democrats who have held them through two or three presidential terms. Rotation in office, provided good men are appointed, is sound republican doctrine.

1866 *N. Y. Times* 29 Aug. 1/5. [Pres. Johnson at Phila.] Is that good old doctrine of rotation in office forgotten?

1874 *Cleve. Leader* 7 July 5/1. Fourteen women clerks fainted on the floor of the Treasury Department upon the general discharge of clerks which took place June 30.... In this country no person can be considered constitutionally qualified for office holding who cannot be rotated out without having a fit.

1881 *Nation* 6 Jan. 5/1. It will be easily seen from all this that when politicians talk of "rotation in office," they do not really mean rotation at all.

rotten borough.

Attested in England as early as 1771 (see Philipson, *Political Slang*, p. 213) *rotten borough* has been used in America to designate a district or state which exercises political control out of proportion to its size or importance:

1864 in *Gt. Deb.* VI.384. When Louisiana is readmitted she will be entitled to seven electoral votes, Tennessee to ten, Arkansas to five, and all Virginia to fifteen. So that by the organization of these four "rotten-boroughs" and unauthorized States there would be secured to Mr. Lincoln not only thirty-seven electoral votes in the presidental election, but ... that number in the Republican nominating convention at Baltimore.

1874 *Cinc. Enquirer* 16 Sept. 4/1. The Republican South is Grant's "rotten borough"....

1885 C. M. Clay *Memoirs* I.240. The rotten borough system of allowing votes in Convention to States which stand no chance of electoral strength....

1899 Robert Grant *Searchlight Ltrs.* 175. Those rotten boroughs have done yeoman service. They are on the tongue of every American citizen for excuses for our national short-comings.

1912 *Rev. of Rev.* XLVI. 7/2. No individual candidate, indeed, is responsible for a system that gives the so-called "rotten boroughs" their enormous voting strength in a Republican national convention.

rounder.

A repeater (q.v.).

1872 *Nation* 4 July 2 ... to superintend the strict registration of voters in advance of the day of election, and to unite in detecting "repeaters" and "rounders."

The word had been used earlier as a synonym for *loafer*, or one who made the rounds of the taverns. For example:

1858 *Ohio State Jrnl.* 6 Oct. 2/3 ... the rounders led on by Dr. Wayne Griswold of infamous notoriety, and long since repudiated by his party....

roundhead.

A Northern unionist; a Southern countercharge to the satirical use of *chivalry* and *cavalier* by Northerners.

1848 in Wilson *Slave Power* II.153 [Joseph L. White, N.Y., at Buffalo Convention]. Beware! The blood of the Roundheads is aroused.

1864 Sumner *Works* XI.449. I know not if the armies of the Union now fighting the world's greatest battle for Human Rights, may not be called "Roundheads"; but I am sure that Rebels now fighting for Slavery cannot be called "Cavaliers" in any sense.

The reference is, of course, to the supporters of Cromwell during the English Civil War.

1641? in *N. & Q.* Ser. 10, IX.170. [Cowley's prologue to "The Guardian"]

But our Scene's London now; and by the rout

We perish, if the Roundheads be about.

1642 *Ib.* X.357 [affidavit made on June 16, 1642 by Henry Wills:] ... that Mr. Seldon ... was a man that had more learning than a thousand round-headed Pims.

round robin.

A document having the names of the subscribers arranged in a circle so as to disguise the order in which they have been signed. Originally used by sailors, it may have been a proper name (see quotation of 1671).

1671 Hacket *Abp. Williams* II.177 [*OED*]. These Wat Tylers and Round Robins being driven or persuaded out of Whitehall. **1731** *Gentl. Mag.* I.238 [*OED*]. The Method used by Sailors when they mutiny, by signing their names in an orbicular manner, which they call a round Robin. **1847** Melville *Omoo* XX. I proposed that a "Round Robin" should be prepared and sent ashore to the consul.

The term apparently first entered American politics during the Spanish-American War, when a group of officers in Cuba addressed a letter to General Shafter protesting against the sanitary conditions. Theodore Roosevelt was one of the signers of this letter, which created great public concern for the welfare of the army in Cuba. **1898** *Rev. of Rev.* XVIII.424. The receipt of this order led to the famous "round robin" which was addressed to General Shafter by eight of the officers commanding brigades, divisions, etc., of the army of occupation of Cuba. **1903** Riis *Theodore Roosevelt The Citizen* 196. Until Colonel Roosevelt's round-robin, signed by all the general officers of the army in Cuba, startled the American people and caused measures of instant relief to be set on foot, the fearful truth that the army was perishing from privation and fever was not known. **1900** in Shaw *Cartoon Hist. of Roosevelt's Career* 57. [Cartoon, showing Roosevelt being refused a medal by Secretary of War Alger.]

"You're one of the round-robins; you don't get a medal."

royalist.

A select faction in the Republican party around 1880 who dictated policy: [ ]

c1880 in Pringle *Taft* 59. On the Republican side, a few of the respectables, who would have indignantly rejected illicit profits for themselves, perpetuated the machine. They were called Royalists.... The rank and file of the party resented the superiority of the Royalists. Out of their resentment arose a new group called "Mudsills."

rubber dollar.

Satiric synonym for currency of fluctuating value.

A. The Democratic platform for 1932 contained a plank advocating a price-fixing plank, which President Hoover attacked as tending toward an unstable currency: **1932** Hoover in *N. Y. Times* 5 Oct. 18/6. They [Dems] passed a price-fixing bill creating what might be colloquially called the "rubber dollar."

Roosevelt reacted immediately to Hoover's charge by attempting to ridicule his fears. **1932** F. D. R. in Warburg *Hellbent for Election* 23. The President is seeing visions of rubber dollars. This is only a part of his campaign of fear. **1945** *Fortune* March 111. Suddenly bemused by the idea of the "rubber dollar," he [FDR] torpedoed the London Economic Conference which had been called to deal with tariffs and currencies.

B. Hoover's use of the term may have been patterned on Speaker Cannon's use of *rubber currency* on a similar occasion: **1904** *N. Y. Eve. Post* 22 Nov. 8. Speaker Cannon talked disparagingly of "rubber currency," this being his interpretation of the word "elastic."

rubber stamp.

Applied to one who does not act according to his own judgment but is simply the agent of another:
1919 Thayer *Roosevelt* 334. From the bosom of his family he [Taft] may have heard the exhortation, "Be your own President; don't be anybody's man or rubber stamp."
1925 *Searchlight* Oct. 13/2. The other cabinet members . . . if we except the blundering and unfortunate Wilbur, are useful, tractable fellows of the chief-clerk type of human rubber stamps.
1925 in Lindley *FDR* 248. He termed them [N.Y. legislature] "mere rubber stamps to register other august wills."

During the Roosevelt administrations the close cooperation between the legislative and executive departments often led to the charges of rubber stamp by critics of the New Deal:
1936 Al Smith in Hoover *Memoirs* 26 Jan. III.369. They centered all their powers in the Executive, and that is the reason why you read in the newspapers reference to Congress as the rubber-stamp Congress.
1936 Richard Barry *Theme Song 1936*, 103. Henry the Second [Henry Wallace] invariably approves, and is not this fair exchange? Congress rubber stamped his law and he rubber stamps the friends of his friends in Congress.
1941 in *Jim Farley's Story* 350. "I don't know that Congress is entirely to blame," I said. "When they go along with the administration, they are praised by some people and severely criticized by others as being a 'rubber stamp' Congress."

ruffle(d) shirt.

A member of the wealthy class, especially a member of the wealthy faction of a political party.
A. The term *ruffle shirt* was used

(contemptuously) in the 18th century, to mean a person of wealth and continues to have this general meaning along with the political connotation.
1786 Benjamin Russell in Buckingham *Specimens* II.41.
To sit in the saddle, we've men that know how,
And make all your *ruffleshirts* foot it and bow.
1835 Longstreet *Georgia Scenes* 85. The *ruffled shirted* little darlings of the present day [would be] under the discipline of paregoric.

B. It is in 1836 and the years following that the term is used with great frequency in politics. It probably began to be so used before that time.
1836 *West. Hemisphere* (Cols., Ohio) 20 July 3/2. We have been buffeted, scouted, slandered, abused; our candidates have been persecuted . . . by these ruffle shirts, silk stocking fops and dandies.
1836 *Hamilton* (Ohio) *Intell.* 21 July 2/4–5. The vile *slangwhangers* and *kitchen scullions,* who do the *dirty work* for the Van Buren party in Butler county, are in the habit of dubbing their opponents with the title of "Ruffle Shirt gentry," "silk stocking party" etc. . . . it may be well to inquire *who* are the *"Ruffle shirt and silk stocking gentry"* . . . and to what party do they belong. . . . the . . . haughty ruffle shirt men of Butler County belong to the spoils party.
1836 *Ib.* 18 Aug. 3/3. Elijah Vance of *ruffle shirt* and *wig* democracy was nominated for the Senate.
1836 *Ib.* 1 Sept. 3/2. We knew that a few of the "ruffle shirt" wire workers held a midnight caucus. . . . The leading *ruffle shirt gentry* looked at the two men. . . . Mr. Matthias fell victim to the unprincipled "ruffle shirt" gentry.

That the expression had become hackneyed is made plain in the following quotation:

1839 *Nat. Intell.* 24 Dec. 1/6 . . . he (Mr. Pickens) was but a poor spokesman. He had left out the very essence of a stump speech—the "ruffled shirts—the silk stockings—monied aristocracies—Nick Biddle and the banks."

In 1840 both the political and the non-political aspects of *ruffle shirt* again occur side by side.

1840 Kennedy *Quodlibet* 158. If he [a merchant] . . . makes a little fortune, we call him a . . . "Ruffle Shirt."
1840 *Ohio Confederate* 18 June 2/3. "Ruffle Shirt Gentry"—Who are they? . . . So far as I can discover, the Tories are quite as fond of sporting ruffled shirts, silk stockings, and other expensive finery, as the Whigs. . . . Now I have no objection to any person's dressing as expensively as his finances will allow, whether he be Whig or Tory; but I think it unfair in the latter to find fault with the former, for a practice of which they themselves are guilty, if there is any guilt in the matter.

rugged individualism.

Coined by Herbert Hoover in the 1928 campaign in a speech at Madison Square Garden, October 22:

in *Newsweek* 10 April (1937) 3. We were challenged with a peacetime choice between the American system of rugged individualism and a European philosophy of diametrically opposed doctrines—doctrines of paternalism and State socialism.
1928 Norman Thomas in *Nation* 7 Nov. Mr. Hoover calls his capitalism "rugged individualism" and professes to find some peculiar virtue in the wasteful and chaotic mismanagement of coal, in our frantic real-estate speculation. . . .
1931 *Wash. Merry-Go-Round* 184. Mr. Hoover once used the resounding expression "rugged individualism." He had no intention of applying it to the Senate Insurgents.

rule of terror.

1876 *Harper's W.* 24 June 510/2. No one can live safely in many districts of the South who is an ardent advocate of Republican principles, who insists that all the people shall be educated, and the right of suffrage be secured to all. Should he avow such opinions, he is liable to be shot at from lonely places, . . . he will be driven from his farm by threats of whipping and silenced by a rule of terror.

See REIGN OF TERROR.

rule or ruin.

Dryden in *Absalom and Achitophel* Part I, 1. 174:
Resolv'd to ruin or to rule the State.

In American politics the phrase was a charge against the Whig party:

1836 *Western Hemisphere* 2 Nov. 2/5. "Rule or ruin" is the bandit motto of the coalition.
1840 *Ohio Statesman* 17 April 2/5. A great many are leaving the Federal Bank "rule or ruin" party.
1840 *Rough-Hewer* 219/1. "Our party right or wrong" is their animating principle; "rule or ruin" is their aim.
1843 *Lima* (Ohio) *Porcupine* 27 May 3/2. His operations have been on the same principle upon which he and his coadjutors have always worked—"rule or ruin."

Later applied to other factions and policies:

1857 *Grand Rapids Eagle* in Streeter *Pol. Parties* 273 . . . a mistaken and deluded faction in Kansas, who would rule or ruin.
1880 in Hayes *Diary* 11 June III.601. [Likewise] the defeat of the rule-or-ruin Senators, who usurped the power of the people.

rump (Congress).

Reminiscences of the English Rump Parliament occur sporadically in America before the Civil War:

1837 in Byrdsall *Loco Foco* 178. Hence the Equal Rights Party became divided within itself; the majority for union [with Tammany] called the opposing minority Rumps, and the latter called the majority Buffaloes.

1838 *New Yorker* 17 Feb. 764/1. If such doctrines are correct, what prevents Congress from declaring itself perpetual—a rump Parliament—and then asserting, as they have in the present instance, that, so long as that decision remains unrescinded, the constitutional power of the states to hold their regular election is suspended, and their laws nullified?

1838 in Woodley *Stevens* 98. The Hopkins House had continued to gather in the House Chamber and the Cunningham House, or "Stevens Rump," met at a hotel room until it was locked out....

In 1860 following the exodus of the Southern delegates from the Democratic Convention at Charleston, a second convention met at Baltimore.

1860 *Xenia Fairchild* 9 May 2/1. The best thing that the Rump convention can do upon its reassembling at Baltimore on the 18th of June, will be to take up Gen. Houston and run him to save the Union "and whip the politicians."

1860 *Ib.* 27 June 2/1. Since the adjournment of the Rump Convention, Senator Fitzpatrick has declined accepting the nomination for Vice President on the Douglas ticket.... Douglas—the candidate of the Rump Convention.

In 1866 the Democrats characterized Congress as a "Rump Congress" because they believed it did not represent all the states:

1866 *Wash. Morning Chronicle* 24 Feb. 2/3 [from the *Chic. Trib.*]. He echoes, in measured but no less positive phrase, the Copperhead cry that the present Congress is a "Rump Congress!"

1866 *N. Y. Trib.* 27 Feb. 4/2 [from the *World*]. They have proclaimed the present Congress to be a Rump Congress, and the Radicals ... to be Disunionists.

1866 *Nation* 8 March 294/2 ... the practice pursued by the World of keeping the term "Rump Congress" as a standing head for its report on Congressional proceedings, give us a little glimpse of the pit which our enemies would fain prepare for us.

1866 Nasby *Swinging Round the Cirkle* 188. Do yoo bleeve the present Congress a rump...?

Later example:

1948 *Cols. Dispatch* 14 July 1. Rebellious states' rights Democrats will hold their own "rump" convention at Birmingham, Ala., this week-end, according to plans made today.

run ahead of the ticket.

To win more votes than the rest of the candidates on a party's ticket.

1840 *Ohio State Jrnl.* 2 Dec. 2/4 ... General Harrison constantly runs ahead of his ticket.

running mate.

Usually the vice-presidential nominee—the second horse in the party's stable.

1900 *Rev. of Rev.* XXI. 7/2. Men of all parties will admit that Mr. Root's name would add positive strength, and that a better man could hardly be selected as Mr. McKinley's "running mate."

run without weights.

In a political campaign, to have no vote-losing encumbrance, either of candidates or of platforms.

In horse racing, handicaps are adjusted by adding weights to the fastest horse.

1874 Wilson *Rise and Fall* II.517. The Republicans, not hampered by a Southern Wing with its prescription and proscription, and "running without weights"....

S

sacred cow.

A newspaper term, a metaphor obviously based upon the sacred cows of India, which refers to the preferential treatment—or even silence—given to certain public figures and establishments.

1926 *Emporia Gazette* 30 March. Every office has its sacred cows, people and things that must be handled in the news gingerly, and with care.
1940 Stokes *Chip off my Shoulder* 171. He ...was too curious about the steel trust in which Harding's friend, Judge Elbert H. Gary, was such a power, as well as about other sacred cows of Republicanism.
1946 Seldes *In Fact* 3 June 3. Herbert Hoover's reward for representing big business during his White House term, even though it meant a ruinous depression, has been the role of "sacred cow" in most of the nation's newspapers...to be mentioned only in glowing terms...all criticism played down or suppressed.
1946 White *Autobio.* 132. So the county commissioners who dispensed the county printing were sacred cows.
1950 Lattimore *Ordeal by Slander* 125. It is a little incongruous to think of a sacred cow being handled with kid gloves, but that was the kind of handling that Budenz got.

saddle, in the.

A. To be in office or to have control of the government; the power and authority associated with being in the saddle are like that of an experienced horseman: "no seat is so secure as a firm one in the saddle" (John Hinds, *Rules for Bad Horsemen,* 1830).

1801 *Federalism Triumphant* 6. The Democrats will bawl out for energy, they being in the saddle, will be all spirs [*sic*].
1805 in W. C. Bruce *John Randolph* I.268.

As Mr. Jefferson is again seated in the saddle for four years....

B. One of the historic sayings of Bismarck:

1867 in Büchmann *Geflügelte Worte* 528. Setzen wir Deutschland, so zu sagen, in den Sattel! Reiten wird es schon können.

saddle bag resolutions. [ ]

1858 *Ohio St. Jrnl.* 25 Jan. 2. Mr. Knapp of the Ashland Union is down upon the Democrats of the Legislature for passing what it calls "a series of saddle bag resolutions" upon Kansas affairs. The issue between Judge Douglas and the Democratic party is of such a nature as to admit of no compromise.

Sag Nichts.

Name of a Democratic faction in the 1850's.

This group apparently originated during 1854 or 1855 in opposition to the Know Nothings (q.v.).

1855 *Cleve. Herald* 9 Jan. 2/2. Sag Nicht— There is nothing like fighting a foe with its own weapons. As a sort of back fire the Loco-foco party have instituted a secret order in their ranks, the object of which party is to play the part of *ferrets* and smell out the Know Nothings. This order, "Sag Nicht" is now in session in conjunction with the Democratic Convention at Columbus.
1855 *Ib.* 31 March 2/1. The *Plaindealer* belabors the "Know Nothings," but is as whist as a mouse about the secret political society of its own [Dem.] party—the "Sag Nicht." The *Leader* denounces the "Know Nothings" as a "secret cabal," but is silent as to its pet order the "Know Somethings." ... Know Nothing, Know Something, Sag Nicht, Nix-cum-arous, it's all Dutch as sour-krout [sic] to us.
1855 *Ib.* 4 April 2/3. The *Times* of the afternoon of the same date [April 3] says: "We stated in yesterday's paper that during the forenoon a bitter feeling was manifested by the Sag Nichts in the Eleventh

Ward, towards the few Americans stationed at the polls.

The Sag Nichts order, being in opposition to the Know Nothings, was naturally in favor of the naturalized citizen.

1855 *Ohio St. Jrnl.* 15 May 2/1. Sag Nicht —That secret order of Foreigners, Catholics, and locofoco office seekers. . . . **1855** *Ravenna* (Ohio) *Camp. Dem.* 6 Aug. 3/3. We knew that the editor of the *Sentinel* was a Sag Nicht but we did not know that he had joined the Order of Know-Nothings, and that his paper was to be an organ of that Order as well as of the Sag Nichts! **1855** *Ib.* 13 Aug. 2/2. A secret political association, known as the *Sag Nicht* association, is now in operation, as a co-worker with the Slave power. . . . What Jesuitism is to the Catholic Church . . . *Sag Nichtism* is to the slavery politics of the United States. **1855** *Ib.* 13 Aug. 3/1. The Know Nothings South are intensely Pro-Slavery, and there have the sympathy and co-operation of the Pro-Slavery "Sag Nichts" and in Louisiana there exists a sort of *Know-Nothing-Sag-Nicht* order, to which Catholics are admitted as members. **1855** *Hickory Flail* 22 Aug. 2/2. We are not, and never have been, members of any secret political organization, nor do we believe there is a *Sag Nicht* order in this County, unless the Know Nothings have stolen the name.

saloon party.

A variation of the Republican charge associating the Democratic party and liquor. (See WHISKY DEMOCRAT, BOURBON.)

1932 *New Rep.* 13 July 234/1. The Republicans will of course argue that the Democratic party is the saloon party, bent upon restoring the unrestricted sale of liquor.

Salt River.

Usually used in the phrase "row up Salt River" or "go up Salt River." To suffer political defeat.

The phrase is commonly explained as referring to an event in the life of Henry Clay [*DAH*]. He is said to have failed a speaking engagement in Louisville because a boatman, supporter of Jackson, rowed him up Salt River rather than up the Ohio. The date of the alleged incident is given as either 1828 or 1832. Mencken [*Am. Lang. Suppl.*] doubts the explanation without considering it entirely impossible; on the other hand, Botkin [*Treas. of Am. Folklore*] declares it "too full of geographic and logical improbabilities to credit." The latter view is borne out by the linguistic facts.

The earliest occurrences suggest that the expression was known before 1828 and clearly show that it was in use before the election of that year.

1828 *Cong. Deb.* 2 Feb. 1341. But, sir, I will venture to say this, that, in playing this game, if the Secretary of State is not influenced by the same courtesy which governed the courtiers of the great Frederick, never to beat the monarch at chess, that he could give the President twenty-nine, and, as they say in Kentucky, "row him up salt river." **1832** Mrs. Trollope *Domestic Manners* II. 117. [A story she found in a newspaper when she arrived in 1828.] This was one of those threats which in Georgia dialect would subject a man to "a rowing up Salt River"; and, accordingly, down leaped our driver from his box, and peeling himself for the combat, he leaped about the vehicle in the most wild-boar style.

A circumstance which must have contributed greatly to the popularity of the phrase is that "the redoubtable Salt, the river of Roarers," as Bird calls it, always figures in typical brags of the river boatmen or the backwoodsmen.

1828 (Hamilton, Ohio) *West. Intell.* 26 Dec. 1/4. A "Salt River Roarer." One of these two fisted backwoodsmen, "half horse, half alligator, and a little touched with the snapping turtle."

1835 *Knickerbocker* V.403. They [speeches in Congress] are chiefly made up of extracts from the common school collection of lessons for reading and speaking, sprinkled with scraps of dog-latin, and a sort of patois, called Salt-river roaring.

1837 Bird *Nick of the Woods* 49. " 'Whar's your buffalo-bull,' he cried, 'to cross horns with the roarer of Salt River? . . . Ar'n't I a ring-tailed squealer? Can go down Salt on my back, and swim up the Ohio! Whar's the man to fight roaring Ralph Stackpole?' "

In the 1830's the phrase becomes increasingly popular in politics:

1832 *Washington* (Ohio) *Herald* 17 Nov. 3/4. Thank a kind Providende [sic], that with all the cold blooded machinations and guilty intrieges [sic] of the adversary, the Jackson boys of Ohio have been enabled to give them another ride "up Salt River."

1836 *West. Hemisphere* 21 Sept. 3/1. The Whig Orator's of Cincinnati "Rowed Up Salt River."

1837 *Annals of Cleve.* 25 July. We anticipate a triumphant Whig victory, in which event some of the western wilds, probably the Salt River country, is to rejoice in the presence of Mr. Francis Thomas the Maryland Jacobin. The hardy western men will row him as far as he likes "up Salt River."

1838 *Ohio St. Jrnl.* 10 Oct. 3/1. Tumblebug Benton rolled through this city on Saturday morning, hard after Amos Kendall and Obadiah Brown—all bound for Salt River.

1838 *Alex. West. Mess.* 21 Nov. 4/1. All those 'ere passengers what's agoin' to take passage up Salt River, in the steamer Minority, on Monday next, will please step to the Cap'ns office and settle.

1838 *Ohio St. Jrnl.* 7 Nov. 2/4. Result of

the Election in Ohio.—We have met the enemy and—We Are Theirs! . . . We had heard of the head waters of Salt River, but never before have we been blessed with such an intimate personal knowledge of the peculiar scenery in that very interesting region! We cannot say that upon the first view we are so well pleased with the Salt River country into which the merciless locofocos have rowed us, as to desire a permanent residence. *It is a proper bad country.*

Salt River figured prominently in the songs of the Log Cabin campaign of 1840:

1840 in Norton *Tippecanoe Songs* App. 15.
So here's three cheers for honest Tip,
We've got the locos on the hip—
We'll row them all far up Salt river,
There let them stand to shake and shiver,
    Hurrah, hurrah, hurrah!

1840 *Niles' Reg.* 7 Nov. 159/3. Joe Hoixe then sang the song of "Up Salt River,". . . .

1840 *Ohio Statesman* 19 June 3/6.
Democrats, you must all remember,
It's a faction we've to fight in November;
I expect you know what's to do—
Row up Salt River old Tippecanoe.

Later examples, many of which show how elaborate the metaphor of the voyage can become:

1842 *Albany Argus* 18 Sept. 2/5. The flood of light which the rising sun of democracy in Maine is casting on the haziness of whiggery, must dissipate the "fog" in which the men of the Eve. Journal have been so long groping, and enable them to set their compass and lay their course for "salt river."

1844 *Whig Battering Ram* 9 Aug. 2/5. A sudden gust arising to the dismay of the Locofocos, their Polk and Dallas, braking its hold, took a straight shoot and was borne on the wings of the wind far away towards Salt River.

1844 *Ib.* 20 Sept. 41. It would be advisable for them to . . . start without delay for the headwaters of Salt River, before the country is so much crowded in those parts, that they will have to cry "for a lodge in some vast wilderness."

1852 in Minnegarode *Presidential Years* 292.

For in spite of all endeavor,
Hasty soup and fuss and feather. [Gen. Scott],
They must hurry up Salt River
When November's ides are past.

1868 *Cong. Globe* 3593/1. I offer the following amendment to the amendment: For the improvement of the navigation of Salt River, that the dreary passage up the rapid and turbulent waters of this great national highway be rendered less grievous to the motley crowd of involuntary exiles, who, about November next, will be seeking "some sequestered spot" where a "white man's Government" may be maintained in its purity.

1880 in J. Cutler Andrews *Pittsburgh Post Gazette* 218. For Salt River. The River Boat Democracy left its Wharf Tuesday, Nov. 2, 1880, bound up Salt River in search of the late lamented Samuel J. Tilden.

The spirit of fun and play which is implicit in the use of the phrase from its first occurrence is probably also responsible for the obscene variation which when it appears in "Little Orphan Annie," a comic strip favorite, becomes "up Mud Creek, without a paddle." [*Col. Dispatch* 14 Aug. 1949.]

Sam.

The Know Nothing party; a member of that party.

The name may be assumed to be an abbreviation of Uncle Sam and an allusion to the strong nationalistic sentiments of the party organization. The coupling with Sambo —an abolitionist— (see 1855 quote) is probably not to be taken as suggestive of its origin.

1854 in Desmond *Know-Nothing Party* 54. Those inducted into the first degree do not appear to have been informed as to the name of the order. They were brought into "the august presence of Sam."

1854 in Isely *Horace Greeley and the Rep. Party* 82–3. The followers of this new party were disciplined into lodges, where secret rituals, captivating the gullible, were performed. A stranger met on the street was tested with the query, "Have you seen Sam?" If one of the select, he would return the password.... if a non-member became curious and tried to pry into the forbidden, he was frozen with a cold, "I know nothing." This bewildering response bestowed upon these misguided patriots an appropriate appellation, "Know Nothings."

1854 in *Ib.* 112. "Sam" is *everywhere*, is directed by his Anti-Slavery friends, & is a good fellow.... Seward *must* see *Sam*, as soon as he can, or he *cannot succeed*—at any rate *in the West.*

1854 Henry A. Wise in *N. Y. sw. Trib.* 24 Nov. 7/2 ... the sky must fall and catch Know Nothings, before the times of Revelations are out, and the Pope catches "Uncle Sam."

1854 *N. Y. sw. Trib.* 5 Dec. 4/1. We should not wonder if he [H. A. Wise] sees Sam in his travels through Virginia this canvass.

1855 R. B. Hayes *Ltrs.* I.483. Yesterday was a political day, very squally times, "Sams" and "Sambos," Whigs and Locos, etc. etc., all squabbling.

1855 *Olympia* (Wash.) *Pioneer* 6 July. It is a common thing to hear men boast that some fellow has "seen Sam" or is "Right on the Goose."

sand lot (in various compounds).

Characterized by rough, powertactics, as those employed by Dennis Kearney, who rose to prominence on the sand lots on the outskirts of San Francisco.

1878 *N. Y. Trib.* 14 Aug. 4/3 Sandlot political science. Mr. Kearney, the "sandlot orator" of California ... came East with the prestige of a victorious leader. **1880** *Harper's W.* 3 April 211/3. The manly and resolute position against the "Sand Lot" sedition taken by the Reverend John Hemphill. ... He declared in his pulpit that the Sand Lot terrorism must cease. ...

Also sandlotter.

1880 *Puck* 23 June 279/2. It may please sandlotters; but decent people prefer a President who isn't so new to his business. ...

sans culotte.

Like *Jacobin, sans culotte* was used first in reference to the French Revolution and later as a synonym for *radical:*

1794 Erskine *Sp.* II.127. The London Corresponding Societies, the only avowed sans culottes in the metropolis. ... I fear you are somewhat short of the true sans culotte liberty.

1801 Adams *Works* IX.583. The doctrines of sans-culotteism are productive of more plagues than those of Sir Robert Filmer, while they last.

1809 Fisher Ames *Works* 221. The sans-culottes, or rabble, and people of small property, who were violent revolutionists, paid nothing; while the rich were arbitrarily, and without any estimation or rule, assessed at pleasure.

1811 Graydon, *Memoirs of a Life* 335. [the arrival of Genet] with liberty caps, and other wretched trumpery of sans culotte foolery!

satellite.

A follower; later applied to nations.

A. The earliest English use of the term—antedating even the astronomical development of the 17th century—implies that the original satellites were official attendants of a person of high rank.

c1548 Hall *Chron. Rich.* III 52b [*OED*]. Environed with his satellytes and yomen of the crowne.

B. The derogatory connotations seem to be American, growing out of the discontent of the Revolutionary period.

1776 Paine *Works* II.136. In no instance has nature made the satellite larger than its primary planet; and as England and America ... reverse the common order of nature, it is evident that they belong to different systems: England to Europe—America to itself.

1793 Washington in Leary *Freneau* 235. Beware of "court satellites," the "mushroom lordlings," who have deceived you.

1831 Benton in *Gt. Deb.* XIII.71. Every planet must have its satellites; every tyranny must have its instruments; every knight is followed by his squire. ... Just so of this imperial bank.

1834 *Niles' Reg.* 20 Sept. 37/1. Resolved, That in the "Jackson gold," now ... "disencumbered" of the glorious cap of liberty, and gilding the palm of rewarded satellites, we perceive only another "experiment" of the executive.

1860 Stevens in *Cong. Globe* 585/2. I withdraw it ["parasite"], and simply use the word satellite—revolving of course, around the larger body, as according to the laws of gravitation they must—and that is not offensive.

1925 Coan *Red Web* 187. The timidity and impotence of intimidated and panic stricken administration senators and congressmen lent zest to the operations of the triumvirate on the committee, pep to their satellite cheer-leaders.

1952 Stevenson *Major Camp. Sp.* 250. A few peddlars of hate and fear would be of little consequence if they had not been welcomed as satellites by Senator Taft and included in the leadership of this strange crusade.

C. Reference to countries under the domination of a major power, particularly Russia.

1946 Arnall *Shore Dimly Seen* 147. It is not necessary to predicate our national foreign policy upon accords that involve the maintenance of undemocratic regimes in countries that have become satellites of other "great powers."

1952 Stevenson *Major Camp. Sp.* 275. I have negotiated face to face with the Russians and their satellites in San Francisco, London and New York.

satrap.

A. Originally a governor of a province in the ancient Persian monarchy; but in the Reconstruction Period a satirical designation for the military governors in the South.

1866 *Impeachment of Andrew Johnson* I.300. I could have remained at the capital with fifty or sixty millions of appropriations ... with my satraps and dependents in every township.

1866 in *Cinc. Comm. Campaign Special* 22 Oct. 56/5. Mr. Johnson ... said that, with the forty or fifty millions of dollars placed at his disposal, under the Freedman's Bureau bill, with his satraps scattered throughout the land, he could make himself a dictator.... Satraps, you know, are Turkish officers who are liable to lose their heads by the scimiter (!) if they do anything to displease the Sultan.

1868 DeForest *Union Officer* 39. My satrapy ... contained two state districts or counties....

1868 *Harper's W.* 4 Jan. 2/4. The Democratic party will go into the election clamoring for its [reconstruction] repeal, and insulting Sheridan and all the "satraps" who enforced the law.

1874 *N. Y. World* 10 Aug. 2/6 ... miserable scallawag and oppressive black satrap.

B. In later uses it is a term for subordinate party leaders:

1938 in Salter *Am. Politician* 245. Within limits, and with due consideration for the intimate problems of his local satraps, he [Farley] has tried to pick the better brands of Democratic horsemen.

sauerkraut money.

A facetious reference to currency which became a great local concern (see quote). ¿

1896 in *Milwaukee Jrnl.* 10 July (1953) ... 1896, when thousands of Milwaukeeans voted in a congressional race on the basis of "sauerkraut money." The fermented cabbage issue got its start at a meeting of the Liberal club that October, where the speaker was the Democratic candidate, Robert Schilling, one of the most colorful state politicians of the day.... In his speech, he dilated on his theory of money, pointing out that the Republicans' sacred gold standard was just an arbitrary choice of metals. In fact, he said, it didn't really matter whether money was made of "gold, silver, copper, paper, sauerkraut or sausages." That's all his opposition needed. They treated the quotation as a serious explanation of Schilling's monetary beliefs, instead of the figure of speech he intended. Schilling, they said, was a fool and a charlatan who would issue sauerkraut for money if elected. "Schilling and sauerkraut" was the slogan they adopted, and it worked.

scab.

Since certain skin diseases commonly called scab (see *OED;* Osborn, *King James,* p. 514, 1658, ... he died of the Scab) were considered to be contagious, persons having this ugly disease were often ostracized by society. Early American uses of the term for strikebreakers or independent laborers indicate clearly that *scab* applied to their being avoided by society as though they were lepers:

1806 in Commons *Doc. Hist.* III.73. They told me if I did not come to the body, I was liable to be scabb'd.... Their meaning was, that if I did not join the body, no man would set upon the seat where I worked; that they would neither board or work where I was unless I joined.

1806 *Ib.* III.79 . . . when I first fell in company with him he would not speak to me because he knew I was a scab.

1806 *Ib.* III.83. Mr. Recorder directed Mr. Ryan to be sworn, which being done, he declared that he heard George Alcorn say, a scab is a shelter for lice. . . .

1871 *N. Y. Times* 8 Nov. 4/1. Tweed will doubtless boast of his majority in the district which his organ, the World, calls a "loathsome scab."

1892 Tucker *Instead of a Book.* If, after that, any laborers shall interfere with the rights of their employers, or shall use force upon inoffensive "scabs". . . .

scabbery.

1905 Brissenden *IWW* 66. It was, of course, realized that outside of all unions stood the overwhelming majority of all working men, and, as Daniel DeLeon put it, these men did not "propose to go into these organizations run by the Organized Scabbery, because they had burned their fingers thus enough.

1908 *Gt. Issues and Nat. Leaders of 1908* 226. [Socialist Labor party platform] . . . The nomination under such circumstances of Debs is an attempt to sugarcoat the Hanford scabbery. To endorse Debs would, therefore, be to endorse Hanford's scabbery.

scalawag.

A Southerner who supported the Congressional plan of reconstruction.

A. Although prominent in Southern politics of the Reconstruction Period, the word is probably of Northern origin. Bartlett, 1848, has:

Scalaway. A favorite epithet in western New York for a mean fellow; a scapegrace.

Somewhat later we find *scalawag* to mean a worthless piece of cattle:

1854 *N. Y. Trib.* 24 Oct. 8/3. The market is not a lively one and good beeves do not sell for a price to justify feeders in making good beef. The truth is that the number of miserable "scallawags" is so great, that like the bad portion of the biped race, they tend to drag down all above themselves to their own level.

If the derivation from the place name Scalloway [*Webster New International Dictionary,* 1934] is correct, this meaning is the primary one. In this case the word must originally have referred to the dwarf cattle raised in the Shetlands. Spitzer's etymology that connects *scalawag* with Old French *esclavage* offers great phonetical difficulties.

1864 Parton *Butler in New Orleans* 122. The country around it [Ft. Monroe], on the main land is level . . . ; the roads, miserable cart tracks; the cattle "scallawags," the people ditto.

1872 *House Report* 42nd Cong. 2nd sess. No. 22 pt. 1, 297. The name originated in a fellow being kicked by a sheep so that he died. He said he didn't mind being killed, but he hated the idea of being kicked to death by the meanest wether in the whole flock—the scalysheep. We mean by scalawag a meaner man than a carpetbagger.

B. Already in 1854 the word occurs in Northern politics. The exact meaning is hard to find but the tenor of the following article seems to indicate that the prevailing idea is that of mongrelism:

1854 *Wash. Daily Union* 19 Sept. 3/2 [from *Vermont Patriot*]. The few "national whigs" returned begin to feel uneasy, while the "striped whigs" and the "scaliwags" are fearful of trouble from the men they have attempted to swallow.

C. Whether there is any connection with the later political use is uncertain since all the examples from the Civil War period are non-political in nature.

1862 *The Haversack* 25 Oct. 3/1.
> Your campaign's a fizzle
> You cussed skallywag.

1862 Wells *Army Life* 66. The 7th Cavalry don't acknowledge the Michigander troopers to be more than the equals of Jeff. Thompson's scalawags.

1863 Kelso *Stars and Bars* 76. Companies of armed men, gangs of ruffians, gentlemen and scallawags,... white trash and black trash, were pouring into town from every quarter.

1864 *U. S. Service Mag.* II.40 ... poor, sick, weak heroes, the amiable public think them; "bummers" and "scallywags," in the elegant and expressive language of the army surgeon.

D. The specialized Southern meaning of the post-war period is clearly established in the following quotations:

1866 *Wash. Morn. Chron.* 7 April 1/3. Whenever a white man appeared to vote [in Alabama], every one of these infuriated devils ... set up a yell, calling him "white negro," "Low trash," "Scalwag," "Mean White," etc.

1868 *Harper's Mon.* XXXVI.713. Southern men who side with the Republican party are called "Scalliwags."

1868 in *Wash. Morn. Chron.* 20 Feb. The negroes were warned of this in time but many preferred to go with the scallawags and carpet-baggers.

1871 in *Gt. Deb.* VIII.199. Those who were born in the South and remained faithful to the Government, or have since joined the Republican party, are stigmatized as the "scalawags," as low persons of the baser sort, disgraced and degraded by every opprobrious epithet, and all of this execrable Billingsgate is reechoed, with additions, in the North.

1874 *N. Y. World* 14 August 6/6. Beyond a doubt the united carpetbagdom and scalawaggery of the South will give Morton a brave reception.

scarecrow.

A bugbear; a false charge used to frighten for political effect.

c 1824 Van Buren in Lynch *Epoch* 302 ... what has, with some propriety, been called the scarecrow of the Constitution—the power of impeachment.

1830 *N. Y. Sentinel* 16 June 1/2 ... the cries of Infidelity and Agrarianism are mere political scare-crows, such as were formerly set up to terrify the democrats of 1801.

1856 *Ashland Times* Oct. 2/5. A Loco Foco Scare Crow [accusation of forging tickets] was issued on the election morning by the Democratic Central Committee.

1856 *Ohio State Jrnl.* 23 Oct. 2/1. The disunionists of the South ... and their scarecrow battalions.... the pauper aristocracy of Carolina and Virginia.

scholar in politics.

A phrase applied to Henry Cabot Lodge and later to other highly educated men who became prominent in politics.

1888 *N. Y. World* 8 Oct. 4/6. The artiodactyl, ungulate mammal of the genus *Sus* has succeeded the scholar in politics. The Hog is on deck!

1892 *Nation* 22 Sept. 211/3. This was the work of Henry Cabot Lodge, the "scholar in politics."

1892 *Ib.* 20 Oct. 294/1. The best that can be said of this confusion of the two Woolseys is that it was a fearful blunder for a "scholar in politics" to make.

1903 *Ib.* 9 July 24/2. Another Scholar in Politics.... But Congressman Littauer is a shining example of a scholar in public life.

schoolhouse campaign. [ ]

in *Cyc of Am. Govt.* I.209/2. The so-called "schoolhouse campaign" of 1876, conducted throughout the rural districts of several western states, was strictly educative in purpose and did much to develop sound views upon problems pertaining to the currency. Neighborhood meetings were held in country schoolhouses, usually addressed by some one personally known to the audience and able to understand and often to remove the difficulties in the minds of those who sincerely desired to vote intelligently upon intricate and far-reaching questions.

scission.

Older term for secession (q.v.) :
1798 letter in Jefferson *Memoirs, Corr. and Misc.* III.394. But if on a temporary superiority of the one party, the other is to resort to a scission of the Union, no federal government can ever exist.
1865 John P. Kennedy *Mr. Ambrose's Ltrs.* 9. It was at that time [Hartford Convention] that the word "secession" itself first became familiar as a term of our political vocabulary. Before that date Mr. Jefferson called it "scission"; and, by the by pronounced it to be incompatible with any government.

scoot.

To abstain from voting: [ ]
1874 *Frank Leslie's* 11 July 274/3. The thirty-six Senators who voted against confirmation, and the several who "scooted"....

scratch.

Although documentation is lacking, it seems that originally *scratching* was used in its literal sense, as a synonym of *erasing:*
1881 Shapley *Mulhooly* 104. The Scratcher, who would not hesitate at any time to erase from his ticket the name of an improper candidate improperly placed upon it. He often said, "The Independent Voter and the Scratcher are the country's safest, cheapest and best doctors."
1888 Lane *America.* Scratchers, voters who erase from the ticket the name of any candidate for whom they do not wish to vote.

However, already in 1841 the word appears as a synonym of *splitting the ticket* (q.v.) apparently without connotations of what must have been its original meaning.
1841 *Whig Almanac* 3. Messrs. Ritner and Shulze, the Harrison Senatorial Electors, were scratched by a number of voters.
1853 *N. Y. Times* 26 April 2/4. On a stormy day, by a little manoeuvering and a good deal of scratching they can elect their Supervisor, Clerk and constable.
1854 *Cleve. Plain Dealer* 4 Oct. Vote the Whole Ticket.... Let there not be a scratch upon it.
1854 *Sandusky Comm. Reg.* 27 July 2/2. Every foreign name will be scratched on every Ticket.

Later examples show scratching to be a thoroughly "polarized" word: while to the orthodox party man and to the machine politician scratching is foolish and sometimes almost equivalent with treason, to the independent it stands out as a meritorious act.
1860 *Boston Transcript* 17 Nov. 4/5. Let every voter exercise the divine right of scratching.
1872 *Harper's W.* 322. We have often enough in these columns advocated the unalienable right of scratching, and we certainly hope that no man will consent to vote for a rascal because he has been regularly nominated.
1879 *Nation* 23 Oct. 265 ... he endorsed Mr. Cornell, ridiculed scratching as "voting in the air" and raised again "the Strong Man cry."
1889 Shapley *Mulhooly* 58. A scratcher is a traitor to us.

secesh.

Jocular nickname for a Southerner.
1861 in *War Ltrs. of Wm. Thompson Lusk* 54 ... to our imagination every strip of woods contained a body of "secesh" infantry.
1862 *Toledo Blade* 18 Jan. 2/3. Mr. "Secesh," in getting out of the hack, fell upon his drawn knife....

secession.

The withdrawal of a state from the Federal Union.

A. There is a long English tradition preceding the use of the term in American politics. In England *secession* is found frequently in discussions of the relations of church and state. (See *OED*.)

B. After the founding of the American Union *secession* (and *secede*) are commonly mentioned as the right of an individual state, particularly during the Nullification crisis of the 1830's. However, even at this time, we find objections to this doctrine and the use of the word. (See Webster, 1833 f.)

1795 in *Ltrs. of N. Webster* 438. Notice is hereby given, That in case the treaty entered into by that d—d Archtraitor J—n J—y with the British tyrant should be ratified, a petition will be presented to the next General Assembly of Virginia, their next session, praying that said state may secede from the Union....

1825 Jefferson *Works* I.20. Possibly their colonies might secede from the Union.

1830 *Cong. Deb.* 948/2. Make good the charge, prove the injury, and they [the people of N.Y.] will consent to the secession [of S.C.] to-morrow.

1833 Webster *Works* III.454. *Accession*, as a word applied to political associations, implies coming into a league, treaty, or confederacy, by one hitherto a stranger to it; and *secession* implies departing from such league or confederacy. The people of the United States have used no such form of expression in establishing the present government.

1850 *Ib.* V.361. Peaceable secession is an utter impossibility.

1850 *Ib.* V.361. I hear with distress and anguish the word "secession".... Secession! Peaceable secession! Sir, your eyes and mine are never destined to see that miracle!

1851 *Ib.* II.591. I hear the cry of disunion,

secession. The secession of individual States, to my mind, is the most absurd of all ideas.

C. The Civil War Period, of course, marks the culmination of the secession controversy. The term, although widely used, was held by some to be too mild to refer to Southern action, thus suggesting a general widening of meaning.

1859 *Harper's Mon.* XX.256. Governor Gist, of South Carolina, in his Message, advocates the secession of the South from the Union, in case of the election of a Republican President.

1860 *Burlington* (Vt.) *W. Sentinel* 14 Dec. in *Northern Editorials* I.195. There are many words in use in our country which have different meanings in different parts of our land.... An instance of this is the word *secession*.... In the North (we mean thereby the States having voted for Lincoln in the late election,) it means, if we are to judge from the republican press, just nothing at all. At best, with the republicans, it means an attempt on the part of the South, to scare the North by a threat of disunion or *secession*, which the republicans think, speak of, and treat as mere gasconade.... On the other hand, the southern States ... give a deep, and we may say with propriety, an *awful* significance to the word. There, it means no more or less than a dismemberment of the United States of North America, peaceable if soon yielded, forcible if not.

1861 Greeley *Am. Conflict* I.358 n. He [Calhoun] did me the honor to give me much of his confidence, and frequently his Nullification doctrine was the subject of conversation. Time and time again have I heard him ... defend it on constitutional grounds, and distinguish it, *in that respect*, from the doctrine of Secession. This last he never, with me, placed on any other ground than that of revolution.

1861 *Cols. Gazette* 28 June 2/3. Now they have secured thousands of sympathizers

by calling their treason secession, and all over the north and west editors and others are talking of "secession" and "secessionists" instead of rebellion and traitors. Why do we permit ourselves to be hoodwinked by the use of terms. It is certainly easier to say rebel or traitor than secessionist, and rebellion than secession; then why not do it?
1862 Christy *Pulpit Politics* 530 . . . I think South Carolina mistook her remedy—secession, and not nullification, ought to have been her watchword. . . ."

secret ballot.

A vote which is unknown to any except the person casting it.

The term was originally peculiar to American politics since the evidence in the *OED* shows that in English usage any election in which a ballot vote is cast is by its very nature secret. Our earliest quotation is apparently not in conflict with this meaning, *secret* applying to the composition of the ballot, rather than to the casting of it. In the later uses, however, it is obviously synonymous with *secret voting*.
1805 Dallas *Life* 228. The members who remained delivered a prepared & secret ballot for a new candidate to fill the executive chair.
1835 *Cong. Globe* 23rd Cong. 2nd Sess. 165/1. He [Vanderpael] asked upon what principle the practice of here giving a secret ballot vote could be justified?
1850 in *Butler's Book* 114. The Coalition party obtained ascendancy in the legislature elected in 1851, because in 1850 we had passed an act "For the conduct of Elections," always known by the name of the "Secret Ballot Law."
1853 Rev. Dudley Tyng *An Add. on the Legal Prohibition of the Traffic in Intox. Liquors* (Cols., Ohio) 1 Feb. 22. In Mass. . . . it was passed by both houses with a submission to the people in open ballot;

& being vetoed by the Gov. through preference of the secret ballot, it was passed again . . . [ref. to "Maine Law"].
1855 in Overdyke *Know Nothing Party* 65. A man may flatter himself with being able to strike down his bosom friend where the secret ballot exists, but this will not be so easy in the Old Dominion, where every voter must speak out his choice.
1893 Davenport *Caste* 44. Republicans were cheered, and said: "This means the quiet vote. The secret ballot is with us. . . ." The Democrats said: "The secret ballot is with us this time. . . ."

sect.

See CHURCH.

seesaw bill.

Reference to the ambiguous terms of the Kansas-Nebraska bill: [ ]
1854 Benton in Wilson *Slave Power* II. 398–9. It is a bill of assumptions and contradictions, assuming what is unfounded and contradicting what it assumes,—a balancing every affirmation by a negation. It is a see-saw bill; not the innocent see-saw which children play on a plank stuck through a fence, but the up-and-down game of politicians, played at the expense of the peace and harmony of the Union. . . . It is an amphibological bill, stuffed with monstrosities, hobbled with contradictions, and badgered with a proviso.

segregation.

Long used in English theological issues:
1532 More *Confut. Tindale Works* 428/1 [*OED*]. Those holye consecrate companyes, the tone segregate from paynims by the sacrament of baptysme, the tother segregate fro the laye peple by the sacrament of order.
1662 Hibbert *Body Divin.* II.36 [*OED*]. Let the separatist . . . through his sullen segregation . . . be a thief to himself.

And in genetics, following Mendel's statements of 1865:

1909 Bateson *Mendel's Prin. Hered.* 11. This phenomenon, the dissociation of characters from each other in the course of the formation of the germs, we speak of as segregation.
1915 Quick *Brown Mouse* 46. It was what we breeders call a Mendelian segregation of genetic factors that had been in the waltzers and albinos all the time....

A. Segregation turns up in the Communist Party platforms of 1928 and 1936 but seems to go out of use, and when revived is in connection with the Japanese.

1928 Communist Plat. in Porter and Johnson *Nat. Party Plat.* 318. Abolition of all laws which result in segregation of Negroes.
1936 *Ib.* 359. Segregation and discrimination against Negroes must be declared a crime.
1939 in Bradford Smith *Americans from Japan* 245. "The time has come to burn a few of our bridges behind us," the writer continued. "Endless treatises on Japanese art will not solve the problem of segregation.
1943 *Ib.* 310. In July 1943 the United States Senate passed a resolution urging segregation of the "disloyal" residents.... Tule Lake was designated the segregation center....

B. The term received greatest prominence in connection with events leading up to the Supreme Court decision of May 17, 1954, in which segregation (of negroes) in the public schools was declared unconstitutional.

1940 Helm *Truman* 137. They [negroes] have been forced to live in segregated slums, neglected by the authorities.
1948 *Toledo Blade* 11 Sept. 4/2. The two groups of Negro pupils were denied admission by Gloucester and King George County school authorities, who cited the state's segregation laws.... Governor Tuck called for the utmost calmness and tolerance in handling the problem of equalizing public school facilities. His statement said segregation in schools will continue to be observed in accordance with the state constitution.
1953 *Nation* 17 Jan. 48/2. The prophets of doom who say the end of segregation will mean blood flowing in the streets had ample opportunity to make the gathering prove their thesis.
1953 *Ib.* 31 Oct. 350. Everywhere I went [in the South] I heard anxious speculations about what will happen if the Supreme Court outlaws segregation in the public schools.
1954 *N. Y. Times Mag.* 25 April 10/1. Justifiably, most of the emphasis has been on the unfortunate impact of discrimination and segregation on the Negro community. But it should be remembered that segregation is a two-edged sword that cuts both ways.
1954 Chief Justice Warren in *Newsweek* 24 May 25/2. We conclude that in the field of public education the doctrine of "separate but equal" has no place.... Therefore, we hold that the plaintiffs ... are by reason of the segregation complained of deprived of the equal protection of the laws guaranteed by the Fourteenth Amendment.
1954 *New Rep.* 31 May 6/1. Probably no decision ever rendered by the Supreme Court was better tailored to its purpose than the historic ruling against racial segregation in the public schools.

C. An isolated quotation, suggesting that the origin of the current meaning may be found in the Reconstruction Period:

1884 Morgan *Yazoo* 331. The tendency of the "African Methodist Episcopal Church" to segregation.... the "purely Yankee ticket" in Yazoo, in the fall of 1867, allied with the element favoring segregation.

self-government.

Lieber, *On Civil Liberty and Self-Government,* states correctly that the word, a translation of Greek *auto*, originated in the sphere of ethics and, to begin with, meant self-control (see *OED,* s.v. example from 1734). The following quotation is on the borderline between the ethical and political meanings of the word:

1776 Price *Observations* 3. It should be observed, that, according to these definitions of the different kinds of liberty, there is one general idea, that runs through them all; I mean, the idea of self-direction, or self-government.

The same work, however, uses *self-governed* in a clearly political sense:

9 ... in a great state, all the individuals that compose it cannot be admitted to an immediate participation in the powers of legislation and government, yet they may participate in these powers by a delegation of them to a body of representatives. —In this case it is evident that the state will be still *free* or *self-governed.*

Even Jefferson in his first known use of the word refers to the individual rather than to the body politic:

1789 Letter to Madison in Foner *Basic Writings* 589. What is true of a generation all arriving to self-government on the same day, and dying all on the same day, is true of those on a constant course of decay and renewal, with this only difference.

But not much later, he writes:

in Lieber *On Civil Liberty* 247. the residuary rights are reserved to their own self-government.

1811 Jefferson *Works* XIII.72 ... but the mass of our citizens is firm and unshaken. It furnishes as an incident, another proof that they are perfectly equal to the purposes of self-government.

A new variation of meaning develops around 1850 in connection with the theory of popular sovereignty; at that time a narrowing of meaning takes place, giving to *self-government* the sense of right of the territories to make their own laws.

1850 in *Cong. Globe* 808/3. The exercise of this power of self-government is not revolutionary, as it has been called, but strictly conservative—conservative of the existence of society, and of the relations with the parent country.

1850 Douglas in Flint *Douglas* II.29 ... for, when we decide that the wisdom of our revolutionary fathers was foolishness, and their piety wickedness, and destroy the only system of self government that has ever realized the hopes of the friends of freedom, and commanded the respect of mankind, it becomes us to wait patiently until the purposes of the Latter Day Saints shall be revealed unto us. For my part, I am prepared to maintain and preserve inviolate the Constitution as it is. . . .

1854 Douglas in *Gt. Deb.* IV.270. Those measures [Comp. of 1850], therefore, abandoned the idea of a geographical line as the boundary between free States and slave States ... and, in lieu of that, substituted a great principle of self-government which would allow the people to do as they thought proper.

Ib. IV.277. Now, when that has been abandoned, when it has been superseded, when a great principle of self-government has been substituted for it, I choose to cling to that principle.

1858 in *Lincoln Encyc.* 252/2 ... squatter sovereignty, otherwise called "sacred right of self-government," which latter phrase, though expressive of the most rightful basis of any government, was so perverted in this attempted use of it as to amount to just this: that if any one man chooses to enslave another, no third man shall be allowed to object.

During the post-Civil War years, *local self-government* was used in opposition to the Northern reconstruction policy:

1876 Hayes *Diaries* III.329. I don't like the phrase, by reason of its Democratic associations, which you use—"local self-government"—in that connection. It seems to me to smack of the bowie-knife and revolver. "Local self-government" has nullified the Fifteenth Amendment in several States.

In recent times, the general meaning comes into its own again:

1905 Roosevelt *Works* XVII.337. The noblest of all forms of government is self-government; but it is also the most difficult.
1911 *Ib.* XV.548. You cannot give self-government to anybody. . . . You give him the chance to obtain self-government, but he himself out of his own heart must do the governing. He must govern himself. . . . That is what self-government means.
1923 *Rev. of Rev.* LXVIII.229/2. Our system of local self-government furnishes countless training-schools, working all the time, to prepare men for service in representative capacities.

A humorous variation, indicating the ever present tendency to ridicule a popular concept:

1861 Lowell *Writings* VI.109. The Southern army will be fighting for Jefferson Davis, or at most for the liberty of self-misgovernment.

senatorial courtesy.
See COURTESY OF THE SENATE.
c 1877 Hoar *Autobio.* II.45. What was called Senatorial Courtesy required every Senator belonging to the party in the majority to support every other in demanding the right to dictate and control the executive and judicial appointments from their respective States.
1880 *San Diego Daily Union* 7 Feb. 1/1. It is reported that President Hayes is nettled at the rejection of the nomination of Horton to the San Francisco Collectorship, and is reported to have said last night that he did not intend to yield his convictions to what is termed "Senatorial courtesy."
1881 *N. Y. Trib.* 23 May 5/2. "Senatorial Courtesy." [head]

1906 Peck *Twenty Years of the Republic* 360. Finally, the ramifications of so-called "senatorial courtesy" traverse party lines and create among the members of the Senate an esprit de corps, which is often stronger than the dictates of party loyalty.

sepoy.
One who revolts, either against his party or his nation.

The use of the term in 1858 is due to the influence of the Sepoy Mutiny in India in 1857–8. The derogatory connotations—not found in earlier English usage—undoubtedly arise from the close association with *mutiny*.

1858 *Ohio St. Jrnl.* 7 Jan. 2/2. The St. Louis Democrat regards Bigler of Pa., as the "only Administration Sepoy from the North that has not revolted."
1862 in Sidney Edgerton *New Conspiracy*. Why, then, do we hear this talk of peace with these Sepoys, who murder our wounded soldiers in cold blood . . . ?

sham democracy.
This term was applied to the Democratic party prior to the Civil War in derision of their professed adherence to the tenets of democracy while at the same time they supported measures in favor of slavery:

1852 *Scott Battery* 20 July 1/2. Mr. Faulkner . . . went over to the camp of the Sham Democracy.
1852 *N. Y. Times* 23 Sept. 4/5. When the Sham Democracy had satisfied themselves who this Pierce was. . . .
1856 *Ohio St. Jrnl.* 13 Aug. 2/2. The sham-Democracy attempt to ridicule the Republican speakers, by styling their addresses from the stump "shrieks for freedom."
1857 *N. Y. Trib.* 24 June. Sham Democracy . . . seems incapable of letting the Black Race alone, whence result infinite

confusions, hypocrisies, solecisms, and mulattoes.

See SLAVOCRACY.

shell game.

A political trick or subterfuge:

1904 White *Editor and His People* 265. He worked a shell game on the President by which Burton got Roosevelt's signature to an endorsement of a Midway show at St. Louis....

shelve (put on the shelf).

To put in a position of inactivity or uselessness.

A. Used in England since 1575; in political uses:

1740 Croker in Boswell *Johnson* [*OED*]. His friend General Oglethorpe, who, after acquittal by a court-martial, was (to use a vulgar but expressive phrase) put upon the shelf.

For other examples, see *OED*, SHELF I.d; SHELVE v.4.

B. In American politics:

1840 *Cinc. Gazette* 13 July 2/5. The Loco Focos of Michigan have wisely concluded to lay on the shelf Mr. Crary, the present member of Congress.

1860 *Cong. Globe* App. 444/3. And, perhaps, in this honorable trait of his political character may be found one, if not the chief cause of his indecent shelving at Chicago by the representatives of a party which owes to him all its claims to national strength at the present day.

1899 Roosevelt *Ltrs.* II.1122 ... the general opinion was that it would not be a wise move for me personally, as I would simply be shelved as Vice-President and could do nothing....

See SIDETRACK.

shingle clapper.

A yes man or claquer.

The backwood audiences may have used shingles to add volume to their support.

1844 in Mitgang *Lincoln As They Saw Him* 45. The "shingle clappers" by whom he was surrounded, no doubt, received it with implicit faith and credit; but what must have been Mr. Lincoln's opinion of the intelligence of his auditory if he expected them to swallow that?

shiny hat brigade. [ ]

c 1870 in Werner *Tammany Hall* 170. These men who held sinecures and received presents from Boss Tweed were known as the "Shiny Hat Brigade"....

shirt sleeve diplomacy.

See 1914 quot.

The association of shirtsleeves and honest work is found early:

1864 Sala in *Daily Telegraph* 27 Sept. The people are going to elect shirt-sleeve aldermen that work all day.

Conflicting evidence from the phrase's period of greatest popularity, however, makes it difficult to choose between the shirtsleeves of John Hay and the rolled-up sleeves of Theodore Roosevelt as the particular mode which gave its name to a style of diplomacy.

1904 Sullivan *Our Times* II.628. Two new phases for American diplomacy were current: "shirt sleeves," meant to describe Secretary of State John Hay's directness; and "hair-trigger," meant to lampoon Roosevelt's promptness and forcefulness.

1905? in *Shaw Cartoon History of Roosevelt's Career* 120,149. [Two cartoons showing TR rolling up his sleeves; others picture him with sleeves already rolled up.]

1905 *Nation* 13 July 27/1. Manner counts immensely in diplomacy; ... Of course, the more brutal offences of the "shirt-sleeves" epoch will not now be repeated, but the better-mannered period has its temptations.

1908 *Pall Mall Gaz.* 20 April 2/2. The Congressmen have a preference for what they picturesquely describe as "Shirt-sleeve Ambassadors"—men who they think will labour for their country's interests and scorn social fascinations.

1910 *Nation* 5 May 447/1 . . . he [Taft] upholds Knox's policy in Nicaragua, by inference even to that shirt sleeves diplomacy denunciation of Zelaya which is unparalleled in the history of our State Department.

1911 R. H. Davis *The Consul* 30 . . . "inside" stories of great occasions, ceremonies, bombardments, unrecorded "shirt-sleeve" diplomacy.

1914 *Cyc. of Am. Govt.* III.308. Shirt Sleeve Diplomacy. A title which has been given to some of the diplomacy of recent years which has disregarded much of the circumlocution and indirectness of earlier practice and has stated clearly the purpose of the negotiation and the methods by which a state proposed to attain the purpose. This term has been particularly applied to the diplomacy of the United States from the late years of the nineteenth century.

shoestring district.

A long and narrow congressional district gerrymandered to secure a majority for a party which would be outvoted in a normally laid out district; particularly the 6th district in Mississippi.

1878 *Cong. Rec.* App. 478/2. I will promise to meet him on the northern border of "the shoe-string district."

1880 *N. Y. Trib.* 15 July 4/5. This is the famous shoe-string district which the votarious General Chalmers has succeeded in currying of late by means of the most shameless fraud and bulldozing.

1884 G. B. Raum *Existing Conflict* 313. The celebrated "Shoe-string" district, which extended almost from the Tennessee line along the frontage of the State on the Mississippi River to the Louisiana line, was created [in 1875]. It contained a Republican majority of about 15,000.

short boys.

A New York faction of toughs, active in party fights.

1851 Strong *Diary* II.48. German loaferism warring with the Aaron Burrs of New York, the gutterhorn soaplocks and short-boys of the wharves and their Irish allies.

1851 *Harper's Mag.* III.276/1. A large number of Germans . . . were attacked by a gang of desperadoes from New York, known as "Short Boys."

1854 Bungay *Off-Hand Takings* 321. The members of the Convention had the Governor of the State tempting them on with the spoils in front, and the Short-Boys of New York pricking them up with bowie-knives in the rear, and yet they failed to harmonize.

1880 *Cong. Record* 12 April 2327/1. We should protect the ballot-box from violence, . . . from the "short boys" and "dead rabbits" of this country.

short-hair.

A member of a faction of the Democratic party composed of workers and ex-fighters.

The terms *short-hair* and *swallow-tail* were two factions of the Democratic party which arose out of a reform movement within the party.

c1874 in Werner *Tammany Hall* 289. Early in John Kelly's administration of Tammany Hall, the organization had split into two factions, popularly known as the "Swallow-Tails," consisting of the rich men of Tilden's group . . . and the "Short-Hairs," who were the working men and pugilists led by Morissey.

1876 *Cinc. D. Gazette* 27 June 1/1. The anti-Tilden New Yorkers began to realize the fact last night that the rowdy or *short hair* element of their forces was disgusting the country delegates and reacting in Tilden's favor.

Some carry-over into later years is observed:

1894 Stead *If Christ Came to Chicago* 36. Mayor Hopkins was elected by the *silkstockings* on the one hand and the *short hairs* on the other.

short horns.

See COLOGNE WHIGS.

shot-gun.

Northerners referred to the instances of intimidation of the negroes in the South following the Civil War as the "shot-gun policy," and any election victory of the Southern democrats was labelled as "shot-gun politics," "shot-gun rule," etc:

1876 *N. Y. Trib.* 3 Nov. 4/2 . . . during his "shot-gun canvass" he has not seen "a single gun or saber in the possession" of the rifle clubs. . . .

1880 *Cong. Record* 1450/1. The shot-gun policy which worked so well in 1876 and secured such grand results for the democracy, has been continued up to the present time.

1884 *Cleve. Leader* 2 Oct. 5/4. The ballot box stuffers and shotgun politicians of the south. . . .

The Democratic Party was itself stigmatized as *Shot-gun Democracy.*

1876 *N. Y. Trib.* 2 Nov. 1/1. Ex-Governor Randolph of New Jersey appears as the latest apologist of the "Shot-gun" democracy of South Carolina.

1878 *Nation* 21 Nov. 312/1 . . . to collect "outrages" for him, and to launch an occasional volley of abuse at the "shot-gun Democracy."

shoulder hitter.

Roughs who hung around the polls and were often paid to influence voting; also over aggressive political language or action.

1852 *N. Y. Trib.* 23 Aug. 7/4. The shoulder-hitters of the [Empire] Club

gathered around. . . . one of the shoulder-hitters struck him a violent blow.

1857 *Ann. of Cleve.* No.1518. They [anti-Wood men] feel that the "empire city" will now be able to wipe off the disgrace upon her fair escutcheon caused by the increase of crime consequent upon complicity of Wood with the shoulder-hitters, gamblers, grogshop-keepers, proprietors of houses of ill-fame, and fag ends of creation.

1867 *Cong. Globe* 10 Dec. 102/1. Are we so used to Presidential shoulder-hitting, that we will neither fend off nor strike back?

1871 Strong *Diary* 7 Nov. IV.397. "Mike Norton," a shoulder-hitter and king of the repeaters, elected in the Fifth District.

1879 *Cong. Globe* 16 June 2026/1. The statute requires that the juryman shall be intelligent, of good moral character; but the man who selects him may be a shoulder-hitter in the purlieus of the streets of New York.

1879 *N. Y. World* 12 March 4/3. If Grant or some other Republican is preferred, the sooner the untamed South strikes out from the shoulder the better.

shriek (-er).

A noisy partisan of the abolition cause:

1857 *Ohio Statesman* 8 May 2. The decision of the Supreme Court, pronounced by Judge Brinkerhoff in the Poindexter case, this morning, was a regular political abolition "shriek."

1857 *Ib.* 5 May 2. [reference in editorial to "freedom shriekers," that being a Democratic name for the Republican agitators in Kansas.]

1857 *Ib.* 17 Oct. 2. Ohio Shrieks for Freedom. [head]

Siamese twin.

A close association of persons or of measures.

Chang and Eng (1811–74), the "original" Siamese twins, created great attention throughout the world and particularly in America during their exhibition here.

1832 Weed *Autobio.* I.413. We [the Anti-Masons and Nat. Republicans] were styled by the Jackson men throughout the canvass the "Siamese twin Party." **1832** in Gammon *Pres. Camp.* 146 ... the Democratic press which referred to the coalition [Anti-Mason and Nat. Rep.] as the "Siamese Twin Party," on account of the peregrinations about the State of Davis and Weed. **1836** Mrs. Child *An Appeal* 108. This [preservation and extension of Southern policy] has principally been accomplished by yoking all important questions together *in pairs,* and strenuously resisting the passage of one, unless accompanied by the other.... The admission of Maine into the Union as a free State and Missouri as a slave State, were two more of these Siamese twins, not allowed to be separated from each other. **1836** *Ib.* 212. If the Southern politicians are determined to make a Siamese question of this also—if they insist that the Union shall not exist without slavery—it can only be said that they join two things that have no affinity with each other, and which cannot permanently exist together.

sick man.

Found in European politics as early as 1683 (see Büchmann, *Geflügelte Worte,* 494).

A. In 1853 the phrase was used in a much noticed conversation between Czar Nicholas I and Sir G. Seymour. (According to *OED,* 21 Feb., but according to Büchmann, 9 Jan.)

B. Shortly after, *sick man* turned up in American politics, occasionally referring to Mexico but more generally to the South.

1859 S. S. Cox *Eight Yrs.* 129. Mr. Boyce. Mexico is our "sick man." Mr. Cox. Yes; she is to America what Turkey is to Eu-

rope. If she is not healed of her wounds and set upright on her progressive path, she will become not the "sick man" merely, but the dead man, whose very corpse will arrest our steps, taint the air, and poison our own political system. To save her, she must be inoculated with American energy. **1860** in Wilson *Slave Power* III.32. It [Washburn and Tappan's Report] styled the Southern States "our sick man," for whose cure the proposed nostrums were "perfectly idle".... **1868** Schurz *Writings* I.456. The South is our "sick man." For his disease we must find a remedy, and the remedy we select must correspond with a careful diagnosis of the ailment.... But, unfortunately, the "sick man" has been operated upon by Democratic doctors once more. **1884** Morgan *Yazoo* 338. The "sick man of the South" is very sick indeed, but it is only a question of endurance, my brother.

sideshow.

A secondary or irregular convention; also any convention because of its hoop-la and other similarities to a circus sideshow.

1872 *Cinc. Enquirer* 3 Sept. 2/6. Blanton Duncan's Sideshow Convention. [head] **1876** *Ann. of Cleve.* No. 1462. Mr. Watterson can train in no Republican side-show this year. He lives in a Bourbon State and must stick to the straight Democratic creed. **1892** Sotheran *Greeley* 165. But, apparently, as if to hurt Greeley's chances of election, the Democratic Party endorsed him and then through "a side-show" nominated Charles O'Conor as a third candidate. **1939** Michie *Dixie Demagogues* 7 ... the sideshow politician who believes that 90 per cent of the American people vote their prejudices.

sidetrack.

A. The verb *to sidetrack* as a railroad term occurs as early as 1877:

Dacus *Gt. Strikes* 32 ... suddenly one of the strikers named Wm. Vandergriff ran forward and seized the switch-ball for the purposes of opening it to "side-track" the train.

B. A metaphor in 1875 uses the idea of sidetracking in a political sense, but not the word; a second in 1878 combines the metaphor and the noun *sidetrack.*

1875 in *Cong. Record* App. 4/2. We propose not to be turned off the track and switched off by mere questions of technicality, by merely legal questions.
1878 *Harper's W.* 21 Sept. 746/3. The literary examination, however, has the undeniable and extraordinary merit of "shunting" the Honorable Jones, M.C., upon a side track.

C. 1. As a political term, *to side-track* became popular in 1900 when Senator Thomas A. Platt conceived the idea of getting rid of Theodore Roosevelt as governor of New York by making him run for the vice-presidency:
N. Y. Trib. 13 Feb. 7/3. Governor Roosevelt's political friends believe he put an end today to Senator Platt's scheme to "sidetrack" him by bringing about his nomination for Vice President.
Ib. 13 June 13. [The pictorial representation of *sidetrack* is shown in a cartoon in which Platt is throwing the switch for the oncoming Roosevelt engine.]
Nation 28 June 491/3 ... Roosevelt's intimate friends, who denounced the plan of the boss to "side-track" the Governor for having been too independent....
1935 Chamberlain *There is No Truce* 135. When the crafty Platt side-tracked him in the vice presidency, destiny intervened and raised him to the supreme office.

C. 2. We find *sidetrack* referring to questions not connected with Roosevelt:
1900 *Cleve. Leader* 30 May 7/1. Bill Providing for Extradition of Criminals from United States to Cuba Sidetracked.
1900 *N. Y. Trib.* 18 June 1/6. Republican leaders from other States have taken up with all seriousness the project of side tracking Woodruff.
1960 *Detroit News* 16 Aug. 10 A/1. Democratic leader Johnson (Tex.) put the Senate on a 12-hour work day today in an effort to sidetrack political feuding on side issues....

See SHELVE, KICK UP STAIRS.

signs of the times.

A phrase used in order to recommend certain measures as timely or appropriate.

A. Biblical:
Matthew 16:3. O ye hypocrites, ye can discern the face of the sky; but can ye not discern the signs of the times?

B. Political:
1828 *Ohio St. Jrnl.* 8 May 3/3. If the "signs of the times" do not miserably fail us, Gov. Trimble can out-run any Ebony candidate that can be started in the state.
1829 *Workingman's Adv.* 14 Nov. 3/5. A Sign of the Times.—The following toast was given.... May the rights acquired by the one be secured by the lights conferred by the other.
1855 *Ann. of Cleve.* No. 2525. This I regard as one of the signs of the times, as politicians phrase it, and a most significant sign it is.
1864 in Barnes *Weed* 448. The political "signs of the times" are full of hope and joy.

silent vote.

The vote which had been hoped for but was never cast.
1848 *Cinc. Campaigner* 30 Sept. 1/2. At the next election the silent vote for Van Buren will be immense.
1875 *Cinc. Enquirer* 4 Oct. 4/1. The "silent vote" will be given to William Allen this year.
1880 *N. Y. Times* 19 Oct. 1/5. The "silent vote," as it is called, is what will tell in November.

1934 Carter *New Dealers* 279. It is possible that he feared the "last minute" swing of the "silent vote," which had won lost elections for the Republicans before.

silk stocking.

A person of wealth (contemptuous). See RUFFLED SHIRT.

The term *silk stocking* used as a label of contempt is to be found as early as 1798:

Ann. of the 5th Cong. 1948. If they wished to place them in a ridiculous point of view or to procure for them the name of the *Silk Stocking Company,* or any other term of derision, they could not take a more effectual course to obtain it.

1812 in Jefferson *Writings* XIII.163. What, then does this English faction with you mean? . . . They think they will be happier in an association under the rulers of Ireland, the East and West Indies, than in an independent government. . . . But I trust that such perverseness will not be that of the honest and well-meaning mass of the federalists of Massachusetts; and that when the questions of separation and rebellion shall be nakedly proposed to them, the Gores and the Pickerings will find their levees crowded with silk stocking gentry, but no yeomanry; an army of officers without soldiers.

The term *silk stocking* was also used as a noun:

1894 Stead *If Christ Came to Chicago* 36. Mayor Hopkins was elected by the *silkstockings* on the one hand and the *short hairs* on the other.

1903 *Independent* 12 Nov. 2663/1. The mass of voters look on him as a "silk stocking"—one who neither understands nor sympathizes with their life.

In 1914 the *Cyclopedia of American Government* defined *silk stocking* (n.):

III.309/1. A derisive appellation bestowed by the practical politicians upon those citizens of wealth and high social position

who occasionally interfere in politics in support of some reform measure or candidate.

This term is usually to be found used attributively in such expressions as *silk stocking gentry, silk stocking fop, silk stocking Republican:*

1840 *Cinc. D. Gazette* 26 Aug. 2/2. Mr. Grundy had alluded in his speech, to the Baltimore Convention of Whig Young Men, as being composed of the "silk stocking gentry."

1840 Lincoln in *Uncollected Works* I.545. They came like the rush of the mountain torrent. . . . They came not like "the silk stocking gentry" (as they are frequently called by their opponents;) but as farmers, mechanics, etc.

1840 *Little Magician* 24 June 3/5. The silk stocking tippies are all now in motion With coaches and log cabins moving afar, etc.

1884 *N. Y. World* 11 March 2/2. "You say that the silk-stocking Republicans are using the bulldozing business," remarked the reporter.

1913 Roosevelt *Autobio.* 63. I was a Republican from the "silk stocking" district, the wealthiest district in New York.

1913 *Ib.* 86 . . . the "silk stocking" reformer type, as Abraham Lincoln called it.

1946 W. A. White *Autobio.* 82. There the Democrats nominated a good old Tennessee silk-stocking Democrat, something of an orator.

1946 *Ib.* 84. Nasby even hooted at old-fashioned, silk-stocking Democrats, of which group my father was one.

silver grays.

Members of the conservative wing of the Whig Party around 1850.

A. It is commonly assumed that the nickname originally alluded to the silvery hair of Francis Granger of New York, Harrison's running mate in 1836. This is not absolutely correct. It is true that at the Utica Convention of 1850, Granger said:

N. Y. Trib. 18 Oct. 5/2. I shall gladly fight on in this cause so long as I shall live, and ask no higher post than the proud one of a private in the Silver Grays.

B. This event certainly helped to popularize the word, but Granger did not coin it.

1850 *N. Y. Trib.* 21 Oct. 4/2. We have no course left but to repel, as we here do, its charges that we have spoken of the "Silver Grays" in the language of the Five Points.

1850 *Ib.* 22 Oct. 4/5. The Express commends the Address of the "Silver Grays" at Utica, in the following terms.

As early as 1836 "Silver Gray" was the name of an organization within the Whig Party comprising men over sixty years of age:

1836 *Lexington Observer* 2 Nov. 3/5. Silver Greys. . . . a meeting of all the Whigs of the county over sixty years of age. . . . When the men whose heads are silvered with age and when the youth with their active energies come to the rescue, we cannot fail of Victory.

C. While in many cases, ironical or derogatory party names have been taken up in good earnest by the people against whom they had been coined, the tendency in the case of Silver Grays is clearly the opposite one. Probably due to the pro-slavery attitude of this group, its name loses the connotation of venerable and becomes synonymous with *old fogy* and similar terms.

1853 in Foner *Douglass* II.247. The Silver Gray Whig shakes hands with the Hunker Democrat, the former only differing from the latter in name.

1858 *Ohio Statesman* 29 Sept. 2/2. Tom

Corwin is an old dilapidated, antiquated silver-gray Whig.

cf. COTTON WHIGS, WOOLLY HEADS, SHORT HAIRS.

sit-down strike.

American reports of the strikes which were prevalent throughout France in the summer of 1936 described them with such terms as *barricaded in, encamped, crossed arms strikes* (see *N. Y. Times,* 27 May, 1 June), and later *stay-in* strikes.

1936 *N. Y. Times* 28 June 11/1. Lillé and Roubaix were without newspapers because of a "stay-in" strike of linotype operators.

1936 *Ib.* 1 July 5/4. A "stay-in" strike was begun by some of the artists, the orchestra, the chorus and the mechanical staff [of the Opéra-Comique].

By January, 1937, however, *sit-down strike* was in widespread use.

1937 *Ib.* 1 Jan. 1/8. 33,400 Men Are Made Idle; "Sit-Down" Strikes Close 7 General Motor Plants. [head]

1937 *Ib.* 2 Jan. 10/2. "Sit-Down." Whatever may be the merits of the controversy between the General Motors Corporation and the strikers, it has at least become clear that the "sit-down" strike is a formidable weapon, and one toward which . . . the general public must soon adopt a definite policy.

1937 in Cross *Conn. Yankee* 355. I want you to understand, sir, that there will be no sit-down strikes in Connecticut so long as I am Governor.

1944 *Life* 4 Sept. 25. The sit-down strike was copied from Paris, France, salesgirls, who remained all night in a department store [in 1936].

sixth columnists.

Gossips and defeatists. Apparently coined by Franklin D. Roosevelt.

1942 *Time* 6 April 13/2. Phrase-fancier Franklin Roosevelt had picked up a new one: sixth column. He used it at a press conference to denounce gossips and defeatists who spread rumors planted by enemy agents.
1942 Hoover *Add. Speeches* 167. Or at least they are under suspicion as being appeasers, compromisers, various obnoxious bipeds, reptiles, and Cliveden sets, Nazi sympathizers and Sixth Columnists. ... From the philosophical viewpoint, I would like to see the Sixth Columnists given a little more liberty. They are defined as the ones who discuss the war or speculate or even criticize in private conversation.

A booklet of the Promotion Department of the Liberty Mutual Insurance Company of Boston, published in July, 1942, and directed at carelessness in industry was entitled "Smash the 7th Column and Help Win the War."

See also FIFTH COLUMN.

skiddonians.

Members of a faction led by Thomas Skidmore, an advocate of land distribution.
1830 *Workingman's Adv.* 5 June 2/1. Sam and I are also called Radicals and Skiddonians.

skillet (tote one's own).

To act independently of party affiliations:
1850's in H. W. Grady *Life* 248. Stephens having a campaign right on him, and being pressed to locate himself, said he was neither Whig nor Democrat, but was "toting his own skillet," thus introducing that homely but expressive phrase into our political history.
1893 Simkins *Pitchfork Ben Tillman* 207. When asked, "Whom do you favor for governor, Tillman or Sheppard?" he re-

plied evasively, "I am a George Tillman man and tote my own skillet."

sky skimming.

A humorous term applying to the high-flown oratory characteristic in the latter half of the 19th century.
1874 *N. Y. World* 25 Sept. 8/1. It [Conkling's speech at Utica convention] was also intended to furnish the text for all the "sky-skimming" and spread-eagle orators on that side.

See SPREAD EAGLE.

slackwater politics.

Little political activity. In rivers and streams a deep, navigable slackwater is produced by a series of dams or locks.
1884 Julian *Recoll.* 372. Although this transition [from revolutionary period to orderly administration of affairs] has given birth to an era of "slack-water politics," it has gradually brought the country face to face with new problems....

slambanger.

A. For a short time a synonym for *locofoco.*
1837 *N. Y. Herald* 1 Nov. 2/1. On Monday, those valuable democrats, Slam, Bang, & Co., held a meeting at Tammany Hall, of which we gave a full account yesterday, doing justice to little Cain, but forgetting to mention that several other "Slambangers," such as Col. Ming, Major Carr, and Mr. McKeon also made speeches, and good ones too.
1838 *Ann. of Cleve.* No.1815. The "Slam Bang" order in New York do not like Gov. Marcy, and would prefer a little rotation in office.

B. The phrase is an interesting example of the suggestive force of connotations attached to personal names.

1837 Bryant *Prose Works* Dec. 8 II.385. Mr. Van Buren has issued his message, and the Whig journalists have answered it with the phrase "Slam, Bang, & Co." 1842 Byrdsall *Loco Foco Party* 134. Levi D. Slamm had been previously known as a useful man at drawing up resolutions, and also as a secretary at many of the Loco-Foco meetings. Shakespeare says that a rose by any other name would smell as sweet, but it was exactly the reverse with Mr. Slamm, for with any other name he would not have acquired the same renown. With this name the N. Y. Herald did much for him by adding Bang to it for the sake of ludicrous euphony; hence Slam Bang & Co became its favorite designation for the Equal Rights Party.

slate.

List of candidates.

The probable origin of the political slate in the use of the common school slate on which to write the list of prospective candidates is cited by Walsh:

Handy-Book of Lit. Curio. 1014. The origin of the phrase is unknown, but it is suggested as probable that at some early stage of the practice a slate was used as a convenient instrument upon which to make the list, from the ease with which names could be erased from it and added to it. . . .
1842 *N. Y. Trib.* 24 Jan. 3/1. The Regency are obliged to put them on the *slate* to be rid of them, and then rub their names out at leisure. . . .
1844 in *Am. Hist. Assoc. Pub.* II.56. He does not know the condition of things in relation to the presidential slate.
1858 *Ann. of Cleve.* No.2852. The Republicans at their conventions, have named their slates of nominees in four Ohio counties.
1860 Lincoln *Papers* I.232 . . . to call Ills, Ind, Penna and N.J. Delegates together to harmonize between you and Cameron, such a move would appear like a "Slate" and Seward is too potent here to attempt

such a meeting, his friends would probably Slate us, if it were done. . . .
1863 Halpine *Miles O'Reilly* 69.
To the Albany chiefs the War Democrats spoke,
Ere you play the old game, there are slates to be broke;
. . . .
And after November's slate smashing grand row,
We'll, with gaiety, make you our very best bow.
1878 *Harper's W.* 16 Nov. 906/4. It was a sharp and characteristic jest that Mr. Richmond was willing to leave the unimportant nominations to be made by the Convention. The rest were upon "the slate," and delegates inquired anxiously whose names were written there, that they might know how to vote.
1878 *Puck* 21 Aug. 2/1.
Freely inscribes on the political scroll—
In vulgar parlance better known as "slate"—
The name of each and every candidate
Whom it may strike his fancy to extol—

The pictorial value of the slate to suggest a list of names is clearly shown in a series of Nast cartoons and in others.

1876 *Harper's W.* 24 June 505. [shows Nast finishing his "Republican Slate" of Fish and Hayes]
1876 *Ib.* 8 July 545. [After the Convention, Nast triumphant with his slate under his arm; the name of Fish crossed out.]
1878 *Ib.* 23 Feb. 156. [Nast sitting in one corner of his cartoon holding "My Slate" on the currency problem.]
1898 *Rev. of Rev.* XVII.31. [Two cartoons showing Croker's influence in N.Y. politics. In one, Mayor Van Wyck is writing "Croker" on a slate while sitting on Croker's knee; in the second Croker himself has just written a large question mark on the slate.]

slaughterhouse.

The Whig Convention of 1848, so called by Horace Greeley:

1848 *N. Y. Trib.* 14 June. The Philadelphia Slaughterhouse . . . a slaughterhouse of Whig principles.
1849 *Akron Dem. Standard* 8 Nov. 2/3. When the Convention at Philadelphia (designated by Greeley as the "Slaughter House of principle") . . . . He was hostile to the Philadelphia "slaughterhouse" nomination.

slave (compounds and derivatives).

The following list is supplementary to that in Mathews, *Dictionary of Americanisms,* either as additional entries or as earlier examples:

Slave Democracy:

1854 *Ohio St. Jrnl.* 7 July 2. If there be one thing more absurd than another in the new doctrines broached by the Slave Democracy, it is that of "Squatter Sovereignty" in the Territories.
1855 *Lancaster* (Ohio) *Eagle* 9 Aug. 2/6. The charge . . . that we are the "Slave Democracy" is false.

slavedom:

1862 Mrs. French *Slavery in S. C.* 32. [The cradle] is high and elegant and so provided that the stinging insects of slavedom should not reach one babe; while another, because darker, is thrown by the Christian mistress into the irresponsible hands of the worst of men.

slave-hound Cabinet:

1877 *in Puck* April No.4, 8–9. Such a Cabinet—a slave-hound Cabinet—to pilot this ship, tossed on the hot indignation of twenty million Northerners and the tireless hate of ten millions at the South.

slaveocracy:

1856 *Ohio St. Jrnl.* 7 July 2/2. He expects to be a candidate of the Slaveocracy for Congress in this district.

slaveocrat:

1842 Birney *Ltrs.* 666,688 . . . Slaveocrats in Georgia. . . . A desperate effort is making by the Slaveocrats to prevent Giddings' reelection.

slavocratic:

1851 *N. Y. Trib.* 17 April 4/2. It is certain that the more ardent and slavocratic Southrons hanker for that lovely and fertile island [Cuba] as a new slave State in this Union, and that they will not easily resign the hope of getting it.

slave oligarchy:

1862 Christy *Pulpit Politics* 539. The enemy was conquered. At their feet lay the carcass of that odious slave oligarchy, which, for so long a period, had ruled our country, ruled Northern men, and tyrannized over both.

slave party:

1823 *Cinc. Nat. Rep.* 8 Aug. 2/3. And the *slave* party, and the *anti-slave* party . . . are the only parties whose views and interests are widely variant.

slave power:

1840 *The Liberator* 23 Oct. By the slave-power, I mean, however, not only the actual slaveholding community, but the slaveholding *spirit,* which, fostered by prejudice, and interests, pervades the whole Union.
1844 *Cinc. W. Herald and Philanthropist* 16 Sept. The Force which has ruled our country so long, we called the Slavepower. It consists of the associated wealth of a class of slaveholding monopolists, who constitute about a sixty-sixth part of the population of this country.
1846 *in Mangum Papers* IV.508. A new State, which has been constitutionally admitted into the Union, not by *"slave power,"* but by the votes of the *free States.*
1849 *in* "Warrington" *Pen Portraits* 28 May 43. We shall try to persuade the people that it is high time the rule of the slave-power was discontinued. . . .
1857 *Cinc. Daily Comm.* 12 March. There is such a thing as the Slave Power. It has marched over and annihilated the bound-

aries of the States. We are now one great homogeneous slaveholding community.

slavery.

Represented as the necessary consequence of oppressive British measures, *slavery* is, together with *slave* and *enslave,* a frequently used catchword in writings both before and during the Revolution.
1765 in Becker *Pol. Parties in N. Y.* 17 Oct. 29 ... a meeting called of "friends of liberty and the English constitution," in order to form "an association of all who are not already slaves, in opposition to all attempts to make them such."
1773 in *Ib.* 6 Dec. 105. Therefore, to prevent slavery ... we, the subscribers, being influenced from a regard to Liberty and disposed to ... transmit to our posterity those blessings of freedom which our ancestors have handed down to us, ... do ... agree to associate together under the name and stile of the Sons of Liberty of New York.
1774 in *Ib.* 12 April 109. "Every friend of his country" was summoned to attend at Marray's Wharf at that time, in order that he might see "with his own eyes, their detestation of the measures passed by the ministry to enslave the country."
1774 *Ib.* 17 Sept. 147. These resolutions declared that the coercion acts were a gross violation of the constitution. ... that they be regarded as the "attempts of a wicked administration to enslave America."
1775 Seabury in *Ib.* 17 Jan. 175. To you, gentlemen, ... the good people look for relief ... from this intolerable state of slavery.

slow bell campaign.

A railroad metaphor which appeared during the campaign of 1948, perhaps motivated by Truman's "whistle stop" campaign (q.v.) :
1948 *Nation* 16 Oct. 422/1. Slow-Bell Campaign in the Northwest.... [Brakeman

on Great Northern] "You used to see the coaches full of Roosevelt buttons and the Pullman fares wearing the latest Republican decorations.... Now you don't hear folks mention the election. This campaign is sure proceeding under a slow bell.

slush fund.

A. Originally money collected in the army and navy from the sale of grease and other refuse and used to purchase luxuries for the men.
1864 *Rio Abajo Press* 5 July 2/2. The polite Commissary informed us that they received twelve dollars a barrel for the grounds, and thus added materially to the "slush fund."

B. Also an appropriation of Congress to be administered by the Secretary of the Treasury at his discretion.
1874 Kellogg in *Cong. Record* 17 April 3166/1. It was a matter of economy and good judgment ... to consolidate all these offices into one bill, and dispense with what has been received out of ... the "slush fund." ... We have had this "slush-fund" since 1866.

C. Later, funds used for campaign expenses.
1894 C. Clark in *Cong. Record* 904/1. [Cleveland] was not elected in 1888 because you had got the "fat fried" out of your manufacturers; because of pious John Wanamaker and his $400,000 of campaign slush funds, and because of men like to him. ...
1920 *Cols. Citizen* 27 Aug. 1. Cox May Bare More Slush Fund Proof [head] ... to prove his charge that the Republican leaders are raising a campaign fund of "at least $15,000,000."
1924 Rogers *How We Elect* 44. If I was running for office I would rather have two friends in the counting room than a Republican Slush fund behind me.
1927 *Searchlight on Congress* March 4/1. The attitude of "Dave" Reed toward "the slush fund" committee headed by the

other Reed, "Jim" of Missouri, exemplifies the situation as to present Pennsylvania Senatorial intellectuality.

1937 *Am. Sp.* XII.7–8. New Dealers were using [in 1936] appropriations as giant slush-funds, it was charged.

small potato.

A. Used to minimize the importance of a person or an issue:

1840 *Ohio Statesman* 9 Dec. 3/1. This is the "small potatoe" business of all tyrants and senseless demagogues. It is thousands for hard cider and coonskins, but not a cent for printing.

1840 *N. Y. Mirror* 405/3. It is with your little politicians—the "small potatoes" of partisanism—we have to do at present.

1844 in *Mangum Papers* IV.5. I shall without further preliminary make you acquainted with the low, *small* potatoe conduct of Loco foco Henshaw.

1852 *N. Y. Times* 19 Oct. 1/3. The Captain went on to state ... that he would not have come there, had not some of the small potato politicians of his party seen fit to leave his name off the posters.

1858 *N. Y. Trib.* 1 Jan. 1/5. Judge Douglas may be a small potato, but in the present ticklish posture of the Democratic party, the loss of even a small potato may result in starvation and death.

James Buchanan is reported to have used the phrase in a speech in Congress during the debates on the Bank in the late 1830's:

in Cox *Why We Laugh* 140. Mr. Buchanan's playful wit shone ... and then drew him [Clay] and his party in the pleasing posture of demanding a bank anyhow, even though its exchanges should be made in bacon hams, and its currency be small potatoes.

James Gordon Bennett is also credited with an early use of the term:

c1839 in Christman *Tin Horns and Calico* 38. Bennett ridiculed the Governor's appeal to the farmers as the "small potato proclamation" and the tenant uprisings as the "small potato war."

1839? *N. Y. Herald* in *Ib.* 323.

To Small Potatoes we will send
For troops these Dutch to fight....

smoke filled room.

Harry M. Daugherty in *The Inside Story of the Harding Tragedy* (p. 303) denies the story of the smoke filled room:

A direct outgrowth of the Fable of the Senatorial Clique is the amazing yarn that has gained wide currency to the effect that Harding was chosen by a powerful group of United States Senators who met in the smoke-filled room of Colonel George Harvey at the Blackstone Hotel an hour before he was nominated.

Whatever Daugherty's reasons may have been for the denial of the story, it is on record that the phrase was actually used in connection with Harding's nomination and may even have been mentioned months before the Republican convention of 1920:

Stimpson *Am. Politics* 366. At five o'clock on the morning of June 12, 1920, Simpson filed a story beginning: "Harding of Ohio was chosen by a group of men in a smoke-filled room early today as Republican candidate for President."

W. A. White *Autobio.* 584. We had been warned five months before the convention by Harry Daugherty, an Ohio lobbyist, that Harding would be nominated in a "smoke-filled room" after the delegates had been allowed to play for a while with their own candidates.

1935 Chidsey *Gentleman from N. Y.* 282. It is not true that all Republican Presidential nominees since the Civil War have been selected by a few men in a smoke-filled hotel room at midnight. Surely this was not the case in 1880—and not simply because Senator Conkling would not tolerate cigar smoke, but even more because he wouldn't tolerate any dealing with the enemy.

snap convention.

A convention held with only a brief advance notice; usually with the purpose of packing the later regular one with delegates favorable to a particular faction or person.

A. Snap convention undoubtedly belongs to the group of terms, all compounds, with *snap* (meaning quick), to be found in politics as early as 1841.

1841 *Cong. Globe* App. 42/3. This extra session of Congress called in time of peace to take snap judgments on the American people.
1854 *N. Y. Trib.* 2 Aug. 7/3. Now, these meeting are the easiest things in the world—they are nothing but snap meetings, and they show nothing more clearly than the weakness of the slaveites.

B. Identified with the N.Y. Democratic convention of 1892.

1892 *Nation* 4 Feb. 79/1. The meeting of Democrats in this city on Friday evening, which resulted in a formal protest against the Hill "snap" Convention....
1892 *Ib.* 11 Feb. 97/3. Mr. Hill continues to neglect his duties ... in order to "set up" the caucuses which will send delegates to his "snap" convention of February 22.
1892 *Ib.* 18 Feb. 121/1. That is a condemnation of Hillism, as exhibited in seat-stealing and snap-convention-calling, which is not to be misunderstood.

Later example.

1896 *Nation* 20 Feb. 150/1. We are now within four months of the Republican national convention, and the choice of delegates has already begun, "snap" conventions having been held in some Congressional districts of New York, Pennsylvania, and two or three Southern States.

soak the rich.

A slogan during the early years of the New Deal. (See 1935 *Lit. Digest* quot.) Whether the policy may be attributed to Huey Long or to LaFollette is unimportant in considering the term, as it seems obviously the creation of the press opposing Roosevelt's measures in 1935.

1935 *New Rep.* 11 Sept. 121. Soaking the Poor [head.]. ... We have heard a great deal about soaking the rich.
1935 in *Lit. Digest* 14 Dec. 6/3. Soak the Rich (Antonym, Soak the Poor) — Newspaperese for a system of taxation founded upon the absurd and revolutionary theory that a man should be assessed taxes in proportion to his ability to pay.
1935 Warburg *Hell Bent for Election* 72. He [FDR] thought he was being "clever" when he tried to steal Huey Long's thunder by suddenly coming out with his "soak the rich" tax message.
1935 in Stokes *Chip* 419. Huey's "Share the Wealth" crusade was responsible for what the newspapers called the "Soak-the-Rich" tax bill of the Roosevelt administration which boosted surtaxes on the very wealthy to their all-time peak.
1935 in Creel *Rebel at Large* 290. His so-called "soak the rich" program.
1936 in *Am. Sp.* XII.7. The New Dealers' *Soak the rich* theory meant in reality, *Soak the thrifty,* the Republicans said.
[?] W. S. Sayre in Salter *Am. Politician* 146. There was a disposition [in the first New Deal Congress] to adopt the "soak the rich" features of the La Follette tax plan.

The close connection of the policy with Huey Long may be seen from the following quotations, suggesting that *soak the rich* may have been used first in a Louisiana reference.

1935 in Stokes *Chip* 402. He [H. Long] gave them a cause—"Share the Wealth."

1935 Long in Davis *Huey Long* 299. I had been in the United States Senate only a few days when I began my effort to make the battle for a distribution of wealth among all the people a national issue for the coming elections. On July 2, 1932... I heard Franklin Delano Roosevelt, accepting the nomination... use the following words: "Throughout the nation, men and women, forgotten in the political philosophy of the Government for the last years, look to us here for guidance and for a more equitable opportunity to share in the distribution of the national wealth.

sober second thought.

Behind the phrase are reminiscences from classical authors like Tacitus' remark that the Germans discussed public affairs at their banquets but made decisions only after a night's rest had restored them to sobriety (*Germania*) and Valerius Maximus' anecdote about the woman condemned by Phillip of Macedonia while he was drunk and who later appealed to Phillip the sober. (*Lib.* VI, c.2)

In 1788 Fisher Ames wrote "I consider biennial elections as a security that the sober second thought of the people shall be law." ("On Biennial Elections")

The phrase became very popular after William Allen had used it in his remarks on Van Buren's message of December, 1838:

1838 *Wash. Globe* 26 Dec. in Lynch *Epoch and a Man* 443... yet he, almost alone, amidst the general consternation, amidst the desertions of the venal and the shrieks of the timid, stood unappalled—confiding, as he ever has done, and ever will, in that "sober second thought" of his countrymen, which is "never wrong, and always efficient."

In the following years the phrase was occasionally attributed to Van Buren himself:

1840 *Georgia Jrnl.* 21 Jan. 3/1. Was the "sober, second thought," about which Mr. Van Buren prates so much, brought into requisition?

1840 *Harrison Dem.* 12 May 4/1. Indeed! has not the declaration of their President, that he relies on the "sober second thoughts" of the people to sustain him become the boast of his party orgins [sic]?

Later example:

1917 White *The Old Order Changeth* 248. This national public sentiment is not the belief of our rich men, nor of our slums.... It is calm crowd judgment, amalgamated in the heat of discussion, but cooled in sober second thought.

social democracy.

Although the German *Sozialdemokrat* is first attested from 1849 (Ladendorf, p. 290), the American *social democracy* antedates not only this usage but the American term *socialist* as well. The phrase seems to have originated with Orestes Brownson: ¿ in Van Deusen *Greeley* 45. After the campaign [of 1840] was over, he showed a poorly disguised contempt for Orestes Brownson's appeal to Democrats to resort to first principles and raise the standard of social democracy.

1840 *Ohio Statesman* 10 Dec. 3/2... we do not profess to know exactly what "social democracy" is.

1842 *Sketches of Mike Walsh* 27 Nov. 81. There were several fine fellows—social Democrats—Subterraneans, if you will—rich and poor, but all gay larks—no distinction.

Probably more under the influence of German *Sozialdemokratie* than of Brownson, since any connection between the two is unlikely, later organizations adopted the title as their party designation, as for example:

1874 in Foner *Hist. of Labor Movement* I.449. The Social-Democratic Party of North America, founded in 1874 by the Lassalleans, emphasized in its original platform that workingmen must concentrate their efforts upon political action.
1898 in Brissenden *IWW* 44. It was in this same year that the Social Democratic party (which became the Socialist party three years later) was organized in Chicago.

socialism.

For a presentation of the much-discussed origin of *socialism* and *socialist,* we refer to "The Evolution of the Socialist Vocabulary" by Arthur E. Bestor, Jr. (*Journal of the History of Ideas,* June, 1948) where an additional bibliography on the subject is given. *Socialist* seems to have first appeared in England in the *Cooperative Magazine* of November, 1827, while *socialisme* was used in French periodicals in 1831. The actual word *socialism* did not appear in England until 1837 in the *New Moral World.* (*OED*)

To begin with, the meaning of the word seems to be rather vague:
1842 Stein *Der Socialismus und Communismus* 130. Das Wort selbst hat noch keine feste technische Bedeutung; bald wird es für alle Bestrebungen, materielle wie intellectuelle genommen, die auf die Verbesserung der gesellschaftlichen Zustände hinzielen, bald ist es allein die Schule der Fourieristen, die ihre Theorie die Science sociale nennen.
1953 Cole *Socialist Thought* I.308. The word "Socialism" did not up to 1848 usually conjure up in men's minds the idea of a political movement—except to the extent to which Louis Blanc and

Pecqueur in the 1840's gave it this connotation in France. It suggested a "social system" rather than a political demand....

It is significant that the 1840 edition of Lieber's *Encyclopedia Americana* does not contain an entry under *socialism* nor under *Fourierism.* Nor does Horace Greeley, one of the earliest apostles of American socialism, use the term in his early articles on the movement. Instead, he speaks of *Fourierism, Association.* It is apparent, however, that two of these terms were closely associated in America since Emerson writing in 1842 (*Dial,* III.86–89) discusses Fourierism but calls the disciples socialists. The 1848 edition of Webster states:
Socialism. A social state in which there is a community of property, among all the citizens—a new term for Agrarianism.

From the rich collection illustrating the later history of *socialism,* we select only those quotations which indicate the author's attitude toward the term, some agreeing with the statement of Engels, others opposing it as a term of reproach:
Bestor "Evol. of Soc. Vocab." 291 [Quoting Engels, preface to Communist Manifesto, 1888 ed.]. Thus in 1847, Socialism was a middle class movement, Communism a working class movement. Socialism, on the continent at least, "respectable"; Communism was the very opposite.
1856 Sotheran *Greeley* 8 July 36n. We never objected to the designation of Socialist when it was a term of reproach and opprobrium....
in Nevins *Cartoons* 101. ["Worship of the North" by Adalbert Volck. The nation's youth is shown being sacrificed on an

altar built of the stones of "negro worship," "spirit rapping," "free love," "witch
burning," "socialism," "atheism," "ra-
tionalism," and "puritanism."]

1875 Weed in Barnes *Weed* 30 Jan. 513.
Let it be remembered always that the
real purpose of these combinations—for
which we are unhappily indebted to the
worst specimens of English, French, and
German radicalism—is, first as "socialists"
and then as "communists," to sow the
seeds of agrarianism and infidelity among
us.

1878 *Harper's W*. 31 Aug. 686/1. It
[the Democratic party] is evidently conscious that the Nationalists, or Socialists,
or Greenbackers, or Communists, or however they may be called, are largely drawn
from its ranks, and it fears to alienate
their support.

1878 *Cols. Dem*. 1 Dec. 1/3. Savage Socialists Who Slaughter the Kings. [head]

1896 Bryan *First Battle* 81. A poor man
is called a socialist if he believes that the
wealth of the rich should be divided
among the poor, but the rich man is
called a financier if he devises a plan by
which the pittance of the poor can be
converted to his use. . . .

1909 Roosevelt *Works* XVIII.563. Socialism . . . is blind to everything except the
merely material side of life. . . . it is a
form of communism with no moral foundation, but essentially based on the immediate annihilation of personal ownership of capital, and, in the near future,
the annihilation of the family, and ultimately the annihilation of civilization.

1913 *Ib*. XXII.551. Because of things I
have done on behalf of justice to the
working man, I have often been called a
Socialist. Usually I have not taken the
trouble even to notice the epithet. I am
not afraid of names, and I am not one
of those who fear to do what is right
because some one else will confound me
with partisans with whose principles I
am not in accord. Moreover, I know that
many American Socialists are high-minded
and honorable citizens, who in reality
are merely radical social reformers. . . .
None the less, without impugning their

motives, I do disagree most emphatically
with both the fundamental philosophy
and the proposed remedies of the Marx-
ian Socialists.

1929 Al Smith *Up to Now*. During 1914
and 1915 a decidedly reactionary element
in the legislature . . . had been actively
bent upon attempting to stop what they
called socialistic legislation.

1945 *Chicago Trib*. 27 July. "Socialism"
has recently come into favor with American Communists as a substitute for "communism."

Solid South.

The complete alignment of the
Southern states supporting the
Democratic party following the
Reconstruction.

On January 26, 1830, Daniel
Webster said,

Speeches II.294. As to manner how, the
gentleman already sees that it was by
voting in a solid column for the required
relief.

This suggests that the use of *solid*
in politics meaning unamimous or
with an overwhelming majority
may have been taken from military
language, a possibility further supported by the following:

1855 in Foner *Business & Slavery* 114. We
are now beaten by the solid vote of the
City of New York, against which the
country will organize and recruit an army
of freemen to besiege and conquer the
Sebastopol.

Already before the Civil War we
find occasional phrases pointing to
Solid South.

1856 *Annals of Cleve*. 9 Aug. He [Fill-
more] cannot carry a single state for the
South is solid for Buchanan.

The phrase itself was used by Colfax in 1858:

in Hollister *Colfax* 137. When the solid
South in the House and a score of North-

ern Democrats dare to vote *NO* on a resolution approving existing laws against the African slave trade.

The term gains importance in 1876 when the possibility of the Southern states turning unanimously to the Democratic party appeared on the political horizon. **1876** *Harper's W.* 26 Feb. 162/2. State after State has been conquered from the majority by violence, and we are no longer left in doubt as to the purpose thus to establish a solid South in the interest of the Democratic party.

As Professor Acheson Hench pointed out in a paper read at the MLA Convention in Detroit, 1951, the phrase was given currency by General Moseley in a letter of August 6, 1876, which caused quite a sensation because the old guerrilla leader came out for the Republican ticket headed by Hayes. Moseley ltr 6 Aug. in *Cinc. Commercial* 16 Aug. 2/5. But suppose, Hayes is elected with a solid South against him—what are you going to do then? *Harper's W.* 26 Aug. 691/2. Of course, we must recognize *the Solid South* as the core of the Democratic party. . . . The Solid South is the Southern Confederacy seeking domination of the United States through the machinery of the Democratic party. 15 Sept. in Adams *Storrs* 189. Is this Democratic party, characterized to-day by being a solid South, is that party, which for years and years has waged relentless war against the national life, to be trusted with its old doctrine still fresh upon its lips, and its old bitterness still lingering in its heart? *N. Y. Trib.* 19 Sept. 4/6. The claim of a "solid South" is likely to do the Democrats full as much harm as good. They originated the expression, and the Republicans are using it with great force

against them, chiefly because of Democratic efforts to keep it "solid." *Ib.* 6 Oct. 4/3. *A Solid South.* . . . A solid South means complete denial to the colored voters of that freedom of choice which the Constitution guarantees to them as to all other citizens.

Its popularity was reinforced by Nast cartoons during the campaign, in which he constantly refers to the Solid South, characterizing it as a wolf, a snake, etc. *Harper's W.* 21 Oct. 860. A Solid South. 21 Oct. 845. "The Solid South"—Gaunt and Hungry [as a wolf]. 28 Oct. 872–3. The Boast of a Solid South. 4 Nov. 883 [as weight unbalancing a scale]. 4 Nov. 892–3 [as a cannon]. 4 Nov. 896 [as a snake].

The phrase remains unchallenged for almost fifty years. For a few years *Solid North* was offered as its counterpart. **1877** *N. Y. Trib.* 7 July 4/3. "The Solid South" was the great fact brought out in the last Presidential election. **1878** *Puck* 20 Nov. 2/1. The President is going to fling the Bloody Shirt to the breeze, and array a Solid North against a Solid South. **1878** *Harper's W.* 24 Aug. 666/2. We have read with regret some things in Mr. Foster's speech upon his renomination to Congress in Ohio. He recommends a solid North as a cure for a solid South. **1880** *N. Y. World* 3 Nov. 1/2. Garfield carries probably the Solid North excepting New Jersey, California, and Oregon. **1880** *Nation* 11 Nov. 340/1. When the "Solid North" shall offer to the "Solid South" the complete retirement of "machine" and "bloody shirt" politicians . . . then will "fidelity to Democracy" and a "Solid South" pass as quickly and irrecoverably away as the dreams of a night. **1890** Hilary A. Herbert *Why the Solid South.* (Baltimore.)

1927 *Mirror of the Year* 19. The obstacle presented by the existence of the Solid South to the idea of nominating Governor Alfred E. Smith.
1952 *New Rep.* 17 Nov. 10/2. The "Solid South" myth is past.

sons of the wild jackass.

A nickname for the independents.

A. Of the several places in which the Bible mentions wild asses, Job 24:5 is probably the one that is behind the use of the term in American politics:

Behold, as wild asses in the desert, go they forth to their work; rising betimes for a prey: the wilderness yieldeth food for them and for their children.

B. In a letter of John Hay to Theodore Roosevelt in 1890, we find:

Roosevelt *Autobio.* 266. You have already shown that a man may be absolutely honest and yet practical; a reformer by instinct and a wise politician; brave, bold, and uncompromising, and yet not a wild ass of the desert.

Another possible source might be found in the following quotation:

Bryan *First Battle* 455. I remember that a few years ago a Populist in Congress stated that the small burros that run wild upon the prairies of South America form a group, when attacked by a ferocious animal, and, putting their heads together and their feet on the outside of the circle, protect themselves from the enemy. But he added that the advocates of reforms sometimes showed less discretion, and, turning their heads toward the enemy, kicked each other.

C. It seems likely that there is a connection between these early uses of *wild ass* and the phrase *sons of the wild jackass* which Senator Moses of New Hampshire

launched on a successful career in 1929:

1929 Moses in Moos *Republicans* 365. Mournfully I prophesy that the progress of these sons of the wild jackass who now control the Senate will probably go forward to complete consummation.
1932 Tucker and Barkley *Sons of the Wild Jackass v.* This term, an excellent example of the caustic wit and epigrammatic ability of the brilliant Senator, was seized upon with avidity by the newspapermen present, who realized its news value, and the next day "Sons of the Wild Jackass" was given a front page spread by many of the leading newspapers throughout the country.

Soon afterwards one of the insurgents, George W. Norris, used the words good naturedly about himself in a parody describing the "murder" of Joseph Grundy:

in Neuberger and Kahn *Integrity* 146–7.
Look, in this place ran Caraway's dagger through.
See what a rent the envious Borah made.
Through this the son of a wild jackass stabbed,
And, as he drew his cursed steel away,
Mark how the blood of Grundy followed it,
. . . .
For when the noble Grundy saw the jackass stab
Ingratitude more strong than traitors' arms
Quite vanquished him; then burst his heart,
And in his mantle, muffling up his face,
The great Grundy fell.
[Neuberger and Kahn's presentation gives the erroneous impression that the incident took place in the early twenties.]

sorehead.

A disgruntled politician; a bolter. (See *Am. Sp.*, Oct. 1952, 167ff.)

A. Apparently derived from the phrase "as mad as a bear with a sore head" which is found in political language as early as 1836:

Ohio People's Press 29 June 3/3. The *Globe* grumbles like a bear with a sore head.

B. *Sorehead* is found as a political term on various occasions, particularly when a third party movement was being initiated. Among the most prominent of these are:

(1) 1848, the Free Soil Party.

1848 *Albany W. Argus* 12 Aug. 253/3. As no other selection could be supposed so well to represent such a Conventicle of "sore heads," it is perhaps quite as well it sho'd take that direction as any other.

1848 *Ib.* 23 Sept. 363/2. I have just returned from a ringed, striped and speckled "sore-head" demonstration at Sharon Springs.

1849 *Democracy Untrammeled* (Rossville, O.) 27 Sept. 2/4. The renowned and valorous Capting growls at the "Independents" like a bear with a *sore head*. ... He has exhibited strong symptoms of the "swell head" ever since!

1850 *N. Y. Trib.* 3 Oct. 4/4. Be wise, then O sore-headed friends! [bolters at Syracuse Convention] and remember that He who fights and runs away. ...

(2) 1854, the Republican Party.

1854 *Ohio St. Jrnl.* 8 April 2/1. They certainly do not take the Statesman, up there in Molly Stark, or they would have known that Leiter was only a sorehead, and broken-down politician, and cast-off democrat. They have a good many of that sort, up in those parts.
[See also April 20, 1854, edit., "Seven Kinds of Soreheads" 2/1.]

1854 *Ohio Statesman* 3 July 2/2. ... Bankites, Abolitionists, Free Soilers, soreheads, etc., are expected to fall in gracefully [with plans for a "People's Party"].

1854 *Ottawa Free Trader* 5 Aug. in Beveridge *Lincoln* III.264n ... Whigs, abolitionists, know nothings, sore heads, ... and fag ends in the country under a common name.

1856 *Cleve. Plaindealer* 18 Sept. 2/1 ... they [abolitionists] will slink back into their original insignificance and be heard of no more only as a party of sore heads, "shreakers," and professional agitators.

1856 *Ib.* 20 Sept. 2/1. Sore-heads Soaking. Our Yankee sore-heads from New England, who have led off on that "Sick list" which made such a blow in the Fusion papers not long since, begin to attract attention where they came from.

1861 *Vanity Fair* 11 May 219/1. General Webb was one of the Great Disappointed —felt like a hungry bear with a sore head.

(3) 1872, the Liberal Republican Party.

1872 *Harper's W.* 23 March 226/1 ... Republicans selfishly estranged from their party and known as "sore heads."

1872 *Ib.* 8 June 442/2 ... Mr. Greeley's actual support in the Republican party is limited mainly to the noble army known as "soreheads."

1872 J. A. Logan in *Shawneetown Merc.* 20 Sept. These liberal sore-heads are just using you as a *Democratic cat's paw*.

1879 *Harper's W.* 11 Oct. 802/3. The Republican dissenters are undoubtedly liable to be called deputy Democrats, and a sore-headed squad, and canting reformers, and prigs altogether too good for this world, and Pharisees, and political Miss Nancys, and impractical fools, and milk-whey politicians, and crotchety, and "cranky" and "unco guid," and theorists, and doctrinaires, and puling sentimentalists, and dress-parade statesmen, and juvenile Republicans, and female lunch parties, and all the other familiar and well-worn names which are always showered upon such dissenters.

(4) 1884, the Mugwumps.

1884 *Harper's W.* 8 March 156. Messrs. O'Brien and Co. say, as they said in 1879 and 1882, that the other Republicans are merely goody-goodies and canting soreheads, who sniff and kick until election day comes and then vote the straight ticket.

sovereign, sovereignty.

The idea that supreme sovereignty resides in the people did not seem to prevail in the minds of the Revolutionary leaders. John Adams probably took a more advanced view than most of his contemporaries when he spoke of a shared sovereignty:

1790 J. Adams *Works* IX.564. Our new government is an attempt to divide a sovereignty; a fresh essay at *imperium in imperio*. It cannot, therefore, be expected to be very stable or very firm.
1790 *Ib.* VI.415. Whenever I use the word *republic* with approbation, I mean a government in which the people have collectively, or by representation, an essential share in the sovereignty.

Sam Adams' reply to this statement must probably be considered a minority statement:

1790 in J. Adams *Works* VI.421. A republic, you tell me, is a government in which "the people have an essential *share* in the sovereignty." Is not the *whole* sovereignty, my friend, essentially in the people?

The French Revolution is clearly responsible for the radical theory of the people as the supreme authority of the state. The constitution declares (III, 1) "... la conséquence trés juste que la où est le peuple, la est le souverain" (Brunot, IX. pt. 2. 724) .

Very early the controversy about the French Revolution carried the idea to England:

Mackintosh *A Defence of the French Revolution*, in *Misc. Essays* 448/2 ... as a direct emanation from the sovereignty of the people, it ("the supreme magistracy") is as legitimate in its origin as in its administration.

The event that popularized the new concept in America was probably Genet's imbroglio with Washington during which he declared that the president was not the sovereign and allegedly threatened to appeal to the true sovereigns, the American people. (Minnegarode, *Friend of France.*)

In a letter to Jefferson of Sept. 18, 1793, Genet wrote:

Persuaded that the sovereignty of the United States resides essentially in the people and in its representation in the Congress....

It is unlikely that this was Genet's first use of the expression.

The *National Gazette* had used the phrase somewhat earlier:

in Gordy *Hist. of Pol. Parties* 163. The people are his (Genet's) friends or the friends of France. She will have nothing to apprehend, for as yet the people are the sovereign of the United States.

And we find it from American sources of the 1792:

Barlow *Pol. Writings* 203. Letter to the Citizens of Piedmont. A whole people is essentially sovereign ... and the same sovereign people can at any time change its form.

Opponents of the new idea frequently took up the words *sovereign* and *sovereignty* in order to criticize and ridicule.

1799 Cobbett *Ltrs.* 38. Yesterday all my goods sailed for New York, so that they are no longer, I hope, within the grasp of the sovereign people of Pennsylvania.
1807 *Salmagundi* 41. The mob is called the sovereign people.
1837 Hone *Diary* 245. The ceremony (inauguration) was conducted as usual in the presence of ... as many of the "sovereigns" as could gain admittance to the presence of their "servant."

On the other hand, the serious use of the terms continued:

1799 Fisher Ames *Works* 100. The time to do this is at the elections. There, if anywhere, the sovereignty of the citizen is to be exercised.

1827 Alexander Everett *America* 76. The fundamental principle, or ... the mainspring of our political machine to which all others are subordinate and secondary, is the sovereignty of the people.

in Hoar *Autobio.* I.153n. Shortly after Burlingame came into active life, he made a journey to Europe. The American Minister obtained for him a ticket of admission to the House of Commons. He was shown into a very comfortable seat in the gallery. In a few minutes an official came and told him he must leave that seat; that the gallery where he was was reserved for Peers. They are very particular about such things there. Burlingame got up to go out when an old Peer who happened to be sitting by and had heard what was said, interposed. "Let him stay, let him stay. He is a Peer in his own country." "I am a Sovereign in my own country, Sir," replied Burlingame, "and shall lose caste if I associate with Peers." And he went out.

Toward the middle of the nineteenth century, both the serious and the satirical concepts of sovereignty were well enough established to furnish the foundations, respectively, of the ideas of popular sovereignty and of squatter sovereignty. (q.v.)

Spartan band.

At a banquet in honor of Andrew Jackson in New York, February, 1819, a toast was given to the "Spartan band of modern story— the Volunteers of Kentucky and Tennessee at New Orleans." The sensation created at the same banquet by Jackson's toast to DeWitt

Clinton must have made it the topic of the day and probably contributed to the popularization of the phrase. (Parton, II.561) Later *Spartan band* was repeatedly used as a name for small but determined political groups.

A. The followers of Wm. C. Rives were given that name:

1837 in *Madisonian* 30 Sept. 1/6. Whatever may now be said of the "Spartan band" of Conservatives by the unprincipled demagogues of the day, the time is not far distant when they will be hailed as the Saviours of the Democratic party.

1839 in *Cong. Globe* 30 Jan. Sir, let me tell that gentleman to pause and count the cost before he becomes Conservative. Is he in a proper state of mind to join that little "Spartan Band," who have periled all for their country?

1839 in Simms *Whig* 135. "Spartan Band number 2."

B. Mike Walsh and his followers:

1842 in *Sketches of Mike Walsh* 88. "Well," said I to myself, "Here's Mike Walsh ... the President of the 'Spartan Band'—the champion of the shirtless ... the advocate of the houseless ... the idol of the Subterraneans...."

1842 *Ohio St. Jrnl.* 13 July 1/7 ... Mike Walsh and about thirty of his New York "Spartan Band."

1842 *N. Y. Trib.* 17 Sept. 6/5. The Spartan Band followed with a flag inscribed "Free Sufferage," a style of spelling not generally used, but apparently preferred by these modern heroes of Thermopylæ.

C. Northern partisans of the Confederate cause:

1860 in Wilson *Slave Power* III.69. We have a Spartan Band in every Northern State.

Later:

1885 *Nation* 8 Oct. 289/3. The Mugwumps of Baltimore, of whom there is a Spartan Band....

speak German.

See quot.

1943 E. Gordon *Wrecking the 18th Amend.* 198. The Tammany Society was, of course, out in full strength with everything alien that could be mustered,— Polish Falcons, United Hungarian Societies, County Tipperary men,...Unaffiliated German-Americans, ready, at the drop of a hat, "to speak German at the ballotbox" (that is, vote for beer) as they had been admonished by their leaders.

spiked helmet democracy.

German members of the Democratic Party.

The Franco-Prussian War widely covered by news articles and pictures had made America familiar with the German helmet.

1878 *Ohio St. Jrnl.* 13 Aug. 2/3. The Spiked Helmet are singing the Wacht am Rhein with terrific vigor.

spit on the platform.

The acquiescence of the Baltimore (Whig) Convention of June, 1852, in the Fugitive Slave Law drew a violent protest from Horace Greeley:

N. Y. Trib. 22 June 4/6. But by "the question thus settled," the plank evidently means to cover all questions relative to Slavery.... All this is alike futile and preposterous—we defy it, execrate it, spit upon it.
1852 Strong *Diary* II.98. [Scott] won't be helped by Horace Greeley's editorial of this morning, wherein he repudiates and spits upon the plank of the platform which affirms the Fugitive Slave Law.

During the following years *to spit upon the platform* becomes a common phrase, meaning either to disagree violently with a platform or to make light of platform statements and campaign promises. Oc-

casional protests about the crudeness of the phrase did not hurt its popularity.

1852 *Cleve. Plain Dealer* 16 July 2/1. Greeley spits on the Whig platform, Webb expectorates on the Whig candidate, and Medill says that "Scott could have torn open the jaws of Gen. Jackson and spit down his throat" if he had chosen to do so.
1852 Lincoln *Works* II.14...but where among his [Douglas'] millions of friends can a single one be found who is supporting him because he understands him to defy, and spit upon, the Whig platform?
1852 Julian *Recoll.* 35...thus anticipating the sickly political morality of 1852, when so many men of repute tried in vain to save both their consciences and their party orthodoxy by "spitting upon the platform and swallowing the candidate who stood upon it."
1852 Blaine *Twenty Years* I.104. Supporting the candidate and spitting on the platform became the expressive if inelegant watchword of many Northern Whigs.
1856 *Middletown* (N.Y.) *Banner of Liberty* 13 Aug. 258/3. Whilst a number of the Know Nothing party and presses of the South have given in their adhesion to the Philadelphia platform, there is a very respectable number of them that refuse to swallow it, and some go so far as to "spit upon it," as a cunningly devised trick to get them in alliance with the Black Republicans.
1876 *Cinc. Enquirer* 3 July 4/6. Some Western Democrats are disposed to pick out some planks of the platform and spit upon them.

spoils (-men, party, system).

See SPOILS (TO THE VICTOR BELONG THE).

1826 Cobbett *Hist. of the Reformation* 31 [*OED*]. Away with this shameful calumny, the sole object of which is, and always has been, to secure a quiet possession of the spoils of the Catholic church, and of the poor.

1835 Crockett *Van Buren* 58. His views reach no higher than . . . to hold out "the spoils of victory" as a temptation to membership, to perfect a party drill.
1839 in *Cong. Globe* App. 374/3. These are the men who live by the trade of politics. Their object and their aim is self-aggrandizement. They go for the "spoils" of office.
1840 in Norton *Tippecanoe* App. 7.
  While Martin on his downy bed
  Could dream of naught but spoils.
1863 *N. Y. Trib.* 24 Jan. 3/1. How memory paints the future of their dreams and how the "stealings," or "spoils," as it is now more mildly drawn, fill up the foreground.
1871 Schurz in *Gt. Deb.* IX.311. You have learned that the offices of the Government are mere "spoils," "public plunder," that . . . they are regarded as conquests, the conquest of a party; as "berths". . . . And you have learned more: how current these words "spoils" and "plunder" have become in the mouths of the people, so that we have lost all senses of their fearful meanings.

spoilsmen.

1840 in Norton *Tippecanoe* App. 19.
See the spoilsmen and leg treasurers, treas, treas,
All in a stew,
For well they know they stand no chance
With Tippecanoe, etc.
1840 *Ib.* App. 20.
Reform the reformers and sweep out corruption,
Let tyrants and spoilsmen, with faces of gloom,
Hear the rumblings and throes of the earthquakes eruption,
The voice of a nation deciding their doom.

spoils party.

1836 in *Mangum Papers* V.605. The party has acquired the appropriate and significant appellation of "the spoils party."
1840 in *Cong. Globe* App. 426/2. "The spoils party"; and what would the hungry Federal office seekers be, if they were to get all the offices and spoils! would they not be "the spoils party" too. . . .
1840 *Georgia Jrnl.* 7 Jan. 3/3. We have nailed to our "masthead" the name of one more to be revered . . . than either the candidate of the "Spoils party" or the hero of Tippecanoe. . . .

spoils system.

1838 in *Cong. Globe* App. 378/3 . . . if I should tell you that these defalcations constitute a portion of the "spoils system" —that system which has been to this Administration what his flowing locks were to Samson—the secret of his strength; if I should tell you all this, I should tell you no more than I conscientiously believe.
1838 in Mayo *Pol. Sketches of Wash.* 40. Mr. Jefferson . . . authorized a friend to compromise with the federalists for . . . a guarantee against the spoils system.

spoils, to the victor belong the.

A. Although there are many connotations of *spoils* in American politics, the dominant one is that referring to the Roman plunder of war. This is particularly clear in the following:
1830 J. S. Johnson in *Cong. Deb.* 299/2. The country is treated as a conquered province, and the offices distributed among the victors, as the spoils of the war.

B. Marcy's use of the phrase *to the victor belong the spoils* in the debate over the nomination of Van Buren as minister to England was responsible for the great vogue of the phrase and for its application to the Democratic party in particular.
1832 *Cong. Deb.* 1325. If they [politicians] are successful, they claim, as a matter of right, the advantages of success. They see nothing wrong in the rule, that to the victor belong the spoils of the enemy.
1832 *Niles' Reg.* 1 Sept. 8/2 [following

the account of Marcy's speech]. Judge McLean, who retired from the place of postmaster general because he would not be an agent in giving to the victor the spoils of the enemy—alias, dismiss persons from office for opinions's sake ... said. ...

1838 in *Cong. Globe* App.383/2. Since the avowal of that unprincipled and barbarian motto that "to the victors belong the spoils," office, which was intended for the use and benefit of the people, has become but the plunder of the party.

1840 Clay in Norton *Tippecanoe* 202. If we acted on the avowed and acknowledged principle of our opponents, "that the spoils belong to the victors," we should indeed be unworthy of the support of the people.

In later examples the phrase is given a much wider application:

1889 Farmer *Americanisms* 508. "To the victor belong the spoils" is apparently the watch-word of most American politicians.

1899 in Werner *Tammany Hall* 336. To the party belong the spoils.

spot resolutions.

Historians (e.g. Beveridge, II. 132) frequently use this designation for the resolutions Lincoln introduced in the House on December 22, 1847:

1847 Lincoln in *Gt. Deb.* II.374. First. Whether the spot on which the blood of our citizens was shed, as in his message declared, was or was not within the territory of Spain, at least after the treaty of 1819 until the Mexican Revolution. Second. Whether that spot. ... Third. Whether that spot. ...

No contemporary use of *spot resolution* has been found; however, *spotty resolutions* occurs along with a great number of other derisive uses of *spot* and *spotty*.

1848 *Bellevue Adv.* in Beveridge *Lincoln* II.135. Resolved, that Abe Lincoln, the author of the "Spotty" resolutions in Con-

gress against his own country—may they be long remembered by his constituents, but may they cease to remember him, except to rebuke him.

1848 *Ill. St. Reg.* in Riddle *Congressman Abraham Lincoln* 38. Therefore henceforth will this Benedict Arnold of our district be known here only as the Ranchero Spotty of one term.

1848 *Ill. St. Reg.* in *Ib.* 37. This fever does not prevail to any very alarming extent in Illinois. The only case we have heard of that is likely to prove fatal, is that of poor "spotty Lincoln," of this state. This "spotty" gentleman had a severe attack of the "spotted fever" in Washington City not long since. ... We have not heard of any other person in Washington being on the "spotted list"—and it is probable that the disease died with the patient.—What an epitaph: "Died of the *Spotted Fever.*" Poor Lincoln!

Evidently these slurs had not lost their efficacy at the time of the Lincoln-Douglas debates:

1858 *Chic. Times* in Sparks *Deb.* 190. He [Lincoln] lost all his natural powers, and it was discovered that whenever he moved about the stand there was a leak from the roof or elsewhere. The leak seemed to be confined to the "spot" where Lincoln stood.

spotted pig party.

A faction of the Democratic party during the campaign of 1836. [ ]

1836 *Western Hemisphere* 10 Aug. 3/1. Judge White, as the chosen of "the spotted pig party," (so aptly christened from his speech in which he described a renegade, by way of showing that he never could become one) ....

1836 *Castigator* 17 Aug. 2/4. The late election in Louisiana, has resulted in the total route of the White spotted pig party.

See WHOLE HOG.

spread-eagle.

The spread eagle symbol used on the official seal of the United States on coins, flags, etc. is of course a fertile topic of 4th of July speeches and similar oratory. It is also popular as the mast-head of newspapers and on banners used in election parades.

1840 in Norton *Tippecanoe* 264. The second (banner), a spread-eagle on white ground bearing in its talons, "Harrison and Reform," and underneath the celebrated watchwords of the Emperor Constantine, "In Hoc Signo Vinces."
1840 *Cinc. Gazette* 3 Oct. 2/4. The Mississippi Delegation came next. Her banner was a Spread Eagle, with Shield and a stalk of Cotton in its talons.
1868 *Wash. Morning Chron.* 9 Jan. 2/3. Dick Merrick, of Ill.... exhumed one of his old 4th of July orations, which he delivered in regular spread-eagle style.

Very early the spread eagle takes on a more pointed political meaning as a symbol of territorial expansion.

1807 *Nat. Intelligencer* 16 Jan. Robert Fulton toasted the American eagle's spreading wings.
1823 Holcombe and Skinner *Hendricks* 31. ... we have seen ... the eagle of liberty expand his wings over a sister continent [South America].

Shortly before the Civil War spreadeagleism became the hallmark of the tendencies of Young America (q.v.) as expressed in *SpreadEagleism* by G. F. Train (New York, 1859). From this book we quote:

88. Our former townsman, Mr. G. F. Train, has recently made a tremendous spread-eagle speech in England. [from *Boston Gazette,* 1856?]
vii. The Illustrated London News gives me a column and a half on Young America. The editor thinks I shall make no more books. Perhaps I should have followed his suggestion, had he not furnished me with a title for another: "Spread-Eagleism."
xiv ... spread-eagleism, which is only a modern word for the Monroe doctrine.

These tendencies identified with rabid patriotism were continued in uses in which the American was compared to the eagle spreading his wings as a symbol of prowess:

1862 Bob Hart *Plantation Songster* 13. All you'ver got to do is to come to the polls, put your tickets in the box, an' like the American Eagle which roosted on the head of Queen Victoria, we'll spread our wings and shout to the bammy breezes, "Mustum in parrofacit perse!"
1874 Nichols *Am. Life* 484. With all his glorifications and spread-eagleism, the American has much less of calm conceit and solid self-satisfaction than his insular progenitor.

The popularity of *spread-eagle* is attested by its use in other fields. Its application to ministerial oratory—

1858 *Harper's W.* 28 Aug. The sermon was a splendid failure,—a much ado about nothing,—and is yet laughed at as the "Spread Eagle sermon."—

may have been influenced by references to such Biblical passages as Jeremiah 48:40.

For thus saith the Lord; Behold, he shall fly as an eagle, and shall spread his wings over Moab.

The idea of bombast and high-flown ventures was also carried over into the commercial world where we find *spread-eagle* referring to a particular kind of speculator:

1870 Medbery *Men of Wall Street* 86. One modification of this is the Spread Eagle, formerly a highly popular style of speculation with capitalists who had plenty of money and a wide awake broker.

square deal.

A slogan characterizing the administration policies of Theodore Roosevelt.

In his *Autobiography* Lincoln Steffens gives the following account of a conversation between Theodore Roosevelt and himself:
506. I accused him of this superficiality once during his first term, when he was keeping his promise to carry out McKinley's policies. That was his excuse for doing "nothing much." He was "being good" so as to be available for a second term.

"You don't stand for anything fundamental," I said, and he laughed. He was sitting behind his desk; I was standing before it. He loved to quarrel amiably with his friends, and it was hard to hit him. So now, to get in under his guard and land on his equanimity, I said with all the scorn I could put into it, "All you represent is the square deal."

"That's it," he shouted, and rising to his feet, he banged the desk with his hands. "That's my slogan: the square deal. I'll throw that out in my next statement. The square deal." And he did.

What did he care how I meant and used it? He knew how it would be taken; he felt in his political sense how all kinds of people would take it as an ideal, as a sufficient ideal, and out he threw it; and he was right. "A square deal," a phrase shot at him in reproach and criticism, he seized upon and published as his war cry; and a good one, as it proved.

Roosevelt himself used the phrase countless times:
1903 *Works* XVIII. We must see that each is given a square deal, because he is entitled to no more and should receive no less.
1907 *Ib.* XXII.560. When I say "square deal," I mean a square deal to every one. . . .
1910 *Ib.* XIX.16. I stand for the square deal. But when I say that I am for the square deal, I mean not merely that I stand for fair play under the present rules of the game. . . .

However, neither Steffens nor Roosevelt invented the term, as it is found in the political vocabulary much earlier:
1878 *Puck* 6 March 3/1. The Silver Bill has passed. But it was not a square deal.
1879 *Ib.* 16 July 2912. What we ask is for fair play—for a square deal, between man and men.
1893 Champ Clark in *Cong. Record* 2667/1. What I want is a square deal and a fair "divy" all around.

squatter sovereignty.

In a Senate speech of 27 June, 1848, Calhoun criticizes Cass's theory of "popular sovereignty":
Cong. Globe App. 871/1. The first half-dozen of squatters would become the sovereigns, with full dominion and sovereignty over them; and the conquered people of new Mexico and California would become the sovereigns of the country as soon as they became the territories of the United States, vested with the full right of excluding even their conquerors.

It is among the ironies of history that by this speech the great champion of slavery furnished its opponents a means to offset the suggestive power of the slogan, *popular sovereignty*. But the derogatory term *squatter sovereignty* must have been used before 1852 when Cass said:
1852 *Cong. Globe* 784/2. A few words more, sir, as to California, and what has been called "squatter sovereignty." . . . As to the term . . . one of two things is inevitable: either the people of California had the right to establish a government for themselves, without reference to "squatter sovereignty" or "landlord sovereignty," or. . . .

The term continued to be used so long as the conflict over slavery in the territories remained an issue:

1854 *N. Y. Trib.* 18 Feb. Whenever these men are pressed on the point of whether they mean to reorganize the rights of the people of the territories, they invariably turn up their noses at the suggestion, repudiate the idea, and derisively characterize it as "squatter sovereignty."

1858 *Marshall* (Mich.) *Statesman* 28 July 2/2. At that time, Judge Douglas and James Buchanan, not relishing the homely name "squatter" given it by Cass, had it baptized and christened with the ad captandum euphonious and beautiful name of "Popular Sovereignty."

1858 Lincoln at Quincy in Sparks *Deb.* 431. Judge Douglas has sung paeans to his "popular sovereignty" doctrine until his Supreme Court, cooperating with him, has squatted his squatter sovereignty out. But he will keep up this species of humbuggery about squatter sovereignty. He has at last invented this sort of do-nothing sovereignty—that the people may exclude slavery by a sort of "sovereignty" that is exercised by doing nothing at all. Is not that running his popular sovereignty down awfully? . . . The Dred Scott decision covers the whole ground, and while it occupies it, there is no room even for the shadow of a starved pigeon to occupy the same ground.

1859 *Xenia* (Ohio) *Torchlight* 7 Sept. 1/4. Then we had Douglas' wonderful "Squatter Sovereignty"; Brandeth's Pills were nothing in comparison.

1863 Heartsill *1491 Days* 102. Bob and I was compelled to abandon our Squatter Sovereignty principles, and turn over our pre-emption rights to the ship carpenters.

stab in the back.

To attack treacherously:

1863 in Sandburg *War Years* II.423. Shall men [Northern "rebel" leaders] who are getting rich off the Government patronage, who sleep quietly and peacefully in their beds because we watch here in the cold and wet, stab us in the back and denounce us?

1878 *Harper's W.* 10 Aug. 626/2. The prostitution of their [officers of the custom House] patronage to the service of any man is a "blow," and "a foul blow," "an insult," "a treachery," "a defiance," "a stab in the back," "an outrage," and "a persecution," toward all the people for whose benefit the office exists.

1888 Barnum in Eli Perkins *Thirty Years of Wit* 131 . . . because I love those noble Democrats who, when we were soldiering, cursed old Abe Lincoln and stabbed us in the back.

It is uncertain whether there is any connection with the German *Dolchstoss in den Rücken,* a phrase used to describe the effect of the Revolution of 1918 on the army.

See KNIFE, FIRE IN THE REAR, TOMA-HAWK.

stalking horse.

Not, as may be assumed, a metaphor of the turf, but of the hunt. The stalking horse was originally a horse trained to offer concealment to its rider so that he could get within close range of his quarry; later a portable device was substituted for the horse. (See *OED*) Thus the phrase designated an issue or a person that served as a screen or camouflage.

1777 Moore *Ballads of the Revolution* 170.
Religion too is often made
A stalking horse to drive the trade.

1800 Bishop *Connecticut Republicanism* 50. Multitudes of rational men are for destroying that kind of religion which is made a foot-ball or stalking horse, and which operates only to dishonor God and ruin man.

1846 *Niles' Reg.* 2 May 129/2. The 54–40 doctrine is a mere stalking horse.

1866 *Harper's W.* 226/2. He [Johnson] must know that they would willingly use him as a wedge to split the Union party, as a stalking horse to their own purposes,

as a spring-board to leap into power.
1872 in Nevins *Fish* 598. I look upon him
[Greeley] as the stalking horse of the
secessionists.
1880 *N. Y. World* 25 June 4/2. A great
body of men in earnest do not care to
waste their time in watching transparent
and trifling tricks of men who advance
successive stalking horses to conceal their
real purposes.
1912 LaFollette *Autobio.* 586. My answer
was that my candidacy should not be
made a shield and cover for Roosevelt;
that if he was to be a candidate, he
should come out in the open; that I
would never consent to be a stalking
horse for Roosevelt or any other man.

The special meaning cited in
Smith, *Dictionary of American
Politics,* seems to be of comparatively recent origin:
A candidate who is put forward by the
party organization or in the interest of
another candidate, for the purpose of
dividing the opposition, and who with-
draws when the purpose is accomplished.

stalwart.
Attested in American political
usage since 1856:
1856 *Ohio St. Jrnl.* 24 Oct. 2/2. The mil-
lenium of politics came upon us—the
straight waistcoat of the bigotted in nationalism and religion has been stretched
so as to compass the stalwart form of the
demagogue, whose hopes of victory lay on
the humbugging process by which he
could gather in the Irishmen and the
priest ridden.
1864 Adams *Emery A. Storrs* 4 July 45.
... the cause of the Union, the cause of
good government everywhere, upheld by
the strong arms of the stalwart sons of
the Northwest, thank God, moves gloriously and nobly on.

It gained political importance
through a letter by Blaine to the
Boston Herald, in which he objected to Hayes's southern policy.

1877 *N. Y. Trib.* 12 April 5/5. Boston,
April 11. The Herald will publish the
following tomorrow: To the Editor of the
Herald: ... I trust also that both Governors [Packard and Chamberlain] know
that the Boston Press no more represents
the stalwart Republican feeling of New
England on the pending issues than the
same press did when it demanded the enforcement of the Fugitive Slave law in
1851. Very respectfully, J. G. Blaine.
Augusta, Me., April 10, 1877.
1881 *Nation* 16 June 415/2. The epithet
"Stalwart" as applied to a class of politicians was first used by Mr. Blaine in 1877
to designate those Republicans who were
unwilling to give up hostility and distrust
of the South as a political motive. In the
present contest at Albany it has by a curious transformation been appropriated by
the followers of Mr. Conkling to distinguish politicians faithful to his Machine.
...All reference to the South has
dropped out of the term. In fact, the
Albany row is everyday adding to the
political nomenclature.

The word, according to *OED,* re-
juvenated by Walter Scott, an author highly valued by Blaine (cf.
Gail Hamilton, *James G. Blaine,*
p. 191), was taken up by his followers and probably helped on its
way by the ridicule cast on it by
his enemies. [ ]
1878 *Nation* 30 May 350/1 ... he [Hayes]
will soon dismiss the odious Schurz and
the renegade Key, and put "stalwart" men
in their places.
1878 *Harper's W.* 6 July 526/2. Strange as
it may seem, although the general
[Butler] is asserted to be one of the most
stalwart of Republicans, there are a great
many sincere, original and unswerving
Republicans who would vote against any
Republican candidate, however regularly
nominated, if they knew that he was a
stalwart Republican of the Butler brand.
1878 *Ib.* 13 July 546/4. The Iowa platform
is called stalwart and radical.
1878 *Ib.* 20 July 566/2. Now he [Butler]

and his friends are nothing if not party men. They are described with unction as "stalwart" Republicans.

1878 *Nation* 19 Dec. 378/1. Mr. Blaine's speech on Wednesday week in the Senate had at least the merit of bringing out the true nature of the Southern difficulty as it lies in the mind of that section of the Republican party known as "Stalwarts."

1879 *Harper's W.* 1 March 162/1. The party has thus chilled and alienated an important if not vital support, and some of its members seem to have supposed that its power might be retained by describing those who especially sustained the errors by which it was weakened as "stalwarts." Meanwhile the painful and obvious truth is that the party is not so stalwart as it was. . . .

1879 *N. Y. Trib.* 5 June 4/6. It will be a tremendous chorus of stalwart Republican music. . . .

1880 *Punch* 19 May 185/1.

There was an old stalwart named Blaine,
Who hailed from the region of Maine.
  When he felt badly hurt
  He would cry "Bloody Shirt"—
And slay over the already slain.

1881 *N. Y. Trib.* 28 May 4/4. The advocates of the Hayes policy immediately [in 1877] tossed the word "stalwart" back and forth in terms of ridicule, and made merry over it, as they thought, at Mr. Blaine's expense. As usual, Mr. Blaine stood his ground, and his phrase soon took its place in the political nomenclature of the day.

The proposal of a third term for Grant brought about a narrowing of the term in that its advocates limited *stalwart* to a degree that even excluded the original user of the word:

1878 *Nation* 4 July 1/1. It [the convention] was made the means by the Illinois "Stalwarts" of bringing forward Illinois' Favorite Son, Gen. Grant, as a party candidate for 1880.

1878 *Ohio St. Jrnl.* 12 Aug. 2/3. Yet the stalwart Grant Republicans denounced

the present President for doing precisely what the late President proposed to do.

1879 *Nation* 27 Nov. 355. There is a most painful doubt spreading among the Stalwarts as to whether General Grant is a Stalwart after all.

1880 *Cleve. Leader* 31 May 1/4. The Sherman men, Blaine men and Edmunds men are all stalwarts; why should they not support Grant?

1881 Hayes *Diary* 23 Oct. IV.48. Most of them are malignant Stalwarts.

1881 *Nation* 29 Dec. 506. If, as is thought by some of President Arthur's friends as well as his opponents, it is his purpose to turn the old third-term or "Stalwart" faction, which now forms only a small minority of the party, into a majority. . . .

1884 *Harper's W.* 716/2. Mr. Blaine was [in 1880] the leader of the Half-Breed Republican faction as General Grant was the chief of the Stalwarts.

1884 *N. Y. Trib.* 3 Jan. 4/3 . . . while the Stalwarts were indeed stalwart, they were not the only ones entitled to that designation, which was first used in a letter to the Tribune, by a Republican, who was not a so-called Stalwart in a broad sense and not a factional one.

Quite commonly historical works consider *stalwart* and *half-breed* as contrasting words. They were so only after the beginning of 1881 (see HALF-BREED). The theory that both terms were coined by Conkling (Chidsey, *Gentleman from New York,* p. 277) is incorrect.

At the beginning of the twentieth century *stalwart* was revived in Wisconsin where it applied to the opponents of the LaFollette party:

1901 in LaFollete *Autobio.* 242. The newspapers on the morning of January 9th contained the startling announcement that the "Stalwart" Republicans (as the machine element of the party now for the first time called themselves) were in control of the senate and that they proposed to fight the administration measures. **1904** *Cleve. Leader* 18 June 1/2. The "stalwarts," so-called, were opposed to the La Follette men.... John Olin ... made the first speech for the "stalwarts," the Anti-La Follette side.

stampede.

A sudden rush to the support of a candidate or a measure.

A. The Mexican-Spanish *estampida* meaning "the rush of panic-stricken cattle" is found in various forms in the early 19th century, popularized by the growing interest in the territory of the Southwest.

1826 *Va. Herald* 14 Oct. 2/1. Instantly this prodigious multitude ... took what the Spanish call the "stompado."
1834 *U. S. Exec. Doc.* 2nd Sess. 23 Cong. I.74. A stupid sentinel last night ... alarmed the camp and set off in a stampedo the rest of the horses.

B. As a political metaphor *stampede* is first used to describe a rush or panic caused by a critical event:

1846 in *Cong. Globe* 549/1. Who had forgotten the perfect panic we were in on the Thursday before she [the *Cambria*] sailed? It was a sort of senatorial *stampede*. It was contagious.
1860 E. Kirby Smith in Nevins *Lincoln* II.130. Was not the stampede of the Southern students from Northern colleges a beautiful thing.
1856 *Greenville* (Ohio) *Jrnl.* 30 July 1/4. Nothing but party discipline prevents a perfect democratic stampede in New Hampshire.

C. However, at almost the same time the term was used in a sense in which the action toward was the important element of the rush.

1854 *N. Y. sw. Trib.* 24 Nov. 4/1 ... all attempts, by reason or argument, to stay the stampede toward the Mysterious

Order, are as futile as they would be in stopping a prairie-fire.
1855 *San Diego D. Union* 1 July 2/4. The Stampede in Tennessee [for Know-Nothingism] [head].
1881 *N. Y. World* 3 Feb. 1/6. The [N.Y.] Assembly was stampeded today into passing the Anti-Telegraph Consolidation bill.

D. This latter development resulted in the specific political meaning which is still the predominant one in politics: a rush in a convention to the support of a particular man.

1872 in Lloyd *H. Dem. Lloyd* I.32. A furor, artificial at first, became real and ended in a stampede, which resulted in the nomination of Mr. Greeley.
1876 *N. Y. Times* 10 June 1/1. It is well known that many nominations, both in State and national Conventions, have been made by what is known as stampedes. A candidate runs ahead of all competitors, but while yet far short of the required number of votes, some County or State which has not kept tally supposes the Plurality man to be nominated, and wishing to be on the winning side changes to him.
1880 *N. Y. Trib.* 26 May 4/5. That hoped-for third-term stampede didn't reach Louisiana, evidently.
1880 *Cleve. Plain Dealer* 9 June 1/1. As state after state *stampeded* from Blaine and Sherman to Garfield the wildest excitement reigned in the hall.
1880 *N. Y. Trib.* 24 June 4/2. They raise a suspicion, however, that an attempt will be made to-day to stampede the Convention for the "old ticket".…
1888 *N. Y. Trib.* 15 June. Mr. Smith was asked whether he looked for the nomination of Blaine after all by a sudden outbreak of feeling, as is so often predicted. He said he did not. In any event it would not be a stampede.
1922 Morgenthau *Life-time* 147. In three quarters of an hour we had corralled our delegates safely out of the path of the Clark stampede. They sat immovable in the face of the frenzy of the crowd. When

the Clark demonstration had subsided, and the next ballot was taken, the Clark managers had a rude awakening: the result was practically unchanged.

stand on the record.

In campaign oratory, to point to good actions of the past or to re-affirm one's belief in those meas-ures or policies.

Probably based upon the older phrase to *stand upon the platform* (see PLATFORM), but surely influ-enced by the change of names of the official accounts of Congress to *The Congressional Record,* often called merely, *The Record* (see *DA*).

1904 *Omaha Bee* 16 Aug. 4. The republi-can campaign book stands upon...a record of promises made good.

1924 La Follette in White *Politics* 321. I am a candidate upon the basis of my public record....I shall stand upon that record exactly as it is written....

stand pat (stand patter).

To accept the *status quo.*

On February 28, 1896, Speaker Joe Cannon said:

Cong. Record 2268. The proposition was fought bitterly in the House; but the Senate stood, if the gentlemen will allow me the expression, pat;...[Johnson]... why should not the House "stand pat" as the Senate did?

The introduction of this poker term into politics thus can not be attributed to Mark Hanna, al-though his use of the phrase in 1902 is responsible for its popu-larity:

1902 *Cleve. Plain Dealer* 28 Sept. 1/7. [Reporting Hanna's speech the preced-ing day at Akron.] About a year ago it was my privilege to attend the opening meet-ing of the Republican party, and after

thinking and looking over the situation, I came to the conclusion—"Let well enough alone." That was the whole chapter: that is all there was in the campaign of interest to you. Now I say stand pat.

The following discussion shows that the term was still not well enough known to pass without a word of explanation:

1902 *Cleve. Plain Dealer* 29 Sept. 4/2. The player "stands pat" when he declines to discard from his hand, and draw other cards, and the supposed earning quality of such a hand is superior to that of three aces. According to the rules of the game it is perfectly honest, however, for a player to hold a pat hand when it has little or no value, and if successful in scaring his opponents into laying down their hands he wins the bank or "pot." This is, we are informed, called a "bluff." Thus it will be seen that Dr. Hanna in his Akron speech invented a singularly appropriate figure of political speech.

Hanna in *Cinc. Enquirer* 3 Oct. 6/4. "When I told the people to 'stand pat' it was merely to use a familiar saying to express the situation," he said. "I have been told that this is a phrase used in the game of poker; but everybody under-stands it just the same...."

Ib. 6 Oct. 4/1. Senator Hanna probably got the suggestion of his "stand pat" speech from some fellow who played poker; but the Senator didn't know that, of course.

The term later became a synonym for *conservative republican* and *reactionary:*

1909 Butt *Taft and Roosevelt* I.140. It looks as if the Aldrich school and the standpatters in the House were in abso-lute control.

1911 *Rev. of Rev.* XLIII.339/2. Socialism is now impossible just as the old stand-pat reactionism is impossible.

1916 Wilson *New Freedom* 33, 45. The American people are not naturally stand-patters. Progress is the word that charms their ears and stirs their hearts.... The

stand-patter doesn't know there is a procession.
1920 *Ltrs. of William A. White* 204 ... a lot of old high-binder standpatters who haven't had an idea since the fall of Babylon. ...
1960 *Time* 11 April 28/1. Stand-pat, hold-the-line thinking is not enough to meet the great challenges confronting the American people at home and abroad.

star chamber.

Secret, inquisition-like proceedings. Abolished in England in 1641, the Court of the Star Chamber had become notorious during the reigns of James I and Charles I for its injustice and oppressiveness:
1655 Fuller *Ch. History* IX.187 [*OED*]. The most sturdy and refractory Nonconformists ... were brought into the Star-Chamber, the power whereof was above dispute.
1764 Churchill *Gotham* II.490 [*OED*]. Curs'd Star-Chambers made, or rul'd the law.

In America:
1700 *Virginia Gazette* 22 March in Miller *Origins of Am. Revolution* 305. A libell curse on the Star Chamber law.
1735 in Moss *Am. Metropolis* II.38 [Zenger trial]. These are Star Chamber cases, and I was in hopes that practice dead had been with the Court.
1907 in *Gt. Deb.* XI.323. Letters from a number of Federal Judges have come to me approving this bill, stating that ... star-chamber proceedings ought to be stopped. ...
1912 Taft in Rosewater *Back Stage* 31 May 90. But it is important that the public should know that there are no star chamber proceedings and that they shall have access to the evidence upon which you act, through the newspapers.

starvation wages.

A phrase of labor or liberal groups implying that wages are not high enough for proper sustenance.

A. As an effective slogan against Business, *starvation wages* may be better explained by a brief look at the interesting history of *starvation*. This term—the second noun added to the English vocabulary by compounding *ation* with a native English verb—was created in connection with a bill in 1775 by which England wanted to counter the rebellion in America by, in effect, starving the Colonies. Thus *starvation* was a word for an aggressive action, withholding food. [See *OED;* M. M. Mathews, *Beginnings of Am. Engl.* 87.]
1778 in *Ann. Reg. Characters* 204 [*OED*]. Behold our ministers ... who talk of peace, of taxes, and starvation.
1791–3 in *Spirit Publ. Jrnls.* 1.260 [*OED*]. *Starvation.* A curious experiment, which, after being tried in America and France, has succeeded tolerably well at home.

B. Starvation wages in American politics.
1874 *N. Y. w. Tribune* 9 Dec. 4/5. Not a school but is besieged by men and women ready to teach at starvation wages. ...
1938 F.D.R. in J. Gould *Homegrown Liberal* 251. We are seeking, of course, only legislation to end starvation wages and intolerable hours.

States Rights Democrat.

Southern Democrat who advocates the supremacy of the rights of the states:
1840 *Rough-hewer* 139/1. There was an immense gathering of state rights democrats at Charleston, S. Carolina.
1858 Bartlett 290. There are two parties in the South, called "National" and "States-Rights" Democrats.

States Rights party.

A Southern Democratic faction:

1833 in *Georgia Jrnl.* 28 April 1840 2/6 [quoting article on meeting at Milledgeville, Georgia, 13 Nov. 1833]. A meeting of persons friendly to States Rights having been called by notice in the Gazettes of this place.... The object of the present meeting is, first to constitute and form one of those associations for the express purpose of counteracting the designs of the Federal party.... To end, they resolve, that the present meeting be organized into an Association, to be denominated "The States Rights Party of Georgia"....

1834 *Reg. of Deb.* III.438. It is the alleged coalition between the national republicans and State rights party.

1840 Webster in Norton *Tippecanoe* 19 Aug. 236. One of the gentlemen of the South, of that nullifying State-Rights party that has absorbed the administration, or been absorbed by it....

1860 *Charleston Merc.* 13 Dec. 3/3. The Picayune ... has heretofore been opposed to the State Rights party.

state socialism.

According to Ladendorf, the German *Staatsozialismus* movement began in the middle 1870's (in 1872 a group of German economists met together at Eisenach to launch the state socialism movement) and in 1877 a newspaper, *Der Staats-sozialist,* was founded to advance their ideas on social reform.

A selective list of American quotations (undoubtedly earlier examples can be found) :

1890 *Contemp. Rev.* LVIII.435,875. State Socialism and Social Reform. State Socialism and Popular Right. [titles of two articles]

1894 Roosevelt *Works* XIV.253. It is to the last degree improbable that State socialism will ever be adopted in its extreme form, save in a few places. It exists, of course, to a certain extent wherever a police force and fire department exist; and the sphere of the State's action may be vastly increased without in any way diminishing the happiness of either the many or the few.

1907 Seitz *Pulitzer* 12 July 315. [A note on Roosevelt's suggestion that a federal receivership be formed for the large tobacco corporations] Receivership colossal. State socialism worse than anything Bryan proposes here, Bebel in Germany, or Jaures in France—worse than anything Debs propounded.

spy ballot.

A phrase used by opponents of the secret ballot.

1888 *N. Y. Trib.* 20 Oct. 6/3. So the Governor [Hill] calls the proposed system the "spy ballot," and seems to think he has coined a name that will bring the idea into popular odium....

stationery.

The alarming extent to which the word *stationery* was used in public accounts in order to cover irregular expenses is discussed in Holst, *Const. History,* II,354n.

1846 Colton *Clay* II.396. [$69,514.78] which, divided among 242 members of the House, shows, that the cost of stationery, for each member of the 25th Congress, for a period usually of about nine months, was $287.25.

A few illustrative examples of the euphemistic qualities of the word:

1837 in Buley *The Old Northwest* 31 Oct. II.233 ... it ["Junto" in Mich.] had allowed Mason $500 for rent and $58 for "stationery" at groggeries.

1853 *N. Y. Trib.* 19 Feb. 4/3. In the House ... the Civil and Diplomatic bill came up again in Committee, where it appeared that the appropriation for the expenses of the two houses of Congress reached upwards of $1,186,000, of which $12,500 are for newspapers, $28,000 for stationery (?) and $10,000 for folding.

1860 *Cleve. Herald* 13 June 2/2. The Democratic prints, among their other falsehoods in reference to "Honest Old Abe," have charged that whilst member of Congress he drew on the Contingent Fund for the value of three pairs of boots, under the head of Stationery.

1860 *Lebanon* (Ohio) *Western Star* 14 June 2/2. The Statesman, Enquirer, and other smaller Democratic sheets, have been charging Lincoln with having three pair of boots charged to the Government in his stationery account while in Congress.

1862 *Cols. Gazette* 9 May 3/3. In the annual report of the receipts and disbursements of the City of Columbus for the year ending April 4, 1862, under the head of Miscellaneous, may be found the following record of the disposition made of a certain portion of the public funds: Paid for cigars for Dayton Zouaves, while aiding as Police Guard in May, 1861, $4. Can it be possible that we have in the public service of our city an official who is not aware that it is a well established rule among politicians, never to let such an item appear in an official report? that when public money is spent by an office holder for Cigars, Whisky, Lager Beer, Schweitzer cheese and the like and an official report is to be made, that the term Stationery shall embrace them all.

1866 Parton *Topics of the Times* 379. Nor can we give details of the manner in which mean men steal from the price of the school-children's copy-books and slate pencils, nor open up the enormous and complicated cheat which is covered by the word "stationery."

1876 *Cinc. Comm.* 17 Aug. 5/2. "Mr. Hanna, Mr. Pry says he didn't get any hardware." "Did you ask him if he got any whiskey? . . . That is what he got and charged it as hardware. Now, my friends, that is what they are calling stationery—knives, gold-pens, pocket-books, and scissors."

stay at home.

Pertaining to those persons who do not exercise their right to vote.

1855 *Marshall* (Mich.) *Dem. Expounder* 6 Dec. 2/1. The New York Day Book dubs this the great "stay-at-home party."

1880 *N. Y. Times* 22 Oct. 1/7 . . . the Republicans will get large accessions from the lukewarm, "stay at home" Republicans as well as from the Democrats.

steal one's thunder.

The origin of this expression is attributed to an anecdote of the Restoration stage. A type of thunder invented by John Dennis for one of his plays was used without permission by a rival company. He is reported to have said: "See, how the rascals use me! They will not let my play run, and yet they steal my thunder!" (See Bartlett, *Quot.*) In American politics politicians have frequently cried that their thunder has been stolen when the opposition claims credit for a popular law or action. An early and widely known usage seems to have centered around Daniel Webster:

1847 in Wilson *Slave Power* II.124. I do not quite consent that they shall undertake to appropriate to themselves all the benefit and honor of it [Wilmot Proviso]. Allow me to say, sir, it is not their thunder.

1850 Douglas in *Ib.* March I.263 . . . in 1847, when Mr. Webster claimed it as his invention, and entered a caveat against its use, as stealing his "thunder."

1852 Parker *Additional Sp.* 117. He [Mason] introduced the Bill. Mr. Webster seized it, made it his "thunder" on the 7th of March, 1850.

1852 in *Gt. Deb.* IV.220 [cartoon]. Webster Stealing Clay's Thunder While Foote Is Talking the Senate to Sleep.

Other examples:

1861 Vallandigham in *Cong. Globe* 453/2. This thunder is not Republican thunder, and the gentleman cannot be allowed to steal it.

1867 in Barnes *Weed* 458 [Weed editorial] ... remembering that in 1828 Tammany Hall took the wind out of the sails of the Clintonian party by making General Jackson, an active Clintonian, its candidate, I determined that the adversary should not steal our thunder a second time.

1874 in *Cong. Record* App.423. Our democratic friends have stolen our thunder—they have gobbled our carpetbaggers.

1907 Bryan *Commoner Condensed* VI.361. They have stolen our thunder—why don't they steal our lightning, and not be satisfied with mere noise?

steamboat election (vote).

Trial elections held on Ohio and Mississippi river boats:

1844 *Niles' Reg.* 25 May 196/2 ... from the common mode of testing the success of candidates for the presidency, to wit—by steamboat elections—he, Smith, will beat all the other aspirants to that office, two to one.

1848 *Old Zack* 19 Aug. 1/4. Straws.—For a while the Locofoco papers ventured to publish steamboat votes. ... A vote was taken on the Steamer Fairmount on her trip to Pittsburg.—This is the vote: Taylor 75, Cass 37, Van Buren 4.

steamroller.

That the steamroller was a center of attention—and thus a likely source of metaphor—is seen from an early description.

1878 in Chamberlain *No Truce* 114. One morning in 1878 the peace of the community was shattered by the appearance of a juggernaut that clattered its way over the unpaved streets with protestations of escaping steam and grinding gears. It was a steam roller, the first to be seen in those parts. The whole town [Auburn, N.Y.] came out to jeer the operator.

The steamroller as a symbol of ruthless convention tactics was

frequently mentioned in newspapers during the weeks preceding the Republican convention in July, 1952. At that time the public was reminded by some writers that the phrase dated back to the convention of 1912 when the Taft forces were accused of using steamroller tactics against the supporters of Theodore Roosevelt; however, the phrase is somewhat older. It seems that it was first applied to the political methods used by Russia:

1902. *Munsey's Mag.* XXVI.489. She [Russia] sought to achieve her end by means of the "steam roller" of the concert of Europe.

1906 *Westminster Gazette* 16 June 15/1. In the Caucasus, as in Finland, she has adopted the steamroller policy, and by crushing national aspirations has estranged possible loyalists.

Mencken's undocumented statement that "the word was invented by Oswald Schuette, Washington correspondent of the *Chicago Inter-Ocean,* to designate the rough devices used to force through the nomination of William H. Taft as the Republican presidential candidate in 1908" may, however, be correct in so far as "invented" can be replaced by "first applied to American politics." From that year we have the cartoons:

1908 in *Rev. of Rev.* XXXVIII.11. [Uncle Sam is shown speaking to Taft, who is seated at the throttle of the "Steamroller" headed down the "Road to Prosperity." Uncle Sam says, "If you can smooth out this road, William, I can rest easy."]

1908 *Ib.* XXXVIII.165. The Prohibitionist "Steamroller."

Neither of these cartoons refers to convention politics, but in *Back*

Stage Victor Rosewater states, in reference to the 1912 convention: 92. It was over the operation of this rule that the howl about "the steam roller" was originally raised, although the phrase had been used in the same fashion by "the allies" during the contest scrimmages four years earlier, and was kept a-going through the convention.

In 1910 the steamroller turns up as a synonym of *big stick:*

1910 *N. Y. Times* 29 Sept. He [Roosevelt] used the steamroller and the big stick when it came to the nomination.

1910 in La Follette *Autobio.* 650. Once in control they would be able to steam-roll Roosevelt's nomination.

1910 *Ib.* 658. Whether one is on top of or under the steamroller influences somewhat one's point of view.

A poem from the *Baltimore Sun* (quoted in Rosewater, 93) shows the popularity of the term:

The Steam Roller
Oh, they threw the throttle open
And they jammed 'er full of coke
And they watched 'er as she gathered up
    her steam.
A lot o' men were hopin'
That she wouldn't stir a stroke
When they jerked the rope and let the
    whistles scream.

Some parts of her were shattered
And her flues were full of soot
And the rivets rattled loosely in her
    frame.
She was rusty. She was battered.
But she gave a mighty toot
And the old machine was working just
    the same!

During the first Franklin D. Roosevelt campaign the word comes into frequent use again on the Democratic side, when the adherents of Roosevelt were accused of steamroller tactics. Describing a committee meeting of 1931, Jim Farley says:

Behind the Ballots 76. The opponents . . . were led by Senator Joseph T. Robinson, Senate Democratic Leader, who delivered a sizzling attack on Raskob in which he accused the chairman of attempting to steam-roller the party.

1960 *Time* 11 April, 29/1. Liberal, Manhattan-rooted Rocky had steamrollered upstate Conservative Walter Joseph Mahoney out of the G.O.P. gubernatorial nomination.

step across the platform.

A euphemism for *spit upon the platform* (q.v.) .

1876 in Garfield *Works* 29 July II.374. We denounced the platform upon the instant, and took what care we could that Lamar's speeches upon his national reputation should not ruin our canvass. We called upon the people to "step across the platform". . . .

still hunt.

A campaign characterized by secrecy and undercover maneuvering. [See *Am. Sp.,* XXVII, Oct. 1952, 160ff.]

A. As a type of hunting which called for great stealth, stillhunting was not highly regarded by some sportsmen, who felt an unfair advantage was being taken of the animals.

Frank Forester *The Deerstalker* 46. "They wun't have no huntin' here nohow, 'Less it's still-huntin'."

1833 Crockett *Eccentricities* 67. *Still hunting* is with all hunters a favorite amusement. . . . There are many modes practiced by a wary hunter of approaching game, even in an open field, which are attended with success. One will steal up while it is feeding—remaining perfectly still, and personating a stump when it becomes the least alarmed. . . . The object which he wishes to shoot becomes familiarized to the stump, as it supposes, and the hunter approaches as near as he wishes. . . .

1839 C. F. Hoffman *Wild Scenes in the Forest and Prairie* I.87. The Deer-stalkers, or "Still-hunters" as they are called in this part of the country, are very inveterate against those who hound the deer.

B. An occasional metaphorical use may be found in politics before 1876.

1844 *Frankfort Commonwealth* 15 Oct. 3/1. The Locos are perfectly organized and ready. They are operating secretly— engaged in what they call *still-hunting* and *bush-whacking.*

C. In the Hayes-Tilden campaign *still hunt* becomes one of the chief epithets hurled against the Tilden forces. The Democratic campaign manager, Abram S. Hewitt, who hoped to win praise for Tilden's investigations of the Tweed Ring, said:

1876 *Cong. Record* 14 Aug. 5654/b. Governor Tilden for more than three years, like a sleuth-hound upon the scent, followed these people patiently, secretly, diligently. . . . I know how he tracked these people to their dens of iniquity and finally dragged them forth to public execration.

Almost immediately Republican speakers and writers, recognizing the possible derogatory connotations of such undercover activities, turned the phrase against Tilden:

1876 *N. Y. Trib.* 28 Aug. 4/4. It will be well for the Republican managers to bear in mind that a "still hunt" is Gov. Tilden's favorite campaign method.
1876 *Cinc. Comm.* 13 Sept. 4/1. The managers of the Democracy did not feel that even with their solid South, securely held with pocket pistols, they could afford to lose the October States, and Tilden set about to console himself and prepare for victory by a "still hunt" in Vermont and Maine.

In Nast cartoons:

1876 *Harper's W.* 9 Sept. 733. Governor Tilden's Democratic "Wolf (Gaunt and Hungry") and the Goat (Labor) . [Quotes passage from Hewitt's speech.]
1876 *Ib.* 16 Sept. 764. No "still hunt" Mr. Tilden.
1876 *Ib.* 23 Sept. 769. "Still Hunt"-ing. [title] "Like a hound upon the Scent." [Tilden as a fox hunter on a "Usufruct Reform" hobby horse.]
1876 *Ib.* 30 Sept. 789. An "Aggressive" "Still Hunt." "Governor Tilden has for years, like a hound on the scent, followed the members of the Ring patiently, secretly, and diligently,"—Mr. Hewitt.

However, a widening of meaning is indicated by its references to other campaigns and personalities:

1876 *N. Y. Trib.* 30 Aug. 4/6. The "still hunt" has begun in Ohio. The *Cleveland Leader* has caught sight of the "barrel" of money and raises the alarm.
1876 *Cinc. Comm.* 15 Sept. 4/2. The still hunt with the pocket-pistol in behalf of the Democratic candidates will be thoroughly done in the Solid South.
1878 *Indianapolis Jrnl.* in *Cinc. Enquirer* 17 Oct. 4/8. Those Republicans who went on a still-hunt are still hunting.
1880 *N. Y. Trib.* 6 May 4/4. The briskest thing in politics now is Tilden's still hunt.
1884 *Harper's W.* 1 Nov. 716/1. Indeed, the campaign of the voters who will decide the election has not been a "still hunt" but a silent reading and thinking.
1886 Poore *Perley's Rem.* 332. Yet never did a wily politician more industriously plot and plan to secure a nomination than Mr. Buchanan did, in his still-hunt for the Presidency.
1887 *Louisville Courier-Jrnl.* 5 May 4/2. The G.O.P. on a Still Hunt For a National Leader For the Battle. [title]

D. In the intervening years *still hunt* continued to be associated with Tilden:

1878 *N. Y. Trib.* 8 May 4/5. It is an opportune moment to remember that Mr.

Tilden is the inventor of the "still hunt" method of political warfare.

1878 *Harper's W.* 28 Sept. 766/3. Messrs. Tilden and Hendricks and Thurman, with their "still hunts," and the miserable mousing tricks of their agents, and their "straddles" and "somersaults" from "coin" to paper money, and all their breathless eagerness to snatch the prize of the Presidency, are humiliating figures in American public life.

stock.

The political capital of a potential candidate, based both upon his popular appeal and his status with leading politicians.

One of the terms from the sphere of business (see LAME DUCK, etc.) that became popular in American political metaphors in the 1830's.

1836 *Scioto Gazette* 23 March 4/3. The rapid advance of Jackson stock in the political market presented too splendid a speculation to be eluded by such jobbers as the house of Van Buren & Company....

1876 *Cleve. Leader* 17 June 1/4. Hayes stock is strong.

stool pigeon.

A prominent public figure who is used as a decoy to attract voters to a party, just as wooden stool pigeons had been used by hunters to deceive various birds:

1830 *Workingman's Gazette* 1 Dec. 79/2. A wag who keeps an oyster cellar in Newark, advertises, among other things, ... stool pigeons trained to catch voters for the next Presidency.

1841 J. Alliano *Chron. of Ohio.* And Wilson, whom we thought to have made a bait and an enticement even as the idle youths bait and entice the pigeons in the field, even him they deride and hold in scorn, and say of him, "Is he not the stool-pigeon of John the Big and of Sam the Seizer?"

1848 *Ann. of Cleve.* No. 1126. Thus has Horace Greeley his reward, which consists in being made the stool pigeon for Taylorism, hunkerism, in the 6th congressional district of New York.

1876 *Ib.* No. 2803 ... Tilden and his stool pigeons.

1908 W. A. White *Ltrs.* 88 ... all over the River counties they think you (J. L. Bristow) are Long's stool pigeon.

straddle.

To take an equivocal position on an issue or question.

It is clear that the political use of *straddle* rests upon two basic metaphors: *A.* straddling of the fence and *B.* standing with the feet resting on two objects, especially two horses as in the case of the bareback rider. In the following list no attempt is made to separate the metaphorical elements.

1837 Neal *Charcoal Sk.* 133 ... sometimes I was a-one side, sometimes a-t'other, and sometimes I straddled till the election was over, and came up jist in time to jine the hurrah.

1839 *Cinc. Gazette* 24 Jan. 2/2. Upon the matter properly before the Chamber, he [Green] was a little in the sitting a-straddle of a rail vein.

c1842 in *Prenticeana* 110. A writer in the "True Whig" justly represents Mr. Tyler as standing with "a foot on one boat and a foot on the other." The writer forgets to add, that the boats are getting farther and farther apart. Although his Accidency's legs are not of the shortest, his straddle is becoming inconveniently wide. He will soon be as badly split up as his party is.

1848 *Boston Courier* in *Buckeye Eagle* 4 Oct. 1/4. These two planks are so far asunder that we imagine a person must make an uncomfortable straddle of it who attempts to stand upon both.

1858 in Sparks *Deb.* 374. [banner: Douglas riding "Popular Sovereignty" and "Dred Scott" horses.]

1872 *Harper's W.* 527. [cartoon: Greeley as bareback rider.]
1874 *Ann. of Cleve.* No. 2408. It is rumored that Barnum sent his agent to negotiate with the editor of the Herald. The object of this was to exhibit Barnum as the champion straddler; in his act Barnum carries inflation on one shoulder and non-inflation on the other.
1874 *Ib.* No. 2409. The name of the venerable dame [*Herald*] should have been "The Straddler" because she is so constantly on the fence on nearly all important questions.
1875 *Ib.* No. 3240.
There was once a Governor named Hendricks.
Who was celebrated for his end tricks.
His love was immense for a seat on the fence,
This political straddler named Hendricks.
1878 *Harper's W.* 28 Sept. 766/3. Messrs. Tilden and Hendricks and Thurman, with their "still hunts," and the miserable mousing tricks of their agents, and their "straddles" and "somersaults" from "coin" to paper money, and all their breathless eagerness to snatch the prize of the Presidency, are humiliating figures in American public life.
1878 *N. Y. Trib.* 29 March 4/5. Whenever Mr. Randall doesn't straddle a question, he gets on the wrong side of it.
1880 *San Diego Daily Union* 5 Sept. 1/3. For once in his life, therefore, Hendricks didn't straddle. He put both feet down on the wrong side, and tipped the whole party up.
1884 *N. Y. Trib.* 29 March. It [Dem. party] discarded all its distinctive issues but the tariff; and when it was compelled to decide whether it would make an old-fashioned fight upon that . . . it merely straddled the fence.
1896 *Rev. of Rev.* XIV.285. [cartoon: Bryan on "Democracy" and "Populism" donkeys]
1900 *Ib.* XXII.160. [cartoon: D. B. Hill on "Gold Democracy" and "Silver Democracy" donkeys, each going in a different direction]

C. To secure passage of a bill by bi-partisan support:
1905 Phillips *Plum Tree* 33. Such measures are usually "straddled" through a legislature,—that is, neither party takes the responsibility, but the boss of each machine assigns to vote for them all the men whose seats are secure beyond any ordinary assault of public indignation.

The metaphor may have been reinforced by another type of straddling peculiar to the frontier:
1843 Carlton *New Purchase* I.86. This delicate performance of wagons [driving over stumps] is called—straddling, and is done by the rough ones without fear; other vehicles utterly refuse to straddle.

See ON THE FENCE.

straddle bug.
The straddle bug is a long-legged beetle, but it is obvious that the following political metaphor is a pun derived from *straddle* plus (gold) *bug* (q.v.) .
1896 T. B. Reed in Stimpson *Politics* 333. McKinley isn't a gold-bug, McKinley isn't a silver bug, McKinley's a straddle-bug.

straight-out.
The first issue of the *Straight-Out Harrisonian* published at Columbus, Ohio, on May 1, 1840, calls attention to the fact that the terms *straight-out* and *straight-outism* were not known in the political vocabulary before 1840:
1/2. Straight-outism is a new word in our vocabulary. . . . To our Chillicothe brothers belongs the parentage of our new order. . . .
A campaign paper of 1844 further explains the origin of the word:
1844 *Whig Battering Ram* 20 Sept. 2/1. The word straightout, which of late years has become so popular, was originated by a worthy mechanic of Chillicothe, in this

State, by the name of Benjamin Taylor. Soon after the nomination of General Harrison (1839) at the Harrisburg convention, numbers of the former friends of Van Buren, perceiving the superior excellence of his competitor for the Presidency, were induced to unite with the Whig party in advocating his claims.

Mr. Taylor was one of the first to set an example so worthy of imitation. . . . He did this openly, and boldly, and as he declared on that occasion went "for no half way measures"—he left "the foul party Straight-out to join the supporters of the patriotic Harrison."

Ib. 27 Sept. Correction.—In our notice of the derivation of the term Straightout, we inadvertently accredited its origin to one Benjamin Taylor, of Chillicothe. It should have been Benjamin Thompson, a tailor by trade. The latter was the gentleman who first used that popular phrase.

A Democratic paper's definition is a burlesque counterattack against the effectiveness of the straight-outs:

1844 *Ohio Statesman* 8 May 3/3. A friend of ours a day or two since, gave the definition of this word,—"A man who is so drunk that he can't curl up is a straight-out."

There is no lack of evidence from 1840 that *straight-out* referred to former Democrats who were supporting Harrison:

1840 *Tippecanoe Banner* (Maysville, Ky.) 27 Oct. 2/3 . . . the number of "Straight-outs" who declared for the Whig cause.

Later examples also suggest the bolting nature of the straight-outs: (See below 1872 Blaine.)

1891 *World Almanac* 75/2. South Carolina, Democratic "Straight-out" State Convention . . . put a ticket in the field in opposition to the regular (Tillman) Democratic ticket.

There are, however, quotations which show the straight-outs to be the regular party members:

1874 *N. Y. Trib.* 7 Oct. 1/6 . . . These gentlemen will throw their influence in favor of a unification of races in politics, and if necessary, will hold a convention in opposition to the straight-out Democratic and Radical Republican nominating bodies.

1882 *Nation* 3 Aug. 85/1. The Virginia Straight-out Republican Committee decided . . . not to call a State Convention.

In 1872 the Anti-Greeley Democrats were known as "Straight-out Democrats."

1872 in Blaine *Twenty Years* II.534. Early in that month a body of Democrats, who declined to accept Mr. Greeley, and who called themselves "Straightouts" held a convention at Louisville. . . .

1872 in Cooper and Fenton *Am. Politics* II.53a. Democratic (Straight-out) Platform, Louisville, Ky., September 3.

strawslide.

Apparently nonce coinage parodying *landslide:*

1948 *Newsweek* 20 Sept. 28/2. Dewey by a Strawslide [based on pre-election polls].

straw votary.

1928 *New Rep.* 24 Oct. 271/2. I see where the straw votaries of the Literary Digest give the G.O.P. the big edge. . . .

straw vote.

A trial vote.

A. The term undoubtedly refers to the old adage "straws show which way the wind blows" found in English literature as early as the seventeenth century (John Selden's *Table Talk*):

Take a straw and throw it up into the air, —you may see by that which way the wind is.

B. In American political usage we find many examples of the expression as headings for articles in which the results of a trial vote are given:

1817 *Adv. of the People* 23 April 2/2. Straws show which way the wind blows.
1840 *Rough-hewer* 159/3. On the school section in the same township there are 18 legal voters, and among them there is not a solitary whig. "Straws show which way the wind blows" as Uncle Tobey said when the breeze capsized his hat.
1856 *Warren* (Ohio) *Sharp-shooter* 1 Aug. 2/2. Straws show which Way the Wind Blows. [head]

C. The earliest example of *straw vote* is 1866, but the evidence of the popularity of the practice suggests that the term is much older:

1866 *Cleve. Leader* 6 Oct. 4/2. A straw vote taken on a Toledo train yesterday resulted as follows; A. Johnson 12; Congress, 47.

See STEAMBOAT ELECTIONS.

strike (bill).

A method of obtaining money by threatening to pass legislation opposed by lobbies or corporations; based upon the formula of *gold* or *silver strike:*

c1870's in Werner *Tammany Hall* 177. The method of the Black Horse Cavalry at Albany was to introduce a bill which struck at the interests of some large corporation, or the Tweed combine, and which was known as "strike" legislation. The bill progressed in the Committee of the Whole, and indications were that it was likely to pass. Then the Cavalry waited, and if the agents of the corporation, or the agents of Tweed, or Tweed himself did not pay the amount they wanted, the bill was advanced further. The corporation paid and the bill was never heard of again.
1871 *N. Y. Times* 25 Dec. 4 . . . one-half of the measures will be nipped in the bud; while jobs, "strikes," and corrupt bills of all sorts will issue from the hands of the committees, and lumber up the files of members.
1913 Roosevelt *Works.* XX.72. The blackmailing, or, as they were always called, the "strike" bills, could themselves be roughly divided into two categories: bills which it would have been proper to pass, and those that it would not have been proper to pass.
1921 Orth *The Boss and the Machine* 123. With the tremendous increase of business after the Civil War, New York City became the central office of the nation's business, and many of the interests centered there found it wise to have permanent representatives at Albany to scrutinize every bill that even remotely touched their welfare, to promote legislation that was frankly in their favor, and to prevent "strikes"—the bills designed for blackmail.

striker.

A. A desperado associated with Murrell in his land-thievery in the Old Southwest.

c1836 Howard *Hist. V. A. Stewart* 92. They . . . gave him the two degrees, and the signs by which they were distinguished. He first received the sign of the striker, and afterward that of the grand counsellor. . . . 103. The first mystic sign which is used by this clan was in use among robbers before I [Murrell] was born.
1838 Simms *Richard Hurdis* 184. "Barret," said the one ruffian to the other, "we must see who it is that volunteers to be our *striker.* He has a ready hand, and should be one of us, if he be not so already." *Ib.* 363. I showed him the first two signs of the club—the sign of the *striker,* and the sign of the *feeler*—the first being that of the common horse-thief or mail robber; the other that which empowers a member to probe the nature of the man he meets, and secure him . . . to the uses of the brotherhood.

B. An unprincipled speculator.

1860 in *Covode Invest.* 791. Answer. I think he was looked upon more as an attorney in such matters than as a capitalist. Question. Was he not looked upon as what is termed a "striker?" Answer. I would rather not answer that question.

C. A political henchman. Applied to those who do the intimidating and general dirty work for major politicians or bosses, the term still carries the opprobrious connotations associated with Murrell's band of murderers and robbers.

1855 *Sons of Sires* 90. The "strikers" are a bold class of marauders, who "come down" upon a candidate for a place ... with threats that if he does not give it, they will be down upon him in the Primary Elections.
1872 *Harper's W.* 402/4. The convention ... was captured and controlled by the most notorious political jobbers and strikers.
1872 *N. Y. Trib.* 2 Oct. 4/2. The "Apollo Hall Democracy," as they call themselves, are nothing more nor less than "Jimmy" O'Brien's strikers for Grant.
1874 Nichols *Am. Life* 313. He came to Washington a senator. During his term he visited New York, where he held a public reception in the Governor's Room of the City Hall, and shook hands with his old friends of the fire department and the rowdies and strikers of the political party of which he was an ornament.
1878 *Harper's W.* 14 Dec. 986/4. The Republican party in the city of New York is controlled by political strikers and "heelers" of the kind that carried this vote, and who are endearingly known as "the boys."
1880 *Cleve. Plain Dealer* 24 June 2/1. At the Republican convention almost through one entire week the Grant bullies and the Blaine strikers, howled and roared.
1880 *N. Y. Trib.* 2 Oct. 1/1. You're a dirty political striker, that's what you are.

1884 in *Rep. Conv.* 100. He [Hawley] is a reformer; and he believes not in the reform by which "heelers" and "strikers" and "bummers" control the politics of certain sections.

stump (n.).

The rostrum or platform for making a campaign speech.

A. In the colonial period of America a stump left standing in a clearing provided a natural platform for sermons and other addresses to an assembly.

1716 in Ann Maury *Memoirs Hugenot Family* 276. I went down to the Saponey Indian town ... There is in the centre of the circle a great stump of a tree; I asked the reason they left that standing, and they informed me it was for one of their head men to stand upon when he had anything of consequence to relate to them, so that being raised, he might the better be heard.

B. Inevitably the stump became the political rostrum.

1840 Thomas *Rem.* I.100. On entering, we had observed rather an unsightly stump in our host's [Daniel Drake's] reception room, but it soon became manifest that there was both humor and design in it. The Doctor had resolved on both giving and getting a stump speech, and therefore providently supplied himself with the stump of the Buck Eye tree—a tree from which Ohio derives the name of "the Buck Eye State." In the course of the evening the Doctor regularly mounted the stump, and delivered an address. ...
1903 Turpie *Sk.* 290. Two or three times in the beginning I have spoken literally from the stump—not a bad stand, but it has its limitations. The speaker from the stump was obliged to be careful of his steps, and guarded in his movements; otherwise he lost his balance and fell, although there was nothing very perilous to his person in such a fall; still he seldom recovered from the effects upon the audience produced by it.

C. With rapidly expanding industrialization and the steady disappearance of the frontiers, modern campaign methods were adopted with the stump replaced by scaffolding, town halls, and railroad platforms; but the term remained.

1863 Russell *Diary* 179. "We do not require a press, because we go out and discuss all public questions from the stump with our people," said Mr. Wigfall.

1866 Lowell *Works* VI.325. Mr. Johnson is the first of our Presidents who has descended to the stump, and spoken to the people as if they were a mob.

1876 *Cinc. D. Gazette* 16 June 2/4. [Hawley's speech on Resumption Act] But I am not desirous to be tied upon the *stump* to the advocacy of that bill.

1884 Blaine *Congress* 148. In the first debate, where Douglas had the opening, he had, in the popular judgment, rather worsted Mr. Lincoln. His greater familiarity with the arts if not the tricks of the stump had given him an advantage.

1896 Bryan *Battle* 125 . . . the fact that a campaign is carried on through the press and upon the stump. . . .

1932? in Cross *Conn. Yankee* 235 . . . this year things were not going very well for him on the stump.

1939 Michie *Dixie Demagogues* 7. The demagogue is able to win the votes of those who crowd to his stump for the simple reason that he gives voice to their inarticulate thoughts and emotions.

1960 *Time* 7 March 16/1. Both prefer to ring bells and shake hands on street corners than to get up on the stump.

stump (v.).

To make a speechmaking campaign tour.

1838 *Hamilton* (Ohio) *Intell.* 23 Aug. 3/1. "Stumping it" is a new game for candidates for Governor in Ohio, and we very much doubt whether the "Experiment" will be sanctioned by a dignified people.

1838 *N. Y. Herald* 29 Oct. 2/5. Mr.

Speaker Polk is *stumping* it about the State of Tennessee.

1876 *Harper's W.* 20 May 402/3. The argument for Mr. CONKLING in the State Convention was that he was upright and able; that he had supported the Republican policy in Congress, and had brilliantly stumped the State in 1872.

1879 *Nation* 6 Nov. XXIX.301. Mr. Sherman went about the country stumping with Dutcher, the Appraiser, to whom he had granted leave of absence for the purpose.

stump (adj.).

stump man.

1840 Kennedy *Quodlibet* 98. Agamemnon Flag, who was the only stump man on the ticket, (Schoolcraft and Short having expressly stipulated that they were not to be called on to speak in the canvass) . . . .

stump orator (-y).

1840 *Georgia Jrnl.* 22 Sept. 3/4. They [Calhounite Van Buren men] head all the conventions and Van Buren barbecues; they are the *stump orators,* through whose ability, integrity, and consistent republicanism, the independent people of Georgia are to be brought into Martin's fold!!

1856 Goodrich *Recoll.* 125. This Abraham Bishop . . . grew up a democrat and became an able and skillful stump orator. He is said to have originated the electioneering apothegm—"one doubt loses ten votes!"

1879 *Nation* 10 July XXIX.20. In so far as the controversy has furnished material for stump oratory in the fall elections, it cannot be denied that the Republicans have the best of it.

1938 Farley *Behind the Ballots* 25. He had . . . an ability to explain campaign issues in simple homely phrases unrivaled by any stump orator of the day.

stump speaker.

1862 Edmund Kirke *Among the Pines* 187. Stump speaker was a term given to a person making a political speech during the Civil War.

1866 Welles *Diary* II.594. He [Seward] said the President was doing good and was the best stump speaker in the country. The President should not be a stump speaker.

1880 *Cinc. D. Gazette* 9 June 1/5. His [Garfield's] effectiveness as a *stump* speaker has been manifested by invitations to participate in the campaigns of most of the States, East and West.

stump speech.

1823 *Delaware Patron* 30 April 3/2. Mr. Clay . . . is making an electioneering tour through the Atlantic cities. At Philadelphia he received the compliment of a public dinner, at which he drank a toast, and made a stump speech.

1833 A. Greene *Yankee Among the Nullifiers* 15. The following is an extract from his stump speech. . . .

1840 J. Q. Adams *Memoirs* Sept. X.352. Mr. Webster and Mr. Saltonstall were there, and a stump-speech scaffold.

1841 in *Georgia Jrnl.* 3 Aug. 1/1 [Meriwether in HR, 30 June]. The gentleman from Maine announced to us in advance, that his purpose was not to make a "stump speech": that his sole object . . . was to present a *fair view* of this measure to his constituents. . . . had the gentleman's speech been addressed . . . from a *stump* as the forum, his manner and his matter would have eminently entitled his remarks to the classification he seems so much to repudiate.

1861 Chesnut *Diary* 120. Yancey will have no mobs to harangue. No stump speeches will be possible, superb as are his of their kind.

stump candidate.

One supported by a faction or group of irregulars of a party.

1842 *Bro. Jonathan* II.4 . . . elect the regular ticket! If not, elect the stump candidate, and let the country perish!

1850 *N. Y. Trib.* 12 Oct. 4/1. We are informed that the Conservative portion of the Locos in the 1st Congressional District in this City, chagrined by the successful packing of the Hart party, have determined to run Gen. Hiram Walbridge as a stump candidate for Congress.

1858 *N. Y. sw. Trib.* 27 July 2/1. So Gerrit Smith is to be run as a stump candidate for Governor.

1880 *N. Y. Trib.* 7 Oct. 4/4. A few individual bolters . . . may set up for themselves and run as "stump" candidates; but the majority will be quickly cuffed back into the traces again.

stumper.

A stump speaker.

1849 *Knickerbocker* XXXIV.513. The best "stumpers" are not always the best qualified for the business of the state.

1856 *Cleve. Plaindealer* 15 Oct. 2/1. The State was literally flooded with electioneering pamphlets and papers and the very ground was trod up with political stumpers.

1875 *N. Y. Trib.* 1 Oct. 4/3. Two Kinds of Stumpers [head].

1880 *Cleve. Plaindealer* 9 June 2/2 [edit.]. The real fun of the campaign will begin when the Republican *stumpers* allude to "civil service reform."

stump tail.

A. One of the Western animal metaphors associated with paper currency:

1857 in Fowler *Ten Years in Wall Street* 112 . . . his own private opinion was, the bank was a "wild-cat," and the currency was "stump-tail and red dog."

1861 *Chic. Trib.* 22 May 4. "Stumptail" currency:—At the outbreak of the Civil War, those bank notes secured by Southern state bonds and depreciated Northern issues were called "stumptail" and were, as the name denotes, circulated at a discount. . . .

1874 *N. Y. Times* 14 July 2/4. The Democracy, throughout the country, is by no means a unit for Government notes, and the only refuge is in State banks of issue, if national banks are stricken down. With the West, Indiana has not entirely forgotten the ante-rebellion stump-tail days, and the Republican portion of the present system....

B. Also a faction favoring this type of currency:

1860 *Stark Cty.* (Ohio) *Republican* 13 June 2. The "stump tails" absquatulated and have determined to hold a convention of their own.

submission(ist).

177? Wirt *Henry* 23 March 141. There is no retreat but in submission and slavery. **1798** Jefferson *Ky. Resolutions.* Resolved, That the several States composing the United States of America, are not united on the principle of unlimited submission to their general government....

Even before the nullification crisis *submission* was used in the South to brand those who favored too lenient an attitude toward the tariff question:

1828 *Mangum Papers* I.339. We find ourselves placed in this awful dilemma, either to submit patiently to the operations of this [tariff] act, or to resist or counteract its influence. Submission will add greatly to the distress and embarrassment under which the people of the South already labour, and will go very far toward completing our ruin.

Concerning nullification:

1833 *Sumterville* (S.C.) *Whig* 5 Jan. in *Niles' Reg.* 19 Jan. 332/1...it is not the union men generally—the spiritless submissionists, as they have been scornfully termed—but chiefly the brave spirits, the pinks of chivalry, the fire and brimstone-eaters, who have suddenly been enlightened as to the vast advantages of the western country.
1834 *Savannah Georgian* 8 July 2/6. The Nullifiers call us Submissionists.

In the decade before the Civil War *submissionist* designated those opposed to secession:

1849 in Shryock *Georgia & the Union in 1850* 208 [based on account in *Savannah Georgian*]. Hill's silence and evasiveness proved him the "Submissionist candidate."
1850 Ranck *Brown* 76 [from *Miss. Free Trader*]. Hereafter in arguing the matter, we will term the two parties Secessionists and Submissionists, for we believe those are the only issues before the country.
1850 *Ib.* 108. $1\frac{9}{20}$ths of the old state-rights group are submissionists.
in Wilson *Slave Power* III.183. Let the border States submit to the Abolition rule of this Lincoln administration if they like; but don't let the miserable submissionists pretend to be deceived.
1862 Hunnicutt *Conspiracy* 27 May 332. This word submission has for nearly the last two years produced a greater terror over the Southern people than any other word to be found in the English language or in any language in the world. Submission! Submission to whom?...But let us examine and see who are the submissionists.

Occasionally the term was applied to the Northern Peace Democrats:

1862 *Ann. of Cleve.* No.2473. The English journals are not blind to all the bearings of political movements in the United States. Some of them have a proper appreciation of the Peace Democrats or submissionists.

subsoil.

To prepare the way for a campaign by secret, under-cover maneuvering.

A. The term, used in English agricultural terminology at least as early as 1840, was prominent in America in the campaign of 1872, when Horace Greeley's varied fields of interest were the objects of severe ridicule by opposition editors. His view on farming was one of the targets:

1872 Chamberlain *Struggle of '72* 492, 496. Mr. Greeley's great hobby as an agriculturist is deep plowing. He will not stop a barley-corn short of thirty inches; and the brindle steers that perish in the attempt to haul subsoil plows through the stoney hard-pan....

... he [Greeley] concluded with the statement that if the Emperor William said that subsoil plowing was not good in light soil, or that guano was better than bone-dust, he was "a liar, a villain and a slave!"

B. The metaphorical application of the word is to be found only a few years later.

1874 *Nation* 22 Oct. 267. This process of subsoiling has no reference to influencing the opinions or wishes of the body of voters. It consists in making secret combinations and arrangements among persons who hope to get ... offices and posts, ... log-rolling with them, and organizing and drilling the paid workers in secret squads.
1876 *Ib.* 10 Feb. 92/2. That a vigorous effort will be made to prepare the Convention for its perpetuation there is little doubt. The work of "subsoiling" is going on now. The "pre-primaries" have been held long ago.
1884 *Ib.* 30 Oct. 364/3. They [Blaine agents] are subsoiling a little for the Irish vote and labor vote, but are expending most of their money and strength upon New Jersey and Indiana.
1903 Hoar *Autobio.* I.189. A good many Anti-Slavery men ... joined the [Know Nothing] movement simply in order that they might get rid of the old parties, and prepare the State as with a subsoil plow for a new one.

Subterranean Democracy.

A faction within the Democratic party in New York City.

1842 in *Sk. of Mike Walsh* 18. I know that we, the Subterranean Democracy, possess the power, if we will but exercise it, of

breaking up every species of cliques, dictation and party management in the Democratic party.
1842 *Ib.* 78. The traveling community to me have always appeared ... as distinct and different from the masses of the people, as the old clo'dealers of "New Jerusalem," alias Chatham street, are from the "Subterraneans."
1844 *Wash. Intelligencer* 15 Aug. 3/4. Is it to be the leader of the Subterraneans, who some time ago told us of "the codfish aristocracy" of Democracy?
1874 Wilson *Slave Power* II.399. The "subterranean" Democracy of the city of New York found a fitting exponent in its member, Michael Walsh.

The name may have been suggested by living habits:

1852 *N. Y. Times* 27 Oct. 2/4. Subterraneanism, as it exists in N.Y., is not known there [Phila.]. No people, not even the vilest, ever live in cellars.

subversive.

A. In 18th century English usage referring to a measure which is hostile to accepted rights or principles.

1764 Dickinson *Writings.* II.174. Resolved. ... That the levying of Taxes upon the Inhabitants of this Province in any other Manner, being manifestly subversive of public Liberty, must of necessary Consequence be utterly destructive of public Happiness.
1794 Erskine *Sp.* II.476. Whether in seeking to interfere practically in an alteration of the constitution, they have manifested ... a spirit inconsistent with affection for the government, and subversive of its authority.
1794 *Ib.* III.80. Subversive of the known and acknowledged liberties of England.

B. Almost the same general usage is found in America. Often the word is synonymous with *unconstitutional.* The 1836 quotation, however, foreshadows *C.*

1798 Gallatin in *Gt. Deb.* VII.65. That principle was subversive of the principles of the Constitution itself.

1814 Res. of Conn. Legis. in Dwight *Hartford Conv.* 336. And whereas the principles of the plan and bill aforesaid, are, in the opinion of this assembly, not only intolerably burdensome and oppressive, but utterly subversive of the rights and liberties of the people of this state, and the freedom, sovereignty, and independence of the same....

1823 *Cinc. Nat. Rep.* 20 June 2/5. There is nothing so subversive of the genuine principles of Republicanism....

1836 *Ann. of Cleve.* No.887. A meeting of the inhabitants of the township of Euclid was held ... for the purpose of expressing their sentiments in regard to certain persons who are visiting this place promulgating doctrines, we think, subversive of the best interests of our country.

1860 Dem. Platform in Stanwood *Hist. of Pres.* 284. Resolved, That the enactments of state legislatures to defeat the faithful execution of the fugitive slave laws are hostile in character, subversive of the Constitution, and revolutionary in their effects.

C. In the 20th century the rise of Russian communism led to a specialized application of *subversive:* designating activities directed at the overthrow of the government.

1925 Coan *Red Web* 188. He [Atty. Gen.] was convinced that it was sought for no reason except to supply ammunition for the cause of red radicalism and to reveal to the leaders of various subversive movements just what the government knew about their intrigues against the government.

1952 Stevenson *Maj. Camp. Sp.* 275. The Federal Government must use all its resources to expose and identify communistic activity ... and to protect our institutions from communistic espionage, sabotage and subversion.

1954 James Burnham *Web of Subversion* 32. The general public first heard of the existence of the web of subversion during the summer of 1948. On July 31 of that year, Elizabeth Terrill Bentley testified at length before an open session of the House Committee on UnAmerican Activities.

succotash party.

A fusion party in Iowa. (See MERMAID, MONGREL, CHOW CHOW.)

1878 *N. Y. Trib.* 27 Dec. 5/2. In Iowa the Democrat and Greenback combination is called the succotash party. The reference, of course, is to the mixed corn-and-beans character of the combination. It is almost too good a name for such a mess.

sugar.

Money used for campaign purposes.

Apparently first used in connection with the notorious campaign in Indiana in 1880.

1880 *N. Y. Times* 19 Oct. 1/5. Mr. Jonathan Scoville ... has put a bung in his barrel since the Indiana election, and the "sugar" does not flow as freely as it did.

1882 *Judge* 4 March 2/3. Some allusion was made there [Dorsey Dinner] by General Arthur to the influence of "sugar" in bringing about the great victory. Every man in possession of a slang dictionary knows that the word "sugar" thus used signifies money.

This usage of *sugar* obviously existed in the slang vocabulary and is derived from the older verb "to make agreeable":

1613–18 Daniel *Coll. Hist. Eng.* 51 [OED]. To baite the people, and sugar their subjection.

sulphurcrat.

A portmanteau creation designating a Democratic sulphur lobbyist who was regarded as acting like a Republican:

1936 Michie *Dixie Demagogues* 42. Whatever lip service Lobbyist Miller may give the Democratic Party, his actions in Texas affairs have been such as would shame the most reactionary Republican. "Sulphurcrat" is the only term adequate to define Miller's political stripe. . . .

Sunday School.

Epithet ridiculing idealistic politicians, especially those who advocated Civil Service reform.

1878 *Harper's W.* 4 May 346/1. By ridiculing reform, and scoffing at pacification, and sneering at the President as a goody-goody Sunday-school superintendent.

1878 *Ib.* 13 July 546/4. He [Smyth, chmn. N.Y. Rep. Com.] trusted there would be no more Sunday-school and silly civil service reform under this Administration.

1878 *Ib.* 27 July 587/1. These were all inventions of the glory-to-God-regards-to-Babcock statesmen, who especially abhor goody-goody and Sunday-school politics, which is their name for whatever threatens their ascendency.

1878 *Nation* 1 Aug. 61/2. The passage in which he [the President] says, "Let Mr. Tilden have the place by violence, intimidation, and fraud, rather than undertake to prevent it by means which will not bear the strictest scrutiny," would, however, have been read with much amusement by the two Chandlers. This is what statesmen of that school call "Sunday-school politics."

1878 *Harper's W.* 3 Aug. 606/4 . . . the ex-Senator (Mr. Conkling) can expect nothing else than to be accounted a goody-goody, and a Sunday-school politician and a Pharisaic prig, by every "practical" politician who desires "Glory to God, respects to Babcock."

1878 *Ib.* 7 Dec. 966/2. Every patriotic man concedes the wisdom of recalling the country to the spirit and the methods of the Constitution, and it is under such a course that the North becomes once more probably Republican. But those who have sneered at it as cowardice or Sunday-school imbecility, and who are surely drifting behind the real sentiment of the country, naturally struggle to wrest the

frauds and violence in the Southern States into a justification of the Republican opposition to the Administration as treacherous.

1884 *Cleve. Leader* 2 Oct. 4/2. That class of philosophers whom Ben Butler some years ago designated as Sunday school politicians.

1888 *Nation* 5 July 3/1. The dismissal of Mr. Seth Low of Brooklyn by the *Tribune* as a "Sunday-school politician," because he cannot swallow the Republican platform, is simply a renewal of the war on the "Pharisees and hypocrites" and "mollycoddles" which followed the bolt against Blaine in 1884. . . . the Sunday-school, as a place in which the duty of following conscience without regard to consequences is taught, has become a synonym with them for cant and humbug, and serves as a term of reproach.

superserviceable.

A henchman: [ ]

1872 *N. Y. Trib.* 1 June 6/2. Never weary in ill-doing, Gen. Butler and his band of superserviceables rallied all their cohorts in the House yesterday, in an attempt to pass the Force Bill.

swap horses.

A. Widely attributed to Abraham Lincoln, the phrase "don't swap horses while crossing the stream," or a variant of this formula, may be found much earlier in American political lore. The following quotation suggests that the anecdote had a long tradition behind its adoption into the political vocabulary.

1846 *Hamilton Intell.* 10 Sept. 2/2. No Time To Swap Horses. There is a story of an Irishman who was crossing a stream with mare and colt when finding it deeper than he expected, and falling off the old mare, he seized the colt's tail to aid him in reaching the shore. Some persons on the bank called to him, advising him to take hold of the mare's tail, as she was the ablest to bring him out. His reply was, that it was a very unseasonable time for swapping horses.

It seems to be something like this with Judge Vance.... [He] prefers the sure support of the judicial colt, to the chance of grasping the Congressional mare, which he would much prefer. He will accordingly cling to the colt's tail, under the full persuasion that this is no time for swapping horses.

Lincoln's usage, however, is undoubtedly responsible for the popularity of the phrase and probably for its modern meaning—referring to changing incumbents during a crisis or in the middle of a long-range program. There are three versions of Lincoln's statement to the Union League Committee in June, 1864:

1864 in *N. Y. Trib.* 10 June 5/2. I have not permitted myself, gentlemen, to conclude that I am the best man in the country, but I am reminded in this connection of a story of an old Dutch farmer, who remarked to a companion once that "it was not best to swop [sic] horses when crossing streams."

1864 Lincoln *Works* II.98. I have not permitted myself, gentlemen, to conclude that I am the best man in the country; but I am reminded in this connection of an old Dutch farmer who remarked to a companion once that "it was not best to swap horses when crossing a stream."

1864 in Tarbell *Lincoln* III.194 ... they have concluded that it is not best to swap horses while crossing the river, and have further concluded that I am not so poor a horse that they might not make a botch of it trying to swap.

Later examples and variants:

1864 Heartsill *1491 Days* 215. But this is no time for "Swapping horses," this little squad must get out of here, and that quick.

1880 *N. Y. World* 10 Oct. 6/4. It is not safe to swap horses while crossing a stream....

If the Republican generals blundered so egregiously in laying out the original plan of campaign why should the rank and file feel any more confidence in their new strategy and tactics.

1882 Wilkins *Cloverdale Mystery* 24. At this time there must be no change of horses, for Senator Hamblin has served his constituency faithfully.

1900 *Rev. of Rev.* XXI.270. The Argument Against "Swapping Horses." [head]

1900 *Ib.* XXI.405/2. Although Lord Lansdowne at the head of the war office continues to be unpopular, the sentiment now is that there must be no swapping of horses in the middle of the stream.

1932 *New Rep.* 22 June 141/1 ... the campaign will have been launched on the general philosophy of "don't change barrels while going over Niagara."

swartwout.

To abscond to avoid prosecution.

1838 in Poore *Perley's Rem.* 128 ... Old Hickory closed the case by bringing his fist down upon the table and exclaiming: "By the Eternal! Sam. Swartwout *shall* be Collector of the Port of New York!" He was appointed ... and he "Swartwouted" (to use a word coined at the time) to avoid a criminal prosecution.

1838 Van Buren in *Cong. Globe* 21/1. I hereby transmit a special report, made to me by the Secretary of the Treasury, for your consideration, in relation to the recently discovered default of Samuel Swartwout, late collector of the customs at the port of New York.

1839 *Alex W. Messenger* 10 July 2/7. The editor of the Picayune complains that his washerwoman has Swartwouted (absconded) with twelve of his shirts.

1840 *Cong. Globe* App. 376. He was taken up—examined—and sure enough the money was found in his possession. Well, sir, this was too bad—something must be done—it must not go abroad that a Whig had been Swartwouting, and they tried to prevail upon him to avow himself a Democrat.

1840 *Ohio St. Jrnl.* 17 Dec. A Swartwouter Caught.—We sometime since copied from a Michigan paper an account of the Swartwouting Sheriff of Oakland county in that State.

1841 *Georgia Jrnl.* 17 Aug. 2/2. What will Webster do now with his dictionary? He [Swartwout] has made a new verb, thus, To Swartwout, v.a. to absquatulate, run away, evaporate, back out, mosey, cut stick, mizle, slope, slant, cut dirt, make tracks, take the sabine slide, and disappear.

1852 *Ohio St. Jrnl.* 4 Nov. 2. Our opponents will now rot again in power and the spoils for which they have so long struggled. The Swartwouts are again at the National crib.

1869 Curtis *Orations* II.11. He got an office and he gave a new word to the language. He became collector and he "Swartwouted"; that is, he put the money in his own pocket instead of in the Treasury.

sweat a barrel.

A campaign euphemism: probably, to supply whiskey for electioneering purposes, as the second quotation suggests.

1856 *Cleve. Plaindealer* 18 Sept. 2/3. Lt. Gov. Ford, of Ohio, is spending his time principally in Pa. since the nominations were made.... He promised to "sweat a barrel" in last year's campaign, and we suppose he will be bound to go a couple of barrels, at least, in this.

1864 in Grinnell *Men and Events* 295. I know that it was said liquor was poured out by the barrel against me in my district during the last election. Thank God, I have no desire to belong to a party that cannot come into power except upon a whiskey barrel.

swing around the circle.

The tour around the country which a politician makes to look over the political situation and pull his forces together for the approaching election is generally accepted as having started with President Johnson's "swing around the circle" in September, 1866. Most historians and lexicographers attribute the origin of the phrase to Johnson, and although Milton (*Age of Hate,* p. 726) states that the phrase was known in Tennessee as early as the Jackson period, there is a present lack of contemporary documentation.

Perhaps Milton's statement is based upon such evidence as the following quotation:

1803 Shipp *Wm. H. Crawford* 51. I did hear Mr. W. H. Crawford say that you went 'round the circuit, or part of the circuit, with Judge Griffin for the purpose of influencing the grand juries to procure recommendations of favor of the Judge.

However, the circumstances surrounding the use of *swing around the circle* have been largely ignored, and it has been assumed that Johnson referred to his trip through the Midwest in the fall of 1866. His first known use of the phrase occurred in February of the same year and he alluded not to a tour but to the union of states:

in McPherson *Pol. Manual* 58. Now, as we swing around the circle of the Union, with a fixed and unalterable determination to stand by it, if we find the counterpart or duplicate of the same spirit that played to this feeling and these persons in the South, this other extreme, which stands in the way, must get out of it, and the Government must stand unshaken and unmoved on its base.

His comparison of the United States to a circle is repeated in later speeches, one made on the day his trip began:

N. Y. Trib. 30 Aug. 8/3. I took my position in the Senate of the United States and assured them ... that this Union was perpetual, that it was a great magic circle,

never to be broken.
Ib. 4 Sept. 5/2. I hand over to you the Union of these States; not a semicircle. No, but a complete circle of States, and along with them the Constitution.

Although it is entirely possible that President Johnson used the term in an informal and unreported speech at the time of his Chicago trip, until such evidence is uncovered, we must attribute *swing around the circle* in its present meaning to Petroleum V. Nasby, who wrote a humorous and fictitious chronicle of the President's trip. In a letter dated September 4, he reports the following statement:
Nasby *Swinging Round the Cirkle* 206. "I know it wood," replied Johnson; "but where kin we find sich a one? I hev swung around the entire circle, and heven't ez yet seen him."

Although we have found no use of the phrase describing the trip, Nasby ridicules Johnson's frequent use of "swinging round the circle."
Nasby *op. cit.* 211. At this pint I interrupted him. I told him that he hed swung around the cirkle wunst in this town, and ez yooseful ez the phrase wuz, it might spile by too much yoose.

The phrase became a fixed part of the political vocabulary and continued to be identified with Johnson for many years.
1872 *San Diego Daily Union* 20 Aug. 2/2. Boutwell made it part of his impeachment tirade against Andrew Johnson, that he permitted his secretaries to participate in the "swinging around the circle" campaign.

However, it was applied to trips taken by other politicians as well:
1869 Peck *Terence McGrant* 27 ... until me Cousin Ulissis gets through swinging around the circle.

1909 *Rev. of Rev.* XL.414. [cartoon entitled "A Swing Around the Circle" lampooning Taft's appeal to various sections of the country on the tariff question.]

Swiss (press).

The memory of the Swiss mercenaries hired by the French court and other European monarchs is apparently behind its use in American politics:
1824 *Cinc. Nat. Rep.* 23 Nov. 2/4. They [Caucus Junto of Ohio] seem to be sensible that the very lean plurality which has been obtained over the Jackson ticket, with the aid of the Swiss [Adams faction], does not redound much to their credit.
1828 *Nat. Rep.* in *Liberty Hall* (Cinc.) 10 April 3/1. Every assertion therein made [in coffin handbills] against the motives and honorable conduct of Gen. Jackson has long since been proved to be false, and this the Coalition and their Swiss Corps of mercenaries, know.
1828 *Ib.* 17 April 1/1. "The late election of city and town-ship officers in Cincinnati, has been made the occasion for the grossest misrepresentations by the Swiss corps, of the popular sentiment of this city in relation to the next Presidency."... *Swiss corps*. ... Why are such epithets employed?
1834 *Niles' Reg.* 4 Jan. 308/1 ... sustained by the combined operations of the Swiss press of the United States.
1844 in *Mangum Papers* IV.31. What can John C. Spencer and all the rest of the Swiss Corps—who came amongst us for spoils. ...

syndicalism.

According to Cole (*Socialist Thought*, II.328):
In the 1880's Syndicalism had still to emerge as a clearly defined doctrine.... After the legalizing statute of 1884 Trade Unions grew fast, and in 1886 a national Trade Union Congress at Lyons set up a Fédération Nationale de Syndicats.... At the next Congress, in 1887, the syndicats

declared in favour of collective ownership of the means of production, and also began to discuss the question of the general strike, which was to play so important a part in the theory of Syndicalism at a later stage.... the French Syndicalist movement which reached its height in the first decade of the twentieth century.

American papers in noting this later French movement still felt it necessary to offer some sort of explanation of the term:

1909 *Rev. of Rev.* XL.91f. The crisis which has been reached [in France] is due to the fact that "the case of 'syndicalism' against capital has become the case of the wage-earners against the modern principles of the State." Syndicalism is not to be confounded with British or American trade-unionism.

However, the word was occasionally applied to labor movements in the United States:

1913 *Pol. Science. Qrtly.* XXVIII.451. In a general way, "syndicalism" has become familiar to American readers. It is understood to be a revolutionary labor movement, which aims at the abolition of the wage system through "direct action" culminating in the "general strike."...The most effective organization of American syndicalism today is the Industrial Workers of the World, with headquarters in Chicago.... 478. The first meeting of the Syndicalist League of New York City was held in December, 1912. There are leagues in many other cities, and "The Syndicalist League of North America" exists at least on paper.

T

taffy.

Flattery or misleading political promises; similar to *soft soap:*

1879 in *Cong. Record* 462/1. [I wish to prevent them from] denouncing me as the coadjutor of the South, distributing "taffy" to the South.

1879 *Puck* 15 Oct. 503/2. Meanwhile Mister Kelly is giving his followers taffy.

1879 *Ib.* 5 Nov. 555/2. Many an untutored Indian has worn his belt of scalps more proudly because of the taffied eloquence of Mr. C. Schurz....

1880 *N. Y. World* 15 June 4/3. General Garfield is a skilfull maker of philanthropic political "taffy."

1880 *Cleve. Plain Dealer* 17 June 1/3. He [Garfield] is serenaded according to agreement and gives taffy to the gathering.

1880 *N. Y. Trib.* 13 July 4/5. John Kelly is too old a politician not to understand the difference between taffy and spoils.

1890 in *Cong. Record* 8041/1. Flattery, as [Cummings] suggests, means "taffy," and sometimes it means a little more than that.

talkathon.

See WALKATHON.

1952 *Life* 25 Aug. 35. Political candidates of 1952, if they have iron constitutions and brass lungs, can avail themselves of a brand-new weapon, the Talkathon. Theoretically it is simple: the aspirant for office sits before a radio microphone and a battery of telephones, and as questions come in over the phones he goes on answering them and answering them and answering them. In practice, candidates have found it necessary to engage a Miami advertising man named Bob Venn, who not only has a staff and technical know-how, but has applied for a trademark on the title, "Talkathon." Venn unveiled the Talkathon in May in the Florida primaries, helped get his man Brailey Odham an impressive 328,000 votes, though he lost.

1952 *Ib.* 8 Sept. 42. In his aggressive attack on McCarthy, Schmitt has broken all existing records for the new trademarked "Talkathon"...finally extending it in Milwaukee to a full 26 hours.

McCarthy countered by focussing his ridicule in a parody of the term:

1952 *Life* 8 Sept. 42. He admitted he was worried about the effect of what he called the "smearathon."
1954 *New Rep.* 17 May 5/1. The *Talkathon* may soon provide one answer to the high cost of politicking over radio and television.

tapeworm ticket.

A ballot devised to find out if purchased voters kept to their bargain. [ ]
1875 in *Cong. Record* 1890/2. I exhibit a ticket prepared in the City of Washington and sent to Mare Island in my own district, known in California as the "tapeworm" ticket, which is three inches in length, one-16th of an inch in width.... **1878** in *Ib.* 6 Feb. 804/2. Gentlemen will remember those tickets which were exhibited here some time ago, called "tapeworm tickets.".... These small tickets were given to a certain class of voters, and as they were put into the ballot-box the employers of the voters could easily tell whether such tickets were voted or not. **1882** *Harper's W.* 28 Jan. 50/3 ... the trick of the "tape-worm tickets," as they were called, which resulted in a law requiring uniform ballots [in San Francisco]....

tariff for revenue only.

A Democratic slogan expressing the party's opposition to the high protective tariff.
Henry Watterson reported the Democratic platform of 1880 in which the phrase occurs:
in Stanwood *Hist. of the Presidency* 413 ... and a tariff for revenue only.

That Watterson is responsible for its origin is evident from remarks which he made later:
in *Marse Henry* II.133. All seemed to me lost save honor and conviction. I had become the embodiment of my own epigram, "a tariff for revenue only."

This particular feature of the Democratic platform of 1880 plagued the candidate, General Hancock, who was satirized in both editorial and cartoon for his obvious lack of information on financial matters. A cartoon by Nast (*Harper's W.*, November 13) shows Hancock asking Senator Randolph of New Jersey, "Who is Tariff, and why is he for revenue only?"
The formula *tariff for revenue only* had appeared earlier than 1880:
1870 *Gt. Deb.* XII.140. He [Winans of Ohio] said it might happen that even in a tariff imposed only for the purpose of revenue some benefit or good might come to some interest of the country; ... His doctrine is this: a tariff can only constitutionally be laid for revenue.
1876 Democratic Platform in Stanwood *Hist. of the Presidency* 376. We demand that all custom-house taxation shall be only for revenue.
1881 *N. Y. Trib.* 18 Jan. 4/3. "I cannot tell a lie! I did it with my little tariff for revenue only plank in the platform."

Tartar.

Designating a radical member of a minority faction:
1864 *Cinc. Comm.* 13 May 2/3. A National Convention of the long-haired Tartars of Northern radicalism has been called.... **1864** *Ib.* 31 May 3/5. The Tartars Assembled.

See LONG-HAIR; CALMUCK.

telepolitics.

1942 *New Rep.* 7 Sept. 271/1. Telepolitics —long distance politicking—is trying to win Texas primaries in the Hotel Astor in New York.... These telepoliticians....

tennis cabinet.

Variant of *kitchen cabinet* (q.v.).

1931 *Wash. Merry-Go-Round* 105–6. Half an hour later, he [H. L. Stimson] appeared on the White House tennis court. ... Next morning the newspapers published a detailed account of the importance which Mr. Stimson attached to his membership in the "Tennis Cabinet."

terrapin (system).

Goodrich (in *Recollections,* 578n.) gives the historical background of the term:
When the Non-intercourse act [1809]—the last of the so-called "Restrictive Measures," and which by way of ridicule had been nick-named the "Terrapin System," was repealed—Dwight wrote the following. ...

> Mourn! sons of democratic woe!
> In sadness bow the head:
> Bend every back with sorrow low
> Poor TERRAPIN is dead.

Since the last verse of the poem refers to the gerrymander, it can not be older than 1812. The political use of *terrapin,* however, can be assumed to be somewhat older.
1808 in Robinson *W. R. Davie* 386. War points to incalculable evils, and the Embargo, or Terrapin [to] hostilities.

While it is quite probable that the point of comparison between the terrapin and the embargo that kept the American merchant fleet tied to its ports was partly furnished by the animal's policy of avoiding danger by drawing in its head, another possible origin is suggested by the discovery of some humorist that *embargo* spelled backwards reads *o grab me.* A cartoon of 1813 pictures the o-grab-me as a snapping turtle grabbing a sailor by the seat of his pants, thereby preventing him from getting his merchandise to his ship. The memory of these conditions may be behind the use of the turtle as representing the East in a cartoon of 1829. (See Murrell, *Hist. Am. Graphic Humor* I.67, 112.)

terrorism.

Terrorism has not been found before 1858 in American sources, but it is no doubt much older. (The *OED* has *reign of terrorism* from 1795.)
1858 *At. Mon.* I.113/1. Every form of terrorism (in Kansas), to which tyrants all alike instinctively resort to disarm resistance to their will, was launched at the property, the lives, and the happiness of the defenceless settlers.
1868 *Harper's W.* 5 Sept. 563/2. Political Terrorism [head of article treating with Democrat tactics to win Southern elections]
1876 *Ib.* 3 June 443/3. The people of the United States will be very slow to commit the national power to a party which sends Hill and Tucker to Congress, which contains the spirit and furnishes the men for negro terrorism. ...
1876 *Ib.* 3 June 443/2. It is an old issue, indeed, but it is still vital, and it will be vital so long as the Democratic party shows itself anxious only to put the negro in the wrong, and to excuse or justify white terrorism under the plea of carpetbaggery and ignorance and rascality.

thimblerigging.

In England the term occurs in the gambler's vocabulary in the first quarter of the 19th century. Its metaphorical use in American politics may be found as early as 1842:
N. Y. w. Trib. 21 May 5/3. Thimblerigging [head]. The game of Political Thimblerigging now carried on in this City is strikingly in character. Loco-Focoism in our City Offices is the operator; the three thimbles are Mayor Morris, ex-Alderman Shaler, and the Loco-Foco Inspectors of

the Sixth Ward. They are turned up one after the other, but the ball does not manifest itself.

1848 *Xenia* (Ohio) *Torchlight* 10 Aug. 3/2. E. S. Hamlin . . . has for weeks been engaged in the business of political thimble-rigging over the State of Ohio.

1872 Russell *Henry Demorest Lloyd* I.38. No more of these false guides for me; no more thimblerigging in politics—I am going in (if at all) for a straight persistent fight. . . .

1878 *N. Y. Trib.* 26 July 4/4. Alexander Stephens is amusing Georgia Democrats by calling the leaders of the fraud hunt "thimbleriggers."

thinking committee.

Satirical allusion to advisers of General Harrison in the campaign of 1840.

1840 *Rough-hewer* 123/1. General Harrison and his Thinking Committee. [head] The following dialogue from the Pennsylvanian places the answer of Gen. Harrison's thinking committee in its true light: . . . General Harrison—What do I think . . . Do you want me to think myself to death? Here, committee, what do I think about these things? . . .

third party.

A minor party formed in opposition to the two major ones.

1. Against the Federalists and Democratic-Republicans:

1801 Fisher Ames *Works* II.138. He is a very weak or very presumptuously vain man, who can think of organizing a third party.

2. Against the Democrats and Whigs:

1840 *Ohio St. Jrnl.* 21 Oct. 3/2. Let them see that the names of Harrison and Tyler are not placed over the Third Party electors.

1844 Webster *Springfield Speech.* I speak to the Third Party as they are called, if any be here.

3. Against Democrats and Republicans:

1878 *Harper's W.* 7 Sept. 707/1. Under all the forms of the "third party" movement, whatever name it may take, one thing, and one thing only, is evident—the conviction that the remedy for hard times is a larger amount of paper currency issued by the government. . . .

Thomas Jefferson Proviso.

A suggested name for the Wilmot Proviso.

1847 in *Cong. Globe* 377/3. It should be called, known, and distinguished as the "Thomas Jefferson proviso." He, sir, was its author.

1849 William Jay *Rev. of Mex. War* 186 . . . the northern Democrats endeavored to shelter themselves from the reproaches of their southern friends by calling their proposal "the Thomas Jefferson proviso," its language being copied from the ordinance for the Government of North-Western territory, originally drafted by Mr. Jefferson, in 1784.

306.

The 306 stalwarts (q.v.) who supported Grant for a third term at the 1880 Republican convention; later, a political club.

1880 *N. Y. World* 3 July 1/4. The Republican National Committee Organizes with a Very Mild Concession to the "306." [head]

1880 *N. Y. Times* 19 Oct. 1/5. There is also another unique organization here [Buffalo], composed largely of young men, known as "306." . . . it only means the 306 solid votes that Gen. Grant received at the Chicago Convention.

See OLD GUARD.

329. ¿

1885 *Mag. Am. Hist.* April 396. During the presidential campaign of 1880, these numbers were chalked by Democrats on every wall, door-step, and fence in the land. Mr. Garfield, the Republican candidate, had been charged with having received a bribe of $329 worth of Credit Mobilier Stock.

thug ticket.

Slate of candidates in New Orleans which was supported by the underworld element of the city.

1860 *Cong. Globe* 439/1 . . . his prominence in aiding in the inauguration of the thug ticket with the notorious Ben Harrison at the head of it.

ticket.

A. The original sense in English seems to be "a written notice for public information" (see *OED*). The connection between this use and the American one is shown by the following quotation. However, the list which was publicized throughout the country was later the ballot which was cast in the election.

1755 *Hist. Rev. Penn.* Every one votes as he pleases, the election being by written tickets, folded up and put in a box.
1765 S. Purviance, Jr. in Hart *Source Book* 127. As soon as your ticket is agreed on, let it be spread through the country, that your party intend to come well armed to the election. . . . and further, I would report it, that not a Mennonist nor German should be admitted to give in a ticket without being sworn that he is naturalized and worth £50, and that he has not voted already.

B. The current meaning of a list of candidates put up by a party or faction has long been the dominant one in American politics.

1711 in *Penn-Logan Corr.* II.438. Chester [Pa.] carried their ticket entire.
1796 Hamilton *Works* X.164. We believe, confidently, our election in city has succeeded; the other party, however, also claims success. Our Senator ticket seems admitted on both sides to have prevailed.

1800 Bishop *Conn. Republicanism* 58 . . . 20,000 votes in favor of the democratic ticket.
1818 Fearon *Sk.* 142. An announcement, called "The Ticket," issues from this Caucus a few days before the election; in this case there were three of these "tickets" severally headed, *Federal, Republican,* and *Democratic.*
1835 Crockett *Van Buren* 102. It is said the Clark party, in the face of all the facts I have mentioned, as well as against their notorious opposition to him in the last election for the same office, in which they had an organized ticket against him, are now about to support this same Van Buren. . . .
1848 *Free Soil Banner* 21 Aug. 3. Ohio, Wisconsin and the New England States will probably vote for the Free Soil Ticket.
1860 *N. Y. Trib.* 3 Jan. They didn't like some one who was on the Republican ticket.
1889 Farmer *Americanisms* 533. A list of candidates placed in nomination for office, as the "Democratic ticket," the "Prohibition ticket," etc. A "straight ticket" comprises all the regular party nominations. A "split ticket" represents different divisions of a party. A "mixed ticket" combines the nominees of different parties. A "scratch ticket" is one from which one or more names have been erased.

Tilden and reform.

A. A Democratic slogan of 1876.

1876 *Harper's W.* 3 June 443/1. The cry of Thurman and reform, Hendricks and reform, Bayard and reform, has no meaning whatever. But Tilden and reform will have a real significance to many more than the Democratic party, and we think, if the party managers are wise, they will not fail to raise it.
1876 *Ib.* 11 Nov. 906/2. "Tilden and Reform" can be successful only by fraud at the North and force in the South and the inflation sentiment in the West. . . . Under the cry of "Tilden and Reform.". . .

B. In 1878 when the Democratic part in the fraudulent dispatches

of 1876 was made public, the slogan was revived by the Republicans to mock Tilden and his party.
1878 *Harper's W.* 2 Nov. 866/2. "Tilden And Reform."... Will it not possibly occur to them that a man who was chairman of the Democratic State Committee during all the ascendency of Tweed, and who took no public stand against him, was not a man to represent to intelligent New Yorkers the cause of political purity and reform?... 867/2 Since the foregoing article upon "Tilden and Reform" was in type, Mr. Tilden has published a general and explicit denial of all guilty knowledge of the cipher telegrams. **1878** *Ib.* 2 Nov. 869. [Nast cartoon showing Tilden as a "Cipher Mumm (er) y"] Tilden and Reform.

timber.

Men who are regarded as potentially good candidates.

A. The building term is adapted by Bacon to the political vocabulary.
1607–12 Bacon *Ess., Goodness* 206. Such disposicions are ... the fittest tymber to make great Pollitiques of.

B. In American politics:
1833 Beriah Greene in Wilson *Slave Power* I.249. If there is not timber amongst ourselves big enough to make a president of, let us get along without one. **1837** *Ohio St. Jrnl.* 18 Oct. 3/2. The Vanocracy of Champaign were so scarce of timber out of which to manufacture a representative.... **1880** *Cleve. Plain Dealer* 20 June 1/4. The situation now so chaotic arises from the fact that there is a superabundance of timber. **1896** *Rev. of Rev.* XIV.424. There are sharp eyes looking out on all such occasions for presidential timber, and "fool friends" unable to contain themselves. **1914** White *Editor and People* 32 ... he is everlastingly and preëminently N.G. as gubernatorial timber—full of knots, warts, woodpecker holes, and rotten spots.

1923 *Rev. of Rev.* LXVIII.229. He [McKinley] had been patient, impartial, unselfish throughout the convention, and seemed like a piece of well-seasoned presidential timber. **1924** Rogers *How We Elect* 33. Talk about Presidential Timber, why, Man, they had whole Lumber Yards of it here.

time serving.

Describes politicians motivated only by their own self interests.
1807 *Weekly Inspector* 366. Our time-serving politicians (some calling themselves federalists, as well as others) have strove long to catch the gale of popular applause, by pretending to be peculiarly hostile to Great-Britain. **1836** Mrs. Child *An Appeal* 138. The time-serving class—so numerous in every community,—who are always ready to flatter existing prejudices, and sail smoothly along the current of popular favor, join it [American Colonization Society], of course.

time to unload.

A phrase, attributed to President Grant, advising the casting out of certain undesirable party officials.
[ ]
1875 *N. Y. Trib.* 12 Feb. 6/3. Following the elections of 1873 the President was delivered of a Delphic utterance in interpretation of the results; and the men who kow tow around him hastened to give it to the country. He said it was "time for the party to unload." **1876** *Ib.* 4 March 6/3. Time to Unload. [head] But we think not enough stress has been laid upon the wise and pointed utterance in the title of this article, which is also one of the President's [Grant's], and one of his pithiest and best. It was delivered, if we remember rightly, about the time the Republican party began to stagger under the weight of the Crédit Mobilier disclosures....

tin pan.

Whig nickname for the caucus of

the Ohio Democracy; a caucus in general.

A. There are several conflicting suggestions as to the origin of this name, two of them centering around the Tontine, a Columbus coffee house:

1835? in Lida Rose McCabe *Don't You Remember?* 73. [Democrats served oysters in tin chafing dishes, Locofocos served mush and milk.] For ten years, thereafter, the Democratic party was known all over the State as the tin pans, and ever after the name clung to the coffee house.

1839? in A. G. Riddle *Life of Benj. F. Wade* 136. An elevated Whig member of the house, in his exhilaration on the floor one day, irreverently called it [Tontine Coffee House] Tin Pan, and so it was ever after known.

Another offers a more metaphorical origin:

1842 *Cinc. D. Gazette* 14 Sept. 2/3. The History of A Tin Pan [series of articles, signed "A Hard Worker"]. In Ohio this system [log rolling] is brought to great perfection by a contrivance which is very appropriately called the *Tin-pan.* You that are farmers have often seen a swarm of bees sailing through the air in search of a habitation, kidnapped by a fellow who beats on a tin-pan, and pelts them with clods of dirt, until the insects are so confused with noise and dust, that they settle down and suffer themselves to be covered with a box. The man with the tin-pan carries them off and sets them to work for him. It is just so with the members of the Legislature when they arrive at Columbus. The State Printer, Auditor, and a few others commence beating a tin pan, and throwing dust in the eyes of the new members of the party, until the whole are driven into a box prepared for them.... To lay aside this figure, the Tin Pan is a secret society, into which the leaders of one party and the members of the Legislature of that party are admitted ...

Early quotations from politics definitely point to the Tontine as the headquarters of the state Democrats.

1836 *Ohio People's Press* 25 May 4. The Tin Pan. [head] ... This must be the place that has been so often spoken of under the name of the "Tin Pan."

1836 *West. Hemisphere* 6 July 2/6 ... made a desperate charge on the Tin Pan, (according to Whiggery, the head quarters of the democracy,) but ... the concern was found empty.

1837 *Ohio St. Jrnl.* 27 Oct. 2/3. The Tinpan. Our neighbor Pike of the TINPAN, is renovating and fitting up his famous establishment in superior style, preparatory to the annual gathering together of the brethren of the faith, in December.... The power of the Tinpan utterly prostrated.

1836 *Ohio St. sw Jrnl.* 8 April 1/1. When "tin pan" politicians or drunken vagabonds resort to such means for the purpose of exciting the prejudices, and inflaming the passions of the ignorant and uninformed against a candidate....

B. The Democratic caucus:

1836 *Ohio St. Jrnl.* 30 Aug. 3/2 ... higher honors than those of which he was deprived last winter by a mandate from "the Tin Pan."

1839 *Cinc. D. Gazette* 14 Feb. 3/1. The Michigan Locofocos do not yield to caucus as obediently as our Ohio Tinpans.

1839 *Ohio St. Jrnl.* 26 Nov. 2/1. This cabal or caucus, more recently designated by the sonorous appelation of "Tinpan." ... ... and a severe pledge was extracted from each Tinpanner to enforce in the Legislature what the majority of the Tinpan should decree.... In the next Legislature, or rather Tinpan ...

1840 *Cinc. D. Gazette* 7 Sept. 1/2 ... the members of "Holy Midnight Tinpan" who last winter read the *"Test Oath"* to the candidates for Judgeship at Columbus.

C. Referring to the Whig caucus:

1840 *Ohio Statesman* 7 Dec. 2/4. All had been settled on Saturday night last in *Tin pan,* by these *anti-caucus* politicians; but, most unfortunately, the "bottom was knocked out" on the first trial. A Mr. Birney . . . was nominated in the "whig tin pan" on Saturday.

1843 *Ib.* 20 Dec. 3/3 . . . no sooner do the Whigs get here with a majority in the House, than they meet in caucus or "tin pan". . . .

1844 *Ib.* 20 Feb. 3/4. The coons have had a terrible time in tin pan, and are afraid to go into the elections.

1844 *Ib.* 27 Feb. 3/1. Tin-Pan Lyrics. [2 campaign songs]

(#1) There's hell among the whigs,
       The coons begin to roar;
       Jo Hawkins' sow & pigs
       Are tusking Duncan's bore.
       The de'il has set them kicking
       And smashed the old tin pan
. . . .
(#2) Oh what is the matter, my darling?
       Is the bottom of the tin-pan out?

1844 *Ib.* 9 Dec. 2/3 . . . there is a third house, on the corner of High and Broad streets over which *still* floats the tattered banner of Clay and Frelinghuysen, known to all the boys in the city, as the "whig tin pan," . . . where may be seen, going in and out, the Whig Central Committee, and *their* representatives in the General Assembly.

D. Tinpanning—caucusing in general.

1838 *Ib.* 22 Jan. 2/5. Federal Tinpanning. How often have the people of this state heard the hypocritical cry of federalism about *"Tinpanning"* and *caucusing*—how the Democrats would meet *out* of the Legislature, nominate their candidates, and then convene *in* it and merley [sic] record their edicts!

1840 *Ib.* 9 Dec. 3/3 . . . such a "pipe laying" system of tinpanning as the reformers of the House of Representatives have adopted, is a disgrace to the *caucus.*

1843 *Ib.* 15 Dec. 2/7 . . . the practice of "tin-panning," or submitting to a caucus the consideration of a matter which is about to be acted upon in the Legislature. . . . At the coon-skin fandangoes of 1840, they [Whigs] sung the "dy-

ing groans of the tin pan," and carried a tin vessel, with the bottom bursted out of it, upon a pole . . . and falsely professing that they would condemn as an abuse, and correct what they termed a corrupt practice in legislating.

1855 *Ravenna* (Ohio) *Campaign Dem.* 17 Sept. 2/4. When the article appeared in our columns, charging the Sag-Nichts of Ravenna with having tinpanned the nomination of David Johns for Commissioner, it was met with flattest denial.

tomahawk.

To defeat by treacherous means.

1880 *Cleve. Leader* 1 June 1/5. General Beatty is waging an active, earnest and effective war against John Sherman, and Charley Moore has his tomahawk already red with the blood of Jake Donaldson and raised to cut, if possible, into nobler game.

1898 *Milwaukee Sentinel* 12 Jan. 6/2. There is also a disposition manifested on the part of some to tomahawk him.

1928 Allan Franklin *Trail of the Tiger* 149. Tammany's rule or ruin tiger . . . inaugurated the method of tomahawking candidates who did *not* obey the wishes of the Boss.

See also KNIFE; STAB IN THE BACK.

Tom Tinker's men. [ ]

Whiskey men (q.v.).

1794 John Shippen in Balch *Ltrs. & Papers* 302. It is surprising and laughable, that in this country, every body tells you they were forced by threats to go to such and such place, and they talk violently against the proceedings of Tom Tinker's men, (for that is the name of the Whiskey-boys now,) and when you ask them, where are the persons that threatened them, and that were principals, "Oh! they are run off"; which is not altogether untrue, for numbers have fled, but numbers of those that remain are as guilty as they.

1885 *Mag. Am. Hist.* April 396/1. During the Whiskey Rebellion . . . the house of an obnoxious official was pulled to pieces by a mob whose members gave out they were "mending it." Mending and "tinkering" being interchangeable terms, the members dubbed themselves "tinkers," and "Tom the Tinker" was shortly evolved as the popular watchword of the first rebellion against the United States Government.

torchlight (meeting, procession).

An outdoor political event illuminated by flaming torches.

1837 *New Yorker* 441/3. A Loco-Foco "torchlight meeting," auxiliary to the larger concern in Tammany, was held in the Park on Thursday evening.

1842 *Ann. of Cleve.* No.1941. The Whigs of Cleveland and Ohio cities will have a grand Torch Light procession this evening.

1844 *Whig Battering Ram* 23 Aug. 3/4. The Locofocos of this city . . . announcing a grand torch-light procession.

1856 *Middletown* (N.Y.) *Banner of Liberty* 56/1. Midnight—torch light procession; kettle drums; serenade; make a speech, great cheering; rotten egg hits me in the eye; general fight; spanners, brick bats, clubs, banners, torches and fists.

1858 *Miss. Republican* 31 Aug. in Sparks *Deb.* 194. But a new feature has here been introduced into the reception. By the side of every main street there are flaming torches, each with a living bearer. . . .

tornado.

The earliest known American use of the term is from the 18th century.

1780 *Phil. Trans.* LXX.493. A tornado last night, with a deal of rain, thunder, and lightning.

Numerous political examples are to be found in the early decades of the 19th century.

1828 *Mangum Papers* I.321. If you delight in storms and tornadoes—you might be gratified here [Washington]—there is scarcely a day—which does not elicit angry feelings in debate.

1836 *West. Hemisphere* 26 Oct. 1/6. As Popular As a Tornado. The popularity of a Tornado is new to us as it probably is to a majority of our readers. But a letter incorporated in an editorial article of the Baltimore Patriot, informs us that in Penn. the "popularity of Gen. Harrison is like that of a tornado!" The comparison is certainly a queer one. There never were two things more unlike than a tornado and the petticoat hero; the one surprises, and the other, as at Tippecanoe, is surprised.

1837 *New Yorker* 553/1. When the Albany Argus and other journals of that stamp simultaneously exclaim, "A tornado has swept over the State," they can mean nothing else than this.

However, the popularity of *tornado* in the political vocabulary seems to begin with the campaign of 1840, along with other names for natural forces of devastation. (See AVALANCHE, WHIRLWIND, PRAIRIE FIRE, EARTHQUAKE.)

1840 *Log Cabin* 15 Aug. 2/3. The Harrison Tornado is Sweeping over Kentucky and Indiana.

1840 Kennedy *Quodlibet* 209. The Log Cabin instantly became the representative of a sentiment, and a word of power, and in a perfect tornado of enthusiasm, was raised in every village, hamlet and meeting ground in the land.

The effect of the word in 1840 was undoubtedly strengthened by accounts of a particularly destructive tornado which swept through Mississippi in the early spring.

1840 *Frankfort Commonwealth* 19 May 2/6. We are indebted . . . for the following particulars of the destruction of a great portion of Natchez, by one of the most appalling tornadoes with which the Mississippi has been visited within the recollection of the oldest inhabitant. . . .

3/2. The awful tornado that has desolated Natchez is the great topic of conversation.

Later political occurrences:

1844 *Ohio Coon Catcher* 17 Aug. 1/3.

Coons all dead—curled up by a Democratic tornado.

1844 *Wash. Globe* 7 Sept. 855/4. There were seven States that gloriously resisted the hard-cider tornado, and gave their votes in 1840 to the democratic candidates.

1846 in Nason *Wilson* 84. Confident that in five-years our cause will sweep through the country like a tornado. We shall carry every free State with a whirlwind: it will go like the fire over the prairies of the West.

1848 *N. Y. Herald* 8 July 1/3. A tornado of enthusiasm is sweeping down all remnants of opposition to Gen. Taylor.

1860 Barr in *Cong. Globe* App. 442/3. We shall not, therefore, be driven from our safe Democratic moorings by the fitful gusts of a tornado that springs from the miasma and swamps of contracted and almost unknown localities; it may spend its fury in vain, unless, perchance, it should, by the attraction of affinity, be wafted across the bay, and float over the neighboring city of rowdyism and plug-law; it can neither affect nor taint the healthy Democratic atmosphere of Virginia and can do but little harm outside her borders.

Tory.

Like *Whig* (q.v.), *Tory,* taken over from English party life, underwent a specialization of meaning before and during the War of Independence. Originally applied to what we now would call "conservatives," it became more and more the name of Americans opposed to independence. In the process it acquired the character of a derogatory word.

1765 Adams *Works* II.168. I began to suspect a Tory sermon, on the times, from this text, but the preacher confined himself to spirituals. But, I expect, if the tories should become the strongest, we shall hear many sermons against the ingratitude, injustice, disloyalty, treason, rebellion, impiety, and ill policy of refusing obedience to the Stamp Act.

1769 *Boston Gazette* 24 April 3/2. Keep your Rights out of Sight, and you may have any Thing you please. A Tory.

1775 *Boston Evening Post* 6 March. Our meek and tender lambs, the Tory Refugees, who have fled to this town for protection, are incessantly inculcating ... that the people of this province are a set of timid mortals.

The word remained in use in the post-Revolutionary period, as an epithet for the Federalists in their opposition first to Jeffersonian principles and later to the policies which led to the War of 1812:

1807 *Weekly Inspector* 366. Those who maintain different principles, are tories of a very vile species—They are French tories—they are jacobin tories—they are Bonaparte's tories.—They are pursuing measures, and are the advocates of principles, which would place the world at the feet of France.

1810 Jefferson *Writings* XII.373. The toryism with which we struggled in '77, differed but in name from the federalism of '99, with which we struggled also; and the Anglicism of 1808, against which we are now struggling, is but the same thing in still another form.

1812 *N. Y. Evening Post* 28 Oct. 2/4. The war-hawks of that vicinity ... began abusing him with the usual slang of Federalist, old Tory, &.

Somewhat later there is a tendency toward the identification of *tory* with what was later to be called "conservative," especially in Federalist campaigns:

1823 *Cinc. Nat. Rep.* 22 April 1/1. The Bucktails and Clintonians have for a long time filled New York with their contentions, and have fought as if they were whig and tory, instead of belonging equally to the old republican party.

1824 *Ib.* 1 Oct. 2/1. Republicans of Ohio, keep a bright look out for Caucusites, Tories, and office hunters.

1824 *Ib.* 31 Aug. 1/1. The former cannot conceive that Toryism may not be Federalism. . . .

The attempt of the anti-Jacksonians to saddle the Jackson party with *tory* is described under *Whig.* During the Civil War *tory* was used in both the North and the South; to Northerners with Southern sympathies and to Southerners who stood by the Union.

1861 Brownlow *Sketches* 91. The South can look upon you in no other light than as a traitor and a Tory, and the twin brother of Andrew Johnson.

1861 Gen. Jeff. Thompson in Logan *Gt. Conspiracy* 364 [Proclamation of 31 Aug.]. I . . . will make all tories [Unionists] that come within my reach rue the day that a different policy was adopted by their leaders.

1862 *Cleve. Leader* 3 Dec. 2/1. Fernando Wood, leader of the tories in New York.

1862 *Ashland* [Ohio] *Times* 18 July 2/1 [edit.]. How the Tories talk.
8 Aug. 2/2.
To be a democrat is to be a secessionist.
To be a democrat is to be a traitor.
To be a democrat is to be a tory.

1866 Reid *After the War* 402. If you fetch any d— tories heah, that went agin their State, and so kin take the oath, . . . 'twill soon be too hot to hold 'em.

According to Mencken (*Am. Lang. Suppl.* I.299) *tory* was used "in 1896 for advocates of the gold standard, and in 1933 for persons who refused to accept the New Deal."

Later example:

1912 Roosevelt *Works* XVII.252. It [Dem. Platform on States rights] is sufficiently unreasoning to satisfy every rural Tory in the country, every man who believes that . . . we can get back to the conditions of the fifties.

[trade names.]

Under *advertisements* (q.v.) political trade names were mentioned as devices to attract buyers. To these examples add:

1844 *Coon Dissector* 14 June 2/2. Clay pencils.

1840 *Straightout Harrisonian* 7 July 4/5. Straight-Outs and Harrisonians! Look well to the basis upon which you STAND. The Subscriber has on hand and for sale at his Shoe Store a fine supply of Gentlemen's Tippecanoes. A splendid summer article. Also—Nullifiers, Monroes, Slippers, &.

1840 Parton *Greeley* 181. There were Tippecanoe medals, Tippecanoe badges, Tippecanoe flags, Tippecanoe handkerchiefs, Tippecanoe almanacs, and Tippecanoe shaving-soap.

1856 *Bellefontaine* (Ohio) *Republican* 7 March 4/4. Young America Excelsior Corn and Cob Mill.

Occasionally the names were applied for satirical purposes:

in Congdon *Reminiscences* 26. I doubt if any public man was ever more thoroughly hated than General Jackson was then in Massachusetts. We even named a cutaneous complaint contracted in barbers' shops after that much admired and much abused hero. Then there was a particularly disagreeable square-toed boot which we called the Jackson.

1846 *Cleve. Herald* 28 Jan. 2/2 . . . what hatters call a "Tyler cap," to be worn either side out.

See DOLLY VARDEN.

tramp (party, vote).

A term known in England since the 17th century but which came into vogue in America in the 1870's:

1883 in *Cong. Record* 1678/2. Under your protective-tariff system . . . on every hand are counted the "tramps," a name that was never heard of until this high protective system brought into existence the class which it describes.

1888 in *Ib.* 153/1. For a number of the years since 1870, the country has been filled with "tramps."

1894 in *Ib.* 1748/2. It [the protective system] has helped to envest anthropology with new interest by adding to its classifications the "snob" and the "tramp."

Thus: Tramp party:

1878 *N. Y. Trib.* 30 Aug. 4/2. New Jersey also has a Tramp party. Its official name— "The National Greenback-Labor party"— is too long and meaningless for use.

Tramp vote:

1878 *N. Y. Trib.* 30 May 4/6. The democrats make a bald bid for the tramp vote when they try to muzzle the army that it cannot suppress riots.

treasury leeches.

1828 *Georgetown Castigator* 18 March 3/2. "Treasury leeches" (by which I mean men who disregard the welfare of the people, and seek office and emolument merely for the money they derive from them) are seen to spring up and monopolize power.

See PAP.

treasury rat.

Office holder or spoilsman who robs the public crib. (q.v.)

c1848 Prentice *Prenticeana* 162. Perhaps it is not strange that these treasury-rats have an antipathy to the wife of the patriotic old farmer-President [Taylor]. Probably said rats have in mind the fate of the three blind mice—

       —"The farmer's wife, She cut off their tails with a carving knife."

1823 *Cinc. Nat. Rep.* 19 Aug. 4/1. He [an astrologer] states, that the steel trap is prefigurative of the terror which the election of the people's candidate will be, to treasury rats—the trap is a thing per-

fectly harmless, except to dishonest fingers.... it means those treasury rats who have so long lived upon the public money by dishonest means.

trimmer (trimming).

One who vacillates in his party allegiance, always favoring that which has most to offer him personally.

A. The nautical phrase *to trim the sails* so as to get the greatest advantage of the wind is behind the political use of the term. *Trimmer* became widely known in England as applied to Lord Halifax (1680–90), who accepted the epithet in the sense of "one who keeps even the ship of state." (See *OED*)

B. In America the derogatory meaning prevails throughout the word's history.

1765 Adams *Works* II.167. Let the towns and the representatives therefor, renounce every stamp man and every trimmer next May.

1789 Foner *Jefferson Basic Writings* 576. I am neither federalist nor antifederalist; that I am of neither party, nor yet a trimmer between parties.

1802 in *Dem. Rev.* I.231. An accommodating trimmer, who would change with times and bend to circumstances for the purposes of personal promotion.

1807 *Weekly Inspector* 255. Cheetham is wheeling and wheedling, and twisting and trimming, at a fine rate.... But, we believe he will blunder into the right path at last, as respects national defense.

1830 *Workingman's Adv.* 29 May 3/4. To put down political trimmers—those who make politics a trade.

1844 *Dem. Rev.* XV.326. Clay ... forever trimming his sails afresh to woo to them every stray breeze of seeming popularity.

1858 Richardson *Secret Service* 312. Lincoln ... who without "trimming" enjoyed the support of the many-headed Opposition in Illinois.

1869 Curtis *Orations* II.14. The victory of the other party—in which case all the trimmers and camp-followers of the victors will enter upon the spoils.

1880 *Cleve. Leader* 3 June 1/3. The Grant men delegates, alternates and trimmers were taking not only second but third, fourth and even fifth choice on yesterday.

Trojan horse.

A politically dangerous gift; a trap.

1837 in Dickey *Prentiss* 85. He cannot so easily introduce this Trojan horse within these walls [seating of contested members in Mississippi House]. I for one will hurl a spear against its hollow sides.

1847 *Niles' Reg.* 18 Sept. 47/1. Like the Trojan horse, this fatal gift of Mexican territory is fraught with danger and death.

1867 Dennett *Hay* 18 March 278 ... in which he compared the Johnsonian policy to the Trojan horse and himself to the sagacious Laocoon.

1880 *Harper's W.* 481. [cartoon: Hancock as a Trojan horse.]

1944 Hoover *Add. upon the Am. Road* 249. Already the New Dealers have planned a large number of Trojan Horses labelled "Liberalism" and "Freedom" stuffed with a mixture of totalitarian economics and with doubtful statistics.

It is obvious from several of the above quotations that many politicians were familiar with Virgil and Greek legend. Compare:

1802 Hamilton *Works* VII.244. To admit foreigners indiscriminately to the rights of citizens ... would be nothing less than to admit the Grecian horse into the citadel of our liberty and sovereignty.

troughsman.

A subordinate politician who depends upon sharing in the government moneys or the "public crib" or "trough."

1904 *Nation* 23 June 500/2. The grafters ... comprise ... a number of lesser persons spoken of as "troughsmen." These used to be called "henchmen," then "heelers," but the newer word may be accepted without cavil.

1904 Lynde *The Grafters* 153. He filled the vacancies with political troughsmen.

twisting the lion's tail.

Humorous allusion to American defiance of the British lion's might.

1889 Roosevelt *Ltrs.* I.157 ... just at present our statesmen seem inclined to abandon the tail of the lion, and instead are plucking vigorously at the caudal feathers of that delightful war-fowl, the German eagle—a cousin of our own bald-headed bird of prey.

1898 Dinsmore in *Gt. Deb.* III.199. Indeed that pre-eminent twister of the British lion's caudal appendage, Senator Henry Cabot Lodge, of Nahant ... , is not to be satisfied with the one island of Cuba in the West Indies. ...

1898 Schurz *Writings* 24 April V.465 ... for the present attitude of Great Britain will no longer permit the American demagogue to seek popularity by twisting the British lion's tail.

1915 Page *Ltrs.* II.123. While our Irishmen have been leading us to twist the lion's tail, we've been depending almost wholly on English ships.

1954 *Nation* 2 Jan. 2/2. Twisting the Lion's Tail. [McCarthy and Brit.-China trade]

Earlier similar phrases to express American disdain for British power:

1846 Shaw *Lincoln Cartoons* I.123 ["Gen. Bunkum"] ... here's a bird that will cut your British lion's liver out, and eat it cold without sugar, by thunder!!!

1846 *Ohio Statesman* 23 Feb. 2/5. Your fathers shook the lion's mane.

1872 *Harper's W.* 6 July 521. [cartoon showing Grant with his foot on the lion's tail.]

two dollars a day and roast beef.

One of the Whig slogans in the campaign of 1840, created to attract the votes of the laboring classes.

1840 *Niles' Reg.* 19 Sept. 44 [Inscription on banner of Bunker Hill Convention].

> Matty's policy: fifty cents a day,
> And French soup!
> Our policy: two dollars a day,
> And roast beef.

1844 *Whig Battering Ram* 18 Oct. 2/3. Two Dollars A Day And Roast Beef.... The Statesman has asserted that the above was the inscription upon banners borne in almost every whig procession during the campaign of '40. We deny the assertion.

Tylerize.

A few weeks after assuming the Presidency, John Tyler was at loggerheads with other members of the Whig party because of his support of certain Democratic policies. During his term the breach widened and many regarded him as no longer a Whig. Thus *to Tylerize* became a term meaning to forsake the party to which one owes allegiance or office.

1848 *Maysville* (Ky.) *Campaign Flag* 8 Sept. 3/5. You can't come it—we've been Tylerized once.

1851 *Oregon Statesman* 6 June 2/6. It will be seen from our Telegraphic despatch that the President has Tylerized at last and in earnest.

1860 *Cols. Gazette* 25 May 2/3. Is it probable that Mr. Lincoln, if he is elected, will undertake to Tylerize the Republican party by ignoring its strong active men, and creating a party himself out of the weaker elements and fossil remains?

1877 *N. Y. Trib.* 12 April 5/1 ... the leaders who have arrayed themselves against the Administration mean to make it surrender or Tylerize it.

U

ukase.

A command or decree, felt by the opposition to be similar to the oppressive *ukaz'* of the Russian Czars.

1867 *Harper's W.* 22 June 386/1. "Despotic Ukases" [head] ... The orders of the commanding Generals [in the South] are "despotic ukases" [according to Democratic papers].

1872 Durbin Ward *Sp.* 104. The judgments of the courts are constitutionally the final arbitraments of litigated rights, but Radicalism, through a subordinate lieutenant, revokes them by a military ukase.

1895 Altgeld *Live Questions* 459. Under this procedure a federal judge ... can on motion of some corporation lawyer issue a ukase which he calls an injunction forbidding anything he chooses to and which the law does not forbid.

ultramontane.

In church politics long used in France and Germany to refer to the Italian control of the papacy; and in Italy to designate all outside attempts to seize power. The term was frequently used in American politics in the 1870's to apply to the close association of the Democratic party and the Catholic Church. The doctrine of papal infallibility announced in 1870 and the struggle in New York between the state and the church over public education helped to renew the term and its sinister connotations.

1875 *Harper's W.* 9 Oct. While the editors of the ruling section of the Democratic party are crying out for the destruction of the whole system of public instruction, while from Oregon to Massachusetts, every Roman Catholic *ultramontane* is a democrat....

1875 *Ib.* 16 Oct. Not a word is suffered to escape the lips of Democratic orators of the fact that their party is founded upon a solid basis of *ultramontanism.*

1876 *Ib.* 18 March 226/2. Between the Congress of 1863–64 and the Congress of 1875–76 a resemblance exists that is not altogether accidental.... To both the Democratic Representatives came borne into power by a sudden uprising of the ultramontane population of the large towns. It was observed that in all the elections of 1862 the ultramontane element was singularly active.

1876 *Ib.* 2 Sept. It was upon the *ultramontane* population of New York (Irish) that the indiscreet utterances of the Democratic leaders in Congress or in their public and private meetings, produced the most dangerous effect.

un-American.

A. The term does not always necessarily apply to politics.

1817 Birkbeck *Notes on a Journey in America* 23. Ninety marble capitals have been imported at vast cost from Italy, to crown the columns of the Capitol, and shew how *un*-American is the whole plan. There is nothing in America to which I can liken this affectation of splendor, except the painted face, and gaudy head-dress of a half-naked Indian.

c1848 in *New Yorker* 14 Feb. 1948, 17/1. About a hundred years ago, George Palmer Putnam, the publisher, visited London and while there paid some royalties to Elizabeth Barrett. Mr. Robert Browning, an outspoken poet of the day, heard about the incident and expressed great surprise that Mr. Putnam's firm, Wiley & Putnam, had not pirated Miss Barrett's work, as was the custom at that time. Said Browning, "Wiley and Putnam are fine fellows, who do a really straightforward, un-American thing."

B. The following list of political usages shows the great variety of opinions and measures that have been branded as *un-American* or *anti-American* in earlier instances

before the term was fixed. Among the earliest uses in politics is its application as a criticism of the self-styled American Party.

1841 *Mangum Papers* V.637. This hateful doctrine of repudiation, and the still more anti-American doctrine ... of the repeal of charters.

1844 *Am. Volunteer* 16 May in Geary *Third Parties* 96. Misguided men assuming the title Native American, but un-American at heart, breathing destruction on those not born here, denouncing a whole religious community and all professing a particular faith have been joined with the Whigs.

1850? Seward in Sanderson *Republican Landmarks* 200. It is sufficient for me to say that, in my judgment, every thing is un-American which makes a distinction of whatever kind, in this country, between the native born American and him whose lot is directed to be cast here by an overruling Providence....

1855 Henry Wise in *Sons of the Sires* 201. So far as it opposes our naturalization laws, it is not only against state policy, but against Americanism itself. In this it is especially anti-American.

1855 *Ann. of Cleve.* No. 2803. But several ... have no sympathy with the "Un-American" and "Un-Republican" principles of that order.

1856 *Middletown* (N.Y.) *Banner of Liberty* 47/1. I confess that I have been much alarmed at the political aspect of demagogism in our country, but have been lead to thank God and take courage at the signal defeat of the anti-American party....

1870 *N. Y. Times* 7 Jan. 4/5. It [*N. Y. Trib.*] stigmatizes its opponent as false to his party, or as "un-American"—its two favorite and well-worn labels.

1876 Garfield in *Garfield-Hinsdale Ltrs.* 343. I have been very hard at work, trying to master the complicated problem of Louisiana politics. I have been in what seemed a different world from ours—a world in which the modes of thought and action are, in many respects, un-American and un-Republican.

1876 *Harper's W.* 26. Feb. 162/1. So, in regard to municipal government, it is a widespread conviction that the suffrage for municipal purposes exclusively should be confined to the tax-payers.... But there is very little public and direct discussion of such opinions, because they are thought to be un-American.

1878 Curtis *Orations* II.131. I venture to say that nothing is more un-American than the present practice. Under the system of patronage as now administered the public service is the monopoly of a few men of the dominant party in every State.

1896 Dem. plat. in *The Parties and the Men* 444. It [gold monometallism] is not only un-American, but anti-American....

1903 in Mitchell *Organized Labor* 189. The task of pulling up root and branch the un-American institution of trade unionism as at present conducted.

1917 in *Roosevelt Cyc.* 13/2. Everything is un-American that tends either to government by a plutocracy or government by a mob. To divide along the lines of section or caste or creed is un-American. All privileges based on wealth, and all enmity to honest men merely because they are wealthy, are un-American—both of them equally so.

1921 *Sel. Ltrs. of W. A. White* 220. To make a case against a birthplace, a religion, or a race is wickedly un-American and cowardly.

1924 LaFollette in White *Politics: The Citizen's Business* 317. We are unalterably opposed to any class government, whether it be the existing dictatorship of plutocracy or the dictatorship of the proletariat. Both are essentially undemocratic and un-American.

1948 *New Yorker* 14 Feb. One questionable thing about the House Committee on un-American Activities is its name.... The word "un-American," besides beginning with a small letter and gradually working up to a capital, is essentially a foolish, bad word, hardly worth the little hyphen it needs to hold it together. Literally, nothing in this country can be said to be un-American. "Un" means "not," and any-

thing that happens within our borders is American, no matter what its nature, no matter how far off the beam it may be.

The following quotation points to the conditions under which the term probably had its origin. The activities of Alexander Hamilton to which Garfield alludes have not been fully investigated.

1880 Garfield *Works* I.xix. More than a hundred years ago, a young student of Columbia College was arguing the ideas of the American Revolution and American Union against the un-American loyalty to monarchy of his college president and professors.

Uncle Tomism.

This and other coinages (*Uncle-Tomitude, Uncle Tomized, Uncle-Tomific;* see *DA*) indicate the popularity of *Uncle Tom's Cabin,* both in America and abroad.

1853 *N. Y. Trib.* 21 Feb. 4/3. Europe has achieved the luxury of a new sensation in the reception and digestion of Mrs. Stowe's great work.... Even our Diplomacy stands aghast at the rushing, swelling flood of Uncle Tomism which is now sweeping over the continent.

unconstitutional.

The word is used in 18th-century England in the sense of "not in harmony with, or authorized by, the political constitution; at variance with the recognized principles of the state" (*OED*). Naturally the meaning "at variance with the regulations laid down in a written constitution" does not attach to the English word, which refers to binding practice rather than to legal acts; neither could it prevail in American usage before 1787. Wherever American writers use it before this period, it has necessarily the English sense.

The word became prominent in American politics in connection with the Stamp Act of 1765 and similar matters.

1765 Carter *Corr. of Gen. Gage* 12 Oct. I.69–70. [Question which congress was debating was not one] of the inexpediency of the Stamp Act, but that it is unconstitutional, and contrary to their Rights, Supporting the Independency of the Provinces, and not subject to the Legislative Power of Great Britain.

1765 Adams *Works* 14 Oct. III.465. We shall confine ourselves, however, chiefly to the act of Parliament, commonly called the Stamp Act, by which a very burthensome, and, in our opinion, unconstitutional tax, is to be laid upon us all. . . . We take it, clearly, therefore, to be inconsistent with the spirit of the common law, and of the essential fundamental principles of the British constitution. . . .

1765 Dickinson *Writings* 19 Oct. II.195. The invaluable Rights of taxing ourselves, . . . are not, we most humbly conceive, unconstitutional, but confirmed by the great Charter of English liberty.

1768 *Ib.* II.312. There is another late act of parliament, which appears to me to be unconstitutional, and as destructive to the liberty of these colonies, as that mentioned in my last letter; that is, the act for granting the duties on paper, glass, etc.

1770 J. Quincy in Harlow *Sam Adams* 157. The holding the General Court, from its antient [sic] and proper station, is unwarrantable, unconstitutional illegal and oppressive.

1774 in West *Source Book* 422. All which statutes are impolitic, unjust, and cruel, as well as unconstitutional, and most dangerous and destructive of American rights.

1774 in Davidson *Propaganda in the Am. Revolution* 61. Those [resolutions] that were drawn up in the summer of 1774 all professed loyalty to George III but declared the Intolerable Acts "unconstitutional, oppressive, and tyrannous."

1786 in Coxe *Judicial Power* 234f. Judge Cooley observes that this [Trevett *v.* Weeden, Rhode Island, 1786] was the first American case in which a law "was declared unconstitutional and void." [Based upon report in *Providence Gazette,* October, 1786]

After the Constitution came into existence all important measures were debated upon the question as to whether they were constitutional or not, a development clearly foreseen by the *Federalist:*

1788 *Federalist* 295. The truth is, that this ultimate redress may be more confided in against unconstitutional acts of the federal than of the State Legislatures.

Following is a selection in which various issues are held to be unconstitutional by one group or another:

1789 Madison in *Hist. of Congress* 13 May 339. I understood it had been intimated that the motion was inconsistent or unconstitutional.

1798 in Koch *Jefferson and Madison* 191. Taylor's change restored Madison's original wording [of Virginia Res.], inviting the states to "concur with this commonwealth in declaring as it does hereby declare, that the aforesaid acts are unconstitutional."

1803 in *Gt. Deb.* II.110. It has been argued that the bill [Louisiana Purchase] ought not to pass because the treaty itself is unconstitutional. . . .

1814 *Niles' Reg.* 5 March 6/2. The committee are of opinion that the late act laying an embargo is unconstitutional, and void in divers of its provisions; not upon the narrow ground that the constitution has expressly prohibited such acts, but upon the more broad and liberal ground that the people never gave a power to congress to enact them.

1816 Clay in *Gt. Deb.* XIII.60. I infer either that the legislature did not believe a bank to be unconstitutional or that it had formed no opinion on that point. . . .

1828 Calhoun *Works* VI.2. [South Carolina Exposition] . . . the result, on full investigation, is a unanimous opinion that the act of Congress of the last session, with the whole system of legislation imposing duties on imports,—not for revenue, but the protection of one branch of industry at the expense of others,—is unconstitutional, unequal, and oppressive, and calculated to corrupt the public virtue and destroy the liberty of the country. . . .

1836 Leggett *Pol. Writings* 31 Dec. II.157. A Writer . . . has undertaken to prove the unconstitutionality of the restraining law, on the ground that it is a violation of that clause of the federal constitution which declares that no state shall grant any title of nobility.

1861 *Northern Editorials* II.718. It is simply the Republicans fighting for the unconstitutional Chicago platform.

1862 Christy *Pulpit Politics* 480. The pretense that such a purchase and admission into the Union are unconstitutional, is the only plausible justification for the otherwise treacherous or fanatical cry of Disunion, which so often deafens our ears.

1864 in *Lincoln Cyc.* 383. I felt that measures otherwise unconstitutional might become lawful by becoming indispensable to the preservation of the Constitution through the preservation of the nation.

1896 *Nation* 2 July 3/1. Judge Wright of the Illinois Circuit Court has declared unconstitutional and void the State law requiring the national flag to be displayed over every schoolhouse.

1911 *Roosevelt Cyc.* 18 Nov. 595. For the Supreme Court to nullify an act of the Legislature as unconstitutional except on the clearest grounds is usurpation.

This list could be greatly enlarged by following the indications given in Swisher, *American Constitutional Development*, 1943.

In some cases objections to the constitutionality of a measure were not based upon a supposed violation of the U.S. Constitution—or any constitution.

1857 Sandburg *Prairie Years* II.37. The bridge was built, even though the Chamber of Commerce of St. Louis voted . . . that a bridge across the Mississippi River was "unconstitutional, an obstruction to navigation and that it was the duty of every western state, river city, and town to take immediate action to prevent the erection of such a structure."

This leads to instances in which there is a complete degeneration of meaning.

1848 *Carpet-bag* II.3/3. Doughnuts, sir, is unconstitutional; and I'll just tell you why.

1868 Sumner *Works* XVI.341. Yes, it is the old Democracy, . . . after thwarting every measure for its [Rebellion] suppression as "unconstitutional," from the Proclamation of Emancipation to the firing of a gun or the condemnation of Vallandigham,—after interfering with enlistments also as "unconstitutional," . . . champions the Lost Cause.

1876 *Harper's W.* 19 Feb. 142/3. If a strict constructionist wants a measure to succeed, it is constitutional, and if he does not want it, it is unconstitutional.

under dog.

As a name for the downtrodden, neglected individual or class, the term has become increasingly popular in the vocabulary of many politicians asserting their loyalty to the underprivileged but numerically powerful lower classes.

Under dog was apparently first used in a poem by David Barker (See *Marietta Republican*, 22 July, 1859, 1/1).

1892 Walsh *Lit. Curiosities* 243. The phrase "the under dog in the fight" seems to be a modern one, and may have been derived from the once well-known song by David Barker, which ran as follows:

. . . .
But for me,—and I care not a single fig
  If they say I am wrong or am right,—

I shall always go in for the weaker dog,
 For the under dog in the fight.
1900 *Rev. of Rev.* XXII.177/1. The man who managed and voted in that convention represented, consciously or unconsciously, the under-dog elements of society —the elements which are in a state of discontent.
1907 in Heaton *Cobb of The World* 71. A Democrat who is a Democrat from principle instinctively sympathizes with "the under dog."
1926 Sullivan *Our Times* I.10. A certain mood that was prevalent in America in 1900, a mood of championship for the under dog against the upper, a disposition of the average American to see himself as an under dog in economic situations and controversies in his own country.
1932 Carter *What We Are About to Receive* 57. Cockleburr Bill Murray, Governor of Oklahoma, is being put forward as a Jacksonian populist and will receive strong backing from the poor white, hillbilly, down-and-out, under-dog element which undermines the political pretensions of the stately orators of the Solid South.
1934 Carter *New Dealers* 374. And when Al [Smith]—who once was the hero of the under-dog—lines up with the New York plutocracy, he can no longer work his old magic on his followers.
1956 *New Rep.* 16 Jan. 7/2. Is the ancient gibe to be revived that liberals will rally only to the cause of the under dog?

The Union as it was and the Constitution as it is.

A Democratic slogan of 1864.

1864 in Logan *Gt. Conspiracy* 548. He [Powell] professed that he wanted "the Union to be restored with the Constitution as it is."* [footnote] ... This phrase slightly altered, in words, but not in meaning, to "The Union as it was, and the Constitution as it is," afterward became the shibboleth under which the Democratic Party in the Presidential Campaign of 1864, marched to defeat.
1864 Thad. Stevens in Logan *Gt. Con-*

spiracy 561. All this struggle by calm and dignified and moderate "Patriots"; all this clamor against "Radicals"; all this cry of "the Union as it Was, and the Constitution as it Is"; is but a persistent effort to reestablish Slavery, and to rivet anew and forever the chains of Bondage on the limbs of Immortal beings.
1864 Robert C. Winthrop in *Dem. Camp. Doc.* No.9. At another we have heard open declarations from the high places of the land, that we never again were to be permitted to have "the Constitution as it is and the Union as it was." Good Heavens, what else are we fighting for?

The formula with variations existed several decades earlier:

1844 *Kennebec Jrnl.* in *Frankfort Commonwealth* 15 Sept. 1846. [If Clay is elected] we shall have the Union as it is.
1844 *Buckeye Eagle* 11 Sept. 2/2. [Whig banner] The Union As It Is; No Annexation.
1844 (Col. Ohio) *Facts for the People* Aug. 4/3. The democrats decide to preserve THE CONSTITUTION AS IT IS.
1850 in Foner *Business & Slavery* 48. Let no man who is not known to be firmly and resolutely opposed to all further agitation, who is not known to be an ardent supporter of the Constitution AS IT IS, be entrusted with political power.
1851 in *Ib.* 78. It [Union Safety Com.] has encouraged the Union men of both parties, so that in the Legislature, and in future conventions, they will speak out, and speak plainly in favor of the Union as it is, the constitution as it is, and the Compromise as it is.

Union hater.

A Republican who placed his abolition views above the preservation of the Union:

1858 *At. Mon.* II. 758/1 ... he [Cushing] assures us that there are thirty million Americans who stand ready "to devour and swallow up" the "handful of negrophilist Union-haters."

Union lover.

Like *Union saver* (q.v.) an ironical term applied to those who wanted to save the Union at any price:

1863 Beecher *Patriotic Add.* 85. There were the few men of the South, and the Union pronounced anti-slavery men of the North, and the few pronounced slavery men of the South, and the Union lovers (as they were called during the latter period) attempting to hold the two together, not by a mild and consistent adherence to truth plainly spoken, but by suppressing truth and conviction, and saying "Everything for the Union."

Union saver (Union saving).

An ironical term applied to both Northerners and Southerners in the decade prior to the Civil War who tried to prevent the dissolution of the Union by a policy of appeasement or by a professed love of country based upon the *status quo.* The term was probably in use as early as 1850, although our actual quotations begin only with 1853.

in Wilson *Slave Power* II.311 [writing of events after the passage of the Fugitive Slave Act]. Dr. Cheever, did not leave his hearers in doubt as to what laws they should obey. To the "Union-savers" of that day, who counseled submission for the sake of harmony and peace....

1853 *Ann. of Cleve.* No.2425. Inasmuch as A. H. Stephens, Daniel S. Dickenson, Robert Toombs, Rufus Choate, Lewis Cass and other "Union savers" are invited to take part in the proposed convention, we are led to suppose that it is to be an intensely Hunkerish, pro-slavery party, which expects to save the Union by promptly catching runaway slaves, suppressing the finer emotions of humanity, and opposing all schemes of progress.

1853 *N. Y. Trib.* 5 March 6/2. The Legislature of Illinois, wherein the spirit of Union-saving and hostility to agitation reigns supreme, has just passed an act to forbid and punish the immigration of Negroes and Mulattoes into that State.

1854 *N. Y. Trib.* 24 Nov. 4/2. Suffice it that the Know-Nothing movement is in the hands of the Union-savers of 1850....

1854 *Harper's Mon.* IX.402. "Union Saving" has for some time past been a byword and a reproach.

Union shrieker.

Synonym for *Union saver.*

1863 Hunnicutt *Conspiracy Unveiled* 129. And when they would speak as they always did, of the "Union-shriekers," the "followers and admirers of old Abe Lincoln"....

United Roses. [ ]

1870 *San Fran. Golden Era* XX.69/4. Tennessee has a secret society of colored men known as "The United Roses of Old John Brown."

the unterrified.

A nickname for an ultra section of the Democratic party, almost synonymous with *hard (shell)* (q.v.).

A. Milton says in *Paradise Lost* (v.896):

So spake the Seraph Abdiel, faithful found;
Among the faithless faithful only he;
Among the inummerable false unmoved,
Unshaken, unseduced, unterrified,
His loyalty he kept, his love, his zeal.

That the political use of *unterrified* goes back to this passage is more than likely since not only the earliest application to politics is a direct quotation from *Paradise Lost* but also some of the later quotations couple *unterrified* with *unseduced:*

1823 DeWitt Clinton in *Cinc. Nat. Rep.* 16 May 2/5. In the midst of senseless clamor, and malignant denunciations, you [N.Y. friends] continued

> "Unmoved, Unshaken, unseduced, unterrified"....

1840 *Democratic Rev.* VII.290. Through all this tempest Mr. Van Buren remained calmly at his post at the helm of the state, alike unterrified and unseduced. **1841** *Ann. of Cleve.* No.1494. It [Whig press] is unseduced and unterrified.

B. To begin with, *unterrified* is not a party name but rather an honorary epithet:

1839 *Cong. Globe* App.185/3. I take leave, in his [Rives] own strong language, to say that I *too* am an "unterrified" Senator of the unterrified Commonwealth of Virginia.... **1840** *Ann. of Cleve.* No.1755. Vermont never has bowed the knee, and never will. Faithful and bold—unsubdued and unterrified!

It is more than doubtful whether Thornton is right in giving 1832 as the earliest date of *unterrified* as a party name. He quotes from an 1860 edition of Seba Smith's *Downing Letters* (equal to *Thirty Years out of the Senate*):

Mr. Van Buren was taken up by the "unterrified Democracy" to run as Vice-President on the ticket of "old Hickory."

But this is from a footnote added in this late edition and not to be found in the earlier ones. Only from 1840 on is the word unambiguously used as a party faction name:

1840 in *Rough-hewer* 12 Sept. 263 ... the immense procession of wagons ... filled with the unbought and unterrified democracy of Tompkins. **1840** Kennedy *Quodlibet* xx.... the indefeasible, unquestionable and perpetual right of succession to the Presidential Chair, claimed by and asserted for the candidate of the great, unterrified, New Democratic school of patriotic defenders of the spoils.

1842 *Ohio St. Jrnl.* 5 Oct. 1/2. The "unterrified" Democratic Whigs of Richland assembled in large numbers.... **1848** *Ib.* 11 Jan. 2/3. It might have been supposed that the "unterrified" would at least have listened quietly to his [Tappan's] suggestions. **1849** *Cinc. Daily Gazette* 26 May 2/3. The Wails of the "Unterrified." Yes, the "unterrified democracy," as they called themselves.... **1853** *Syracuse Jrnl.* 20 Oct. The "Unterrified" held their ratification on Tuesday evening. [Contributed by Constance Robertson, author of an historical novel, *The Unterrified.*] **1855** *Ravenna Campaign Dem.* 10 Sept. 3/1. The Unterrified Slice and the Terrified Slice of the Democratic party. **1868** *N. Y. Times* 2 Sept. 5/2. The "Unterrified" Terrified. [head]

C. As seen from these examples the word is mostly used sarcastically. Its quick deterioration is shown by its being coupled with *unwashed* (q.v.).

1853 *Weekly Oregonian* 8 Jan. At this point a great portion of the unwashed, as well as the "unterrified" left the hall. **1854** *Ib.* 22 April. Brother Waterman must have help. Come, ye unwashed and unterrified to the rescue.

unwashed (great unwashed, unwashed democracy).

A. Although Brewer's *Reader's Handbook* attributes the phrase to Burke, no quotation has been offered to justify this claim. In the first recorded example, the use of quotation marks implies that the term was known as a synonym for the lower class in England before 1833.

1833 T. Hook *Parson's Daughter* II.119. The "fat and greasy," and the "great unwashed," bowed and smiled their best.

... But the bright-eyed wives and daughters of the gentleman "soap and tallow line,"... looked on, and in "their looking, looked unutterable things"....
1841 in Hodder *Shaftesbury* 181. My popularity, such as it is, lies with a portion of the "great unwashed."

B. In America the phrase is found as both adjective and noun, with and without *great* but always referring to those who supported the Democratic party.
1844 in Julian *Recoll.* 40. They [Whigs] insisted that ... the larger element of ignorance and "unwashed" humanity, including our foreign-born population, gave victory to Mr. Polk.
1845 *Ann. of Cleve.* No.1437. The "unwashed" hailed the addition of Texas to the union.
1857 *Ib.* No.1538. The great unwashed Democracy assembled in terrific numbers at the old court house.
1876 S. S. Cox *Why We Laugh* 147. Over in Simpson County, I was compelled to sleep in the same bed with this distinguished nominee, this delight of his party, this wonderful exponent of the principles and practices of the unwashed Democracy, and in the morning I found myself drunk on corn whisky.
1876 *Cinc. D. Gazette* 24 June 1/4. Gathering of the Clans of the Great Unwashed. [St. Louis convention]
1884 *Cleve. Leader* 11 Oct. 4/7. Thomas A. Hendricks Addresses the Great Unwashed at Cincinnati. [head]
1946 W. A. White *Autobio.* 61. When election time came around, this black abolition Republican, who was my mother, and this Stephen Douglas Copperhead Democrat who was my father, still unwashed, still voting for Jackson, had their purple moments.

upas tree.

A Javanese tree which yields a poisonous juice.

Used metaphorically in England from early in the 19th century.

1818 Byron *Childe Harold* iv.cxxii.
This uneradicable taint of sin,
This boundless upas, this all-blasting tree.
1824 *Westminster Rev.* April 464. That Upas tree, which has since borne all the bitter fruits of Turkish oppression.
1833 *Blackwoods* XXXIII.88. Hang out your rags on the infidels' Upas tree, Root and branch dripping with poison and blood.

Used in American politics occasionally to stigmatize various oppressive measures such as slavery, the national bank, etc.
1819? in Halleck, *J. R. Drake* 340
There's magic in the robe of power
Ennobling everything beneath it.
Its spell is like the Upas' bower
Whose air will puff up all that breathe it.
1834 *N. Y. Courier and Enquirer* 5 April 2/3. The friends of the Kitchen Cabinet dread these discussions, on the subject of Executive usurpations, as they would dread, if within its atmosphere, the Bohon Upas of Java.
1840 *Dem. Rev.* VII.292. He [Van Buren] saw that the whole [economic depression] had its primary origin in the radical viciousness of that fatal paper-money banking system which has grown up, like a Upas tree, to poison the atmosphere of the land which it overshadows....
1840 *Fillmore Papers* II.209. The *Extra Globe* is a perfect Bohon Upas in the field of truth and virtue. Its noxious leaves are falling in every town and hamlet....
1864 Bret Harte *Works* VIII.20. ["The Copperhead"]
There is peace in the swamp, though the quiet is death,
Though the mist is miasmia, the upas-tree's breath,
Though no echo awakes to the cooing of doves,—
There is peace; yes, the peace that the Copperhead loves.
1874 *Cong. Record* App.147/2. The repeal of these obnoxious measures [tariff], which, like the baleful bohun-upas, sheds its seductive, but poisonous perfume on

all around, is imperatively demanded.
1891 *Nation* 12 Nov. 366/3. So that we
think we can confidently assure our Republican contemporaries that they cannot
get rid of their Bosses without laying the
axe to the *root* of that upas tree, the
spoils system.

usufruct.

The temporary use or enjoyment
of property or office.

A. In American diplomatic language:
1846 Polk *Diary* I.161. He thought the
Brittish [sic] title under the Nootka
Sound Treaty was a mere usufruct and
conferred no claim....

B. After Samuel J. Tilden used
the term in his letter of acceptance
in 1876, the opposition frequently
satirized both his scholarship and
his wealth by labelling him "Usufruct" or "Usufructuary."
1876 Tilden in Appleton's *Ann. Cyc.*
790/2. The public interest in an honest,
skillful performance of official trust must
not be sacrificed to the usufruct of the incumbents.
1876 *Harper's W*. 16 Sept. 749 [cartoon].
Exile Tweed to Usufructuary Tilden. 764
[cartoon]. Usufructuary Tilden.
30 Sept. 789 [cartoon: Tilden as hound
with "Usufruct" collar.]
8 Oct. 865 [cartoon: barrel "Usufruct
from Tilden."]

V

Vanocrat.

Nickname for supporter of Mar-
tin Van Buren: Van (Buren) +
(Dem) ocrat.
1840 in Julian *Recoll*. 19.
  Ye jolly young lads of Ohio,
  And all ye sick Vanocrats, too,

Come out from among the foul party,
  And vote for old Tippecanoe.
1840 in Norton *Tippecanoe* App. 40.
Then let us stick to him young, old, and
  all,
And like old Proctor's men, Matty must
  fall;
Turn, then ye Vanocrats, fear not their
  sneers,
Harrison, Harrison—give him three
  cheers.
1840 *Harrison Dem*. 14 July 3/3. Vano-
crat Arguments [head].

vassal.

One of the many terms of contempt used in the South to designate the Union armies.
1862 Heartsill *1491 Days in the Confederate Army* 68. Lincoln has ordered his
hords of Northern Vassals to invade our
Confederate Government and force us
into submission.

See HIRELING, MINION, MYRMIDON.

vest pocket vote.

An early and rudimentary form
of secret voting.
in Kerr *John Sherman* I.24. At this election [1854] there was practiced, perhaps
for the first time what afterwards came to
be known as vest pocket voting. Voters in
large numbers would approach the polling places with their tickets folded in
their vest pockets, and without giving the
electioneers about the polls an opportunity to address them, would hand their
tickets to the election judges.
1888 *N. Y. Trib*. 27 Oct. The vest pocket
vote will be important this year in this
State. There will be many Democrats,
faithful to their party on National issues,
who will yet have too much self-respect to
vote for David B. Hill. There are Democrats who want to vote against Cleveland, but who will hardly like to do it
openly. The Republicans must see that
this is made easy for them.... There will
be many ... men who will not care to apply to Republicans for ballots, and who

will not be in a way to get them without doing so. A very simple method of meeting this want will be for every Republican paper in the State to print the Republican ticket, being careful to have it properly "backed," so that any person desiring to do so can cut it out and vote it. In this way any Democrat who wants to vote [Republican] ... can get a ballot, which he can slip into his vest-pocket and make use of on Election Day without any of his Democrat friends being the wiser.

viceship.

The vice-presidency.

1831 *Liberty Hall* 22 Sept. 1/2. And the great demagogue of Missouri, too, is indisposed to recognize the right of Pennsylvania to the Viceship.

Vigilance Committee (and related terms).

The earliest organizations of this type seem to have been directed against the abolition movement.

1826 *Mangum Papers* I.293. Philadelphia, whence this committee of superintendence and vigilance emanated.
1831 *Boston Transcript* 17 Oct. 2/2. The "Vigilance Association of Columbia,". . . have offered a reward of fifteen hundred dollars for the apprehension and prosecution to conviction of any white person who may be detected in distributing . . . [abolitionist literature].
1835 Garrison *Garrison Story* I.519. The slave States . . . have organized Vigilance Committees and Lynch Clubs.

Later, various organizations, similar to the Regulators (q.v.) adopted the names "Vigilance Committee," "Vigilante," etc.

1836 *Scioto Gazette* 27 July 2/1. Many of our political friends in the county as well as in town, are desirous that Committees of Vigilance should be appointed in each township, or in each school-district if thought proper, whose duty it shall be to disseminate correct information among the people, touching the candidates before them.
1851 *San Francisco Herald* 1 July 2/2. A large number of the Vigilance Committee proceeded yesterday to the County Prison, by invitation of the Sheriff.
1852 Letts *Calif. Illus.* 54. They consequently organized themselves into what was termed a "Vigilance Committee," with the determination of bringing every suspicious person to a strict account.
1852 Royce *Calif.* 323. We have a Committee of Vigilance who are determined that, until a different state of things exists, they will not disband, but will punish in the most exemplary manner all and every high-handed offense against life and property.
1858 *Toledo Blade* 2 Jan. 2/3 [from Lawrence, Kansas, December 24, 1857]. To stop these depredations [by ruffians] the Free State men organized a Vigilance Committee.
1874 Foote *Casket* 163. When about sixteen years ago the second vigilance committee was organized in San Francisco, the Governor ... sent General Sherman ... instructions to put down the forces of the committee at all hazards.
1874 *N. Y. Times* 6 July 4/7 ... Gov. Coke, of Texas, has been issuing proclamations, telling the vigilants that they must not lynch accused men any more.

VIP.

1944 *Collier's* 26 Feb. 73. VIP* means Presidents, Prime Ministers, Secretaries of State, Diplomats, Senators, Secretaries of War, and Navy, Generals, Admirals, Technicians.
* VIP is Army's language for "very important people."
1945 *Fortune* Aug. 161. Very important people, or "Vips," usually travel in plush C-54's.... A brigadier general is reasonably sure to be considered a Vip; with colonels it is touch and go. Foreign dignitaries are always Vips, and the status is usually accorded high government officials, ranking editors and publishers, and movie stars.

VIPI.

See VIP.

1945 *Fortune* Aug. 210/2. A "V.I.P.I.," the very top drawer in the command's aristocracy of passengers, is a Very Important Person Indeed.

visible admixture.

A. A mixture of races.

1831 *S.C.Ct. Appeals Rep.* II.558 [*DA*]. Where there is a *distinct* and *visible* admixture of negro blood, the individual is to be denominated a mulatto, or a person of color.

1860 *Sandusky* (Ohio) *Comm. Reg.* 19 July 2/3. "V. A." in Virginia. [title]

B. Bills introduced to exclude persons of mixed blood from citizenship.

1868 *Ann. of Cleve.* No. 2611. The Democrats have tried to get the visiable [sic] admixture bill passed, but as yet it is not a law.

1868 *Cong. Globe* 2452/2 [*DA*]. The whole question of the "visible admixture" law ... is one of the most ... characteristic chapters in modern Democratic history.

visionary (adjective and noun).

Long used in England, the term has retained its derisive connotations in American politics.

1770 Burke *Works* I, 124. [*Pres. Discont.*]. If a man happens not to succeed in such an enquiry, he will be thought weak and visionary.

1776 Paine *Works* II.136 [*Common Sense*]. To say they will never attempt it again is idle and visionary; we thought so at the repeal of the Stamp Act, yet a year or two undeceived us.

1811 *Balt. Fed. Republican* 29 Oct. in Mayo *Clay* 400. Even Editor Hanson of "Pickering's Gazette" professed to hope that a stand would be taken after "years of self-immolation upon visionary experiments."

1836 Byrdsall *Loco Foco* 66. [If] business cannot prosper but at the sacrifice of the rights of the people, If so, then is a democratic government only fit for the region of Utopia, and democrats are visionaries.

1840 Steenrod in *Cong. Globe* 17 April ... a system not to be supported by any correct principles of political economy—a gross delusion, the dream of a visionary.

1905 Brissenden *I.W.W.* 94. Even Daniel DeLeon had nothing but contempt for "the visionary politician, the man who imagines that by going to the ballot box and taking a piece of paper—throwing it in and then rubbing his hands and jollying himself with the expectation that through that process, through some mystic alchemy, the ballot will terminate capitalism and the socialist commonwealth will rise like a fairy out of the ballot-box."

vote-gett(er, -ing).

The primary attribute of any candidate.

1905 Bohn in Brissenden *I.W.W.* 95. Socialist to the core must the new economic organization be—and when the June convention has painted the skull and crossbones on the door of "pure and simpledom," that last working-class compromise with capitalism, there will probably issue a political organization strong in numbers, but stronger in principle, because raised by the revolutionary spirit high above "mere vote-getting subterfuge."

1933 Guilfoyle *Forgotten Man* 39. The Senator [Walsh] had been the most popular vote getter in Massachusetts over a long period of years.

1936 *Rev. of Rev.* XCIV.15. Lehman the Vote Getter. 16. He [Farley] had come to the conclusion that Mr. Lehman—unsurpassed vote-getter—would have to sacrifice his personal preferences this year in the interest of the President and the New Deal.... [caption:] Governor Lehman of New York, Empire State's most potent vote getter, yields to the blandishments of Farley, Wagner, and Robinson.

The degree to which vote getting may be predicted is suggested by the following burlesque:

1912 *Cinc. Enquirer* 23 June 15/4 ... Mr. Harmon has the flannel suit vote almost solidly.... Gaynor has the button vote. It is sharply and celluloidly for him. ... The hat band vote is undoubtedly for Dr. Woodrow Wilson.... and he is a close second in the button vote.... The map vote is for Champ Clark.... [his] managers were wise in canalling this vote early in the day.... The lithograph vote and the brass band vote are hopelessly split up ...

vote yourself a farm.

A slogan of the Anti-Rent party (q.v.) in New York in the 1840's; also a political faction.

1845 in Foner *Labor Movement* 11 Oct. I.186 [based on quotations from *Young America*]. In 1845, the walls of New York were plastered with circulars bearing the title, "Vote Yourself a Farm."

in Barnes *Weed* 141n. "There used to be at that time [1847] in New York (he added) a political sect called the 'Vote-yourself-a-farm' party."

1848 *Old Zack* 1 July 2/1 ... it [a meeting] was convened for the double purpose of forming an Anti-Slavery and Vote-yourself-a-farm Club....

1851 Smith *Thirty Yrs. Out of the Senate* 338 ... the Union Safety Committee party, and the regular Free-Soil party, and the regular Vote-yourself-a-Farm party.

voting cattle.

In 1831 James Gordon Bennett wrote:

Memoirs of Bennett 127. What have we? An organized corps ... buying men and votes as cattle in the market.

For several decades after this date American examples are missing but it must have been frequently used since several German authors refer to it as characteristically American:

1856 Frobel *Aus Amerika* I.500. Es ist bei der Herrschaft solcher Grundsätze kein Wunder, dass die fremdgeborenen Bürger sich bei ihren politischen Herren und Meistern den Ehrennamen *voting cattle,* d.h. Stimm-Vieh zugezogen haben.

1858 *Columbus Westbote* 30 Sept. 2/1. Die Ritter von der deutschen republikanischen Presse sprechen von "voting cattle!" und rümpfen die Nase über deutsche Landsleute die mitrichtigen Tact, der demokratischen Partei ihren Gestutzung geben.

in Ladendorf *Hist. Schlagwörterbuch* 303. Stimmvieh dringt als eine verächtliche Bezeichnung kritikloser Wählermassen in den sechziger Jahren des 19. Jahrhunderts von Amerika herüber nach Deutschland und wird in gleicher Bedeutung besonders zum politischen Lohnwort. Blankenburg, Die innern Kämpfe der nordamerikanischen Nation (1869) S.41 berichtet über Deutsche und Iren in Amerika: "Die Eingewanderten wurden mit dem Namen Stimmochsen (voting cattle) belegt, was sie natürlich nur noch mehr anregte, mit der demokratischen Partei zu gehen."

American examples:

1857 *Ann. of Cleve.* No.1464. A great majority of these voting cattle are foreigners ... who are so completely under the control of corrupt fuglers of the party that they will even turn out at the "firing of a gun."

1860 in Carpenter *Causes of the War* 5 Oct. 27/1 [from *Chic. Trib.*]. Taken altogether, the squatter reception, last evening, fell below what had been promised, but furnished an instance of what a few determined wire pullers can do with a few hundred *voting cattle.*

1874 De Forest *Honest John Vane* 27. The veteran leaders in politics saw that the "cattle" as they called the common herd of voters, were determined for once to run the party chariot.

walkathon.

A technique of soliciting votes by going from door to door. See TALKATHON.

1954 *Cols. Citizen* 31 Oct. 1. Republicans led by President Eisenhower and Democrats led by Adlai Stevenson countered each other today with unusual "talkathons" and "walkathons" in last minute get-out-the-vote bids for control of congress. The Republicans did it by telephone; the Democrats by doorbell ringing.

In the 1930's walkathons were one of the popular endurance fads, along with dance marathons and flagpole sitting.

1932 *K. C. Times* 20 Feb. 26. Sure a hick town is a place where they have enough superhicks to put on a walkathon.

walking corpse.

A name proposed for defeated congressmen.

1925 *Searchlight on Congress* March 19. This has been called the "lame duck" session. It might as properly be called "the session of the walking corpses."... Many had been condemned to "political death" by the voters. But their official burial, under the Constitution, could not take place till the 4th day of March, 1925. Nor could their bodies, under the Constitution, lie in a political morgue till that day should come.... Walking corpses may well become malodorous. It is a revolting figure of speech. For that reason it is better to continue to use the pleasantly satirical term "lame ducks"....

walking delegate.

A labor union official who acts as a business agent for the union, enforcing rules, arranging contracts with employers, etc.

1892 Howells *Quality of Mercy* 131. She decided that he must be a walking-delegate, and that he had probably come on mischief from some of the workpeople in her father's employ.

1902 *World's Work* IV.2428/2. Each local union has the regular officers including the important business agent (once called

"walking delegate," a name now generally discarded).

1903 in Mitchell *Organized Labor* 216. Shall employers be permitted to conduct a lawful business in a lawful way without the dictation of walking delegates from irresponsible and lawless unions?

1903 *Nation* 3 Sept. 180/2. The conviction and sentence of Parks, the walking delegate, for extortion have aroused public interest extraordinarily.

1904 *Weber's W.* 5 Nov. 1. May 7, 1903, four walking delegates, representing the four unions to which the union workmen of the Kellogg shop belonged, called upon the company officially and presented drafts of a written agreement....

walk over (v. and n.).

To win an election with little effort.

A. In horse racing it has long been the tradition that a superior horse which often has no opposition must only walk around the track to be the winner of the race.

1823 "Jon Bee" *Dict. Turf* "To walk over" another is...to set him at naught, as a racer which is so vastly superior to other cattle that none dare start, and he walks over the course.

B. In politics:

1834 *Niles' Reg.* 1 Nov. 130/1. We agree ...that he should be allowed "to walk over the track"—"unopposed."

1836 *Ann. of Cleve.* No. 882. Old Tippecanoe is walking over the course.

1836 *Louisville Jrnl.* 21 Sept. 1/4. In Maryland, on the 6th inst., the Whig nag walked round the course. The Van Buren pony ran at the top of his speed, and was beaten by two whole lengths after all. Let him be used hereafter for a dray-horse.

1844 *Nat. Intell.* in Minnegarode *Presidential Yrs.* 236. Clay will have only to walk over the course.

1867 in Dennett *Hay* 293. He is not a Grant man but he says the General has no fight to make—will walk over the course.

1874 *N. Y. Times* 10 Sept. 1/7. Upon his

[Tilden's] ... leaving the track clear for a walk over by Church, depended Democratic hopes.

1880 *N. Y. World* 23 Sept. 4/3. The Republicans ought to have a "walk-over" in October.

1885 *Puck* 23 Sept. 50/1. We don't expect —we don't want—a walk-over in this contest.

1912 *Harper's W.* 29 June 11/1. Looks as if Bryan had a walkover.

war to the knife.

Unflinching hostility or opposition.

A. In a note to canto I.lxxxvi of "Childe Harold" (1812) —

Such be the sons of Spain, and strange her fate.
They fight for freedom who were never free;
. . . .
Back to the struggle, baffled in the strife,
War, war is still the cry, "War even to the knife!"—

Byron says, "War to the knife. Palafox's answer to the French general at the siege of Saragoza."

B. The saying became popular all over Europe, and in America we find it applied to politics, enlarged by the addition of "knife to the hilt."

1837 in *Cong. Globe* App. 20/2. The bill has been denounced in advance upon this floor, and war to the knife has been declared against it.

1842 in Hellon and Butler *William Bollaert's Texas* 49. General Houston has issued a proclamation to the volunteers which, as it does not breathe "War to the Knife" and "Onwards," makes the President unpopular with the War Party.

1844 Duncan in *Wash. D. Globe* 6 Jan. 22/2. We have heard them declaring "war to the knife and the knife to the hilt," dissolution of the Union and all that sort of thing.

1844 *Ib.* 12 Jan. 43/2. He [C. M. Clay] is, in fact, one of his most devoted political partisans, and has *literally* carried the party war around Ashland to the knife—and from the point to the hilt. It was this Mr. Clay who cut Mr. Brown to pieces with a Bowie knife.

1847 in *Mangum Papers* V.25. Who are the principal "War to the knife" men in your body for instance?

1856 Lovejoy in Bigger *Gibson* 255. If I use my Sharp's rifle, I will shoot in God's name. I am for war to the knife, and knife to the hilt, if we are forced to make it so.

Warm Spring Indians.

A faction of the Republican party in Mississippi. [ ]
See MODOC

watchdog of the treasury.

A person, usually a member of the House of Representatives, who tries to limit the expenditure of public money.

1827 *Spirit of Seventy Six* 29 March 3/4. The watch-dogs of the Treasury ... have made loud and grievous complaints about the waste of public money in purchasing a Billiard Table.

1853 *N. Y. Trib.* 10 Jan. 4/5. The economists of the House (and there is really a handful of members who strive to guard the Treasury on all occasions) might put a stop to such voting by boldly exposing its enormity.

1853 in *Cong. Globe* 11141/1. If I were to select the man in this House who was the most faithful watchdog over the Treasury of the U.S., I would select the gentleman from Alabama.

c1866 Kerr *Sherman* I.229. Mr. Holman was given the sobriquet of "watch-dog of the Treasury," and he was justly entitled to it.

1884 *Boston Jrnl.* 20 Sept. Cleveland ... gave a promise of his ability to become the watch-dog of the United States Treasury.

Also designates persons who guard other expenditures and revenues:

1874 *N. Y. World* 25 Aug. 2/2. Four trunks came with her.... Yesterday, on examination they were found to contain a large quantity of kid gloves and black silks carefully covered with wearing apparel. It is hinted that overtures to mislead the watch-dogs of the revenue were made.
1874 *Cinc. Enquirer* 22 Sept. 4/1. Mr. Sater is represented as a great watchdog of the County Treasury.
1947 *Toronto Daily Trib.* 21 Dec. 12/1. [Vishinsky] spoke for more than 90 minutes, raking the United States for ... proposing that the assembly send a semi-permanent UN "watchdog" commission....

waxface.

A doughface (q.v.) .

1855 *Ann. of Cleve.* No.2553. Let the dirt-eaters and *waxfaces* unite their forces.

See also NOSE OF WAX.

wayward sisters, depart in peace.

The slogan of the peaceable secessionists of the North, generally attributed to General Winfield Scott in a letter to Seward written March 3, 1861:

1861 Scott in Elliott *Scott* 3 March 698. Say to the seceded States, Wayward Sisters, depart in peace!

However, there are suggestions that the phrase was invented by other public figures:

Isely *Greeley* 305. Greeley's basic condition for peaceable secession was a solemn and deliberate judgment on the part of the people of the slave states. For this reason, such eye-catching quotations as "Wayward sisters, depart in peace" is to distort his intent. [Referring to editorial following election of Lincoln.]
Wilson *Slave Power* III.32. Mr. Corwin, in opening the debate, said he should confine himself mainly to "an explanation of the motives which have induced the committee to make the recommendations of the report.... To pacify and persuade

the 'wayward sisters' to return to their allegiance...."

We have not found any contemporary evidence for either of the preceding quotations, but we do know that fragments of the phrase were used before Scott's letter:

1848 *Ohio St. Jrnl.* 9 May 2/2. That man who dared to stand up in an assembly of the citizens of his State, and threaten to eke out, the scanty support ... *let him depart in peace.*
1860 *N. Y. Trib.* 9 Nov. 4/2 ... if the Cotton States shall become satisfied that they can do better out of the Union than in it, we insist on letting them go in peace.
1860 in Greeley *Am. Conflict* 9 Nov. I.334. Cooperation with our Southern sisters has been the settled policy of South Carolina for at least ten years past.
1860 *Wash. Nat. Rep.* 26 Nov. in Perkins *North. Editorials,* I.192 ... a State whose people are desirous of dissolving their connection with the Federal Union should be permitted to "go in peace"....
1861 *Col. Capital City Fact* 9 Feb. in Perkins *Ib.* I.352. Her [S.C.] sister conspirators are no less determined in their treason than she. Let them go, if they will, where they will.
1861 in *Appleton's Annual Cyc.* All we [the South] ask is that we be allowed to depart in peace.

weasel word, phrase.

A word or phrase which by its ambiguity destroys the clarity or force of a statement.

Popularized by Theodore Roosevelt, who frequently illustrates the metaphor, and in a later writing (see 1919 quot.) attributes the phrase to Dave Sewall of Maine.
1912 Roosevelt *Works* XIX.350f. With a cautious accompaniment of weasel phrases each of which sucks the meat out of the preceding statement.... "by legislation that will not injure or destroy legitimate industry." This is as fine an example of a

weasel phrase as could ever be imagined. **1916** *Ib.* XXIV.483. One of our defects as a nation is a tendency to use what have been called "weasel words." When a weasel sucks eggs the meat is sucked out of the egg. If you use a "weasel word" after another there is nothing left of the other. **1919** Roosevelt *Maine My State* 19. It was from Dave that I heard an expression which ever after remained in my mind. He was speaking of a local personage of shifty character who was very adroit in using fair-sounding words which completely nullified the meaning of other fair-sounding words which preceded them. "His words weasel the meaning of the words in front of them," said Dave, "just like a weasel when it sucks the meat out of an egg and leaves nothing but the shell"; and I always remembered "weasel words" as applicable to certain forms of oratory, especially political oratory which I do not admire. **1943** Cross *Conn. Yankee* 232 ... Roraback insisted upon a verbose prohibition statement in a vague platform which, appropriating an animal that Theodore Roosevelt introduced into politics, I described as weasel words. Each sentence was a weasel to kill the sentence immediately preceding, until a reader reached the last sentence which I myself dispatched. All the words then lay dead, void of meaning. **1946** Alinsky *Reveille for Radicals* 28. Liberals in their meetings utter bold words; they strut, grimace belligerently, and then issue a weasel-worded statement "which has tremendous implications, if read between the lines." **1954** Barkley *That Reminds Me* 142. No grounds for accusing the Democratic party of using weasel words in its prohibition plank.

The expression, however, is recorded as early as 1900:

1900 *Cent. Mag.* June "And like most platforms ... it contains plenty of what I call weasel words." " ... weasel words are words that suck all the life out of the words next to them, just as a weasel sucks an egg and leaves the shell. If you heft the egg afterward it's as light as a feather, and not very filling when you're hungry; but a basketful of them would make quite a show, and would bamboozle the unwary."

wet blanket.

The metaphorical use of *wet blanket* may go back to the use of the dampened blanket or sheet as a fire extinguisher, but it is probable that the revived interest in the cold water cure in the 1830's and '40's (see Cruikshank, *Comic Almanack,* frontispiece) is responsible for its popularity in the political vocabulary.

1844 *Ohio St. Jrnl.* 24 Aug. 2/2. Easily Satisfied—A Torchlight Procession—A Wet Blanket! [rain] **1848** Seba Smith *Thirty Yrs. Out of the Senate* 311 ... if I can make our friends show a bold front for Cass there, it will be such a wet blanket for the Whigs that they'll give it up. **1848** *Ann. of Cleve.* No.1079. The nomination of Taylor fell like a "wet blanket" on the Whigs of the Reserve. **1868** Hayes *Diary* 14 July III.54. Yes, hurrah for Seymour and Blair! The thing is a wet blanket here to our Democrats.

wheelbarrow government. [ ]

1885 Crafts *Sabbath for Man* 288. The political code now in vogue ... leads to a wheelbarrow government, carried on ... by the people pushing them [the legislators] from behind.

wheel horse.

A party member who can be depended upon for loyal support and hard work.

The wheel horse in a team is that which is hitched between the shafts and thus has a greater share of the load than the leader.

A few representative references from politics:

1848 *Marion Eagle* 14 June 2/2. He

[Cass] has been the very wheel horse on which the party have relied to carry through all their great measures.

1856 *Greenville* (Ohio) *Jrnl.* 1 Oct. 2/4. The party were represented fully, by the leaders, and the rank and file from the "wheel horse" down to the second-hand "lackeys" who do the "small work" on all occasions.

1860 *Stark Co.* (Ohio) *Republican* 1 June 1. For many years he was the "wheel horse" of the Whig party of Illinois, and was on the electoral ticket in several Presidential campaigns.

1876 *Cleve. Leader* 25 May 4/1. St. Louis Convention will be managed under the two-thirds rule. This will be likely to shut out the *wheel-horses* like Tilden, Hendricks and Thurman.

1886 Poore *Perley's Reminiscences* 176. He was another "wheel horse" of the Whig party.

1904 Lynde *The ,Grafters* 19. Wheelhorses who came at the party call.

1947 Carlson *Plotters* 26. In the American Nazi underworld he [Thomas Dixon] was called Chief New Moon.... When [*Bundesführer* Fritz] Kuhn was arrested and New Moon's real name made public, he [Dixon] lost his job. After that, he became a regular wheelhorse for the hate-mongers.

1960 *Detroit News* 16 Aug. A22. Almost always heretofore Senator Kerr has been a dependable wheelhorse of the Democratic leftwing.

Whig.

British party names, "Whigs" and "Tories," were, of course, used by the colonial sympathizers of each party in the pre-Revolutionary period. In 1752 there existed a Whig Club in New York (Becker, *History of Political Parties,* p. 49). A newspaper, the *American Whig,* was started in 1768 (*OED*). The approaching crisis brought about a change of meaning in so far as "whig" became a name of the independence party, while the Tories were identified with the Loyalists (q.v.).

1771 in Harlow *Samuel Adams* 165. It is a great detriment to the Whig cause that there is but little honor amongst them but little dependence to be had one upon another. ...

1774 Capt. Evelyn *Memoir* 28 [*DA*]. They are distinguished here by the name of Tories, as the Liberty Boys, the tarring and feathering gentlemen, are by the title of Whigs.

1774 Adams *Familiar Ltrs.* 7. Dr. Gardiner ... brings us news of a battle at the town meeting, between Whigs and Tories.

In consequence of the success of the Revolution, *whig* emerged from the war as a term of honor, while *tory* became strictly opprobrious. When the Democratic party was founded, there was no contrast between *whig* and *democrat*. Prominent members of the new party were proud to claim the designation "whig" for themselves, trying at the same time to stigmatize their Federalist opponents as "tories":

1801 in Parton *Jackson* III.93 ... believing, as I do, that any citizen who does obtain the suffrage of the freemen of Tennessee, must be a character, the composition of which is virtue, talents, and the true whig principles of seventy-six; in short, sir, that he must be a republican. ...

1823 Jefferson in *Ltrs. and Times of Tyler* 477n. The Tories are for strengthening the executive and general government. The Whigs cherish the representative branch and the rights reserved by the States as the bulwark against consolidation.

See TORY, 1807, 1810.

On the other hand, there is no lack of evidence for the derogatory use of *whig* in the other camp:

1800 Cobbett *Ltrs.* 118. The damnable heresy of Whiggism seems to be confined to the despicable rump, which is aptly enough denominated a "club."

1809 in Cutler *Life of Ephraim Cutler* 11 Aug. 93. He ... took up a vile Democratic paper called "The Whig"....

1809 *Chillicothe Supporter* 3 Nov. 3/1. The original tories were a set of savages who robbed in the country, in Ireland; while the Whigs, or *wigs*, were town pick-pockets, who frequently changed their wigs, for a disguise....

The use of *whig* as the name of the party opposed to the Democrats seems to have its roots in the Southern nullification movement of 1832:

1832 *Charleston Merc.* in Cole *Whig Party in the South* 18 ... all the printers throughout the State shall designate the friends of the State by the proud name of *Whigs*, and the friends of Andrew Jackson and of consolidation by the name of Tories.... Every man now in South Carolina is a whig or a tory.

1832 *Ib.* in *Niles' Reg.* 29 Dec. 287. This unhappy old man [Jackson] has been suffered by his advisers to arrogate the power to coerce a state of the confederacy. ...He has attempted in this proclamation to intimidate the whigs of South Carolina....

In 1834 it became the official name of the anti-Jackson party at the suggestion of Gen. James Watson Webb, editor of the *New York Courier and Enquirer:*

1834 *Courier and Enquirer* 1 April 2/1. The time for action is at hand. Our liberty is threatened—our birthright is in danger—and we must rally under the ever memorable designation of Whig and Tory.—From this time forward let us have no more of Jackson-men, Clay-men, Van Buren-men, Webster-men or opposition-men; but let us like our fathers who arrayed themselves manfully against the usurpations of the British King, assume the justly merited title of WHIGS, and give to all who aid or abet the executive usurpations the equally appropriate name of Tories.

Ib. 2 April 2/1. Great Whig Meeting.... Philip Hone was called to the chair, and ... adverted to the proposal of the Editor of this paper yesterday morning, to apply the names of Whig and Tory to the two parties now arrayed against each other, and illustrated the peculiar appropriateness of those terms, as forceably indicating the principles by which they were respectively governed. He closed by recommending that the meeting should adopt the name of Whig for the party which they represented, and apply that of Tory to the other—a proposition which was received with rounds of applause.

Within two weeks the name "whig" had been widely accepted:

1834 *Niles' Reg.* 12 April 101/2. In New York and Connecticut the term "whigs" is now used by the opponents of the administration when speaking of themselves, and they call the "Jackson men" by the offensive name of "tories."

In the following years we find the same reactions to the terms which we had observed in the earlier period, the Whigs approving their name and its historic associations, the Democrats rejecting both "tory" and the "mis-appropriated" "whig." Among the weightiest of the voices supporting the name was that of Calhoun, who in 1834 said:

in Parton *Clay* II.129. I can not, however, but remark, that the revival of the party names of the revolution, after they had so long slumbered, is not without a meaning. ... Gentlemen ought to reflect, that the extensive and sudden revival of these names could not be without some adequate cause. Names are not to be taken or given at pleasure. There must be *something* to cause their application to *adhere*. ... What is there in the meaning of Whig and Tory, and what in the character of the times, which has caused their sudden revival as party designations? I take it, that the very essence of toryism—that which constitutes a tory—is to sustain *prerogative* against *privilege*—to support the executive against the legislative department of the government, and to lean to the side of power, against the side of liberty—while the Whig is, in all these particulars, of the very opposite principles. . . . I am content with that [name—Whig] which designates those with whom I act. It is, at least, an honest and patriotic name. It is synonymous with resistance to usurpation—usurpation, come from what quarter, and under what shape, it may.

In a less philosophical way, the newspapers of the times comment along the same lines:

1838 *Hamilton Intelligencer* 16 Aug. 2/2. The two great divisions of Party in the republic at the present moment are Whig and Tory. . . . the party of the Legislature and the party of the Executive—the friends of the People & the friends of the President.

On the Democratic side the claim to the name of "Whigs" is branded as a fraud:

1835 in Beveridge *Lincoln* I.172 . . . a blazing Democratic resolution was introduced into the House [Ill.] denouncing "the false and arrogant claims of the Webster, White, and Harrison party to the exclusive use of the ancient and honorable name of Whig."

1836 *Niles' Reg.* 5 Nov. 150/2 . . . over the combined forces of anti-masons' traitors, apostates and mis-called whigs.

1840 *Ohio Statesman* 2/3. A Name Stolen. . . . The whigs, falsely so called, are making strong efforts here to make an impression on the public mind, that what is now called the whig party, is the old democratic party of the times of Jefferson!! . . . they would try to steal the name of democrats from us.

With the disintegration of the Whig party in the 1850's, the name ceased to be a living party designation. Since then it has existed only as an historical word. Its death is recorded.

1854 *Wash. Union* 6 July 2/6. Dissolution of the Whig Party. . . . Such a thing as the national whig party does not exist.

1854 *Ib.* 28 July 3/2. Neither convention [in Ohio and in Indiana] mentioned the name whig once. They consider the whig party defunct.

In fact, due to the realignments of the period *whig* had come to have a very vague meaning:

1856 "Warrington" *Pen Portraits* 6 Nov. 225. The name of "Republican" has the great merit of meaning very little; being, in that respect, almost equal to "Whig," which meant nothing at all.

whirlwind.

A devastating political movement. One of the many metaphors from nature popular in the campaign of 1840.

1840 *Richmond Whig* 11 Sept. 1/3. "Whirlwind" in Vermont. . . . O.K. . . . Vermont reporting.

1840 *Ann. of Cleve.* No.1734. The prairies are on fire, and the whirlwind they create will be felt east of the mountains, before the Washington soirees of next winter have commenced.

1855 *Ib.* No.2752. How the whirlwind sweeps! Union and action will ensure a like success in every Free State.

1876 *Cinc. Daily Gazette* 29 June 2/5. He would sweep them both by a whirlwind of majority.

1880 *Cleve. Plain Dealer* 3 June 2/1. If the Democrats are wise and nominate Payne as I think they will, he'll sweep this state like a whirlwind.

whirlwind campaign.

A fast, extensive campaign, usually characterized by long trips and many speeches.

1896 *Rev. of Rev.* XIV.519/2. His [McKinley's] speeches have been prepared in advance, and have been punctuated with statistics and precise statements of fact which a "whirlwind campaign" from a train platform would not allow.
1924 *Cleve. Plain Dealer* 27 Sept. 1/8. [Al Smith] Promises He'll Make Whirlwind Campaign. [head]

whiskey Democrats.

The assumption that the participants in the Whiskey Rebellion were called Whiskey Democrats rests on an 1863 quotation [*DA*] that probably does not reflect contemporary usage. According to Sandburg the Democratic party in Illinois was known as the "Whiskey Party" in 1853 (*Prairie Years,* I.44). *Whiskey Democrat* as a party nickname is attested from 1882 on but is probably much older.

The background of the word is the widespread opinion that more than any other party the Democrats were addicted to the use of whiskey:

1854 *Peru* (Ind.) *Daily Union City* 18 Aug. 2/2 . . . that sentiment dear to every democrat, "Whisky and Democracy, now and forever, one and inseparable."
1861 Hingston *Genial Showman* 53. Later in the day I called at the Democrat office, and offered five dollars for a puff which I wished to be inserted. Messrs. Hughes and Harney not only accepted it, but volunteered to treat me with whisky in return for my fair dealing. As a rule, out West, I always found the democratic editors to be better patrons of whisky than the republican ones. There is a vein of whisky running through Western democracy, as characteristic of the genial democrat as the "blue blood" is of the Vere de Veres of Aristocracy.

1878 *Cinc. Enquirer* 18 Sept. 4/1. Milk and water having been suggested as a proper Republican beverage . . . the good old Democratic whisky which Democrats are not ashamed to drink or ashamed to say they are fond of.
1882? in W. A. White *Autobio.* 82. Whereupon the convention nominated George W. Glick—a man whom my father called a "whiskey Democrat from Atchison."

whiskey men.

Participants in the Whiskey Insurrection, western Pennsylvania. [ ]

1794 Balch *Ltrs. & Papers* 299. [John Shippen to his father, 31 Oct.] At Carlisle, (I believe) one or two persons were taken hold of as Whiskey-men, (for that is our term,) but at Bedford, twelve or fifteen were taken prisoners. . . .

whispering campaign.

Although Harry M. Daugherty in *The Inside Story of the Harding Tragedy* (p. 60) says—

At every election in which Harding was a candidate for office, from the beginning of his career in 1898 as a State Senator till his last campaign, this foolish lie was revived by the opposition in a whispering campaign.—

there is no evidence to suggest that it was used as early as 1898 in American politics; however, there is the fact that our first quotation does refer to the campaign of 1920, which links the phrase directly with Harding:

1920 *Nation* 10 Nov. 517/1. The scandalous underhandedness of the whispering campaign of the Democrats. . . .

In later campaigns the term was used to denote the undercover tactics of the opposition, usually directed at some alleged personal characteristic.

1928 *Nation* 19 Sept. 263. The Hoover Whispering Campaign.... Hoover's campaign strategy requires that he do nothing, say nothing, which might in any way distract attention from the real Republican campaign—the under-cover attack on Governor Smith.
1929 Al Smith *Up to Now* 410 ... I was probably the outstanding victim of the last half century of a whispering campaign.
1932 *Rev. of Rev.* LXXXVI. 17/1. Nothing else has been so hard for Mr. Hoover to bear as to have opposing politicians foment whispering campaigns about his indifference to human misery....
Ib. LXXXVI. 18/1. It was a whispering campaign that came near fixing it in the minds of the American people that Theodore Roosevelt did his work ... under alcoholic stimulation [in 1908].

We must be prepared to find the term much earlier, since already in 1811, Randolph said:

in Bruce *Randolph* 754n. All the initiated have been busily at work like moles underground, and this has been and is their plan of operation; to assail me by every species of calumny and whisper, but Parthian-like never to show their faces or give battle on fixed ground.

whistle stop.

Operational or flag stops on a railroad; in politics a campaign characterized by brief speeches at each of these unscheduled stops.
1948 *N. Y. Times* 7 Sept. 18/8. Truman To Speak At "Whistle Stops"... President Truman told a railroad station crowd here [Toledo] tonight that "before this campaign is over I expect to visit every whistle stop in the United States."
1950 *Newsweek* 22 May 19. Whistle-Stop Harry Rides Again. [head]

white Charley.

An ultra Whig. [ ]

1842 in *Cong. Globe* App. 74/2. One word further upon the subject of a coalition between the Administration and the Democrats. I see no signs of such a union. There seems to me as much prospect of the ultra Whigs—the "White Charlies"—coalescing with the Democrats, as there is of Tyler and his friends.

White Feather party.

During the Civil War a nickname for Peace Democrats.

The white feather as a symbol of cowardice attested in England since 1829 is supposed to have its origin in the cockpit, a white feather in the plumage of a fighting cock being considered a sign of inferior breed. (*OED*)
Already in 1835 the phrase *to show the White feather* turns up in American politics.

Crockett *Life* 249. The Little Flying Dutchman will no doubt calculate upon having a true game cock in Mr. Huntsman, but if he doesn't show them the white feather before the first session is over....
1854 letter in Pike *First Blows* 13 May 226. Pray you admonish Northern members that such as show the white feather will be exposed; they are all watched.

In 1861 it must have been quite common to refer to the advocates of peace at any price as *white feathers;* otherwise a cartoon in *Vanity Fair,* IV.132, could not have been understood. It shows a cannon ball fired from a confederate gun and wearing a false face crowned by a white feather. The title is "The White Feather Movement."
1861 *Ashland Times* 17 Oct. 2/1. The Judge and the Union men were surprised when they found he was nominated ... by the White Feather party.

1862 *Toledo Blade* 16 Jan. 2/2. A Response to the "White Feathers." [Democrats in Ohio legislature.]

The term seems to have been short lived; it was probably killed by the competition of *copperhead* (q.v.) .

Cf. PLUMED KNIGHT.

white legs.

See CHARCOALS.

white line (liner).

Advocating government by members of the white race only.

Its origin in the early Reconstruction Period is found in the segregation of voters:

1871 *Cong. Globe* App. 291/3. They had [in Virginia] two lines of voters, in hostility to the spirit of the fifteenth amendment, a white line, and a colored line.

Later *white line* became an official organization, first started in Louisiana. [ ]

1874 in Garfield *Works* II.367. "The White Line."—This interior organization has not yet assumed definitely, in the State of Mississippi, such precise form and so distinct an existence as in the State of Louisiana, but is, unquestionably, an extension into Mississippi of the "White League" organization, whose headquarters are in New Orleans.

1876 in *Ib.* II.374. In their party powwow of that day, disregarding the deep undercurrent of public opinion, they declared by formal resolution against the White Line policy.

1876 Morton in *Cong. Record* 497. The inflexible purpose of the "white-line" democracy of the South is the destruction of the political rights of the negro.

1876 Morton in *Harper's W.* 26 Feb. 162/2. In many of the Southern States the policy is openly avowed of seizing all power into the hands of the white race, and depriving the colored people of their

political and civil rights. With this policy, commonly known as the white line, it is believed the Democracy sympathize in every Southern State.

1876 *Lebanon* (Ohio) *West. Star* 25 May 1/6. The White Liners of Louisiana are getting in their word. The Presidential election is approaching and the negroes must be terrified into submission.

1880 in Adams *Emery A. Storrs* 216. It [home rule] means the White-Liner and the Ku-Klux at home; it means the argument of the shot-gun; it means the persuasion of Chisholm and Dixon and hundreds of others by the gentle methods of assassination.

white man's government.

On February 15, 1851, the fugitive slave Shadrack was rescued in Boston in defiance of the Fugitive Slave Law. Alluding to the prominent part that colored citizens played in his rescue, Henry Clay said on February 18:

1851 in *Cong. Globe* 597/1 . . . the question which arises is, whether we shall have law, and whether the majesty of the government shall be maintained or not; whether we shall have a Government of white men or black men in the cities of this country.

The term *white man's government* was current during the Civil War and in particular during the Reconstruction Period:

1862 Wilson *Slave Power* III.334. Among the loudest, if not the most potent, voices raised against it [Trumbull bill] was that of Garret Davis of Kentucky, . . . advocating in most offensive terms, the theory of "white man's government."

1862 Blaine *Twenty Years* I.436. They [Pennsylvania Democratic Convention] further declared that "this is a government of white men and was established exclusively for the white race."

1868 "The White Man's Flag" [Campaign song].

Come then, all free-born patriots,
  Join with a brave intent
    To vindicate our Father's choice
A White Man's Government.
1868 *Harper's W.* 12 Sept. 579/3. [Arkansas Convention, Jan. 17] A white man's government in a white man's country.
1868 *Ib.* 5 Sept. 568. This Is A White Man's Government. [Cartoon, showing Irish Five-Pointer, Confederate, and 5th Avenue Capitalist standing with their feet on a prostrate negro soldier.]

white man's party.

See WHITE MAN'S GOVERNMENT.
1860 Foner *Douglass* II.515 ... the sun of science and civilization has risen too high in the heavens for any party to stand long on the mean, narrow and selfish idea of a "white man's party."
1860 Greeley *Overland Journey* 37. They must be harsh, and cruel, and tyrannical, toward the unfortunate blacks as possible, in order to prove themselves "the white man's party."
1874 *Ann. of Cleve.* No.3868. In Louisiana a "white man's party" is being formed "to arm and protect itself against lazy blacks."
1874 *Cleve. Leader* 2 July 4/1. The New Orleans Republican gives publicity to a wide spread rumor to the effect that the demagogues are at work forming a white man's and black man's party in Louisiana, to oppose each other in the coming elections.
1892 in Hicks *Populist Revolt* 239. The Democratic party at the South is something more than a mere political organization striving to enforce an administrative policy. It is a white man's party, organized to maintain white supremacy and prevent a repetition of the destructive rule of ignorant negroes and unscrupulous whites. ...

white necktie faction.

Politicians of elegant dress and manners.
1884 *N. Y. World* 12 March 1/5. "The boys" achieved a victory which sent the bankers, brokers, merchants and white necktie faction to the rear.

See BAND BOX STATESMAN, SILK STOCKING.

white nigger.

An intensified variation of *white slave* (q.v.), a white person doing hard manual work.
1841 *N. Y. American* 28 Dec. 2/5. The Northern Whigs in the house are getting a little tired of the unseasonable and insulting rant, in which, as at the last session, Mr. Marshall contemns the hard-working free electors of the North as "white niggers," as if they were the counterpart of his miserable slaves.
1854 *Peru Daily Union City* 9 Oct. 2/1 ... they will be executed in spite of White Niggers or Black Niggers.
1860 Stoddard in *Vanity Fair* III.269/1. O, White niggers, mudsills, Northern scum, Base hirelings, hear me, and be dumb.
1871 Eggleston *Hoosier Schoolmaster* 52. Ole Miss Meanses white nigger, as some them called her, in allusion to her slavish life.

Even *nigger* alone can be used to apply to a white person:
1837 Bird *Nick of the Woods* 179 ... I'm her dog and her niggur from now to etarnity. ...

In the *DA* quotation from *Nick of the Woods* the exact meaning of *white nigger thief* is not clear:
Ib. 96 [the negro, Emperor, speaking]. "'Top, massa! 't ar Captain Stackpole, what stole Brown Briery! Reckon I'll touch the pony on the rib, hah? Hanging too good for him, white niggah t'ief, hah!"

white slave.

Ever since the days of the first Congress, allusions to the laboring classes of the North as *white slaves* are frequently used by the defenders of negro slavery:
1789 in *Hist. of Congress* 13 May 337 ... he hoped it [motion on importation tax] would comprehend the white slaves as

well as black, who were imported from all the jails in Europe.

1819 in *Gt. Deb.* IV.50. What comparison did he [Clay] make between the "black slaves" of Kentucky and the "white slaves" of the North ...?

During the Missouri debate of 1820 John Randolph seems to have used the expression so impressively that it was remembered long afterwards:

1846 *Hamilton* (Ohio) *Intelligencer* 30 July 2/5. John Randolph said twenty-six years ago that the South would govern the North by their white slaves....

Other examples:

1830 *Niles' Reg.* 16 Jan. 341/2 ... the "peasantry," or "white slaves," as it is the slang of the aristocracy of the day to call all persons who earn an honest living by the labor of their hands.
1836 *West. Hemisphere* 19 Oct. 1/6; 2/3. White Slavery. Harrison and White Slavery. [heads]
1845 *Ann. of Cleve.* No.1512. The Northern doughfaces of the party have yielded all to the South, until the chivalry feel that they have a sort of divine right to lord it over white as well as black slaves.

Notice that in this last example the word has taken on a new shade of meaning in that it refers to Northern politicians subservient to the South.

Another variation of meaning, *white slave* equaling white person actually reduced to the legal status of a slave, is attested by:

1856 *Marshall* (Mich.) *Statesman* 22 Oct. 1/7. White Slaves Next [editorial on suggestion of Robt. Wickham of Ky. to make slaves of the Irish and Germans].

After the Civil War the word survived as a designation of the downtrodden laborer

1892 Louis A. Banks *White Slaves or The Oppression of the Worthy Poor*. Boston.

Already in 1857 *white slavery* is used for prostitution:

W. Acton *Prostitution* 94. The natural question why does not this woman escape from this white slavery is best answered by other queries, whither can she fly, what can she do?

This use was taken up in the days of the agitation leading to the passage of the Mann Act, as described by Mencken:

Am. Language Suppl. I.300. The legend that white-slave traders infested the primitive movie parlors of the land, and fetched their recruits by injecting morphine into their arms, was set afloat c. 1910, and soon won millions of believers.... The culmination of the frenzy came with the passage of the Mann Act in 1910.

In England *white slavery* is not attested as a phrase before 1835. Therefore it may be assumed from its occurrence in the early congressional debates that it was of American origin. [ ]

white tile party.

The Liberal Republicans of 1872; a humorous allusion to Horace Greeley's white hat.

1872 *N. Y. World* 28 July 2/2. Mr. Greeley's supporters being known as the "white tile" party, it is proposed to distinguish the adherents of the present stable administration as the hoss tile party.

whitewash.

To cover up mistakes or faults, either public or private, which would be political liabilities.

A. Found in English politics:
1764 H. Walpole *Mem. Reign Geo. III*

II.35. A poet and an author will go as far in white washing a munificent tyrant.

B. The derogatory connotations are evident throughout American political history.

1795 Freneau *Poems* III.127. To court!—Return to Britain's tyrant reign, whitewash her king, and scour her peers.
1819 Randolph in Bruce *Randolph* I.445. ...the old minority men, whitewashed into courtiers.
1828 *Ohio St. Jrnl.* 17 April 3/3. Nelson Patterson, Esq. the Secretary of the famous white-washing committee....
1828 *Ky. Reporter* 30 April 2/4. All attempts hitherto made to whitewash his [Jackson's] blood-stained character have failed.
1828 *Cinc. Liberty Hall* 24 April 3/3. He [Rev. Doctor Ely] has become a sort of pious whitewasher to Gen. Jackson....
1836 *Niles' Reg.* 16 Jan. 329/2. It would appear to us, that the character of Aaron Burr, and all his associates...is "whitewashed" and redeemed by recent events.
1842 Byrdsall *Loco Foco* 115....which turned out to be one of the veriest bank white-washing committees that ever was chosen.
1865 in Sumner *Works* XIII 48....the whitewashing menage of Franklin Pierce with regard to the committee in Kansas.
1866 Pres. Johnson in *N. Y. Times* 22 Feb. 4/7. I have been accused of whitewashing.
1945 Norris *Fighting Liberal* 109. Sec. Ballinger was to be vindicated; the investigators were to apply a copious coat of whitewash.
1946 *PM* 14 March 7. Truman's Whitewash Note to Pauley Makes Political Ammunition for GOP. [head]

C. Punning reference to Hugh L. White of Tennessee, who broke with Jackson over Van Buren's suitability as a presidential candidate, and to Whitelaw Reid.

1835 *Globe* 29 April. We believe that no party among the People except the Nullifying party, will support Judge White. They want *Whitewashing*.

1872 *Harper's W.* 31 Aug. 665. [cartoon: Greeley using "Whitewash Reid" brush to apply "reform whitewash" to Tammany tiger.]

whole hog, to go the.

To support a candidate or measure without reservations.

A. A plausible explanation of the origin of the phrase "go the whole hog" is given by Thomas Hamilton:

1833 *Men and Manners in America* 18. Jackson For Ever. Go The Whole Hog! When the sphere of my intelligence became enlarged with regard to this affiche, I learned, that "going the whole hog" is the American popular phrase for Radical Reform, and is used by the Democratic party to distinguish them from the Federalists, who are supposed to prefer less sweeping measures, and consequently to go only a part of the interesting quadruped in question. The Go-the-whole-hoggers, therefore, are politicians determined to follow out Democratic principles to their utmost extent, and with this party, General Jackson is at present an especial favourite. The expression, I am told, is of Virginian origin. In that State, when a butcher kills a pig, it is usual to demand of each customer, whether he will "go the whole hog"; as, by such extensive traffic, a purchaser may supply his table at a lower price, than is demanded of him, whose imagination revels among prime pieces, to the exclusion of baser matter.

This suggestion is borne out by other references:

1832 in Clay *Sp.* II.114. The senator modestly claimed only an old smoked, rejected joint; but the stomach of his excellency yearned after the whole hog!
1836 *Lebanon* (Ohio) *Western Star* 24 Nov. 3/1. Some of our citizens has caught the pork panic which is raging throughout the State, and are going the entire swine in this business. Pork is now selling from three, to four dollars and fifty cents,

for cash up, and no grumbling at that. Let them go "the whole hog" while they are about it.

B. The phrase became closely identified with the Democratic party during the Jackson era.
1828 *Baltimore Republican* 16 Feb. 2/3. If I am not greatly mistaken, Kentucky "will go the whole hog" for Jackson.
1828 *Cinc. Liberty Hall* 3 April 3/1. I find it impossible to "go the whole hog" in the cause of "the Hero of New Orleans"....
1828 *Ib.* 25 Sept. 3/3 ... they did not know who were the persons comprising the Jacksonian, or "whole hog ticket"....
1830 *Workingman's Adv.* 3 April 2/1 ... in true Jacksonian phrase, he "goes the whole hog"....
1834 Van Buren in Jackson *Corr.* 22 July V.275. I have sent them a whole hog toast.
1834 *Ann. of Cleve.* No.473. McLane has privately resigned his office, for even he is troubled with digesting the "whole hog."
1836 *Scioto Gazette* 23 March 1/2. I am nateirally all the way from Old Kentuck. I not only approve the great leading precept in her own native science, "down horse and up stump," but with her I go it, from snout to tail, "the whole hog."
1840 Kennedy *Quodlibet* 51 ... thoroughbred, whole hog Democrats, sworn to follow the new democratic principle through all meanderings....

C. Euphemistic variations leaving out or replacing the word *hog* (cf. *nigger in the woodpile*) :
1828 *Ky. Reporter* 30 April 2/4. His [Jackson's] Partizans now go the whole on another tack....
1833 *Sketches of Crockett* 40. Didn't I go the whole animal?
1835 *Knickerbocker* VI.439. I have before me, for example, a late number of the Logtown Universal Advertiser and Entire-Swine Despatch.
1840 *Valentine Vox* xlii. Then of course you mean to go the whole quadruped.
1842 Hood *Comic Annual* 171. The Quaker, being over rigidly denied the pig-

ments, was the very man to go the whole hogments.
1848 Burton *Waggeries* 22. We go the hull shoat with them.

wide awake.

The earliest use of *wide awake* in politics points clearly to Irving's Rip Van Winkle. At some time during the tariff controversy (around 1828) a South Carolinian succeeded in attaching the epithet "Rip Van Winkle" to the "Old North State" (North Carolina) :
1829 *Shelbyville* (Ky.) *Adv.* 5 Dec. 2/4. Wm. C. Preston, of South Carolina, in one of his furious tirades, applied to the State of North Carolina, the somewhat degrading epithet of "the Rip Van Winkle of the South."

By contrast the idea of being awake or wide awake was soon introduced:
1834 in Lefler *North Carolina* 241. The state of North Carolina, so long taunted as the Rip Van Winkle of the confederacy, has at last been awakened.
1834 *Niles' Reg.* 8 Nov. 148/2. North Carolina, like Virginia, has been taking a long nap, while other states were "wide awake."
1840 in Norton *Tippecanoe* 27 ... and when the election returns come in, said Mr. Cherry, they will show that "old Rip is wide awake again."

The next step is the frequent use of *wide awake* in headlines describing growing political interest in this or that district:
1836 *Ohio People's Press* 22 June 1/5. Clinton County Wide Awake.
1852 *Western Reserve Chron.* 20 Oct. 3/3. Newton Wide Awake.

Wide awake as the name of political organizations is usually considered as a feature of the first Lincoln campaign, but before that period it was used by the Know Nothings:

1854 *N. Y. Trib.* 4 Sept. 1/5 ... a party of "Wide Awakes," as they are called, went down for the purpose of sustaining the preacher.... The Police force of the First Ward and the "Wide Awakes" finally succeeded in scattering the Irish.

1860 *Ashland Union* 5 Sept. 1/7. The Wide Awakes. Under this name the Republicans are organizing political clubs throughout the country.... The gentlemen of the Wide Awake Club who are now so zealously blowing their horn, do not appear to know what historical reminiscences are attached to their name. The title ... first acquired notoriety in 1855, when it graced those bands of nativists, who somewhat later acquired such celebrity under the name of Know Nothings.

1860 *Ib.* 3 Oct. 3/4. Origin of the Wide Awakes.... A madman calling himself the Angel Gabriel held forth for several Sundays in succession in front of the City Hall and other public places in this city and Brooklyn.... The advocates of free street preaching, who formed the body guard of the Angel and his horned clerk, wore mostly a species of drab felt hat, and their watchword was "Wide Awake," from which they and their soft supercapillary integuments received the denomination of "Wide Awakes." The hats retained the title.

(Concerning the Angel Gabriel, he is apparently the only angel who edited a newspaper. See Monaghan, *The Great Rascal,* pp. 206, 305.)

In 1860 the Wide Awakes are mentioned so frequently that a few quotations will suffice:

1860 Flood *Nat. Dem.* 12 Oct. 1. The Wide Awakes made a fine show in their procession. The number of torches, 1627 by actual count, seemed to put the different streets in a blaze of light.

in Schurz *Reminiscences* II.194 ... "Wide Awake" companies with their glazed capes and caps ... sprang up all over the land as by magic.

The characteristic uniform of the Wide Awakes is shown in Shaw's *Cartoon History of Abraham Lincoln,* II.61, 105, 106.

wigwam.

A hall or building serving as the headquarters or meeting place for a party.

A. Originally the building erected by the Tammany Society of New York:

1787 in Kilroe *St. Tammany* 120. The members of St. Tammany's Society in the City of New York are requested to meet at their wigwam.

1868 *Harper's Mon.* 567. The new Tammany Hall, or "wigwam" as it is styled— for the "order" professes to be composed of Indians—was formally dedicated.

B. Applied to the buildings of other parties:

1855 Anon. *Sons of the Sires* 86. There was scarcely a redeeming trait left in the character of those who ruled the old wigwams.

1860 *Ashland Times* 30 Aug. 2. The Republican Association of the District has a Wigwam, and big meetings are held in the capacious hall.

1880 *Cinc. D. Gazette* 14 June 6/1. The new wigwam of the Fourteenth Ward Garfield and Arthur Club was handsomely decorated with flags.

C. Also found occasionally to refer to a private home which houses the head of the party.

1829 in Bayard Smith *Forty Yrs. Wash. Soc.* 283. Everyone thinks there is great confusion and difficulty, mortification and disappointment—at the Wigwam—as they call the General's [Jackson's] lodgings.

1835 *Mich. Whig* 15 Jan. 3/3. The recent measures of the Whigs have introduced confusion into the Jackson whigwam [sic].

wild-eyed.

Though *wild-eyed* is found in English literature as early as 1817 (Shelley, *Revolt of Islam,* iv.xx) it is probable that its use in William Allen White's widely discussed editorial, 1896, "What's the Matter with Kansas?" is responsible for its entry into American politics:

We have another shabby, wild-eyed, rattlebrained fanatic who has said openly in a dozen speeches that "the rights of the user are paramount to the rights of the owner...."

1915 H. Quick *Brown Mouse* 118. I guess that's so—to a wild-eyed reformer.
1931 in *Wash. Merry-Go-Round* 226. In a few minutes a long-haired, wild-eyed professor came rushing into the barn to acknowledge the parentage of the little child he called "Oleo."
1932 *New Rep.* 10 Aug. 332/2. He [Norman Thomas] is not one of your wild-eyed Reds.

windypendent. [ ]
1884 *Ohio St. Jrnl.* 11. Sept. The effect of the so-called "great Republican revolt" of the year is not yet apparent. Oregon, Vermont, and Maine have spoken, and the lines are solid everywhere. The Windypendents made a good deal of noise, but it was nothing else.

wire puller.

One of the many terms adapted from the terminology of puppetry into the vocabulary of politics. The *motif* is found in 18th century English cartoons and other political writings:

1767 *Pol. Reg.* in Wright *Caric. Hist.* 306. [cartoon showing Bute controlling puppets by wires.]

1801 Fox *Sp.* VI.449. How do I know that I can place the least reliance upon any treaty made with men who, indeed may be mere puppets moved by wires, in the hands of others.

The expression, *wire puller,* however, seems to be an American creation:

1823 *Cinc. Nat. Rep.* 24 June 2/3 ... we are taught to despise ... the grand operator, the chief juggler, who sits behind the scenes, and moves the wires.
1839 Clark in *Cong. Globe* 30 Jan. Let there be attached to the internal clockwork of these figurantes, a wire, to be touched by some faithful devotee of the President. Perhaps my honorable colleague, the chairman of the Ways and Means, and the venerable gentleman from New Hampshire, as they are about to disencumber themselves of the robes of office, might be appropriately selected for this duty, to be denominated Executive wirepullers general, at a respectable salary, which is the cream of an official joke.
1852 *Am. Whig. Rev.* 176/2. There is but one other example of a complete appropriation of the suffrage of one half the nation by two or three wire-pullers, and that was the nomination of Polk by the same Convention.
1855 Greeley in Parton *Greeley* 180. Wirepulling is a sneaking, bad, demoralizing business, and the people hate it.
1869 Barnum *Struggles* 616. I was a party man, but not a partisan, nor a wirepuller.... On arriving at Hartford the night before the session began, I found the wire-pullers at work laying their plans for the election of a Speaker of the House.
1876 *N. Y. Times* 23 May 4/1. A car-load of wire-pullers were to be at Springfield to-day, to influence the course of the Illinois Republicans.
1912 La Follette *Autobio.* 46. There was no influence they did not use; no wires they did not pull.
1931 Steffens *Autobio.* 275. Parker, a new type to me, ... the man who liked to sit back and pull wires just to see the puppets jump.

wires.

Political manipulation or techniques of influence.

1828 (Batavia, Ohio) *Spirit of the Times* 13 Sept. 3/2. And we already see measures taken in our own section of the country, by a few master spirits who move the political wires, to extend the strife in some shape or other beyond the day of election. **c1836** Crockett *Life* 276. The showman set his wire to work, just as "the Government" does the machinery in his big puppet show. **1876** *Harper's W.* 27 May 418/1. What a contrast, and how favorable to our time, between the action of the Secretary of the Treasury, Mr. Crawford, and the Secretary of the Treasury, Mr. Bristow! Mr. Crawford had his agents and his "wires" and his "pipe" in every State.... **1880** *Cleve. Leader* 2 June 1/4. He says it looks to him as though Grant's wires were so laid as to catch the nomination.

wire worker.

A political manager, mainly of the lower grade:

1823 *Cinc. Nat. Rep.* 4 Nov. 1/1. At present they [the people] are made the puppets of intrigue and corruption, and moved north or south, east or west, in quest of a candidate, as the chief wireworkers behind the curtain determine.... **1828** *Liberty Hall* 4 Sept. 1/5. By common consent, Doct. M'Nairy has been exalted to the enviable distinction of chief wireworker for the coalition in this place. **1836** *Calumet and War-Club* (Springfield, Ohio) 17 Aug. 3/1. The dissolution of the first cabinet of President Jackson, effected through the intrigue and machinations of Martin Van Buren, exhibits one of the rarest instances of skill in political wire working. **1840** *Cong. Globe* App.429/2. Such is the secret mandate of the State Convention wire-workers—such is the secret mandate of the wire-workers of the National Harrisburg Convention. **1860** *N. Y. Trib.* 18 Sept. All around us—in Penn., in New Jersey, in Mass. and else-

where, little knots of party wire-workers are sitting up late o'nights in tavern private parlors, desperately intent on some sort of Fusion that will take their respective states from Lincoln and send three or four of the fusers to Congress.

See PUPPET, JUGGLER.

Wisconsin idea.

The philosophy of the Progressive Movement, its foremost leader being Robert M. La Follette of Wisconsin.

1912 Charles McCarthy *The Wisconsin Idea.* [title] **1940** Stokes *Chip* 199. There he [LaFollete] had originated reforms which... have made that state a laboratory of social and economic experiment. In 1906 when he was sent to the United States Senate he got his opportunity to fight for the "Wisconsin idea," as it was characterized, on a national scale. **1952** Stevenson *Major Camp. Sp.* 224. The Wisconsin idea—the faith in the free mind and in the application of reason to government—was one of the hopeful ideas of our country.

wiskinski.

One of the Indian terms designating an official—apparently the treasurer—of the Society of Tammany.

1843 *New Mirror* 15 April 18/2. They were placed in charge of the Wiskinski of the wigwam. **1877** *N. Y. Trib.* 17 April 4/4. It is the Sagamore and the Wiskinskie whose mysterious functions puzzle us. **1879** *Puck* 8 Jan. 2/1. Then why should not Kelly, and Spinola and the Wiskinski dance a break-down before their final break-up? And, by-the-by, who or what is a Wiskinski? Considering the occupation of the principal members of Tammany, ought he not rather to be called the whisky-skin-ski? **1881** *N. Y. Trib.* 25 Oct. 4/4. It has been used to send out its "Wiskinskie" armed with a book in which were written the names of contractors, supply-men and of-fice-holders bound by feudal ties to render financial service to the "Boss." The con-tractors and supply-men went in fear of the Tammany Controller, and the office-holders charged off their assessments in some mysterious manner upon the tax-payers.

1905 Riordan *Plunkett* 99. Dan Donegan, who used to be the Wiskinskie of the Tammany Society, and received contribu-tions from grateful office holders.

woodpecker ticket. [ ]

1872 *Ann. of Cleve.* No.2497. Missouri Democrats add the last touch to the "sore-head" nominees by calling them the "Woodpecker ticket." What a name to go down in history!

wool hat.

A. A coarse, woolen hat worn by the lower classes:

1856 *Ency. Brit.* 8th ed. XI.240/2. Wool hats are made entirely of coarse native wool and hair stiffened with glue. Before the emancipation act these hats were largely exported for negroes' wear.

B. In politics, a nickname for the Democratic party:

1828 *Western Intelligencer* (Hamilton, Ohio) 3 Oct. 3/1. Thus has Mr. Woods endeavored to gain the votes of the wool hats as he terms his Jackson friends in Washington.

1830 *Am. Sentinel* 27 Aug. 2/2. Formerly the supporters of General Jackson were said to be the rowdies, the wool hats, the filthy mechanics, &c.

1836 *Western Hemisphere* (Cols., Ohio) 27 July 2/6. The "wool hats" as the aris-tocracy stigmatize the democrats, are mus-tering for the fight.

1836 *Ib.* 3 Aug. 1/7. The very men whom a few years ago they called the "ragged wool hat boys" and "Tories," they are now seeking to attach to their [Whig] party!! But the "wool hat boys" will row

this silk stocking, kid glove and shirt tail aristocracy up Salt River this fall.

Attempts were made to turn this slogan against the Whigs:

1836 *Hamilton Intelligencer* 29 Sept. 2/5. ...it is the Colonel of the Great Crossings alone who covets the woolen fabric.

1840 *Cong. Globe* App.435/1. The log cabin, and its wool hat inmates, will find themselves in the vocative....

woolly heads.

Originally a nickname for Ne-groes; in politics those who sympa-thized with the Negro, particularly within the Whig party.

1827 Cooper *Prairie* xv. Some people think woolly heads are miserable, working on hot plantations under a broiling sun.

1851 in Wilson *Slave Power* II.355. He [Dodge of Iowa] also charged them with "panting for the experiment" of introduc-ing "black-skinned, flat-nosed, and woolly headed senators and representatives...."

1852 *Scott Battery* 14 Sept. 1/4.
The Butler pony is on the track,
    And the Loco team will have to back—
    "Although his head's a little woolly
Vallandigham will find him a 'Bully.'"

1853 *N. Y. Trib.* 3 Jan. 6/1. Senator Soulé thinks Cass, Slemens, Downs and others of the same ilk little better than Federalists died in the wool. "Wooly-heads" he would not call them, for that would be libel.

1853 *Knickerbocker* XLIII.653. "Woolly-Heads" were "about," and "far off the coming shone" of dignified "Silver-Grays."

1854 *Weekly Cleve. Plain Dealer* 1 Nov. 4/2.... the Tribune, Journal, Buffalo Ex-press and that woolly class of papers repudiate the Know Nothings and stick to Clark.

1854 Bungay *Off-Hand Takings* 316. Dan-iel S. Dickinson is an "Old Hunker," dyed in the wool, although not a "woolly head."

1855 *Lancaster* (Ohio) *Eagle* 9 Aug. 2/1. The Woolly Head Mass Meeting. [head]

woolly horse.

Nickname for the Republican party in 1856 and later.

The word originated in a publicity hoax of P. T. Barnum's. He had on mere speculation bought a horse in Cincinnati which was small with no mane and very little hair on its tail but was covered with thick, curly hair like sheep's wool. The continuation of the story is given in Barnum's own words:

1854 *N. Y. Leader* 11 Nov. 3/4. Just at this time, in 1849, Col. Fremont and his party were reported to have been lost among the Rocky Mountains; the public were greatly excited. . . . Now came the chance for the woolly horse. It was duly announced, that after three days chase upon the borders of the River Gila, an animal had been captured by the quartermaster of Col. Fremont's party, who partook of the nature of the buffalo, antelope, and camel. This story was so far true, that I was myself the quartermaster who captured him, and I charged a quarter for the sight.
1850 *N. Y. Trib.* 29 Oct. 4/3. Some of those who are now riding the Woolly Horse as hard as they did, in the hope of sudden riches, may in like manner be dismounted.
1856 *Cinc. Gazette* 24 June 2/3. They call us a "woolly horse" party. Well, we have one thing in common with the woolly horse—our candidate can run.
1856 *Cleve. Plain Dealer* 2 July 4/3. Col. Fremont is distinguished for three particularly glorious achievements viz. 1. the discovery of Barnum's celebrated Rocky Mountain wooly [sic] horse. . . .
1856 *Ib.* 5 Aug. 2/2. It seems this wonderful Woolly Horse, this "astonishing animal," was made up of about as many incongruous parts as the party which is now running after him. There is no doubt that this bobtailed buffalo one horse party, with the "haunches of a deer, and the tail of an elephant" is "nature's last."
1856 *Ohio Statesman* 21 Sept. 2. All at once the Fremont stumpers have found it necessary to deny that their party is an Abolition party. They feel the weight of

carrying Hale, Giddings, Fred Douglass, &c., on their backs, and are struggling like an overloaded Woolly Horse to throw a part of the load off.
1859 *N. Y. Trib.* 25 Jan. 7/4. So you are from that great Wooly-horse State [Penn.]. You are all Black Republicans there.
1863 *Vallandigham Songbook* 19.
John Brough the wooly horse has tried
  A few days, a few days
To office Johny wants to ride
  But Val is coming home.
[Brough, the Republican candidate for governor of Ohio, was a longtime Democrat who had joined the Republicans only recently.]

woolly Whig. [ ]

1854 *Ohio St. Jrnl.* 1 Sept. 2/2. We were met almost uniformly with the remark . . . "You at the West were better situated to meet this issue than we are." If the speaker was a Wooley Whig, he would refer to the position of the Whig party in the State. If a Soft Democrat, then there was the General Government, forbidding the idea of abandoning a triumphant national organization.

workies.

An organization of working people.

This word seems to have developed either in 1829 or 1830 and was applied to a party which called itself the Working Man's party.

1830 *Workingman's Adv.* 8 May 3/4 . . . the laboring class of community, whom the Argus and its Co-Courier of New York abuses, ridicules and insults with the epithet of "workies."
1830 *Ib.* 29 May 3/4. Working Men. A party under this name has lately spread terror among the aristocracy of the state of New York. . . . The Jackson party are making great efforts to put them down. They hate the *Workies* and *Anties*, as they call them.

1830 *Ib.* 5 June 1/5... such terms as "workies," "unmannered slaves"... are the courtly epithets bestowed upon those who have joined in a holy resistance against fraud and force.
1830 *N. Y. Sentinel* 26 June 1/3. [fr. *Am. Spectator*] The New Party—the workies! That is a dwarfish name.—We do not like it.
1839 *Buckeye Whig* 9 Aug. 2/1. We are not in the habit of writing popularity seeking eulogisms upon our brother workies....

The term apparently died out quite soon after this, enjoying about ten years' popularity.

Y

yeomanry.

The farmers.

The quotations from 1845 and 1890 indicate how the appeal could be made to win the farm vote.

1790 in Tolles *Logan* 101...an independent yeomanry—such as our American farmers ought to be—gentlemen cultivating their own estates.
1798 in Link *Dem. Rep. Societies* 205. The spirit of Yeomanry Meetings pervades almost every part of the Union.
1832 *Boston Liberator* 1 Dec. 191/3. There is actually a scheme on foot for transporting to the shores of Africa a large portion of the yeomanry of this country! And why? Because it is said they can never attain to respectability or happiness here—among their own countrymen!! Hail Columbia! happy land!
1840 Kennedy *Quodlibet* 139. His hypocritical boast of Independence will be scowled upon by every honest eye and spurned by every honest tongue which are to be found amongst the high-minded

New Light Yeomanry of Quodlibet, Bickerbray, Tumbledown, and the adjacent parts.
1845 Lyon *Govt. of U. S.* 53. They [politicians] treat them, invite them to their political meetings and club-rooms, and introduce them to their orators and slangwhangers; who immediately give them the first lesson, consisting in calling them free men, the yeomanry, the sinews and backbone of the country, the real sovereigns and support of the country.
1846 *Frankfort Commonwealth* 15 Sept. 1/4. You see before you, gentlemen, the embodiment and personification of Democracy—the proud representative of the flat-footed, square-shouldered, hard-fisted, dirty-faced, square-toed, cotton-shirted, wool-hatted yeomanry of Alabama.
1890 Locke *Demagogue* 101. With a crowd of farmers he would make some neat remarks about the antiquity of agriculture ...compliment his hearers as belonging to "that honored class who are the foundation of national greatness, the cornerstone on which our free institutions are built—the bone and sinew of the country, the honest yeomanry who are the pride, as well as the pledge of the perpetuity of our nation.

Yes Man.

A so-called adviser who always approves the policy and actions of his superior.

Mencken's suggestion (*Am. Lang. Suppl.* I.431) that *yes-man* has its origin in German *jaherr* or *ja-ja-Manderl* must be left open.

Sealsfield's reference to the U.S. Congress is too far removed from the first recorded use (1923) of the term in American politics to suggest any direct connection:
1827 Sealsfield *Die Ver. St. von Nord. Am.* in *Am. Sp.* XVI.27.... und der Kongress einen Jaherrn mehr hat.
1923 Rosewater *Behind the Scenes in Politics* 113. I know how easy it would be

to come under the spell of those who were described in the Wilson regime as the Yes-Yes Boys.... 197. The most dangerous group to have around one is a group of worshippers—the yes-yes boys—a group to which all Presidents and all financial giants are peculiarly exposed.

1932 Carter *What We Are About to Receive* 6. He [Hoover] is reported to prefer "Yes Men" around him and is impatient of disagreement.

Young America.

In 1838 Guiseppe Mazzini founded the society *la giovine Italia* and a periodical of the same name, both devoted to the unification and liberation of Italy. During the following years liberal societies all over Europe took names of the same pattern: *la giovine Europa, la jeune Swisse, das junge Deutschland,* etc. In England where some of the societies had their headquarters the name was taken up rather paradoxically by a group of Tories (McCarthy, *History of Our Times,* I.219). There was also a Young Ireland party, followers of O'Connell (McCarthy, I.201). Under these conditions it was hardly more than a question of time when a Young America party should enter the political scene. This seems to have come about in the following way. In January, 1852, the *United States Magazine and Democratic Review* wrote: (12/2)

Let the Baltimore Convention give to this, the young generation of America, a candidate, and we are content.... the democratic nominee for '52 must ... be ... a statesman who can bring young blood, young ideas, and young hearts to the councils of the Republic.

In February the *Democratic Review* (185/2) introduced the formula *Young America:*

We are not for all the young men before the country, but only for the bold, active honor and talent of Young America.

On March 4 (*Cong. Globe,* App. 302/2) John C. Breckenridge, remarking on the January article in the *Review,* used the phrase in an antagonistic spirit on the floor of the House:

I want no wild and visionary progress that would sweep away all the immortal principles of our forefathers—hunt up some imaginary genius, place him on a new policy, give him "Young America" for a fulcrum, and let him turn the world upside down.

From then on the word took roots very fast, both as a term of approval and disapproval. In May, 1852, the *Democratic Review* (393/1) quotes from the *Richmond Examiner:*

Through the ignorance of some and the maliciousness of many, the most absurd and amusing ideas have taken root in the public mind concerning the mission, object, and purposes of that great division which contains the energy, the honesty, and the real experience of the Democratic party, and which have been ridiculously named "Young America."

From the same year we have the following quotations:

N. Y. Times 15 Nov. 4/3. All this may not please Douglas and Young America.

Ib. 16 Nov. 4/4 ... the fillibustering [sic] projects of the Young American Hotspurs. Seba Smith *Thirty Yrs. Out of the Senate* 402. When the old line Dimocrats, North and South, and the Hunkers, and the Barnburners, and the Free-soilers, and the States Rights Dimocrats, and the Union Whigs, and the Secessionists, and the Carolina Nullifiers, and the Old Fogies, and Young America, all get you by the throat. . . .

Both the coupling of Young America and Douglas and the contrast *Young America–Old Fogy* (q.v.) are by no means isolated:

1869 Pollard *Secret Hist.* 36. It may be claimed for Mr. Douglas that he originated the gushing school of "young America," if he did not, in fact, introduce these words for the first time in the political literature of the country.

Young Democracy.

The Young America (q.v.) movement of the 1840's and '50's was also reflected in factions within the parties which endorsed the radical beliefs identified with the expansionist fever of the times.

1844 Whitman in McGrane *Allen* 30 May 99. I considered that you are regarded as the leader of the young Democracy of the Union and one on whom the young Democracy of this Union are determined one day shall fill the Presidential Chair.
1845 in Werner *Tammany Hall* 50. Nine tremendous cheers were given for "Mike Walsh, the poor man's friend" and "Champion of the Young Democracy."
1852 *Cleve. Plain Dealer* 6 Aug. 2/1. The young Democracy must say whether the defeat of Whiggery, this campaign, shall be by a small or by an overwhelming majority.

In later periods the name *Young Democracy* was applied to the liberal wing of the party, usually composed of young men.

1870 *Harper's W.* 627/3. The Young Democracy, as they cheerily call themselves, are organizing for the election. . . . If the Young Democracy break the Tammany Ring they will give us another, of course.

Young Indians.

A group of Whig congressmen who backed Zachary Taylor for the presidency: [ ]

in Poage *Clay and the Whig Party* 152. This triumph [nomination of Taylor by Whigs of Georgia] was the work of Alexander H. Stephens, who in December, 1846, had organized a Taylor club among the members of Congress. Calling themselves the "Young Indians" and working in close cooperation with Crittenden, they originally were only seven in number— Stephens and Toombs of Georgia, Ballard Preston, Flournoy and Pendleton of Virginia, Lincoln of Illinois and Truman Smith of Connecticut.

Young Men's Convention.

A special Whig convention in Ohio, indicative of the rising interest of younger men in politics which culminated in the Young America movement (q.v.).

1836 *Cols. West. Hemisphere* 20 July 3/2. Young Men's Convention. The State Central Committee have appointed a Whig State Convention of Young Men, to be held at Columbus, on the 20th September next.

Young Republican.

1879 *Harper's W.* 11 Oct. 802/2. We observe that the signers of the address are called Young Republicans. . . .
1884 *Ohio St. Jrnl.* 20 June. I know most of the men who attended the Independent meeting in N.Y. on Saturday, and I know that each one represents himself alone. Not one has any constituency behind him. The Young Republicans, I think, will come in line all right by and by.
1950 *Newsweek* 14 Aug. 28. A third wing —made up of young veterans—which informally called itself "The Young Republican Chowder and Marching Society" demanded immediate across-the-board freezing of everything.

young scratcher.

Many New York anti-machine Republicans objected to the nomination of Alonzo Cornell for governor in 1879 and rather than completely switch their party allegiance they were advised by such leaders as G. W. Curtis to scratch their ticket. In a *Harper's Weekly* editorial he writes:

1879 4 Oct. 782/2. To Republicans . . .who are resolved not to vote for Mr. Cornell because they regard his nomination as a blow at the best interests of the party, our advice is not to vote the Democratic ticket, but to make their votes count for Republican principles, and against Republican mismanagement, by scratching the ticket. These "independents," being mostly rising young men in the party, were designated as "young scratchers."

1879 *Nation* 9 Oct. 233/3. These young Scratchers will not be stopped from scratching by hearing that the venerable editor of the Tribune . . . thinks it foolishness.

1879 *Harper's W.* 22 Nov. 918/4. There was no more energetic and efficient body of Republican workers during the late canvass in New York than the Independent Republican Committee, familiarly called the "Young Scratchers."

See SCRATCH, INDEPENDENT, MUGWUMP.

Bibliography

Adams, Isaac. *Political Oratory of Emery A. Storrs.* Chicago, 1888.
Adams, John. *The Selected Writings of John and John Quincy Adams.* Ed. Adrienne Koch and William Peden. New York, 1946.
———. *Works.* Boston, 1850–56.
Adams, John Quincy. *Diary . . .* Ed. Allan Nevins. New York, 1928.
———. *Memoirs.* Ed. C. F. Adams. Philadelphia, 1874–77.
Ade, George. *Artie.* Chicago, 1896.
Alexander, De Alva. *Political History of New York,* 1906.
Alinsky, Saul D. *Reveille for Radicals.* Chicago, 1946.
Allen, Frederick. *Only Yesterday.* New York, 1931.
Allen, Robert, and Drew Pearson. *Washington Merry-Go-Round.* New York, 1931.
———, and W. V. Shannon. *Truman Merry-Go-Round.* New York, 1950.
Allen, William. *Western Democracy.* See McGrane.
Alliano, Jacopi. *Chronicles of Ohio, a Fragment of Cabilistical History.* Columbus, 1841.
Altgeld, John P. *Live Questions.* Chicago, 1899.
Alton, Edmund. *Among the Law-Makers.* New York, 1900.
American Historical Leaflets; Colonial and Constitutional. 36v. New York, 1892–1910.
The American Joe Miller, Philadelphia, 1840.
Ames, Fisher. *Works of Fisher Ames.* Boston, 1809.
Ames, Mary. *Ten Years in Washington.* Hartford, 1873.
Anderson, Edward L. *Modern Horsemanship.* Cincinnati, 1884.
Appleton's Annual Encyclopedia. 1861–1902, New York, 1862–1903.
Arnall, Ellis G. *The Shore Dimly Seen.* Philadelphia, 1946.
Asbury, Herbert. *The Gangs of New York.* New York, 1928.
———. *Sucker's Progress.* New York, 1938.
Asher, Cash. *Sacred Cows, a Story of the Recall of Mayor Bowles.* Detroit, 1931.
Atherton, Gertrude. *Perch of the Devil.* New York, 1914.
Audubon, J. J. *Ornithological Biography.* Boston, 1831–39.
Ayers, James T. *The Diary of James T. Ayers, Civil War Recruiter.* Springfield, Illinois, 1947.

Baker, Osmon C. *Guide-book in the Administration of the Discipline of the Methodist Episcopal Church.* New York, 1855.
Balch, Thomas. *Letters and Papers Relating Chiefly to the Provincial History of Pennsylvania.* Philadelphia, 1855.
Barkley, Alben. *That Reminds Me.* Garden City, New York, 1954.
Barlow, Joel. *The Columbiad.* Philadelphia, 1807.
———. *The Political Writings of Joel Barlow.* New York, 1796.

Barnes, Thurlow W. *Life of Thurlow Weed*. Boston, 1883–84.
Barnum, Phineas T. *The Humbugs of the World*. New York, 1865.
———. *The Life of P. T. Barnum*. New York, 1855.
Barry, Richard. *Theme Song—1936*. New York, 1936.
Bartlett, John R. *Dictionary of Americanisms*. New York, 1849.
Beard, Charles A. *American Government and Politics*. New York, 1931.
Becker, Carl L. *The History of Political Parties in the Province of New York, 1760–1776*. Madison, 1909.
Beecher, H. W. *Autobiographical Reminiscences of Henry Ward Beecher*. New York, 1898.
Bellamy, Edward. *Looking Backward*. Boston, 1888.
Bender, George B. *The Challenge of 1940*. New York, 1940.
Benedict, Almon. *A "Wide Awake" Poem*. Cortland Village, New York, 1860.
Bentham, Jeremy. *Catechism for Radicals*. 1809.
Bentley's Miscellany. London, 1837–68.
Benton, Thomas H. *Thirty Years' View*. New York, 1854–56.
Bernard, D. B. *The Temperance Offering; Containing Addresses, Anecdotes, and Illustrations*. Kirksville, Missouri, 1879.
Beveridge, Albert J. *Abraham Lincoln, 1809–1858*. 4v. New York, 1937.
Bigelow, John. *The Life of Samuel J. Tilden*. 2v. New York, 1895.
———. *Retrospections of an Active Life*. New York, 1909–13.
Bigger, David D. *Ohio's Silver-tongued Orator; Life and Speeches of General William A. Gibson*. Dayton, 1901.
Billings, John D. *Hardtack and Coffee*. Boston, 1888.
Bird, Robert M. *Nick of the Woods*. Philadelphia, 1837.
Birkbeck, Morris. *Letters from Illinois*. London, 1818.
Birney, James G. *Letters of James Gillespie Birney, 1831–1857*. Ed. D. L. Dumond. 2v. New York, 1938.
Bishop, Abraham. *Connecticut Republicanism*. Philadelphia, 1800.
Bishop, Joseph B. *Theodore Roosevelt and His Time*. 2v. New York, 1920.
Blaine, Harriet. *Letters of Mrs. James G. Blaine*. 2v. New York, 1898.
Blaine, James G. *Twenty Years in Congress*. Norwich, Connecticut, 1884–86.
Block, Maurice. *Dictionnaire general de la politique*. Paris, 1873–74.
Bobbe, Dorothie. *De Witt Clinton*. New York, 1933.
Bobolink Songster. 1860.
Booth, Edgar A. *The Mad Mullah of America*. Columbus, 1927.
Bowers, Claude. *Jefferson and Hamilton; the Struggle for Democracy in America*. New York, 1933.
Bowles, Samuel. *Across the Continent*. New York, 1866.
———. *Our New West*. Hartford, 1869.
Brace, Charles L. *The Dangerous Classes of New York*. New York, 1872.
Bradley, Cyrus. *Biography of Isaac Hill, of New-Hampshire*. Concord, New Hampshire, 1835.
Brant, Irving. *James Madison*. Indianapolis, [1921].
Braun, Lily. *Gesammelte Werke*. Berlin, 1923.
Breen, Matthew P. *Thirty Years of New York Politics Up-to-date*. New York, 1899.
Bright, John. *The Public Letters of the Right Hon. John Bright*. London, 1885.
Brisbane, Albert. *Association; or, A Concise Exposition of the Practical Part of Fourier's Social Science*. New York, 1843.
———. *The Social Destiny of Man*. Philadelphia, 1840.
Brisbin, James S. *The Life of James Abram Garfield*. Philadelphia, 1881.
Brissenden, Paul F. *The I.W.W., a Study of American Syndicalism*. New York, 1919.

Brown, Everett S. Ed. *The Missouri Compromises and Presidential Politics 1830–1825*. St. Louis, 1926.

Brown, William. *America: A Few Years' Residence in the United States and Canada*. Leeds, 1849.

Browne, Charles F. *Artemus Ward Complete*. London, 1890.

———. *Artemus Ward, His Travels*. Carleton, New York, 1865.

Brownlow, William. *Sketches of the Rise, Progress, and Decline* . . . Philadelphia, 1862.

Bruce, William C. *John Randolph of Roanoke, 1773–1833*. 2v. New York, 1922.

Brunot, Ferdinand. *Histoire de la langue Française des origine à 1900*. Paris, 1905.

Bryan, William J. *The Commoner Condensed*. New York, 1902.

———. *The First Battle, A Story of the Campaign of 1896*. Chicago, 1896.

Bryant, William C. *Poetical Works*. New York, 1925.

Bryce, James. *The American Commonwealth*. 3v. London, 1888.

Buchanan, James. *The Works of* . . . Ed. John B. Moore. 12v. Philadelphia, 1908–11.

Buckingham, James S. *The Slave States of America*. London, 1842.

Buckingham, Joseph. *Specimens of Newspaper Literature*. Boston, 1850.

Büchmann, Georg. *Geflügelte Worte*. Berlin, 1937.

Buley, Roscoe. *The Old Northwest Pioneer Period, 1815–1840*. 2v. Indianapolis, 1950.

Bungay, George W. *Off-Hand Takings*. New York, 1854.

Burke, Edmund. *Works*. Bohn Stand. Lib. ed.

Burnham, James. *The Web of Subversion*. New York, 1954.

Burns, James M. *Roosevelt: the Lion and the Fox*. New York, 1956.

Butler, Benjamin F. *Autobiography and Personal Reminiscences of Major-General Benj. F. Butler; Butler's Book*. Boston, 1892.

Butt, Archibald W. *Taft and Roosevelt, the Intimate Letters of Archie Butt*. 2v. New York, 1930.

Byrdsall, Fitzwilliam. *The History of the Loco-Foco, or Equal Rights Party*. New York, 1842.

Calhoun, John C. *The Works of John C. Calhoun*. 6v. New York, 1851–56.

Calkins, Alonzo. *Opium and the Opium-Appetite*. Philadelphia, 1871.

Candidates and the Issues. Ed. Mark H. Salt. [N.p.] 1908.

Carey, Mathew. *The Olive Branch*. Philadelphia, 1814.

Carlson, John Ray. *Under Cover*. New York, 1943.

Carlson, Oliver. *The Man Who Made News: James Gordon Bennett*. New York, 1942.

Carlton, Robert. *The New Purchase*. 2v. New York, 1843.

Carman, Harry J. *et al*. *Historic Currents in Changing America*. Chicago, 1942.

Carpenter, Stephen D. *Logic of History*. 2nd ed. Madison, 1864.

Carter, John F. *"The New Dealers"—the Low Down on Higher Ups*. Washington, 1934.

———. *What We Are about to Receive*. New York, 1932.

Cartwright, Peter. *Autobiography*. New York, 1857.

Chamberlain, Everett. *The Struggle of '72*. Chicago, 1872.

Chamberlain, Rudolph W. *There Is No Truce; a Life of Thomas Mott Osborne*. New York, 1935.

Channing, William E. *Complete Works*. Boston, 1886.

———. *The Life of William Ellery Channing*. Boston, 1880.

———. *Memoirs of William Ellery Channing*. Boston, 1850.

Chesnut, Mary B. *A Diary from Dixie*. New York, 1906.

Chester, Leonard. *Federalism Triumphant*. (pamphlet) 1802.

Chidsey, Donald B. *The Gentleman from New York*. New Haven, 1935.

Child, Lydia M. *An Appeal in Favor of That Class of Americans Called Africans*. New York, 1836.

——. *Letters from New York*. New York, 1843.

Childs, Marquis. *I Write from Washington*. New York, 1942.

Chinard, Gilbert. *Thomas Jefferson, the Apostle of Americanism*. Boston, 1939.

Chittenden, Lucius E. *Personal Reminiscences, 1840–1890*. New York, 1893.

Choate, Rufus. *The Works of Rufus Choate, with a Memoir of His Life*. 2v. Boston, 1862.

Christman, Henry. *Tin Horns and Calico*. New York, 1945.

Christy, David. *Pulpit Politics*. Cincinnati, 1863.

Clancy, J. J. *Land League Manual*. New York, 1881.

Clark, Champ. *My Quarter Century of American Politics*. 2v. New York, 1920.

Clark, George W. *The Harp of Freedom*. New York, 1856.

Clark, Thomas D. *Pills, Petticoats and Plows; the Southern Country Store, 1865–1915*. Indianapolis, 1944.

Clay, Cassius M. *The Life of Cassius M. Clay, Memoirs, Writings, and Speeches*. 2v. Cincinnati, 1886.

Clay, Henry. *Speeches*. Cincinnati, 1842.

Cleveland, Grover. *Addresses, State Papers and Letters*. New York, 1909.

Coan, Blair. *The Red Web*. Chicago, 1925.

Cobb, Irvin. *Irvin S. Cobb's Own Recipe Book*. Louisville, 1934.

Cobbett, William. *Letters on the Late War*. New York, 1815.

Cobden, Richard. *Political Writings*. London, 1868.

Cole, Arthur. *The Whig Party in the South*. Washington, 1913.

Cole, George D. H. *A History of Socialist Thought*. London, 1953–.

Colton, Calvin. *The Life and Times of Henry Clay*. 2v. New York, 1846.

Commager, Henry S. *Documents of American History*. New York, 1934.

Commons, John R., et al. *A Documentary History of American Industrial Society*. Cleveland, 1910–11.

Congdon, Charles T. *Reminiscences of a Journalist*. Boston, 1880.

—— and Horace Greeley. *Tribune Essays; Leading Articles Contributed to the New York Tribune 1857–63*. New York, 1869.

Conkling, Henry. *An Inside View of the Rebellion, and American Citizens' Textbook*. Chicago, 1864.

Cook, Joel. *Siege of Richmond*. Philadelphia, 1862.

Cooper, J. C. *The Handwriting on the Wall; or, Revolution in 1907*. St. Louis, 1903.

Cooper, J. F. *The Redskins*. New York, 1846.

Cooper, T. J., and H. T. Fenton. *American Politics*. Philadelphia, 1882.

Cotton, John. *Keys of Heaven*. Boston, 1843.

The Covode Investigation. HR. 36 Cong. 1st Sess. Rep. no. 648.

Cox, S. S. *Eight Years in Congress, from 1857 to 1865*. New York, 1865.

——. *Why We Laugh*. New York, 1876.

Cozzens, F. S. *Sayings, Wise and Otherwise*. New York, 1880.

Creel, George. *Rebel at Large; Recollections of Fifty Crowded Years*. New York, 1947.

Crippin, William G. *Green Peas Picked from the Patch of Invisible Green, Esq.* Cincinnati, 1856.

Crissey, Forrest. *Tattlings of a Retired Politician*. Chicago, 1904.

Crockett, David. *Col. Crockett's Exploits and Adventures in Texas*. Philadelphia, 1836.

——. *The Life of Martin Van Buren, Heir-Apparent to the "Government."* Philadelphia, 1835.

——. *Sketches and Eccentricities of Col. David Crockett, of West Tennessee*. Louisville, 1833.

Croker, John W. *The Croker Papers*. Ed. L. J. Jennings. 2v. New York, 1884.

Cross, Wilbur. *Connecticut Yankee; an Autobiography*. New Haven, 1943.
Crowther, Samuel. *The Presidency vs Hoover*. Garden City, 1928.
Curti, Merle. *Probing Our Past*. New York, 1955.
Curtis, George W. *Orations and Addresses of George William Curtis*. 3v. New York, 1894.
Cutler, Julia P. *Life and Times of Ephraim Cutler*. Cincinnati, 1890.
Cyclopedia of American Government. *See* McLaughlin and Hart.
Cyclopedia of Political Science. Ed. John L. Lalor. New York, 1882.

Dacus, Joseph A. *Annals of the Great Strikes in the United States*. Philadelphia, 1877.
Dallas, Alexander J. *Life and Writings of Alexander James Dallas*. Philadelphia, 1871.
Dauer, Manning J. *The Adams Federalists*. Baltimore, 1953.
Daugherty, Harry M. *The Inside Story of the Harding Tragedy*. New York, 1932.
Davenport, Benjamin. *The Crime of Caste in Our Country*. Philadelphia, 1893.
Davidson, Philip G. *Propaganda and the American Revolution, 1763–1783*. Chapel Hill, 1941.
Davis, Charles A. *Letters of Jack Downing*. New York, 1834.
Davis, H. Winter. *Speeches and Addresses Delivered in the Congress of the United States*. New York, 1867.
Davis, Matthew L. *Memoirs of Burr*. 2v. New York, 1836–37.
Debs, Eugene. *Speeches of Eugene V. Debs*. New York, 1928.
DeForest, John W. *Miss Ravenel's Conversion from Secession to Loyalty*. New York, 1939.
———. *Playing the Mischief*. New York, 1875.
———. *A Union Officer in the Reconstruction*. New Haven, 1948.
Democratic Party. *Official Proceedings of the National Democratic Convention, Held at New York, July 4–9, 1868*. Boston, 1868.
Dennett, Tyler. *John Hay: from Poetry to Politics*. New York, 1933.
Depew, Chauncey. *My Memories of Eighty Years*. New York, 1923.
Desmond, Humphrey. *The Know-Nothing Party*. Washington, 1905.
DeVere, M. Schele. *Americanisms: the English of the New World*. New York, 1872.
Dickey, Dallas C. *Seargent S. Prentiss, Whig Orator of the Old South*. Baton Rouge, 1945.
Dickinson, John. *The Writings of John Dickinson*. Philadelphia, 1895.
Dictionary of American Biography. Ed. Dumas Malone. New York, 1946.
Dictionary of American English. Ed. Sir William Craigie and James Hulbert. Chicago, 1936–43.
Dictionary of American History. Ed. James T. Adams. New York, 1942.
Dictionary of Americanisms. Mitford M. Mathews. Chicago, 1950.
Dingley, Edward N. *The Life and Times of Nelson Dingley, Jr.* Kalamazoo, 1902.
Dix, Morgan. *Memoirs of John Adams Dix*. 2v. New York, 1883.
Doesticks, [M. Thompson]. *Plur-i-bus-tah*. New York, 1856.
Donnan, Elizabeth, and L. F. Stock. *An Historian's World*. Philadelphia, 1956.
Donovan, Herbert. *The Barnburners*. New York, 1925.
Douglass, Frederick. *Narrative of the Life of Frederick Douglass*. Boston, 1849.
Drake, Benjamin. *Tales and Sketches from the Queen City*. Cincinnati, 1838.
DuBose, John W. *The Life and Times of William Lowndes Yancey*. Birmingham, 1892.
Dunlap, William. *The Memoirs of a Water Drinker*. New York, 1837.
Dwight, Theodore. *History of the Hartford Convention*. New York, 1833.
Dwight, Timothy. *Travels; in New-England and New-York*. New Haven, 1821–22.

Edgerton, Sidney. *Speech of Sidney Edgerton on the New Conspiracy*. Washington, 1862.
Eggleston, Edward. *Duffels*. New York, 1893.

Eggleston, Edward. *The Hoosier School-Boy.* New York, 1882.

Ekirch, Arthur A. *The Idea of Progress in America, 1815–1860.* New York, 1944.

Elliot, Jonathan. *The Debates . . . on the Adoption of the Federal Constitution.* Washington, 1827–45.

Elliott, C. W. *Winfield Scott, the Soldier and the Man.* New York, 1937.

Emerson, R. W. *Complete Works.* Centenary Ed. Boston, 1903–04.

———. *The Conduct of Life.* Boston, 1860.

Erskine, Thomas. *Speeches, with Memoir by Edw. Walford,* reprinted from 1810 ed. London, 1870.

Everett, Alexander H. *America.* Philadelphia, 1827.

Farley, James A. *Behind the Ballots.* New York, 1938.

———. *Jim Farley's Story.* New York, 1948.

Farmer, John S. *Americanisms—Old and New.* London, 1889.

Faux, William. *Memorable Days in America.* London, 1823.

Fearon, Henry. *Sketches of America.* London, 1818.

Federalism Triumphant. See Chester, L.

The Federalist. Modern Library Edition.

Fessenden, Thomas. *Democracy Unveiled.* New York, 1806.

Fidfaddy, Frederick A. *The Adventures of Uncle Sam, in Search After His Lost Honor.* Middletown, Connecticut, 1816.

Field, Al G. *Watch Yourself Go By.* Columbus, 1912.

Field, Henry M. *The Life of Dudley Field.* New York, 1898.

Flint, Henry M. *Life of Stephen A. Douglas.* New York, 1860.

Flint, Timothy. *George Mason, the Young Backwoodsman.* Boston, 1829.

———. *Recollections of the Last Ten Years.* Boston, 1826.

Flower, Frank. *History of the Republican Party.* Springfield, Illinois, 1884.

Flynt, Josiah. *Tramping with Tramps.* New York, 1900.

———. *The World of Graft.* New York, 1901.

Foner, Philip S. *Basic Writings of Thomas Jefferson.* New York, 1944.

———. *Business & Slavery.* Chapel Hill, 1941.

———. *History of the Labor Movement in the United States.* New York, 1947.

———. *The Life and Writings of Frederick Douglass.* New York, 1950.

Foote, Henry S. *Casket of Reminiscences.* Washington, 1874.

Force, Peter. *Tracts and Other Papers.* Washington, 1836–46.

Forman, Samuel E. *The Political Activities of Philip Freneau.* Baltimore, 1902.

Forney, John W. *Anecdotes of Public Men.* 2v. New York, 1873.

———. *Life and Military Career of Winfield Scott Hancock . . . [and] of Hon. Wm. H. English.* Boston, 1880.

Fowler, Richard B. *Alfred M. Landon; or, Deeds not Deficits.* Boston, 1936.

Fowler, William W. *Ten Years in Wall Street.* Hartford, 1870.

Franklin, Allan. *Trail of the Tiger.* New York, 1928.

Franklin, Benjamin. *Complete Works.* New York, 1887–88.

Freidel, Frank B. *Franklin D. Roosevelt.* 3v. [III—*The Triumph*] Boston, 1952–56.

Fremantle, Lt. Col. *Three Months in the Southern States.* New York, 1864.

French, A. M. *Slavery in South Carolina and the Ex-slaves.* New York, 1862.

Fröbel, Julius. *Aus Amerika.* Leipzig, 1857–58.

Funk, Wilfred. *When the Merry-Go-Round Breaks Down!* New York, 1938.

Gammon, Samuel R. *The Presidential Campaign of 1832.* Baltimore, 1922.

Garfield, James A. *The Works of James Abram Garfield.* Boston, 1882–83.

Garfield-Hinsdale Letters. Ed. Mary Hinsdale. Ann Arbor, 1949.

Garland, Hugh. *The Life of John Randolph of Roanoke.* New York, 1851.

Garner, James W. *Reconstruction in Mississippi.* New York, 1901.

Garraty, John A. *Silas Wright.* New York, 1949.

Garrison, Wendell, and Francis Garrison. *William Lloyd Garrison. The Story of His Life.* 4v. New York, 1885–89.

Garrison, William Lloyd. *Selections from the Writings and Speeches.* Boston, 1852.

Geary, Theophane. *A History of Third Parties in Pennsylvania, 1840–1860.* Washington, 1938.

George, Henry. *Progress and Poverty.* London, 1881.

Giddings, Joshua. *Speeches in Congress.* Cleveland, 1853.

Gilbert, Douglas. *Lost Chords, the Diverting Story of American Popular Songs.* Garden City, 1942.

Gilbert, Sir William S. *Plays and Poems of W. S. Gilbert.* New York, 1932.

Gillet, Ransom H. *Democracy in the United States.* New York, 1868.

Going, Charles B. *David Wilmot, Free-Soiler.* New York, 1924.

Goodrich, Charles A. *A History of the United States of America.* Hartford, 1823.

Goodrich, Chauncey A. *Select British Eloquence.* New York, 1853.

Goodrich, Samuel G. *Recollections of a Lifetime.* 2v. New York, 1857.

Gordon, Ernest. *The Wrecking of the Eighteenth Amendment.* Francestown, New Hampshire, 1943.

Gordon, William. *The History of the Rise, Progress, and Establishment of the Independence of the United States of America.* New York, 1789.

Gordy, John P. *A History of Political Parties in the United States.* New York, 1900.

Gosnell, Harold F. *Champion Campaigner: Franklin D. Roosevelt.* New York, 1952.

Goss, Warren L. *The Soldier's Story of His Captivity.* Boston, 1867.

Gould, Jean. Ed. *Homegrown Liberal; the Autobiography of Charles W. Ervin.* New York, 1954.

[Grady, H. W.] *Joel Chandler Harris's Life of Henry W. Grady Including His Writings and Speeches.* New York, 1890.

Grant, Robert. *Searchlight Letters.* New York, 1899.

Gray, J. C., and J. C. Ropes. *War Letters, 1862–65.* New York, 1927.

Graydon, Alexander. *Memoirs of a Life.* Philadelphia, 1811.

Great Debates in American History. Ed. M. M. Miller. 14v. New York, 1913.

Great Issues and National Leaders of 1908. [N.p.] 1908.

Great Political Issues and Leaders of the Campaign of 1900. Chicago, 1900.

Greeley, Horace. *The American Conflict: a History of the Great Rebellion.* Hartford, 1864–66.

———. *Recollections of a Busy Life.* New York, 1868.

———. *What I Know about Farming.* New York, 1871.

Greene, Asa. *The Perils of Pearl Street.* New York, 1834.

———. *A Yankee Among the Nullifiers.* New York, 1833.

Gregg, Alexander. *History of the Old Cheraws.* New York, 1867.

Grinnell, Josiah. *Men and Events of Forty Years.* Boston, 1891.

Groat, George G. *An Introduction to the Study of Organized Labor in America.* 2nd ed. New York, 1926.

Gunderson, Robert G. *The Log-Cabin Campaign.* Lexington, 1957.

Gurowski, Adam. *Diary.* 3v. Boston, 1862–66.

Hale, E. E. *If, Yes, and Perhaps.* Boston, 1868.

———. *Memories of a Hundred Years.* 2v. New York, 1902.

Haliburton, Thomas. *The Clockmaker.* London, 1838.

Hall, James. *Letters from the West.* London, 1828.

Hallam, Henry. *Constitutional History of England.* 3v. New York, 1912.

Halleck, Fitz-Greene. *The Poetical Works* . . . New York, 1869.

Halpine, Charles G. *Poetical Works of Charles G. Halpine.* New York, 1869.

———. *Private Miles O'Reilly.* Carleton, New York, 1864.

Hambleton, James P. *A Biographical Sketch of Henry A. Wise.* Richmond, 1856.

Hamilton, Alexander. *Works.* New York, 1885–86.

Hamilton, Gail. *Biography of James G. Blaine.* Norwich, Connecticut, 1895.

Hammond, Jabez. *The History of Political Parties in the State of New-York.* Albany, 1842.

———. *Life and Times of Silas Wright, Late Governor of the State of New York.* New York, 1848.

Harding, Nelson. *The Political Campaign of 1912 in Cartoons.* New York, 1912.

Harding, Warren G. *Our Common Country.* Indianapolis, 1921.

Harper's Pictorial History of the Great Rebellion. 2v. Chicago, 1866–68.

Harrison, Constance. *The Anglomaniacs.* New York, 1890.

Hart, Albert B. *Sourcebook of American History.* New York, 1925.

Hart, Bob. *Bob Hart's Plantation Songster.* New York, 1862.

Harte, Bret. *Complete Works.* 10v. Cambridge, Massachusetts, 1929.

———. *Gabriel Conroy.* Hartford, 1876.

Harvey, William H. *Coin's Financial School.* Chicago, 1894.

Hay, John. *The Bread-Winners.* New York, 1883.

Hayes, Rutherford B. *Diary and Letters.* 5v. Columbus, 1922–26.

Haynes, Frederick. *James Baird Weaver.* Iowa City, 1919.

Heartsill, William W. *Fourteen Hundred and 91 Days in the Confederate Army.* Marshall, Tex., 1876.

Heaton, John L. *Cobb of "The World."* New York, 1924.

Heckscher, August. *The Politics of Woodrow Wilson, Selections from His Speeches and Writings.* New York, 1956.

Helm, William P. *Harry Truman, A Political Biography.* New York, 1947.

Helper, Hinton. *The Impending Crisis of the South.* New York, 1860.

Herwegh, Marcel. Ed. *1848. Briefe von und an Georg Herwegh.* Munich, 1896.

Hicks, John D. *The Populist Revolt.* Minneapolis, 1931.

Hildreth, Richard. *Archy Moore, the White Slave; or, Memoirs of a Fugitive.* New York, 1855.

Hoar, George F. *Autobiography of Seventy Years.* 2v. New York, 1903.

Hodder, Edwin. *The Life and Work of the Seventh Earl of Shaftesbury.* 3v. London, 1887.

Hoffman, Charles F. *Greyslaer,* New York, 1840.

———. *Wild Scenes in the Forest and Prairie.* London, 1839.

Holbrook, James. *Ten Years Among the Mail Bags.* Philadelphia, 1855.

Holcombe, John W., and H. M. Skinner. *Life and Public Services of Thomas A. Hendricks.* Indianapolis, 1886.

Holinshed's Chronicles. Everyman Ed. London, 1927.

Hollister, Ovando, *Life of Schuyler Colfax.* Chicago, 1887.

Holmes, Oliver W. *Elsie Venner.* Boston, 1861.

Holt, Edgar A. *Party Politics in Ohio, 1840–1850.* Columbus, 1931.

Holzman, Robert. *Stormy Ben Butler.* New York, 1954.

Hone, Philip. *Diary* . . . *1828–1851.* Ed. Allan Nevins. 2v. New York, 1927.

Hoover, Herbert. *Addresses Upon the American Road.* New York, 1938.

———. *Memoirs.* New York, 1951– .

Hosmer, John. *A Trip to the States in 1865.* Missoula, Montana, 1932.

Howard, H. R. *The History of Virgil A. Stewart.* New York, 1838.

Howard, Perry H. *Political Tendencies in Louisiana, 1812–1952*. Baton Rouge, 1957.
Howe, Henry. *Historical Collections of Ohio*. Cincinnati, 1847.
Hudson, W. C. *Random Recollections of an Old Political Reporter*. New York, 1911.
Hunnicut, James. *The Conspiracy Unveiled*. Philadelphia, 1863.
Hunt, Leigh. *Autobiography*. London, 1928.

Irving, Washington. *A History of New York*. 2v. New York, 1809.
——, *et al. Salmagundi*. New York, 1807–08.
Isely, Jeter. *Horace Greeley and the Republican Party, 1853–1861*. Princeton, 1947.

Jackson, Andrew. *Correspondence of* . . . Ed. J. S. Bassett. 7v. Washington, 1926–35.
Jackson, J. Hampden. *Clemenceau and the Third Republic*. London, 1946.
James, Marquis. *The Life of Andrew Jackson*. Indianapolis, 1938.
——. *The Raven; a Biography of Sam Houston*. Indianapolis, 1929.
Jameson, John, and J. W. Buel. *Encyclopedic Dictionary of American Reference*. Boston, 1901.
Jay, John. *Correspondence and Public Papers*. New York, 1890–93.
Jay, William. *A Review of the Causes and Consequences of the Mexican War*. Boston, 1849.
Jefferson, Thomas. *Memoirs, Correspondence, and Miscellanies*. Charlottesville, 1829.
——. *Writings*. New York, 1892–99.
Jenkins, John S. *History of Political Parties in the State of New York*. Auburn, New York, 1846.
——. *The Life of James Knox Polk*. Auburn, New York, 1850.
[Johnson, Andrew.] *The Great Impeachment and Trial of Andrew Johnson, President of the United States*. Philadelphia, 1868.
Jones, John B. *Wild Southern Scenes*. Philadelphia, 1859.
Jones, William. *Mirror of Modern Democracy*. New York, 1864.
Julian, George W. *Political Recollections, 1840 to 1872*. Chicago, 1884.
——. *Speeches on Political Questions*. New York, 1872.
July, Robert. *The Essential New Yorker, Gulian Crommelin Verplanck*. Durham, 1951.

Kellogg, Robert. *Life and Death in Rebel Prisons*. Hartford, 1865.
Kelso, Isaac. *The Stars and Bars*. Boston, 1863.
Kendall, Amos. *Autobiography*. Boston, 1872.
Kennedy, John P. *Memoirs of the Life of William Wirt*. Philadelphia, 1849.
——. *Mr. Ambrose's Letters on the Rebellion*. New York, 1865.
——. *Quodlibet*. Philadelphia, 1840.
Kent, Frank R. *Political Behavior*. New York, 1928.
King, Rufus. *Life and Correspondence*. New York, 1894–1900.
Kingsley, Charles. *Alton Locke, Tailor and Poet*. New York, 1850.
Kirke, Edmund. *Among the Pines*. New York, 1862.
——. *Down in Tennessee, and Back by way of Richmond*. New York, 1864.
Kirkland, Caroline. *Forest Life*. New York, 1842.
——. *A New Home—Who'll Follow?* New York, 1839.
Kirkland, Joseph. *The Captain of Company K*. Chicago, 1891.
Koch, Adrienne. *Jefferson and Madison; the Great Collaboration*. New York, 1950.
Koenig, Louis W. Ed. *The Truman Administration, Its Principles and Practice*. New York, 1956.
Ku Klux Klan Report. Washington, 1872.

Ladendorf, Otto. *Historisches Schlagwörterbuch*. Strassburg, 1906.
LaFollette, Robert M. *Autobiography*. Madison, 1912.

Lane, Marcus. "American Political Catchwords" in *America: a Journal for Americans.* 13 Sept.–8 Nov., 1888.

Lattimore, Owen. *Ordeal by Slander.* Boston, 1950.

Leary, Lewis. *That Rascal Freneau, a Study in Literary Failure.* New Brunswick, N.J., 1941.

Lee, John H. *The Origins and Progress of the American Party in Politics.* Philadelphia, 1855.

Lefler, Hugh T. *North Carolina History Told by Contemporaries.* Chapel Hill, 1934.

Leggett, William. *A Collection of the Political Writings of William Leggett.* New York, 1840.

Lester, Charles E. *Life and Public Services of Charles Sumner.* New York, 1874.

Lever, Charles J. *The Works of Charles Lever.* New York, 1880.

Lewis, Alfred H. *The Boss, and How He Came to Rule New York.* New York, 1903.

———. *The Sunset Trail.* New York, 1906.

Lieber, Francis. *Encyclopedia Americana.* 1st ed. Philadelphia, 1853.

———. *On Civil Liberty and Self-Government.* Philadelphia, 1853.

Liebling, Abbott. *Mink and Red Herring.* New York, 1949.

Lillard, John F. *Poker Stories.* New York, 1896.

Lincoln, Abraham. *Works.* Nat. Ed. New York, 1905–06.

Lincoln Cyclopedia. Compiled by Archer H. Shaw. New York, 1950.

The Lincoln Papers. See Mearns, D. C.

Lindley, Ernest K. *Franklin D. Roosevelt; a Career in Progressive Democracy.* Indianapolis, 1931.

Link, Eugene. *Democratic-Republican Societies, 1790–1800.* New York, 1942.

[Littell, William.] *Reprints of Littell's Political Transactions.* Louisville, 1926.

Lloyd, Caroline. *Henry Demarest Lloyd, 1847–1903.* New York, 1912.

Lloyd, Henry D. *A Sovereign People; a Study of Swiss Democracy.* New York, 1907.

Lodge, Henry C. *Life and Letters of George Cabot.* Boston, 1877.

Log Cabin Song Book. New York, 1840.

Logan, John A. *The Great Conspiracy.* New York, 1866.

Longstreet, Augustus. *Georgia Scenes.* Augusta, 1835.

Longworth, Alice. *Crowded Hours, Reminiscences of Alice Roosevelt Longworth.* New York, 1933.

Loth, David G. *Public Plunder; a History of Graft in America.* New York, 1938.

Lowell, James R. *My Study Windows.* Boston, 1871.

———. *Political Essays.* Boston, 1889.

———. *Writings.* Boston, 1890.

Luetscher, George. *Early Political Machinery in the United States.* Philadelphia, 1903.

Lusk, William. *War Letters of Wm. Thompson Lusk.* New York, 1911.

Luthin, Reinhard. *American Demagogues: Twentieth Century.* Boston, 1954.

Lynch, Dennis T. *An Epoch and a Man: Martin Van Buren and His Times.* New York, 1929.

Lynch, William O. *Fifty Years of Party Warfare.* Indianapolis, 1931.

Lynde, Francis. *The Grafters.* Indianapolis, 1904.

Macaulay, Thomas B. *Speeches and Poems.* New York, 1880.

McClure, Alexander. *Colonel Alexander K. McClure's Recollections of Half a Century.* Salem, Massachusetts, 1902.

McCormac, Eugene. *James K. Polk. A Political Biography.* Berkeley, 1922.

McDuffie, George. *Speech of Mr. McDuffie on Internal Improvements.* Columbia, South Carolina, 1824.

McGrane, R. C. *William Allen: a Study in Western Democracy.* Columbus, 1925.

McKenzie, Frederick. *"Pussyfoot" Johnson, Crusader—Reformer—a Man Among Men.* New York, 1920.

MacKenzie, William L. *The Life and Times of Martin Van Buren.* Boston, 1846.

Mackintosh, Sir James. *The Miscellaneous Works.* New York, 1854.

———. *Vindiciae Gallicae: Defence of the French Revolution.* Dublin, 1791.

McLaughlin, A. C., and A. B. Hart. *Cyclopedia of American Government.* New York, 1914.

MacMaster, John Bach. *A History of the People of the United States.* New York, 1883–1913.

McPherson, Edward. *A Handbook of Politics for [1868–1894].* Washington, 1868–94.

———. *Political Manual.* Washington, 1866–67.

Madison, James. *The Papers of James Madison . . . Being His Correspondence and Reports of Debates during the Congress of the Confederation, and . . . in the Federal Convention.* 3v. Washington, 1840.

———. *Writings.* New York, 1900–10.

Mangum, Willie P. *Papers.* Ed. H. T. Shanks. Raleigh, 1950–   .

Mann, Arthur. *Yankee Reformers in the Urban Age.* Cambridge, Massachusetts, 1954.

Marshall, Thomas R. *Recollections of Thomas R. Marshall . . . a Hoosier Salad.* Indianapolis, 1925.

Martineau, Harriet. *Retrospect of Western Travel.* London, 1835.

[Massachusetts Acts]. *The Acts and Resolves . . . of the Province of Massachusetts Bay.* Boston, 1869–1922.

Mather, Cotton. *Magnalia Christi Americana.* Hartford, 1853.

Mathews, Mitford M. *The Beginnings of American English.* Chicago, 1931.

Matlack, Lucius C. *The Antislavery Struggle and Triumph in the Methodist Episcopal Church.* Cincinnati, 1881.

Maurice, A. B., and F. T. Cooper. *The History of the Nineteenth Century in Caricature.* New York, 1904.

May, Earl C. *The Circus from Rome to Ringling.* New York, 1932.

May, Samuel J. *Some Recollections of Our Antislavery Conflict.* Boston, 1869.

Mayes, Edward. *Lucius Q. C. Lamar: His Life, Times and Speeches, 1825–1893.* Nashville, 1896.

Mayo, Bernard. *Henry Clay.* Boston, 1937.

Mayo, Robert. *Political Sketches of Eight Years in Washington.* Baltimore, 1839.

Mearns, D. C. *The Lincoln Papers.* 2v. New York, 1948.

Medbery, James K. *Men and Mysteries of Wall Street.* Boston, 1870.

Melville, Herman. *Omoo.* New York, 1847.

———. *Redburn.* New York, 1849.

Men and Issues of 1900. Ed. James P. Boyd. [N.p.], 1900.

Mencken, H. L. *The American Language.* New York, 1936. Suppl. 1945; 1948.

———. *Making a President.* New York, 1932.

———. *Newspaper Days, 1899–1906.* New York, 1941.

Merriman, George S. *The Life and Times of Samuel Bowles.* New York, 1885.

Michael, George. *Handout.* New York, 1935.

Michie, Allan, and Frank Ryhlick. *Dixie Demagogues.* New York, 1939.

Miller, Joaquin. *Life Amongst the Modocs.* London, 1873.

Miller, John C. *Origins of the American Revolution.* Boston, 1943.

Milton, George. *The Age of Hate: Andrew Johnson and the Radicals.* New York, 1930.

Minnegarode, Meade. *Jefferson, Friend of France, 1793.* New York, 1928.

Mitchell, John. *Organized Labor, Its Problems, Purposes and Ideals.* Philadelphia, 1903.

Mitgang, Herbert. Ed. *Lincoln as They Saw Him.* New York, 1956.

Mockridge, Norton, and Robert Prall. *The Big Fix.* New York, 1954.

Moore, Frank. *The Rebellion Record: a Diary of American Events.* New York, 1862–71.
———. *Songs and Ballads of the American Revolution.* New York, 1856.
Moos, Malcolm. *The Republicans: a History of Their Party.* New York, 1956.
Morford, Henry. *Shoulder Straps.* Philadelphia, 1863.
Morgan, Albert T. *Yazoo.* Washington, 1884.
Morgenthau, Henry. *All in a Lifetime.* New York, 1922.
Morris, B. F. *The Life of Thomas Morris.* Cincinnati, 1856.
Morris, Gouverneur. *The Diary and Letters of . . .* 2v. New York, 1888.
Moser, Johann J. *Europaische Volkerrecht.* 1750.
Moss, Frank. *The American Metropolis from Knickerbocker Days to the Present Time.* 3v. New York, 1897.
Moton, Robert R. *What the Negro Thinks.* Garden City, 1942.
Murray, Amelia M. *Letters from the U.S., Cuba and Canada.* 2v. London, 1856.
Murrell, William. *A History of American Graphic Humor.* 2v. New York, 1933–38.
Muzzey, David. *James G. Blaine.* New York, 1934.
Myers, Allen. *Bosses and Boodle in Ohio Politics.* Cincinnati, 1895.
Myers, Gustavus. *The History of Tammany Hall.* New York, 1901.

Nasby, Petroleum. *Struggles of Petroleum V. Nasby.* Toledo, 1880.
———. *Swinging Round the Cirkle.* Boston, 1867.
Nason, Elias. *The Life and Public Services of Henry Wilson.* Philadelphia, 1876.
National Clay Minstrel. Philadelphia, 1844.
Neal, John. *Brother Jonathan.* Edinburgh, 1825.
Neal, Joseph. *Charcoal Sketches, or Scenes in the Metropolis.* Philadelphia, 1843.
Neuberger, R. L., and S. B. Kahn. *Integrity: the Life of George W. Norris.* New York, 1937.
Nevins, Allan. *The Emergence of Lincoln.* 2v. New York, 1950.
———. *Hamilton Fish: the Inner Story of the Grant Administration.* New York, 1936.
———. *Ordeal of the Union.* 2v. New York, 1947.
———, and Frank Weitenkampf. *A Century of Political Cartoons.* New York, 1944.
Newell, Robert H. *The Orpheus C. Kerr Papers.* New York, 1863.
Nichols, George W. *The Story of the Great March.* New York, 1865.
Nichols, Thomas. *Forty Years of American Life.* London, 1874.
Nicolay, J. G., and John Hay. *Abraham Lincoln: a History.* New York, 1890.
Northern Editorials on Secession. Ed. Howard C. Perkins. 2v. New York, 1942.
Norton, Anthony B. *The Great Revolution of 1840. Reminiscences of the Log Cabin and Hard Cider Campaign.* Mt. Vernon, Ohio, 1888.
———. *Tippecanoe Songs of the Log Cabin Boys and Girls of 1840.* Mt. Vernon, Ohio, 1888.
Norton, Charles L. "Political Americanisms" in *Magazine of American History.* 1884–85.
Nourse, Edwin G. *Price Making in a Democracy.* Washington, 1944.
Nye (Bill) Edgar W. *Forty Liars and Other Lies.* Chicago, 1882.

O. Henry. *Cabbages and Kings.* New York, 1904.
———. *Roads of Destiny.* New York, 1909.
Oberholtzer, Ellis. *The Referendum in America.* New York, 1911.
Old South Leaflets. Boston, 1896–   .
Olmstead, Frederick. *The Cotton Kingdom.* 2v. New York, 1861.
Orth, Samuel. *The Boss and the Machine.* New Haven, 1921.
Otis, James. *Vindication* (1762) ; *Rights of British Colonies* (1764) ; *Considerations* (1765) ; *Vindication of British Colonies* (1765) ; *Brief Remarks* (1765) in *U. of Missouri Studies* IV (1929) .

Our National Leaders of 1904. Springfield, Massachusetts, 1904.

Overdyke, William D. *The Know Nothing Party in the South.* Baton Rouge, 1950.

Owen, Robert D. *Twenty-seven Years of Autobiography: Threading My Way.* New York, 1874.

The Oxford English Dictionary. Ed. Sir James Murray *et al.* [Oxford.] 1884–1933.

Padover, Saul. *Jefferson.* New York, 1942.

Page, Charles A. *Letters of a War Correspondent.* Boston, 1899.

Paine, Albert B. *Th. Nast, His Period and His Pictures.* New York, 1904.

Paine, Thomas. *The Works of* . . . 3v. Philadelphia, 1854.

Parker, Theodore. *Additional Speeches, Addresses, and Occasional Sermons.* Boston, 1855.

——. *Life and Correspondence of* . . . Ed. John Weiss. [N.p.] 1864.

The Parties and the Men, or Political Issues of 1896. [N.p.] 1896.

Parton, James. *General Butler in New-Orleans.* Boston, 1864.

——. *The Life and Times of Aaron Burr.* New York, 1858.

——. *The Life of Horace Greeley.* New York, 1855.

——. *Topics of the Time.* Boston, 1871.

Paulding, James K. *Chronicles of the City of Gotham.* New York, 1830.

——. *Letters from the South.* 2v. New York, 1817.

——. *The New Mirror for Travellers.* New York, 1828.

——. *Westward Ho!* New York, 1832.

Peck, George W. *Adventures of One Terence McGrant.* New York, 1871.

Peck, Harry T. *Twenty Years of the Republic, 1885–1905.* New York, 1906.

[Penn-Logan Correspondence.] Historical Society of Pennsylvania. *Memoirs,* IX–X.

Perkins, Eli. *Thirty Years of Wit.* New York, 1891.

Perkins, James H. *The Memoir and Writings of James Handasyd Perkins.* Boston, 1851.

Philipson, Uno. *Political Slang, 1750–1850.* Lund, 1941.

Phillips, David G. *The Plum Tree.* New York, 1905.

Phillips, Wendell. *Speeches, Lectures, and Letters.* Boston, 1884.

Phillips, William. *The Conquest of Kansas.* Boston, 1856.

Pike, James S. *First Blows of the Civil War.* New York, 1879.

Pittenger, William. *Daring and Suffering.* Philadelphia, 1864.

Pittman, H. D. *The Belle of the Blue Grass Country.* Boston, 1906.

Platt, Thomas C. *The Autobiography of Thomas Collier Platt.* New York, 1910.

Poage, George. *Henry Clay and the Whig Party.* Chapel Hill, 1936.

Poetry of the Anti-Jacobin. The Anti-Jacobin or Weekly Examiner. 2v. 4th ed. London, 1799.

Der Politische Thierkreis. Strassburg, 1800.

Polk, James K. *Diary.* 4v. Chicago, 1910.

Pollard, Edward. *Life of Jefferson Davis, With a Secret History of the Southern Confederacy.* Philadelphia, 1869.

——. *The Lost Cause; a New Southern History of the War of the Confederates.* New York, 1866.

——. *Southern History of the War. The First Years of the War.* New York, 1863.

Pollard, John G. *A Connotary; Definitions not Found in Dictionaries.* New York, 1935.

Poore, Benjamin Perley. *Perley's Reminiscences of Sixty Years in the National Metropolis.* Philadelphia, 1886.

Porter, Kirk, and Donald Johnson. *National Party Platforms, 1840–1956.* Urbana, 1956.

Porter, William T. *A Quarter Race in Kentucky, and Other Sketches.* Philadelphia, 1846.

Post, Lydia. *Soldiers' Letters from Camp, Battlefield and Prison.* New York, 1865.

Post, Waldron. *Harvard Stories.* New York, 1893.

Powell, Lyman P. *The Social Unrest.* New York, 1919.

Prentice, George D. *Prenticeana; or, Wit and Humor in Paragraphs.* Philadelphia, 1871.

[Pres. Messages.] *A Compilation of the Messages and Papers of the Presidents, 1789–1897.* Comp. James D. Richardson. 10v. Washington, 1896–99.

Price, Richard. *Observations on the Importance of the American Revolution.* London, 1784.

Price, William. *Clement Falconer; or The Memories of a Young Whig.* Baltimore, 1838.

Pringle, Henry. *The Life and Times of William Howard Taft.* 2v. New York, 1939.

Quick, Herbert. *The Brown Mouse.* Indianapolis, 1915.

Quincy, Edmund. *Life of Josiah Quincy of Massachusetts.* Boston, 1867.

Ranck, James B. *Albert Gallatin Brown, Radical Southern Nationalist.* New York, 1937.

Raum, Green Berry. *The Existing Conflict between Republican Government and Southern Oligarchy.* Washington, 1884.

Record of Hon. C. L. Vallandigham. Columbus, 1863.

Register of Debates. 3v. Washington, 1834.

Reid, Whitelaw. *After the War.* Cincinnati, 1866.

[Republican Party.] *Official Proceedings of the Republican National Convention . . . 1884.* Minneapolis, 1903.

Reynolds, John H. *The Fancy.* London, 1820.

Rhodes, James F. *History of the United States from the Compromise of 1850.* New York, 1900.

Richardson, Albert D. *Beyond the Mississippi.* Hartford, 1867.

———. *A Personal History of Ulysses S. Grant.* Hartford, 1868.

———. *The Secret Service.* Hartford, 1865.

Riddle, Donald W. *Congressman Abraham Lincoln.* Urbana, 1957.

Ridpath, John. *The Life and Work of James A. Garfield.* Cincinnati, 1881.

Riis, Jacob. *How the Other Half Lives; Studies among the Tenements of New York.* New York, 1890.

———. *Theodore Roosevelt, the Citizen.* New York, 1904.

Riordon, William. *Plunkett of Tammany Hall.* New York, 1948.

Robertson, William. *The History of America.* Philadelphia, 1812.

Robinson, Blackwell P. *William R. Davie.* Chapel Hill, 1957.

Robinson, William. *Jeffersonian Democracy in New England.* New Haven, 1916.

———. *Thomas B. Reed, Parliamentarian.* New York, 1930.

Rogers, Will. *Autobiography.* Boston, 1949.

———. *How We Elect Our Presidents.* Boston, 1952.

[Roosevelt, Franklin D.]. *F.D.R. His Personal Letters.* Ed. Elliott Roosevelt. 2v. New York, 1950.

———. *Public Papers and Addresses of . . .* Comp. Samuel I. Rosenman. 13v. New York, 1938–50.

Roosevelt, Theodore. *Letters.* Ed. E. E. Morison. Cambridge, Massachusetts, 1951– .

———. *Theodore Roosevelt Cyclopedia.* Ed. A. B. Hart and H. R. Ferleger. New York, 1941.

———. *Works.* Memorial ed. New York, 1923–26.

Root, Elihu. *Addresses on Government and Citizenship.* Cambridge, Massachusetts, 1916.

Ropes, Hannah. *Six Months in Kansas.* Boston, 1856.

Rosewater, Victor. *Back Stage in 1912.* Philadelphia, 1932.

Rush, Benjamin. *Letters.* Ed. L. H. Butterfield. 2v. Philadelphia, 1951.

Russell, Charles. *Blaine of Maine. His Life and Times.* New York, 1931.
Russell, William. *My Diary North and South.* London, 1863.

Sala, George. *My Diary in America in the Midst of War.* 2v. London, 1865.
Salisbury, William. *The Career of a Journalist.* New York, 1908.
Salter, J. T. *The American Politician.* Chapel Hill, 1938.
Sandburg, Carl. *Abraham Lincoln: the Prairie Years.* New York, 1926.
——. *Abraham Lincoln: the War Years.* New York, 1939.
Sanderson, John. *Republican Landmarks.* Philadelphia, 1856.
Sargent, Epes. *The Life and Public Services of Henry Clay.* Auburn, New York, 1852.
Scherr, Johannes. *Michel.* New York, 1871.
Schurz, Carl. *Life of Henry Clay.* Boston, 1887.
——. *The Reminiscences of Carl Schurz.* New York, 1909.
——. *Speeches, Correspondence, and Political Papers of Carl Schurz.* New York, 1913.
Scott, John. *Paris Revisited, in 1815, by way of Brussels.* Boston, 1816.
Scott, Leroy. *The Walking Delegate.* New York, 1905.
Scott, Walter. *Autobiography of Sir Walter Scott, Bart.* Philadelphia, 1831.
——. *The Journals of Sir Walter Scott.* New York, 1890.
Sedgwick, Catherine. *Tales and Sketches.* Philadelphia, 1835.
Seitz, Don C. *Joseph Pulitzer, His Life & Letters.* New York, 1924.
Seldes, George. *The Facts Are.* [In Fact, Inc.] New York, 1942.
——. *Witch Hunt.* New York, 1940.
——. *You Can't Print That!* New York, 1929.
Seward, William H. *Autobiography, from 1801 to 1834.* New York, 1877.
——. *The Works of . . .* 5v. New York, 1884.
Shapley, Rufus. *Solid for Mulhooly.* Philadelphia, 1889.
Shaw, Albert. *Abraham Lincoln.* 2v. New York, 1929.
——. *A Cartoon History of Roosevelt's Career.* New York, 1910.
Sheahan, James. *The Life of Stephen A. Douglas.* New York, 1860.
Sheridan, Richard B. *Speeches of the Right Honourable Richard Brinsley Sheridan.* 3v. London, 1842.
Sherman, John. *John Sherman's Recollections of Forty Years in the House.* Chicago, 1895.
Sherman, William T., and John Sherman. *The Sherman Letters.* New York, 1894.
Sherwood, Robert E. *Roosevelt and Hopkins, an Intimate History.* New York, 1948.
Shinn, Charles H. *The Story of the Mine.* New York, 1897.
Shipp, John. *Giant Days; or, the Life and Times of William H. Crawford.* Americus, Georgia, 1909.
Shryock, Richard. *Georgia and the Union in 1850.* Durham, 1926.
Siebert, Wilbur. *The Underground Railroad from Slavery to Freedom.* New York, 1898.
Simkins, Francis. *Pitchfork Ben Tillman, South Carolinian.* Baton Rouge, 1944.
Simms, Henry. *The Rise of the Whigs in Virginia. 1824–1840.* Richmond, 1929.
Simms, William G. *Richard Hurdis.* Philadelphia, 1838.
Smith, Alfred E. *Up to Now; an Autobiography.* New York, 1929.
Smith, Bradford. *Americans from Japan.* Philadelphia, 1948.
Smith, Edward C. *Dictionary of American Politics.* New York, 1924.
Smith, James M. *Freedom's Fetters; the Alien and Sedition Laws and American Civil Liberties.* Ithaca, 1956.
Smith, Seba. *Jack Downing Letters.* Philadelphia, 1845.
——. *My Thirty Years out of the Senate.* New York, 1859.
Sons of the Sires, by an American. Philadelphia, 1855.

Sotheran, Charles. *Horace Greeley and Other Pioneers of American Socialism.* New York, 1892.

Sparks, Edwin E. *The Men Who Made the Nation.* New York, 1901.

———. *Address of Dr. Edwin E. Sparks . . . on the Subject of Robert Morris . . . before the Altoona Railroad Club on January 19, 1910.* (N.p. 1910?)

Sparks, Jared. *The Lincoln-Douglas Debates of 1858.* Springfield, Illinois, 1908.

Stanwood, Edward. *A History of the Presidency.* Boston, 1912.

———. *A History of Presidential Elections.* Cambridge, Massachusetts, 1884.

———. *James Gillespie Blaine.* Boston, 1905.

State Trials for High Treason. London, 1794.

Stead, William T. *If Christ Came to Chicago!* Chicago, 1894.

Steele, John. *The Papers of John Steele.* Ed. H. M. Wagstaff. 2v. Raleigh, 1924.

Steffens, Lincoln. *The Autobiography of . . .* New York, 1931.

Stein, L. *Der Socialismus und Communismus.* Leipzig, 1842.

Stephens, Alexander. *A Constitutional View of the Late War Between the States.* 2v. Philadelphia, 1868–70.

Stevenson, Adlai. *Major Campaign Speeches.* New York, 1953.

Steward, Mother. *Memories of the Crusade.* Columbus, 1888.

Stimpson, George. *A Book About American History.* New York, 1950.

———. *A Book About American Politics.* New York, 1952.

Stokes, Thomas L. *Chip off My Shoulder.* Princeton, 1940.

Stone, Edwin M. *The Life and Recollections of John Howland.* Providence, 1857.

Stowe, Harriet B. *Uncle Tom's Cabin; or, Life among the Lowly.* New York, 1884.

Streeter, Floyd. *Political Parties in Michigan, 1837–1860.* Lansing, 1918.

Strong, George T. *Diary.* Ed. Allan Nevins and M. H. Thomas. 4v. New York, 1952.

Sullivan, Mark. *Our Times; the United States, 1900–1925.* 6v. New York, 1926–35.

Summers, Festus P. *William Wilson and Tariff Reform, a Biography.* New Brunswick, 1953.

Sumner, Charles. *His Complete Works.* 2v. Boston, 1900.

Sumner, William G. *The Forgotten Man, and Other Essays.* New Haven, 1918.

Tarbell, Ida. *The Life of Abraham Lincoln.* New York, 1900.

Taylor, B. L., and W. C. Gibson. *The Log of the Water Wagon.* Boston, 1905.

Taylor, Carl C. *The Farmer's Movement, 1620–1920.* New York, 1953.

Taylor, John. *An Enquiry into the Principles and Tendency of Certain Public Measures.* Philadelphia, 1794.

Thacher, James. *A Military Journal.* Boston, 1823.

Thayer, William. *Theodore Roosevelt, an Intimate Biography.* Boston, 1919.

Thomas, Ebenezer. *Reminiscences of the Last Sixty-five Years.* Hartford, 1840.

Thompson, R. W. *History of Protective Tariff Laws.* Chicago, 1888.

Thornton, John. *The Pulpit of the American Revolution.* New York, 1860.

Thornton, Richard. *An American Glossary.* 2v. Philadelphia, 1912. Suppl. in *Dialect Notes* VI (1928–39).

Three Years among the Working Classes in the United States during the War. London, 1865.

[Tipton Papers.] *The John Tipton Papers.* 3v. Indianapolis, 1942.

Tocqueville, Alexis de. *De la Democratie en Amerique.* Bruxelles, 1835.

Tourgee, Albion. *An Appeal to Caesar.* New York, 1884.

———. *Bricks without Straw.* New York, 1880.

———. *A Fool's Errand.* New York, 1880.

———. *Hot Ploughshares.* New York, 1883.

Train, Arthur. *Yankee Lawyer, the Autobiography of Ephraim Tutt.* New York, 1943.

Train, G. P. *Spread-eagleism*. New York, 1859.
Trial of Andrew Johnson. 2v. Washington, 1868.
Trollope, Mrs. Frances. *Domestic Manners of the Americans*. New York, 1901.
Trowbridge, John T. *My Own Story*. Boston, 1903.
———. *The South: a Tour of Its Battlefields and Ruined Cities*. Hartford, 1866.
Truesdale, John. *The Blue Coats, and How They Lived, Fought and Died for the Union*. Philadelphia, 1867.
Truman, Harry S. *Memoirs*. Garden City, 1955–56.
Trumbull, James H. *The Origin of M'Fingal*. Morrisania, New York, 1868.
Tucker, Benjamin. *Instead of a Book, by a Man Too Busy to Write One*. New York, 1893.
Tucker, Ray, and F. R. Barkley. *Sons of the Wild Jackass*. Boston, 1932.
Tumulty, Joseph. *Woodrow Wilson As I Know Him*. Garden City, 1921.
Turpie, David. *Sketches of My Own Times*. Indianapolis, 1903.
Twain, Mark, and C. D. Warner. *The Gilded Age*. Hartford, 1874.
Tyler, Lyon. *The Letters and Times of the Tylers*. 3v. Williamsburg, 1896.
Tyler, Royall. *The Contrast*. Philadelphia, 1790.

Usher, Ellis. *The Greenback Movement of 1875–1884*. Milwaukee, 1911.

Van Buren, Martin. *The Autobiography of . . .* Washington, 1920.
Vandenberg, Arthur. *If Hamilton Were Here Today*. New York, 1923.
Van Deusen, Glyndon. *Horace Greeley, Nineteenth-century Crusader*. Philadelphia, 1953.
"Vigilans." *Chamber of Horrors*. New York, 1952.

[Walsh, Mike]. *Sketches of the Speeches and Writings of Michael Walsh . . . by a Committee of the Spartan Association*. New York, 1843.
Walsh, William. *Handy-Book of Literary Curiosities*. Philadelphia, 1925.
Warburg, James. *Hell Bent for Election*. New York, 1936.
Ward, Durbin. *Life, Speeches and Orations of Durbin Ward of Ohio*. Columbus, 1888.
Ward, John. *Andrew Jackson, Symbol for an Age*. New York, 1955.
Warren, Charles. *Jacobin and Junto*. Cambridge, Massachusetts, 1931.
"Warrington." [W. S. Robinson] *Pen Portraits*. Boston, 1877.
Washington Merry-Go-Round. See Allen, Robert.
Watkins, Gordon. *An Introduction to the Study of Labor Problems*. New York, 1922.
Watterson, Henry. *The Editorials of . . .* New York, 1923.
———. *"Marse Henry"; an Autobiography*. New York, 1919.
Webb, Beatrice. *The Cooperative Movement in Great Britain*. London, 1891.
Webb, Sidney, and Beatrice Webb. *Industrial Democracy*. London, 1897.
Webber, Charles W. *Tales of the Southern Border*. Philadelphia, 1853.
Webster, Daniel. *Works*. Boston, 1851.
Webster, Noah. *Letters*. Ed. Harry R. Warfel. New York, 1953.
Weed, Thurlow. *Autobiography*. Boston, 1883–84.
Welch, F. G. *That Convention; or, Five Days a Politician*. New York, 1872.
Welles, Gideon. *Diary*. New York, 1911.
Wells, David. *Practical Economics*. New York, 1885.
Werner, M. R. *Barnum*. New York, 1923.
———. *Tammany Hall*. Garden City, 1928.
West, Willis. *A Sourcebook in American History to 1787*. Boston, 1913.
Weston, Florence. *The Presidential Election of 1828*. Washington, 1938.
Whipple, Wayne. *The Story-Life of Lincoln*. Chicago, 1908.
White, Laura A. *Robert Barnwell Rhett*. New York, 1931.

White, William A. *The Autobiography of William Allen White.* New York, 1946.
――――. *The Editor and His People.* New York, 1924.
――――. *The Old Order Changeth.* Milwaukee, 1917.
――――. *Politics: the Citizen's Business.* New York, 1924.
――――. *Selected Letters.* Ed. Walter Johnson. New York, 1947.
Whitlock, Brand. *The 13th District.* Indianapolis, 1902.
Whittier, John G. *The Writings of* . . . Riverside ed. 1895.
Wilkins, W. A. *The Cleverdale Mystery.* New York, 1882.
William Ballaert's Texas. Ed. W. E. Hallon and Ruth Butler. Norman, Okla., 1956.
Williams, James. *Rise and Fall of "The Model Republic."* London, 1863.
Williams, Samuel. *The Natural and Civil History of Vermont.* Walpole, New Hampshire, 1794.
Williamson, William. *The History of the State of Maine.* Hollowell, Maine, 1832.
Willkie, Wendell. *An American Program.* New York, 1944.
Wilmer, Lambert. *Our Press Gang.* Philadelphia, 1859.
Wills, Charles. *Army Life of an Illinois Soldier.* Washington, 1906.
Wilson, Harry. *Somewhere in Red Gap.* Garden City, 1916.
Wilson, Henry. *History of the Rise and Fall of the Slave Power in America.* New York, 1872–77.
Wilson, William. *Cabinet Diary of W. L. Wilson, 1896–1897.* Ed. Festus P. Summers. Chapel Hill, 1957.
Wilson, Woodrow. *The New Freedom.* New York, 1913.
――――. *The Public Papers of* . . . 6v. New York, 1925–27.
Wiltse, Charles. *John C. Calhoun.* 3v. Indianapolis, 1944–51.
Wirt, William. *The Life of Patrick Henry.* New York, 1831.
Wise, John. *A Vindication of the Government of New-England Churches.* Boston, 1772.
Withington, Leonard. *The Puritan.* Boston, 1836.
Wittke, Carl. *Tambo and Bones.* Durham, 1930.
Wolcot, John. *The Works of Peter Pindar, Esq.* London, 1812.
Woodley, Thomas. *Great Leveler; the Life of Thaddeus Stevens.* New York, 1937.
Wooley, Solomon J. *Life, Recollections and Opinions of* . . . Columbus, 1881.
Wright, Thomas. *Caricature History of the Georges.* London, 1867.

The Yankee in London; or, a Short Trip to America. Philadelphia, 1826.
"Young Sam"; or, Native Americans' Own Book! New York, 1855.

Zachariah Chandler; an Outline Sketch of His Life and Public Services by the Detroit Post and Tribune. Detroit, 1880.

The manuscript was edited by Alexander Brede and the book was designed by Richard Kinney and Edgar Frank. The type face used is Linotype Baskerville, cut by Mergenthaler Linotype Company and based on a face originally designed by John Baskerville between 1750 and 1758.

This book is printed on Warren's Olde Style Antique White Wove paper made by the S. D. Warren Company and bound in Columbia Mills' Riverside Linen. Manufactured in the United States of America.